T5-ADM-708

REPORT

ON THE

SHIP-BUILDING INDUSTRY OF THE UNITED STATES.

BY

HENRY HALL,
SPECIAL AGENT.

Reprinted from a copy in the collections of the
G. W. BLUNT WHITE LIBRARY
MARINE HISTORICAL ASSOCIATION
MYSTIC SEAPORT, CONN.

Reprinted from the edition of 1884, Washington, D.C.
in which this volume appeared as the final section
of Volume 8 of the Tenth Census published
by the Department of the Interior, Census Office.
First LIBRARY EDITIONS edition published 1970
Manufactured in the United States of America

INTERNATIONAL STANDARD BOOK NUMBER: 0-8432-0013-8

LIBRARY OF CONGRESS CATALOG NUMBER: 76-126718

**LIBRARY EDITIONS, LTD.
NEW YORK, NEW YORK 10013**

Macdonald
Maritime History
Series

REPORT ON THE SHIP-BUILDING INDUSTRY OF THE U.S.

BY

HENRY HALL

Macdonald and Jane's
London

Reprinted from a copy in the collections of the
G. W. BLUNT WHITE LIBRARY
MARINE HISTORICAL ASSOCIATION
MYSTIC SEAPORT, CONN.

Reprinted from the edition of 1884, Washington, D.C.
in which this volume appeared as the final section
of Volume 8 of the Tenth Census published
by the Department of the Interior, Census Office.
This edition first published 1970 in the United States
of America
First published in Great Britain 1974

ISBN 0 356 04760 1

MACDONALD AND JANE'S
ST. GILES HOUSE, 49-50 POLAND STREET, LONDON W1A 2LG
Printed in the United States of America
Bound in Great Britain

TABLE OF CONTENTS.

	Page.
LETTER OF TRANSMITTAL	v, vi
CHAPTER I.—FISHING-VESSELS	1–45
CHAPTER II.—MERCHANT SAILING VESSELS	46–95
CHAPTER III.—SHIP-BUILDING ON THE OCEAN COASTS	96–143
CHAPTER IV.—STEAM VESSELS	144–195
CHAPTER V.—IRON VESSELS	196–222
CHAPTER VI.—CANAL-BOATS	223–233
CHAPTER VII.—UNITED STATES NAVY-YARDS	234–241
CHAPTER VIII.—SHIP-BUILDING TIMBER	242–249
CHAPTER IX.—STATISTICS OF SHIP-BUILDING	251–265

LETTER OF TRANSMITTAL.

NEW YORK, *November 30, 1882.*

Hon. CHARLES W. SEATON,
 Superintendent of Census, Washington, D. C.

SIR: I beg to submit a report on the ship-building industry of the United States.

The work of this investigation began in November, 1880, in the city of Bath, Maine, at which place the greatest number and the largest and finest wooden vessels in this country are built. It was found almost at once that the only means of getting full, reliable, and accurate statistics of the ship-building industry would be by personal visitation of the various ship-building localities of the country. After a thorough study of the state of the industry in Maine, the whole coast southward to Norfolk, Virginia, was visited, every ship-yard, repair yard, boat-shop, and important establishment being entered on the way. All the different establishments scattered along the Hudson river were then visited, and after that the boat-yards of the Erie canal and the ship-yards of the northern lakes all the way from Oswego, New York, to Manitowoc, Wisconsin. The statistics of the industry at Green Bay, Wisconsin, were obtained by correspondence. Letter-writing was, however, seldom resorted to, as one day spent in a ship-yard in personal contact with builder, engineer, and workmen, and in the inspection of such books, draughts, and models as one would be permitted to see, was worth four weeks' correspondence by mail. After a visit to the lakes, several weeks were spent on the Monongahela, Allegheny, Kanawha, Ohio, and Mississippi rivers in gathering the statistics of barge and steamboat building and in learning by actual observation what was going on in the yards. Two months were then spent on the Pacific coast in personal visits to all the different ship-building localities in California and on Puget sound and the Columbia river, Humboldt bay and Coos bay alone excepted, data from the two bays being obtained by correspondence. With regard to the Gulf of Mexico and the south Atlantic coast, the statistics of the industry were obtained through the medium of the local census agents and the local collectors of customs, and were verified by means of data prepared by leading and well-informed shipwrights in Charleston, South Carolina; Key West, Florida; New Orleans, Louisiana; and Galveston, Texas.

Great pains have been taken to verify the facts and statistics presented in this report. A large number of small builders keep no accounts other than rough memoranda on a board, no copy of which is retained after the boat or vessel in hand is completed, or, at any rate, nothing better than equally rough notes jotted down in a pocket memorandum book, which are not complete when entered, and are almost unintelligible in a year's time. Vessel builders trust to their memory and judgment in some things to an extent hardly paralleled in any other trade, and it frequently happened that those who had completed vessels of considerable size in the census year, having no accounts, and not having charged their memories with details, were unable to tell the quantities of materials that had entered into the construction of the vessels or how much money had been paid out for labor in building them. In such cases a careful calculation of the quantities of materials was made, based upon the size of the scantling in the vessels and the style of fastening adopted, and a result was then reached which, when corrected by the recollections of the builder, was practically correct. Results arrived at in this manner were compared with data obtained directly from the books of more careful builders, a large number of whom cheerfully submitted their private accounts for the inspection of the agent of the Census Office; and it is believed that by the continual employment of both of these checks upon the returns of the small builders, and by taking the returns of the larger establishments directly from their books, exaggeration has been avoided and substantial accuracy reached.

On the whole, the ship-builders of the country have assisted in the collection of facts about their industry with great heartiness. A few were sensitive and suspicious, owing to the fact that they had not been making money for a few years; but the great majority gave such practical and sufficient help as to secure the faithful and complete collection of the statistics required. A number of them have taken considerable trouble to supply information for this report. The Census Office is particularly indebted to the following persons:

L. W. Houghton, of Bath, Maine, for facts concerning cost of materials, cost of ships, and methods of building in former years.

William Rogers, of Bath, Maine, for historical and other valued information.

LETTER OF TRANSMITTAL.

Pattee & Rideout, draughtsmen, of Bath, Maine, for models of old cotton ships and freighting vessels.

Edward O'Brien, of Thomaston, Maine, for information as to the days of labor required for the building of great ships.

Mrs. Donald McKay, of Hamilton, Massachusetts, for data in relation to the famous clipper ships built by her husband during his lifetime.

Hiram Lowell & Son, of Salisbury, Massachusetts, for models of fishing boats and historical information.

William H. Webb, of New York, for historical data in regard to the ship-building of New York city.

Gildersleeve & Sons, of Portland, Connecticut, for historical data.

William Cramp & Sons, of Philadelphia, for draughts, etc., of iron vessels.

The Harlan & Hollingsworth Company, of Wilmington, Delaware, for information in regard to iron vessels.

Robert Ashcroft, of Baltimore, for draughts and models of the clipper vessels of that port.

Emerson Rokes, of Baltimore, for facts about the white-oak supply of the Maryland and Virginia peninsulas.

B. Hufty, deputy collector at Crisfield, Maryland, for models of bug-eyes, and data in regard to them.

T. Quayle & Sons, of Cleveland, Ohio, for data in regard to wooden propellers on the lakes.

Frank E. Kirby, C. E., of Wyandotte, Michigan, and H. D. Coffinberry, of Cleveland, Ohio, for full information about the iron steamships of the lakes.

Joseph P. Rogers, of Cincinnati; James Howard, of Jeffersonville, Indiana; J. L. Shallcross, of Louisville, Kentucky; and Thomas P. Morse, of Saint Louis, for valuable data in regard to modes of building, cost of construction, and achievements of vessels on the Ohio and Mississippi rivers.

Middlemas & Boole, of San Francisco, designers and shipwrights; Matthew Turner, of San Francisco, yacht builder; and J. J. Holland and C. W. Townsend, of Portland, Oregon, for draughts and data relative to Pacific coast vessels.

Commodore Phelps, United States navy, for facts concerning the teredo and the strength of Pacific coast woods.

Constructor George W. Much, of Mare Island navy-yard, for draughts of vessels.

Constructor Samuel M. Pook, of the Washington navy-yard, for strength and weight of American ship-building woods.

Professor C. S. Sargent, of Brookline, Massachusetts, chief special agent of the Census Office on forestry, for data in regard to weights of American ship-building woods and the supply of ship timber.

W. W. Bates, of Chicago, for historical data.

Hon. N. B. Walker, chief of the tonnage division of the Treasury Department, for valuable tables showing the ship-building of the United States from 1797 down to 1882, being the first complete statement ever prepared for publication.

A large number of others have aided in the collection of special information of much value in the preparation of this report.

Respectfully, yours,

HENRY HALL,
Special Agent.

SHIP-BUILDING INDUSTRY OF THE UNITED STATES.

Chapter I.—FISHING VESSELS.

Fishing vessels properly come first in any account of the American ship-building industry. In the United States there are owned at the present time more than 51,000 boats and vessels which are regularly engaged in fishing either along the different coasts of the country, or on the banks of Newfoundland, or in the distant latitudes near the north and south poles, where they go for the noblest game the sea contains—the whale, the seal, and the sea lion. This multitude of boats, sloops, schooners, and ships gives constant employment to more than 101,000 hardy and energetic men in the catching and curing of fish and to thousands of people on shore in the various trades concerned in the building, fitting out, repair, and maintenance of vessels, and half a million of our population are afforded a livelihood by the fishing enterprise of the country. The boats put out from hundreds of capes and harbors, in fair weather and foul, and encounter much toil and danger, facing both bravely, and push their ventures under circumstances that would often completely check enterprise in the merchant navy. This rough but fascinating service trains hundreds of excellent new sailors annually, fitting them to go on the larger vessels of the merchant branch of our marine and enabling them to command, if required. It also makes hundreds of new carpenters and builders every year on shore, a large part of them getting their first acquaintance with the forms and the methods of framing and planking vessels in constructing some modest and clumsy boat during the rainy days or in wintry weather, for their own use when the fishing season next arrives, their unpretending efforts in this direction fitting them afterward for the skillful building of larger and more pretentious craft. It is not the least of the good things accomplished by the fishing fleet that it supplies the people with a vast quantity of cheap and delicious food; but that is mentioned only by the way. Fishing vessels are the starting point of our ship-building and merchant service, as they have been, historically, in the case of every nation which has been conspicuous upon the sea; and the experience of the United States is so like all the other important maritime nations of the earth in this respect that the similarity is too remarkable to be passed by without notice.

The first fishermen of whom we have any account were a race of people who settled on a forlorn portion of the Mediterranean coast, in a little territory, 200 miles long, cut off from the interior by rugged and heavily wooded mountains, which ran parallel with and not far from the coast. The land could not support the natives in agriculture, and they lived in part by fishing off shore in row-boats. Fishing villages were scattered along the coast of Phœnicia in large numbers as early as 1500 B. C., and had a large fleet of small boats, built from the strong and light timber of the country. The marketing of the surplus product of the fisheries, and the desire to buy grain and other needed commodities, led to expeditions along the coast to distant localities. This was the beginning of the far-reaching commerce of the Phœnicians, which did not pause until vessels had been sent as far northward as the British isles and as far southward as around the lower cape of Africa; it also made them the vessel builders of their age, and converted several fishing towns into large commercial cities.

The Carthaginians, who were colonists of the Phœnicians, began to build boats and to fish from the first, as their forefathers had done, and afterward to trade, and were the common carriers of the western part of the Mediterranean for several centuries.

Fishing boats were the small beginning from which sprang the sailors and the towering ships of the Barcelonians in Spain, the wonders of their day, in the early part of the Christian era.

The eminence of the Italians as builders of great vessels took its rise from the fisheries of the Adriatic sea. The ravages of the barbarians of the north, who made frequent invasions into Italy after A. D. 400, having driven a large number of people from the mainland to the islands which subsequently became the city of Venice, the settlers built boats for fishing purposes, and soon began to trade with the mainland and with Greece. Thinking only of subsistence, these islanders created by their modest efforts a race of brave sailors and a great fleet of boats, and in due time became the principal ship-builders of the world, their fleets assisting in all the crusades and their vessels being bought or borrowed by every nation of their time which had need to make a demonstration of any magnitude by sea.

The Portuguese also began their maritime career as fishermen. The busy trade of the early nations of Europe swept past their doors continually, but they took no part in it until, after many generations, they began to fish and had built sail-boats and small vessels large enough to go to the North sea and bring their catch safely home. The early commercial treaties of the Portuguese were made to protect their sailors and vessels in the northern fisheries, it being one of their great industries, the country not being so well adapted to agriculture as to other pursuits; and not until after the reign of a king who flourished from A. D. 1279 to 1325, who brought people from Genoa to teach the art of building great ships and planted royal forests of useful timber, did the Portuguese begin to trade, explore, and conquer.

The fisheries of the north of Europe, and the abundant growth of cheap and good timber, made maritime and trading nations of every people in that part of the earth except the French. The latter occupied a fertile and delightful region, which fully employed the population at home. The Dutch became the foremost of the fishing nations. They had an immense fleet of small sailing boats and busses of their own construction and a great seafaring population of daring men, ready for any service. About 1360 they discovered the art of salting and curing fish, which enabled them to make long voyages for the sale of their staple, just as it did afterward in the case of the Americans. With the rise of industry at home this discovery brought them at once into a large and profitable foreign trade, and by 1580 they were the principal carriers of the north of Europe. By 1650, according to the histories, they had 3,000 vessels and 50,000 men fishing off the coasts of Great Britain, 9,000 vessels to market the fish, and 8,000 more which their owners were employing exclusively in general trade, and had taken possession of India, were pushing out to every part of the world, and were the commercial masters of the sea. One of their cities was built upon the immense mass of herring bones accumulated by the industry of several generations, very much as the little modern fishing town of Crisfield, in Maryland, has been built upon the immense bank of oyster shells thrown into deep water by her fishermen, which now affords a strong foundation for a whole town to stand where formerly vessels rode safely at anchor.

England felt the need of ships for defense from the earliest times; and, recognizing the fact that the best way to get them was to make it profitable for the people to build, she encouraged her fishermen by every means in her power. Her general trade was almost wholly carried on by foreigners, but at any rate she might have a fishing fleet. A great many regulations were made; bounties were given, with various special privileges; and, in addition thereto, in the sixteenth century the people were required by law to abstain from meat on two days of each week and sometimes 153 days in the year, in order to make a profitable market for fish and to foster the creation and maintenance of a large native marine. These regulations had the desired effect. Large numbers of boats and vessels were built yearly for fishing purposes, and the native ship-building industry of England received its start and derived a great deal of its early vigor from the construction of small smacks and fishing boats.

America has followed the path of all of her predecessors; and it was the steps she took in this direction which led originally both to the possession of her large fleet of fishing boats and vessels and to her success in the field of general nautical enterprise. The following statement of the details concerning the fishing fleet in the census year of 1880 has been prepared by the fishery branch of the census, in charge of Professor G. Brown Goode, of the Smithsonian Institution, at Washington:

States and Territories.	NUMBER OF PERSONS EMPLOYED.			APPARATUS AND CAPITAL.					Value of minor apparatus and outfits.	Other capital, including shore property.
	Total.	Fishermen.	Shoresmen.	Vessels.			Boats.			
				Number.	Tonnage.	Value.	Number.	Value.		
The United States	131,426	101,684	29,742	6,605	208,297.82	$9,357,282	44,804	$2,465,393	$8,145,261	$17,987,413
New England states	37,043	29,838	7,205	2,066	113,602.59	4,562,131	14,787	739,970	5,038,171	9,597,335
Middle states, exclusive of the Great Lake fisheries.	14,981	12,584	2,397	1,210	23,566.93	1,382,000	8,293	546,647	674,951	1,822,480
Southern Atlantic states	52,418	38,774	13,644	3,014	60,886.15	2,375,450	13,331	640,508	1,145,878	4,789,886
Gulf states	5,131	4,382	749	197	3,009.86	308,051	1,252	50,173	52,823	134,537
Pacific states and territories	16,803	11,613	5,190	56	5,463.42	546,450	5,547	404,695	467,238	1,330,000
Great lakes	5,050	4,493	557	62	1,768.87	183,200	1,594	83,400	766,200	313,175
Alabama	635	545	90	24	317.20	14,585	119	10,215	7,000	6,400
Alaska	6,130	6,000	130				3,000	60,000	7,000	380,000
California	3,094	2,089	1,005	49	5,246.80	535,350	853	91,485	205,840	307,000
Connecticut	3,131	2,585	546	291	9,215.95	514,050	1,173	73,585	375,535	457,850
Delaware	1,979	1,662	317	69	1,226.00	51,600	839	33,227	70,324	113,080
Florida	2,480	2,284	196	124	2,152.97	272,645	1,058	28,508	39,927	65,037
Georgia	899	809	90	1	12.00	450	358	15,425	18,445	44,450
Illinois	300	265	35	3	209.73	8,500	101	2,000	11,900	61,000
Indiana	52	45	7	1	21.90	2,500	15	1,650	20,210	5,000
Louisiana	1,597	1,300	297	49	539.69	20,821	165	4,800	18,000	50,000

FISHING VESSELS.

States and Territories.	NUMBER OF PERSONS EMPLOYED.			APPARATUS AND CAPITAL.						
	Total.	Fishermen.	Shoresmen.	Vessels.			Boats.		Value of minor apparatus and outfits.	Other capital, including shore property.
				Number.	Tonnage.	Value.	Number.	Value.		
Maine	11,071	8,110	2,961	606	17,632.65	$633,542	5,920	$245,624	$934,593	$1,562,235
Maryland	26,008	15,873	10,135	1,450	43,500.00	1,750,000	2,825	186,448	297,145	4,108,850
Massachusetts	20,117	17,165	2,952	1,054	83,232.17	3,171,189	6,749	351,736	3,528,925	7,282,600
Michigan	1,781	1,600	181	36	914.42	98,500	454	10,345	272,920	60,900
Minnesota	35	30	5	1	33.59	5,000	10	900	3,760	500
Mississippi	186	110	76				58	4,600	1,600	2,600
New Hampshire	414	376	38	23	1,019.05	51,500	211	7,780	60,385	89,800
New Jersey	6,220	5,659	561	590	10,445.90	545,900	4,065	223,963	232,339	490,000
New York	7,266	5,650	1,616	541	11,582.51	777,600	3,441	289,885	390,200	1,171,900
North Carolina	5,274	4,729	545	95	1,457.90	39,000	2,714	123,175	225,436	118,950
Ohio	1,046	925	121	9	359.51	38,400	487	29,830	253,795	151,775
Oregon	6,835	2,795	4,040				1,360	246,600	245,750	639,000
Pennsylvania	552	511	41	11	321.99	10,500	156	13,272	40,538	55,500
Rhode Island	2,310	1,602	708	92	2,502.77	191,850	734	61,245	138,733	204,850
South Carolina	1,005	964	41	22	337.32	15,000	501	9,790	25,985	15,500
Texas	601	491	110				167	15,000	4,400	23,000
Virginia	18,864	16,051	2,813	1,446	15,578.93	571,000	6,618	292,720	560,763	489,636
Washington	744	729	15	7	216.62	11,100	334	6,610	8,648	4,000
Wisconsin	800	730	70	11	220.25	26,700	319	24,975	145,165	26,000

The first step in the development of the fishing business of America, and the attendant ship-building industry, was that which led to the crossing of the Atlantic by European fishing craft and the planting of small establishments on shore by their crews. At the time of the settlement of the north Atlantic coast fish were in great demand abroad and brought high prices. In 1497 Cabot made known in Europe that the ocean in the neighborhood of the northern part of this continent was full of fish of a size then seldom seen in the old country. Here, he said, "were great seals, and those which we commonly call salmons, and also soles above a yard in length; but especially there is a great abundance of that kinde which the savages call baccalos, or codfish." When this information was printed in London the news spread to every part of Europe, and there was great excitement among fishing merchants and the owners of fishing vessels. In 1504 several Normans and Biscayans crossed the ocean in craft dangerously small for that voyage and took cargoes of cod, which they carried back for sale. The great banks of Newfoundland, 200 miles broad and 600 miles long, were soon discovered. By 1517 there were 50 European vessels on the spot taking fish, and by 1540 there were establishments on shore at Newfoundland for salting and drying what they had caught. From that day to this the banks have been annually resorted to by large numbers of vessels, and the coast has been occupied by fishermen. In 1577 the French had 150 sail on the banks, and there were between 300 and 400 in all on the spot. By 1600 the English were sending out 200 vessels annually, and were employing fully 10,000 men as catchers and curers; and as they had now become familiarized with the idea of crossing the Atlantic, the large profit they found in the business made their fishing expeditions to America a regular feature of British enterprise. In 1602, 1603, 1605, and 1606 several explorers who had pushed on past the banks to the mainland of America discovered that cod could be taken close inshore to what is now Maine and Massachusetts in six or seven fathoms of water which were far larger and better than those caught off Newfoundland, where the depth was forty-five or fifty fathoms; and it was also found that six or seven cod would make a quintal in New England, when, by reason of their smaller size, twice that number were required at Newfoundland, while the shares of common fishermen earned only £6 or £7 each at Newfoundland, against £14 in New England. The reports brought back by these explorers were so satisfactory that they greatly increased a desire then felt in England for colonizing the mainland of America with fishing stations. Merchants found it expensive to add twenty men to the company of a vessel and carry them across the ocean and back again, paying and maintaining them all the while, simply to employ them on shore in curing and packing the fish caught by the regular force of the vessel, as it was cheaper to establish villages on shore, where the fish would be cured by the residents and the expense of doubly manning the ships thus be avoided. The desire to found fishing colonies in New England became strong, and the grant made by James I, in 1606, to the Plymouth company was largely with that idea in view. In a brief time the coast from Newfoundland to the capes of Virginia was planted with a succession of little villages of several different nationalities, the people of which were more or less engaged in the catching of fish.

So far as the English fishing merchants were concerned, their object in aiding the establishment of colonies in New England was to save the expense of the double manning of their ships and to secure permanent drying stations on shore, where their people and apparatus would be protected against the hostility of the Indians. But the planting of the new colonies had an effect not foreseen by them. The people left behind in the New World, finding the land unfit for high cultivation and able to live easily by following the trade they already knew so well, began to build boats and go fishing on their own account. A fisherman is always half a ship-builder by the nature of his calling. A few ship-carpenters besides had been sent over to the villages in Massachusetts by members of the home company, and the art of building sail-boats was almost the first industry after house-carpentry introduced into the colony. The result was unexpected, and the people of the Massachusetts towns soon owned a large number of fishing boats of their own construction. The country was covered with excellent timber, and vessels were cheaply built. One merchant was fishing with 8 boats at Marblehead as early as 1634, and Portsmouth had 6 great shallops, 5 fishing boats, with sails and anchors, and 13 skiffs in the trade as early as 1635. Canoes were owned everywhere. By 1645 they had sent a "ship and other vessels" from Boston to the banks to fish, Lechford stating in his "Plain Dealing; or, News from New England" that at this time the people of the colony "were building of ships, and had a good store of barks, catches, lighters, shallops, and other vessels". The English government was troubled by this multiplication of fishing craft, and in 1670 an order was issued by the lords of trade and plantations to capture and burn the boats and break up and destroy the boat fisheries of New England. This had some effect, but not much, as the fishermen went on building boats and taking fish; and as the years went by those who were prosperous built larger vessels and pushed out to the banks, while others went out for whales and seals, following their game from one latitude to another until they reached the impenetrable regions of the north and south poles. Vessels were sent out to New York and Virginia, to the West Indies and other islands of the Atlantic, and finally to Europe, to market the products taken from the sea, and their masters brought back the commodities of the lands they visited to sell at home. Afterward many of the vessels went regularly into trade, masters and men being recruited from the fishing fleet. A great and valuable foreign commerce was the result of their operations, and this, reacting upon the ship-building industry at home, made it an active and prosperous business within a hundred years of the time of the first permanent settlements.

While a few trading vessels were built at an early period in the history of the colonies, the number was not for fifty years large enough to give regular employment anywhere to a great number of men. The main stay of the industry, that which enabled men to learn and practice steadily the trade of a ship-carpenter, was the fishing business, and all the early builders learned their art in the construction of boats for that branch of the service. It was the fishing business also which, in large part, supplied the captains and crews of the trading ships, when any of that class were built.

The first vessels sent to America to fish were among the largest of their time in the merchant service of England, France, and Portugal; but, large as they were relatively, they were small compared with those which are sent out in this age for voyages across the Atlantic. As illustrating the size of those early vessels, it is stated that of the 1,232 sail which in 1582 comprised the whole marine of England not over 217 were over 80 tons actual burden; that is to say, not over 75 feet in length by about 23 feet in breadth, and about 10 feet deep in the hold. Fifty of the larger class were sent to Newfoundland annually, so that one-fourth of the whole merchant navy of England fit for distant voyages was employed in the American fisheries. In 1603 England had four vessels, each of which exceeded 400 tons burden. The ships of the discoverers of America were surprisingly small. Columbus made his first voyage in vessels the largest of which was between 150 and 200 tons burden. The Santa Maria was a decked vessel, and, in accordance with the models of that age, must have been about 100 feet long, 29 feet wide, and about 12 feet deep in the hold. The other two, the Pinta and the Nina, were "light barques", or "caravels", decked only at the ends, open amidships, but having cabins and quarters at the bow and stern for the crew and officers respectively. The foremast carried one large square sail; the mizzen carried a lateen sail, attached to a yard which was suspended from the mast by the middle at an angle of about 45° with the horizon; the sail was triangular in shape, and was the fore-and-aft canvas of barks and ships in the sixteenth century. The bowsprits on the vessels of Columbus probably carried no canvas; if they did, the sail was a square one, hung from a sprit-sail yard underneath the bowsprit, which raked high, so as to carry the sail up to where it would take the wind.

Gosnold's expedition in 1602 was made in the "small ship" Concord. Pring explored the waters of Maine in 1603 with the bark Speedwell, of 50 tons, and the Discoverer, of 26 tons. John Smith's fleet in 1606 was composed of a pinnace or long boat of 20 tons and two vessels of 40 and 100 tons respectively. The Mayflower, small as it was, was a large vessel for the times.

It is hard to identify the rig of these early vessels by their names. The term "ship" is now used to designate a vessel of three masts, square rigged throughout, and the term "bark" means a large vessel square rigged on the fore and main masts, but carrying only fore-and-aft canvas on the mizzen. Two or three centuries ago, whatever the size or rig of the vessel, it was called a "ship", in the general sense of the word, as often as by its own class name. There is an English official list of the vessels of the Cinque Ports made in 1587, in which the following expressions occur:

Deal hath small barks from the burthen of 3 tons to 5 tons	5
Walmer hath small barks from the burthen of 2 tons to 3 tons	4
Ramsgate hath small barks from the burthen of 5 tons to 19 tons	12
Dover hath ships and small barks from the burthen of 12 tons to 120 tons	26

In the list are also mentioned "Small boats of the burthen of 5 tons"; "one small bark of the burthen of 20 tons;" "small barks and boats from 2 tons to 25 tons apiece;" "small boats from 14 tons to 20 tons;" and "ships and small barks from 6 tons to 8 tons". In an old lawsuit, the record of which is still preserved, a small sloop was described variously as a "ship", a "boat", and a "vessel". In all vessels bearing more than one mast the mizzen-mast appears always to have carried a lateen sail, while those forward of it carried square sails. The difference between a "bark" and a "ship" seems to have been at first one of size only, the ship being the larger. When tonnage grew large, ships probably carried three masts, with two square sails on each of the forward masts and a lateen sail on the mizzen. A bark was a smaller vessel, usually with two masts, but sometimes three, with one or two square sails on the forward spars, as before, and a lateen sail aft. The tons of burden above referred to were the actual tons weight of cargo the vessels were able to carry.

The accompanying (Fig. 1) is the "light bark" or "caravel" of the fifteenth century, as shown by a drawing at Venice.

The boats carried by the vessels of that day were the pinnace, or long boat, and the chaloupe, or shallop, both open boats, mounting several pairs of oars, and fitted with small masts and sails, which could be put up at pleasure. The pinnace was long, sharp, and fast, often carrying 25 men, and was much used by early discoverers in exploring the coast. The shallop, a more or less capacious barge, was handy and safe, and was the more popular style of boat. Shipwrecked mariners often decked the pinnace and set sail in it for distant places. The shallop became the boat in common use for fishing and coasting in the early days of the settlement of America, though many widely different styles of boats grew out of it in the course of time.

Fig. 1.—CARAVEL OF THE FIFTEENTH CENTURY.

It is now proposed to describe, as fully as this report will allow, the different classes of vessels used in America for fishing purposes, the kinds of wood put into them, the manner of building them, and the places where they are and have been built.

NEW ENGLAND FISHERIES.

The first boats used by the settlers in fishing were wooden canoes, made by the Indians. In Maine these canoes were usually made of the bark of birch trees, sewed on ribs of ash wood, and made so light that an Indian would carry on his head for several miles one which would hold eight or ten persons, while in Massachusetts they were usually made from the trunk of a large tree. Wood (1634) says:

> Their Cannows be made either of Pine trees, which, before they were acquainted with English tooles, they burned hollow, scraping them smooth with clam shels and Oyster shels, cutting their outsides with stone hatchets: These boats be not above a foot and a halfe or two feete wide, and twenty foote long. Their other Cannows be made of thinne Birch rines, close ribbed on the inside with broad thinne hoopes, like the hoopes of a tub; these are made very light, a man may carry one of them a mile, being made purposely to carry from River to River and bay to bay to shorten land passages. In these cockling fly-boates, wherein an English man can scarce sit without a fearefull tottering, they will venture to sea, where our English Shallope dare not beare a knot of sayle; scudding over the overgrowne waves as fast as a wind-driven ship, being driven by their paddles; being much like battledoores; if a crosse wave (as is seldome) turne her keele upside downe, they by swimming free her, and scramble into her againe.

The majority of canoes would carry only four or five men; the larger ones, twenty, thirty, and even forty men; and they were round-bottomed and very crank. The bodies of the log canoes were straight, the ends sharp, and the fore foot and heel cut away as in a modern whale-boat. Their narrowness gave them great speed, and three men, with paddles, could drive them faster than a shallop could be propelled with eight oars. An Indian, by going into the woods and giving his time to it, would make a canoe in ten or twelve days.

When the English settled at Plymouth, Salem, Ipswich, Portsmouth, and other places on the New England coast they bought these strong and handy boats in large numbers, both for fishing in smooth waters and for crossing streams and visiting their neighbors, and nearly every family in towns like Salem owned its canoe, as every farmer to-day does his horse. Canoes were the universal oyster boats for the first fifty years on the whole American coast, and were so well adapted to that use that they are still so employed by American oystermen in many localities.

It is not probable that log canoes ventured more than 2 or 3 miles from shore, and then only in calm weather, as they could not be launched through the surf nor taken into very rough water. A larger class of boats was required for taking cod and for other work in the open sea. The first ones were ships' boats left behind by the vessels which visited the coast; but in 1624 boat-building began regularly at Plymouth, some ship-carpenters having been sent over for the purpose. Two chaloupes, or shallops, were built, one of them afterward making a voyage as far eastward as the Kennebec. They were open boats, like others of their class, having, however, a little deck amidships, to keep the crew dry. In 1625 one of these boats was sawed in two and lengthened 5 or 6 feet by putting in more frames amidships. A deck was laid the whole length of the boat, and she did the colonists good service for at least seven years afterward. A great many shallops were built in subsequent years, as there was need for them at Salem, Ipswich, Gloucester, Medford, Portsmouth, and the other settlements all along the coast. Some were used for trading purposes, but the majority were fishing boats. They usually carried one mast, with one sail hoisted from the deck; but in the larger ones, instead of fitting the shallop with a tall mast and a large sail, the owners usually followed the safer and more convenient plan of adding another mast with its own sail (Fig. 2). Two small sails were more easily handled than one large one, and in a fresh wind the after sail could be lowered and the boat allowed to scud under the foresail alone. The ancient shallop probably carried lug sails, as in the illustration herewith.

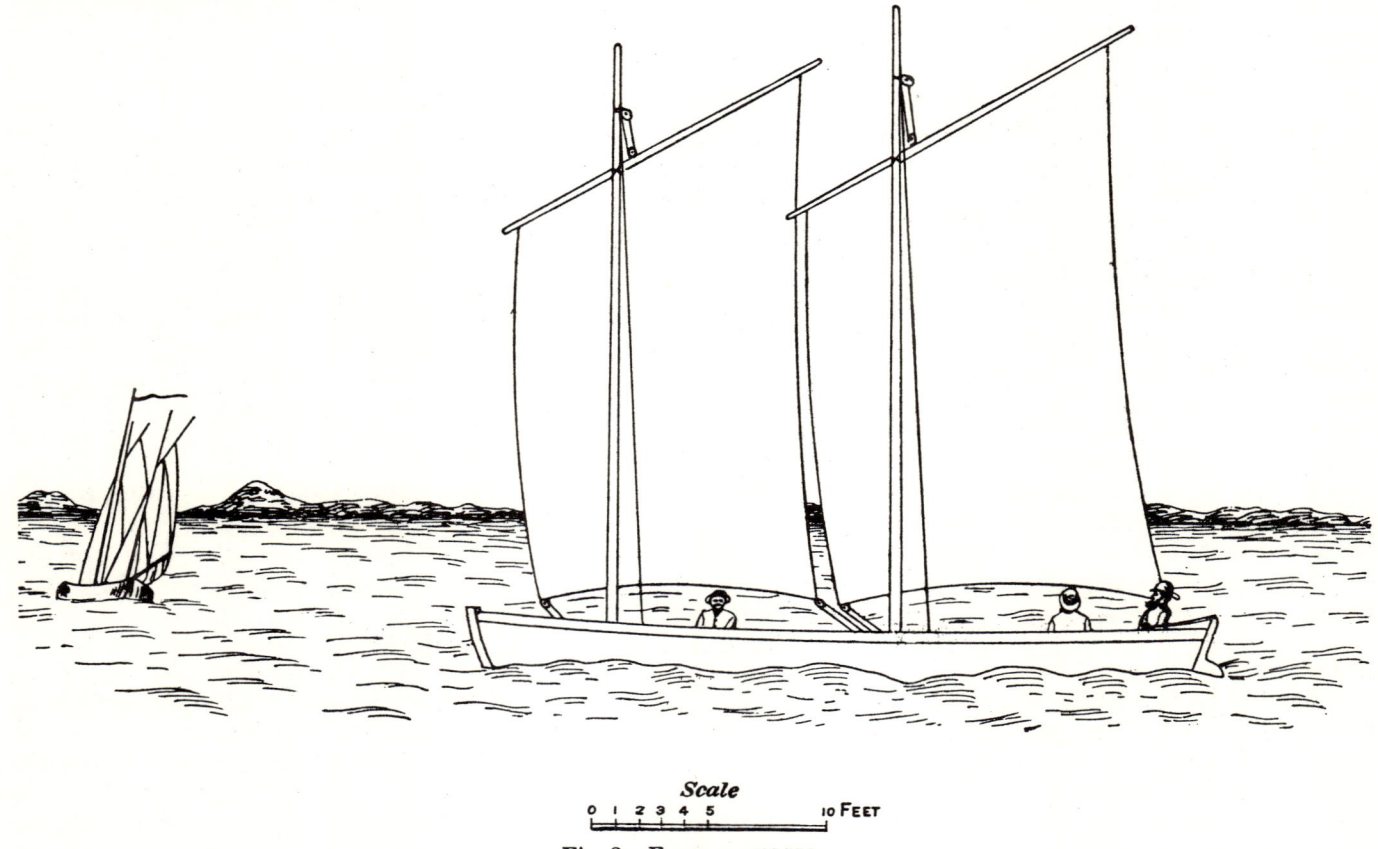

Fig. 2.—FISHING LUGGER.

A great many shallops were built in the winter time by the fishermen and their sons, who thus employed their idle season with useful work. The lumber for the boat was gathered little by little, a good deal being cut in the common woods and some picked up on the beach, so that it cost them next to nothing, and the boat, when built, was found to have cost them little more than the outlay required for nails, paint, iron fittings, blocks, cordage, and canvas. These boats were constructed in door yards, often in barns, and sometimes in the woods 2 or 3 miles from the water, whither they were dragged on sledges of timber. The home company sent over a number of shipwrights among their early dispatches of emigrants; many others came voluntarily among the crews landed from the large fishing vessels from England; and boat-building became an established industry in nearly every village in twenty years after the landing at Plymouth.

The first vessels sent from New England to the banks to fish set sail in 1645, and comprised "a ship and other vessels", their rig not known; but a style of smack which became popular as soon as something larger than the shallop was required was the "catch", or "ketch". The Dutch called them the "pinkie", a name borrowed from the Mediterranean and meaning a hull round at both ends, the outside planking ending on the stem and on the stern-post, in distinction from ships having a broad or "square" stern above the water, which were planked straight across. The "pinkie" hull was popular with the Dutch, and there is reason to believe that the hulls of the vessels in the northern fisheries of Europe were of that class. The first catches carried one mast amidships, with a large square sail. Afterward a small mizzen was added away aft, the mainmast being planted in that case

FISHING VESSELS.

one-ninth or one-tenth of the vessel's length forward of amidships. The mizzen-mast carried a lateen or a lug sail, which is a lateen with one-half of the forward part cut off. The mainmast bore two square sails, perhaps three. The popularity of the ketch was due to its simplicity of construction, as no ingenuity was required in framing either the bow or the stern and the planking was easily put on. It was a good sea boat, pretty fast and safe on account of its breadth of beam, easily handled, and, when required for the coasting trade, was useful for its great capacity, the bottom being broad and round. The probate records of Suffolk county, Massachusetts, indicate that ketches and shallops constituted the whole fleet of the fishing merchants up to about 1700. The ketches were 9 or 10 feet deep in the hold, drew 7 or 8 feet water, were decked throughout, had cabins aft, and were built of white oak, except the deck and cabin, which were of white pine, and the masts, which were usually of spruce. The broadest part of the hull was two-fifths of the vessel's length from the bow.

Salem was the principal center for the building of ketches, and it is said that the people of that town clung to the model and rig longer than any other community on the coast, using ketches both in fishing and in general trade. The average size was about 30 tons register, but a few were as large as 80 tons; the majority were below 30 tons, and cost about £3 5s. per ton to build.

The accompanying illustration (Fig. 3) represents an English ketch of 1692 with the bulwark pierced for eight light guns and the top sides curved home above the load-line, after the fashion of the times, so as to bring the weights further inboard, and thus maintain the vessel's stability.

Before the independence of the colonies the ketch had ceased to exist, and had become, through slight modifications of hull and rig, the brigantine of to-day—a class of vessel used only in trade.

Out of the old shallop grew two classes of small vessels which have remained in permanent use. In one of them the two small masts were retained, but were planted a step farther forward, the foremast being set not over 4 feet from the bow, and, in 30-foot boats, the mainmast 10 or 11 feet aft of the foremast, bringing it about amidships. A change took place in the sail. A part of the sail and of the yard forward of the mast was cut completely off, and the end of the yard was shaped to slide up and down the mast, the fore edge of the sail, or the luff, being attached to the mast by wooden hoops, which would also slide up and down with ease. The head of the sail was narrowed, and the foot was spread by means of a "sheet", attached to it at the lower after corner, carried aft and hauled taut. The boat remained open and without deck for many years, was round at both ends, being moderately sharp on the bottom, and the prow was often pointed. These changes in the fishing shallop culminated at Essex, Massachusetts, formerly called Chebacco, the story being that the first Chebacco boat, probably not much larger than the yawl of a modern schooner, was built in a garret, and was taken out of the house through a window and dragged to the water's edge by cattle. The shrewdness of the inventors of this new and handy rig brought a great deal of business to Chebacco, and the Chebacco boats, as they were called (or pinks, from the shape of the hull), became famous along the whole of the New England coast. First used in fishing at Sandy bay, these boats soon came into general use, the majority of them being built in the village in which they originated. They ranged from 3 to 5 tons burden at first, and their owners put out in them to the ledges and shoal grounds for cod, hake, and pollack early in the day, always to return at night; but in later years, especially after the independence of the colonies, they were built larger and decked, and were fitted with a cabin, sometimes being of 30 tons register. When they reached a large size the foot of each sail was fitted with a boom. The Chebacco boats were always framed and planked with white oak, cut from the abundant forests of that timber which grew all around the town, and nothing except heart of oak was used, all of the sapwood of every tree being sawed or hewed off and thrown away. Thus the boats were built of wood which would scarcely perish. The deck beams were usually of oak, but the deck plank and cabin were of white pine, and the masts of white pine or spruce. These boats were often built in the woods, or, at any rate, a long way from the water, and as late as the revolutionary war fishing boats of from 10 to 20 tons were thus built and were dragged to the river by cattle. Though built in Chebacco (or Essex), the boats were chiefly owned in Gloucester, and by 1792 this latter town had 133 boats of this class, registering 1,549 tons, in the shore fisheries; but by 1804 the number had increased to 200, with the tonnage nearly doubled. From 1800 to 1840 the boats were built for $18 a ton, a good price for the times, but much smaller than the builders got afterward. From 1861 to 1865 the price was about $65 a ton, but it is now about $40 a ton.

About 1820 the fishermen began to put bowsprits into the Chebacco boats, shearing off the pointed prow, and calling them "jiggers". The planking of the low bulwark of the boat was carried out beyond the sharp stern 3 or 4 feet and nailed to a short triangular stern-board, like that of a dory. This projection had a seat for the use of the crew, and the boom of the mainsail rested on it while the boat rode at anchor. Fishermen built "jiggers" of 40 tons register for mackerel catching, on account of the abundance of that fish at the time, the first great year being 1825, when one jigger, with 8 men, caught 1,300 barrels of fish; but when the mackerel began to disappear, which was about 1845, the large jiggers disappeared with them. Chebacco boats of moderate size remained in use for many years, but are now obsolete in New England. A few pinks, with bowsprits, are still to be seen occasionally at Gloucester, and especially in the waters around Eastport, Maine, and they are also to be seen, usually without decks and always without projecting prow, but in other respects like the Chebacco boats of the earlier times, at Block island, where they are almost the only style of boat employed (Fig. 4). Full in the forward body, a trifle leaner aft, sailing with a drag of from 2 to 4 feet, broad of beam, and carrying a great deal of stone ballast, they

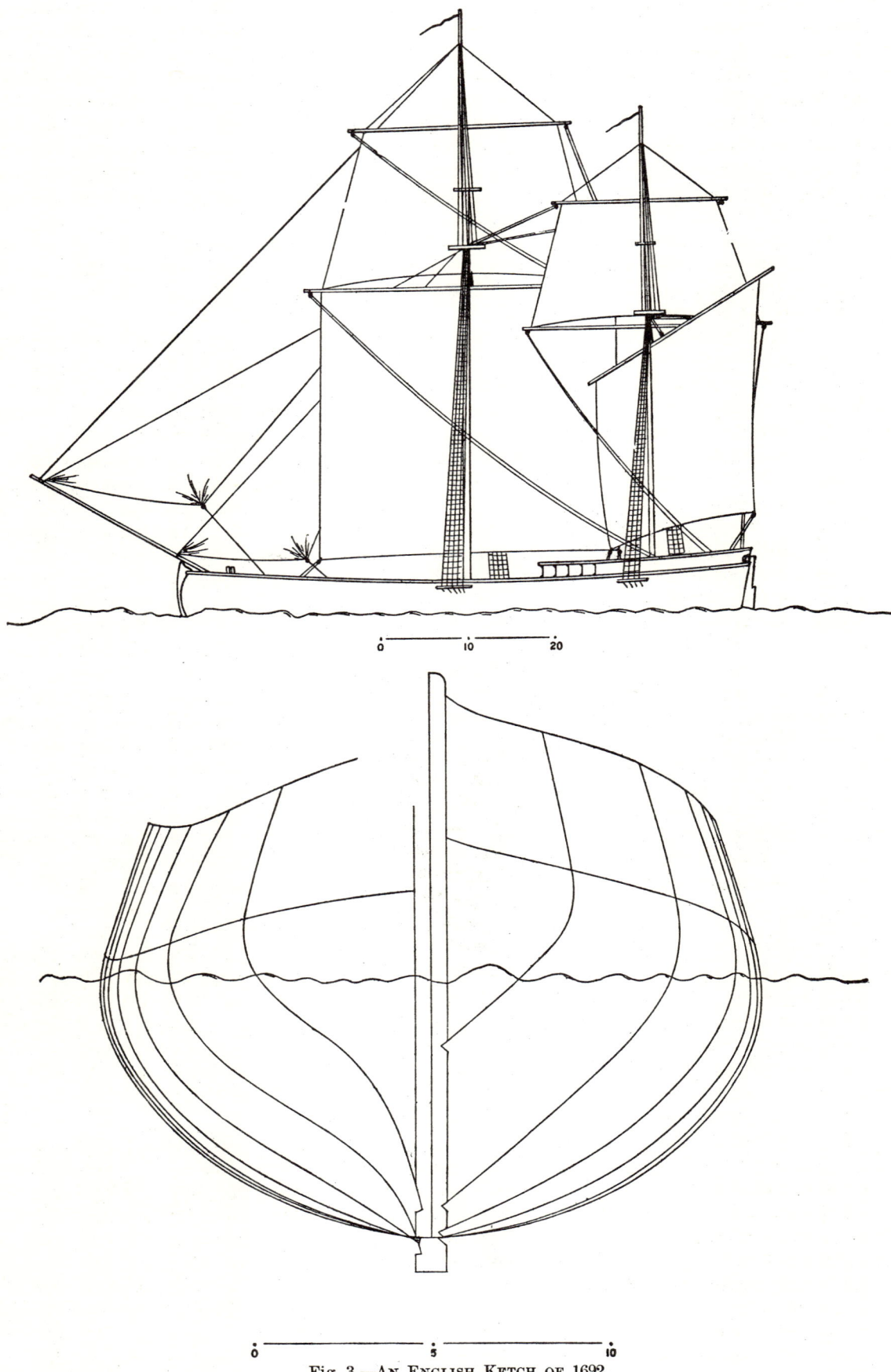

Fig. 3.—An English Ketch of 1692.

MEASUREMENTS.—Length from rabbet of stem to rabbet of stern-post, 60 feet; extreme breadth, 19 feet; depth of hold, 7¼ feet; depth from plank sheer to top of keel, 8 feet. Displacement to 7 feet from top of keel, 138 net tons; coefficient of D., 53 per cent. Register tonnage by modern rule, about 60 tons. Cargo burden, about 80 tons. Fullest part of the body (or midship section), ⅖ length from bow. Weight of vessel, about 58 tons; draught, when light, above keel, 4 feet 2 inches. Center of gravity of vessel, light, 7 feet above the keel; center of buoyancy, loaded, 4 feet 6 inches above the keel, and 21 inches forward of middle of length. A crank vessel, requiring ballast or cargo to steady her.

are a cheap and excellent fishing boat, safe, comfortable, and almost non-capsizable. At Block island, lying 20 miles out to sea from Newport, Rhode Island, the little community of resident fishermen had 100 fishing boats and 200 men employed as early as 1800, as appears from a petition sent by them to Congress in that year, all under 5 tons each. It is probable that the islanders originally built their own boats from the timber which anciently covered their lands in a dense growth, but of late years they have been obliged to send to the mainland to buy, as the island has become entirely denuded of trees of all kinds. The cod banks being within two leagues of the shore, the men go out to them early in the day, returning at dusk, and, drawing up their boats on the beach, fasten them to poles planted in the sand, to protect them from the fury of the waves. The secluded life of the islanders prevented the newer fashioned boats from creeping in among them for any purpose (as

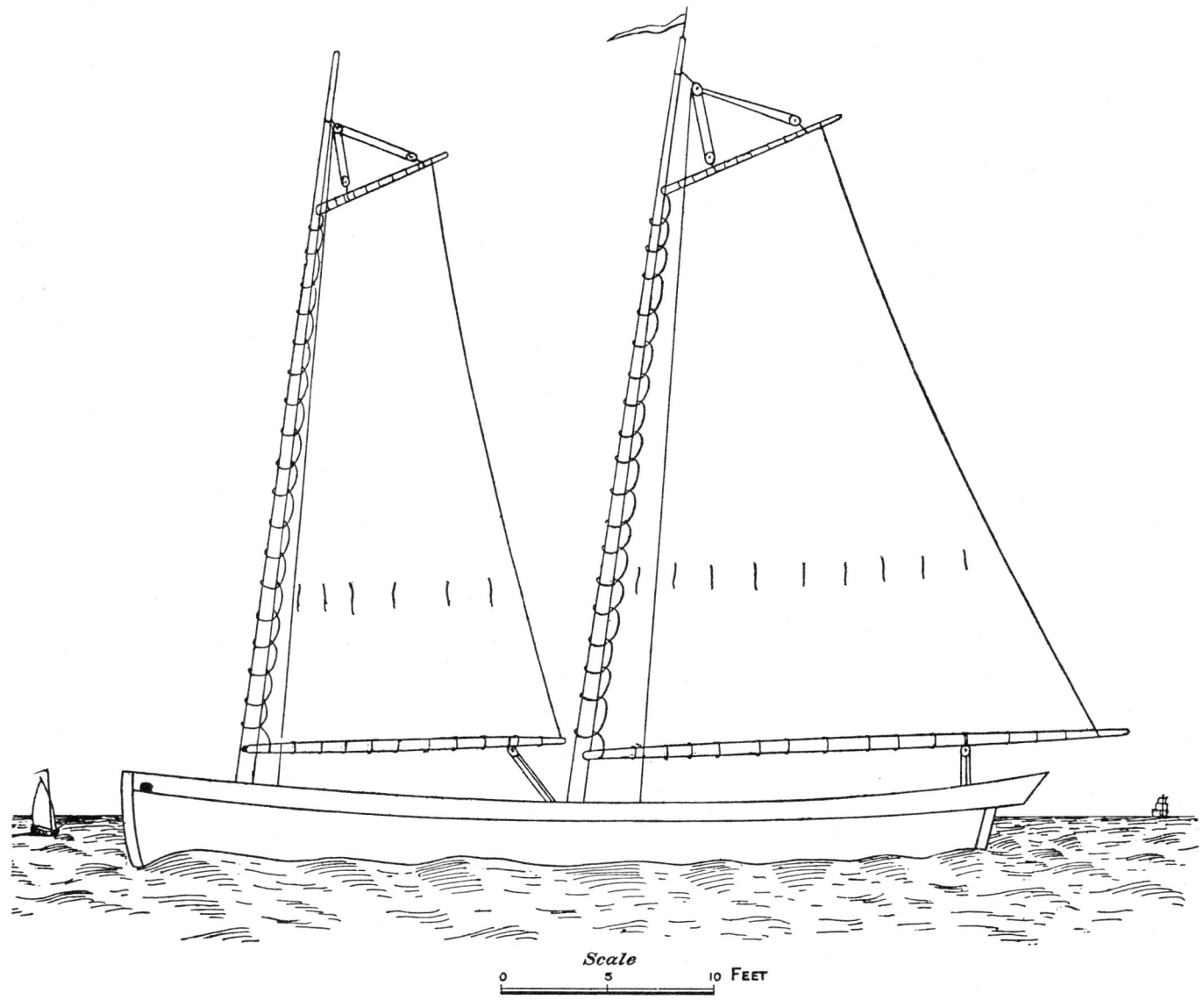

Fig. 4.—CHEBACCO BOAT, OR PINK.

40 feet on load-line; 14 feet beam; 5½ feet depth of hold, registering about 20 tons. Sharp at both ends, with bulwark rising and projecting at stern.

in the case of most of the fishing islands on the northern coast) until about twenty years ago, when people from the mainland began to spend their summers there to enjoy the cool air and the surf bathing. They are now buying boats which are half sloop-yachts and half fishing boats (Fig. 5).

The other style of vessel which grew out of the old "chaloupe", or shallop, was the modern sloop whose name is a contraction of that of the foregoing (Fig. 6). The sloop is a vessel with one mast, spreading a large fore-and-aft sail, the foot of the sail attached to a boom and the head to a gaff, and with a bowsprit spreading a large jib. This class of vessel appears to have been used in America originally for trading purposes; there was certainly a large fleet of them owned in the towns adjacent to Massachusetts bay, employed in freighting fire-wood, hay, and goods along that part of the coast. The hulls were built with broad decks, square sterns, and pretty full models. After the sloop came into existence it was extensively employed in the fisheries, and is now popular among yachtmen, the rig being generally regarded as the handsomest in existence for pleasure boats. When properly designed, the sails present the appearance of a large and showy triangle of canvas, reviving in outline and effect the old lateen sail. The sloop was in vogue at an early day in England, and may have come to America from that source. Square topsails were fitted to the larger sloops in England, and a picture of an English war fleet is extant in which there is a sloop with two square upper sails. In 1714 the Hazard, a sloop, was sent expressly from England to America to carry the news of the accession of George I to the throne and orders for the colonial government. This vessel, after crossing the Atlantic in safety, was wrecked on Cohasset rocks on the 12th of November and dashed to pieces. No papers of any consequence were saved, and of all her company only one man came to land alive. The rig of the sloop was a handy one for boats between 10 or 12 tons register and 30 or 40 tons burden, and came into favor rapidly after 1700, both for large fishing vessels on the New England coast and for trading purposes everywhere in America. Many of the "bankers", and all of the early mackerel boats, were sloops, and the first vessels

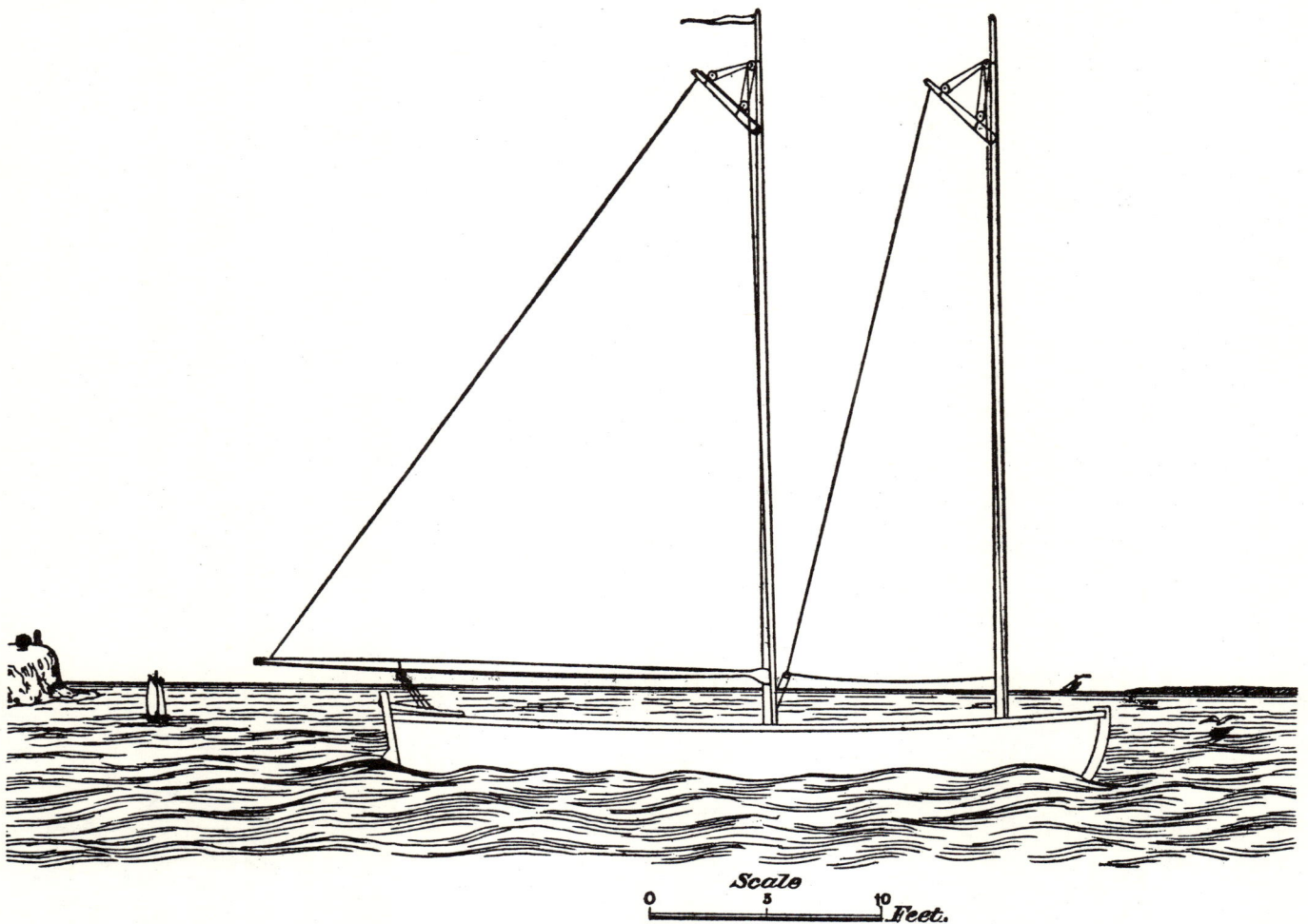

Fig. 5.—BLOCK ISLAND BOAT OF 12 TONS REGISTER.

Keel, 23 feet; length over all, 31 feet; beam, 11½ feet; depth from gunwale to floor, 4 feet 5 inches. Width of main thwart, 10 feet 8 inches; width at forward and after stroke thwarts, 8 feet 7 inches. Masts, 36 and 37 feet, 9 inches in diameter at keel, and 2 inches at head. Gaffs, 4 feet. Boom of mainsail, 23 feet. Foresail has no boom. No shrouds or stays to masts. Two tons of ballast. Keel, 4 by 12 inches. Frames, 2 by 4 inches, spaced 24 inches from center to center. Frames and planking, white oak. Foremast 4 feet from bow; mainmast 10 feet farther aft. These boats are open, but sometimes have a little cabin, which will shelter 6 men.

with which whales were chased out to the Gulf Stream, and thence to distant latitudes, were of this class, the larger ones probably being fitted with a square topsail, to catch the air in light weather. The majority of sloops were not over 10 or 15 tons register, but some were as large as 30 tons. In the little fleet of 10 vessels hurriedly fitted out in Massachusetts, manned by fishermen, the smartest and ablest of sailors then, as now, and sent in 1745 to capture the great fort at Louisburg with its 200 cannon, 3 were Yankee sloops, and of the 34 vessels burned by the British in 1778 at New Bedford at the time of the capture of that town 10 were sloops. Many of the fishing sloops were very fast vessels, and they and their crews were accordingly much in demand during the revolutionary war for privateering, their exploits forming a romantic chapter in the naval history of the United States. The principal places at which sloops were built were Boston, Scituate, Salem, Charlestown, Gloucester, and Newbury, but the boat-yards all along the whole coast began about 1700 to devote considerable attention to this class of vessels, which, as before stated, were employed partly in fishing and partly in trading, entirely superseding in both employments the ancient "catch".

In after years the square topsail was given up and a gaff topsail was bent in its place, being a large triangle of canvas hoisted along the mast above the mainsail, and the jib was divided into two smaller head sails. A great number of sloops were built before the revolutionary war for the open sea fisheries, chiefly at Boston, Charlestown, Scituate, Essex, Salem, Beverly, Marblehead, Gloucester, Ipswich, New Bedford, Portsmouth, and the fishing towns along the coast of Maine. In the cod-fishery Massachusetts alone had 4,000 men and 28,000 tons of shipping before the revolutionary war, the fleet being largely composed of sloops. The great advantages of the sloop were its safety, and particularly its cheapness, arising from the small size of the vessels and from the abundance of native oak and pine near the fishing towns. The fishing vessels built in New England before the revolutionary war cost only one-half what the fir-built vessels of the Baltic did, and the result was that American fishing vessels continually increased in the cod and whale fisheries of the Atlantic, while European vessels continually decreased. Jefferson

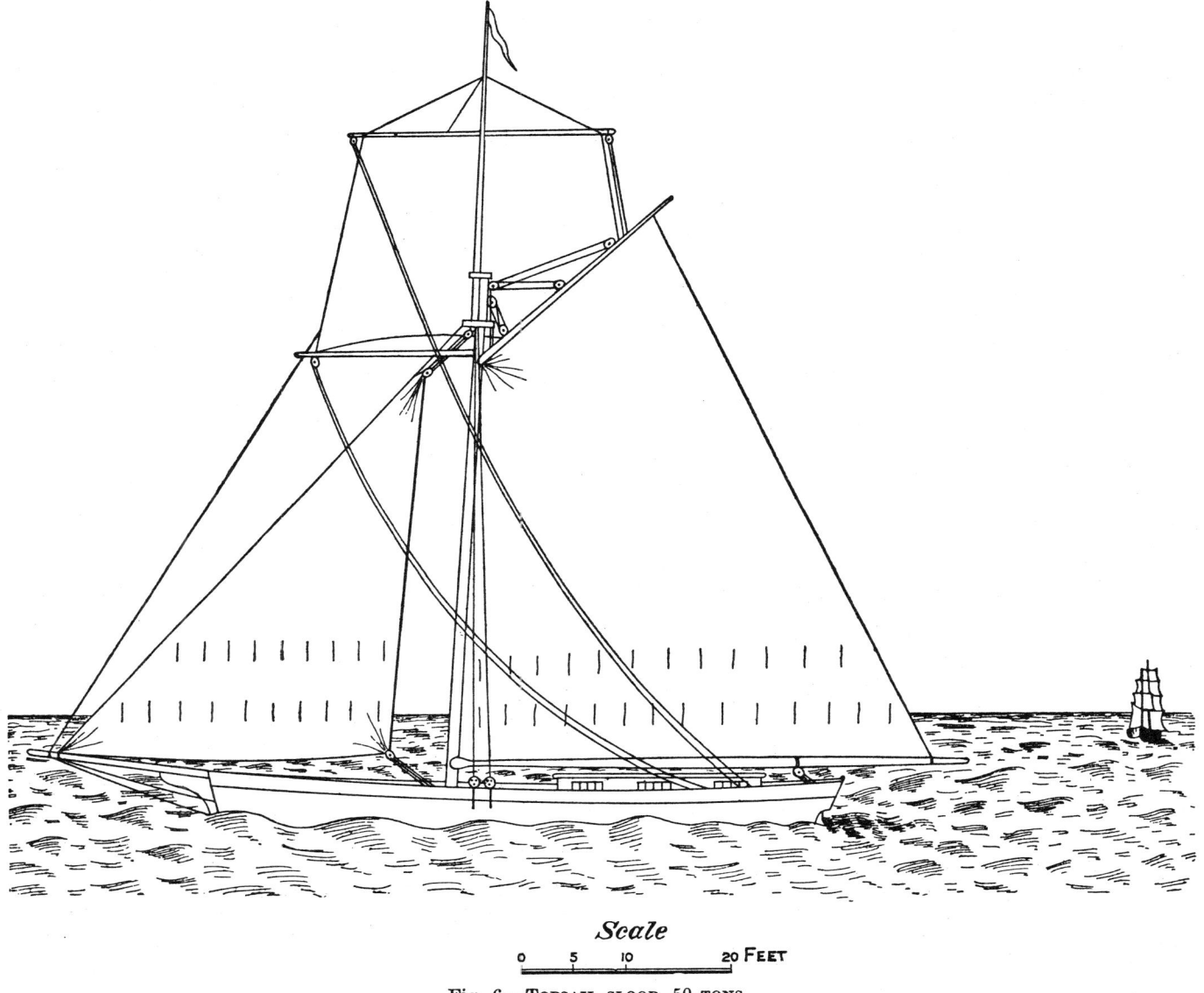

Fig. 6.—Topsail sloop, 50 tons.

reported in 1791 that no other nation except the Americans could make a profit in the Newfoundland fisheries without national aid, and the governmental machinery was invoked to secure the widest possible market for American-caught fish.

Sloops were also largely built at and around New York city for shore fishing, and many are still employed there by the fishermen.

In 1745 Andrew Robinson, of Gloucester, built a vessel with square stern, which was fitted with two masts, bearing a sloop sail on each and a bowsprit with jib. She was sharp on the bottom and fast, and, on being launched, sped over the water so fast from the impetus gained by descending from the ways as to elicit from a bystander the remark, "See how she scoons." "Scoon" was a word used by plain people to express the skipping of a flat stone over the surface of the water when skillfully thrown, and the builder of the vessel, having been somewhat at a loss for a name for the new rig, seized upon the trifling incident referred to and replied, "A scooner let her be," and two-masted vessels, with jibs and fore-and-aft sails, have since been called by that name. The advantage possessed by the "schooner" (as the name is now spelled) is that the canvas of the vessel is divided into a larger number of sails, which are more easily handled than the large sails of a sloop could be, each containing the same amount of cloth. The schooner quickly superseded the sloop in the banks fisheries and in all others requiring voyages of any duration. Carrying twice as many men as a sloop, and making quick trips, a schooner could catch as many fish as two vessels of the other style, and were large enough to carry their own fish to foreign markets. Since the revolutionary war they have been the only vessels employed by Americans in the banks fisheries.

The American fisheries were annihilated during the revolutionary war, and the vessels were captured, the utensils and apparatus destroyed, the ship-yards closed, and both fishermen and carpenters were driven into other employments. The business revived promptly after the peace of 1783 both on shore and out to sea. By 1788 the New Englanders had an aggregate of 540 vessels, registering 19,200 tons, and 3,290 men in the deep-sea fisheries, and for more than half a century, interrupted only now and then by war or by small profits, the business went on increasing steadily. These statistics are from Jefferson's report to Congress in 1791.

The largest schooners were those sent to the Grand Banks, and for many years after 1800 about 70 sail of vessels were annually sent thither, chiefly from Cape Ann. The original "banker" was strongly and substantially built of oak. Her decks and cabins were of pine; her spars of either pine or spruce; her rigging and cables entirely of hemp. The ship-yard was usually located at the water's edge (although a vessel of 100 tons has been built 1 or 2 miles from the water and dragged on sledges over the snow in winter by 200 cattle to a spot suitable for launching), and the ways were planted so that the hull of the new vessel should just escape the water at high tide. The keel was laid of oak or other hard wood. Beginning at the fullest part of the vessel, the frames of the forward body were put in, going forward, and the stem, with its apron, knight-heads, and hawse timbers bolted together, was then raised to its place. The frames of the after body were then raised, and the stern-post, with the frame which belongs to that part of the vessel bolted to it, was fitted to its place. The keelsons were put in, the vessel was ceiled, planked, and decked, and in due time was launched, often with her principal spars in place. The only tools used in the ship-yard were those wielded by hand—saws, axes, hammers, augers, squares, chisels, and calking irons— the largest being the great saw, for cutting timbers lengthwise, worked by two men, one at each end, the timber being placed across two wooden horses, and one man standing on the top of the log, the other in a pit below the surface of the ground. All the beams, planks, keelsons, etc., were carried into the vessel on the shoulders of the men, but the masts were raised and set by means of an extemporized derrick. In model the vessels would be thought uncouth at this day. The bows were nearly as full as half of an apple, the bottom as round as the side of a barrel. They sat low in the water, and there were no bulwarks amidships other than the covering plank, with a chock, which rose in all about 15 inches above the surface of the deck. Aft there was a quarter-deck extending nearly half the length of the vessel and rising 4 feet above the main deck, reached by a flight of steps. The cabin was large, and, as this was before stoves were invented, was furnished with a large fireplace and chimney, the smoke sometimes going out by way of the chimney and sometimes through the open door of the apartment. The masts were rather short, and there was no topmast, except on the mainmast. The bowsprit was set high, sometimes at an angle of about 30°. The cutwater was a large and strong knee, securely bolted to the stem, and served as a means of securing the bowsprit in place, that spar being lashed to the knee with hemp or iron. There was not much beauty to the old-time "bankers", but they were staunch and durable vessels. Built for strength, well calked, and immediately repaired when showing a leak or weakness anywhere, they often lasted for forty or fifty years. The last of them owned at Gloucester was the Manchester, which, after long service on the banks, was sold to go into the coasting trade, and was a successful vessel in that business for more than twenty years. The bankers used to make about three trips a year, beginning in March and ending in November, and then either went into trade or were laid up for the winter.

The clipper schooner succeeded the banker. A few good years, in which fish were plenty and prices profitable, and the anxiety to make rapid trips and as many as possible in one year, led to great improvements in form. The body of the vessel was made leaner and sharper under the water, the bow longer and finer, the run cleaner, and the angle of entrance forward was sharpened from 85° to 45°. The spars were lengthened, and the schooner put under a heavier press of canvas. The clipper fashion is said to have been set at Essex, and the models of the carpenters of that town were so much admired as to bring a great deal of business to their yards. The Essex men have always shown originality in the shapes of their vessels, and have always led every other town upon the New England coast in the production of tonnage for the fisheries. Of the 475 schooners, sloops, and boats

FISHING VESSELS.

owned at Gloucester in the census year, 218 had been built at Essex, 133 only having been built by the Gloucester men themselves. The places where the rest of the Gloucester fleet of 1880 was built will appear in the following statement:

Essex, Mass	218	Belfast, Me	2
Gloucester, Mass	133	Damariscotta, Me	2
Salisbury, Mass	9	Brunswick, Me	2
East Boston, Mass	5	Harpswell, Me	1
Newburyport, Mass	5	Yarmouth, Me	1
Danversport, Mass	4	Wells, Me	1
Chelsea, Mass	3	Portsmouth, N. H	1
Salem, Mass	2	Middletown, Conn	3
Quincy, Mass	2	East Haddam, Conn	1
Medford, Mass	1	Essex, Conn	1
Rockport, Mass	1	Chatham, Conn	3
Ipswich, Mass	1	Noank, Conn	1
Annisquam, Mass	1	New London, Conn	1
Duxbury, Mass	1	Bridgeport, Conn	1
Dorchester, Mass	1	East Haven, Conn	1
Wellfleet, Mass	1	New York	3
Bath, Me	36	New Jersey	1
Boothbay, Me	13		
Kennebunk, Me	9	Total	475
Bristol, Me	3		

As soon as Essex and Gloucester had adopted the fast schooner every other fishing town along the whole coast did the same from necessity, and the new boats superseded not only the bankers, but also the pinks, for shore fishing; so that after 1850 a complete revolution was effected in the character of the fishing fleet of the whole Atlantic coast. Except on the Chesapeake, where a distinct class of vessels, peculiarly local, had been evolved, old fashions lingered only in a few scattered and out of the way places. The fast schooners added greatly to the prosperity of all the fishing towns; the American fishing fleet multiplied rapidly, and the capital invested in fast vessels yielded a far larger return than that put into the slower craft that preceded them. The vessels owned in large towns were provided generally by fishing merchants, who would put the profits of one year into a new schooner, to be added to their fleet the next, and who would fit out annually from three to twelve, and even as many as twenty vessels; but the masters of most of the schooners had shares in the craft they sailed, and hundreds of them came in course of time to possess and sail their own vessels. Builders, sailors, and merchants all became prosperous after the new impetus given to the business by the clipper class of schooners; the fishing towns were filled with neat and comfortable residences, owned by them; and their operations gave rise to shops, lofts, and mills, which made employment for thousands of men in the various arts that a large fishing fleet calls into action. Nearly all the fishing towns in New England made their own sails, rigging and cordage, anchors, and outfit, a contract for a new vessel, therefore, meaning work for nearly all the shops in town. The majority of the villages were supplied with small marine railways, on which regularly twice a year all the vessels of the town were hauled up out of the water for calking and painting and such other repairs as circumstances demanded; and thus there was work both winter and summer. This state of affairs continued, especially in New England, until the operation of the new fishery treaty with Canada brought a blight upon the business by admitting Canadian-caught fish to the United States free of duty.

The early schooners, both bankers and clippers, were from 20 to 40 tons register. The size increased with the growing accumulations of capital, and since 1860 the majority have been built of from 60 to 90 tons register, the fair average being about 75 tons, but many from 100 to 140 tons.

It is remarkable that, while the form and the rig of the schooners have been greatly improved, the manner in which they have been framed and built has scarcely changed in the last hundred years. The measurements, scantling, etc., of a 75-ton schooner are as follows:

DIMENSIONS AND SCANTLING.—Length, 76 feet, from the outside of planking at the bow to the after side of the stern-post, measured along the deck; breadth from outside to outside of planking, 22 feet; depth of hold, 7 feet 8 inches, and molded depth from under side of plank-sheer (top of beam), 8 feet 6 inches; keel, 70 feet long; molded with shoe of 6 inches, 18 inches, and sided 10 inches; stem, 12 feet long, sided 15 inches; stern-post, 10 feet long, sided 15 inches; knee to stern-post on keel, 4 feet 3 inches high, about 12 feet long on keel, and sided 10 inches; keelson, 10 inches square. The ceiling of the hold is 2 inches thick, except on the turn of the bilge, where a few streaks are laid 3 inches thick, and except just under the beams (the clamps), where they are also 3 inches. The outside planking is $2\frac{1}{4}$ inches, with 3-inch fender streaks. The beam knees are sided 5 inches and molded 10 inches in the throat. Beams are 9 inches wide, tapering from 7 inches deep in the center to 5 inches at the ends. Carlines are 4 inches by 6; decking, 3 inches thick. Frames, double, are 14 inches wide and 8 deep over the keel, the depth or molding of the frames tapering thence to the plank-sheer, where it is 4 inches. At the plank-sheer only one of the timbers of each frame rises to form the bulwark of the schooner, this timber, or stanchion, being sided 5 inches and molded 3; bulwark, 2 feet high amidships, 2 feet 6 inches forward; sheer of vessel, 22 inches.

SPARS AND SAILS.—Length of foremast, 69 feet; length of mainmast, 70 feet 6 inches; length of mast-heads, $6\frac{6}{12}$ and $6\frac{12}{12}$ feet; length of topmasts, 35 feet; length of poles of topmasts, 6 feet; rake of masts, $\frac{5}{8}$ inch to the foot; the masts bury below deck 8 feet 6 inches;

from knight-heads to center foremast, 21 feet; from center foremast to base of mainmast, 27 feet; from center mainmast to center of taffrail, 36 feet; length of bowsprit outboard, 21 feet; center line of bowsprit strikes stern-post above keel 4 feet; length of jib-boom outside cap, 13 feet; length of fore boom, 23 feet; length of main boom, 57 feet; length of fore gaff, 23 feet; length of main gaff, 25 feet.

The spars, with the bill for labor in making them, cost about $300.

Mainsail: Hoist, 46 feet; foot, 55 feet; head, 24 feet; after leech, 60 feet; containing 2,015 square feet of area and 410 yards of canvas.

Main gaff topsail: Hoist, 36 feet; after leech, 31 feet; foot, 24 feet; area, 350 square feet; canvas, 70 yards.

Foresail: Hoist, 46 feet; head and foot, 22 feet; after leech, 51 feet; area, 940 square feet; canvas, 190 yards.

Fore gaff topsail: Hoist, 36 feet; after leech, 34 feet; foot, 23 feet; area, 340 square feet; canvas, 70 yards.

Staysail: Fore leech, 15 feet; after leech, 36 feet; head, 31 feet; foot, 24 feet; area, 550 square feet; canvas, 115 yards.

Jib: Fore leech, 60 feet; after leech, 44 feet; foot, 46 feet; area, 840 square feet; canvas, 175 yards.

Flying-jib: Fore leech, 68 feet; after leech, 40 feet; foot, 32 feet; area, 350 square feet; canvas, 75 yards.

Jib-topsail, or balloon jib: Fore leech, 84 feet; after leech, 42 feet; foot, 50 feet; area, 805 square feet; canvas, 165 yards.

Riding-sail, or lug-sail: Area, 450 square feet; 90 yards of canvas.

Total sail area, 6,640 square feet, or 1,360 running yards of canvas, to which add about 60 yards for linings; cost of the suit, about $570.

[The sails vary in area somewhat on different vessels of the same tonnage, as the masts are planted at slightly different distances apart and the topmasts are shorter or longer, but the variation is seldom more than 50 yards of canvas either way.]

Blocks, etc.: 16 double and 46 single blocks; 24 6-inch and 8 4-inch dead-eyes; 36 21-inch and 16 10-inch mast hoops; 24 24-inch, 30 18-inch and 40 16-inch jib-hanks; 2 topmast balls. Average cost of blocks, etc., for a two-topmast schooner, about $140.

A schooner of this size will carry, in addition to what is mentioned below, two chains from 30 to 45 fathoms long each, if fitted out for mackerel fishing; but if fitted out for cod or halibut fishing she will have from 225 to 425 fathoms of best 8½-inch or 8¾-inch manila cable and three anchors, one of them being carried on deck for use in case one of the others should be lost. The following is the hemp standing rigging, the table giving the circumference and the fitted lengths ready to go on the vessel:

	Lengths, in feet.	Circumference, in inches.		Lengths, in feet.	Circumference, in inches.
Jib stay	88	8¾	Maintop-mast stay	38	2¾
Foremast shrouds, each	54½	6¾	Bowsprit foot-ropes, each	24	2¾
Mainmast shrouds, each	56½	6¾	Main-boom foot-ropes, each	26	2½
Bowsprit shrouds, each	28	5	Counter stay (foretop-mast)	37	2½
Spring stay	25⅜	5	Maintop gallant stay	41	2
Flying-jib stay	108	4½	Foretop gallant stay	133	2
Flying-jib guys, each	35½	4	Flying-jib foot-ropes, each	15	2¼
Foretop-mast back stays, each	86	3	Jib topping-lift	36	3
Maintop-mast back stays, each	88	3	Fore-boom topping-lift pendant	24	3
Foretop-mast shrouds, each	32	2¾	Main topping-lift pendant	57	4¼
Foretop-mast stay	129	2¼	Main-boom topping-lift pendant	30	4½
Maintop-mast shrouds	32	2¾	Flying-jib topping-lifts pendant	15	3½

The following are the circumferences and lengths of the manila running rigging:

	Lengths, in feet.	Circumference, in inches.		Lengths, in feet.	Circumference, in inches.
Main sheet	132	3	Flying jib sheets, each	60	2¼
Cat stoppers	27	3	Fore staysail halliards	120	2¼
Main topping-lift runner	18	3	Topsail sheet	114	2¼
Fish-hook	12	3	Crotch tackles, each	48	2¼
Fore and main lanyards, each	30	3	Main topping-lift, fall	96	2¼
Fore-peak halliards	318	2¾	Topsail halliards	114	2
Fore-throat halliards	264	2½	Main-peak downhaul	126	1¾
Fore sheet	96	2¾	Fore-boom topping-lift	156	2
Main-peak halliards	324	2¾	Fore-peak downhaul	60	2
Main-throat halliards	270	2½	Topsail back	60	2
Jib halliards	180	2½	Reef tackle	96	2
Jib sheet	60	2½	Main-peak whip	144	2
Jib downhaul	87	2	Fore-peak whip	138	2
Main-staysail halliards	165	2½	Jib-peak whip	138	2
Main staysail sheet	60	2½	Jib-topsail halliards	258	1¾
Main-boom tackle	108	2½	Jib-topsail downhaul	108	1½
Flying-jib halliards	198	2¼	Jib-topsail sheet	72	2½
Flying-jib downhaul	105	1¾	Topsail clew-line	138	1¾
Jib topping-lift	156	2¼			

Weight of tarred hemp, 1,330 pounds; weight of manila cordage, 890 pounds. Cost, about $440, including rigger's bill of $100 for fitting and setting up.

The practice has been in vogue for the builder to contract to furnish only the hull and the spars of the vessel, the sails being furnished by another contractor. The cordage is bought by the owner from the manufacturer or from

FISHING VESSELS.

a ship-chandlery store, and is fitted to the vessel by a rigger, whose bill is almost exclusively for labor, and the chains and anchors are bought from either a shop or a store. The fine carpentry work on the cabins is done by a joiner; the iron ballast, often costing $500, is purchased from the mill, and when the sails, rigging, cabins, chains, anchors, and ballast have been purchased the main features of the outfit of a fishing schooner have been provided, the rest of the outfit consisting of a large lot of small articles, costing in all from $400 to $600.

Many of the fishermen sail with no foretop-mast, this being thought to be a snugger and safer rig, the rolling and pitching of a fishing boat being severe upon all the top hamper. In such cases the "top bills" of the vessels are lessened somewhat.

The following statement, taken from the books of a leading sail-maker in a fishing town in New England, shows the yards of canvas in schooners of different sizes, the first cost, the yearly amount spent for repairs of sails, and length of time the suits of sails last:

In what fishery.	Tonnage of schooner.	Yards of canvas in sails.	Cost of suit.	Yearly amount for repairs.	Life of a suit of sails.
					Years.
Halibut, the year round	95	1,350	$600	$100	2
Mackerel and herring, the year round	93	1,338	600	70	2½
Halibut, the year round	83	1,380	570	100	2½
Mackerel and herring, the year round	83	1,380	570	50	2½
Mackerel, the season	80	1,349	650	50	3
Bank fisheries, the season	75	1,360	570	100	3
Mackerel and shore, the season	72	900	470	80	2
Bank fisheries, the season	65	850	570	83	3
George's banks, the season	60	800	500	70	2
Do	56	750	450	60	2½ to 3
George's banks and shore, the year round	48	700	340	50	2½ to 3
Shore, the year round	40	640	300	40	2½
Do	32	550	250	40	2½ to 3
Do	28	500	240	30	2½ to 3
Do	26	460	200	30	2½ to 3

The differences between vessels of nearly the same size are due to the lack of foretop-mast on some of them, and to the use of light canvas in some cases and of heavy canvas in others.

The manner of building a 75-ton schooner in the New England yards is as follows: All the plank, and a good deal of the square lumber, such as is used in keelsons, beams, and stern-posts, are bought from the lumber-yard in the town, or in the most favorable market near by and sent to the town by coasting vessel or by railroad. The frame timber is obtained in two ways: Either it is bought at the nearest saw-mill in the flitch, that is, in heavy plank sawed only on two sides, the bark of the tree remaining on the other two edges, and drawn to the yard on wagons or sleds, according to the season, when the crooked pieces of the frame, stem, etc., are hewn from it with broadaxes; or the cheap pine board patterns of the crooked pieces are given to a contractor, who makes a business of getting out frames in the woods in Delaware, Maryland, or Virginia. In that case the contractor goes to the scene of his operations in the winter time, fells the trees, hews the frames from the trunks on the ground on which they fall, marking each separate piece when finished, and brings the whole frame to the yard in New England by coasting vessel in the spring. The contractor pays about $3, but sometimes from $4 to $6 per thousand board feet for the white oak standing in the woods, and it costs him about $9 a thousand to fell the trees and hew out the frames, besides an additional charge for hauling out of the woods. Freight to the north is about $7 a thousand, and by the time the timber is delivered in the ship-yard the frame has cost the builder about $34 per thousand board feet. The white pine used for decking and houses costs him about $35 a thousand, and the pitch-pine, for beams, keelsons, and other uses, $25 a thousand.

The keel is stretched on a series of blocks made of cheap timber, and such of them as have to be split out are usually hemlock or spruce. The declivity toward the water is usually about five-eighths of an inch to the foot. A keel 73 feet long would be made of two pieces, with the ends united by a horizontal beveled joint, or scarf, about 6 feet long, strongly bolted with round iron. Owing to the fact that single sticks of timber of the right curvature long enough to reach from the keel to the main rail cannot be obtained for the ribs of the vessel the frames have to be made of several pieces. A frame is composed of eleven pieces, the first being the "floor timber", 7 inches wide and 8 inches deep, tapering toward the ends, which is laid across the keel, extending each way as far toward the bilge as the natural crook of the log from which it is cut will allow. Abutting against each end of the "floor timber" is another curved stick, or "futtock", which carries the sweep of the frame farther on upward, and against the end of that another futtock, or "top timber", as in the illustration on page 16, which carries it to the plank-sheer on either side of the vessel, the frame tapering gradually from the keel to the plank-sheer. This collection of pieces makes one-half of the frame. In front, and strongly fastened to them by treenails of oak or locust, are the pieces composing the other half of the frame, which break joints with the pieces first mentioned. There are, first, two "navel timbers" abutting over the keel; then a "futtock" adjoining each navel timber; then a "stanchion", which rises to the main rail and supports the planking of the bulwark of the vessel. As the frame is thus double, it measures over the keel 14 inches by 8. The pieces are laid together and treenailed on the ground, and the completed frame is then raised to its place by a derrick and held up by shores. The arrangement of the frame is shown in Fig. 7.

In a schooner of 75 tons there are about 27 frames, spaced 24 inches from center to center, the first one being set up about 6 feet from the stem at the water-line. After these frames are set up, and each is fastened to the keel with 1-inch iron bolts about 2 feet long, the stem, with the hawse timbers and knight-heads bolted to it solidly, is raised and bolted to the keel. Then the stern-post is set up, the deadwood is placed at the stem and stern, upon which the extreme forward and after frames, or "cants", are stepped, and then the keelson is laid, bolts 1 inch thick and about 20 inches long are driven through each frame into the keel, and these bolts often go clear through the keel and are clinched on the under side by spreading the ends with a hammer. The forward cants are usually four or five in number, and are of the same size as the frames of the "square body", so called; but the bottom ends are tapered to suit the model of the vessel, and are bolted with $\frac{7}{8}$-inch iron to the deadwood. There are five or six after cants, which are secured in the same way. After the frames are all up, three sets of ribbons, or strips of wood, are run around the vessel lengthwise and nailed to the frames, to hold them steady and in proper position while being planked, one of these ribbons being fastened at the head of the navel timbers, another on the bilge, and the third at the gunwale. The planking and ceiling generally go on at the same time, but in many cases the ceiling is put in first, and is fastened with spikes. The planking is fastened to the frames with

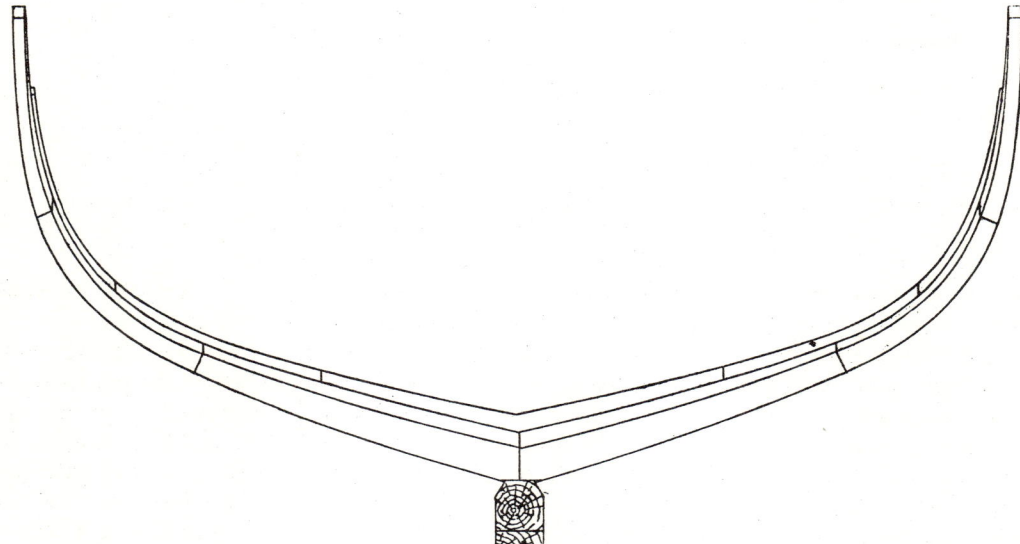

Fig. 7.—MIDSHIP FRAME OF A 75-TON FISHING SCHOONER.

oak or locust treenails, 4 in each frame, one-half of the treenail going through frame and ceiling, and is clinched at each end by driving wooden wedges into the treenail. The ends of the planking are fastened by two 5-inch spikes of galvanized iron and one $\frac{5}{8}$-inch galvanized iron bolt, going through, and clinched inside over an iron ring. Each plank of the "bends" is bolted to every set of timbers, this being called "bend bolting". The beams are put in about 4 feet from center to center, and are bolted to the clamps, or piece of thick ceiling, with $\frac{3}{4}$-inch iron, there being four $\frac{3}{4}$-inch bolts through each lodging knee into the beam and about six through the body of the knee into the side of the vessel. The deck planking is laid nearly straight fore and aft, but aft it follows the sweep of the sides of the vessel somewhat. The decking is 3 inches thick, 5 or 6 inches wide. Two 5-inch spikes are driven through each plank into every beam, the heads countersunk, and the holes plugged with wooden plugs set in white lead. On the top of the main rail, at the bow, is placed a wooden chock 5 inches high, tapering to 3 inches aft, and $5\frac{1}{2}$ inches thick, tapering to 4 inches aft. This chock extends from the bow to the fore-rigging. The taffrail varies from 14 to 18 inches in width on the main rail; the top rail is 9 inches wide. The houses are the last thing built. The whole of the top and outside of the vessel is duly planed, the deck oiled, the hull calked and painted, and the schooner is then launched (Figs. 8 and 9). At present, it is more frequently the case that fishing schooners are launched before the spars are set.

If there are ship-chandlery stores and sail and rigging lofts in the town the new schooner is placed alongside of a wharf and fitted out at once, but in many towns near cities as large as Rockland, Portland, Gloucester, Boston, and New York the schooner is placed in tow of a tug and sent to the city, where she gets her spars, sails, rigging, anchors, hawsers, boats, and all the paraphernalia of her outfit. It costs from $50 to $100 to tow a new schooner to the nearest large city, but, as a rule, outfits can be purchased there relatively so cheap as to warrant

FISHING VESSELS.

this expense. The use of the steam tug has within the last twenty-five years extinguished the sail and rigging lofts, anchor shops, and chandlery stores of a large number of vessel-building towns along the Atlantic coast by concentrating the outfitting business in the large cities.

From first to last, about thirty distinct trades are concerned in the collection of the material for a fishing schooner and the construction of a vessel. The largest part of the cost is for material. Fishing schooners were built in the census year for from $55 to $65 per register ton. The cost of a 75-ton vessel was about $5,000; the amount paid out in the ship-yard for labor of building was about $1,900.

The outfit of such a vessel for a five-weeks' mackerel trip for a crew of master and 14 men is:

- 1 seine, costing $850.
- 40 hogsheads of salt, $70.
- 1 seine-boat, $225.
- 400 barrels, $400.
- 4 barrels of flour.
- 2 barrels of beef.
- 100 pounds of pork.
- 120 pounds of sugar.
- 25 gallons of molasses.
- ¼ barrel of beans.
- 25 pounds of dried apples.
- 25 pounds of cornmeal.
- 10 gallons of kerosene.
- 10 pounds of coffee.
- 50 pounds of lard.
- 60 pounds of butter.
- 10 bushels of potatoes.
- 1 bushel of pease.
- 10 pounds of rice.
- 50 pounds of oatmeal.
- Other small stores, costing about $40.

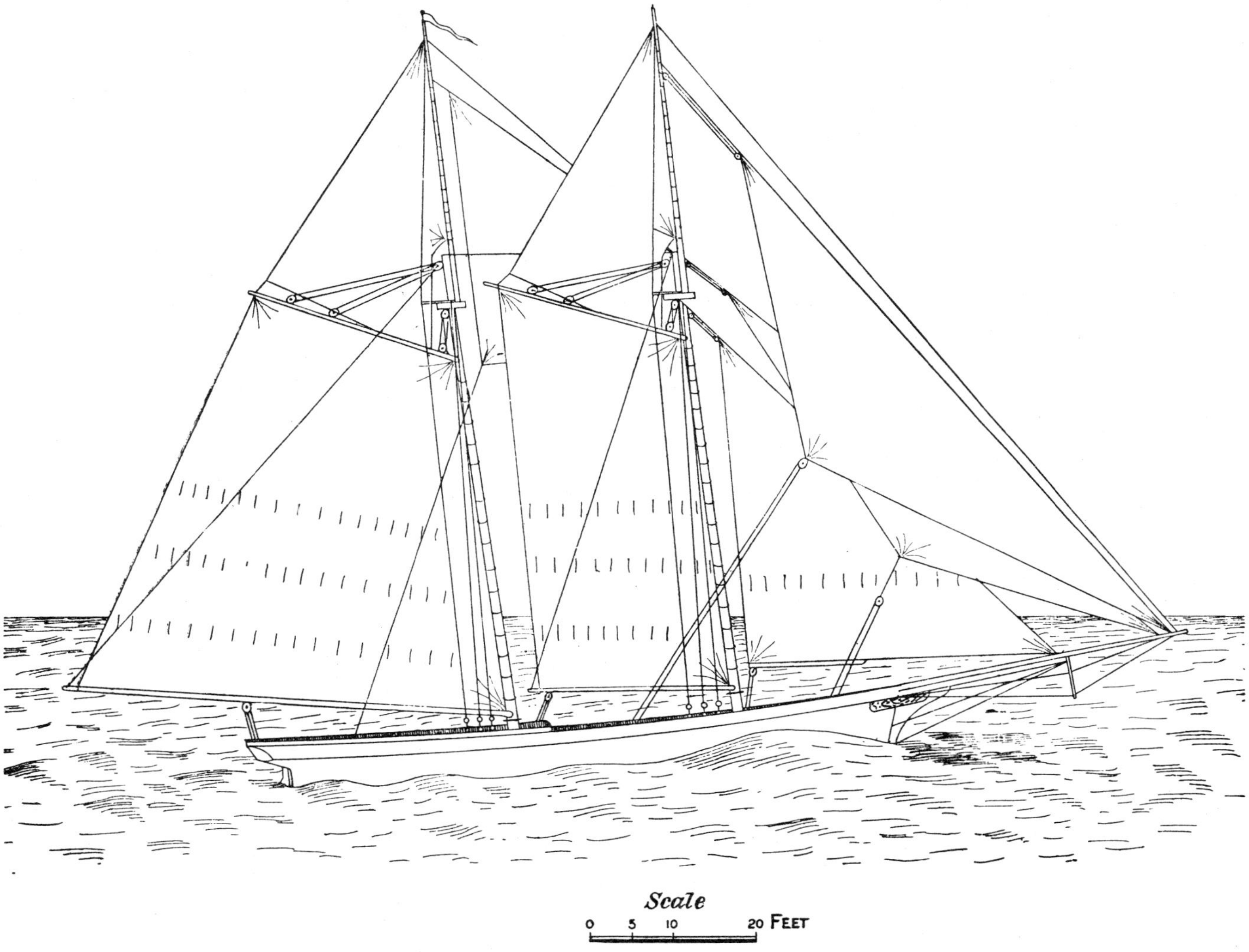

Fig. 8.—NEW ENGLAND CLIPPER FISHING SCHOONER.

75 tons, 76 feet long, 22 feet broad, and 7⅜ feet deep in the hold. Draught, forward, about 4 feet + the keel; aft, about 6 feet + the keel. Coefficient of D., to 6 feet from keel amidships, 0.39; to 5 feet from keel amidships, 0.33. Total displacement to 5 feet draught above keel, 89 net tons. Angle of entrance at bow, 40°.

It ought perhaps to be stated that the shallowness of the clipper schooner and the smallness of its under water midship section are doubtless the causes of a large proportion of the terrible losses of life and capital that yearly afflict the fishing communities of New England, especially Gloucester. Captain J. W. Collins, with others, have been trying for some time to induce the people engaged in the business to build deeper vessels for the winter fisheries.

The fishing smacks built on the Connecticut coast for the Long Island and New York fisheries are clipper schooners carrying light poles for topmasts, but often with no foretop-mast at all (Figs. 10 and 11). They usually have no jib-boom. The rig is adopted for its convenience, but, as a rule, the vessels do not remain out over night.

However, they are able vessels, and sometimes are out a week without making harbor, especially in the spring and summer time. They are of smaller tonnage than the New England schooners, though deeper, and usually range from 20 to 45 tons register. Usually they have a well amidships, into which the fish are thrown, to be brought to market alive. A fair specimen of this class is the Elisha A. Baker, built in 1848 at New London, which is 65 feet long over all, 17 feet 10 inches broad on the beam, and has an 8-foot hold. Amidships, the well is 18 feet long and 5 feet high, with access into it through a 4-foot hatchway on the deck, covered with a wooden grating, the curb of the well lengthening fore and aft, so as to make an 8 by 4 feet opening. There is a bulkhead across the vessel in the middle of the well, while on top, and under deck, is an ice-house extending the whole length of the well. Forward of that is a little bait pen, and still further forward, reaching to the bow, is a forecastle and bait room 5 or 6 feet high, under which ballast is stowed. The mainmast steps on the after end of the well. The steerage is just aft of the mainmast, and the cabin, 12 feet long, aft of that, with a companion-way at its rear. The stove is in the forward end of the cabin, and ballast is stowed under the floor of the cabin. At the mainmast the deck rises 6 inches for a quarter-deck. The stern-post rakes about 4 feet to the head of the rudder-post, and the stern overhangs 6 feet from the cross-seam. A smack of this class has a broad keel and draws about 7 feet forward and 8 feet aft. It generally carries a yawl at the stern and two dories on deck.

A large number of these little smacks are owned in New York city and vicinity by fishermen who bring their fish to Fulton market for sale. They are now generally built all along Long Island and in Connecticut, and

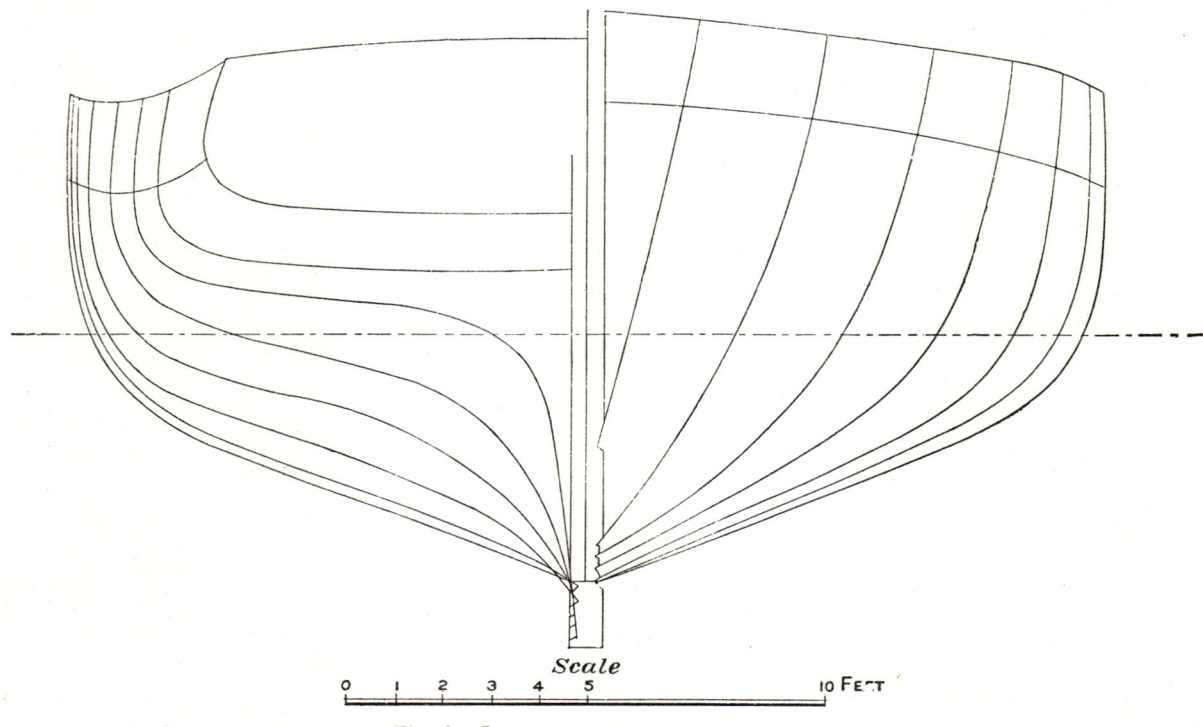

Fig. 9.—LINES OF THE FISHING SCHOONER.

being made of oak, locust, and the best pine, they do good service for from twenty to forty years. Formerly they were built in the ship-yards of New York city, where large numbers of smacks, both sloops and schooners, of great beauty of model have been constructed. Forty years ago the smacks of New York city were built with a tumble home to the top side, as in the illustration, and the bow raked sharply. The sides are now perpendicular amidships above the water, as in New England. The high price of labor in New York city has driven the business of building them out to country towns, as before stated. The smacks add little to the tonnage of the merchant marine of the United States, but their number is so great that they give employment to large numbers of carpenters on shore and of sailors on the deep. Any man who can build one of them right can build a good wooden ship of 2,000 tons register; and as long as they are built in large numbers the United States will not lack a handful, at least, of competent carpenters and builders.

In place of the schooners used on the New England coast for the capture of menhaden to make into fish-guano and oil there has been employed during the last five years a number of small-sized fishing steamers. These fishing steamers are sloop-rigged, but carry tug-boat engines and screw propellers. Seven were built at Boothbay and Kennebunkport, in Maine, and Noank, Connecticut, during the census year, ranging from 80 to 145 tons register. The hulls cost from $5,000 to $7,000, and the boilers and machinery from $6,000 to $10,000 each. The machinery, with propeller, weighs about 30 tons. Steamers have virtually superseded sailing craft in this particular employment.

FISHING VESSELS.

A brisk business is done in New England in building boats for fishing schooners. Formerly fishing was done entirely with hand-lines over the side of the vessel, and then the schooner only needed a yawl; but the method has changed during late years, and now the crew take along a number of small boats, and when they reach the cod grounds they scatter away in them from the vessel, each boat on "its own hook", and after a load is obtained the boats return to the schooner. This new method has developed the business of boat-building immensely, not only making a demand for what is needed to fit out new schooners, but also supplying the shop steadily with large orders in behalf of vessels already in commission. Fishing on the banks is a stormy and perilous occupation, as a great deal of heavy weather is encountered and the decks of the schooners are often swept clean of nearly everything on board by huge seas. There is a continual loss of boats in that and other ways, and the result is that a schooner seldom sets sail from the home port for a fishing trip without first having to buy from one to five or six boats for the occasion.

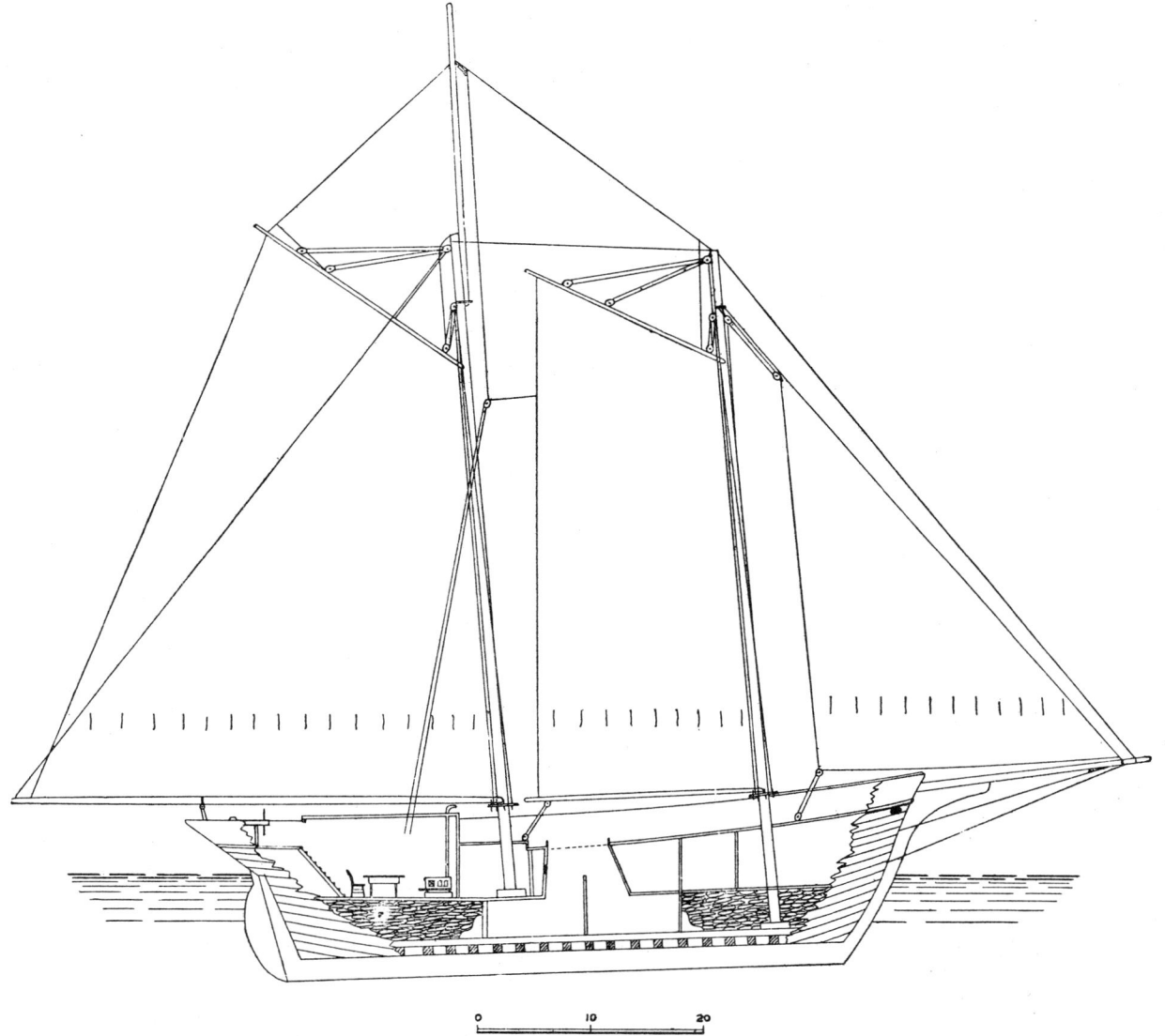

Fig. 10.—NEW YORK FISHING SMACK, 45 TONS REGISTER.

The boat now used is the "dory" (Fig. 12), a Yankee invention of most excellent qualities. It is built in five different sizes, designated by their length on the floor, viz: 12, 13, 14, 15, and 16 foot boats. The different sizes are used in different fisheries, the small sizes being used for hand-line fishing, the others for haddock trawling, and the largest of all for halibut. The boats carried by any one schooner are usually of the same size, for the reason that when the thwarts are removed the dories of a special size will stow away within one another in a "nest". Five or six boats will thus occupy on deck no more space than one boat. Sometimes one larger or one smaller dory is carried, and in that case it has to go at the top or the bottom of the nest. Experience has taught the best shape and sheer for a dory, and this admirable boat has reached almost perfection of form. The boats are swift, easily handled, capacious, and safe, and, if properly handled, are hard to capsize. Occasionally one will be tripped by a wave, but such an occurrence is rare; and there have recently been three instances in which some daring sailors crossed the Atlantic ocean to England in one of them.

The regular builders of dories are found at Cundy's Harbor and Portland, Maine; Seabrook, New Hampshire; and Salisbury, Newburyport, Essex, Beverly, and Gloucester, Massachusetts; but numbers of them are built in a small and scattered way all along the New England coast down as far as New York city by farmers and fishermen. The principal center of this industry is Salisbury, Massachusetts, where there are seven shops, each producing from 200 to 650 dories every year. About 200 are built at Gloucester yearly, 75 in Portland, 75 in Cundy's Harbor, and from 20 to 50 in each of the other places named. The large builders have the advantage of being able to buy a car-load of lumber at a time, by which means they get it cheaper and can sell their boats at a lower price. At Salisbury, in the census year, the stock for a dory did not cost more than $12 on the average, the expense of labor in building being $5 or $6. The boats sold for $18, $20, and $25 each. The business in the shop is organized in a way not seen in any other branches of boat-building, except in the few establishments (not exceeding twenty in the whole country) where ships' boats are built on a large scale. Each man has a special task to perform, as the getting out the boards for the floor, the planks for the sides, the frames, or other pieces, the fitting of the several parts of the boats into place, or the painting and finishing. Each one is paid by the piece, and the result is seen in a degree of rush and hurry in the large shops not noticed in other branches of the art. The boats are built in winter time, and the active work of the men serves to keep them warm in spite of the rather excessive ventilation of the barn-like buildings.

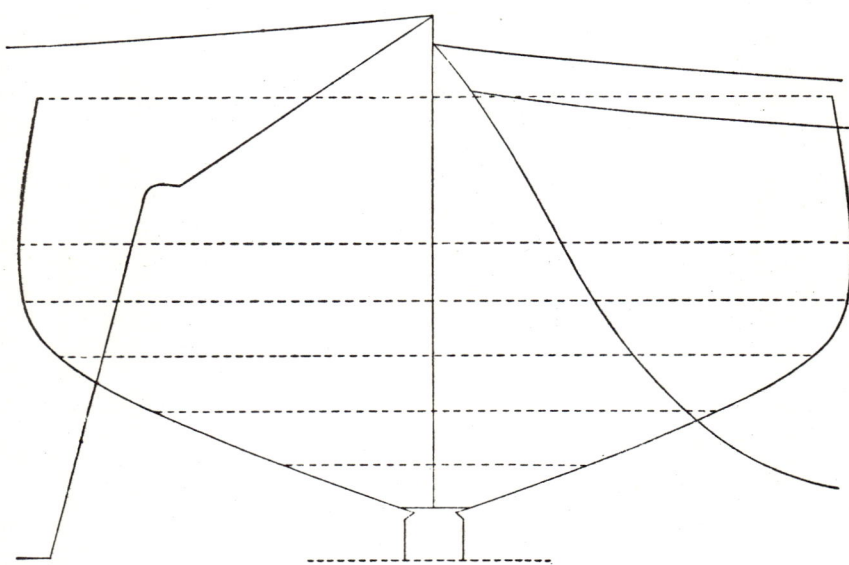

Fig. 11.—Outlines of midship section, bow, and stern of the sloop-smack "Prouta", built in New York in 1842.

The frames of the dories are spaced from 27 to 30 inches apart. They are of white oak, and are cut from natural crooks when the stuff can be obtained; but owing to the difficulty of obtaining the large supply of natural elbows required a patent iron dowel has been invented for uniting two sticks of oak into an elbow, and frames thus united are almost exclusively put into boats in the large shops. In making the dory the first step is to cut out the floor of the right length, width, and outline from two or three $\frac{7}{8}$-inch white-pine boards, grooved and jointed at the edges. The boards are driven tightly together and fastened by laying floor strips of oak across them midway between the places for the frames and nailing them strongly to the boards. As the bottom of the boat is to be given 3 or 4 inches sheer, the next step is to lay the floor on a row of blocks having just the sheer required. It is held in place firmly by poles reaching to the ceiling of the room. The frames having been meanwhile made, are put into position on the floor of the boat and nailed. The stem-post, with its knee, is placed, as is also the narrow V stern-board and its knee. The planking is of white pine about five-eighths of an inch thick, and is cut from planed boards with the aid of a wooden pattern or mold, the edges being beveled so as to lap. There are three streaks on each side of the boat. Builders are guided by personal taste in deciding whether to make the upper of the three planks of the side or the bottom one the widest, the practice varying; but a wide upper streak is held to make a handsome boat. The lower board is the first one put on, and is held to the frames by carpenters' set-screws until fastened. The other boards are then put on in order, being nailed to the frames, the stem-post, and stern-board, and to each other where their edges lap. The boats have about 14 inches sheer, but when built for use near shore and in comparatively smooth water they can be somewhat less crooked on top than that.

Thirteen-foot dories have two thwarts, with parting boards or bulkheads under them, to keep the fish from shifting about, and one pair of oars. A narrow batten, or "rising", is fastened to the frames for the thwarts to rest upon. Fifteen-foot or trawl dories have three thwarts and three parting boards, with two pairs of oars. The space aft of the after parting board is occupied by buoy lines, anchors, etc., and the seats are usually on the first, second, and third timbers. The bow and stern rake considerably. The top length of a 13-foot boat is 15½ feet; of a 15-foot boat, 19¼ feet. The sides flare from 12 to 15 inches amidships. Dories are very light for their size, the 13-foot size weighing about 180 pounds, the 14-foot 190 pounds, and the 15-foot 250 pounds. They float like an egg-shell on top of the water, drawing from 3 to 5 inches only, and it is possible to load them down to within 6 inches of the gunwale in safety.

A variety of other boats are built along the New England coast for fishing, some to go with vessels, others for alongshore use, primarily intended for rowing, but often having also some sort of a small fore-and-aft sail, with a pole for a mast that can be unshipped and taken down readily. The shore boats are for lobstering and fishing with hand-lines, seining, etc. They are regularly framed keel boats, usually open, and are sometimes clinker built and sometimes sharp at both ends. The seine boats are always sharp at both ends; they are rather full on the floor amidships, are well modeled at the ends, and are given a good sheer. On the coast of Maine some of the shore boats have a little cuddy forward, in which is placed a stove, to keep the men warm in winter, and also to prevent the lobsters

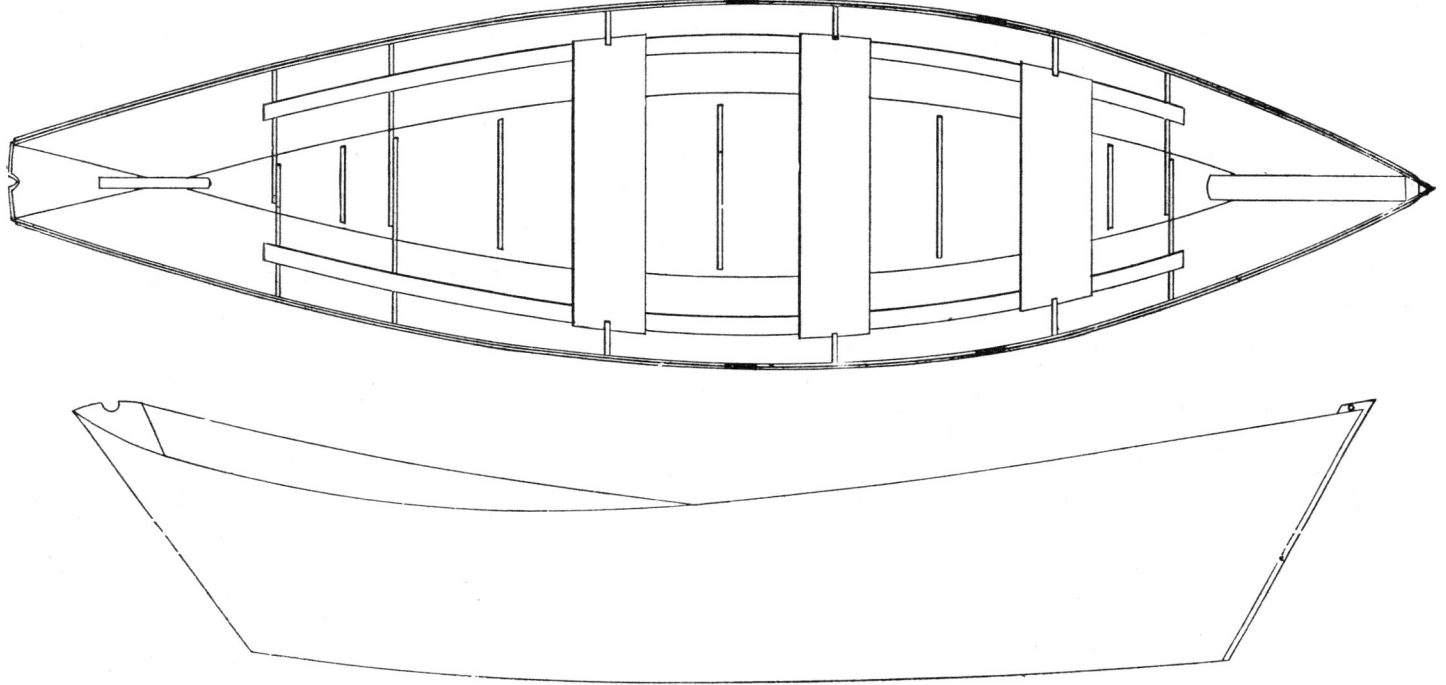

Fig. 12.—15-FOOT FISHING DORY.

19 feet 4 inches long over all; 22 inches deep; 31 inches wide on the floor; 5 feet 3 inches wide across the gunwales; 14 inches flare. Weight of boat, 250 pounds. Will float at 3¼ inches draught of water. At 9 inches draught will carry 1,200 pounds; at 13 inches draught, 2,000 pounds.

from freezing until they can be brought to shore and sent to market. The general model of the open boat is a legacy from early times. It came into existence at a very early period, owing to the exigencies of the peculiar calling in which it is employed, which has compelled the shore fishermen to adopt a boat suited to flat beaches and having the properties of light draught, buoyancy, stability, and stowage capacity for fishing apparatus and fish. The object of building the boats with sharp ends is to enable fishermen to launch and land through the surf with facility and to handle the boat in rough water with safety. The New England fishermen of to-day have been accustomed to this general model from childhood, and they pin their faith to it with the utmost tenacity. It is the model which forms the basis of the admirable boats used in the United States life-saving service. The crews of the life stations have been largely recruited from the sea-coast fishermen, and the bureau at Washington gives them the model they know so well and can handle with such remarkable skill. Whale and seine boats are the largest of this class of boats used in the fisheries. The seine boats of Gloucester are extremely handsome specimens of workmanship, and are now built 36 and 40 feet long; but the usual size is 34 feet long, 7 feet 10 inches wide, and 33 inches deep. They are fuller than a whale-boat, and can carry a net 200 fathoms long and 1,000 meshes deep. Extensive use is made of this class of boats in shore fishing. They consume a great deal of material in building, namely, 600 board feet of cedar, 230 feet of oak, 250 feet of white pine, 70 pounds of iron nails and bolts, 75 pounds of iron fittings, and 35 pounds of paint, and are expensive boats, costing from $200 to $250. The model bears so close a resemblance to that of the whale-boat that the one illustration, given elsewhere, will do for both.

Many keel-boats were formerly built in New Hampshire and elsewhere for Labrador fishing, but the business has declined of late years. In one shop in Seabrook, New Hampshire, that used to build a hundred boats per annum, only five were constructed in the census year.

On the Connecticut shore a large fleet of small flat-bottomed fishing boats are employed, called "sharpies", which have a family resemblance to the dory. These are fully described under the heading of "Oyster boats".

WHALING VESSELS.—The whale fishery was actively pursued in Europe before the settlement of America, the Biscayans and Basques being the first to capture this gigantic fish. Their earliest exploits were on their own coasts; but, becoming expert in handling the whale, they followed their game to the north of Europe by the middle of the fifteenth century, and in 1578 they had 25 large sailing vessels in the business. The Dutch, following the example of the Biscayans, also went into the business, and about 1650 had 200 vessels in this fishery, while the people of Hamburg had 350. The English also sent out whaling vessels, and by the time the coast of New England was settled the commercial value of the whale was thoroughly understood. The early visitors to America had a sharp eye to business opportunities, and finding that the whale was a native of the American coast they made repeated mention of the fact in the several reports of their voyages.

The first whaling in America was limited to securing such specimens of the fish as had died a natural death and had drifted ashore, cape Cod, the Massachusetts coast northward, Nantucket, Rhode Island, and Long Island being the principal localities where this business was carried on. Drift whales, as they were called, were always the property of the public, and the colonial government, the township where the whale came ashore, and the finder of the game divided the oil, etc., equally. The active pursuit of this profitable fish began, however, within twenty years after the landing at Plymouth. The first organized work appears, from the report of Mr. Starbuck, published in 1878, to have taken place on the eastern end of Long Island, at Southampton. Encouraged by the example of the Indians, who occasionally put out from the shore in their log canoes and attacked a whale with spears and arrows, the settlers built boats suitable for the purpose and chased every whale blowing in sight of land that it was possible to get. On Long Island, and afterward at Nantucket, a regular lookout was kept on shore. A mast was set up, and a watch kept from a platform built upon it; boats were kept in readiness to launch; and when a whale was seen to spout an alarm was sounded by shouting or by blowing a horn, and the boats were manned and launched and sent out in eager pursuit of the game. In calm weather these boats would sometimes venture almost out of sight of land—a dangerous proceeding, as it often proved—and many times they could scarcely reach the shore again. On one occasion 30 boats were out from Nantucket for whales when it began to blow and snow, and it was only after long and hard rowing and a desperate struggle with wind and tide that they reached land again in safety.

The boats first used were shallops, built after the fashion of ships' boats, but sharper. The first requisite in a whale-boat was speed, with its consequent ease in rowing, and the object was gained by making the shallop long and narrow, with keen ends and a sharp floor. The bow raked considerably, after the universal fashion of the day in vessels large and small, and the stern was sharp, but had a post or skag, on which the rudder was hung. It is probable that by the year 1700 this boat had reached nearly the form it keeps to-day; and by the time of the revolutionary war, large and a double-ender, it was a style of boat famous for its speed, lightness, and capacity. The accompanying cut (Fig. 13) is of a boat built in 1789 which nearly resembles the whale-boat of to-day.

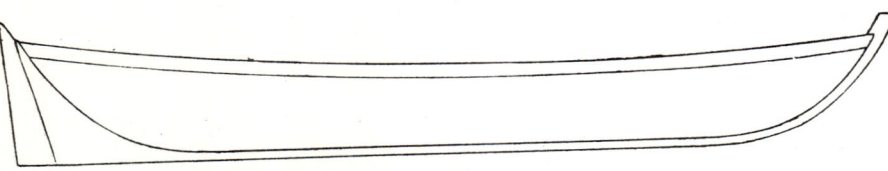

Fig. 13.—WHALE-BOAT OF 1789.

Whale-boats played a part in the war for independence, their size and speed making them useful to the Americans for warlike service, short expeditions, and quick surprises. The British took pains to destroy as many of them as possible in their raids on the Rhode Island, Massachusetts, and Long Island towns, and Sag Harbor, Newport, Warren, Rhode Island, Martha's Vineyard, Nantucket, and New Bedford suffered heavily from the capture and burning of large numbers of whale-boats, as well as of whaling vessels.

Living on an island, the people of Nantucket were obliged by necessity to own shipping for communicating with the main land. As early as 1694 they were buying sloops of from 15 to 25 tons measurement in Scituate, Salem, and Boston, and later at Newport and other towns in Rhode Island, the sloops thus obtained being used in cruising a little off shore for whales as early as 1712. In 1715 Nantucket had six small sloops, which in that year got 600 barrels of oil and 11,000 pounds of bone, worth £1,100. The catching of a sperm whale excited the people of Nantucket greatly, and they began at once to "whale out in the deep" with larger vessels for that species of the fish. Sloops of 30 tons were fitted out for cruises of about six weeks each, carrying two whale-boats, one with which to chase the fish, the other for use in case of accident to the first boat, and with only hogsheads enough in the hold to contain the blubber of one whale. Whenever a prize was caught they sailed for home again, and, unloading the sloop, they left the blubber ashore to be tried and immediately put to sea again. The people of Nantucket soon took the lead in whaling, it being their only means of support, and by training they became more expert and successful than their neighbors on other coasts. Sloops were also sent out from cape Cod, Sag Harbor, Boston,

FISHING VESSELS.

New Bedford, Rhode Island, Martha's Vineyard, New York, and Williamsburg, Virginia, along from 1750 to 1760, and from 1760 to 1775 whaling vessels grew in size and multiplied rapidly. It is not known definitely when the schooner was first employed in whaling, but that style of vessel was adopted as soon as whalers began to visit the West India islands and remained longer than six weeks at sea, as it was then necessary to have something larger than a sloop of 30 tons. Schooners are mentioned as early as 1760, and they soon superseded sloops for distant voyages. A number of brigs were added to them as early as 1770, and small barks were soon added. Voyages were then from two to ten months in duration. In 1770 Nantucket had 120 sail of from 75 to 110 tons register engaged in whaling. This fleet had grown in 1775 to 150 vessels of from 90 to 180 tons. In all the colonies at the outbreak of the Revolution there were owned 360 whaling vessels, registering 33,000 tons and employing 4,700 men at sea, besides the large number of people on shore who were building them, fitting them out, and repairing them. The vessels in the Greenland fisheries were of about 65 tons register, and it cost to build and fit them out about $3,000 each. The larger schooners, and the brigs and barks that sailed to the south Atlantic, were of 140 tons register on the average, and cost $6,500 each. The Revolution nearly destroyed the whale fishery of America, and in 1788 there were only 80 whaling vessels in the United States. This did not crush the spirit of the whalemen, however, and after the war the first vessel that carried the American flag into Great Britain was the Yankee whaler Bedford, which sailed up the Thames to London. After 1812 the business revived and increased steadily in importance until 1858, when there were over 700 American whaling vessels at sea, of 198,000 tons register, employing 17,000 men. The greater number of the vessels were rigged as barks and ships, and were each of 400 tons register; the others were brigs and schooners, the sloop having ceased to be used as a whaler shortly after the revolutionary war. Owing to the large size of these vessels, they were unable to enter many harbors where whalers had been fitted out in previous years, and the business had become concentrated at New Bedford, New London, and Sag Harbor, where the water of the harbors is deep. There was afterward some whaling from New York.

Whaling boats and vessels have been built chiefly at Nantucket, Newport, New Bedford, New London; Sag Harbor and Greenport, on Long Island; Provincetown, and Boston, and at a number of small villages along that coast which have carried on whaling to a small extent. Within the last 40 years the larger whaling vessels have frequently been built in Maine, and they are now built in Maine almost exclusively, chiefly at Bath.

Whale-boats continue to be built in New London, New Bedford, and Fairhaven, and at Provincetown and other places on cape Cod. The form and all the details of these craft have been closely studied, and the experience of 220 years has led to the production of a class of boats equaled nowhere in the world for their strength, lightness, speed under oar or sail, and seaworthy qualities. The model is substantially the same wherever in America the whale-boat is built. The early boats could not have been longer than from 15 to 20 feet. They were carried on the deck or at the davits of sloops and schooners, and 15 feet was probably the most convenient size. In later days they grew to 25 feet, barks and ships having from four to six of these boats at the davits when on the fishing grounds. They were narrow, and could have been placed inside of one of the boats now used. The whale-boat of to-day (Fig. 14) is either 28 or 30 feet long, 5 feet 8 inches or 6 feet wide across the gunwales, and from 24 to 26 inches deep amidships, with 16 inches sheer. It is sharp at both ends, with hollow lines forward and aft and a rather flat floor amidships; is fitted to be rowed with five or six oars, and is steered with an oar, put out aft over the stern. Formerly it carried a pole mast 12 feet long, with a small sail about three cloths wide; but now that the fish have become shy and are easily frightened by the splashing of the oars this boat is handled chiefly with the aid of the sail. It carries a 24-foot mast, mounted upon a hinge, so as to be conveniently raised and lowered, and has from 35 to 55 yards of canvas. A sprit sail is sometimes used, but as a rule the whale-boat has a regular sloop sail, with the boom reaching out over the stern, and sometimes a jib and a gaff topsail are added. Now that sails are employed so largely, the model of the boat has been altered slightly to correspond, and it has been widened several inches and made a trifle more full forward, so as to bear up under a press of canvas. A great many boats are also fitted with a center-board about 8 feet long and a rudder, which can be easily removed when desired. When under sail a boat is ballasted by five or six men sitting on the weather gunwale. Thus fitted out, a whale-boat can live in any weather, almost beat a ship for speed, and can cross the Atlantic ocean in perfect safety. It costs $90 or $100 to build a whale-boat, the material costing $45 or $50, and from 20 to 25 days of labor of a single man is required for its construction. To rig the boat costs $30 or $32, viz: 5 oars, $8 50; 24-foot mast, with sail, $8; mast hinge, $4; mast fasteners, $3 25; rowlocks, $6 50; jib and topsail, about $3 more. A large and specially fine whale-boat complete has cost as high as $212.

The stem, stern-post, keel, frames, and gunwales are of white oak; the thwarts, 5 or 6 in number, and the seats at each end, are of white pine; the planking is of white cedar, half an inch thick; and the keel is 9 or 10 inches wide amidships when pierced for a center-board, tapering to 4 inches at the ends, and is 2 inches thick. The keel is laid on building blocks on the floor of the boat-shop, and the stem and stern-post, with aprons, are fitted to their places with a scarf on the keel and secured in an upright position temporarily by wooden shores from the ceiling of the shop. Several molds of cheap 1-inch pine boards are then set up at intervals along the keel, the profile of each being a fac-simile of the section of the boat at the point where it stands. The molds are kept in place by narrow ribbons or battens (extending the whole length of the boat), which are nailed to them and to the stem and the stern-post. The outside shape of the boat is thus reached in skeleton form. The frames are not put in first, as in vessel building; they are put in last. The planking goes on first. Two gunwale streaks of oak are first put on each side of the boat, each one lapping over the streak below it, after which five or six streaks of cedar planking are placed on each side of the boat, completing the shell from keel to gunwales. The edges of these lower streaks abut squarely against one another, and are fastened, after the molds are removed, by running a batten 2 inches wide on the inside of each seam the whole length of the boat and fastening the edge of each plank at each seam to the batten by a row of nails driven clear through and clenched on the inside. The shell is completely built and

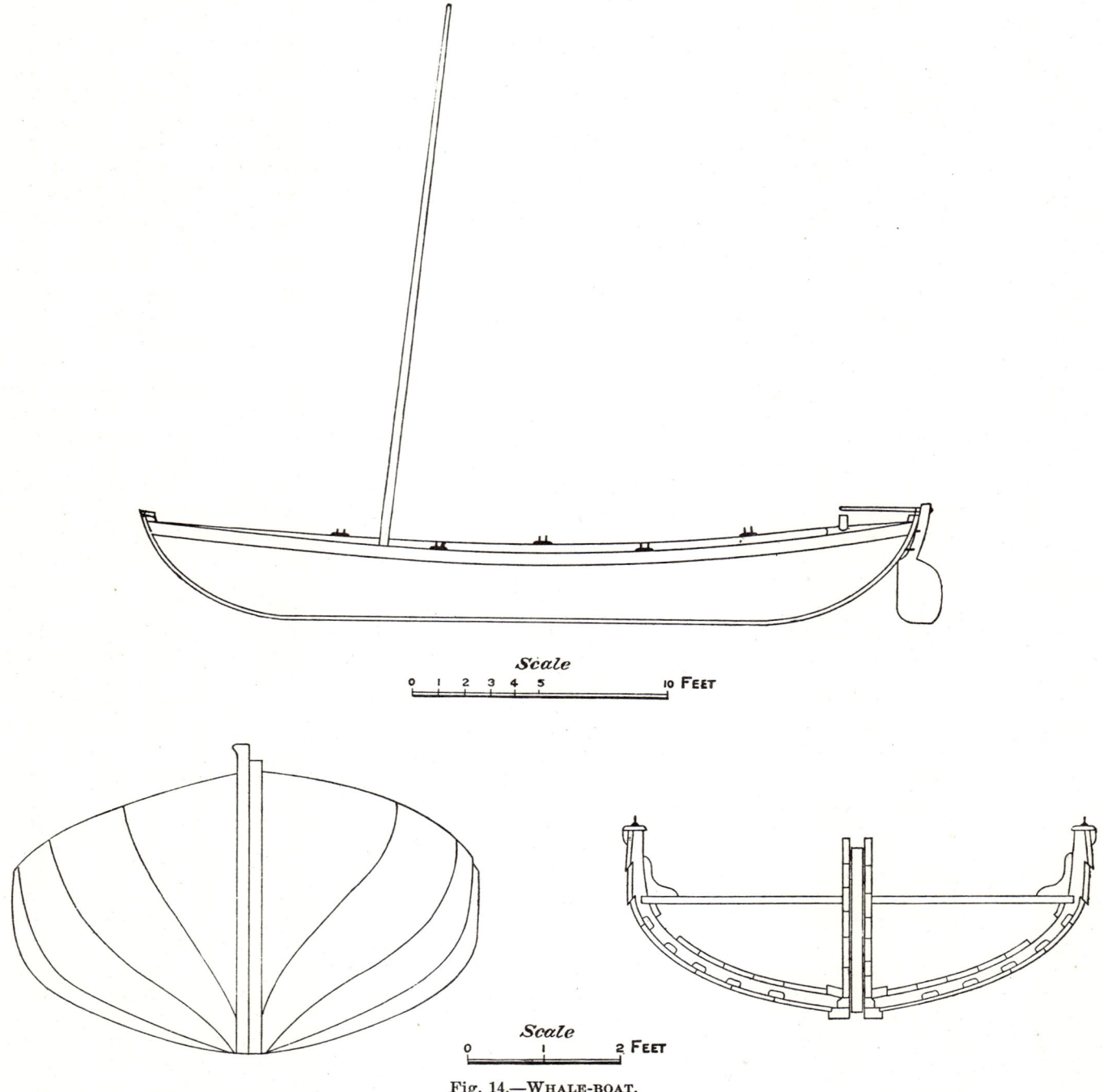

Fig. 14.—WHALE-BOAT.

30 feet long by 6 broad and 26 inches deep; 30 inches molded. Displacement to 19 inches draught of water above the keel, 7,100 pounds. Weight of boat with fittings, about 1,100 pounds. Coefficient of D., 43 per cent; angle of entrance at bow, 33°.

nailed before the transverse frames are put in, and the battens serve the double purpose of calking each seam and of forming a light and admirable system of longitudinal frames. Planks long enough to reach the whole length of a 30-foot boat cannot often be obtained; and if they could, it would make a great waste of material to cut them out from the boards, as each streak has to have a certain amount of curvature to fit conveniently to the curved surface of the boat. Each streak of planking is therefore made of two pieces, lap-jointed, the joints of one streak being carefully arranged so as to come nearly in the middle of the streaks above and below it. The ends of the planks are strongly nailed to the stem and stern post, and the garboard-streak is well fastened to the keel.

The frames are put in next. They are single frames, extending in one piece from keel to gunwale, and are made of oak, bent to the right curvature on molds after being thoroughly steamed. The outside edge of each frame is notched, so as to fit over the batten and laps of the planking. They are fastened with copper or composition nails, driven through the planking and clinched on the inside over disks or rings of the same metal. The frames are spaced from 9 to 18 inches apart, and a light keelson of oak is laid to cover and secure the heels of the frames. The boat is floored across the bottom and part way up the sides with pine. The thwarts, of pine, are then laid; the ends rest on a batten nailed to the frames, and are also secured with small cedar knees. If there is a center-board, the well for it is made in the same manner as all other center-board wells, large and small. An upright post is set in each end of the slot through the keel and nailed in place, and is then planked up the sides to the top of the posts. The mast step, rail, oar-locks, the bit of decking at the bow, the snubbing post, rudder hangings, and other finishing touches, are then added, and the boat is complete. From 150 to 200 board feet of oak, from 550 to 700 feet of cedar, and about 200 feet of pine, with 18 or 20 pounds of nails and 20 pounds of iron fittings, are required for the building of a whale-boat. The lumber wastes from one-fourth to one-third in cutting up. The boats are painted either a white or lead color.

The business of boat-building requires but little capital, a cheap shed near the water and $100 worth of tools and apparatus being all that is required. At the same time the business is a profitable one, and in every town that built whale-boats during the busy period, when over 3,500 hung at the davits of the whaling fleet in the service and several hundred new ones were called for every year, the builders were a prosperous class of men. William Smith, of New Bedford, and others each built from 100 to 120 boats a year, employing several of the finest mechanics, and not only paid high wages to the men, but received for their own work the very best compensation. The reduction of the whaling fleet to about 170 vessels, carrying not over 900 boats and requiring not over 150 boats yearly, has extinguished a large number of the boat shops which were active 30 years ago, and left those which are still open struggling to get along in a business in which there is sharp competition and little more to be made than a moderate day's wages all around.

In whaling vessels, as in boats, speed has always been desired; but seaworthiness has been the prime requisite, and schooners, brigs, barks, and ships have all been built with the latter quality chiefly in view. Large capacity has never been demanded, and whaling vessels have seldom exceeded from 250 to 400 tons register. Before the last war the whole fleet did not contain more than 20 vessels that approached 500 tons each, and it is believed that there was only one, the ship George Washington, which was as large as 600 tons. Those now employed are each under 500 tons, the size preferred being from 300 to 400 tons (Fig. 15). The problem which has occupied the builders has been how to make a strong, dry, seaworthy, good-going vessel, looks and every quality not specially needed in the whaling business being passed by. Above water the hulls have accordingly had a clumsy shape, owing to the large square stern, the full, round, flaring bow, and the large cut-water and figure-head; but under water they have always been of a well-considered and often extremely good model, sometimes quite sharp, both on the floor and at the ends, and never very full, a little narrower than merchant freighting vessels, deep, with the broadest beam, well forward of amidships, averaging two-fifths the length from the bow. Of late years lighter sterns, handsomer bows, and smaller cut-waters have been introduced; and the whaler has become as neat looking a vessel as any in the merchant navy, while retaining its satisfactory speed and good qualities in a sea way.

The New London, New Bedford, and Sag Harbor builders have always prided themselves upon the staunchness and durability of their vessels, as no material except the best was ever put into them. Whalers were usually constructed of oak throughout, except the beams, decking, and houses; and timber or planking with a flaw of any kind was instantly thrown away. Every bolt, rope, sail, seam, or part of the vessel on which its strength and safety and the lives and success of the crew depended has always been attended to with a degree of care not known in any other branch of the ship-building industry. The calking of the seams of the hulls was done with peculiar thoroughness, and the system of "heaving down" the vessel—that is, pulling her over on one side so as to strain open the seams on the other, which were then thoroughly calked, the hull being afterward coppered—was often practiced at New Bedford. The George Howland and the Roman were vessels thus treated, and it is said they sailed for 18 years without recalking. The length of life of the whalers has been remarkable, forty years being a usual and sixty not an uncommon age for them to attain; but they have been known to do good service for over seventy-five years, the ship Maria, of 202 tons, built in 1782, being one of the vessels of noted longevity.

The following specifications will show the scantling, etc., of a whaling bark of 310 tons, two decks, now in the service, a fair specimen of its class:

Length on deck, 115 feet. Breadth from outside to outside of planking, 27 feet. Depth of hold, 16 feet. The keel is of rock maple, in two lengths, sided 13 inches, molded 29, with a 3-inch shoe in addition. Stem, stern-post, apron, knight-heads, transom, and counter timbers of the best white oak; stanchions the best white oak, and to be made half tops. The floor timbers of the frame, white oak, with some maple; first and second futtocks and half of the forward and after cant frames of white oak, the remaider being of hackmatack; top timbers one-half oak, the others hackmatack. The frames are sided over the keel 22 inches and molded 13, being spaced 6 inches apart; at the gunwale they were molded 6¼ inches, diminishing to that point by nearly a true taper. Keelson, 14 by 14 inches, with a rider keelson 12 by 12 inches and a sister keelson each side of the main 6 by 10 inches, all well bolted through frames and into the keel with 1¼-inch galvanized iron bolts, and through the scarf of the keel with yellow metal bolts. The outside planking was of pitch-pine, except where a twist occurs, when the best oak plank was used. Garboards, 5, 4, and 3 inches thick; bottom plank, 3 inches; wales, 4 inches, fastened at the butts with metal bolts, and elsewhere with oak and locust treenails, those of locust driven clear through and wedged at both ends. Ceiling of pitch-pine, 3 inches thick on the floor, 5 inches on the bilge; two sets of clamps, 5 inches thick, under the lower deck beams; ceiling of sides to the main deck 3½ inches, with two streaks of 4½-inch clamps under the main-deck beams. Water-way on the end of the lower deck beams 8 by 10 inches, and on the upper deck 8 by 12. Lower deck beams, pitch-pine, 10 by 13 inches, secured at the

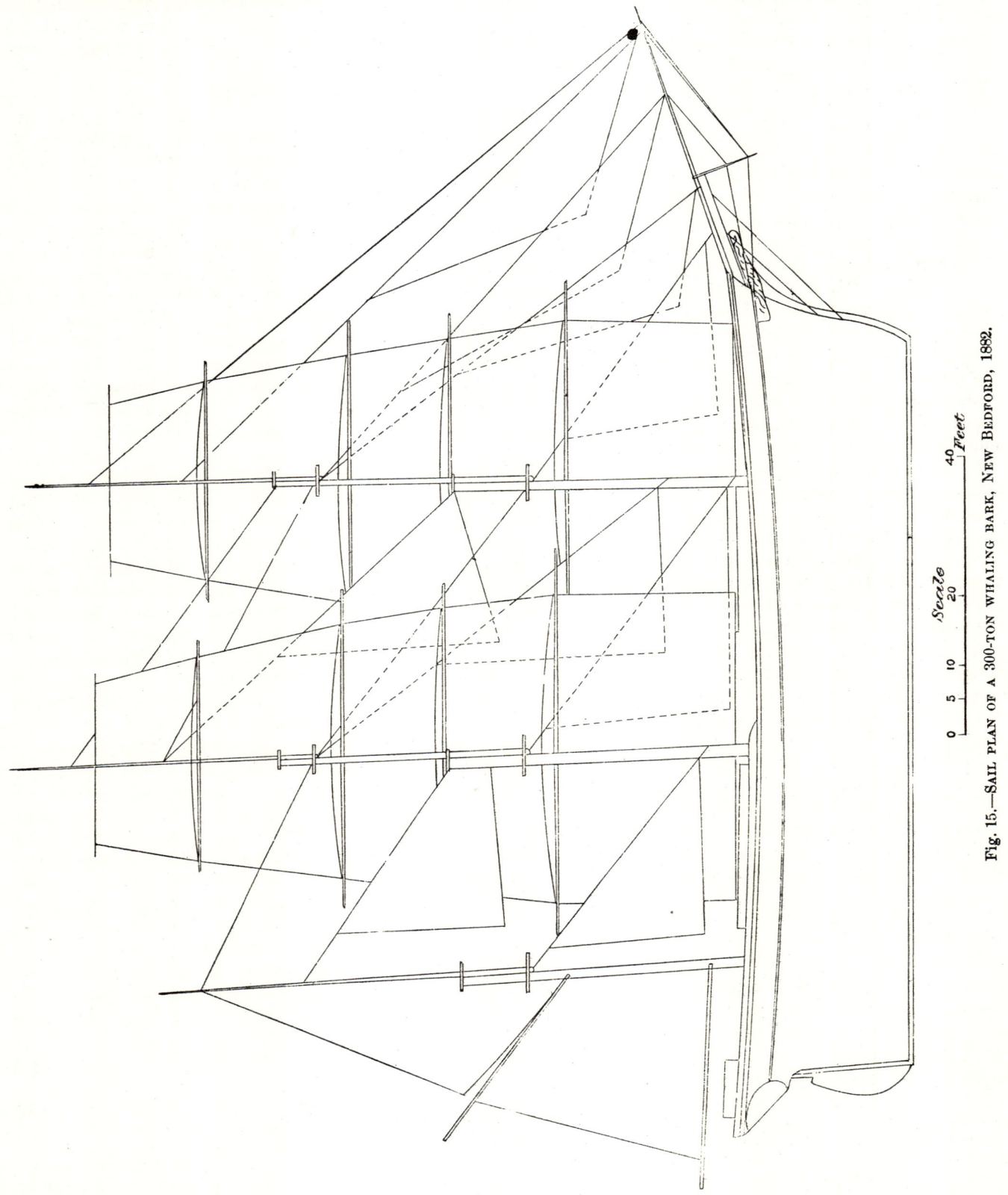

Fig. 15.—Sail plan of a 300-ton whaling bark, New Bedford, 1882.

ends by one hackmatack hanging and two horizontal or lodging knees, sided 7 inches. Lower deck plank 3 inches, same wood as beams. Main-deck beams, 8 by 12 inches at center, 7 inches thick at the ends, secured with three hackmatack knees at each end. The beams abut against a timber at each end, are bolted to the clamps, and are spaced about 56 inches apart. Knees are bolted heavily to beams, clamps, and frames adjoining. Main-deck plank, 3-inch white pine, of the best quality, the seams calked and pitched, with two spikes in each beam, the heads countersunk and the holes filled with wooden plugs, set in white lead. Plank-sheer and main rail, 4¼ inches thick, with "monkey" bulwark on top of rail. The bulwarks to be tight forward, but with gangways amidships, as is usual in whalers, and lower bulwark boards, hung on composition hinges. A small top-gallant forecastle deck at the height of the main rail, for working the anchor, etc. A forecastle house for the crew and cook at the the foremast, with a hurricane deck for the boats. The cabin aft, with skylight. Cut-water and billet-head of modern style; square stern, with spread eagle for ornament. Windlass bitts, 9 feet long, with 24-inch patent windlass gear; ends straight, with iron whelps. The hull to have two coats of good black paint. Two 8-inch stern and five 6-inch quarter lights. The vessel to be thoroughly salted from plank-sheer to light water mark with rock salt between the timbers before leaving the stocks. Two 1¼-inch iron anchor chains, 90 fathoms each, weighing together 8 tons net. Three anchors, 2,000, 1,600, and 250 pounds weight respectively. Rudder hangings, plates for bobstays and cabin stairs, and rail for cabin gangway of composition and brass. Wheel steering apparatus. The sails of the bark include four headsails (jibs and staysails); a lower, top, top-gallant, and royal sail on the fore and the mainmast, respectively; a spanker and gaff topsail on the mizzen-mast; a maintop-mast, a maintop-gallant staysail, and a mizzen-topmast staysail. The shrouds and great stays of 3½-inch wire rope; the running rigging of best manila. The vessel to be delivered to the owner complete, except the sheathing and coppering of the hull below the water-line, the boats, and the apparatus for trying out the blubber of the whale.

In the main, the scantling and fastening of the vessel are much heavier than would be required in the merchant navy to obtain on the books of the American Shipmasters' Association the class of A1, the highest given by the surveyors of the association.

All whalers are coppered to the load-line, the metal covering the keel, rudder, stem, and stern-post, as well as the planking, the object being to protect the bottom of the ship from the attacks of the teredo (a worm which burrows through the wood and completely honeycombs it with cells), and also to prevent it from becoming incrusted with barnacles and shells, which would greatly retard its motion through the water. The gradual corrosion of the metal by salt water causes the barnacles to shell off as fast as they become attached and keeps the bottom of the ship smooth. It was not until the latter end of the last century that copper was introduced as a means of protecting the immersed part of the hulls of vessels, and the expense of pure copper soon led to substituting in its place an alloy called "yellow metal", which was cheaper and answered the purpose as well. Zinc has also been used; but yellow metal has always been the preference of whalers. The metal is rolled in sheets 48 inches long and 14 inches wide and of a great many different thicknesses, about ten in all, although five only are used on whalers, the thicknesses being indicated by the weight per square foot, a whaler taking 18, 20, 22, 24, and 26 ounce metal. The process of putting on is as follows: The bottom of the hull is first made smooth; and if it is an old vessel, the worn copper is stripped off with chisels and adzes, the sails removed, and the surface of the planking is scraped clean, the old metal and nails being sent off for sale. The hull is then either sheathed with a light planking, or is covered with cement or graved with tar and papered or felted. The oldest fashion with whalers was the use of cement. Sheathing was also in vogue, and is still common; but papering or felting is the new idea, and is extensively practiced, as it is claimed that worms will not go through paper. The sheets of metal are meanwhile being prepared by punching either two, three, or four rows of holes along their edges for nailing them on. The heaviest thicknesses are put on at the bow as far back as the foremast at the load-line, but no farther aft at the keel than the forefoot. The metal of the next weight goes on aft of that, the after boundary of this thickness being a line from the mainmast at the load-line to the heel of the foremast at the keel, and grows lighter yet as the men work aft along the hull. The rudder and keel are both covered with heavy metal. The sheets lap one inch. A bark of 310 tons requires about 1,025 sheets of metal, weighing 6,300 pounds, and 770 pounds of composition nails; cost of metal in the census year at New Bedford, 16 cents per pound; cost of suit, including nails, $1,130; average cost of cleaning off the old and putting on the new metal, about 35 cents a sheet, or $358; but this varies with the amount of tarring and felting required by the fancy of the owner, as it is often as high as 45 cents a sheet.

The weight of copper required to sheathe a whaler varies a great deal. A vessel which is likely to be gone more than two years will take heavy metal, while those sent out for light service, or which are being economically equipped, are clad with lighter suits. The following suits were put on different whalers in the census year:

Weight of metal.	BARKS.				SCHOONERS.		
	440 tons.	420 tons.	310 tons.	380 tons.	180 tons.	130 tons.	66 tons.
	No. of sheets.	No. of sheets.	No. of sheets.	No. of sheets.	No. of sheets.	No. of sheets.	No. of sheets.
18 ounce	300	246	275	....	125	169	....
20 ounce	300	241	275	....	146	97	....
22 ounce	260	289	175	200	120	53	350
24 ounce	298	181	175	200	96	100	200
26 ounce	250	18	125	200	156	82	....
28 ounce	....	....	....	a 450	110	90	....
Total number of sheets	1,408	975	1,025	1,050	753	591	550
Weight of metal in pounds	8,839	5,946	6,300	8,130	5,221	3,835	3,654
Average weight per sheet in pounds	6 3/10	6 1/10	6 1/7	7 3/4	6 9/10	6 1/2	6 5/8

a 150 each of 28, 30, and 32-ounce.

The following is the weight of the different thicknesses of yellow metal and the number of sheathing nails to the pound:

METAL.		NAILS.	
Weight per square foot.	Weight of sheet.	Length in inches.	Number to the pound.
Ounces.	Lbs. oz.		
14	4 1	⅞	230
16	4 11	1	190
18	5 4	1⅛	186
20	5 13	1¼	169
22	6 7	1⅜	112
24	7 0	1½	105
26	7 9	1¾	74
28	8 2	2	64
30	8 12	2½	51
32	9 5	3	35

Whalers usually, but not always, go out with two suits of sails. A 200-ton schooner carries about 1,900 yards of canvas, the suit being worth $900, and a bark of 425 tons about 2,900 yards, worth $1,400. A suit is expected to last two years, and every whaler is expected to spend either $500 for the repair of sails or $1,300 for a new suit, $500 for repair of rigging, besides about $1,400 for recoppering, every time she returns from a two years' voyage, to say nothing of the carpenter work, boat work, etc., which must be done. Whalers are engaged in rough and perilous service, and come back storm-beaten and battered, bringing a vast amount of work for the shops in their native town and rich cargoes of oil and whalebone with which to pay the bills.

Within a few years steam has been employed in whaling with great advantage, in imitation of the Canadians, who have transformed nearly their whole sailing fleet into steamers during the last fifteen years. In July, 1879, the propeller Mary and Helen was launched at Bath, Maine, for Captain Lewis, of New Bedford, being the pioneer of its class. This vessel was 138 feet long on deck, 30¼ feet beam, and 16⅔ feet deep in the hold, registering 420 tons, and was rigged with a full suit of sails, having 2,850 yards of canvas, but carried coal bunkers and a small engine, with a screw propeller capable of driving her at the rate of from 6 to 8 miles per hour. The hull was made a trifle fuller to bear the increased weight. The Mary and Helen was built of oak, yellow pine, and hackmatack, cost $65,000 when ready for sea, and was a successful vessel. With her steam-power she could push her way among the ice floes, and was not dependent on a favorable wind while cruising in the fishing grounds. In June, 1880, the steam bark Belvidere was launched from the same yard in Bath for the same owners. She was 140½ feet long on deck, 31¼ feet beam, and 17 feet deep in the hold, registering 440 tons, and was furnished with a condensing engine, cylinder 22 inches, with 28 inches stroke, and a boiler 12½ feet long and 7 feet diameter, carrying 60 pounds of steam. The first ship was sold to the government for Arctic exploration, and a second Mary and Helen has been built during the present year to take her place. The new bark is 151 feet by 31 feet by 17 feet, registering 508 tons. She is built of white oak, pitch-pine, and hackmatack, has four sets of heavy pointers in the bow, braced across the vessel with heavy timbers, to strengthen her against the shock of ice floes, and carries the usual small propeller engine, and also two donkey engines in the forward house for handling the anchors and for general hoisting.

OYSTER BOATS.

As oystering is an inshore occupation, it only requires a small class of boats. The universal oyster boat was originally the Indian canoe, which was made from a white-pine log. In the beginning the early Americans simply imitated the example of the Indians in taking shell-fish, and oysters and clams were so abundant on the coast of Massachusetts, Rhode Island, and Connecticut that canoes were extensively employed by the white men in collecting them from the date of the very first settlement. This was especially the case on Narragansett bay and along the northern shore of Long Island sound, and the canoe was a good boat for the purpose, on account of its ability to withstand rough usage.

Roger Williams says that canoes were occasionally made by the Indians from the trunks of oak or chestnut trees, these being probably the larger and stronger ones. He says:

I have seen a native go into the woods with his hatchet, carrying only a basket of corn with him and stones to strike fire. When he had felled his tree, being a chestnut, he made a little house or shed of the bark of it; he puts fire, and follows the burning of it with fire in the midst in many places. His corn he boils, and hath the brook by him, and sometimes angles for a little fish. But so he continues burning and hewing until he hath within ten or twelve days, lying there at his work alone, finished, and, getting hands, launched his boat, with which afterwards he ventures out to fish in the ocean.

The Indian canoes were round on the bottom, partaking closely of the shape of the tree, and rarely carried sail. The white men improved the model as well as the methods of making, and generally used the trunk of the pine, on account of the superior lightness of the wood and straightness of the tree. With them the boats were made by hewing out the trunks and shaping the ends with axes, and many of them were used at New Haven to accompany the lighters and sail-boats which brought up the goods from trading vessels arriving at the mouth of the river. Their value is not known, but about 1640 the fine for stealing one was 20 shillings. With the clearing of the timber the use of canoes disappeared on every part of the New England coast, except in Connecticut, where they were favorites with the oystermen for 150 years after the time of the first settlement. Flat-bottomed skiffs came into use along with canoes after a while, but the latter have been built for use at the mouths of the Connecticut and Quinnipiac rivers down to within twenty years of the present time. When pine trees grew scarce builders went to the headwaters of the Connecticut river and made canoes in the winter time, rafting them down stream in the spring, Zebina Allen being noted for the large number that he made and brought down in this way. When that source of supply failed, one of the builders, Mr. John Smith, sought the banks of Cayuga lake, in New York, where large and tall pine trees were abundant, and returned every fall for a number of years with a fleet of from 20 to 30 canoes, which he sold at prices ranging from $30 to $75. Sometimes he made two trips a year, employing a number of men in the business. These canoes were of the shovel-nosed type, so called from

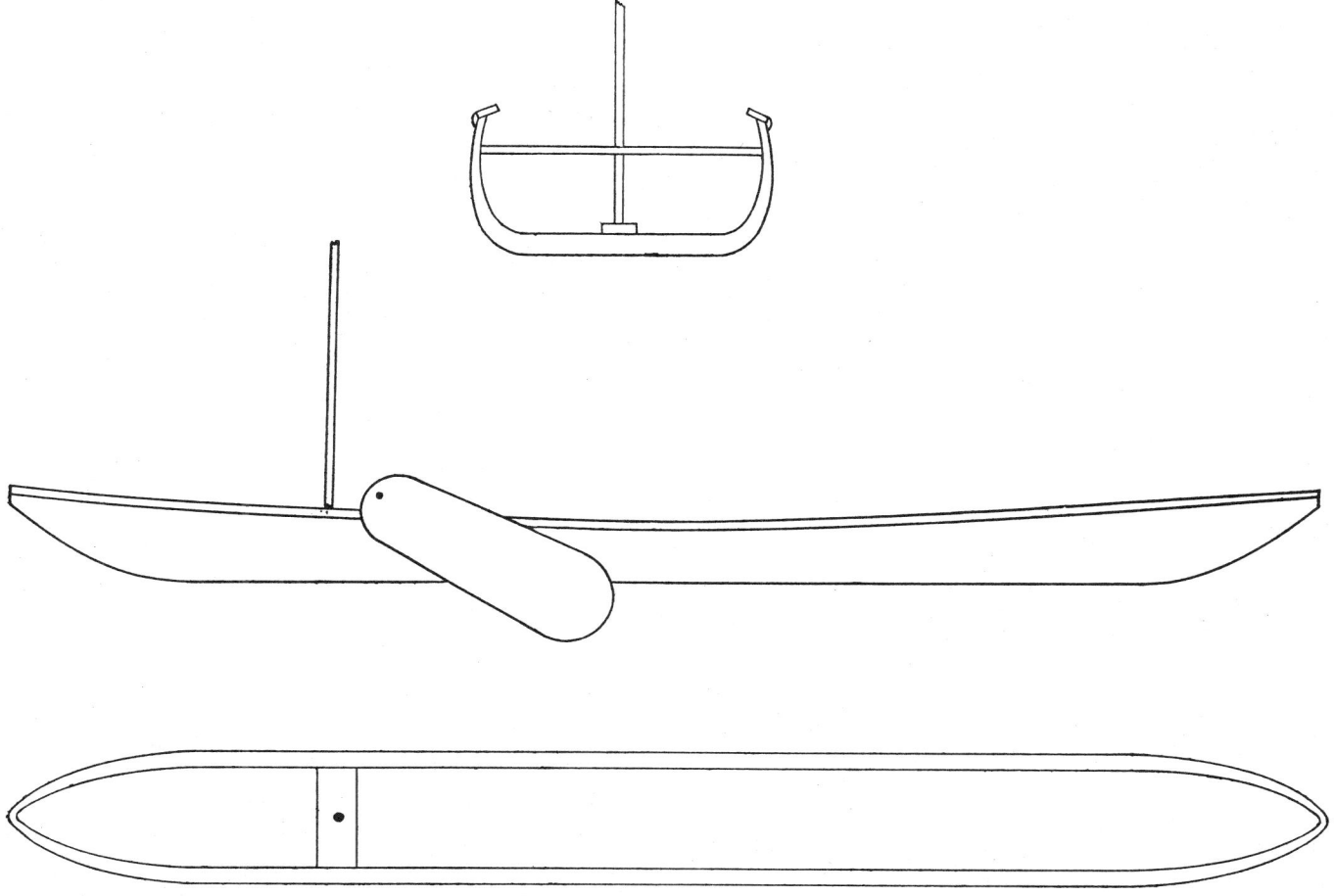

Fig. 16.—CONNECTICUT CANOE.
28 feet long, 3 feet wide, 15 inches deep inside.

the shape of the wooden shovel used in handling grain and flour. They were flat on the floor, having great stability, and were accordingly furnished with one or two light pole masts and sails. The average size was 28 feet in length, 36 or 39 inches beam, and 18 inches in total depth, the wood of the bottom being 3 inches thick, the sides 2½ inches. They were always made from single sticks of white pine, floated at 3 inches draught of water, and were able to carry two men and a ton of oysters in the shell at 9 inches draught. Owing to the flat bottom, and to the fact that three-fifths of all the wood of the canoe was in the thick floor and kept the center of gravity low, they were pretty stiff under a light leg-of-mutton sail. A few dozen of these boats are still seen at Fair Haven, on the Quinnipiac river, some of them being 35 feet long. When under sail they carry a lee board, which is dropped over the side just aft of the mast thwart, and is held by a rope and shifted every time the boat is put about (Fig. 16).

The flat-bottomed skiff followed the canoe. The clumsy shape of the original skiffs is suggested by the name of "New Haven flat-iron boats". They were pointed at the bow, were as broad aft as amidships, and were flat on the floor, with upright sides, having a little outward flare, two or three rowing thwarts, and rowlocks and rudder. They were easily constructed, were cheap and serviceable, and any boy who had learned to handle a hammer, brad-awl, and saw and to drive a nail straight could make one, no other tools being needed. The boards were brought from the lumber yard and were put together on the floor of the owner's woodshed or barn during the season when open-air occupation was light. A great many of these boats were owned by those living near the river side or the coast at an early day, and were used both for fishing and for carrying goods and passengers. When canoes became expensive the skiff came into favor, and as soon as the growth of the oystering business made it necessary to have boats of large size and broad beam an improved skiff became the popular model in Connecticut. The "flat-iron boat" was cheap and safe and drew very little water, which is all that can be said in its favor, as the broad, square stern neutralized the effect of the pointed bow and made rowing a difficult and tiresome occupation. The boat was short and had little capacity; but the remedy for these defects was found in increasing the length and in giving the bottom a gradual round upward at the stern, so as to permit the displaced water to flow in behind the boat easily, as it does behind a keel vessel with a good run, without retarding the forward motion in the slightest degree, and sometimes the floor forward was given a rise of 3 inches to help the speed. The sharper bow and the round upward of the floor at the stern have given this peculiarly American boat its good qualities and its name. It is now universally called the "sharpie" (Figs. 17 and 18), and is so good a fishing boat and so fast a yacht that it has been adopted in a great many other localities throughout the United States where the waters are tolerably smooth and a safe, comfortable, and capacious boat is required. The sharpie is at present the oyster boat of Connecticut, and is also a favorite for all general pleasure rowing on the rivers and lakes of that state. The regular boat-builders at Groton, New London, Norwich, Essex, and other places on the Connecticut river, and at Fair Haven,

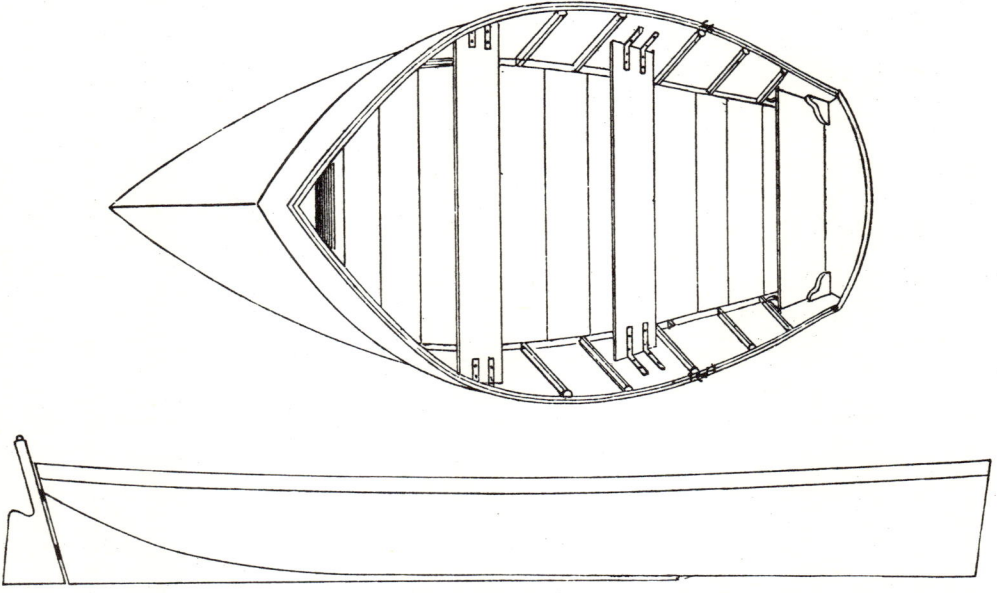

Fig. 17.—Rowing sharpie in Connecticut.

New Haven, Bridgeport, and South Norwalk, make as many as from 10 to 50 of this class of boats a year. A large number are also made by fishermen, one at a time, for their own use, and many are also made every year by young men for pleasure rowing and sailing, some getting out the stuff themselves from the lumber yard of the town, others sending to New York for it. If the immediate construction of a large number of sharpies were demanded by a sudden emergency Connecticut would be found to contain hundreds of young men (mechanics, clerks in stores, students, and others) who could at once build large and excellent boats; in fact, all through the United States the amateur boat-builders are by no means an unimportant element in the population.

The small sharpie for rowing is from 12 to 15 feet long, about 3 feet wide, and 18 inches deep, and has three thwarts. It will carry 3 or 4 men, and costs $20 or $25 to build complete. The bottom is made of 1-inch white pine, the sides of $\frac{5}{8}$-inch pine or cedar, the thwarts of 1-inch pine. The stem, 3 by 4 inches; bilge streak, 1 by 2 inches; frames, 1 by $\frac{3}{4}$ inches; and skag, $\frac{5}{8}$ inch thick, are made of white oak; the knees are of oak or cedar. These boats weigh from 150 to 200 pounds, and about 200 board feet of stuff is cut up in making them. The only tools required by the builder are a hammer, brad-awl, hand-saw, tenon-saw, jack-plane, smoothing-plane, rule, square, bevel, and perhaps a screw-driver, and the addition of a putty-knife and a paint-brush would make the kit complete.

The larger sharpies require no greater outfit of tools on the part of the carpenter, but they do call for more judgment in regard to the keenness of the bow, the rounding up of the stern, and the location of the various parts. Boats from 20 feet in length upward are usually made for sailing. The size used by oystermen would average about 30 feet in length; they vary, however, from 20 to 40 feet. The breadth of the boats is from 0.17 L. to 0.25 L., and the depth amidships about 0.11 L. in small boats and 0.06 or 0.08 L. in large ones, the proportions varying slightly with the fancy of the owners, some wanting large and capacious craft, others fast craft. In the latter case the beam is made narrower. A sailing sharpie carries a pole mast, and if more than 20 or 25 feet long two pole masts, without shrouds, except in a very large one, when one small wire shroud is rigged on either side of each mast. A center-board is generally fitted into a large boat, as also a narrow strip of decking, or wash-board, along by the gunwales, with a low hatch-coaming on the inner edge. The sails are narrow or pointed at the top, and are

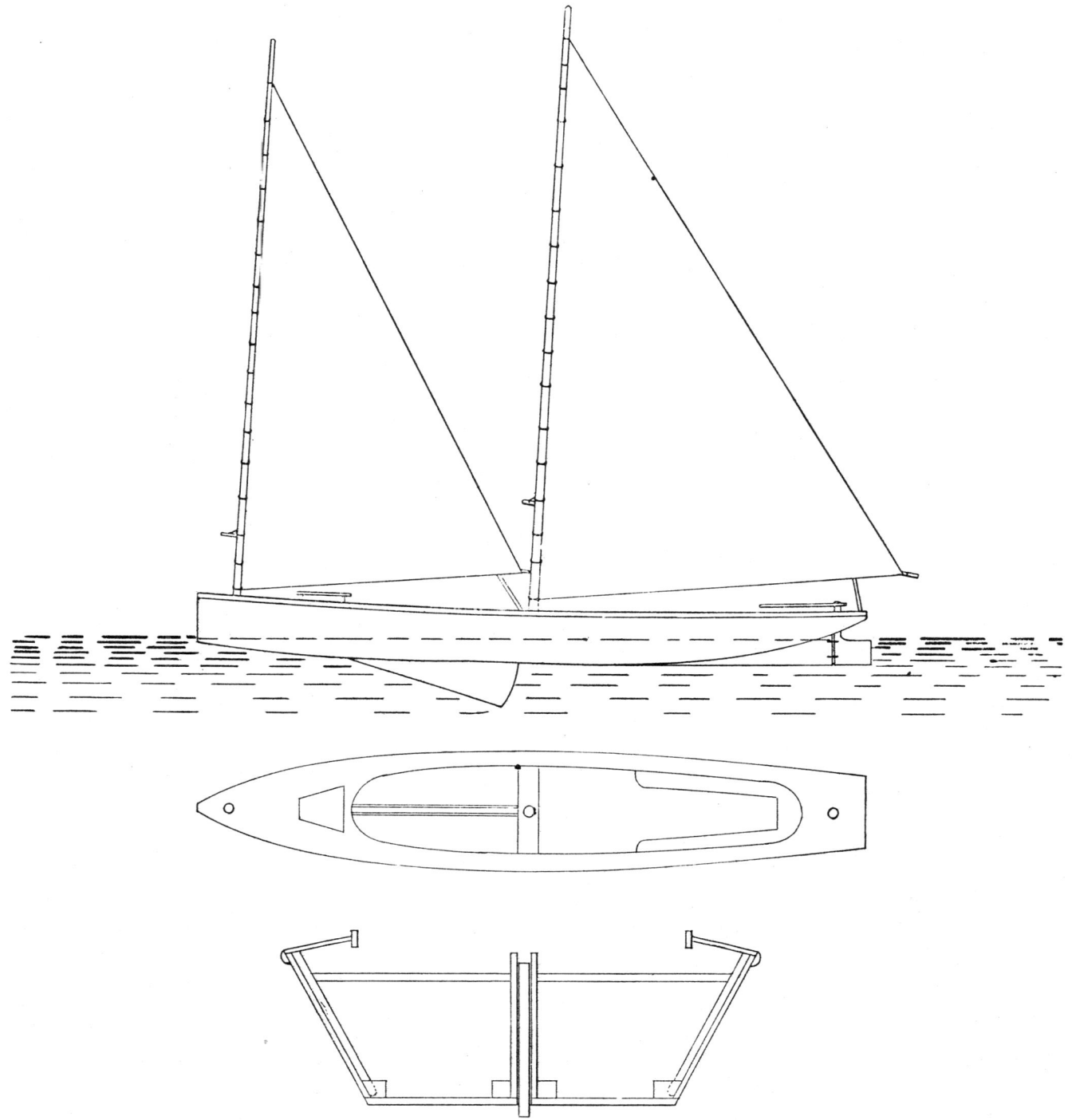

Fig. 18.—SHARPIE 35 FEET LONG, 6 FEET WIDE ON TOP, 4 FEET WIDE ON THE FLOOR, AND 2 FEET DEEP AMIDSHIPS.

spread at the foot by sprits in the smaller boats, but by booms in the larger ones. The sides flare 10 or 12 inches. In small boats the sides are each made of one plank; in deeper ones, of two planks, the sheer being given by the addition of a third and narrow streak forward and aft. They are made throughout of white pine, except the framing pieces, which are of oak or chestnut. The floor is invariably planked across the boat. The capacity and small draught of the sharpie are astonishing, a large one, with the addition of a cabin, and with everything on board, seldom drawing over 3 inches forward and a foot aft. Sharpies are admirably adapted for floating over the bars and shallows of the rivers and coasts of Long Island sound, and are stiff and seaworthy boats. They have been sent out for long cruises, and one drawing 12 inches has sailed in safety to the West Indies. Their speed under sail is one of their good qualities, and when matched against the deep-draught sail-boats and yachts which continually cruise through Long Island sound in the summer time they rarely fail to beat a rival of the same length. The sharpie is pre-eminently an oyster boat, but its speed has led to its introduction into yacht races and to its being now generally debarred from admission into such contests. Many experiments have been made with the model, and light-draught schooners, intended to run in the shallow rivers of the southern states, have been built of 200 tons register for the lumber and other trades; but for large vessels the model has failed to do what was expected. It is now generally understood that a sharpie should not be built more than 50 feet long, but the best results are obtained from 35-foot boats (Fig. 18).

Large sharpies cost from $200 to $400. A schooner-rigged boat of this class, built for racing on the Shrewsbury river, in New Jersey, fitted with cabin and berths, cost $500, the high price being due to the furniture in the cabin. For sharpies used in oystering the cost seldom exceeds $200. The principal place where the sharpie can be seen is is at Fair Haven, Connecticut, where at nightfall in the oyster season nearly 200 of them can sometimes be seen alongside of the wharves.

On the New Jersey coast there is nothing built except fishing and oyster boats, with occasionally a coal barge, from Staten island to the region of Barnegat and Absecom. At Amboy a great many oyster skiffs are employed by the fishermen of that busy locality, and probably 125 of them can be seen every day at nightfall gathering about the landing places on both sides of the Kill at that point. Two or three boat-shops are steadily engaged in their production. Unlike the Connecticut skiffs, these boats are regularly framed, and have a strip of flat bottom, tapering to a point at each end, with clinker-built sides nailed to frame timbers inside, placed about 20 inches apart, the sides being full and round and the stern perpendicular but V-shaped, as in a yawl. There are three sizes of these oyster skiffs, 18, 19, and 20 feet respectively. This is the length of the bottom. The boats over all are 4 and 4½ feet longer. The beam is about 6 feet, and the depth from 20 to 22 inches. The planking is pine or cedar, strongly fastened with copper rivets through each lap; the frames are roots of the white oak tree, selected as having the proper curvature naturally, squared and fitted to their places; and the bottom is floored over and the thwarts made removable, so that a large pile of oysters in the shell can be heaped up in the boat amidships. Most of the skiffs have a pole with small fore-and-aft sail, the mast being planted a little forward of amidships, but not in the bow. When there is a sail, there is generally a center-board also. About 250 feet of cedar are cut up for the planking and flooring. The boats cost $90 and $100 each, and one man with an assistant can make twenty of them in a year. The building of new boats and the repair of old ones is a pleasant and profitable local industry.

Farther down the New Jersey coast the fishermen use a light-draught sail-boat, which, like the dory and the sharpie, is an American invention, and goes by the name of the cat-rigged boat (Fig. 19). In England it is known as the Una boat, from the name of the first specimen of its class seen in England—a yacht built at New York and sent over in 1852. These boats are more complicated in their construction than any others in the oyster service on the northern coast. As a rule, they are built by regular carpenters; nevertheless, in New Jersey, as in New England, amateur boat-builders are numerous, and probably one-third of all the petty craft that sail in and out of the shallow harbors of this part of New Jersey, cruising with the guests at the beach hotels in the summer months and diligently employed in gathering oysters in the fall and winter, are the product of those who build chiefly for themselves. It is the saying in New Jersey that the first thing a boy learns is how to use a gun and go hunting; the next, how to sail a boat; the next, how to build one. A great number of these excellent cat-rigged craft have been made by mere boys, with the occasional advice of older heads.

The frames are cut from cedar roots. There is an abundance of material remaining in the woods, and the roots, being crooked, tough, and light, are desirable for the purpose named. With ax and spade a young man will in one day provide himself with the material necessary to frame a 24-foot boat. He digs out the stumps, sends them to the saw-mill, and has them cut into from three to eight slices, paying ten cents a cut. The stuff for the planking is bought from the nearest saw-mill, and is usually cedar, but sometimes it is oak. The keel and center-work are of oak; the decking of pine. Cedar planking cost $30 per thousand board feet during the census year—an average price—but during the war the price was $55. About seventy-five days' labor is consumed in building a 24-foot boat. The model of the hull is flat and full, the bow sharp, the beam broad, the run lean, and the stern above water is almost perpendicular, V-shaped, and broad on deck, being about two-thirds the width of the main beam. On deck the vessel is about the shape of a flat-iron. The proportions of the boats are, L. by 0.40 to 0.45, L. by 0.10 or 0.125 L. The narrower beam is adopted where speed is wanted. Each boat carries one mast, which steps right in the bow and stands perpendicular, rather inclining to rake forward, if at all, and spreads one large sloop sail, the boom extending several feet over the stern; it is decked over forward, leaving just enough of the center-board projecting beyond the deck to allow of its being worked. The decking is continued aft along the sides of the boat in a strip from 12 to 18 inches wide, and covers a few feet of the stern, leaving a large elliptical cockpit in the after part of the boat, with seats around the side for the passengers, and protected by a 6 or 8 inch coaming from the wash of an occasional wave. Several hundred pounds of ballast, in the form of stones, bars of iron, water casks, or bags of sand, are placed under the flooring of the cockpit and along by the sides of the center-board, and sometimes, but rarely, a cabin is built forward and partly over the cockpit.

FISHING VESSELS. 33

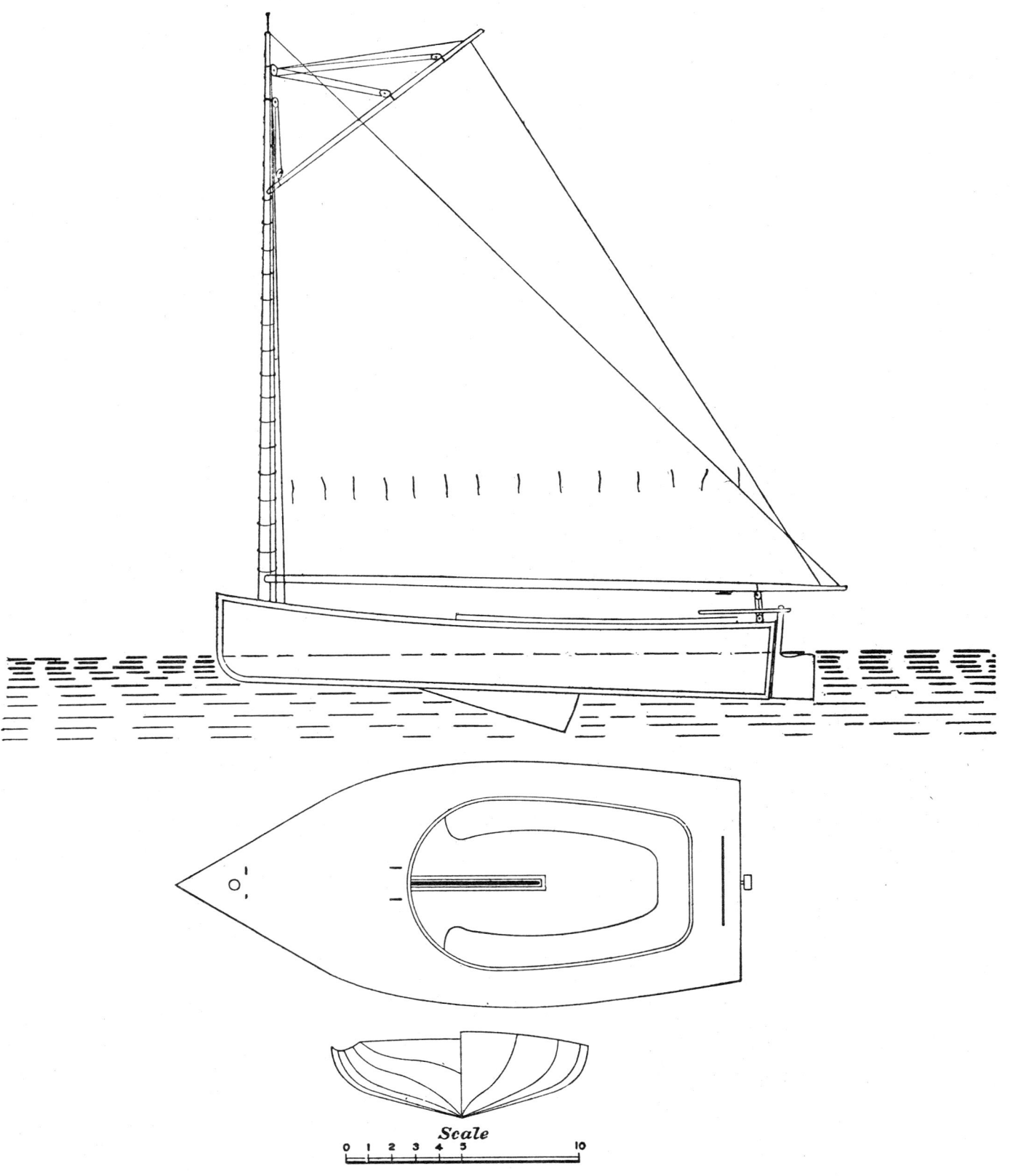

Fig. 19.—CAT-RIGGED BOAT.

24 by 11 by 3 feet. Broadest beam, $\frac{1}{10}$ B. aft of middle. Weight of boat, 1¾ tons. Will carry 3¼ tons on 18 inches average draught of water, and 4¼ tons on 2 feet average draught. Coefficient of D. to 2 feet from keel, 37 per cent.; of load water-line, 65 per cent.; of midship section, 56 per cent. Angle of entrance of load water-line at bow, 55°; of run, 75°; angles of entrance of vertical planes, from 9° to 12°; of run of same, 10° to 13°. Spreads 75 running yards of canvas.

3 S B

As already stated, the principal incentive for the building of these boats is the profitable oyster-fishing on the New Jersey coast; but of late years another has presented itself in the desire to sail on the part of the hundreds of people who frequent the beach hotels in the summer time for the invigoration which the cool air and salt water bring. No craft that skims the water equals the cat-rigged boat for either employment, as it can go almost straight in the eye of the wind, and for shallow waters and crooked channels is unsurpassed. In light airs it will speed by large yachts spreading clouds of canvas, and can beat up against the tide, by keeping close inshore, as no other sail-boat can do. It is manageable in squalls, is seldom capsized, and can carry heavy loads with very slight additions to its draught of water. In New Jersey it is the fashion when an oyster-boat has proved to be fast under sail to enter it in the yacht races in New York harbor, in order to make a record for its benefit; and then, should the boat win, its value, which is only $250 for oystering, would at once rise to $400 or $600 for yachting, and its owner would promptly find a purchaser at a high price.

The construction of a cat-rigged boat is ship-building on a small scale, and the man who can make one understandingly is fit to contract to build a vessel of large tonnage. The ordinary size is 24 feet over all, 11 feet beam, and 3 feet deep, being a little below 5 tons register, and consequently escapes the payment of custom-house fees. There are several hundred men on the sea front of New Jersey (farmers, carpenters, and fishermen) who have all the skill and knowledge which are needed for making this class of boats, and these constitute a reserve force from which good ship-carpenters could be recruited in time of need.

A good year in oystering is always followed by a busy year in the building of these handy and serviceable boats in New Jersey. During 1881 there were being built 8 at West Creek, 7 at Tuckerton, 4 at Greenbank, and others at various places in that region. In the vicinity of Atlantic City and Cape May, and around in the Delaware river, there were many other places at each of which 1, 2, or more boats were being made by both amateurs and regular builders.

The fishing vessels of Chesapeake bay employ large numbers of people on shore and a great deal of small capital in both new and old work. About 175 oyster boats are produced on the shores of the bay yearly, and there are 20 marine railways, costing from $3,000 to $4,000 each, for hauling the vessels out of the water for painting and repair, each doing from $2,000 to $5,000 worth of work yearly. Many of the boats, and indeed all the framed ones, are made in the yards of professional builders; but it is surprising to notice that, after all, about one-half of the whole number annually produced are to be credited to private builders, fishermen mostly, who make their own boats, either in the woods or in their own back yards. Give a fisherman a boat, and let him spend three or four years sailing it on the bay, gathering oysters and fish, loading his boat until its capacity is tested, going with his catch to market, hauling his boat out on the bank two or three times a year, painting it, calking the cracks, repairing it when injured, seeing it, in fact, in all possible lights, and comparing notes with his neighbors, and when the time comes for him to get a new boat the chances are that he will make the boat himself, knowing by that time all there is to know about how to do it; but if he should have it built for him, it will generally be because he is prosperous, and would prefer to spend his time in some other way than in boat-building.

It is on the Chesapeake that the log canoe has retained its greatest popularity in the United States, the preference for this style of boat dating back to the first settlement of the states of Virginia and Maryland. When John Smith arrived in 1609 with the pioneer colony he found the rivers and the bay swarming with dug-out canoes, which the Indians used for fishing, travel, and warfare. In his "Travels and Adventures" Smith says:

Their fishing is much in Boats. These they make of one tree, by burning and scratching away the coales with stones and shels till they have made it in forme of a Trough. Some of them are an elne deep and fortie or fiftie foot in length, and some will beare 40 men, but the most ordinary are smaller, and will beare 10, 20, or 30, according to their bignesse. Instead of Oares, they use Paddles and stickes, with which they will row faster than our Barges.

It was easy for the colonists to buy these boats from the Indians by trading, and they purchased them in large numbers for fishing and for traveling by water, as did their countrymen in New England in other years. The upper Chesapeake region was settled by colonists from England about 1635, and the lower part of the bay by people from the James river about 1650. The islands on the Maryland shore became densely populated early in the history of settlement, especially Smith's, Deal's, and Tangier's islands. From the necessity of their position the people were obliged to have the means of crossing the water, and from the earliest times they bought or made for themselves wooden canoes, each hewn from the trunk of one tree. Almost every family owned one, two, and even three boats, and the men were out in them the greater part of the time, taking the daily meal of fish for the family, traveling to and fro, or sailing off to market somewhere with a canoe loaded down with oysters and fish. A great deal of general trading took place in these boats. The inhabitants of the islands went to church in them on Sundays, and in fact the whole population, white and black, were used to owning and handling canoes, and knew how to make them.

Pitch-pine timber has always been abundant on the bay, particularly on the southern part, and it is from this tree that boats have been made. The supply has lasted for 250 years now, and there are still enough large trees to make all the canoes that are needed. Canoes played a part in the revolutionary war, and from that day to this there has never been any other kind of boat used on the Chesapeake for small fishing and oystering.

The durability of a pitch-pine canoe is great, one well made from a sound tree lasting from 30 to 50 years if cared for and painted every year.

FISHING VESSELS.

The ordinary canoe is 20 feet in length, 4 feet wide across the gunwales, and 18 inches deep inside. It is made from a single log, is straight in the bow, but is pointed at both ends. Formerly 30-foot boats, 5 and 6 feet wide, were also made in one piece. The famous "Methodist canoe", which carried "the parson of the islands" for so many years while visiting the members of his congregation, was one of these boats. The tree from which this canoe was hewn was too large to be useful at a saw-mill, and an Annamessex man finally bought it for $10 and felled it himself, the job occupying nearly three hours. Two logs were cut from the tree and hauled to King's creek, and then towed around to Annamessex, each log making a canoe, the larger one being the boat above referred to. Few of these big trees now exist, and therefore the larger canoes have to be made of more than one stick. When three logs are put into the boat, one is carved to make the keel, floor, stem, and stern, the other two forming the sides to the gunwale. Many are made of 5 and even 7 logs each, and others are carried up on the sides by adding two or three streaks of narrow and heavy plank, which are bolted through into the sides of the canoe. The 35- and 40-foot boats, which have from 6 to 11 feet beam, are generally carved from 5 or 7 logs, with top streaks as above described, the different logs being joined to each other by wooden keys and dowels and by treenails and iron bolts driven in edgewise. None of the smaller boats are decked, but all have an 8- or 12-inch wash-board, with a narrow coaming the whole length of the boat along each gunwale. This top work is supported by light knees spaced from 4 to 6 feet apart; and sometimes short crooked pieces, cut to fit the curvatures of the surface, are nailed along the bilge inside, to strengthen that part of the boat. A 35- or 40-foot boat generally has a short length of decking in the bow, and sometimes a small house. The thickness of the walls of a canoe is as follows: In a 30-foot boat, about 3 inches on the bottom, $2\frac{1}{4}$ or $2\frac{1}{2}$ inches on the bilge, and 1 inch at the gunwale, gradually thickening toward the ends; in the bow, $3\frac{1}{2}$ or 4 inches on the bottom, $2\frac{1}{2}$ to 3 on the bilge, and 2 at the gunwale. In a canoe of smaller size the thicknesses would be in proportion. In a large 7-log canoe building at Point Lookout, Maryland, in the census year, 40 feet long, 11 feet wide at the main beam, and $3\frac{1}{2}$ feet deep amidships, the wood was 5 inches thick near the keel, 4 inches in the bilge, and $2\frac{1}{2}$ and 2 inches at the gunwale, being a little heavier toward the bow. In a large boat there is often, but not always, a center-board, but there is seldom a center-board in a boat of less than 30 feet in length.

In rig these canoes are the most unique and interesting in the United States. A 20-foot boat carries one pole mast, with triangular sail forward of amidships; all others two masts, with triangular sails, the foremast being the tallest and raking $1\frac{1}{4}$ inches to the foot, the mizzen, which is two-thirds the length of the other, raking $1\frac{3}{4}$ inches to the foot. A 20-foot boat has no jib, but in a longer one there is often a 12-foot pole bowsprit, stuck up in the bow at an angle of 40°, with a horizontal line, carrying an odd-looking triangular jib, which is spread by a halliard tied to the mast about three-fourths of the way up from the gunwales (Fig. 20.) When the bow is decked over there is a short horizontal bowsprit with a long and narrow jib. The main and mizzen sails are spread by a sprit, and are furled by taking out the sprit and wrapping the sail around the mast. The rig is a safe and handy one. The center of effort is very low, and a canoe is consequently seldom capsized.

The model gives both speed and capacity. These canoes are very nearly flat on the floor amidships, and a 30-foot boat, weighing 2,000 pounds, will skim over shallows in safety, drawing, with keel, only 12 inches of water. The water-lines are hollow forward and aft, the after body being lean enough to give a drag of 6 or 8 inches. The keel is deepest at the bow, tapering from 5 to 8 inches at the fore-foot to 2 inches at the stern. The broadest beam is usually a trifle forward of amidships; but many place it in the middle of the length, and a few a trifle aft of the middle.

The builders hew out their boats with no other guides than the eye, sometimes aided by a rough draft on a piece of paper, and use no other tools than the ax, adze, square, callipers, two-foot rule, plane, auger, and hammer. A 20-foot boat costs from $50 to $60; but the price increases rapidly with the size, 40-foot boats costing $500 and $600 each.

A great many canoes are now made by farmers and their boys for other purposes than fishing. Near the cities of Baltimore, Annapolis, and Norfolk, and near many bay towns reached by steamboats, there are numerous farms devoted to the raising of melons and vegetables. Boats must be had to carry the produce to market, and rather than buy one the proprietors of these farms will often build; and it often happens that some smart farmer's boy, having thus become initiated into the art of canoe building, will continue the industry as a regular calling. It is usual for the builder of a canoe, professional or amateur, to go into the woods, select his trees, and buy them standing, paying a fixed sum per log, per cord, or per thousand board feet. Logs cost from $3 to $5 each, and the sum of $35 will buy all the trees needed for a 40-foot boat, worth, when finished, from $400 to $500. All the value over $35 is given to the boat by felling the trees, hauling them to a convenient stream, towing them down to the boat-yard, and then expending upon the materials the time and labor of the builder and his men. Sometimes the canoe is carved out of the felled trees in the woods and is hauled down to the water's edge when finished. The outside of the boat is first roughly formed with the ax; the inside is then carved out, the pieces are joined with keys, bolts, spikes, and treenails, and the thwarts, etc., fitted to their places.

A quaint and serviceable oyster boat has been evolved from the canoe by enlarging it, adding a long-pointed prow, and decking it over from end to end, leaving a large hatchway amidships, into which the oysters are thrown, and a smaller one aft for the steersman. There is no bulwark except a simple chock, or water-way, bolted to the top of the gunwales. This boat is the "bug-eye" (Fig. 21), a craft which has now grown so large that it cannot always be

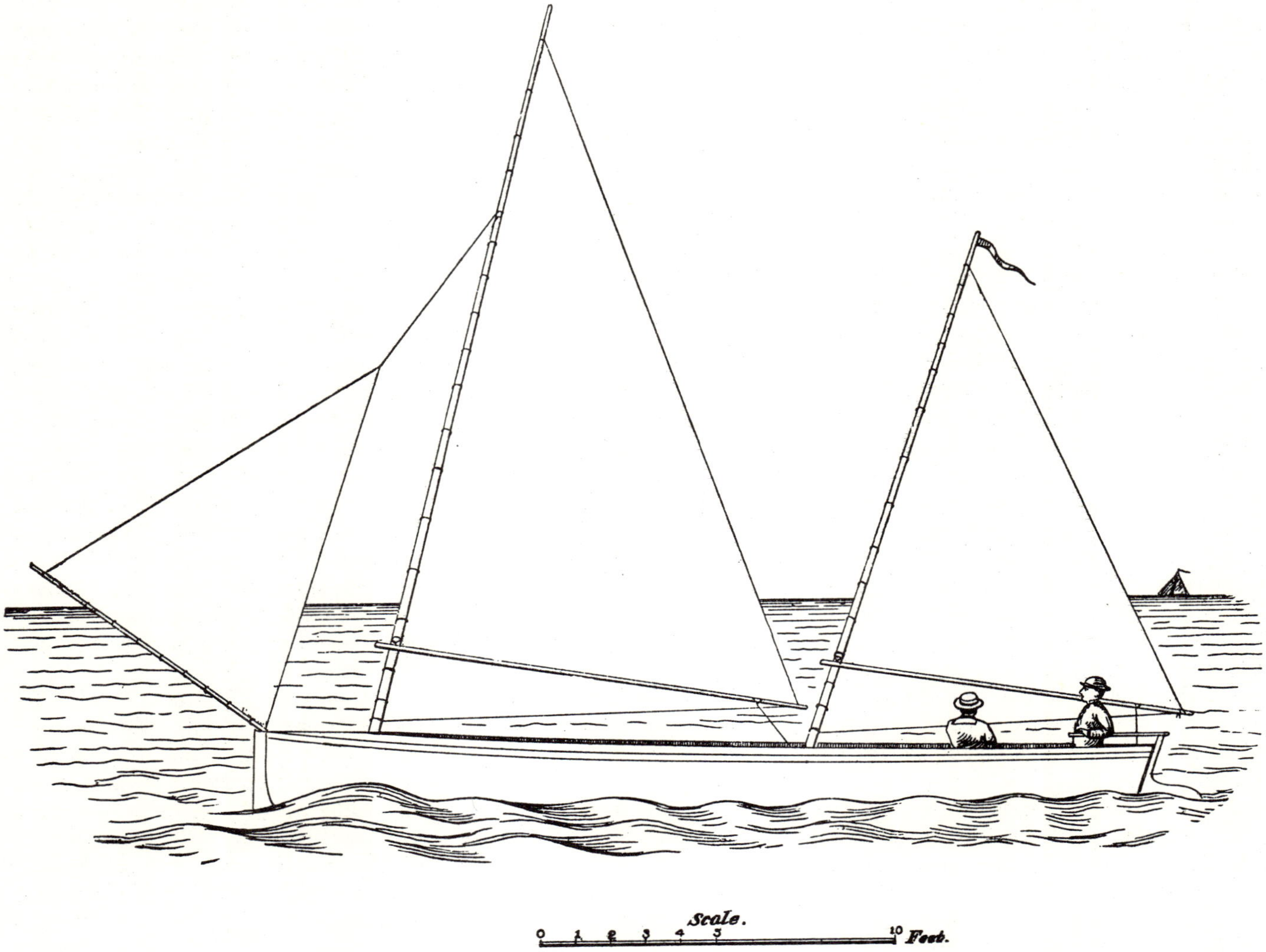

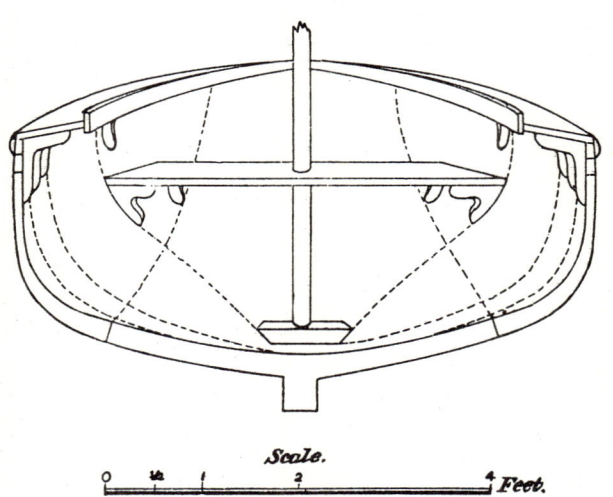

Fig. 20.—CHESAPEAKE BAY CANOE.

30 feet long, 6 wide, and 2¼ deep to top of keel amidships. Coefficient of D. to 18 inches from keel, 44 per cent.; of L. × B. × D. to 2 feet, 51 percent. Weight, 2,000 pounds. Boat will float light at 8 inches draught above keel, and on 18 inches draught will carry 2½ tons. Spreads 65 running yards of canvas. Angle of entrance at bow of load water-plane, 45°; of the planes below, 25°.

made of logs. A large number of "bug-eyes" are in use on the Chesapeake which are regularly framed and planked like other sailing vessels. The 5 and 7 log canoes—at any rate, all above 40 feet in length—are all called "bug-eyes", from their size, but the name itself comes from a peculiarity of the framed boat. The hawse timbers and knight-heads are carried up above the plank sheer, and when painted red the hawse holes look like eyes and the long prow like the beak of some strange insect or bird. In all matters of form and rig the large boat follows closely

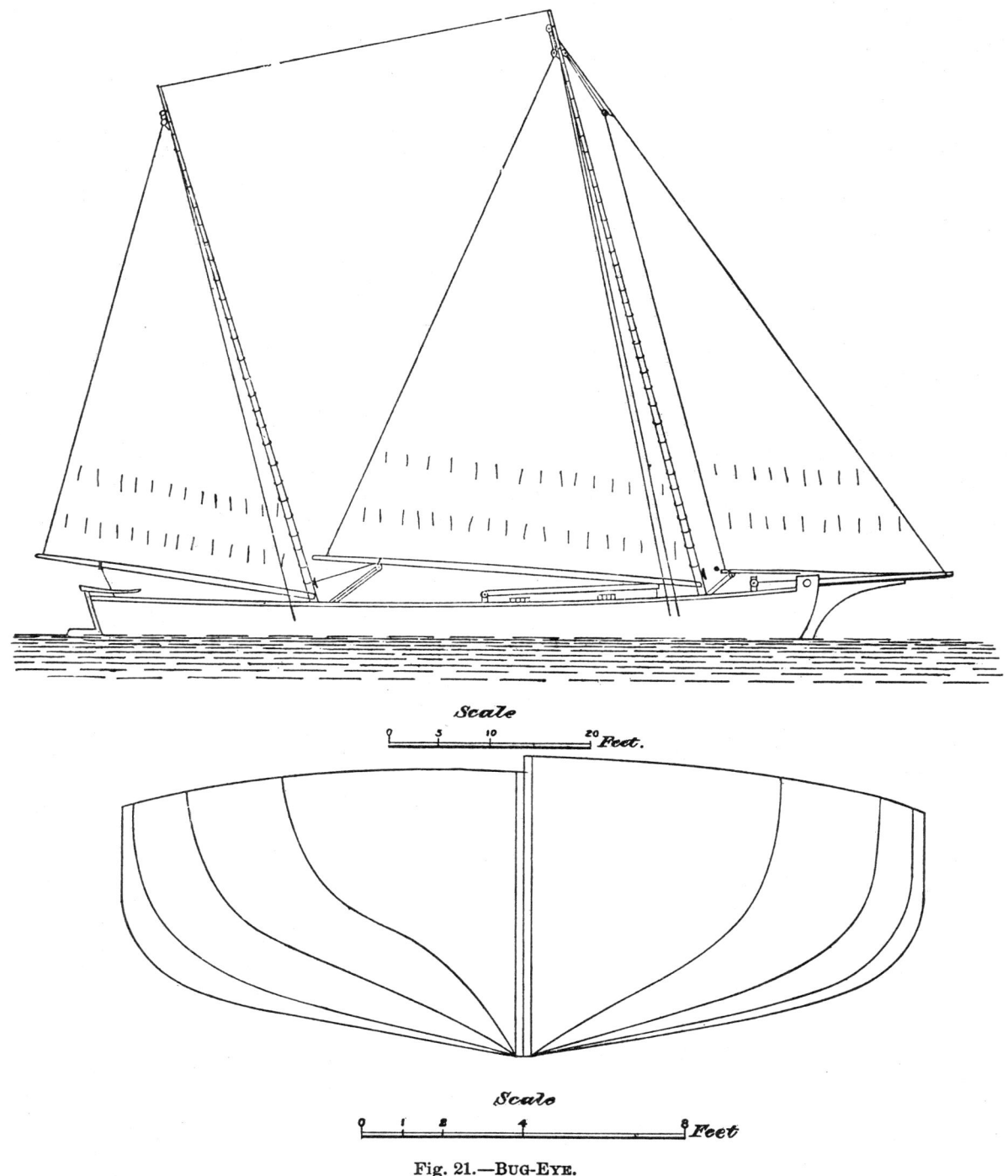

Fig. 21.—Bug-Eye.

72 feet long, 20 feet wide, and 5½ feet depth of hold amidships; molded depth, 6½ feet. Displacement to 4 feet above the keel, 84 tons; 2_{10}^{7} tons per 1 inch of immersion above that plane; coefficient of D., 45 per cent.; coefficient of load water-line, 0.72 per cent.; of midship section, 0.76 per cent. Angle of entrance at bow, 65°; below, 50°; angles of run, 55° and 25°.

all the peculiarities of the canoe. With its large center-board, however, it can sail closer in the wind. The latter boat does better with the wind on the quarter. A few years ago some adventurous Chinamen came to America in a native junk, and the strange rig excited amusement wherever it was seen; but the Chesapeake bay "bug-eye", though a better boat than the junk, is equally as curious and interesting a craft as that which came from the celestial empire.

The average proportions of "bug-eyes" are L. by 0.27 L., by 0.08 L. The boats vary somewhat, however, as will be seen by the dimensions of the following four:

	Length.	Width.	Depth.	Tonnage (approximate).
	Feet.	Feet.	Feet.	
Raven	48	13	3½	8½
Minnehaha	56	11½	2¾	8
Virginia G. Holland	60	18	5	25
Bug-eye now building at Solomon's island, Maryland	72	20	5½	45

The increased tonnage of the larger bug-eyes is due in part to the houses built upon them. Bug-eyes made from logs carry 200 or 300 bushels of oysters each and cost from $600 to $800, while the framed boats cost from $1,500 to $2,500, according to size. Fishermen much prefer those hewn from logs, if they can be obtained, as the hulls are heavier and have greater stability with a smaller quantity of ballast. Each has to carry 2 or 3 tons of ballast, and sometimes more.

The bug-eyes are increasing in size year by year; and it is a singular fact that just as the old "pinkie" sail vessel, inherited from the Europeans, has disappeared from New England, owing to a preference for other boats, a new, original, and purely American "pinkie" has sprung into existence on the Chesapeake, bidding fair to come into great and extended popularity.

The new vessel now building at Solomon's island is of the largest size yet built. As above stated, it measures 72 by 20 feet, being 5½ feet deep. The keel is 64 feet long. It is 14 inches square at the center-board, tapering to 4 inches at each end. The frames are hewn from flitch oak timber 3½ inches thick, the double frame measuring 7 inches by 6 over the keel, tapering to about 3 inches at the gunwale. The keelson is of white oak, 4 by 6 inches, and white-oak boards 2 inches thick are used for planking and ceiling. The deck-beams are of pitch-pine, 5 by 7 inches, spaced 2 feet apart; the decking of 2-inch pitch-pine. There are no bulwarks to a bug-eye, but the boat in question has a wide 4-inch waterway of pitch-pine spiked on top of the frames at the gunwale, with a log or chock, 4½ inches by 6, bolted on top of it. The center-board is 16 feet long. Twelve feet from the bow stands the foremast, 68 feet long, with a 38-foot boom to the sail. The mizzen-mast is 60 feet long, and there is a 14-foot bowsprit, with jib. This vessel is designed to carry 1,400 bushels of oysters, or about 75 tons of cargo, on a draught of 5 feet of water forward and 5½ feet aft.

Oyster canoes are built on nearly all the peninsulas jutting out from the woodland counties of Maryland and Virginia into Chesapeake bay and on the fishing islands. The principal counties are Dorchester, Worcester, Somerset, and Wicomico, in Maryland, and York, Mathews, and Northumberland, across the bay. At Crisfield, in Somerset county, a little fishing town built on a solid bank of oyster shells about 50 rods wide by 150 rods long, there are more than 1,100 fishing vessels owned, 700 of them being canoes not large enough to register at the custom-house. The Crisfield boats have nearly all come from the rivers of the lower Chesapeake. The canoemen are numerous in the vicinity of York, Gloucester, and Pocoson, Virginia. The Pocoson builders make the finest models.

It is a fact of interest that the colored men of the Chesapeake bay region are becoming large owners of oyster boats.

FISHING BOATS IN THE GULF.

The fishing interests of the lower Atlantic coasts, though not so important as those north of the capes of Virginia, nevertheless employ a large number of small vessels. These consist of small sloops and schooners, built for light draught, and large enough to meet the needs of the local markets. In Florida dug-out canoes are seen on many of the rivers. The majority of the 1,058 fishing boats of the state are to be looked for principally at Key West and Cedar Keys and all along the tier of islands that skirt the lower coast. At Key West there are owned about 100 vessels ranging from 5 to 25 tons, costing from $500 to $4,000 each, employed in the sponge business; about 25 vessels of from 35 to 50 tons for deep-sea fishing, with sharp bottoms and wells to carry the fish alive to market, costing from $4,000 to $8,000 each; and about 300 boats of less than 5 tons register, for sponging and other fishing, costing from $100 to $500 each. In addition to this fleet there are about 25 vessels used in farming; that is to say, in freighting the produce of the coast and river farms to market. At Cedar Keys, Apalachicola, and other points similar but smaller fleets are owned. The smallest boats are either cat-rigged or canoe-rigged, and the Chesapeake cut of sail and jib is often followed; the fishing boats which venture much out into the open sea are, however, as a rule, either sloop or schooner rigged, and the larger ones are all fitted for sailing to Havana with their cargoes. These boats meet with much heavy weather, and, on the other hand, are frequently becalmed, and they need both to be good sea boats and to be able to spread enough sail in light airs to carry them as fast as may be under such circumstances. The schooners carry no foretop-masts, imitating in this respect the fashion preferred among fishing smacks at New York. The sponging and farming vessels are usually flat on the floor amidships, with sharp entrance and run, and have center-boards; all the rest are sharp built throughout, are all fast sailers, and resemble northern boats in most respects.

FISHING VESSELS.

The ship-building business in Florida and along the Gulf coast is confined almost entirely to this class of vessels. As is common on all fishing coasts, much of the building and repairing is done by non-professional carpenters; but there are also a considerable number of regular and skillful carpenters, who find constant employment in their trade all through the fishing regions. The reason why these men do not build large vessels is not for the lack of the requisite skill and experience nor the absence of good framing timber, for excellent vessels can be made entirely of pitch-pine, with live oak for the principal pieces. Vessels can be cheaply built, too, on that coast, owing to the low cost of native timber, the drawbacks to extended ship-building being the preference of insurance companies for white-oak framing timber and the fact that shipping enterprise has not yet fully awakened among the merchants of the South.

A number of varieties of wood little known in the north are put into the fishing vessels of the Florida coast. The frames are usually made of Madeira-wood, a light, tough, lasting timber that grows on the keys, and cannot be found so good or in such abundance any nearer to Florida than the Bahama islands. Horse-flesh dogwood, mastic, live oak, and pitch-pine are also put into vessels. The planking and decking are generally of pitch-pine, worth $25 or $30 per thousand board feet; but spruce is preferred for spars. Florida-built boats last about 30 years; with good care, longer.

The proportions of the average boat in Florida are L. by 0.35 L., by 0.11 L. depth of hold; but the beam varies from 35 to 45 per cent. of the length, according to the fancy of the owner. The following are a few of the size built in the census year, the dimensions being those for custom-house tonnage:

SLOOPS.

Length.	Breadth.	Depth.	Tonnage.
Feet.	*Feet.*	*Feet.*	
39.0	13.6	3.6	13.00
26.2	11.5	3.1	5.13
14.2	11.8	2.6	5.90

SCHOONERS.

31.8	15.40	3.80	10.00
39.6	15.00	4.40	13.10
46.8	19.90	4.00	10.80
30.7	10.75	2.75	5.75
37.6	13.00	4.25	12.77
37.5	14.60	6.00	16.80
32.4	10.70	3.30	6.17
28.5	10.30	3.00	5.80
37.5	15.60	4.80	15.36

Farther down the Gulf, especially in the vicinity of New Orleans and on the lakes and rivers surrounding that city, a popular boat with fishermen is the lugger (Fig. 22), and this is the only locality in the United States in which that ancient style of boat is still employed. The cause of this is doubtless the fact that the oyster, fish, and fruit trades demanded the employment of small boats; and these trades are largely carried on by men of Spanish and Italian descent, who have brought to America their ancient ideas and fashions. In modern ship-yards on the Calcasieu, Pascagoula, and other rivers of that region, on Lake Pontchartrain, and at Shieldsboro', Mississippi, large numbers of these little vessels are built every year, some of them large enough to register; but at New Orleans the preference is for Louisiana-built boats, there being an old law which exempts them from tolls and wharfage dues. The framing timber is sometimes but not often live oak, but red cypress and pitch-pine are preferred for the whole vessel. The cypress is light, tough, and durable, and is worth about $22 per thousand board feet; pitch-pine about $25 a thousand.

In model the luggers are sharp, and are mostly keel-boats with a yawl stern. The yard is hung at about one-third of its length on the mast, and experience teaches exactly the right proportions of the sail to go forward and abaft the mast. The yard is secured to the mast by an iron ring, and is hoisted by a halliard, rove through two double blocks, one at the mast-head and one at the yard.

The following are the custom-house dimensions of some of the large luggers built in the census year:

Length.	Breadth.	Depth of hold.	Tonnage.
Feet.	*Feet.*	*Feet.*	
32.6	10.6	3.1	5.31
37.9	11.4	3.4	7.29
36.1	12.1	3.4	7.42
35.1	10.7	3.2	5.42
39.8	12.4	3.6	8.35
37.7	12.2	3.2	7.20

Four schooners were built in Louisiana in the census year of from 8 to 35 tons register.

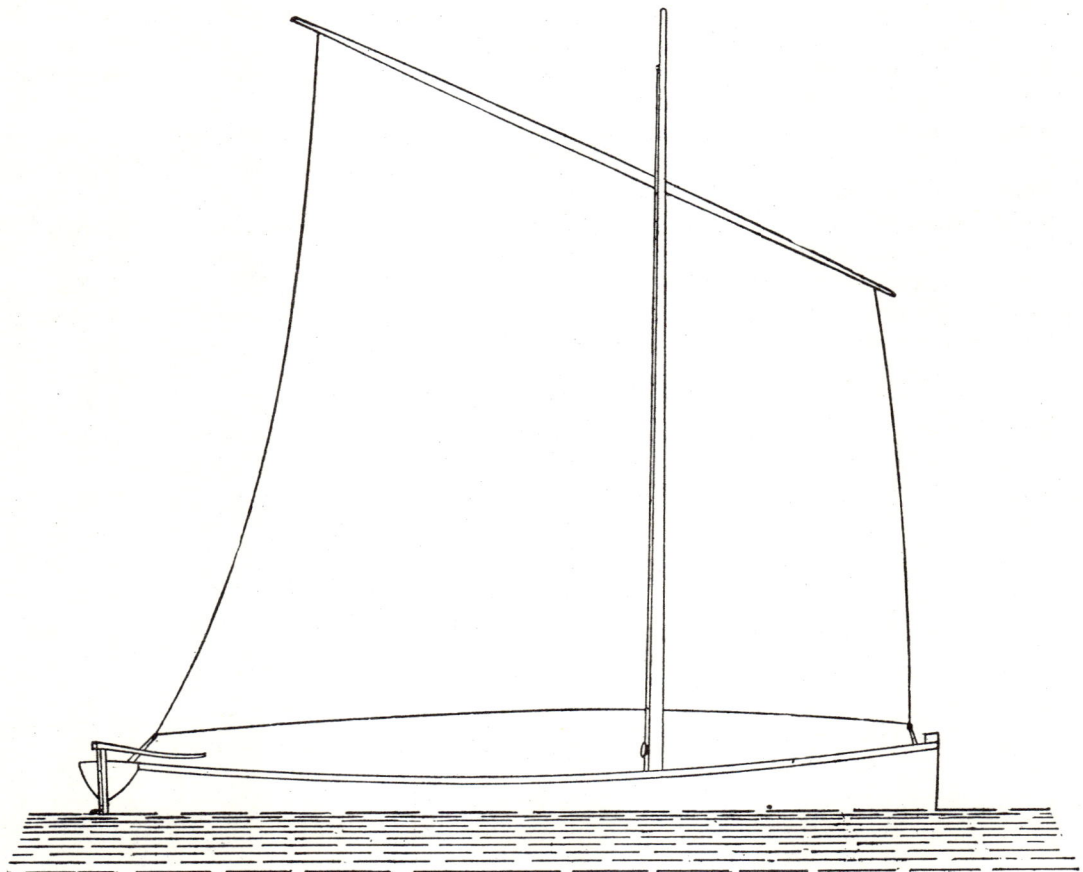

Fig. 22.—LUGGER OF THE LOUISIANA COAST.
35 feet long, 10¼ feet beam, 3¼ feet deep inside.

ON THE PACIFIC COAST.

The lateen sail is seen in America only on the Pacific coast, where it has been introduced by people from Mexico and Central America. The small fishing business of San Francisco is carried on almost exclusively by men of foreign birth, who have brought with them a unique and beautiful style of boat rigged with one mast and a lateen sail (Fig. 23). About fifty vessels of this class are employed in San Francisco bay, each of them just below the size which would make it liable to a tonnage tax, namely, less than five tons. They are from 20 to 35 feet long, have a beam one-third their length, and are from 2½ to 4 feet deep. The model is the nearest approach to a Norwegian pilot-boat of anything built in America for practical use. It is peaked at both ends, and is very sharp on the floor, with hollow water-lines forward and aft and a deep, thin keel. The stem and stern are both perpendicular. The boat is decked and has two hatches, the larger one amidships, into which the fish are thrown, being closed with a hatch-cover when necessary. The apparatus and the "confusion" of small things used by the men are stowed under the forward deck. Aft there is a small hatch, or well, in which the steersman sits. The mast is from 12 to 20 feet in length, and is planted a little forward of amidships, raking sharply forward, after a fashion peculiarly and solely its own. A long, slender yard spreads the sail; but when 30 feet in length the yard is made of two poles, spliced or lashed together at the end. A halliard is tied to the yard somewhat forward of the point where the sail will balance, being about two-fifths of its length from the forward end, and is carried through a sheave in the head of the mast. There is sometimes a bowsprit run out horizontally through a hole in the low forward chock, or gunwale, which is secured with staples, and in this case the boat carries a narrow jib. Rowlocks are placed on each side for 4 or 5 oars. With from 800 to 1,500 pounds of stone ballast aboard in the after hold such a boat dances lightly over any wave, and is good, fast, and seaworthy.

On the Sacramento and other salmon rivers of California quite a different style of boat is in use. There are about a hundred scows on the Sacramento river with houses upon them, in which the fishermen live with their families; but the flat-boat is the popular style, being the old-fashioned fishing punt in principle, flat on the floor, rising at the ends, with the bow and stern square across. The gunwale plan is a rectangle with slightly rounding sides. For description of the flat-boat, refer to the chapter on the vessels of the Mississippi and Ohio rivers.

To complete the review of the fishing vessels of the ocean coasts of the United States the canoes (Figs. 24, 25) of the far Northwest may be mentioned. These are the native boats of the Indians of Puget sound and Alaska, and

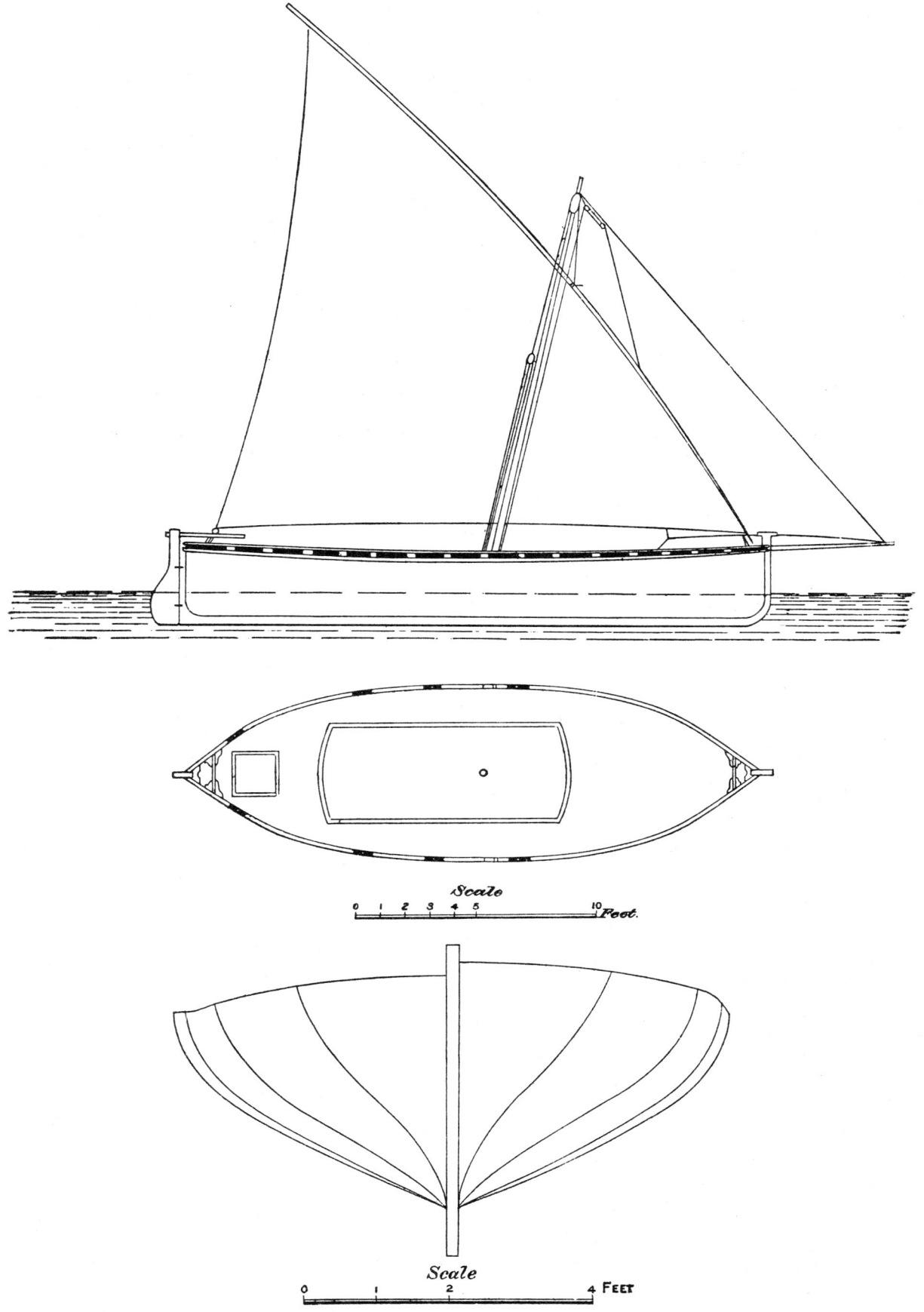

Fig. 23.—SAN FRANCISCO FISHING BOAT.

24 feet long, 7¾ feet wide, and 2¾ feet deep. Weight of boat with outfit and ballast, 2,500 pounds. The boat will float at 14 inches draught above top of keel, and will carry from 1 to 1½ tons of general cargo. Angles at entrance and run, 60°; on the load-line, 30° below; coefficient of D. to ⅗ of depth, 34 per cent.

figure conspicuously in all the boat fisheries of that wild region. The immense war canoe at the Centennial Exhibition, decorated with grotesque images of hideous gods and animals in red, green, blue, and black paint, and now permanently placed in the Smithsonian Institution, in Washington, came from this region, and has the general appearance of all Indian canoes. Its dimensions are: 59 feet in length, 8 feet beam on the gunwale, 4 feet 8 inches in width on the floor, and 3 feet depth amidships. Only war canoes are decorated with painted pictures, however, the fishing boats, as a rule, being simply painted black outside, with green or brown, or no paint at all, inside, while the channel in the peaked prow and the eyes in the prow and stern are painted red. The striking peculiarity in the form of the canoes is the long projecting prow, which bears a quaint resemblance to the outstretched neck and head of a deer. Sometimes the stern is equipped with a similar projection, but usually it is cut off short perpendicularly.

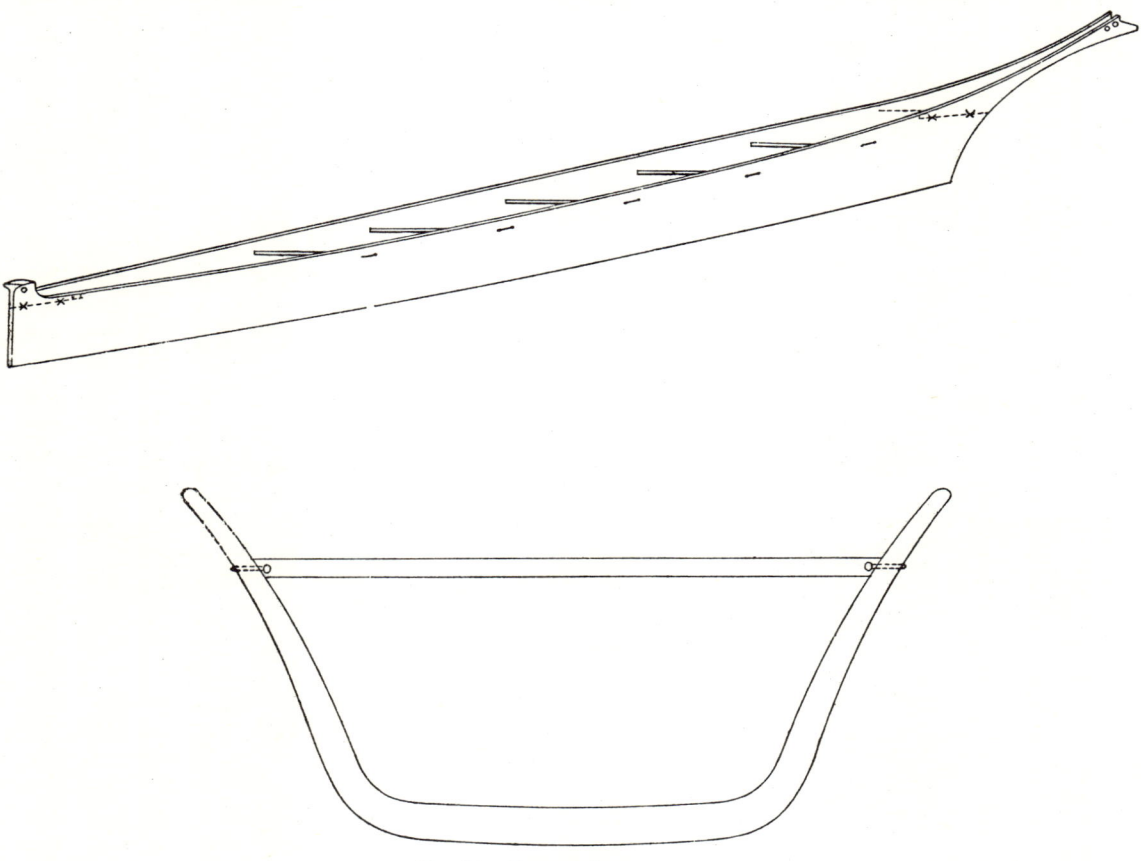

Fig. 24.—PUGET SOUND CANOE.

30 feet long, 4 feet wide on top, 2 feet wide on floor, and 24 inches in total depth, made of a single log of cedar. Boat weighs 800 pounds and floats light on 3 inches draught. Will carry 20 men on 12 inches draught.

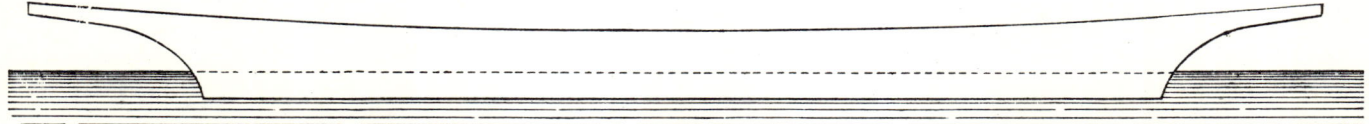

Fig. 25.—PUGET SOUND CANOE.

A form not uncommon for fishing boats.

The Puget sound and Alaskan canoes are hewed from the trunks of the white cedar tree, two varieties of which grow all along the coast from Sitka to California, standing thickly in the fir forests. This tree attains a height of from 100 to 150 feet, and is often 6 and 7 feet, sometimes 8 feet, in diameter near the ground. The wood is white close-grained, elastic, light and durable, the Puget Sound cedar being the lightest and best. It is easily worked, and a boat of any size desired can be carved from a single log. The usual sizes of canoes for shore fishing are from 20 to 30 feet in length, from 3 to 4 feet in width on top and 2 feet on the floor, with a depth of from 20 to 24 inches. The body of the boat to the gunwale is made from one solid log, but the prow and stern pieces are made separately, and are fitted closely to their places and fastened there by means of thongs tied through small holes. There are no thwarts to these canoes, but 4, 5, or 6 round bars of wood, each about 2 inches in diameter, are used in the place of thwarts and are lashed to their places with thongs rove through small round holes, the object being to support the sides of the boat against the dash of waves and the pressure of the water outside. Short broad-bladed paddles

FISHING VESSELS. 43

are used for propelling power, the Indians sitting on mats and blankets, half on the bottom of the boat, half on the gunwales, facing toward the bow, and when driven by three or four muscular pairs of arms these light canoes move with surprising speed. One knows not which to admire the most, the skill which has led to the production of so light, swift, and serviceable a boat by savage men, or the almost incredible endurance displayed by the Indians, who paddle them steadily, while en route to distant points, for from 12 to 15 hours at a time, with no pause whatever, refreshment being snatched in mouthfuls by the men while busily plying their oars. Latterly, the white men's fashions have crept into these canoes to some extent. Many of them are fitted with a pair of short oars, which are plied by a man sitting in the bow; others have a short pole mast forward of amidships, with a small sprit sail; but even if oars and sail be used, the occupants of the boat still line the gunwales after their own ancient fashion and work with the paddles continuously until they reach their destination.

ALONG THE NORTHERN LAKES.

There has always been more or less fishing on the northern lakes; but within the last fifty years the business has grown to be an industry, and of late years it has increased to such an extent as noticeably to affect the inland sales of fish caught in the salt sea. The business is carried on in a multitude of small boats, the majority of them not large enough to register at the custom-house, being of less than 5 tons. Fishing on the lakes is an along-shore occupation. It is not necessary, as a rule, for the men to be out over night in their boats, as they put out from the mouth of the river, or from the bay where they belong, in the early morning, and calculate to be back again perhaps in time for supper. Carried on in this way, the business does not require boats with decks and houses, and the fishing craft of the lakes, therefore, do not as a general rule have either, nearly all of them being open boats. These boats are built chiefly at Ogdensburg, Clayton, Oswego, Charlotte, and Buffalo, New York; Erie, Pennsylvania; Ashtabula, Cleveland, Lorain, Huron, Rocky River, Vermillion, Sandusky, and Toledo, Ohio; Sanilac, Bay City, Alpena, Marquette, and the islands in Michigan; and on Green bay, and at Sheboygan, Manitowoc, Milwaukee, and Racine, Wisconsin; but the business is greatly scattered, and there are few men who construct more than a dozen boats a year. A great many boats are the work of men half fisherman, half carpenter, who make only one boat, or at most two or three boats in a year. It is a modest industry, and is the means of utilizing the spare time of a great many men whose labor would otherwise find only partial employment.

The patterns of boats used on the lakes all come from the sea-coasts, the builders in the majority of cases being eastern born, or of eastern descent. At Erie, Pennsylvania, keel-boats are being built for fishing purposes 28 feet long, 8 feet wide, and 3 feet deep, with a foot sheer, not decked, except sometimes for a few feet at the bow, but with wash-boards the whole length of the gunwales. These boats have perpendicular stems and V-sterns, are round on the floor, and are fitted with center-boards, the bottoms rounding upward aft, as in sharpies and in many racing yachts. They usually have skags to assist in sailing on the wind and also to support the rudders, but in many cases these are omitted. The framing and the center work are of white oak, and the boats are often planked with oak. Their weight causes them to sit low in the water, but they are strong and seaworthy, and can stand a great deal of hard usage. The chief peculiarity is their rig, their generous beam and the stability of the boats enabling them to spread an extra amount of canvas. A boat is accordingly fitted with two tall masts, on each of which is hung a fore-and-aft lower sail and gaff topsail, made into one. A boom spreads the sail below, and a gaff does the same above, the gaff being split in two, one-half going each side of the canvas. The two halves are joined with screw bolts, and thus hold the canvas tightly in their clasp. This rig makes necessary the use of one halliard only, the same rope being used as the downhaul. There is no jib. It is said that this fashion came originally from New York. The boats cost about $250 each.

Along the Ohio coast the sharpie (Fig. 26) is the favorite of the fishermen. This fashion came from Connecticut along with a large percentage of the population of that state. The mouths of the Huron, Black, and other rivers are full of this class of boats, which are pulled up into the bulrushes on the flats when not in use. They are large, open boats, each carrying an anchor and often a chain. The average size of a sharpie is 36 feet long, 10½ feet wide, and 3 feet deep, being thus a fuller, heavier, and more capacious boat than a Connecticut sharpie of the same length. It takes two men 17 days to build one, and its value, when finished, is about $225. While 36 feet is the average and popular length, the boats vary in size, some being not over 24 feet in length and others as high as 42 feet, and cost from $275 to $300 each. The bilge-log, top timbers, stern, and center-board of an Ohio sharpie are made of oak; the planking and flooring are white pine. About 800 feet of pine and 200 feet of oak are cut up in building a boat. The stem rakes a few inches; the sides flare from 10 to 12 inches.

The greatest beam is forward of amidships. Right in the bow there is a stout breast hook, supporting a bit of "ekeing", or a short deck, which in its turn supports the foremast and allows room for working the sail and anchor. A few feet from the bow there is a stout thwart, with a parting board or bulkhead underneath to prevent the fish from sliding about. The center-board is nearly amidships. A strong thwart just aft of the board supports the mizzen-mast, and a few feet farther aft occurs a low thwart with parting-board. The stern is broad and overhanging, and there is a stern seat for the steersman, with a raised platform for his feet. As a rule, the boat has no wash-board. There are two masts; no bowsprit. A 32-foot sharpie is fitted with 36- and 34-foot masts; a 36-foot boat with masts 48 and 46 feet long. The masts rake considerably, and carry the same style of sail as the Erie boats.

The capacity of the Ohio sharpie is quite unusual. It carries from 7½ to 12 tons of pound-nets, fish, and apparatus, besides the crew; and, in addition to its ability in this direction, it is also a very fast and manageable boat.

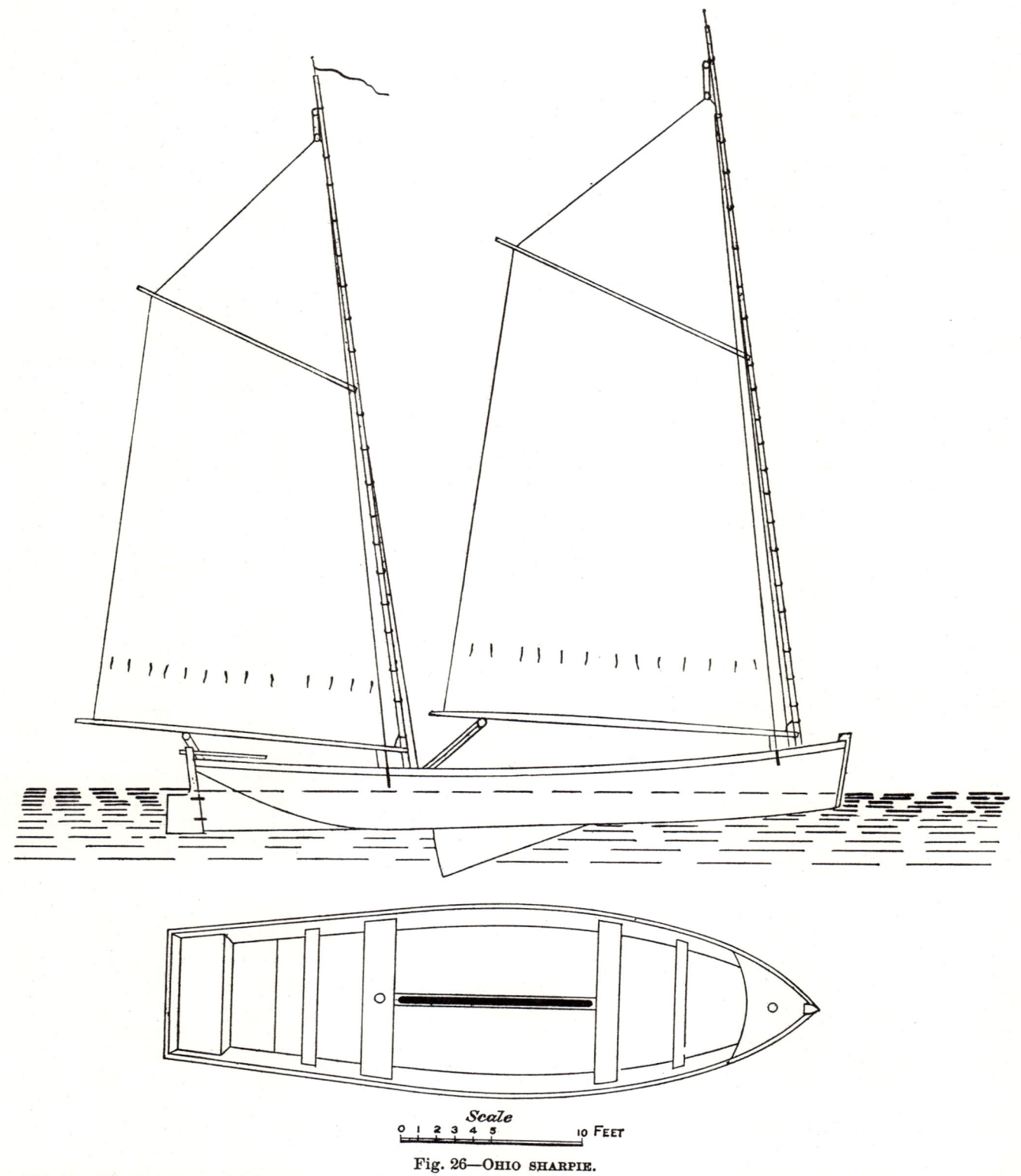

Fig. 26—OHIO SHARPIE.

36 feet long, 10½ feet wide, and 3 feet deep inside. Weight, with sails and rigging, 3,500 pounds. Will carry 8 tons of nets, fish, etc., on 18 inches draught of water.

At Marquette boats are in use that greatly resemble the pink. They are clinker-built, sharp-sterned, and schooner-rigged, and measure from 22 to 28 feet on the keel and from 7 to 9 feet across the gunwales. These boats are from 24 to 32 inches deep, and cost from $200 to $300 each.

Steam has lately come into use at Marquette to a considerable extent, small tugs from 40 to 50 feet long on the keel, 8 to 12 feet beam, and 5 or 6 feet deep, being now employed, and the principal part of the business is carried on there by the owners of these vessels. As the steam tug is not peculiarly a fishing vessel, it will be described elsewhere.

THE BUILDING INDUSTRY.

The preceding pages will show in what a scattered and fragmentary manner the business of building fishing boats and vessels is carried on. The industry is not concentrated in a special class of shops and yards, but is widely diffused among the regular builders of boats and vessels, and some of it is carried on by amateurs. There are few establishments which make a specialty of any branch of fishing-boat building; and as it would be difficult to separate the statistics and details of this line of ship-building from the general work which goes on in behalf of the merchant service, it is deemed best to postpone consideration of the present state of the building industry, so far as fishing vessels are concerned, until the same topic is taken up with reference to wooden merchant vessels.

Chapter II.—MERCHANT SAILING VESSELS.

Wooden sailing vessels for the merchant service comprise the bulk of the tonnage built and owned in the United States. A statement prepared by Mr. T. C. Purdy, special agent of the census for the collection of statistics of steam navigation, shows the following facts concerning the tonnage of the United States in the census year of 1880:

Vessels.	Number.	Tonnage.
Sailing vessels	16,830	2,366,258
Steamers	5,139	1,221,207
Canal-boats	8,771	1,253,688
Barges	5,032	1,331,563
Flat-boats	2,702	220,690
Wharf-boats	145	86,390
Hulks	46	7,638

The fishing fleet comprises about 2,600 vessels large enough to be documented by the custom-houses, registering in the aggregate 120,000 tons. The documented yachting fleet includes 180 small vessels, a total of 4,300 tons. All the rest of the sailing fleet are merchant vessels, employed on the coasts or on the northern lakes, or in foreign trade. There are only five or six iron ships in the whole number, all the rest being timber-built. Americans prefer wooden vessels, and at present they build few others for the general freighting service. For fifty years the largest and best wooden sailing ships in the world have been built in the ship-yards of the United States.

Nature having fitted this continent for ship-building by supplying it with an abundance of good timber, vessels have been built upon our shores from the first year of actual settlement, the first ship, oddly enough, having been constructed to carry a little band of settlers away from an inhospitable region which they wished to leave after their first winter. This vessel was built at the mouth of the Kennebec river, in Maine, a region which has since become famous for its ships, and which is now the leading locality, certainly in America, for the construction of sailing ships. In 1607 a company of English colonists came to Stage island, at the mouth of this river, in the vessels Gift of God and Mary and John to plant a settlement near the fishing grounds of New England. Sir George Popham, Sir Ferdinando Gorges, Sir John Gilbert, and other leading men were identified with this enterprise, and the company of emigrants was composed of Captain Raleigh Gilbert, Edward Harlow, Edward Davis, and about a hundred others. The original purpose was to land on Monhegan island, then, as now, noted for fishing; but finally they went to Stage island and began the settlement. The ships then returned to England, leaving 45 people behind. The severity of the winter discouraged the pioneers, and, growing homesick, they built a vessel in which to return. It was a staunch and excellent little vessel, a two-master, named the Virginia, and in after years this bark made several voyages to the English settlements on this continent. She is said to have been of "thirty tons burden", and judging of her dimensions from the rules for tonnage then in vogue, and also from the relative proportions of the vessels of that day, she must have been about 60 feet long, 17 feet broad on the main beam, and $10\frac{1}{2}$ feet deep in the hold.

The Dutch at New York built the next vessel. The emigrants from Holland in 1614 lost one of their ships by fire, and in 1615–'16, to replace it, Adrian Blok built the small yacht Onrest, of 16 tons burden, which was 38 feet long on the keel, $44\frac{1}{2}$ feet long over all, and 11 feet beam. What is now understood as a yacht is a vessel with a long, sharp bow and sharp floor, designed especially for speed, and used solely for pleasure; but the Onrest was no such craft, the yacht of her time being broad and round, with a bluff bow, and was made for light draught, on account of the shallow water of the rivers and harbors of the Netherlands. This model has been preserved in Dutch drawings. The Onrest was employed for several years in exploring the Atlantic coast from the thirty-eighth to the fortieth degree of latitude. Block island was visited during one of her excursions, and took its name from Adrian Blok.

With the exception of fishing boats and shallops there is no record of the building of any other boats until 1631. In that year, on the 4th of July, the little bark Blessing of the Bay was launched into the Mystic river at Medford for the use of the Massachusetts colony. She was built at the instance of Governor Winthrop, and was finished under his eye, the object being to open communication with the Dutch at the mouth of the Hudson and to trade to various parts of the coast. Governor Winthrop wanted a strong vessel, and she was largely made of locust. The Blessing of the Bay ran to Long Island and other settled localities for a short time and then disappeared from view, and it is possible that she was the unfortunate vessel that was sent by Winthrop and others from Boston to Virginia in 1633 with a load of fish and furs and was wrecked on the capes when near her destination.

The abundance of good timber in New England was a strong attraction to some of the British merchants under whose auspices the new colonies were settled. The forests of England were beginning to be impoverished; timber

MERCHANT SAILING VESSELS.

was dear in the mother land and ships were costly; and the importation of American lumber, particularly of sticks suitable for masts and spars, was encouraged from the earliest years. One of the Massachusetts company, Matthew Craddock, an eminent merchant and ship-owner of London, and president of the company, began an organized effort at ship-building, and it is stated that he "was more forward in advancing out of his substance than any other, being generally the highest in all subscriptions". He never came to the colony in person, but sent over a number of his own men to build vessels and operate for him. Every one of the company who subscribed £50 was to have 200 acres of land allotted to him. Mr. Craddock located his claim on the Mystic river, 3 miles from the infant village of Charlestown, at a place called Medford at the time, and afterward "Neck of Land". Wood says, in 1634, speaking of the Mystic river:

On the East side is Maister Craddock's plantation, where he hath impaled a Parke, where he keepes his Cattle till he can store it with Deere: Here likewise he is at charges of building ships. The last yeare one was upon the Stockes of a hundred Tunne; that being finished, they are to build one of twice her burden. Ships without either Ballast or loading may floate down this River: otherwise the Oyster-banke would hinder them which Crosseth the Channell.

Several vessels of good size were launched from the yard at this spot, and they all went to England to go into the general service of their builder and owner; but as they were not employed on this side of the ocean, there is little record of them.

There was so much large timber of thoroughly good quality, and the wood was so cheap, that vessels could have been built here at a large reduction from the cost in England; an advantage which has never failed to produce striking results when put to proper use. For several years, with the view of taking advantage of the resources of the new territory in this respect, the emigration of shipwrights to America was encouraged, and special privileges were given them, such as exemption from the duty of training and from the taxation of property actually used in ship-building. The inducements offered brought a number of good carpenters to New England, who settled in Boston, Salem, Gloucester, Scituate, and other coast towns and constructed whatever vessels were demanded by the times. But there was no organized effort to develop the industry after the death of Mr. Craddock. Natural advantages go for little without enterprising men to make use of them, and for many years the production of merchant shipping was only of a scattered and modest character. Fishing boats were built in abundance, but trading vessels only now and then, the cost of the latter being about £4 per ton.

After the village of Charlestown, Massachusetts, was planted a small coasting trade sprang up around Boston bay which led to some building. The villages on the bay were without firewood and hay, and sloops and lighters were built to bring these articles from the islands and from the coasts north and south. Many fishing boats were employed in this trade in the winter time; but firewood being a cargo for which they were not well adapted, regular wood boats were preferred, and from a small beginning there soon grew up a large fleet of wood sloops, owned all along the Massachusetts coast, the most of them probably being built at Salem. Six shipwrights had settled in Salem as early as 1629, and three small shallops were built there the same year; and while there were not many vessels demanded, there was nevertheless work enough for a few good men. The industry seems to have thrived in Salem from the start, and the village soon became conspicuous for its ship-yards and for the abundance of vessels produced. Many wood sloops were afterward built on Cape Ann, and Gloucester had 50 in 1706.

The building of merchant vessels is the offspring of a desire to trade. For the first 20 years after the landing of the Pilgrims the colonists thought only of building enough boats to keep the fishermen employed and to carry products along the coast to and from the different towns. The transatlantic trade took place entirely in European ships. About 1640 the colonists began to need large vessels for themselves. They had fish to sell, which the merchants of Barbadoes, Jamaica, Antigua, and other islands wished to buy; and the latter had produce which, on their part, they wished to market in New England. Rev. Hugh Peters, of famous memory, stirred up the people on this subject with great success, and the building of vessels with which to trade with the southern islands followed as a consequence of his efforts. Winthrop writes:

The general fear of want of foreign commodities, now our money was gone and that things were like to go well in England, set us on work to provide shipping of our own, for which end Mr. Peters, being a man of very public spirit and singular activity for all occasions, procured some to join for building a ship at Salem of 300 tons, and the inhabitants of Boston, stirred up by his example, set upon the building of another at Boston of 150 tons.

These two vessels were finished the following year. In 1641 two other vessels were building at Salem, and in 1642 three at Boston, one at Salem, and one at Dorchester. This was the real beginning of ship-building in New England for the general trade. The vessels were successful, and gave the industry a strong impetus. One wide-awake and zealous man woke up the whole coast, and after 1642 a large number of New England towns began to build vessels for distant voyages. That was 240 years ago; and there has been scarcely any change from that day to this in the method of dividing the ownership of vessels among a number of part owners in the general system of framing and planking vessels, or in the terms used to designate the different parts of the structure. The things which have changed in the course of these 240 years are the forms of the hulls, in view of a better knowledge of the scientific principles governing speed and stability in the water, the fashions of sails and rigging, the materials of construction, the cost of vessels, and the devices employed in the ship-yard for saving human labor and for improving its efficiency.

The dawn of the industry in the New World was thought worthy of comment in England, and was referred to in books of travels and in official reports. In *New England's First Fruits*, September, 1642, is the information:

Besides many boats, shallops, hoys, lighters, pinnaces, we are in a way of building ships of an 100, 200, 300, 400 tons. Five of them are already at sea, many more of them in hand at this present.

In Lechford's *News from New England*, London, 1642, it is stated that the people of the provinces were "building of ships and had a good store of barks, catches, lighters, shallops, and other vessels". There is very little in the records to show what the products of the little ship-yards were from year to year. The amount of building up to 1665 was referred to, however, in the report of a committee of the general court of Massachusetts while having that famous legislative dispute with Colonel Richard Nichols, George Cartwright, Sir Robert Carr, and Samuel Maverick:

The number of their ships and vessels, as follows: about eighty from 20 to 40 tons, about forty from 40 to 100 tons, and about a dozen ships above 100 tons.

That more than this number were *built* is certain, for even at that early period the merchants of Barbadoes, Antigua, Jamaica, and the other islands were sending to New England for their vessels, and many were built for them.

About 1670 Sir Joshua Child took alarm at the growth of shipping in America. He declared:

Of all the American plantations, his Majesty has none so apt for building of shipping as New England, nor any comparably so qualified for the breeding of seamen, not only by reason of the natural industry of that people, but principally by reason of their cod and mackerel fisheries; and, in my poor opinion, there is nothing more prejudicial, and in prospect more dangerous, to any mother kingdom, than the increase in shipping in her colonies, plantations, or provinces.

In Connecticut ship-building began soon after the first settlements. The people all provided themselves with fishing boats at the start, and shallops were then built for small coasting and river trade between the different towns. Travel and traffic being by water, on account of the lack of good roads, the shallop, afterward called the sloop, was the universal boat for the purpose, and was generally decked. A few pinnaces, or open long boats (though sometimes decked), were also built, and lighters were made to bring goods from the ships arriving from England up to the river towns. Small as these ships from Europe were, they each drew about 10 feet of water, and could not ascend small rivers. A decree of the general court at New Haven, June 11, 1640, will throw some light on the infant industry of that town. In callings that required skill, among which was that of "ship-carpenters", master-workmen were to be paid not above 2 shillings 6 pence per day in summer, "in wch men may worke 12 howers, butt lesse then 10 howers dilligently improved cannot be accounted nor may be admitted for a full dayes worke, nor in winter above 2s. a day, in wch at least 8 howers to be dilligently improved in worke." Those not master-workmen were to have 2 shillings per day in summer and 20 pence in winter. The order of the court continues: "For goeing with boats of severall sorts, the man not above 2s. a tyde, the whole tyde being dilligently improved, according to the nature of that imploym^t. And for boates, according to their quallity and burden. A lighter of 16 tunne wth a boate or cannow wth her not above 3s. a tide, and one of 12 tunne, with a boate, not above 2s. 6d. a tide. A shallop of 4 tunne, not above 1s. a tide, and so in respective proportio^n. Butt in such raines or stormes that goods cannot be laden without spoyling, nor the boat stirr though the tide serve, no paym^t to be made for the boate in such tides, though the man be paid while he attends the service." The rates for master-workmen were lowered 6 pence a day in 1641. In 1648 a ship was built at New Haven by carpenters, who were brought from Boston for the purpose, and for many years Massachusetts gave to the other coasts of the country the best carpenters they had for ship-building. Hutchinson says that the chief object of the people of New Haven, Guilford, and Milford was trade, and the better to be accommodated they built their houses on small lots of land near the water's edge.

They built vessels for foreign voyages, and set up trading houses upon lands which they purchased at Delaware bay for the sake of beaver, but were unsuccessful, and their stocks sunk very fast, and in 5 or 6 years they were much exhausted. Unwilling to give over, they exerted themselves as a last effort in building a ship for the trade to England, in which they put their whole stock of money, plate, and all the proper goods they could procure, to make a more valuable adventure. In her went passengers Mr. Grigson, one of the magistrates, in order to solicit a patent, and 8 or 10 more considerable persons, who, to use Mr. Cotton's expression, all went to heaven by water, the ship never being heard of after sailing. The loss of this ship entirely broke them up as traders, and they turned to husbandry for their support.

The names of the Swallow and the Fellowship are preserved in the Connecticut records of 1649 as two of the vessels of that date. The unfortunate end of the early ventures in general trade did not, however, stop the building of small vessels in Connecticut, and sloops for coasting and river purposes were built at New Haven and on the Connecticut river in considerable numbers. There was a fine body of excellent timber in the province, white oak, chestnut, pine, and spruce, all of it coming down to the banks of the water-courses, and this was continually resorted to as material for small vessels.

Ship-building at the mouth of the Hudson river began early. The yacht of Adrian Blok has been already mentioned. The directors of the Dutch West India Company were anxious to encourage the starting of ship-yards, and granted many privileges for the purpose. March 10, 1649, it was ordered that only the owners of real estate in New Amsterdam below the Harlem river should have the right to build yachts, sloops, and vessels; but in 1650 new freedom and exemptions were granted, and all who were willing to emigrate to the Hudson river were to have the right, gratuitously, to cut and draw from the public forests as much timber as they should need for the construction of vessels. In 1652 a master ship-carpenter came from Holland expressly to build a ship-house and stocks and go into business; but most of the work done in the early years was at the ship-yard of the company. Private enterprise was long in awakening. The following document has been preserved in the company's records, covering the work done in the years from 1633 to 1638:

RETURN OF THE SHIPS BUILT AND REPAIRED IN NEW NETHERLAND DURING WOUTER VAN TWILLER'S ADMINISTRATION.

Before me, *Cornelis van Tienhoven*, secretary of *New Netherland*, appeared in presence of the undersigned witnesses *Tymen Jansen*, ship-carpenter, about 36 years old, and with true Christian words in stead and under promise of a solemn oath, if necessary, at the request of his Honor, Director General *Kieft*, declared, testified and deposed, that it is perfectly true that he, deponent, during the administration [of Mr. *van Twiller*] has worked as ship's carpenter and has been engaged on all old and new work which Mr. *Twiller* ordered to be made, to wit:

A° 1633 the ship "*Soutberck*" repaired and provided with new knees.
Other carpenters have long worked on the ship "*Hope of Groeningen and Omlanden*".
The yacht "*Hope*" captured A° 1632 by said *van Twiller* was entirely rebuilt and planked up higher.
The yacht "*Prins Willem*" has been built.
The yacht "*Amsterdam*" almost finished.
A large open boat.
In the yacht "*Wesel*" an orlop and caboose were made.
In the yacht "*Vreede*" the same.
The boat "*Omwal*" at *Fort Orange*.
The yacht with a mizzen sold to *Barent Dircksen*.
The wood-cutters' boat.
Divers farmboats and skiffs were sold to various parties.
Also many boats and yawls made for the sloops.
Moreover the carpenters constantly repaired and caulked the old craft.
All of which he, deponent, declares to be true and to have testified and deposed at the aforesaid request to the best of his knowledge without regard of persons but only in the interest of truth. Done at *Fort Amsterdam* this 22d of March A° 1639.

WYBRANT PIETERSEN, } as witnesses.
MAURITS JANSEN,

This is the m ☩ of
TYMEN JANSEN.

After the English occupation of New York ship-building was continued on a small scale. Two ships are known to have been built in 1669, one of 120 tons at New York, and one of about 65 tons at Gravesend, Long Island. In 1678 Governor Andros reports:

There may have lately traded to ye collony, in a yeare, from tenn to fifteen shipps or vessells of about together 100 tunns each, English, New England, and our owne built, of which 5 small shipps and a ketch now belonging to New Yorke foure of them built there.

The record of passes issued by the governor of New York during the years 1678–'80, however, mentions 23 ships as hailing from New York which were probably built in the province, as in several cases not included in the above 23 the entry reads "Ship Beaver, of New York, an *English-built* craft". The description of one of the 23 as "a great square-sterned boat with two bulkheads" gives us an idea on what lines ships were then built. Governor Andros must have been mistaken when making the above statement, or else the trade of New York increased rapidly within a year after he made it; for from June to November, 1681, 154 entries of vessels were made at the New York collector's office, and from November, 1680, to March, 1690, 530 clearances were issued, a large percentage being without doubt New York built ships, including vessels navigating the Hudson and East rivers.

In 1700 there hailed from New York 124 ships of 100 tons and under, ketches, brigantines, and sloops, while Boston had 194, among them ships of 300 tons. Lord Cornbury (governor of New York from 1701 to 1709) found that the war then waging between England and France had a pernicious effect upon the shipping interest of New York, as many New York vessels had been lost, and the continuance of the war did not encourage the owners of ship-yards or capitalists to invest money in such property. His report to the lords of trade and plantations in 1708 tells us how far the shipping of New York had been injured: "There has formerly belonged to this port 32 topsail vessels, besides sloops; now we can't reckon above 28 topsail vessels and sloops." It also informs us that many of the vessels owned by merchants in Jamaica, Barbadoes, and others of the Leeward islands, which were nearly all built in America, came from New York, and that not more than six vessels belonging to the islands were built in the West Indies. The ship-building interest at New York did not recover quickly from the blows inflicted by the war. In 1721 the lords of trade, etc., reporting to the king on the state of the American colonies, say that the vessels belonging to the province of New York are small and not considerable in numbers, being employed only in the carrying trade to the southern islands and neighboring colonies. The transatlantic trade seems to have been carried on by English bottoms, of which 64, with a tonnage of 4,330 tons, arrived in New York from 1714 to 1717. During the same period 63 English ships were cleared from New York for British ports, 464 ships, sloops, and other vessels for the British colonies on this continent and the West Indies, and 118 to other than English ports. A certain percentage of these vessels were built at the port, but the ship-yards languished for many years, their product being principally sloops and small vessels.

It is probable that one strong reason for the dullness in ship-building at the mouth of the Hudson was the activity in New England through all this period. The latter section enjoyed the great advantage of a steady demand for the fisheries and the coasting trade, and its ship-yards had something to do nearly all the time. If the men were not hewing out the timbers and putting together the materials for a new sloop, ketch, or bark, they were apt to be busy repairing an old vessel; and as wages are lower and labor more skillful where work is steady, the New England yards could build better and cheaper ships than those in the other provinces. South of New York there was little or no building in colonial times, and, as above shown, there was not much even at New York. Tonnage was chiefly built in New England, and it is to be regretted that there is little of a definite character on record to show what the production in New England amounted to in that period, the only data that I have been able to find being contained in the colonial archives in the state-house at Boston. The inspection and registry of vessels of 30 tons and upward was ordered in 1698, in imitation of the practice of the mother country. From 1698 to 1714 a registry of vessels was kept, and this record, covering 450 pages of a large ledger, has been condensed and tabulated for this report. The act required:

> That when and so often as any ship or Vessel of Thirty Tuns or upward is to be built and set up in any Town or place within this province [of Massachusetts], before any Plank be brought on the Carpenter or Undertaker shall repair unto one of the Justices of the Peace within the same County, who upon request made is hereby impowered to appoint and authorize one or more able Shipwrights to be Overseers and Surveyors of the s^d Building, and of all the materials and workmanship.

The inspectors were required to survey each plank and timber. Another law for carrying into effect "An act for preventing frauds and regulating abuses in the plantation trade" demanded the registry of the vessels. In their enactments fishing vessels were left out of the account, as they were, as a rule, of less than 15 tons burden. It was therefore substantially the merchant fleet of the time alone which came under the notice of the law. As for the tonnage itself, that was arrived at by a rough estimate of the cargo which could be actually carried, so many tons meaning the actual burden of the vessel. The rule on this subject was established in France in 1681 by order of Colbert. With a view to fixing the relation between capacity of hull and cargo, or burden, the cubic feet of space occupied by a ton of 2,000 pounds was considered as being 42 cubic feet. The average contents of the hull were 45 per cent. of the parallelopipedon inclosing it; and hence the product of the principal dimensions, multiplied by 0.45 and divided by 42, was supposed to represent the actual number of tons weight of goods that would be stowed away in the hull and carried. It was the same as multiplying the length of keel by the breadth and depth, and dividing by 94. The English adopted this plan in substance; but, after all, the rule was so variously applied that the result was indefinite. Besides that, the government officers had one plan, the builders another, and often individual builders had different plans. The owners often had plans of their own, and the same ship which paid duties on 50 tons when importing foreign goods would often be rated at 100 tons when hired as a government transport. This looseness in estimate is seen in the record at the Massachusetts state-house, many vessels appearing several times in the ledger, and often at a different rating each time, the burden varying 10 or 20 tons from the original register, and one extreme case was found where a ship was documented once as of 130 tons and afterward as of 20 tons. The tonnage stated in the register, therefore, can only be regarded as approximate. The dimensions of vessels are not given; such as it is, however, the record remains a valuable one, as showing the production of New England ship-yards from 1696 to 1714, and to some extent for a few previous years. The record, condensed, is as follows, the duplications having been sifted out as far as possible:

Places where built.	SLOOPS.		PINKS.		KETCHES.		BRIGANTINES.		BARKS.		SHIPS.	
	No.	Tonnage.	No.	Tonnage.	No.	Tonnage.	No.	Tonnage.	No.	Tonnage.	No.	Tonnage.
1674.												
Salem			1	15								
1676.												
Beverly					1	34						
1677.												
Lynn	1	15										
1678.												
Charlestown	1	15										
Scituate	1	16					1	35				
England					1	70						
Cork, Ireland											1	90
1681.												
Newbury							1	20				
1682.												
Boston	1	30										
Scituate	1	20										
1683.												
Scituate	1	25										
England											1	70

MERCHANT SAILING VESSELS.

Places where built.	SLOOPS.		PINKS.		KETCHES.		BRIGANTINES.		BARKS.		SHIPS.	
	No.	Tonnage.	No.	Tonnage.	No.	Tonnage.	No.	Tonnage.	No.	Tonnage.	No.	Tonnage.
1684.												
Salem					1	30						
Scituate	1	30										
England			1	60								
1685.												
Boston	1	12										
Lynn	1	15										
Milford, Connecticut	1	14										
Virginia	1	12										
England			1	70								
1686.												
Ipswich							1	30				
Middletown, Connecticut	1	15										
Killingworth	1	10										
Virginia	1	15										
England			1	25	1	30						
1687.												
Salem	2	32			2	50						
1688.												
Salem					1	16						
Marblehead									1	20		
Newport, Rhode Island	1	12										
England											1	80
1689.												
Boston							1	60				
Salem					1	25						
York							1	60				
England											1	90
1690.												
Newbury							1	20				
Providence, Rhode Island	1	10										
New London, Connecticut	1	15										
Pennsylvania	1	20										
1691.												
Boston					1	30						
Salem					1	12					1	170
Lynn	1	10										
Hampton, New Hampshire							2	60				
New Jersey	1	12										
1692.												
Boston									1	35	3	400
Scituate	1	16					1	40				
Amesbury	1	35										
Piscataqua											1	130
Milton											1	300
New London, Connecticut	2	37										
1693.												
Boston							3	120			1	90
Scituate	1	40					1	60				
Salem			1	60			1	40				
Newbury							1	35				
Braintry							1	30				
Milton							1	60				
Hingham	1	20										
Kittery, Maine	1	25										
Rhode Island							1	50				
New London, Connecticut	1	25										
Virginia	1	40										
1694.												
Boston	2	55									3	230
Charlestown	1	30					1	30				
Cambridge							1	45				
Salem	2	50			1	30	3	140	1	60	1	80
Scituate	5	145					2	110	1	70	1	80

SHIP-BUILDING INDUSTRY.

Places where built.	SLOOPS.		PINKS.		KETCHES.		BRIGANTINES.		BARKS.		SHIPS.	
	No.	Tonnage.	No.	Tonnage.	No.	Tonnage.	No.	Tonnage.	No.	Tonnage.	No.	Tonnage.
1694—Continued.												
Newbury	1	30					1	40				
Beverly	1	30			1	25	1	40				
Milton							2	90				
Swanzey	1	40										
Stony Brook	1	20										
Hingham	2	40										
Portsmouth, New Hampshire	1	10										
Rhode Island	1	30										
Long Island, New York	1	30										
Connecticut							1	50				
Milford, Connecticut							2	50				
New York	1	40										
1695.												
Boston	2	38					3	145				
Charlestown	2	45					1	50			1	400
Salem	3	70			1	40	1	20				
Scituate	1	25							1	60		
Ipswich	1	30										
Newbury	3	94										
Bristol	1	10										
Hingham	1	20										
Pemaquid, Maine	1	35										
York, Maine											1	60
Kittery							1	40				
Rhode Island							1	60				
Connecticut	2	45										
Milford	1	30										
Glastonbury	1	15										
England											1	70
1696.												
Captured from the French and Spanish					1	70			1	60	10	1,120
Boston	3	80			1	30	1	45	1	40	2	290
Charlestown							1	50			1	150
Cambridge							2	70				
Salem	1	25			2	50						
Scituate	1	35					1	50			3	280
Gloucester	1	15										
Beverly					1	40						
Plymouth							1	60				
Weymouth									1	50		
Bristol									1	50		
Piscataqua, New Hampshire									1	60	1	110
Hampton, New Hampshire							2	60				
Tiverton, Rhode Island	1	25										
Connecticut	1	30										
Killingworth, Connecticut	1	15										
New London	1	20										
New Haven	1	20										
Milford					1	30						
Stratford	1	10										
New Jersey	1	16										
Maryland	1	20										
England											1	150
1697.												
Boston	2	82					1	60			1	200
Charlestown											4	630
Cambridge	1	18										
Salem	2	45			1	40					1	200
Scituate	2	100					2	120			1	90

MERCHANT SAILING VESSELS.

Places where built.	SLOOPS.		PINKS.		KETCHES.		BRIGANTINES.		BARKS.		SHIPS.	
	No.	Tonnage.	No.	Tonnage.	No.	Tonnage.	No.	Tonnage.	No.	Tonnage.	No.	Tonnage.
1697—Continued.												
Newbury	1	25										
Salisbury							1	30				
Haverhill	1	30										
Plymouth	1	16										
Weymouth							2	110				
Swanzey											1	78
Piscataqua, New Hampshire											2	224
Hampton	1	20										
Rhode Island	1	50										
Providence	1	10										
Connecticut	3	95										
New London	1	25										
Lyme	1	20										
Haddam	1	35										
Guilford	1	25										
Glastonbury	1	50										
Killingworth	1	20										
Milford	1	15										
New Haven	3	86										
Middletown	2	37										
Gardner's Island, New York	1	12										
Southold, Long Island	1	20										
England											1	75
1698.												
Captured from enemy									1	60	3	340
Boston	2	20			3	105			2	125	3	290
Charlestown	2	177										
Salem	2	60			4	130					1	60
Scituate	2	35					3	120			2	200
Newbury	1	30			1	35						
Weymouth							1	40				
Chebacco	1	18										
Plymouth					1	35						
Milton							1	50				
Hampton, New Hampshire	1	30										
Connecticut	2	45										
Bradford	1	12										
Long Island, New York									1	80		
New Jersey	1	12					1	18				
Bermuda	1	25										
1699.												
Captured from enemy									1	60		
Boston	1	25			2	75	4	185	1	60	11	1,160
Charlestown	2	65			1	80					6	680
Medford							1	40				
Salem					9	275			1	80	1	60
Scituate	3	90			1	40	3	135			4	310
Gloucester	1	40										
Chebacco	1	12										
Beverly	1	22										
Lynn					1	30						
Amesbury					1	30						
Newbury	1	30			3	85			1	30		
Weymouth											1	100
Rehoboth							1	30				
Wayland	1	35										
Milton											1	90
Connihasset	1	30										
Taunton											2	200
Hingham	1	45										
Hampton, New Hampshire							1	30				

SHIP-BUILDING INDUSTRY.

Places where built.	SLOOPS.		PINKS.		KETCHES.		BRIGANTINES.		BARKS.		SHIPS.	
	No.	Tonnage.	No.	Tonnage.	No.	Tonnage.	No.	Tonnage.	No.	Tonnage.	No.	Tonnage.
1699—Continued.												
Manchester	1	30										
Maine											1	50
Newport	1	30										
Connecticut	2	50									1	90
New London	1	15										
Hartford	1	30										
England					1	30						
1700.												
Boston	3	87			1	50	1	60	1	35	8	790
Charlestown	4	116					1	50	3	140	3	490
Salem					10	310					1	130
Scituate	3	70			2	60	5	215	1	60	2	146
Gloucester	1	20										
Lynn					1	30						
Ipswich	1	30										
Weymouth											2	175
Plymouth					2	56						
Taunton											1	60
Newbury	2	60			1	20	1	40				
Piscataqua, New Hampshire	2	50										
Newport, Rhode Island	1	40										
New London, Connecticut	1	30					1	50				
Lyme	1	20										
New Haven	1	35										
Guilford	1	8										
Cape Sable	1	12										
1701.												
Boston	3	75			2	75	3	120	2	125	4	540
Charlestown											1	125
Salem	3	76			4	140						
Scituate	4	100					1	60	2	130	1	70
Ipswich	1	30										
Gloucester	2	58										
Newbury							1	50				
Bristol	1	30										
Taunton											1	90
Rehoboth							1	55				
Plymouth	2	50										
Weymouth											1	100
Lynn	1	35										
Milton	1	50										
Kittery, Maine	1	35									2	160
Saco							2	90				
New London, Connecticut	1	25										
Lyme									1	70		
Haddam	1	35										
Guilford	1	16										
Hartford	2	50										
New Haven	1	35					1	60				
Norwalk	1	40										
England											1	110
1702.												
Captured from enemy	2	38									7	816
Boston	5	205					4	195	1	65	2	170
Charlestown											1	80
Salem	1	16			3	75	1	45			1	70
Scituate	2	80					6	270			2	190
Gloucester							2	120				
Newbury	2	55							1	40		
Manamoy	1	20										
Weymouth											1	100
Plymouth	1	25										

MERCHANT SAILING VESSELS.

Places where built.	SLOOPS.		PINKS.		KETCHES.		BRIGANTINES.		BARKS.		SHIPS.	
	No.	Tonnage.	No.	Tonnage.	No.	Tonnage.	No.	Tonnage.	No.	Tonnage.	No.	Tonnage.
1702—Continued.												
Hingham	1	36										
Taunton	1	30					1	60			1	200
Hampton, New Hampshire	1	20										
New Castle, New Hampshire	1	30										
Berwick, Maine	1	50										
York, Maine	1	40										
Connecticut	1	20										
Middletown	1	40										
New Haven	1	26										
Wethersfield	1	30										
England			1	80								
1703.												
Boston	6	130					7	360			6	465
Charlestown											3	320
Medford											1	60
Salem	2	52			2	40					1	150
Scituate	5	146					4	182				
Newbury	2	55										
Amesbury							1	40				
Duxbury	1	35										
Taunton							1	50			2	150
Plymouth	1	30										
Weymouth											1	130
Manchester					1	25						
Piscataqua, New Hampshire	1	40										
Kittery, Maine											1	100
York	2	60										
Hartford	2	56										
1704.												
Captured from enemy (a)	1	15									2	200
Boston	7	225					6	305	1	50	10	840
Charlestown											2	220
Salem	1	30	1	80	1	20					2	250
Scituate	1	35					3	145			2	110
Gloucester	1	35					3	185				
Lynn	1	50										
Rowley	1	25										
Newbury	2	65					1	40				
Amesbury							1	40				
Duxbury	1	35					1	50				
Taunton									1	55		
Bristol	1	15										
Weymouth											1	100
Piscataqua, New Hampshire											2	180
Newport, Rhode Island							1	60				
Long Island, New York	1	15										
Hartford, Connecticut	1	34										
Newcastle, Pennsylvania	1	50										
1705.												
Captured from enemy	1	20									1	100
Boston	2	60	1	50			8	525			8	880
Charlestown	2	55									4	450
Salem					1	25					4	620
Scituate	2	80					6	380			1	90
Gloucester	3	88					4	240			3	270
Newbury	2	60			1	50	2	95				
Plymouth							1	50				
Weymouth											1	120
Hingham	1	30										

a Shallop.

SHIP-BUILDING INDUSTRY.

Places where built.	SLOOPS.		PINKS.		KETCHES.		BRIGANTINES.		BARKS.		SHIPS.	
	No.	Tonnage.	No.	Tonnage.	No.	Tonnage.	No.	Tonnage.	No.	Tonnage.	No.	Tonnage.
1705—Continued.												
Duxbury	1	20									1	75
Taunton	2	55									1	120
Marshfield	1	40										
New Hampshire			1	85							1	80
Exeter							1	48				
Piscataqua							1	40				
Hampton	1	20									1	70
Manchester											2	175
Kittery, Maine											2	450
Bristol, Maine							2	125				
Rhode Island	3	120										
New Haven, Connecticut	1	35										
Middletown	1	50										
Stratford							1	50				
1706.												
Boston	5	165					4	190			6	485
Charlestown	1	35					3	185			2	290
Salem	3	101					4	180			4	770
Scituate	2	70					3	195				
Gloucester	5	185					6	360			1	60
Newbury							2	115			1	100
Haverhill	1	30										
Ipswich	1	30									1	90
Duxbury							2	70				
Plymouth	1	20					1	40				
Hingham							1	40			1	160
Taunton	2	45							1	70	1	90
Bristol	1	35					2	135				
New Hampshire											2	220
Piscataqua							2	100				
New Castle, New Hampshire									1	70		
Manchester	1	34										
Portsmouth											2	155
Kittery, Maine	1	30									5	920
York	1	35					1	60				
Rhode Island	1	30										
Tiverton							1	45				
Connecticut	1	40										
Guilford	1	30										
Milford	1	20										
Glastonbury	1	18										
Lyme	1	15							1	70		
1707.												
Captured from enemy							1	40			1	260
Boston	7	240					6	270	1	60	5	616
Charlestown	1	30					1	60			2	220
Salem	1	15			1	28	1	50				
Scituate	2	60					2	130				
Gloucester	3	90					3	220				
Newbury	3	90					1	30				
Plymouth	1	35										
Duxbury	1	35										
Weymouth	1	40										
Swanzey											1	120
Freetown											1	120
Hingham	1	35										
Taunton	1	40					1	55				
Bristol	1	50										
Hampton, New Hampshire	1	16					1	80				
Kittery, Maine							1	40				
Connecticut	1	35										
New Haven	1	45										
Cow Neck, New York	1	12										

MERCHANT SAILING VESSELS.

Places where built.	SLOOPS.		PINKS.		KETCHES.		BRIGANTINES.		BARKS.		SHIPS.	
	No.	Tonnage.	No.	Tonnage.	No.	Tonnage.	No.	Tonnage.	No.	Tonnage.	No.	Tonnage.
1708.												
Captured from enemy											1	120
Boston	7	245	1	80			2	140			9	1,020
Charlestown											6	685
Salem							1	60	1	60	2	260
Scituate	1	30									1	50
Gloucester							1	40				
Chebacco	1	36										
Ipswich	1	30					1	50				
Hingham	1	30										
Lynn							1	40				
Newbury	3	100					1	60			3	590
Swanzey							1	50			1	170
Duxbury	2	45										
Bristol	2	70										
Taunton							3	200			1	120
Piscataqua, New Hampshire	1	18										
Hampton									1	70		
Portsmouth											1	140
Exeter											1	100
York, Maine	1	35										
Connecticut	2	85					1	55				
England	1	50									1	100
1709.												
Captured from enemy									1	60	4	490
Boston	8	305					4	185			18	1,968
Charlestown	1	40									2	400
Salem	2	55					1	95	1	65	4	500
Scituate	2	50					1	40			1	70
Gloucester	5	128					1	70				
Lynn							1	50				
Ipswich	1	30										
Newbury	1	40					1	20			2	230
Swanzey							2	110				
Duxbury	2	60										
Hingham	1	16										
Taunton	1	25					1	70				
New Hampshire											1	65
Piscataqua			1	80							5	910
Connecticut	1	30										
Bradford							1	55				
Milford	1	40										
Newfoundland	1	40										
1710.												
Captured from enemy											6	900
Boston	7	175					7	360	1	70	18	2,060
Charlestown	1	30					1	50			2	400
Salem	3	90					2	150				
Scituate	1	30					1	60				
Cape Ann	1	25										
Gloucester	6	180										
Lynn							1	60				
Newbury	6	195					1	30			1	200
Duxbury	2	55										
Plymouth	3	75										
Milton	1	40										
Hingham									1	40		
Taunton											1	120
Piscataqua, New Hampshire											2	160

SHIP-BUILDING INDUSTRY.

Places where built.	SLOOPS.		PINKS.		KETCHES.		BRIGANTINES.		BARKS.		SHIPS.	
	No.	Tonnage.	No.	Tonnage.	No.	Tonnage.	No.	Tonnage.	No.	Tonnage.	No.	Tonnage.
1710—Continued.												
Kittery, Maine							2	120			2	360
Rhode Island	1	25										
Newport	1	30										
Connecticut	1	25										
New Haven	1	40										
England											1	110
1711.												
Captured from enemy	3	60									4	350
Boston	7	240					5	285			8	740
Charlestown											2	260
Salem	2	80					1	55			2	170
Scituate	1	30									2	140
Cape Ann	3	90										
Connihasset											1	60
Newbury	4	150							1	40	1	70
Salisbury	1	40										
Lynn	2	75										
Weymouth	1	30										
Plymouth	2	60										
Marshfield											1	70
Bristol	1	50										
Taunton	1	30					1	50			a 3	1,080
Exeter, New Hampshire											1	130
New Castle, New Hampshire											1	70
Newport, Rhode Island											1	55
Tiverton	1	14										
Kittery, Maine	1	25	1	80			1	65			3	470
York, Maine	1	55										
New London	1	40									1	120
Wethersfield	1	45										
1712.												
Captured from enemy	3	72	1	80	1	15					3	310
Boston	10	370					2	130			14	1,355
Charlestown							2	120			1	200
Salem	4	170									1	150
Scituate							3	140				
Cape Ann	1	30										
Newbury	4	145					1	45			3	300
Duxbury	2	50					1	45				
Swanzey	1	35					1	50			1	80
Plymouth	3	100										
Hingham	2	35										
Dighton											1	70
Exeter, New Hampshire	1	30										
Kittery, Maine	3	115					1	50			1	120
Newport, Rhode Island	2	85										
New Haven, Connecticut	1	50										
Fairfield	1	25										
1713.												
Captured from enemy	1	15									1	80
Boston	11	330					5	305			18	1,860
Charlestown	2	75	1	80							6	645
Salem	1	30										
Scituate	1	30									1	70
Ipswich	1	30					1	100				
Gloucester	2	68										
Lynn	1	30										
Newbury	9	275					5	265			3	135
Duxbury	1	30										

a Two of these ships are registered as 600 tons and 400 tons respectively. This is no doubt a great exaggeration.

MERCHANT SAILING VESSELS.

Places where built.	SLOOPS.		PINKS.		KETCHES.		BRIGANTINES.		BARKS.		SHIPS.	
	No.	Tonnage.	No.	Tonnage.	No.	Tonnage.	No.	Tonnage.	No.	Tonnage.	No.	Tonnage.
1713—Continued.												
Rowley	1	35										
Plymouth	1	30										
Marshfield	1	30										
Bristol											2	150
Hingham	1	50										
York, Maine	1	30										
Kittery, Maine	3	150									1	50
Connecticut	1	20										
Haddam	1	25										
1714.												
Boston	9	325									16	1,575
Charlestown	2	65									3	330
Dorchester	1	50										
Salem											1	90
Newbury	3	120					2	70			4	340
Haverhill	1	50										
Plymouth	1	75										
Dighton											1	80
Kittery, Maine	1	30										
York	1	35										
East Haven, Connecticut	1	20										

Of the 1,332 vessels American built in the above list, seven-eighths were owned in Boston. The following 239 were built for foreign owners, every class of vessel being comprised in the list, the majority being ships:

For owners in the British isles	169
For owners in Barbadoes	21
For owners in Antigua	9
For owners in Nevis	7
For owners in Montserrat	11
For owners in Jamaica	6
For owners in Fayal	2
For owners in Madeira	1
For owners in Teneriffe	1
For owners in Oporto Royal	3
For owners in Saint Christopher	9

The names of these early vessels were expressive. Endeavour, Industry, Tryall, Speedwell, Happy Return, Brother's Adventure, Beginning, Blessing, Hopewell, Goodspeed, Unity, and Friendship were popular titles repeated a hundred times in vessels owned on the same coast. A great many were named after members of the owners' families, and a very few had names like Sea Flower, Dispatch, Dove, Lark, Swallow, Swift, and Dragon. Some of the large vessels were named Bedford Galley, Diamond Galley, Leopard Galley, Dudley Frigate, Granville Frigate, and Boston Merchant, Port Nevis Merchant, Antigua Merchant, etc.

Arrivals and departures of vessels were also kept at Boston during the years above named, and show that large sloops left Boston chiefly for points on the American coast. Pinks and ketches were also engaged in the coasting trade, and a few cleared from time to time for Newfoundland, apparently for fishing on the banks. The craft engaged in trading to the West India islands and to Europe were pinks, ketches, barks, and ships, but occasionally sloops sailed for all these destinations.

Small as were the merchantmen of that day, they carried large crews and usually were armed with a number of cannon, a circumstance which affected their form, as they were so round on the floor that the placing of a number of heavy guns on the upper deck was liable to make them crank. A remedy for this was sought in making the hull narrower on deck than on the load water-plane, the top sides often falling home several feet. This brought the deck-weights in toward the center of the ship, and did much toward making her stiff in a sea way. The record of clearances from Boston shows how well armed some of the merchantmen were. A few cases are quoted:

Pink Swallow, for Charleston, South Carolina, 60 tons, 10 men, 2 guns.
Ship Two Brothers, for Jamaica, 140 tons, 19 men, 14 guns.
Ship Swallow, for Barbadoes, 150 tons, 18 men, 12 guns.
Pink Mary, for Barbadoes, 60 tons, 8 men, 4 guns.
Pink Return, for Madeira, 40 tons, 9 men, 4 guns.

Ship Richard, for London, 100 tons, 14 men, 12 guns.
Pink Olive Branch, for Barbadoes, 45 tons, 7 men, 3 guns.
Ketch Hopewell, for Madeira, 40 tons, 7 men, 3 guns.
Ship Trident, for Barbadoes, 140 tons, 15 men, 14 guns.
Pink Richard and Margaret, for Barbadoes, 40 tons, 10 men, 6 guns.
Ship Samuel and Thomas, for London, 120 tons, 16 men, 6 guns.
Brigantine Supply, for Leeward islands, 15 tons, 5 men, 2 guns.
Brigantine Resolution, for South Carolina, 30 tons, 5 men, 2 guns.
Ship James, for Jamaica, 80 tons, 12 men, 7 guns.
Pink Samuel, for Jamaica, 60 tons, 10 men, 6 guns.
Ship Prudent Sarah, 100 tons, 14 men, 10 guns.
Ship Francis and Dorothy, for Nevis, 200 tons, 20 men, 20 guns.
Ketch Fidelity, for Bilbao, 35 tons, 7 men, 2 guns.

The necessity for carrying such an armament on merchant vessels was removed in after years, when America had become a free and independent nation, as much by the treaties and the influence of the United States as by any other cause.

Various contracts for the construction of vessels are on file in the valuable colonial records which are yet preserved in the United States. One of 1661 at Gloucester, Massachusetts, was for a "new ship", 68 feet long on the keel, 23 feet beam from outside to outside, 9½ feet deep in the hold, with two decks. From the mainmast to the forecastle the upper deck was to be 5 feet high, with a fall of 15 inches at the forecastle and a rise of 6 inches at the mainmast for the quarter-deck. The cabin was to be 6 feet high. The price was £3 5s. for every ton of burden, and a part of the payment was to be made with £150 worth of muscovado sugar, reckoned at 2 pence per pound at Barbadoes.

A contract of 1695 at Charlestown, Massachusetts, called for a "new square-sterned ship" of best white or black oak, with pine decks and houses, having two flush decks, a half-deck, round house, forecastle, and head, and of the following dimensions: Keel, 82 feet long; breadth on the frame timbers at the main beam, 25½ feet, with 4-inch plank in addition; depth of hold, 11 feet; rake of stem, 18 feet, 6 feet to be at a foot rise from the keel. Her scantling and details were as follows: Keel, 12 inches square, with a 3-inch shoe; keelson, 12 by 16 inches; stem, either 14 or 16 inches, according as the stuff could be obtained; stern-post, 12 by 24 inches, with a false stern-post of 18 inches to run from the keel to the wing transom; wing transom, 14 by 28 inches; the other transoms, 12 inches; a large knee to unite the stern-post to the keel, with arms 7 and 9 feet long; the floor timbers of the frames to be sided 12 inches at the keel and molded 9½ inches at the floor heads, each timber being 18 feet long; the lower foot-hooks (or futtocks) to fill up between the lower timbers and have a 7-foot scarf, being 12 inches broad over the keel, and running up 2½ feet above the lower or gun-deck; the top timbers, stepping on the lower futtock heads, molded 7½ inches at the heel and 3½ inches at their heads, and sided 7 or 8 inches; between decks, 6 feet high; the outside planking, 3-inch; garboards and channel streaks, 4½ and 4 inches; the lower wales, 7 inches; the ceiling was 3 inches thick, with 2 streaks of 4-inch at the rung-heads, 2 more for middle bands of 4-inch, and a 4- and 5-inch clamp; beams of the gun-deck from 14 to 17 inches broad by 11 inches deep, spaced 4½ feet apart, with carlines, and two knees at each end; water-ways of 4-inch oak, and the rest of the decking 3-inch; the spirketing, 4 by 18 inches; 4-inch clamps to the upper deck; upper deck beams, 9 inches deep and 5 feet apart, with carlines, and with one lodging and one hanging knee; the ceiling between decks, 2½-inch plank; water-ways, 3-inch and 2-inch oak; decking, 2-inch deal; bulwark planking, 2 inches; rails, 4½ inches thick; as many gun-ports as the owners should require; 11-inch wing-transom knees, with arms 6 and 11½ feet long, the other transoms double-kneed with 10-inch knees; beams of the poop-deck, 4½ by 8 inches, with 2-foot spaces between them and 3-inch water-ways; beams of the round-house, 4 by 7 inches, 2 feet apart; 7 breast-hooks, with arms 8 feet long, molded 14 inches; a step for the foremast, 16 feet long, 2½ feet broad, and a similar step for the mainmast; rudder, 18 inches at the head, 20 inches deep, with tiller, drum-head, capstan, and windlass; mainsail and foretop-sail sheet-bits; a pair of small quarter-galleries; bulkheads; a complete set of masts and yards, the vessel finished in all respects down to a cleat, all the materials to be provided by the builder, except iron work, nails, and carvers' and joiners' work; the fastenings to be chiefly with treenails of oak, and the vessel to be built in one year's time. The contract price was £4 5s. per ton, the tonnage to be determined as follows: After multiplying her length, breadth, and half-breadth for the depth, the product was to be divided by 95. £100 was to be paid down on signing the contract, the remainder to be paid from time to time, £200 being reserved until delivery of the ship. Sums amounting to £985 were indorsed on the contract, which, with the £200 on delivery, made the cost of the vessel about £1,185. Her carpenters' measurement was 276 tons; her real carrying capacity was very nearly the same. She would register under our present rules about 180 or 190 tons. She was a two-master, with bowsprit, and was either a brigantine, a brig, or a bark, as the names were then understood. These details give a pretty fair idea of the vessels of her size at that time.

Another contract was for a square stern ship in 1700 at Boston having two decks, a half- or poop-deck, round-house, forecastle, and head. She was to be 72 feet long on the keel, the stem raking 17 feet and the stern-post about 2 feet, 24½ feet wide at the main beam, and 11 feet deep in the hold, with a height of 4 feet between decks. Her scantling were about the same as in the last-named contract. She would have been of about 222 tons, carpenters' measurement, and the contract price was £3 12s. per ton. Money was so scarce in America at this time that it was a common practice to pay for ships in goods, and one has been known to be paid for almost entirely in calicoes.

A third may be mentioned, dated in 1701, for "a new vessel, barque, or brigantine" 45 feet long on the keel, 18½ feet wide, 8½ feet deep in the hold, one deck, 4½-foot waist, quarter-deck, cabin, and forecastle. The stem was to rake 12⅓ feet. There were to be three gun-ports on each side and two in the stern. The contract called for white oak throughout, except for decking and houses, which were to be of white pine. The price was 53s. per ton, carpenters' measurement; and £40 was to be paid down at the signing of the contract, as much more at the laying of her deck, and the rest on delivery of the vessel. She was of about 60 tons.

About the year 1700 the ketch and the pink began to be less preferred than in previous years, and by 1715 they were not built for trading purposes to any extent. These vessels were round-sterned, easy to build, and not expensive, but they lacked a feature much needed in a period when trading ships had to fight: there was no room in the stern for the convenient working of cannon pointing right aft, and the round stern was abandoned for a so-called square stern, which at first did not overhang as in modern vessels. Below water the stern was sharp, but above water it was about the shape of the end of a barrel until it reached the deck, when it ran up with straight sides to accommodate the galleries and houses. While this change was going on the positions of the masts

Fig. 27.—A Snow of the early years of the American Republic.

of the ketch were changed, both being brought farther forward, and the light bonaventure mast aft was enlarged until it became in reality the mainmast of the vessel. This mast carried a lug or lateen sail below and sometimes a square sail above, the foremast having square sails only and the bowsprit two or three jibs and often a sprit sail. A square sheet of canvas hung below the bowsprit on a yard, and thus changed the ketch became a brig or brigantine, and its former name was dropped. The new name was of European derivation. After 1745 the schooner became a popular rig in America for coasting vessels of any size, and also for foreign voyages of moderate length.

One variety of the brigantine was called the snow (Fig. 27), a style of vessel built from time to time from 1700 to 1800, but it might as well have been called a brig as anything else, as its only marked peculiarity was that the fore-and-aft sail on the mainmast was a regular sloop sail, spread by boom and gaff, its luff or fore edge being attached by hoops to a third small mast, placed close to the mainmast and in contact with it, heeling on the deck and having its head attached to the after part of the maintop. Substantially the vessel was what we would call a full-rigged brig, and the name "snow" was never much used. In the expedition from Massachusetts for the capture of the great fort at Louisburg, in Canada, in 1745, the American fleet was composed of 3 ships, 3 snows, 1 brig, and 3 sloops, with a number of whale-boats.

The hulls of that day were round bowed and broad beamed. It was a popular fashion to curve the stem above the hawse holes backward, like the bow of an ancient Dutch galliot, and to dispense with any cutwater or head; but this fashion went out of vogue after independence, as there was little lifting power in such a bow, to say nothing of looks. Americans afterward made their bows flaring at the top. The broadest part of the hull was one-tenth the length forward of amidships. The topsides always had more or less of a fall home, while the fore foot was cut away under water and the stern-post raked 1, 2, or 3 feet.

The sloops of 1700 and for fifty years afterward were large boats for their rig. Whaling and the carrying of firewood along the coast had the effect to develop them, and many cruised back and forth in trade across the Atlantic. It is said that before the Revolution a regulation of England allowed lumber to be imported to the mother country only in sloops, which was one reason for their large size, a sloop built on the Kennebec in 1772 registering 140 tons. These vessels carried one and two square topsails and two jibs when bound on long voyages.

Ship-building flourished at Philadelphia, Baltimore, and Charlestown to some extent before the revolutionary war. Vessels were fitted out by their merchants chiefly for foreign trade, and while not remarkable for number the shipping of these ports was well built and well modeled. Philadelphia was always active in the West India trade, and at one time had almost entire possession of the East India trade to this country.

Each period of our national history has had its peculiarly profitable industry, and before the Revolution ship-building was the one which took nearly the first rank with us. By 1760 from 300 to 400 trading vessels were being built annually in the different provinces, to say nothing of a multitude of small boats for fishing along shore. The coast from New York harbor to Eastport, Maine, was one long row of ship-yards, and wherever there was a village planted by the sea there some vessel was seen in course of construction. Workmen were drawn here from England, much to the disturbance of the master carpenters of that kingdom, and the latter asked parliament more than once in that period not to encourage America in the production of shipping, because of the emigration to which it led. The industry was a valuable one for America, as a large part of the tonnage built was for foreign owners, and the constant exportation of ships brought large sums of money annually to a country where coin was scarce and in great demand. The advantages enjoyed by our ship-builders were, in the first place, cheap timber, low wages, and long days, the men toiling in the yards from sunrise to sunset; and, secondly, the possession of great fisheries, a good foreign commerce, a parliamentary law forbidding foreign-built ships to bring foreign goods to any of our provinces except from their own home ports, and a passion for foreign trade on the part of American merchants, that field of enterprise being the most profitable one in which they could employ their capital. The magnitude that ship-building had attained a few years before the Revolution is illustrated by a report to the house of commons in 1792, in which appears the following information: In 1769 the colonies built and launched 389 vessels, 113 square-rigged and 276 sloops and schooners, of an aggregate burden of 20,001 tons. Of these Massachusetts (including Boston and Salem) provided nearly one-half, New Hampshire and Rhode Island the next largest number, while New York had only 5 square-rigged vessels and 14 sloops and schooners, measuring in all 955 tons. Pennsylvania owned 1,344 tons, Virginia 1,249 tons, North and South Carolina 1,396 tons, and Connecticut 1,542 tons, while Georgia had 1 sloop and 1 schooner, whose combined measure was only 50 tons. In 1769 the entrances to all the ports of the present United States amounted to 332,146 tons and the clearances to 339,302 tons, of which 99,121 tons cleared for Great Britain, 42,601 for southern Europe and Africa, 96,382 for the British and foreign West Indies, and 101,198 for the continent of America and the Bahamas. The aggregate value of the whole imports amounted to £2,623,412, and the exports to £2,852,441, of which Great Britain sent £1,604,975, receiving in return £1,531,516.

During the Revolution ship-building was nearly suspended. English cruisers hovered near our coasts and captured and destroyed large numbers of vessels, the whaling and fishing fleet being almost annihilated. Foreign trade suffered the same fate. Raids were made on various coast towns and the shipping in port was burned; it was not safe to send anything except an armed vessel to sea, and few, except privateers intended especially for preying upon English merchantmen, were fitted out at any American port. A great part of the idle fishing and merchant fleet being employed in privateering in that war, for the time being it was a profitable field for them, and while the losses to their owners were large at times, their gains were sometimes immense, little armed sloops frequently capturing large merchantmen. The ships of one Newburyport merchant who built the first privateer of the Revolution took 23,360 tons of shipping and 2,225 men during her career, the prizes, with their cargoes, selling for 3,950,000 specie dollars. Four frigates and three sloops-of-war were built for Congress, familiarizing our people with the idea of producing powerful vessels of large class, and as the war went along large privateers were built by many merchants, especially in New England, Philadelphia, and Baltimore.

When the war ended many ships were too large for the coasting and other employments in which the bulk of our tonnage had been previously employed, and were no more fit for the small shopping business along the coast and to the West Indies than the great Californiamen of to-day would be for yachting; but while retaining a part at least of their armament, these ships were speedily converted into merchantmen, and were sent, from the necessities of the case, to China and distant parts of the world. It was a Baltimore vessel which, in 1785, sailed into the Canton river and first displayed the new flag there, returning with a cargo of teas, chinaware, silks, etc. In September, 1788, Captain Read, of an American ship, returned to Philadelphia from a voyage to China. The ship Atlantic, of Salem, in 1788, was the first to display the flag in Surat, Bombay, and Calcutta. The peaceful victories of American vessels in the following twenty-five years in the trade to these distant lands sprang, in great measure, from the possession of large privateers at the close of the Revolution, and were also due, in part, to the new conditions under which shipping enterprise had to be conducted after peace was declared. After 1783 American ships were foreign vessels in the eye of British law. Cut off at once from a part of the trade which they had enjoyed before the Revolution, they were compelled to go into the fields of employment which were open to them, and the East India and Asiatic trades being free, our larger merchantmen went into them at once.

Nothing else could have been expected than that American ships should come under the operation of the British navigation act immediately after peace. Nevertheless John Adams and other representatives of Congress were sent to London to endeavor to negotiate such a treaty of commerce as would secure as nearly as possible the advantages which had been enjoyed before the war; but they were unable to negotiate a treaty, and failed even to secure equality as to tonnage taxes. The same repulse was met with at the courts of France and Spain, and the American government was compelled to pass retaliatory laws. The first Congress under the Constitution met in April, 1789. July 20, 1789, two acts became laws which were intended expressly to secure fair play for American shipping abroad. They provided that on each entry from a foreign port an American vessel should pay a tax of 6 cents per ton, a vessel built in America and owned abroad 30 cents per ton, and a foreign vessel 50 cents per ton. Goods imported in American vessels were to pay 10 per cent. less duty, and India and China goods from 9 to 25 per cent. less duty. These laws were effective in securing commercial treaties and enlarging the field of employment for American ships.

The sixteen years that followed, ending with the war of 1812, were perilous times for American ships. English policy excluded us from a profitable trade with the British West Indies, and the same policy led to the searching of our merchant vessels for British subjects, the capture and confiscation of our vessels and cargoes, and the detention of large numbers of them for evasions of English law. England, France, and Holland were at war through a greater part of that time, and this led to other troubles. If the right of neutral nations to trade peacefully with nations with which they were themselves at peace had been fully established, the ships of the new republic would have become the common carriers of the whole world; but to prevent us from gaining that advantage, as well as to injure each other, England and France reciprocally issued a number of famous decrees and orders, each one forbidding trade with her rival, and these orders were vigorously enforced by the detention, seizure, and confiscation of hundreds of American vessels and cargoes and millions of dollars' worth of property—a policy which certainly had the desired effect. In that period ship-building thrived better than did ship-owning. A great many privateers were built, and to replace the large losses of tonnage new vessels had to be produced continually; but there were years when the industry languished, in consequence of the loss of capital and the embargoes and non-importation acts passed by our own government. The news of the peace of 1814 had an instant effect for good. Many privateers were building in Maine, Massachusetts, and elsewhere, and when the news came the ship-carpenters dropped their tools to rejoice over the ending of the disastrous war, but took them up again next day to complete their ships for the new mission of peaceful trade. Ax, hammer, and calking-iron were put to work in scores of yards that had been long lying idle. The maritime world was in excitement, as after so long a paralysis of commerce the ships first in the field were sure to earn the best freights and the cargoes first imported to bring the most profitable returns. Everybody began to think of ships, and in less than a week after receipt of the news of peace ship-building sprang into activity on every part of the coast engaged in the industry.

March 3, 1815, Congress passed a law forbidding any foreign vessel to bring goods to America, except from the country to which it belonged. This act was the legislative weapon by whose unsparing use we were enabled in the course of a few years to obtain from every foreign nation a treaty of reciprocity in trade and to break down, one by one, the vexatious obstructions of foreign law to the free enterprise of American citizens in the carrying trade of the world. The legislative annals of Congress contain the complete record of this struggle and the victory. After 1815 our maritime career was one of great prosperity.

A permanent impression had been made upon the form and rig of American vessels by forty years of war and interference. It was during that period that the shapes and fashions which prevail to-day were substantially attained. The old high poop-decks and quarter galleries disappeared with the lateen and the lug sail on brigs, barks, and ships; the sharp stern was permanently abandoned; the curving home of the stem above the hawse holes went out of vogue, and vessels became longer in proportion to beam. The round bottoms were much in use, but the tendency toward a straight rise of the floor from the keel to a point half way to the outer width of the ship became marked and popular. Hollow water-lines fore and aft were introduced; the fore foot of the hull ceased to be cut away so much and the swell of the sides became less marked; the bows became somewhat sharper and were often made flaring above the water, and the square sprit sail below the bowsprit was given up. American ship-builders had not yet learned to give the vessels much sheer, however, and in the majority of them the sheer-line was almost straight from stem to stern. Nor had they learned to divide the topsail into an upper and a lower sail, and American vessels were distinguished by their short lower masts and the immense hoist of the topsail. The broadest beam was still at two-fifths the length from the bow. Hemp rigging, with broad channels and immense tops to the masts, was still retained; but the general arrangement and cut of the head, stay, square, and spanker sails at present in fashion were reached. The schooner rig had also become thoroughly popularized, especially for small vessels requiring speed, and the fast vessels of the day were the brigs and schooners, which were made long, sharp on the floor, and low in the water, with considerable rake to the masts. The changes made in those forty years of perilous enterprise were chiefly introduced for the sake of speed and ease in handling the sails and the vessel. A merchantman was always liable to be called on to fight or to run away, and quickness in maneuvering and ability to slip away from an armed cruiser were qualities of the first importance. Builders were called on to study models and rig with reference to the needs of the times, and the result was that after the war of 1812 Americans had the ablest and smartest vessels in the world. Many ideas adopted by our builders were borrowed from the French, among whom naval architecture had been most critically and scientifically studied. The French frigates sent to assist us in the Revolution were closely studied, and when taken out of water at Salem and elsewhere for repair their lines were sometimes copied and frequently imitated in American-built ships. Many men-of-war and merchantmen were built on the models of these frigates, and it is possible that a part of the admiration expressed by the French for American frigates built during the Revolution, especially for the Alliance, which was the pride and favorite of our navy, was due to that fact. Our vessels got rid of much of their old clumsy shape and look, and improved materially in speed and beauty and in all other desirable qualities. In the timber employed for building there was no change, except to employ more chestnut, locust, and some live oak, the latter being brought from the south. White oak was the main dependence for frames, center work, outside planking, water-ways, rails, etc., and was much used for ceiling and for beams. Pitch-pine also came into use after awhile, and was first used for beams, afterward for ceiling, and then for keelsons. White pine comprised the rest of the ship, except the upper spars, which were made of spruce, on account of the need of lightening the top gear as much as possible. Treenails, on account of the expense of iron, were liberally used for fastening. The principal part of the iron of our ships had to be imported, and this included not only the bolts, the bar-iron for the fittings of the spars, and much of the other iron work of the ship, but also the rigging chains and the anchors; afterward, when iron chain cables were introduced, they, too, were at first imported. After the termination of hostilities, when our merchant marine had fairly settled down to peaceful enterprise and heavy freighting, our ships lost some of the jaunty character acquired from 1775 to 1814, but that was only because the builders were free to adopt the models best suited to the trades in which the vessels were to be employed, and not because they had forgotten the lessons taught by the previous years of war.

Within a few years after 1814 the foreign carrying trade of America had nearly all been gathered up by home-built vessels, and this was due to the superiority of the ships themselves, the vigor with which our citizens threw themselves into foreign trade, and the protection afforded them by our laws. There were no railroads then, no steamboats, no mines of gold and silver, no cattle ranches, no great and general development of manufacturing industry. Foreign trade was the field for the most profitable employment of our capital, as nearly all our manufactured goods had to be bought in Europe. Travel upon the sea was entirely carried on in sailing vessels. Immigration, which was only at the rate of about 8,000 a year before 1825, rose to over 20,000 a year in 1830, and to 300,000 a year about 1850. The fisheries were prolific and profitable, producing a vast surplus that had to be marketed abroad; and our fertile fields and wonderful forests yielded a great variety of important products, which were in large demand abroad, while on the other hand the teas, coffees, spices, fruits, silks, and wares of the far East were in larger demand among our people. The persistent efforts of the government at Washington having gained, little by little, fair and equal rights for our ships abroad, all the conditions were favorable to foreign trade, and, so far at least as shipping is concerned, our national history from 1814 to 1861 records little except the varying phases of a peaceful development of a profitable foreign commerce, and of the naval art to which it gave steady and paying employment.

Ships naturally took the shapes which fitted them best for the goods they had to carry. The cotton ships were a special class. They were sent out to carry bales of cotton and hogsheads of tobacco from the southern states to Europe and bring back salt, iron, and general manufactures. Great capacity was the prime consideration. Before the powerful compressing apparatus of to-day was invented a gross ton of cotton occupied about 100 cubic feet of space, the reduction to 60 cubic feet being a late achievement. To carry a good cargo of this bulky commodity, therefore, required a large vessel; and as a large ship is expensive, owners prudently studied how to gain the capacity they wanted without at the same time incurring new cost of operation. Tonnage taxes and port charges were the expenses most dreaded, as being the least within the control of owner or master after the vessel was launched. Advantage was taken of the laws for the measurement of vessels to reduce the official tonnage of the cotton ships considerably, (a) and the rule of the law (adopted from the English practice),

---

a May 6, 1864, Congress established a new system of measurement, in accordance with the modern English practice, and American vessels are now measured under the tonnage law of that date. The register length of a vessel is the length from the fore part of planking on the stem to the after part of the rudder-post (after part of the main stern-post in screw steamers), measured on the upper deck, or, in the case of three-deck vessels, on the second deck from below. The beam is the broadest part from outside to outside of planking. The depth of hold is measured from the under side of the deck plank to the floor of the hold. The tonnage of the vessel is only an expression of her actual internal cubical capacity in tons of 100 cubic feet each. It does not express her carrying power; it is merely a standard of measurement. The cubical capacity of the hull is ascertained by what is called "Simpson's one-third rule". The capacity of the houses on deck, the space under the poop-deck, and all other inclosures, is next ascertained, and the total is the vessel's gross tonnage. The adoption of the new measurement law has left builders absolutely untrammeled as to models. It may be stated, incidentally, that the cargo-carrying power of American sailing ships is about 1½ times their register tonnage. A ship of 2,000 tons register will carry about 3,000 tons of dead-weight cargo.

mathematically expressed, was as follows (L being the length from the fore part of the stem to the after part of the stern-post, measured on deck; B the breadth from outside to outside of planking at the broadest part of the vessel; D, the depth of hold from the plank of the deck to the ceiling of the hold, assumed to be ½ B.):

$$\frac{(L - \tfrac{3}{5} B) \times B \times \tfrac{1}{2} D}{95}$$

This was the rule for double-decked vessels. In single-decked vessels the actual depth was taken, instead of considering one-half the beam as the depth; the old divisor of 94 was superseded by 95, the latter being more accurate.

This was very nearly the old European rule for obtaining the actual tons weight of cargo the vessel would carry. It was, at best, only a rough approximation, as the ship often carried more than her official tonnage, often less. The reasonable accuracy of this rule depended entirely on closely following the model of the old merchantmen of about 1700. In those ancient vessels the stem raked forward from the keel about three-fifths of the length of the vessel's main beam, and, as the extreme bow thus had no buoyancy of its own, it was a part of the vessel not appropriated for cargo. The available depth of old vessels was about one-half the beam. A ton of goods occupied from 40 to 42 cubic feet of space, and the rule was an effort to arrive at a fair statement of the tons of goods that could be stowed within a vessel, or the part of the displacement which was due to the weight of cargo alone. Builders of cotton ships were able to turn the inaccuracy of the law to their own advantage and lengthened out the bow under water, so that the deduction of three-fifths of the beam made the tonnage length less than the actual length. They also made the hold much wider at the water than on deck, and much deeper than one-half the beam, and also constructed large poop and top-gallant-forecastle decks, covering nearly the whole top of the ship, open, however, amidships, which were good for the stowage of 200 or 300 bales of cotton, which, nevertheless, escaped tonnage taxation. The result was a roomy ship, with the old-fashioned falling home of the top sides, which passed muster at the custom-house as of far less capacity than she really had. The government did not get its just dues, but shipping was benefited. Boston, Kennebunk, and Bath built a great many vessels of this model, and the builders of those places won the reputation in time of producing the largest ships of a given official tonnage in America. In the tables of tonnage built in the United States from 1814 to 1861 some allowance must be made for this fact, as the actual amount of tonnage produced was larger than the tables show. The bark Saone (Figs. 28 and 29), built at Bath, Maine, in 1846, the model of which has been preserved, is a fair specimen of the "kettle-bottoms", as they were called, of that period.

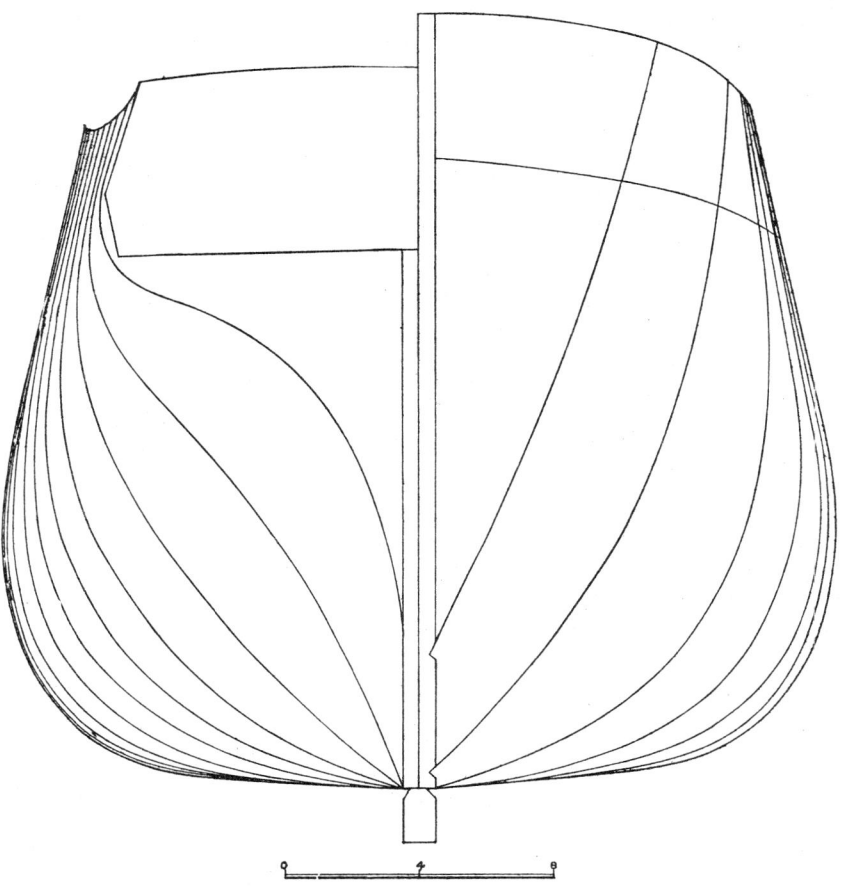

Fig. 28.—Bark Saone, built at Bath, Maine, in 1846, for William A. Rea, of Boston; register, 292 tons.

Length on deck from stem to taffrail, 116⅝ feet; breadth of beam, molded, at upper deck, 21¾ feet; depth, molded, 16¾ feet; swell of sides, 20 inches. First square station, 3 feet from rabbet of stem at rail; Nos. 1 to 7, 6 feet apart; 7 to 8, 9½ feet; 8 to 18, 6½ feet. Coefficient of midship section to 11¼ feet, or about two-thirds depth from keel, 0.89 per cent.; coefficient of displacement, 0.69 per cent. Angle of entrance at bow on load-line, 155°, angles below diminishing to 60°. Angle of run at load-line, 95°, angles below diminishing to 20°. Bark will carry 460 tons of cargo on 14 feet draught of water, reckoned from top of keel.

As no roomy ship could ever be loaded down to her deepest draught with so light and fleecy a cargo as cotton, it was customary to stow away bales in every available sheltered space to be found on board, from the limber strake to the main rail, and even the mess-table in the cabin was often a bale of cotton. No matter how big the cargo, the ship would not be down in the water to her bearings, and would be top-heavy and crank in consequence; so that it was always necessary to carry from 100 to 300 tons of stone ballast for the sake of stability, and even then the "kettle bottoms" were apt to go away over on their sides whenever the wind was abeam and stay there, to the discomfort of all on board. The sailor loves to see a good space between the deck he treads and the water upon which he floats; and whatever beauties the owner saw in a "kettle bottom" that carried a big freight and paid him well, Jack saw none. His preference has always been for a ship that would stand up stiff under sail, and some of the cotton fleet would. They were not all of the model of the Saone. A good many had straight sides, with only enough of a curve home to wear a graceful look and to suit the inclination of the shrouds, and

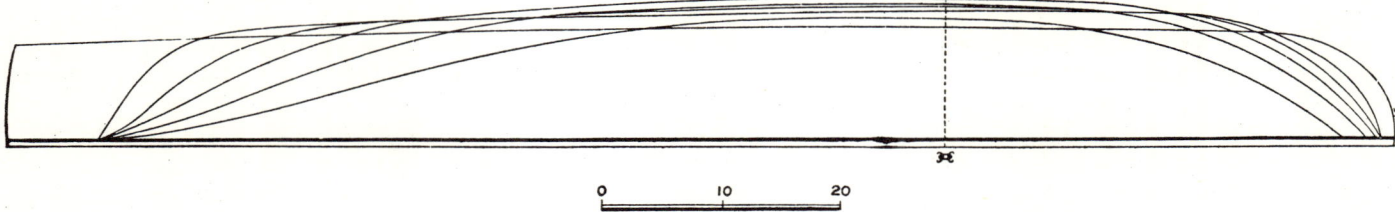

Fig. 29.—HALF-BREADTH PLAN OF BARK SAONE (SHOWING 5 WATER-LINES 3 FEET APART AND LINE OF MAIN RAIL).

often had a longer bow. These were large and fast carriers, and with a large freight on board they sailed well and attained an excellent rate of speed. American cotton ships in time began to do about two-thirds of all the business there was in their line from the ports of the United States, and thronged the wharves of New Orleans, Mobile, Savannah, Charleston, and New York, where the flag of this country is now seldom seen flying from the peak of a transatlantic vessel.

Reference has been made to the evasion of tonnage duties. The success of a ship is necessarily and chiefly due first to a rigid keeping down of all her expenses and to strict economy both in and out of port, and next to her being placed in charge of a good captain and crew, and the adoption of a model which would save taxation was a natural proceeding. It must be said, however, that the burdens of port charges and of taxation in its various forms never weigh hard on shipping unless trade is dull, freights are low, and competition is sharp. No matter how big and costly a ship, no matter what wages are paid or how expensively she is run (and a ship *is* an expensive investment, spending money right and left with a prodigality known in few forms of business), she can carry every burden if trade is good and freights are profitable and spend from 20 to 45 per cent. of her value, as she does, every year, without feeling it. When a ship does make money, it makes it rapidly.

Congress was called upon more than once after 1814 to legislate in behalf of our cotton-carrying fleet. France had considerable tonnage in the trade to New Orleans, and to protect it she enacted a discriminating duty on certain American goods. If brought in a French ship, cotton was to pay $1\frac{1}{2}$ cents per pound less duty, tobacco $1\frac{1}{8}$ cents per pound less, and potash $\frac{55}{100}$ths of a cent less—a discrimination which actually amounted to more than the freight. A French tobacco ship of 300 tons saved about $6,300 on each cargo over what an American vessel had to pay. In 1820 Congress levied a duty of $18 a ton on French vessels in retaliation; a step which secured equality in duties, and soon gave the carrying trade to American ships, by reason of the superiority of the vessels and the management of them.

The bulk of American tonnage during the period from 1814 to 1860 was employed in general freighting and passenger carrying between this continent and the eastern world, and some of it to and from South America. It was into this general trade that the fast privateers of 1812–'14 went after peace, and in which they were steadily engaged until they were worn out, which was in about twenty years' time, when they were succeeded in general freighting by a fuller class of ships, carrying large cargoes and spreading a vast expanse of canvas. It was required that vessels should carry the greatest number of tons of goods on a given draught of water consistent with stability under sail, rolling easily in a sea-way, steering well, and sailing fast, and there was great difficulty in deciding upon a model which would answer all the multifarious demands of trade, as there was such wide variety in cargoes. Sometimes the charter would be for a cargo of railroad iron; sometimes for teas and East India goods; sometimes for grain and flour and naval stores; at other times for a miscellaneous cargo. A good average style of vessel, which would do fairly well under any circumstances, was the best result that could be attained so far as model was concerned, and builders always found it safe to err on the side of capacity to carry a little larger and heavier cargo than was called for. Commerce was growing rapidly. If there was not business enough to guarantee full cargoes when the ship was built, there was apt to be more than enough before the twenty years of her existence should have expired, and no owner ever complained because his vessels carried bigger freights than was expected of them. The tendency was decidedly toward full ships, the old plan being followed of locating the dead flat, or largest section of the ship, at two-fifths the length from the bow. The round floors and the long turn of the bilge, lingering from the preceding century, gradually gave way to flatter floors and a sharper turn of the bilge; the huge swell of the sides was slowly abandoned; figure-heads were left off; the bow was made flaring above water; more sheer was given; the center of buoyancy was moved farther aft; and the handsome freight-carrier used between 1845 and 1860 came into existence in consequence of the successive changes introduced. One sample of this model was the Universe (Fig. 30), built at New York in 1851 to sail between that port and Liverpool, which was one of the first vessels to depart from the old rule of broadest beam at two-fifths the length from the bow, placing it nearer amidships. Her water-lines were hollow forward and aft. The Universe was not a remarkable ship, but her lines have been preserved and are valuable for reference. Reference also is made to the Great Republic, illustrated elsewhere.

The majority of American ship-yards receiving their principal patronage from the merchant owners of this class of ships, the freighter was naturally carefully studied in all its details, and much attention was paid to the subject of strength. European builders gained the rigidity of hull needed to withstand the constantly varying stress brought on the different parts of the ship's length when floating among the waves by strapping the outside of the frame timbers with iron bands extending from a longitudinal iron band bolted to the top timbers down diagonally across the frames to the ends of the floor timbers. These straps crossed amidships in a sort of lattice-work, and were bolted to each other and to the frame at each crossing. From 50 to 100 tons of iron would be put into this work. Straps were also used on the inside of the frames, as also wooden straps and riders; and the same device was adopted in many American ship-yards, particularly at New York, Boston, and Bath. The general plan adopted, however, was one original with American builders, which served the purpose well and has continued in constant use to the present time. The inner planking of the hull, or, as it is called, the ceiling, was made extremely thick on the turn of the bilge, a strip about 10 feet in width being laid with squared logs from 10 to 12 inches thick the whole length of the hold. From this thick stuff the ceiling diminished in thickness to the deck, the planks covering the upright part of the side of the hold remaining, however, of unusual thickness. The water-ways, clamps, and other longitudinal pieces were all made of large dimensions. All this work was fitted to its place with the greatest care, the edges of adjoining pieces faying against each other very tightly. The keelsons were also carried up very high and bolted strongly through and through, and sister keelsons were added. In large freighting ships the iron and composition bolts driven down through the keelson, frames, and keel were often from 9 to 10 feet in length. With

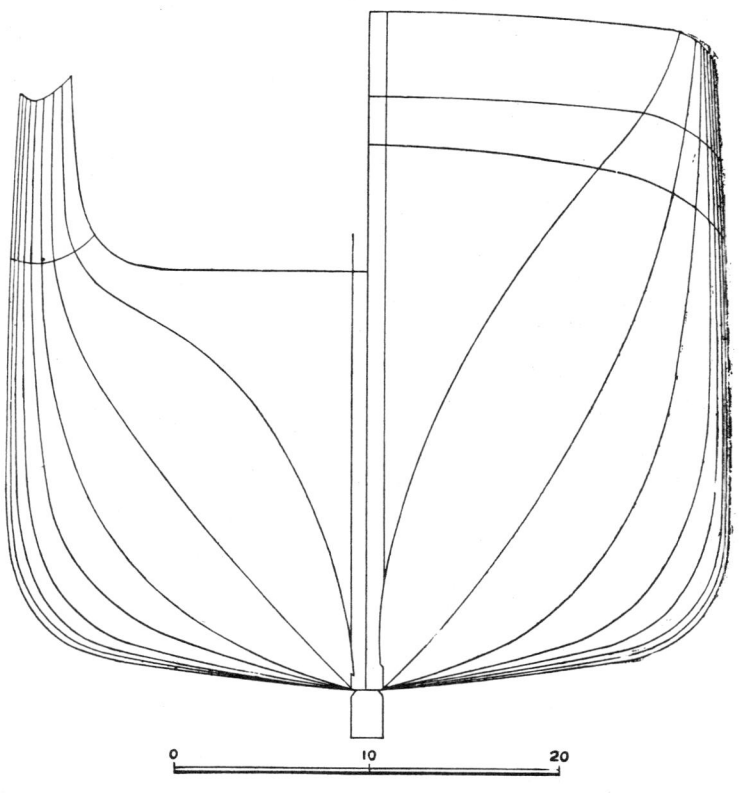

Fig. 30.—FREIGHTING-SHIP UNIVERSE, 1851, AT NEW YORK.

Register tonnage, 1,298 feet. Length between perpendiculars on 15-foot water-line, 175 feet; breadth, 37⅞ feet; depth from plank-sheer to keel, 27 feet. Weight of vessel, about 940 tons net; with anchors, cables, and tank of 2,000 gallons of water aboard, 1,033 tons. Draught, thus loaded, 10 feet 1¾ inches. Capacity between that and 19 feet draught, 1,488 tons net. Coefficient of displacement, 0.67 per cent. Center of buoyancy at 15-feet draught, 8½ feet above keel. Foremast reaches load-line 30 feet from forward perpendicular; mainmast 74 feet aft; mizzen-mast 48 feet aft of mainmast.

such a tremendous backbone, aided by the thick stuff on the bilge and strong clamps and water-ways, wooden ships attained a rigidity and strength never before known, and did not need the aid of iron straps on the frame-timbers, although strapping was sometimes resorted to. This system of heavy scantling became universal in American vessels of every class after 1830. The coasting schooners of to-day are, in consequence, more heavily built than even East Indiamen were before the adoption of this system.

As the weight of additional timber and material was concentrated in the lower part of the hull, the center of gravity of the ship was kept well down (a point of some value) and stability was greatly promoted. A coasting vessel of good model thus built would often sail from port to port, seeking cargo, with the hold entirely empty, without putting aboard a pound of ballast to steady her. A large number of the wooden sailing vessels of the present day in America have this quality, which is valuable at all times, and especially to coasters, because it saves them a great deal of time and money. It is a trait the iron sailing vessel does not possess. The English merchantmen which frequent our ports now, being nearly all of iron, cannot stir without ballast; and they require ballast when laden with cargo more frequently than do our wooden merchantmen.

Good ships are necessary to maritime eminence, but good sailors are equally required. The great prosperity of our shipping from 1814 to 1861 was due in large measure to the excellent personnel of the crews and officers of the merchantmen. These people were recruited in the main from the fisheries and the coasting trade. The majority were American born, having homes and families ashore, and were persons of good principles, abstaining especially from the use of spirituous liquors. Sailors were paid good wages, and the captains were spurred by the payment of a percentage of the freight and passage money as a premium. A good crew means energy on board ship, quick voyages, the saving of time in getting into and out of port, the rescue of the vessel from wreck and injury under trying circumstances, a lower cost of insurance, smaller bills of expense generally, and fewer losses to the owners. The energy and daring of the excellent crews of that period were the admiration of the maritime world, and gifts of plate, the freedom of the city, and other testimonials to their merit were not uncommon. The temperance that prevailed on American vessels was the subject of comment in a report to the British parliament in 1838. The committee said:

> The happiest effects have resulted from the experiments tried in the American navy and merchant service to do without spirituous liquors as an habitual article of daily use, there being at present more than 1,000 sail of American vessels traversing all the seas of the world in every climate, without the use of spirits by their officers and crews, and being, in consequence of this change, in so much greater a state of efficiency and safety than other vessels not adopting this regulation that the public insurance companies in America make a return of five per cent. of the premium of insurance on vessels completing their voyages without the use of spirits, while the example of British ships, sailing from Liverpool on the same plan, has been productive of the greatest benefit to ship-owners, underwriters, merchants, officers, and crews.

A special class of ships which grew up after 1814 were the sailing packets, or vessels carrying both passengers and freight, which cleared from port on regular days in each month and ran back and forth between special points only. When the war ended there were only a few small British ships in the packet service between England and America, and scarce any between America and other parts of the world. Soon after the peace, however, a large number of lines came into existence as a natural outgrowth of the rush of emigration from Europe to America and the general expansion of ocean travel and trade. The carrying of passengers was a profitable business, and there was considerable competition among shipping merchants to get the largest share. None but the best and finest vessels could be used in this business, and the old-fashioned freighting ships, with their small cabins and houses, underwent a considerable change to adapt them to the new state of affairs. A great many houses in Portland, Boston, New York, Philadelphia, Baltimore, Norfolk, Charleston, and New Orleans put their money into ships especially built for the passenger service, and ran them in regular lines to all the ports abroad and on our own coast whither trade and travel chiefly tended. In the coasting trade brigs, schooners, and barks were used, but in the packet service to foreign ports barks and ships only were thought of. The latter were vessels of the largest size, handsomely built and sumptuously fitted up, and carried often from 600 to 1,000 persons and 1,000 tons or more of freight. The lines to Liverpool, Havre, and Australia often comprised 15 or 20 vessels, each of the finest specimens of marine architecture afloat. When the clipper era began the packets improved in speed and made trips across the ocean to Europe and to Australia which it took the steamships years to surpass. These lines were owned chiefly in the north by old shipping houses of great experience and large capital.

It was at New York that the packet business between America and Europe chiefly centered. There were lines from other ports; but New York was the pioneer, and always kept the lead, and had the most and finest packets. The New Yorkers were restless under their dependence on the old English ships sailing to Falmouth, which ran only in the winter time, and besides were slow. In the summer time they sailed from Halifax. It was resolved to run an American line from New York, and a start was made a year or two after the war by Isaac Wright & Co. with the four ships Pacific, Amity, James Cropper, and William Thompson, of from 400 to 500 tons each. These packets constituted the Black Ball line, so called from the round black dot in a white field which was adopted as the pennant of the ships. They were put at once into the packet business to Liverpool, sailing the first of every month, and made the run outward in an average of 23 days and the homeward run in 40 days. The ships were well built, fleet, and handsome, were managed with great energy, and were a success from the start. In about six months four vessels were added to the line, sailing on the 16th of every month, and each vessel made three round trips a year. The Black Ball line remained in existence, though changed in ownership, until the decline of American shipping finally terminated its career, and was one of the last to surrender the field to the new monarch of the sea, steam. A London line followed the Black Ball; then a Havre line was started. In 1821 a second line to Liverpool, called the Red Star, was established, sailing on the 24th of every month, the four ships of this pennant being the Manhattan, Hercules, Panthea, and Meteor. Then Fish, Grinnell & Co. and Thaddeus Phelps & Co. originated the Swallow Tail line, to sail on the 8th of every month.

One of the best of the New York packet lines was John Griswold's, which started in 1823 with the Sovereign, Cambria, President, Hudson, Columbia, Hannibal, Corinthian, and Ontario. In 1837 the number of vessels was increased to twelve.

The New York packets were all superior vessels, and were commanded by a remarkably fine class of men, the best families on the ship-building coasts contributing men to officer these ships. The frequency and regularity of their sailing were strong points. Toward the last there was a packet sailing every five days. No foreign vessel got the mails in those days, as they were all given, at least by the American government, to American packets; and so great was the reputation of these vessels that they were regularly patronized not only by Americans going abroad, but by the West India merchants, Canadians, and even by the English officers of the large garrisons in Halifax and the provinces generally. These packets drove nearly all their foreign rivals out of the business. Many efforts were made to compete with them, but never with any success.

In the construction of these vessels the best talent of the day was employed, and they were generally built for the owners by contractors who had already attained some celebrity. The rivalry of the various lines was keen, and it was this eager competition as much as anything else which led to the continual improvement in models, rig, workmanship, and general excellence of American ships, each new vessel being expected to excel some rival or all the predecessors of its own fleet in some desirable quality. Builders found that more was required of them than at any previous period of their history, and in order to hold their own and maintain the reputation of their yards they were forced to study the scientific principles involved in the form and sparring of ships. After 1815 the designers and builders of packets could not afford to remain in ignorance of the fundamental principles of their art. They did not sufficiently know what made one ship bad and another ship good, and therefore began to study. They sought every source of information. Books were imported from Europe, and many builders went to school to the constructors of the American navy. Delicate tests were made with small models of different forms; fast fishes were cut up and their shapes analyzed; the flow of waves away from the bow of a boat was investigated, and every other conceivable point was looked into. The period from 1815 to 1850 was thus one of study, experiment, and discussion, especially in the large cities; and, in consequence, there grew up a race of acute and daring ship-builders, whose achievements were the wonder of the world, and whose fashions were imitated, both on this and the other side of the ocean, by everybody who built ships.

The qualities desired in a packet ship were strength, speed, stability at sea, ease of handling, easy rolling, beauty of model, and comfort in the passenger accommodations. It must not be supposed that these were all attained at one bound; on the contrary, the best good general model for the packet ship, and the best sizes and dimensions of timbers, were reached only by patient study and slow degrees. A great many bad ships were built before all the questions that interested the building world were decided; but it was the final result of the forty years of study and investigation following the war of 1812 that the sailing ship reached substantial perfection as an ocean carrier, and scarce any advance has been made from that day to this. So well is the art now understood that a ship can be built to perform exactly the service required of it and to meet its owner's expectations fully. What remains to America now to accomplish is, first, to reduce the cost of ships; and, secondly, to handle them in such manner when at sea as to withstand the general competition of other maritime nations.

Down to 1849 packets were either one- or two-decked vessels, with a poop-deck aft and a top-gallant forecastle forward. Those in the service to Europe were of from 900 to 1,100 tons register. The cargo was stored in the lower hold, some of the light freight going between decks if the cargo was a large one. The between-deck space aft was divided into cabins for the passengers; the middle portion was fitted up with kitchens, pantries,

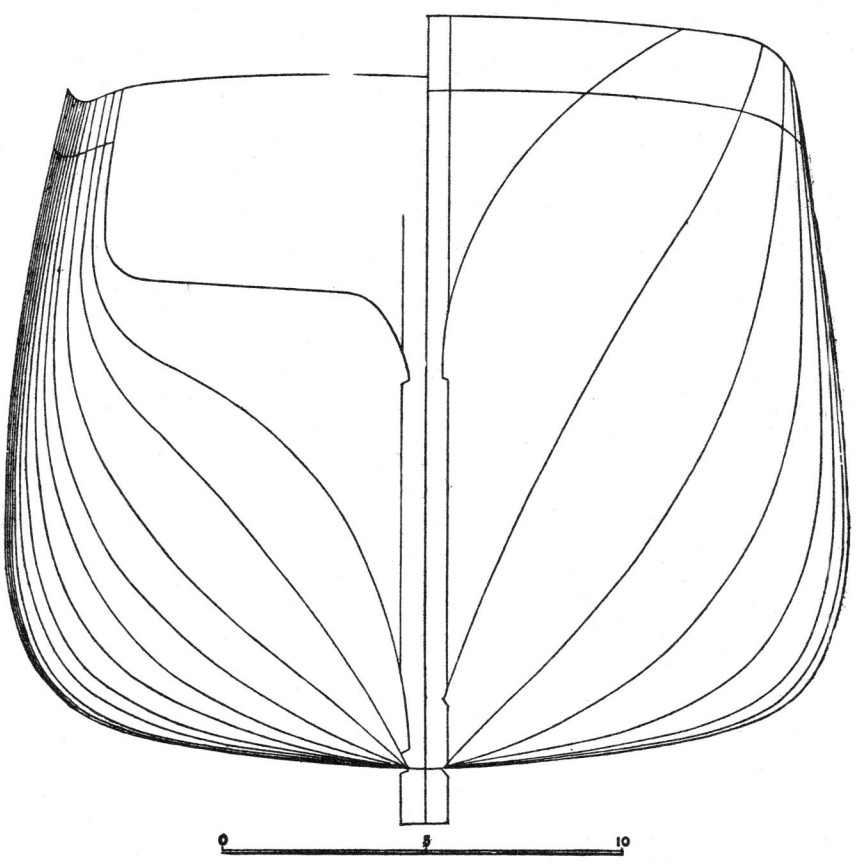

Fig. 31.—Lines of the packet ship Guy Mannering.

etc. The steerage passengers and crew were forward. On deck were houses for the crew and various officers, with others which served as vestibules to the apartments below. The first three-decker was the Guy Mannering (Fig. 31), of 1,419 tons, which was built in 1849 by William H. Webb, at New York—a noble structure and a good ship. Three-deckers, with poop and top-gallant forecastle decks, were afterward the popular style of packet. The Guy Mannering was $190\frac{1}{4}$ feet long, register measurement, $40\frac{1}{4}$ feet beam, and $28\frac{2}{3}$ feet deep in the hold. At 20 feet draught above the keel she would carry 2,400 tons of cargo. Her greatest beam was at $\frac{2}{5}$ L. from the bow. The lower water-lines at bow and stern were concave, and at the plank-sheer and rail the bow was almost round. Her building lines are given above.

The American packets carried the best officers and the largest crews of any ships afloat. They were fast, dry, handsome, and sumptuously fitted up, and were managed with so much energy, care, and ability that they gained a virtual monopoly of the passenger, mail, and express traffic to Europe. They made the best time of any ships afloat, were insured at the lowest rates and earned the highest freights, and superseded nearly all the English, French, and German ships in that business, and their success and fame were the subject of intense envy abroad. After 1830 there were frequent dispatches of rival packets, transient, but all American, from Boston, New York, and Philadelphia to England and other parts of Europe. All the ships sailed with great speed, and made the run across the Atlantic in excellent time. The James Baines ran from Boston to Liverpool in 12 days 6 hours;

the Red Jacket once ran from New York to Liverpool in 13 days 11½ hours; the Mary Whiteridge made the trip from Baltimore in 13 days 7 hours; but the usual time was 19, 20, and 21 days to Liverpool, and from 30 to 35 days homeward. One of the New York packets, the Great Western, sailed regularly from New York on the 4th of March every year with a copy of the President's message to Congress. As they were the noblest ships of their day, the packets had the most dignified names. President, Vanguard, Yorktown, Ivanhoe, Guy Mannering, London, New York, Sovereign, Courier, Orbit, Napoleon, Manhattan, Hercules, Independence, Albert Gallatin, Abbott Lawrence, and United States were the class of titles given them. The ships of one of the New York lines were called after eminent actors.

English steamers were sent out in 1838 and 1840 to compete with these packet lines. The Cunard line began in 1840, backed by a subsidy of £90,000 a year, afterward increased to £145,000. The Americans responded in 1847 with a line of steamers to Bremen, and in 1850 with the Collins line to Liverpool. Then began the era of steam navigation of the Atlantic; but the steamers at first did not display remarkable speed. Under ordinary circumstances their trips across the Atlantic were made only in good average sailing-packet time. Nor did they have great carrying power, as their capacity was occupied with coal and machinery; but they enjoyed the advantage of being able to pursue their course in storms, and in 20 years they had gained so much in speed and carrying power and were so heavily backed with subsidies that sailing ships could no longer compete with them. The United States aided the revolution from sail to steam just enough to destroy her splendid packet lines to Europe completely without replacing them by steamships carrying her own flag. In 1857 all the subsidies to steamers to Europe were withdrawn by Congress, and, in consequence, the Collins and the Bremen lines were taken off. The sailing packets had meanwhile been entirely superseded, and from that day to this the passenger, mail, and express traffic of the Atlantic has been transacted almost wholly in European-built steamships. Sailing packets had disappeared even before the war of 1861, which gave the final crushing blow to the hopes of early American supremacy of the sea. The coast lines of packets were also superseded during the same period by steam vessels.

One peculiarity of this period was the increase in the size of vessels. Referring again to the table of vessels registered at Boston from 1674 to 1714, it will be noted how small were the merchantmen of early days. The fleet with which our forefathers navigated the oceans of the world was composed of little vessels, which would be none too large for the coasting trade now. The three-masted schooners carrying lumber from the southern states to northern ports at the present time would have been regarded then as immense ships. In 1714 sloops were sailing to Europe, and even from the Hudson river to China, and brigs and ships of from 200 to 400 tons were the large merchantmen for the service across the Atlantic and to the East Indies. The lack of capital on the part of our merchants, and the lack of a dense population in the United States, kept the size of vessels down. There was also some timidity on the part of owners and builders with regard to the ability of long ships to live in heavy weather, as they dreaded making the hulls long enough to reach two waves, fearing lest when bow and stern were lifted on different crests the midship portion, being in the trough of the sea, would lack support and be terribly strained. After 1812, however, large ships were demanded. The frigates of the war had done well enough at sea, and owners took courage. Builders were equal to the emergency, and a few large merchantmen were built and sent out, their performance dispelling all fears on the subject of length. Every new experiment in the maritime world was keenly watched by a multitude of eager men, and it needed only the first half dozen of successful ships to prove that the way was clear for all who chose to embark their capital in large vessels. After that the only considerations that governed owners, so far as size was concerned, were their ability to command the capital to build large and the chances of receiving business enough for a big ship. Two of the large ships were the Splendid and the Superior, built in 1822 by Isaac Webb, at New York, for Charles Henry Hall, which were monsters at the time. They were intended for the China and East India trade, but were too large, and it is related that one or both were at one time laid up and partially dismantled because there was not business enough to employ them. Nevertheless, about 1825 the Washington, of nearly 1,000 tons, was built, the largest merchantman of her day, which excited such wonder in foreign ports that people thronged to the wharves to see her. It was many years later before the size of 1,100 tons was attained. In 1841 a bold experiment was made by Clark & Sewall, of Bath, who built the ship Rappahannock, 179.6 feet long, with 37 feet beam, custom-house measurement, and of 1,133 tons, the largest merchantman in the world. Her great size astonished everybody, and it was a general prediction that she would be a failure. It was not believed that there was foreign commerce enough to occupy such a vessel, and it was declared that even the Rothschilds could not afford to own her, and that she would be sure destruction to the fortunes of whoever undertook to employ her. The launching drew a great crowd of people to Bath. The Rappahannock was a bluff-bowed, full and long-bottomed ship, narrower on deck than below, and full-rigged. Her scantling was no larger than that of a 300-ton schooner of the present day, and the fastening throughout would now be considered light. The managing owner of the ship lived in New York, and he did, indeed, have some trouble in providing her with full cargoes. She ran as a packet to Liverpool in the summer time and as a cotton ship from New Orleans in the winter. A good illustration of the limited extent of the export trade of that period is the fact that freights to Liverpool always dropped one-eighth of a penny per pound when the Rappahannock was reported to be coming up to New Orleans, rates in that day ranging from five-eighths to a penny per pound. The ship was a success, living 21 years, and ending her existence in freighting coal to the Mediterranean; she foundered at sea.

MERCHANT SAILING VESSELS.

The following lists of vessels built for a few large shipping houses show the growth in size in sailing vessels for the deep sea after 1814:

VESSELS BUILT BY THE HOUGHTONS, OF BATH, MAINE, FOR THEMSELVES.

Year.	Vessel.	Register Dimensions. Length.	Breadth.	Depth.	Tonnage.	Year.	Vessel.	Register Dimensions. Length.	Breadth.	Depth.	Tonnage.
		Ft. In.	Ft. In.	Ft. In.				Ft. In.	Ft. In.	Ft. In.	
1819	Brig Bolton	72 4	22 9	8 7½	121	1855	Ship Potomac	193 6	36 5	18 2½	1,198
1822	Warren	94 9	23 5	12 3½	214	1856	Pocahontas	193 7	36 4	24 5	1,196
1823	Sublime	93 6	24 6	12 3	249	1856	Rochester	156 8	31 5	21 4	824
1824	Clarissa Ann	97 3	25 3	12 7½	276	1858	Bolton	180 6	34 3	17 0	987
1828	Caledonia	102 0	25 7½	12 9⅞	299	1859	Crescent City	184 6	37 5	24 2	1,205
1832	Ship Cordova	106 1½	26 5½	13 2¾	332	1859	Europa	177 4	36 9	24 2	1,174
1833	Braganza	111 5½	26 6	13 3	353	1860	Persia	182 4	35 2		1,248
1834	Missouri	117 3	27 5	13 8½	399	1860	Caledonia	179 3	37 3	24 0	1,179
1837	Rochester	131 2	30 1	15 5	563	1863	Virginia	177 0	35 5	23 6	1,094
1838	Hanover	135 0	30 8	15 4	577	1865	Scotia	182 6	36 8	24 5	1,171
1840	Bark Clinton	112 8	26 2	13 1	349	1866	China	184 8	38 1	24 2	1,173
1842	Princeton	105 0	25 0	12 6	296	1868	Arcadia	183 1	38 1	24 0	1,234
1845	Ship Charlotte Reed	128 6	28 4	14 2	471	1868	Prussia	184 2	36 6	23 9	1,212
1847	Milan	146 0	32 5	16 2½	699	1870	Austria	198 9	39 0	23 9	1,300
1848	Bark Henry Warren	113 3	26 0	13 0	347	1871	Columbia	205 9	40 0	24 0	1,471
1849	Ship Houghton	156 6	33 1	16 6½	787	1873	Louisiana	202 4	40 0	24 4	1,436
1850	Clara Ann	122 8½	27 5½	13 8¾	421	1874	Geneva	216 4	39 9	24 6	1,535
1851	Pelican State	153 4	33 7	16 9½	849	1875	Bohemia	221 7	40 2	25 5	1,633
1852	Kate Swanton	135 6	28 0	14 0	489	1876	Samaria	247 6	39 1	24 1½	1,509
1852	Northampton	174 9	35 9	23 7	1,130	1877	Armenia	223 3	40 4	25 0	1,698
1853	Shamrock	186 6	36 0	18 0	1,194	1882	Arabia	233 9	43 2	27 6	2,081
1854	Baltic	154 0	36 0	16 6	769						

VESSELS BUILT BY THE SEWALLS, OF BATH, MAINE, FOR THEMSELVES.

[By Clark & Sewall first, and after 1855 by E. & A. Sewall.]

Year	Vessel	Length	Breadth	Depth	Tonnage	Year	Vessel	Length	Breadth	Depth	Tonnage
1823	Brig Diana				199	1863	Brig Glendale	121 9	28 8¾		454
1824	Orbit	83 6	23 7½	11 6½	199	1864	Ship Intrepid	183 6	35 6		1,078
1825	Lewis	93 4	23 5	12 2¾	247	1864	Bark Volant	129 0	29 1		496
1827	Dummer	76 0	22 0	10 1	146	1864	Ship Ocean Signal	193 0	36 9		1,215
1828	Pleiades	98 4	25 0¾	12 8⅞	284	1865	Freeman Clark	190 1	38 5	24 6	1,336
1829	Schooner Emulous	72 0	21 1	7 6½	99	1865	Bark Frank Marion	143 5	31 4	20 4	678
1831	Ship Emperor	105 6½	25 9		314	1866	Ship Matterhorn	189 7	38 3	24 2	1,327
1832	Girard	110 5½	25 3		343	1866	Wetterhorn	151 8	31 5	20 6	698
1832	Tropic	110 10	26 5½		349	1868	Hermon	193 1	38 2½	24 2	1,316
1833	Ceylon	120 0	27 1½		421	1869	Tabor	195 5	36 8	24 5	1,339
1835	Roger Sherman	126 2	29 6		490	1869	Undaunted	207 3	41 1	27 7	1,764
1836	Diadem	140 7⅞	32 1		657	1871	Eric the Red	198 7	41 1	25 9½	1,580
1837	Ville de Paris	130 4	30 2		537	1872	Humboldt	177 6	35 5	22 1	1,018
1840	Pennsylvania	143 8	32 2		677	1872	Carrollton	198 2	39 6	24 6	1,450
1841	Genesee	128 2	28 0		459	1873	Sterling	208 4	42 7	25 11	1,731
1841	Rappahannock	179 6	37 0		1,133	1873	El Capitan	205 9	39 9	24 6	1,493
1843	Bark Detroit	102 0	25 3½		292	1873	Schooner Salilla	128 9	31 6	10 7	312
1845	Ship Macedonia	124 0	27 0¾		414	1874	Ship Granger	209 9	40 0	24 7	1,526
1846	Rio Grande	135 1	29 6		542	1874	Occidental	210 6	39 8	24 7	1,533
1847	Switzerland	134 1	30 6		570	1874	Oriental	220 1	42 2	24 9	1,688
1847	John C. Calhoun	143 11	32 11		708	1875	Continental	220 0	42 2	25 1	1,712
1848	Brig Marcia	86 8	23 2	8 10½	157	1875	Harvester	210 1	39 2	24 0	1,494
1848	Ship William D. Sewall	141 0	32 5		672	1876	Reaper	211 6	39 2	24 0	1,468
1850	Adriatic	147 0	32 8		715	1876	Thrasher	211 9	39 7	24 0	1,512
1851	Sarah G. Hyde	166 9	34 0		890	1876	Indiana	208 9	40 0	23 9½	1,487
1851	Erie	128 0	28 0		458	1877	Challenge	212 4	39 7	23 9½	1,456
1852	Commerce	180 0	36 1		1,085	1878	Schooner Carrie S. Bailey	137 6	32 1	11 7	396
1853	Lady Franklin	138 0	29 5½		549	1878	Ship Chesebrough	212 4	40 0	24 15	1,507
1854	Samaritan	191 3	37 0⅜		1,219	1879	Solitaire	213 7	40 1	24 1	1,531
1855	Holyhead	182 1	36 0		1,099	1880	Thomas M. Reed	227 4	42 4	27 0	1,987
1855	Kineo	159 6	33 7⅞		829	1880	Schooner Belle Higgins	143 1	32 9	11 9	412
1856	Hellespont	159 3	32 3½		767	1880	Kate Markee	142 8	34 2	14 8	503
1857	Leander	166 0	34 2½		896	1881	S. M. Thomas	167 0	35 2	15 0	761
1858	Valentia	158 0	33 2		799	1881	Ship Iroquois	237 1	43 6	28 1	2,121
1859	Villa Franca	170 9	34 1		918	1881	Schooner B. L. Lunt	163 2	35 6	15 6	758
1859	Vigilant	143 2	31 7		652	1882	Ship Henry Villard	219 2	39 8	24 1	1,553
1860	Ocean Scud	181 8	34 6		1,008	1882	Schooner Nora Bailey	145 3	33 0	12 3	448
1862	Vancouver	163 8	36 0		969	1882	Ship W. F. Babcock	240 8	43 8	28 0	2,029
1863	Vicksburg	183 1	36 6		1,130						

VESSELS BUILT BY DONALD McKAY IN EAST BOSTON.

[Custom-house dimensions.]

Year.	Vessel.	REGISTER DIMENSIONS. Length.	Breadth.	Depth.	Tonnage.	Year.	Vessel.	REGISTERED DIMENSIONS. Length.	Breadth.	Depth.	Tonnage.
		Feet.	*Feet.*	*Feet.*				*Feet.*	*Feet.*	*Feet.*	
1845	Ship Washington Irving	150 5/6	33	21	751	1854	Ship Santa Claus	184	38 1/2	23	1,256
1846	Anglo-Saxon	158	35 1/4	21	895	1854	Commodore Perry	212	44 11/12	29	1,964
1846	New World	187	40 1/2	28	1,404	1854	Japan	212	44 11/12	29	1,964
1847	Ocean Monarch	178 1/2	40	26 5/8	1,301	1854	Blanche Moore	220	41 2/3	25 7/12	1,787
1847	A. Z	143 1/2	32 1/6	22	675	1854	Bark Benin	155 1/6	32 1/2	15	692
1847	Anglo-American	149 1/2	32	20 1/4	704	1855	Ship Donald McKay	260 1/2	46	29	2,595
1848	Jenny Lind	141 1/2	28 1/2	22	533	1855	Defender	202 1/2	38 7/12	24 1/4	1,413
1848	L. Z	163 1/4	34 7/12	22 1/2	897	1855	Minnehaha	209	41 5/6	28 1/3	1,695
1849	Plymouth Rock	174 1/4	34 2/3	22 1/2	739	1856	Baltic	187 1/3	39 1/4	24 1/2	1,320
1849	Bark Helicon	128	26 1/2	19 1/3	414	1856	Adriatic	187 1/3	39 1/4	24 1/2	1,327
1849	Ship Reindeer	156 1/2	33 5/12	22	800	1856	Bark Henry Hill	140 1/2	30 1/2	14 1/2	567
1849	Parliament	173	35 1/3	22 1/2	998	1856	Ship Mastiff	168 4/5	36 1/2	22 1/2	1,031
1850	Moses Wheeler	165	33 5/6	23	872	1856	Amos Lawrence	193 3/4	39 1/2	24 1/4	1,396
1850	Daniel Webster	185	37 1/4	34	1,188	1856	Abbott Lawrence	202 1/2	39 11/12	24 1/3	1,498
1850	Stag Hound	209	39 2/3	23 1/2	1,534	1857	Flying Fish	198 1/2	38 1/6	22	1,346
1850	Cornelius Grinnell	182	36 5/12	23 1/2	1,118	1859	Alhambra	174 1/2	37	23 11/12	1,097
1850	Bark Sultana	121 1/3	28 1/3	14 1/2	452	1859	Schooner Benj. S. Wright	84	24	8	107
1850	Ship Antarctic	177	37	23 1/2	1,115		Side-wheel iron steamer Ashuelot. (a)	....	....	....	....
1851	Flying Cloud	229	40 2/3	21 1/2	1,782						
1851	North America	200 1/2	39 2/3	25 2/3	1,464	1861	Iron-clad monitor Nansett (a)	....	....	....	....
1851	Staffordshire	230	41	29	1,817	1865	Propeller (wooden) Treefoil (a)	....	....	....	....
1852	Sovereign of the Seas	258	44 1/2	28 1/4	2,421		Yucca (a)	....	....	....	....
1852	Westward Ho	214	40 2/3	23 1/2	1,650		Sloop-of-war Adams (a)	....	....	....	....
1852	Bald Eagle	215 2/3	41 1/6	23 1/2	1,703	1866	Steamer Theodore D. Wagner	172	27 2/3	21 1/3	607
1853	Empress of the Seas	240 1/2	44 1/6	27 1/2	2,197	1866	George B. Upton	164 1/2	27 2/3	21 1/3	604
1853	Star of Empire	222 3/4	40 7/12	28	2,050	1867	Brig North Star	120	29 4/5	15 3/5	410
1853	Chariot of Fame	222 3/4	40 7/12	28	2,050	1868	Ship Helen Morris	174 1/3	36 1/2	23 2/3	1,285
1853	Great Republic	334 1/2	53 1/2	38	4,555	1868	Sovereign of the Seas	202	41	24	1,502
1853	Romance of the Seas	240 2/3	39 1/2	39 1/2	1,782	1868	Schooner R. R. Higgins	78 1/2	22 7/10	8	90
1854	Lightning	243	42 2/3	25	2,084	1869	Frank Atwood	88	24 1/2	8 1/8	107
1854	Champion of the Seas	252	45 1/2	29	2,448	1869	Ship Glory of the Seas	240 1/6	44 1/12	30 1/2	2,102
1854	James Baines	266	46 7/12	31	2,515						

a For the United States Government.

After the packet came the clipper ship, a vessel intended primarily for freighting, and built to secure the highest possible speed when laden with cargo. The packets were the fast vessels from 1815 to 1845, but after 1845 there grew up various branches of trade in which speed was as important for commercial purposes as it was for passenger travel. For instance, there was the tea trade from China to the United States, in which speed had always been thought essential. The cargoes consisted of teas, spices, coffee, dried fruits, etc., which were liable to deteriorate in a long voyage of four months to the home port, and to shorten the voyage as much as possible was desirable for obvious reasons. Furthermore, there were no telegraph lines and ocean cables in those days, and the uncertainty of the markets made fast trips home from the East Indies very important. Merchants had repeatedly suffered heavy loss, sometimes ruin, by the decline in cotton and other eastern goods brought home by ships during their absence on the voyage out and back, and good ships were therefore always required in that trade. Both in America and in Europe up to 1845 the East Indiamen were, as a rule, the large and fast freighting ships of their day. After 1815 a friendly rivalry broke out among owners of ships sailing to China, and every year races took place homeward with the first offerings of the new crop of tea which had come down to Chinese ports. The shipping houses gave their captains good vessels, and the captains did their part by driving the ships homeward through all sorts of weather, with all the canvas spread that they could carry. Americans earned a world-wide reputation for speed soon after 1814, and finally put the English so much on their mettle that the latter sent out a new and finer class of merchantmen than they had ever before owned to contest for the palm of superiority. The Alexander Baring, John o' Gaunt, Euphrates, Monarch, Foam, and other ships of that class, were equal to any under the flag of the United States in capacity, spread of canvas, and speed. This, in turn, stimulated the pride of the American houses, who responded between 1840 and 1850 with vessels of good and carefully studied form. These vessels sat low in the water, in strong distinction from the fashion of earlier times. The beam was broad, the bow sharp, and the water-lines fine. The masts were tall and raking, and the yards were so long that the ships spread an enormous cloud of canvas in a favoring wind. With these vessels the Americans kept their position ahead of all competitors.

MERCHANT SAILING VESSELS.

The first clippers were built at New York city. The pioneer was the Helena, of 650 tons, built in 1841 for the China trade by William H. Webb, on the order of A. & N. Griswold. Though a good carrier, this beautiful vessel was modeled for speed, and, under the management of Captain Benjamin, made a number of rapid trips and earned a great reputation for the house to which she belonged.

Howland & Aspinwall followed with the Rainbow, of 750 tons, built by Smith & Dimon. The Rainbow was a good ship, and once went to Canton and back in 6 months and 14 days, having spent three weeks of the time in discharging and loading cargo, thus shortening the regular voyage by two months. Brigs and schooners had previously been built for speed and large vessels for burden. The Helena and the Rainbow revolutionized matters. They got better prices for freights than slow ships, and in every respect proved desirable. Other sharp ships soon followed.

In 1844 the Montauk, of 540 tons, was built by Mr. Webb for William S. Wetmore. A. A. Low & Co. then employed Brown & Bell to build the rival ship Howqua, of 706 tons, a very fast and fine vessel, which once ran from Shanghai to New York in 87 days. Not to be beaten, the owners of the Rainbow added to their fleet the famous clipper Sea Witch, of 907 tons, a sharper vessel than her predecessors, with raking bow and stern, fine lines, sharp floor, and remarkable beauty of form throughout, which was intended to beat any ship afloat. She was a fast vessel, a good investment, and a credit to Smith & Dimon, her builders, and once made the voyage to California in 97 days.

The era of sharp ships was now fairly inaugurated, and many of this class were built not only at New York, but at Boston, Philadelphia, and Baltimore. Nearly all the early ones did not exceed 1,000 tons register, but competition and expanding trade led to a great increase in size, and every year saw vessels launched spreading more and more canvas, longer, larger, and faster than ever, and expressly intended to beat everything that had gone before them in the merchant shipping of the world. In ten years after the first clipper the size of 2,400 tons was reached, and there were large numbers built of about 2,000 tons. The exploits of the new ships were amazing, and created the greatest excitement in shipping circles; in fact, they effected a remarkable revolution in the sailing tonnage of the world.

Foreign merchants were by no means idle spectators of what was going on in America, and in 1846 England began to awake to the new and dangerous rivalry from America. Alexander Hall & Co., of Aberdeen, made a specialty of clipper ships, and there were launched from their yard many superior and famous vessels; but the Americans, though hard pressed, were able to maintain the lead, and are entitled to the best record ever made by ships sailing under canvas. There were several famous races home from China between American and English clippers. Once, while a bet was being talked of, the British clippers Chrysolite and Stornaway and the American clippers Race Horse, Surprise, and Challenge engaged in a race from Canton to Liverpool and Deal, and arrived at the home ports as follows: At Liverpool, Chrysolite, in 106 days; at Deal, Stornaway, in 109 days; Challenge, in 105 days; Surprise, in 106 days. The British ship Challenge ran from Shanghai to Deal in 113 days; the American clipper Nightingale in 110 days. These races were claimed by both parties; but the Americans kept the reputation of superiority, and many ships were ordered at our ship-yards on foreign account.

In 1848 an event occurred which gave a great stimulus to the demand for clipper ships. Gold was discovered in California; and as that region was practically as far away as Asia, no vessels could be sent there except those that were large and staunch. A few vessels had found their way to San Francisco before that territory had been purchased, and a number soon afterward. Parcels of gold sent East by way of the isthmus of Panama created a rush of emigration and trade wholly unparalleled in the history of the New World for its sudden rise and great magnitude, and a great part of the freighting tonnage of the eastern states was called on at once to engage in voyages to and from the isthmus of Panama on both sides of the continent, and also in trips to San Francisco around cape Horn. An immense number of people had to be transported to the new territory on the Pacific, and with them all the goods, provisions, furniture, clothing, tools, etc., that they required, including their houses, large numbers of which were made ready in the East, loaded on ships, and sent out entire, ready to be set up. No one in San Francisco wished to be troubled with any more mechanical work than was necessary, and everything that could save labor was done in the East, leaving the emigrants free to make the eagerly-desired, quick, and brilliant fortune in the new El Dorado. By 1850, such was the rush, from 150 to 200 vessels were sometimes at anchor in the bay of San Francisco, where five years before it had been rare to see half a dozen. These were nearly all American vessels, as under our laws none but American ships could bring cargoes from the Atlantic coast. A few packet ships were turned into this new and profitable trade, but the majority were freighting vessels of large size. The time spent in making the run between New York or Boston and the Pacific coast was from 120 to 150 days; but in the summer of 1850 two small tea ships arrived from New York in 100 days. This quick passage caused the merchants of the West to realize the advantage of fast ships, and Alfred Peabody, of Salem, Massachusetts, and J. P. Flint, of Boston, who were on the coast, at once resolved to build clipper ships for the trade. Mr. Peabody started for Boston by way of the Isthmus and arranged with Glidden & Williams and one other firm to build at once the John Bertram, an extreme clipper of 1,100 tons, for freighting to California. The keel was laid in September in East Boston, the ship was launched in 60 days, and in 30 days more she was on her way to California with a cargo at a freight of $40 per measurement ton of 40 cubic feet. In 1879 the John Bertram was still doing well in the merchant service, although then under a foreign flag. This was the first clipper ship built for the California trade; but the clipper Witch of the Wave and four others of the same model, of 1,500 tons each, were built by the owners immediately afterward.

With his beginning the American ship-yards brought out large and fine clippers, exceeding in size and excellence anything ever before seen. Commercial rivalry was strong, not only between the merchants of America, but between them and those of England, and each year ships were ordered to exceed in size and speed everything which had gone before. Merchants realized the benefit of quick returns; owners and builders went wild over the enormous prices paid per ton for freights, and ship-builders could get almost any price for a ship that would meet the requirements of the trade. The goods forwarded were light, and were of such wide variety as not to be brought under any general rule based on dead-weight, and the measurement ton of 40 cubic feet of space was adopted as a basis for freight rates. From $40 to $50 a ton was paid in the first year of the California excitement, although $15 would have been a good profit, and ten years afterward the rate was still as high as $25. Forty dollars a ton would pay a ship to sail for California and then return in ballast for a cargo of goods, as the one freight made a handsome profit on the voyage both ways. Afterward, when rates fell, ships began to sail from California to China for a return cargo of teas and oriental ware, and could thus add to the freight money of from $20 to $30 per ton to California one of from $15 to $25 from China home, making from $35 to $50 per ton of stowage space on the one round trip. Only American ships enjoyed this advantage, for our laws excluded foreign tonnage entirely from all branches of our coasting trade, of which the California business formed a part. Several other influences came into play from 1850 to 1860 to increase the demand for fast ships. Gold had been discovered in Australia, causing a general rush from all parts of the world to that distant continent. Steam began to be employed in crossing the Atlantic, and the yards of Aberdeen and other places in Great Britain began to produce clippers that pushed ours hard in the tea races. Then there was the Crimean war, which broke out in 1854, turning a good deal of the existing tonnage into the transport service, giving a fresh impetus to freights, and making a demand for good ships for general trade. Sailing vessels were paid from $5 to $8 per register ton per month for use as transports during that war; steamers got from $8 to $16 per gross ton per month; timber freights across the Atlantic ran up from $8 to $12 per ton, and even to $14 in some cases; freights from India were from $12 to $20, and ran up to $45 per ton. All these influences combined made the period from 1848 to 1857 one of the greatest excitement and activity in ship-building in the United States. The years 1851, 1852, and 1853 were noted for the fine ships produced, and 1854, 1855, and 1856 have never been equaled in the United States, either for the amount of sailing tonnage built or for the gigantic size and great beauty of the large vessels, and no other age has seen so noble a sailing fleet as that which sprang into existence from the ship-yards of Baltimore, Philadelphia, New York, and Boston in those years of unwonted excitement and prosperity.

The clippers first built had sharp floors and sailed with a drag. Some of them from Baltimore drew 16 feet aft and only 8 feet forward, the midship section, or broadest part of the hull, being at two-fifths the length from the bow, as in the packets and heavy freighting ships. The forward body was full and the after body lean and tapering under water. This was gradually changed in imitation of the fast yachts and pilot boats of New York city, and after 1851 the long, sharp bow was considered the best for speed. The midship section was moved back in a few vessels to the center of length, and the after body was made fuller and more powerful. The ship was then made to sail on an even keel. The bottom was also made fuller. The sharp floor did not give enough cargo capacity; and the sharp bow and stern had so little buoyancy, as compared with the square body or middle portion, that the ends of many clippers sagged and broke down, subjecting them to continual repairs, one of them being compelled to repair to the extent of $15,000 after her first voyage. Besides that, there was a lack of stability in the sharp bottoms. About 1854, therefore, clippers began to be built with full bottoms, retaining the long bow, hollow water-lines, and other peculiarities of the swift model. These were good ships, and the form thus attained has ever since been popular in fast ships. A few draughts (Figs. 32 to 41) will illustrate the changes which took place. The lines of some of these vessels, including some of the most celebrated clipper ships that have ever been built, appear for the first time in this report.

The speed of clippers was remarkable. Six miles an hour was, and still is, a good average rate of speed for long voyages, and nine miles is excellent time, especially for a ship loaded with a full cargo of merchandise. Cargo steamers at this day make no better time. Clippers ran across the Atlantic to Liverpool at an average speed of 9 miles an hour, spurting at the rate of from 10 to 13 miles with the right wind, and on voyages that gave them the advantage of the trade winds they ran for days and weeks in succession at an average speed of from 12 to 15 miles an hour. To sail 300 miles a day was not exceptional. The Red Jacket made 325 miles a day for a week; the Flying Cloud once sailed 427¼ miles in 24 hours; the James Baines, an Australian packet, built by McKay at Boston, once sailed 420 miles in 24 hours; and the Sovereign of the Seas, it is said, while on a voyage from the Sandwich islands to New York, lasting only 82 days, made 437 miles in 24 hours, the fastest time ever made by any vessel, sailer or steamer, on the deep sea. The average time of the fast Atlantic steamers now does not exceed 400 miles a day, and there is no record better than that made recently by the Alaska, which on one occasion made 419 miles in a day. The fast ships gave a great stimulus to trade, and were of vast benefit to commerce.

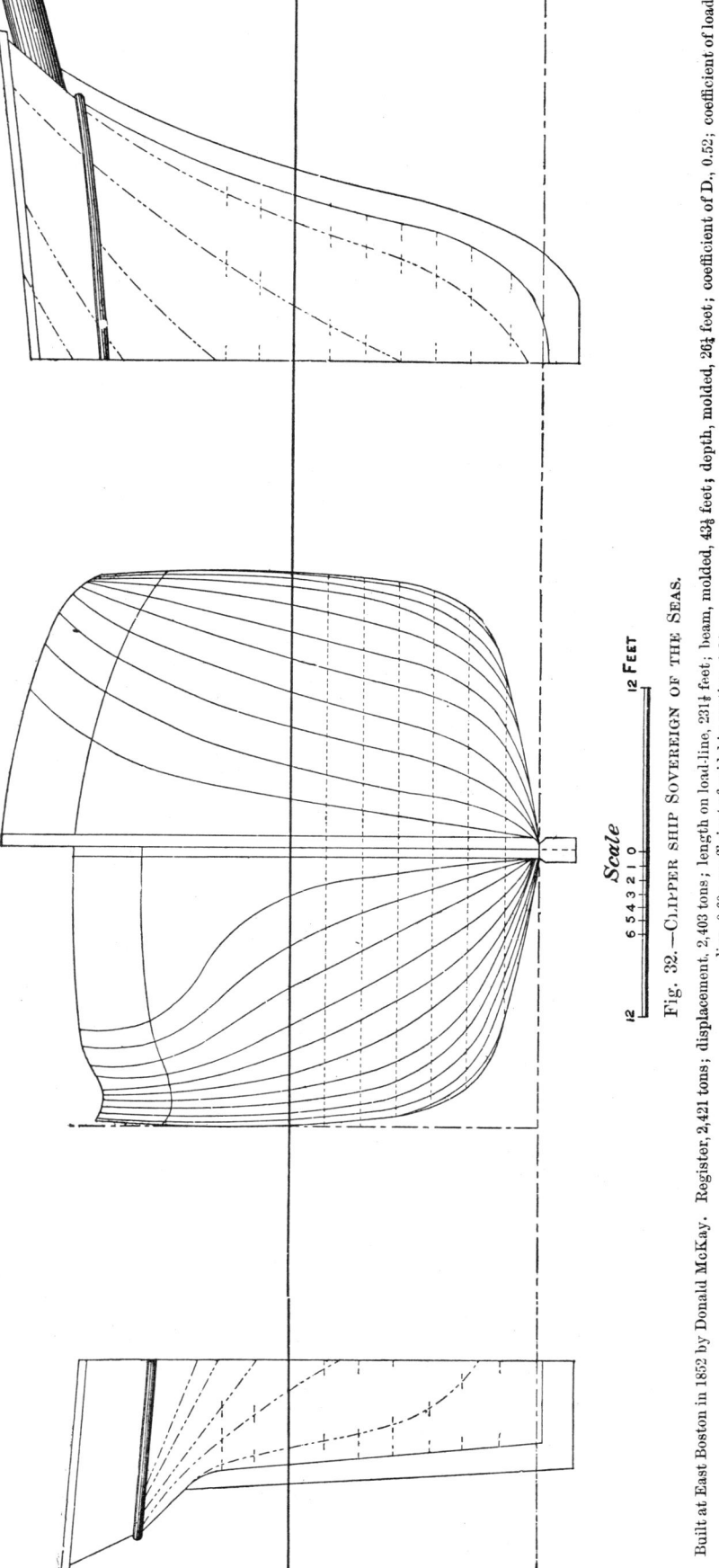

Fig. 32.—Clipper ship Sovereign of the Seas.

Built at East Boston in 1852 by Donald McKay. Register, 2,421 tons; displacement, 2,403 tons; length on load-line, 231¼ feet; beam, molded, 43⅜ feet; depth, molded, 26¼ feet; coefficient of D, 0.52; coefficient of load-line, 0.60; coefficient of midship section, 0.84.

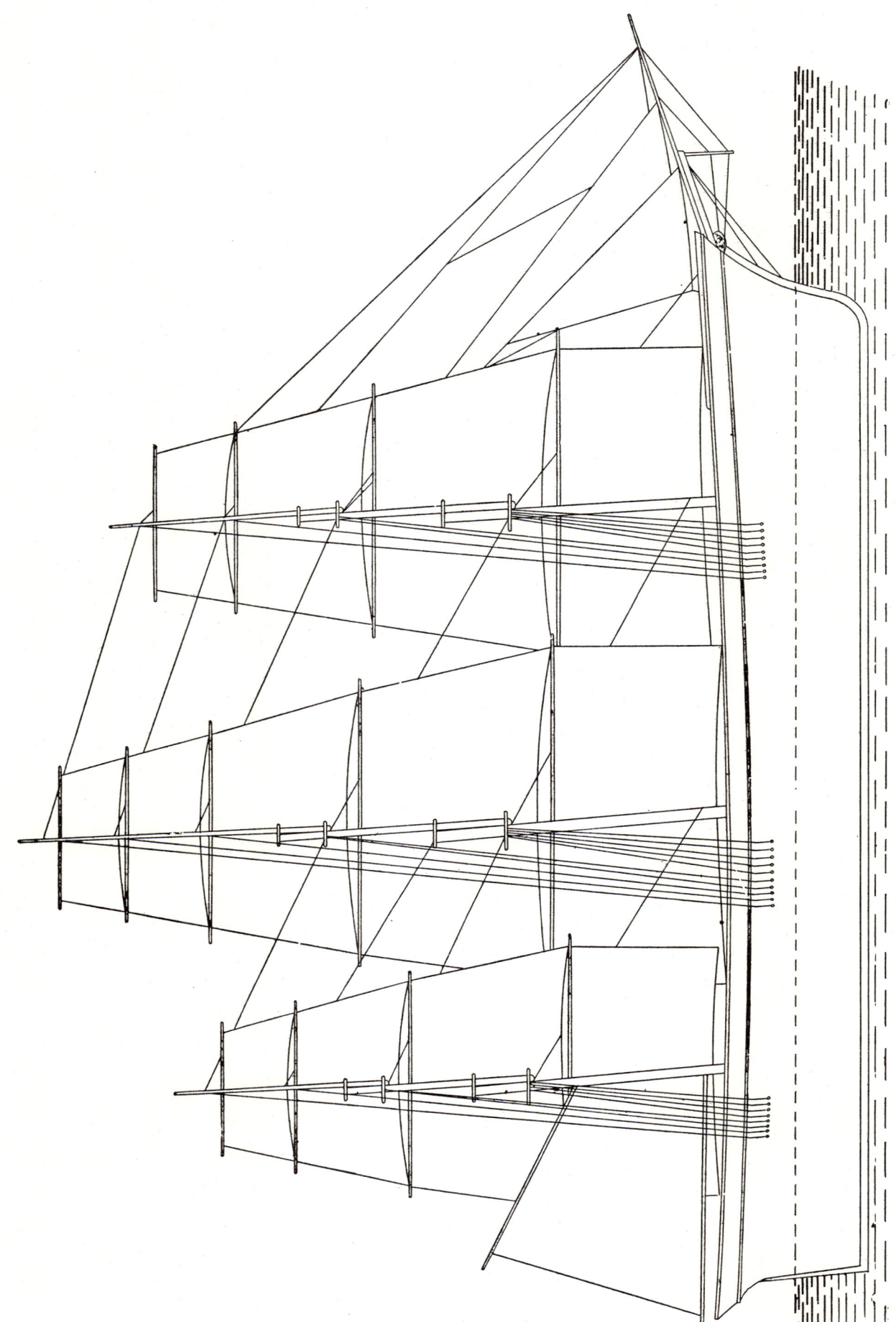

Fig. 33.—Sail plan of the Sovereign of the Seas.
Showing old-fashioned full topsails. Rake of masts, $\frac{1}{4}$, $\frac{1}{2}$, and $1\frac{1}{4}$ inches to the foot, respectively.

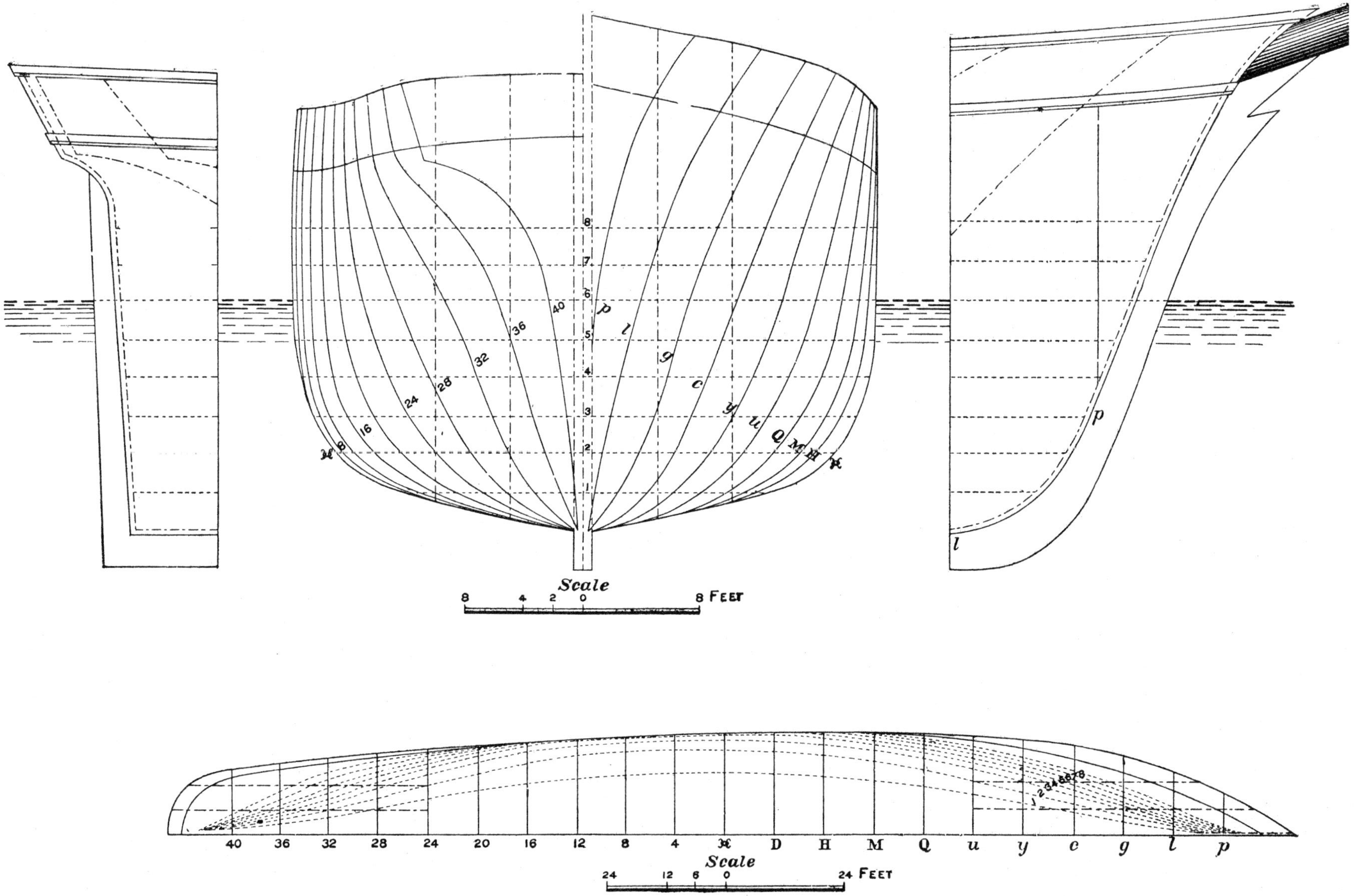

MERCHANT SAILING VESSELS.

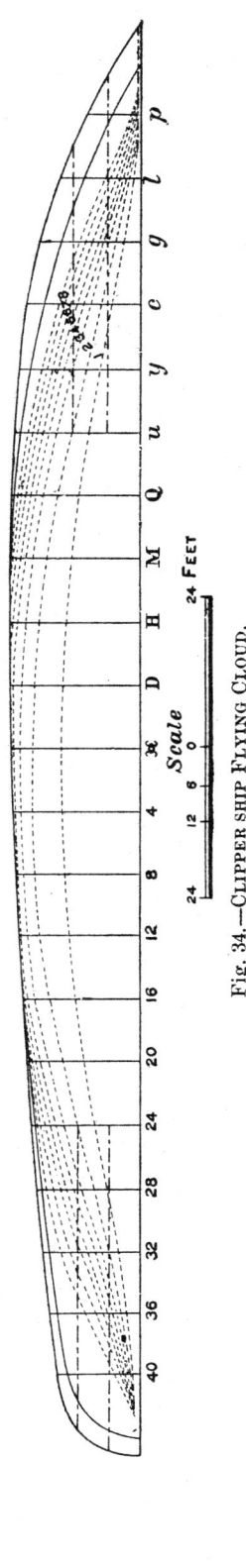

Fig. 34.—Clipper ship Flying Cloud.

Built at East Boston by Donald McKay in 1851. Register, 1,782 tons; displacement at 20 feet, 2,375 gross tons; displacement at 17¾ feet, 1,951 gross tons; displacement per inch at 17¾ feet, 13.91 gross tons; length on deck, 217½ feet; register length, 229 feet; length on load-line, 209¼ feet; beam, extreme, 40⅜ feet; beam, molded, 40 feet; depth, molded, 23¾ feet; coefficient of D., 0.5146; coefficient of load-line, 0.682; coefficient of midship section, 0.82.

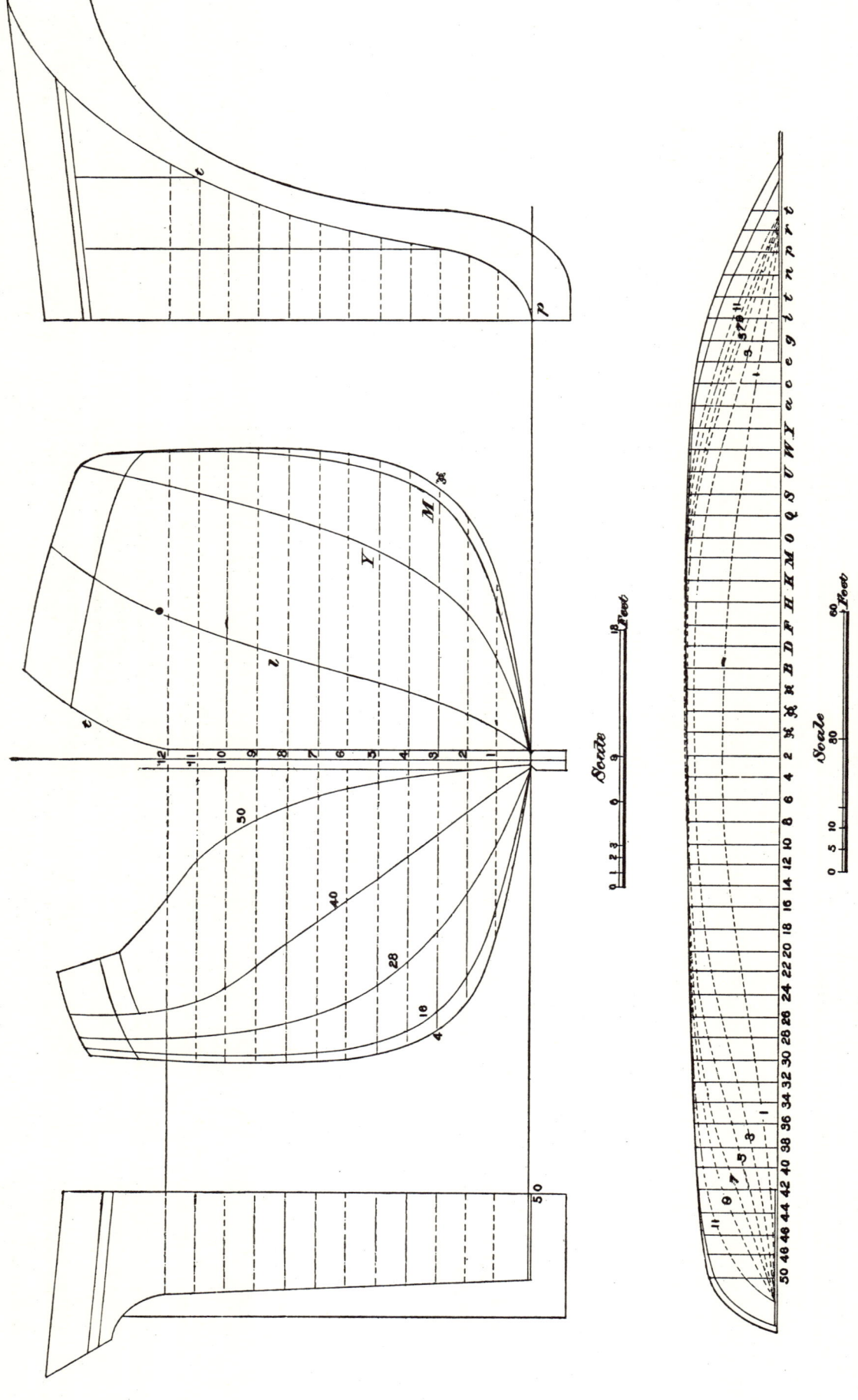

Fig. 35.—CLIPPER SHIP RED JACKET.

Designed by Samuel M. Pook, and built at Rockland, Maine. Register, 2,006 tons; displacement, 3,100 tons gross; length between perpendiculars, 251¾ feet; beam, molded, 42⅜ feet; depth, molded, 26 feet; coefficient of D., 0.54; coefficient of water-line, 0.74; coefficient of midship section, 0.82.

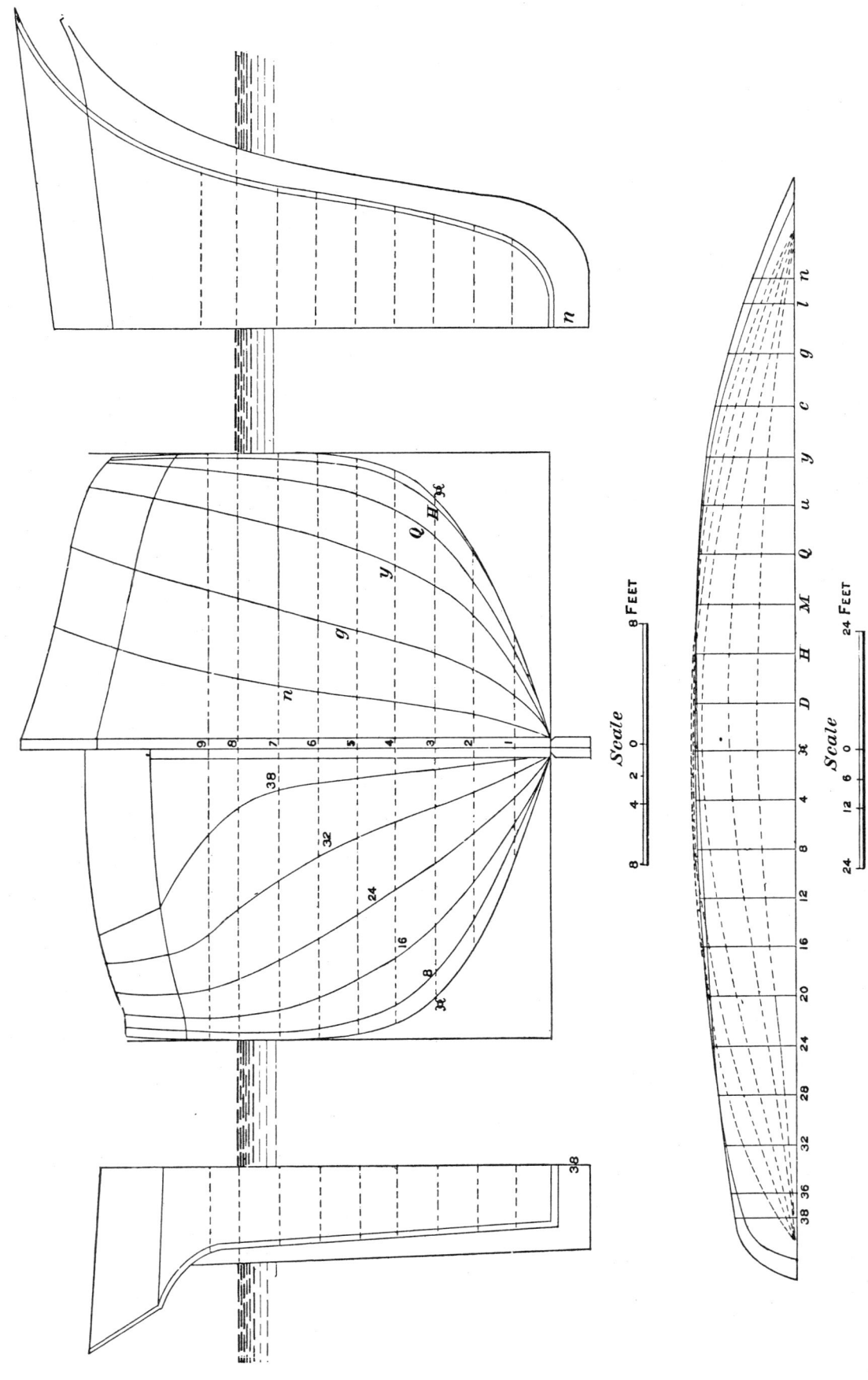

Fig. 36.—Clipper ship Stag-Hound. Register, 1,534 tons. Register dimensions: Length, 209 feet; beam, 39⅚ feet; depth of hold, 21 feet. Built and designed by Donald McKay at East Boston.

SHIP-BUILDING INDUSTRY.

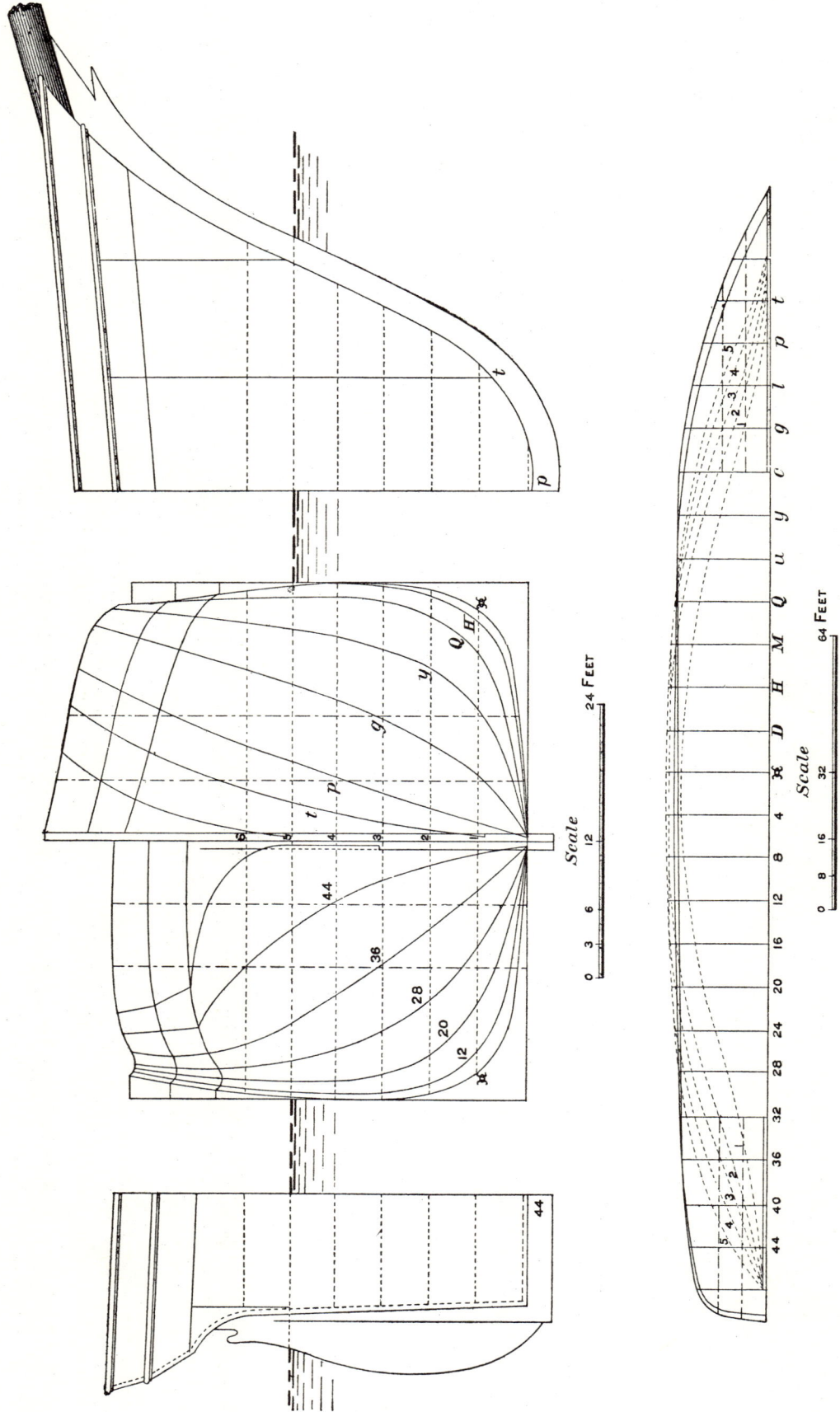

Fig. 37.—CLIPPER SHIP JAMES BAINES.

Built by Donald McKay at East Boston in 1854. Register, 2,515 tons; displacement to 22¼ feet draught, 3,839 tons gross; displacement per inch at load line, 19¾ tons gross; register length, 266 feet; length on load-line, 240 feet; beam, molded, 45 feet; beam, extreme, 46⅞ feet; depth, molded, 30 feet; coefficient of load-line, 0.759; coefficient of midship section, 0.914. coefficient of D, 0.594;

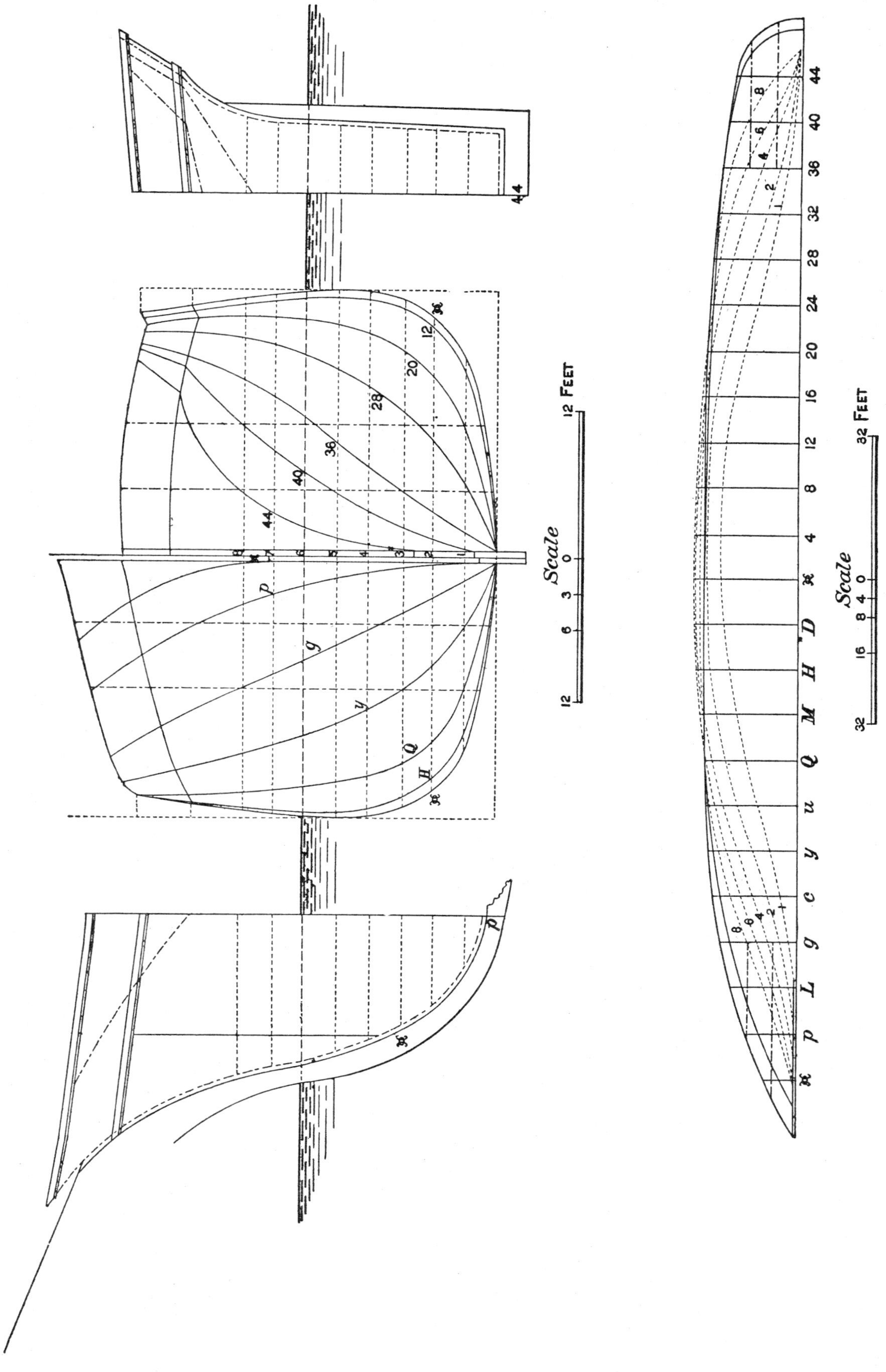

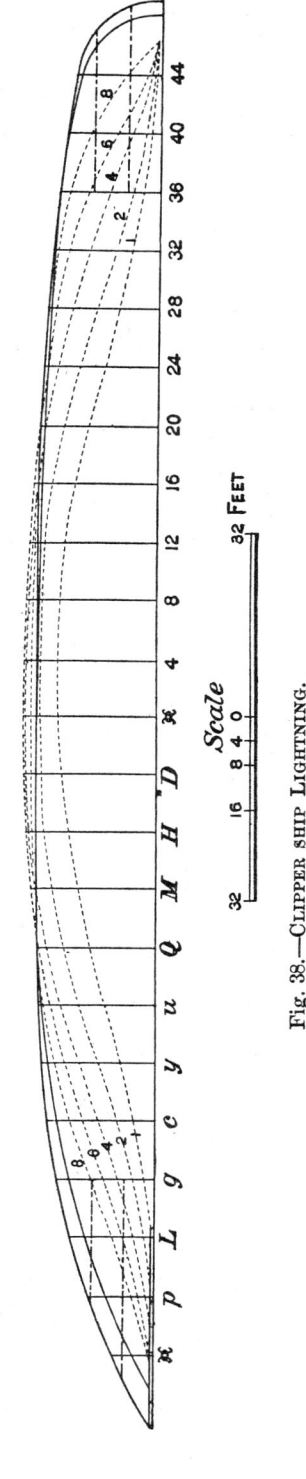

Fig. 38.—Clipper ship Lightning.

Built by Donald McKay at East Boston in 1854. Register, 2,084 tons; displacement at 16¾ feet draught, 2,367 tons gross; displacement per inch at load-line, 16¾ tons gross; register length, 243 feet; length on load-line, 228 feet; beam, molded, 42⅜ feet; depth, molded, 25 feet.

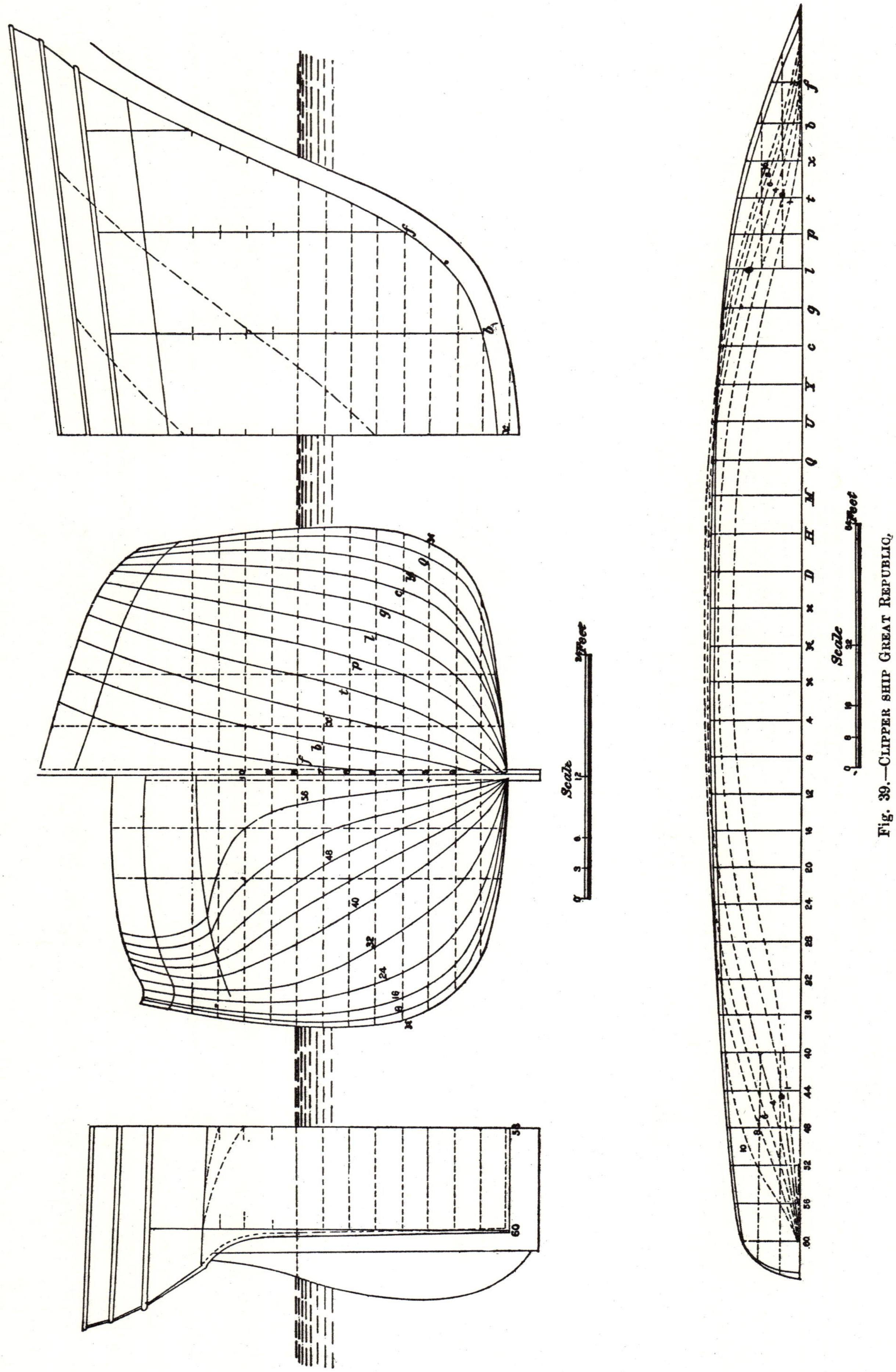

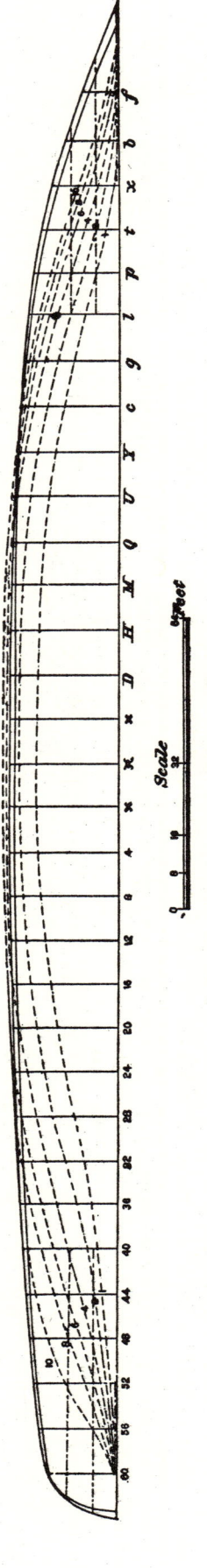

Fig. 39.—CLIPPER SHIP GREAT REPUBLIC.

Built by Donald McKay at East Boston in 1853. Register, 4,555 tons; displacement at 25 feet draught, 5,923 gross tons; displacement at 23 feet draught, 5,273 gross tons; displacement per inch at 23-foot water-line, 26⅔ gross tons; length on deck, 325¼ feet; length on load-line, 314 feet; beam, molded, 49⅔ feet; beam, extreme, 50½ feet; depth, molded, 32 feet.

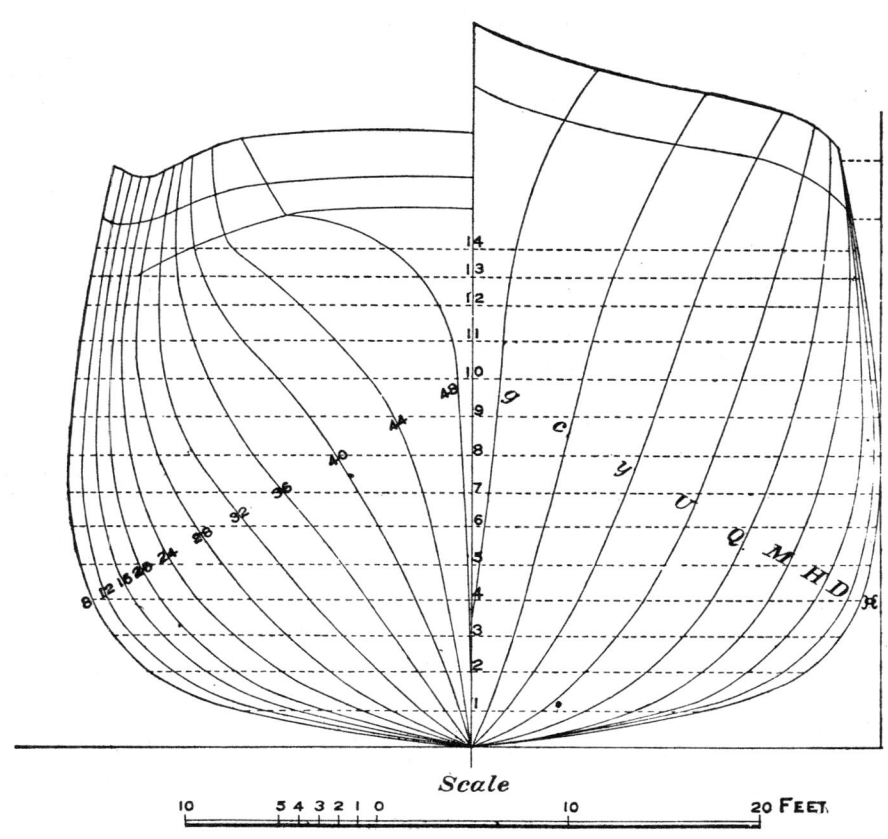

Fig. 40.—CLIPPER SHIP YOUNG AMERICA.

Built by William H. Webb at New York in 1853. 1,962 tons register; length, 236½ feet; beam 42 feet hold, 28¼ feet.

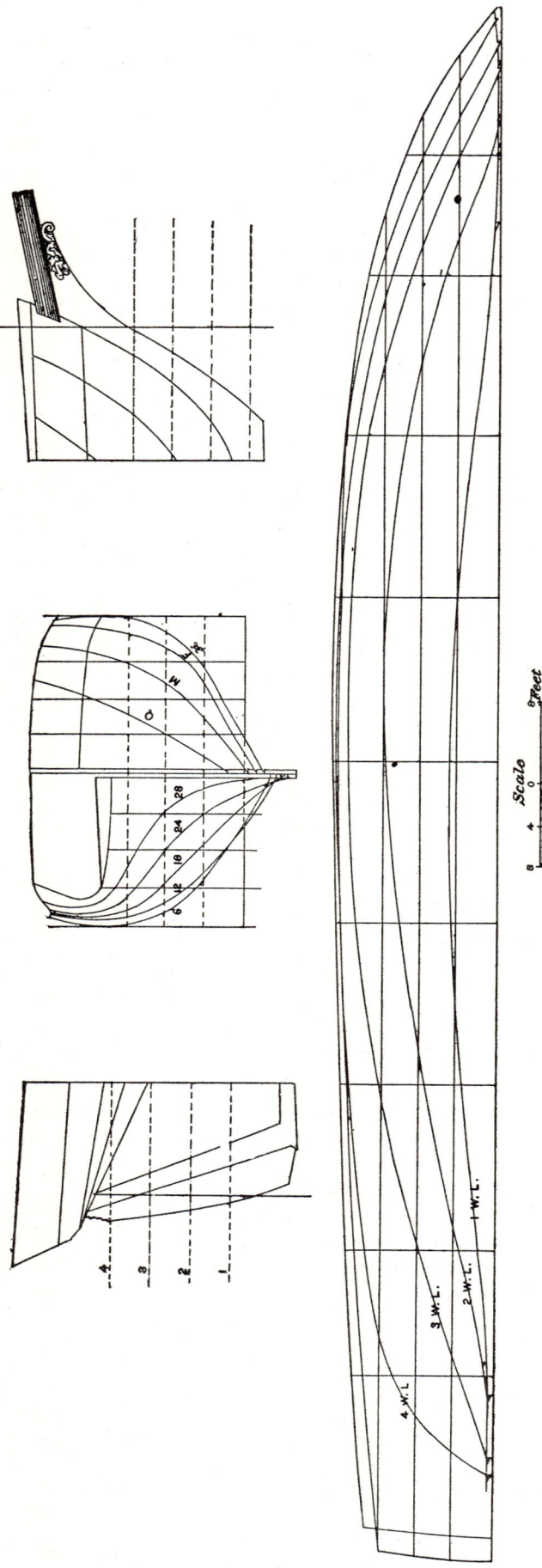

Fig. 41.—Clipper ship Ann McKim. Length, 143 feet; beam, 31 feet; depth, 14 feet.
Built at Baltimore in 1832.

The following are the more important facts relative to the principal clipper ships of the period from 1840 to 1861:

Year when built.	Name of ship.	Place where built.	By whom built.	Registered tonnage.	Dead rise to the foot, in inches.	Length on deck to after side of stern-post.	Depth molded to water-line.	Depth from keel to deck-plank.	Greatest breadth on planking.	Center of buoyancy forward of middle.	Displacement to water-line, net tons.	Cargo at load draught, net tons.	Coefficient of displacement.	Coefficient of midship section.	Coefficient of water-line.	Angle of entrance.	Angle of run.	Remarks.
						Feet.	*Feet.*	*Feet.*	*Feet.*									
.....	Mary Whiteridge.	Baltimore, Md ..	....	......	......	......	......	......	......	....	......	......	....	....	....	....	....	Baltimore to Liverpool in 13 days, 7 hours.
1851	Flying Cloud ...	Boston, Mass....	Donald McKay..	1,782	......	229	......	$21\frac{1}{2}$	$40\frac{2}{3}$	....	......	......	0.51	0.82	0.68	....	....	374 miles in one day; from New York to San Francisco in 89 days, 18 hours; in one day she made $433\frac{1}{4}$ miles, but reducing this to exactly 24 hours, she made $427\frac{1}{2}$ miles.
1851	Gazelle	New York, N. Y.	William H. Webb	1,244	$5\frac{3}{8}$	184	......	$22\frac{8}{12}$	$38\frac{1}{2}$	....	......	......	....	....	....	....	....	Sharp below and broad above.
1851	Comet	....do	....do	1,836	$2\frac{1}{2}$	229	......	$24\frac{5}{8}$	42	....	......	......	....	....	....	45°	75°	Beautiful model and good ship; she made many rapid voyages. Her first voyage was made from New York to San Francisco in 103 days, thence to Hong Kong in 37 days, and on the return she made 332 knots in 24 hours, and 1,512 knots in 120 consecutive hours; from San Francisco to New York in 86 days, and afterward in $76\frac{1}{2}$ days; from New York to Liverpool in 19 days, and from Liverpool to Hong Kong in 84 days.
1851	Invincible	....do	....do	1,769	......	$221\frac{1}{2}$	......	$27\frac{3}{4}$	$41\frac{1}{2}$	....	......	......	....	....	....	....	....	
1851	Challenge	....do	....do	2,006	3	$230\frac{1}{2}$	......	$27\frac{1}{3}$	$43\frac{1}{6}$	....	......	......	....	....	....	30°	34°	A handsome, fast, and good ship; originally oversparred.
1851	Nightingale.....	Portsmouth, N. H.	Samuel Hanscom	1,066	......	178	......	$21\frac{3}{4}$	36	$1\frac{5}{12}$	1,240	......	0.47	0.70	0.74	44°	....	In 1852, on the way home from China, she ran 336 nautical miles in 24 hours; the distance from Batavia roads to London, 13,726 nautical miles, she made in 70 days; in 1854 she ran from New York to Melbourne in 76 days, 16 hours.
.....	Trade Wind.....	....	....	......	......	......	......	......	......	....	......	......	....	....	....	....	....	New York to San Francisco in 75 days; homeward in 84 days.
1852	Sovereign of the Seas.	Boston, Mass ...	Donald McKay..	2,421	25	258	......	$28\frac{1}{4}$	$44\frac{1}{2}$	....	......	......	0.52	0.84	0.60	....	....	From Honolulu to New York she ran 6,245 miles in 22 days; 436 miles in 1 day; for 4 days her average was 398; she made the trip to New York in 82 days.
1852	Flying Dutchman.	New York, N. Y.	William H. Webb	1,200	$3\frac{1}{2}$	$187\frac{5}{8}$	......	$24\frac{1}{2}$	$38\frac{1}{2}$	....	......	......	....	....	....	....	....	She made 4,620 nautical miles in 16 days.
.....	Andrew Jackson	Boston, Mass....	....	......	......	......	......	......	......	....	......	......	....	....	....	....	....	New York to San Francisco in 80 days, 4 hours.
.....	Euterpe.........	Rockland, Me...	....	......	......	......	......	......	......	....	......	......	....	....	....	....	....	From New York to Calcutta in 78 days.
1853	Flying Scud.....	Damariscotta, Me.	Metcalf & Norris	1,713	......	221	......	$25\frac{1}{2}$	41	....	......	......	....	....	....	....	....	From New York to Melbourne in 80 days; is claimed to have run 460 miles in 24 hours, but this is improbable.
1853	Panama.........	New York, N. Y.	Thomas Collyer.	......	......	......	......	......	......	....	......	......	....	....	....	....	....	A fast but wet ship; rolling heavily; from Shanghai to New York in 85 days.
1843	Rainbow	....do	Smith & Dimon.	750	......	......	......	......	......	....	......	......	....	....	....	....	....	
1844	Montauk.........	....do	William H. Webb	540	$2\frac{3}{4}$	127	......	$19\frac{1}{2}$	$14\frac{1}{2}$	....	......	......	....	....	....	70°	55°	
1850	Stag-Hound.....	Boston, Mass....	Donald McKay..	1,534	4	209	......	$23\frac{1}{2}$	$39\frac{5}{8}$	....	......	......	....	....	....	....	....	Sailed from New York to San Francisco in 110 days; her mistake was in lack of stability and capacity.
1853	Young America.	New York, N. Y.	William H. Webb	1,962	2	$236\frac{1}{2}$	......	$28\frac{1}{4}$	42	....	......	......	....	....	....	45°	55°	A very fast and popular ship, which made many rapid voyages. She was always fast. Five trips from San Francisco to New York were made in from 83 to 92 days, and the voyage was once made in 83 days, loaded; five trips were made in from 97 to 101 days. She once ran from New York to Liverpool in 18 days, and back in 23 days; from Liverpool to Melbourne in 81 days; from San Francisco to Liverpool in 102, 103, 105, and 106 days, and one return voyage in 99 days.

Year when built.	Name of ship.	Place where built.	By whom built.	Registered tonnage.	Dead rise to the foot, in inches.	Length on deck to after side of stern-post.	Depth molded to water-line.	Depth from keel to deck plank.	Greatest breadth on planking.	Center of buoyancy forward of middle.	Displacement to water-line, net tons.	Cargo at load draught, net tons.	Coefficient of displacement.	Coefficient of midship section.	Coefficient of water-line.	Angle of entrance.	Angle of run.	Remarks.
1854	Lightning	Boston, Mass	Donald McKay	2,084	228	Feet. 243	Feet. 15½	Feet. 25	Feet. 42¾		2,590		0.52	0.84	0.71	14°		Ran 436 miles in 24 hours, drawing 22 feet of water; from England to Calcutta, with troops, in 87 days, beating other sailing vessels by from 16 to 40 days; from Boston to Liverpool in 13 days, 20 hours; Liverpool to Melbourne, 77 days, back in 64; again in 75 and 65; once in 63.
1854	James Baines	do	do	2,515		266		31	46$\frac{7}{12}$									From Boston to Liverpool in 12 days, 6 hours; from Liverpool to Melbourne in 62¼ days; a return was made in 60 days.
1853	Red Jacket	Rockland, Me		2,006		260		26¾	44	3$\frac{5}{12}$	3,460		0.54	0.82	0.74	42°		From New York to Liverpool in 13 days, 11 hours, 25 minutes; New York to Melbourne, 69 days, 11 hours; from New York to Fastnet Light, 10 days.
	Northern Light																	From San Francisco to New York, 72 days; to Boston, 76 days, 8 hours.
	Dreadnaught	Boston, Mass																Honolulu to New Bedford, 13,470 miles, in 82 days; from Sandy Hook to Liverpool, 13 days, 8 hours.
1869	Glory of the Seas	do	Donald McKay	2,102		240⅙		30$\frac{7}{12}$	44$\frac{1}{12}$			4,000						With 4,000 tons of cargo ran 161 miles a day for over three weeks; from New York to San Francisco in 94 days.

The enthusiasm of the times found expression in the names of the clippers and in the literature of the day, and no title was too grand for a good ship. The song of the day was:

> An open sea and a flowing sail,
> A clipper ship and a driving gale;
> A golden broom at the gallant mast
> That fearless sweeps the ocean vast.

A great many improved appliances were invented for use on the clipper ships, among them the idea of double topsails. Captain R. B. Forbes, of Boston, was the first to divide the enormously large and high old-fashioned topsail and make the lower topsail yard stationary at the cap of the lower mast-head. He made the mast-heads long, to suit the rig. The upper topsail yard kept the place occupied by the original yard, and was raised and lowered in the same manner. This idea was not original with Captain Forbes, for he saw topsail schooners as long ago as 1819 with topsails hoisted on the head of the lower mast and a square sail above on a pole mast; but he was the first to revive the old idea and apply it, in 1841, first to schooners and afterward to ships, to obviate the extreme size to which topsails had grown. Captain Forbes also invented the idea of topmasts fidded abaft the lower mast-head, in order to house them without interfering with the lower yards. This idea did not become popular, but double topsails did after 1850, and are now a common rig throughout the world.

As American clippers gave to their builders a world-wide reputation, this had the practical effect of bringing millions of dollars' worth of business to the United States from foreign countries, especially from the governments of Spain, France, Turkey, Italy, and Russia, and frigates of great size, strength, speed, and cost were built in large numbers for those governments in New York, Philadelphia, Boston, and elsewhere. American ships were in demand in all parts of Europe for the merchant service, and a number of private fortunes were accumulated by builders in filling the profitable foreign orders which were continually coming to this country.

The construction of great ships led to some changes in the manner in which mechanical labor was performed at the ship-yard. In the first place, the labor became differentiated. The old fashion was for the ship-carpenter to be a man of all trades. He would aid in hewing out the frames and setting them up; would line out his streak of planking on the timbers of the ship, dub off the surface of the frames so that the plank might fit truly, put on the plank, bore the holes for the treenails and bolts, fasten the plank, and perhaps even calk the seam; but when business became active this plan would not do, and the work was divided, the separate parts being allotted to different gangs of men, and carpentry, calking, fastening, joining, painting, etc., all became different trades—a system under which time was saved and better work secured. Various devices were introduced to save labor. Previously all the frame timbers were hewed out of the rough log or the flitch plank with broad-axes in the hands of the men, and timbers that needed to be cut lengthwise were sawed through by two men by hand; but Donald

McKay set up in his yard in East Boston a steam saw-mill to perform both of these operations. The saw was hung in such manner that it could be tilted first one way and then another while in motion, and thus all the frames could be sawed out to the proper bevel by three men as fast as twelve men could put them together and set them up. All the heavy sawing being done by steam, the work of the yard was immensely facilitated, and a frame could be got out and put together in less than one-third the time it formerly took. Another improvement was effected by setting up a derrick in the yard to lift the heavy timbers and beams to their places in the ship. That work had previously been done entirely by manual labor, and in building a vessel the master carpenter always required a force large enough at any rate to pick up a large keelson piece or a beam and carry it on their shoulders to its home on the vessel. The heavy ceiling and planking had to be carried from the steam-box to the vessel in the same way. There was an immense loss of time in this clumsy and laborious way of doing business, as all hands had to be called off from the work from time to time, often as much as once an hour, to spend twenty minutes or more in carrying about a huge plank or stick of timber. To change this teams of oxen and horses were brought to drag the pieces about and large derricks were set up, worked by other teams, to lift them to their place. Various other devices were adopted from time to time by smart builders. Treenails were formerly made by hand in the shed on rainy days, and were chopped out of sticks of wood with axes; but a treenail lathe machine was invented to do this work. A machine worked by a hand lever was also invented to cut the long, round bars of iron into suitable lengths for bolts. These bolts had previously been cut by hand with a hammer and cold-chisel. The auger was also improved; and the saving of labor by these various improvements was worth thousands of dollars to the builder of a large vessel, and aided greatly to cheapen the cost of a ship. These improvements were adopted chiefly in the cities of Baltimore, Philadelphia, New York, and Boston, the country towns still adhering to the old-fashioned way of doing things. It was long before Bath, Maine, bought even a bevel saw, and the first that went there was the one previously used by Donald McKay, which was sold after he had built his last ship in 1869. To this day the bevel saw, derrick, and bolt-cutter are unknown in the majority of the ship-yards of the Atlantic coast outside of the five cities above named.

Changes also took place in the kinds of timber used for building ships, as about 1835 the supply of oak timber began to grow scant in New England. Two hundred years of occupation and settlement, with the pursuit of ship-building and other industries, having nearly cleared the primitive forests from such parts of the country as were accessible from water-courses, southern timber was now finding its way plentifully to the northern markets, and between 1830 and 1840 was introduced into the ship-yards. The peninsulas of Delaware, Maryland, and Virginia were overgrown with splendid forests of towering white oak, and the getting out of the timber for the frames of vessels in that region soon became a regular industry. A complete set of patterns, or molds as they are called, having been made for the timbers of the vessel, they were turned over to contractors, who went out into the woods in the winter time with a party of men armed with axes. The party encamped in rough board or log huts, and remained until the trees had been felled and the complete frame of the ship hewn from them. Each piece was then marked, and the whole was hauled to the nearest water-course before the snow disappeared in the spring and put aboard a coasting schooner and sent north. This industry of getting out frames on these peninsulas is still a marked feature of ship-building as now pursued on the north Atlantic coast, nearly all the frames of the large New England ships being now obtained from the region named.

Southern pitch-pine timber was also introduced, the sticks of which could be obtained of such great lengths that they strengthened the ship. This timber was first used for beams and decking and the various longitudinal ties, such as water-ways, clamps, keelsons, etc.; but as soon as the insurance companies were induced to approve of pitch-pine its use also became general for the ceiling and planking of ships, its great length making it desirable for both purposes. Pitch-pine remains the favorite wood for all the parts of a vessel of over 100 tons except the stem, keel, stern-post, and frames, for which oak, hard wood, and hackmatack are preferred. For the masts and spars preference is given to white pine and spruce, but a great many lower masts are made of strips of oak or maple and yellow pine, doweled, bolted, and hooped over with iron. Topmasts and bowsprits are frequently made of pitch-pine sticks.

There was a difference in the cost of ships in this period in favor of American owners. In 1825 a 300-ton ship cost from $75 to $80 per ton in the United States, from $90 to $100 per ton in Canada, and from $100 to $110 per ton in England. In 1847 a large ship, first class in every respect, cost from $75 to $80 per ton here, against $87 to $90 in England.

The interest felt at this day in the ships of the clipper period centers principally in those of the largest size, as large ships alone will now do for transoceanic trade.

The Champion of the Seas, of 2,448 tons, was built by McKay for James Baines & Co.'s Liverpool and Australian line of clippers. This firm owned 20 first-class sail in that trade, and had under charter about as many more. The following are the principal details of this ship: Length of keel, 238 feet; length on deck, 252 feet; extreme beam, 45½ feet; depth of hold, 29 feet; dead rise at half-floor, 10 inches; swell of sides, 10 inches; sheer, 4½ feet. The concavity of load-line forward was 2½ inches, the bow above flaring decidedly outward. Figure-head, a sailor, hat in right hand, left hand extended. Keel, white oak and rock maple, sided 16 inches, the upper part molded 20 inches, the lower 12 inches; false keel, 6 inches; four scarfs, 12 feet in length, fastened with ten 1-inch copper bolts. Stem, white oak, sided 16 inches, molded 20 inches at the head and 26 inches at the foot, in two pieces; main stem bolted to the keel with copper bolts. The gripe of white oak tapered to 4 inches at the front edge. The stern-post was of white oak, sided 16 inches at the keel, 20 inches at the top; molded 24 inches at the keel, 21 inches at the top, and fastened to the keel with 16 bolts of $1\frac{1}{4}$-inch copper. Deadwoods white oak, sided 16 inches, fastened with $1\frac{1}{4}$-inch bolts of iron and copper. The entire frame was seasoned white oak. Room and space, 30 inches; timbers sided 12 and 14 inches over the keel and molded 20 inches, so that the double frame was 26 by 20 inches. The second futtocks sided 12 to 13 inches, and each succeeding shift of timbers diminished in siding to 10 inches at the plank-sheer and 9 inches at the rail. Frames molded 13 inches at the bilge, $11\frac{1}{2}$ inches at the lower deck, 9 inches at the middle deck, 7 inches at plank-sheer, and 6 inches at rail, and tapered truly between these points. Floor timbers 24 feet long, and the timbers of each frame fayed closely from keel to plank-sheer. From four to seven iron bolts in each futtock, from 1 to $1\frac{1}{4}$ inch in diameter. Every second floor was bolted to the keel with $1\frac{1}{8}$-inch copper bolts, driven through and clinched. Cant frames tenoned and bolted to deadwood with $1\frac{1}{8}$-inch bolts. Apron white oak, sided 30 inches at the bowsprit, and fastened to the stem with $1\frac{1}{4}$-inch bolts 18 inches apart. Inner stern-post molded 20 inches at the head, 16 inches at the foot. Stern-post knee, the arms 16 and $7\frac{1}{2}$ feet long, molded 46 inches in the throat. Stern timbers, the two at the side of post 10 by 14 inches, with $1\frac{1}{4}$-inch bolts through the post; other stern timbers 10 by 10 inches. Main keelson pitch-pine, in three tiers, 64 inches deep in all, sided 16 inches, the lower piece fastened to every other floor with $1\frac{1}{4}$-inch copper bolts, the bolts going clean through keel, the second tier with $1\frac{3}{8}$-inch iron bolts, going to within 2 inches of the lower edge of the upper piece of the keel; $1\frac{3}{8}$-inch iron bolts through the upper piece of the keelson down through the navel timbers. Scarfs of keelson, 8 feet; sister keelson, 14 by 30 inches, bolted with $1\frac{1}{4}$-inch iron through every futtock. Ceiling on bilge, and thence to deck, 14 inches thick, bolted to every timber, and fastened edgewise with iron bolts every second frame space, all of pitch-pine. Clamps $14\frac{1}{2}$ inches, bolted edgewise to the next strake below. Beams of lower deck pitch-pine, sided 15 inches, molded 14 inches at middle and $10\frac{1}{2}$-inches at ends. Middle deck beams, sided 15 and 16 inches, molded 15 inches at middle and $10\frac{1}{2}$ at ends; upper deck beams, 16 by 10 inches. Lower deck knees white oak; arms $6\frac{1}{2}$ to 7 and $4\frac{1}{2}$ to 5 feet; sided 11 and 12 inches; 24 inches thick in throat; twenty $1\frac{1}{4}$-inch bolts through each knee; lodging knees, sided 8 inches, molded 30 inches in the throat, eight bolts through each knee. Middle deck hanging knees oak, sided and molded about 1 inch less than above, and arms a foot or two shorter; lodging knees sided 8 to 9 inches. Upper deck hanging knees, hackmatack; arms $4\frac{1}{2}$ feet, sided 10 to 12 inches; 21 inches in the throat; 1 and $1\frac{1}{4}$ inch bolts; lodging knees hackmatack, sided 7 inches. Lower deck water-ways, of pitch-pine, lay flat on ends of beams 14 inches deep, 15 inches wide, 6 feet scarfs, riveted to every timber with $1\frac{1}{4}$-inch iron rivets, and bolted to the clamps; a binding strake, 10 by 12 inches, on beam outside of water-way; deck plank, yellow pine, $3\frac{1}{2}$ inches thick, 6 inches wide; thick strakes in the middle of the deck to receive stanchions, two 14 inches wide by 6 thick. Two standing strakes above water-way, each 20 inches wide and 10 inches thick. Main deck clamps, pitch-pine, 14 by 10 inches; water-way, 15 by 14 inches; binding strake, 12 by 10 inches; deck plank, $3\frac{1}{2}$ inches, 6 and 7 inches wide; thick strakes in middle, 5 inches thick; standing strakes above water-way, two 18 inches wide by 10 inches thick; the upper deck clamps 15 inches wide by 10 thick; water-way 14 inches wide, 12 inches deep, fastened with $1\frac{1}{8}$-inch iron bolts; binding strake, 8 by 10 inches; deck plank, pitch-pine $3\frac{1}{2}$ inches thick by 6 inches wide. Partners of mainmast and foremast, 15 by 15 inches; of mizzen-mast, 14 inches thick by 15 inches wide. Plank-sheer and main rail, 6 by 15 inches. Planking, all pitch-pine; garboard, 15 inches wide, 9 inches thick; the next strakes, 14 inches wide by 8 thick, and 14 inches by 7; bottom plank to bilge, 7 to 5 inches thick; wales, 24 strakes, 7 inches wide, 6 thick; waist plank, $4\frac{1}{2}$ inches thick. The bulwarks, solid like a man-of-war, $4\frac{1}{2}$ feet high, with monkey rail, strapped diagonally on the outside of frames with bands of iron 5 inches wide, $\frac{7}{8}$ of an inch thick, and 38 feet long. Top-gallant forecastle for crew; aft of foremast, a house 50 feet long, 18 wide, $6\frac{1}{2}$ high, with kitchen, second-class cabin, and state-rooms for forward officers. A double staircase from the forward part of the house leads to the deck below. Aft of the mainmast a house 16 feet square, with chief mate's state-room and large staircase leading to the vestibule below, from which the cabins are entered. Aft of the mizzen-mast was a house for smoking-room, to shelter helmsman and approach to staircase to captain's cabin below. All the passenger cabins were below and aft. The after one, 30 feet long, 14 feet wide, and $7\frac{1}{2}$ feet high, had two recess sofas, with costly mirrors, pictures, tables, carpets, gilding, panels, etc. The dining saloon, 40 feet long, was plainly finished, and the pantry, mess-room, bath-room, and other apartments were grouped around the entrance to the dining saloon. The deck forward of the cabins was fitted up for accommodation of the passengers. There were also arrangements below this deck for passengers, for use if needful. Her spars were as follows:

MERCHANT SAILING VESSELS.

	Diameter.	Length.	Mast-heads or yard-arms.		Diameter.	Length.	Mast-heads or yard-arms.
	Inches.	Feet.	Feet.		Inches.	Feet.	Feet.
Foremast	40	63	17	Jib-boom	21	a16, 15, 6	
Foretop	20	47	10	Foresail yard	24½	88	5
Foretop-gallant	15	26		Fore-topsail yard	19½	69	5¼
Fore-royal	13	17		Foretop-gallant	19½	51	4
Fore-royal pole		8		Fore-royal	9	37	2
Mainmast	42	71	17	Mainsail-yard	24½	95	5
Main-topmast	20	50	10	Main-topsail yard	19½	74	5¼
Main-top-gallant	15	27		Maintop-gallant	13½	54	4
Main-royal	13	17		Main-royal	9	42	3
Main-royal pole		12		Cross-jack yard	20	74	4½
Mizzen-mast	36	61	14	Mizzen-topsail yard	15	57½	5
Mizzen-top	16	42	9	Mizzen-top-gallant	9½	42	3½
Mizzen-top-gallant	12	24		Mizzen-royal	7	30	2
Mizzen-royal	10	15		Spanker boom		58½	
Mizzen-royal pole		8		Spanker gaff		42	
Bowsprit	40	a 22		Main spanker gaff		22	

a Outboard.

Mast-heads and yards painted black; lower masts, white; studding-sail booms unpainted, but with black ends; hemp rigging; chains and iron work for bobstays, bowsprit shrouds, martingale stays and guys, topsail sheets and ties, patent trusses, iron futtock rigging, caps, etc.; three backstays on each side to fore and main topmasts; double top-gallant backstays; 12,500 yards of canvas in the sails. This ship was painted black outside and white inside, with blue water-ways.

The Ocean Monarch, of 2,145 tons register, built by William H. Webb, at New York, was 240 feet long over all and 46 feet wide, with 30¼ feet depth of hold, 3 decks, a forecastle for 50 men, two deck-houses, and a large after-cabin. She had 7 hatchways. The keelsons were of five tiers of white-oak logs from 50 to 64 feet long. The side keelsons were 3 logs deep, and were placed at the floor heads. The timbers were of live oak and locust, at least the principal pieces; the rest were white oak and cedar. The frames were spaced 30 inches, and the keel sided 16 inches. The between-deck spaces were 7 and 7½ feet. This ship was double strapped with 4½ by ⅝ inch iron, and could carry 900 passengers and 4,000 tons of cargo. A year after she was built this strong and handsome ship, on account of being improperly loaded, was thrown on her beam-ends in a violent gale, and foundered in consequence.

The Great Republic (Fig. 42), built in 1855 by McKay, was 334½ feet long, with 53½ feet beam and 38 feet depth. For 60 feet from the bow the keel gradually rose from a horizontal line and curved upward into an arch, blending with the stem, and was of rock maple, two tiers, 16 by 32 inches, with five 12-foot scarfs, the end tiers being in six pieces; shoe, 4½ inches. The frame was of seasoned white oak; dead rise, 20 inches. The floor timbers sided 13 and 14 inches, and were molded 22 and spaced 28 inches from center to center; the timbers tapered to the plank-sheer, where they were from 11 to 13 inches in siding and 8 inches in molding. Molding on the bilge 14 inches; at the main deck 12½ inches; and the frames were bolted together and the ends of the timbers wedged. The floors and first futtocks were 25 feet long, and the stem was molded 30 inches at the foot, 26 inches at the head, with the cutwater tapered to an edge. The apron was 51 inches through, with heavy stemson inside, and the bolts in the stem, apron, and stemson were of 1¼-inch copper, and about 6 inches apart. The stern-post was oak, in three upright pieces, molded in all 5½ feet, and was sided 16 inches at the keel and 24 inches at the top. The stern knee was sided 16 inches and molded 36 inches in the throat, with arms 8 and 20 feet in length scarfed to the lower keelson and bolted with copper. The frames on the inside were strapped with iron by braces 4 inches wide, 1 inch thick, and 36 feet long, there being 90 straps on each side of the ship. The keelsons, ceiling, and deck frames were of pitch-pine. The midship keelson was in four tiers, 15 by 60 inches in all, and the sister keelsons in three tiers, the first two of which were each 15 by 15 inches, while the upper one was 12 by 14 inches, and all were wedged, bolted, lock-scarfed, and keyed. There were two 1⅜-inch copper bolts driven through every floor timber and the keel, the first through the timber and keel alone, the other also through the two lower tiers of the keelson, and riveted. Iron bolts were driven through all the navel timbers and keelsons into the keel, and the sister keelsons were bolted diagonally through the navel timbers into the keel and horizontally through the midship keelsons. Whole depth of backbone, 9 feet 10 inches; ceiling (nine strakes), 10 by 12 inches on floor, square fastened through frames and edge-bolted every 5 feet; over the floor heads two bilge keelsons, each 15 inches square and in two depths, square-bolted with 1¼-inch iron through each timber and edge-bolted with 1¼-inch iron; ceiling of floor, 10 inches. The bilge was double ceiled with 6- and 9-inch stuff, square-fastened and edge-bolted at every second beam, the double ceiling extending to a lap-streak, 6 by 15 inches, on which the lower edge of the hanging knees rested. The lower deck clamps, in two depths, were 6 and 10 inches thick; the beams of the lower and main decks 15 by 16 and 18 inches amidships, tapering to 12-inch molding at the ends, there being 38 beams to the lower and 40 to the main deck; while the upper deck beams, forty-one in number, were 12 by 20 inches in the center, tapering to 10-inch molding at the ends, twenty-five of them being double and bolted together, and the spar-deck beams varied in size and were close together, there being eighty-nine of them. The lower- and main-deck hanging knees were of oak, sided from 10 to 13 inches and molded from 22 to 24 inches in the throats; bodies, 5 to 6 feet long; arms, 4 to 4½ feet, each fastened with twenty 1¼-inch bolts; and the lodging knees were also of oak. The upper- and spar-deck knees were of hackmatack, and were all light and diagonal. Between the main and upper decks the ceiling had diagonal braces of pitch-pine from the throat of one hanging knee to the foot of the one next aft, bolted through ceiling and timbers. The lower deck clamps were 12 inches wide, in two thicknesses, 6 and 9 inches; the water-ways 16 inches square, the binding strake 12 by 14 inches, and the standing strake 24 inches wide by 10 inches thick. Main-deck clamps, 16 inches wide, 10 inches thick; water-ways, 16 inches square; binding strake, 12 by 10 inches; standing strakes, 18 by 12 inches thick; filling-in strakes to deck above, 8 inches thick, 14 inches wide. Upper-deck clamps, 12 inches thick, 15 inches wide; water-ways, 12 inches deep, 15 inches wide; binding strake, next the water-ways, 10 by 8 inches. Ceiling up to the spar-deck, 3½ inches; planking of lower three decks, 3½ inches, of pitch-pine; of spar-deck, 3 inches. Plank-sheer at upper deck, 16 by 7 inches; one at spar-deck 7 by 20 inches, having upon it a chock 12 by 6 inches, into which turned stanchions are fitted, supporting a main rail, 3½ feet high from the deck, 5 by 12 inches square. Beam-stanchions of hold, 8 by 24 inches, tenoned into the keelson and strapped with iron to the same; also strapped at the head over the beam and to the heel of the stanchions of the deck above. This system was carried clear to the spar-deck. Planking: First garboard, 10 inches thick, 14 inches wide, bolted clear through into the opposite garboard with 1¼-inch bolts 5 feet apart, and through every third frame into the sister keelson; next strake 9 inches thick, 14 inches wide; the next 8 inches. Bottom plank, 6 inches thick, 14 inches wide, treenailed with 1¼-inch locust through the timbers; butt bolts, 1-inch copper. Bilge planking, 8 inches thick, 12 inches wide, four in number and projecting, square treenailed with 1¼-inch locust, with a copper bolt driven into every fourth timber of the frame. Wales, 6 inches thick, 8 inches wide, double and single fastened. Waist plank, 5 inches thick, 6 and 7 inches wide, treenailed and iron butt bolted; plank above plank-sheer, 4 inches. There were heavy hooks and pointers of white oak, three in the forward hold 30 to 40 feet long and 11 by 12 inches in section, one under each of the decks. The ship had four masts, the after one being called the spanker. The other lower masts were built of pitch-pine, doweled, bolted, and hooped with iron. Her spars were as follows:

	Diameter.	Length.	Length of head or yard-arms.		Diameter.	Length.	Length of head or yard-arms.
	Inches.	Feet.	Feet.		Inches.	Feet.	Feet.
Foremast	44	130	36	Fore upper topsail yard	19	76	4½
Foretop-mast	24	76	12	Foretop-gallant yard	15	62	4
Foretop-gallant	18	28		Fore-royal yard	12	51	3½
Fore-royal	15	22		Fore sky-sail yard	9	40	3
Fore sky-sail mast	11	19		Mainyard	28	120	6
Fore sky-sail pole		12		Main lower topsail yard	24	92	5
Mainmast	44	131	36	Main upper topsail yard	19	76	4½
Main-topmast	24	76	12	Main-top-gallant yard	15	62	4
Main-top-gallant	18	28		Main-royal yard	12	51	3½
Main-royal	15	22		Main sky-sail yard	9	40	3
Main sky-sail mast	11	19		Cross-jack yard	24	90	5
Main sky-sail pole		12		Lower mizzen topsail yard	19	76	4½
Mizzen-mast	40	122	33	Upper mizzen topsail yard	15	62	4
Mizzen-topmast	22	69	10	Top-gallant yard	12	51	3½
Mizzen-top-gallant	16	22		Royal yard	9	40	3
Mizzen royal	10	19	6	Sky-sail yard	6	29	2
Mizzen sky-sail mast	8	15		Spanker boom	11	40	2
Mizzen sky-sail pole		8		Spanker gaff	8	34	8
Spanker mast	26	110	14	Bowsprit	44	a 30	
Spanker topmast	15	40		Jib-boom	22	a 18	4
Foreyard	26	112	6	Flying jib-boom	5	a 14	6
Fore lower topsail yard	24	90	5				

a Outboard.

Fore and main rigging and fore- and main-topmast back-stays, 12½-inch patent hemp rope; fore- and main-topmast rigging, 8-inch hemp; mizzen rigging and topmast back-stays, 11-inch hemp; 8 shrouds on each side, 4 topmast shrouds, 3 topmast back-stays, shifting breast back-stays, double top-gallant and royal back-stays. The lower and topmast stays were double. She had iron futtock rigging, chain bobstays and bowsprit shrouds, martingale stays and guys, topsail sheets and ties, and iron patent trusses and jack-stays. The amount of canvas in her sails was 15,653 yards, and her lower studding-sails were triangular, terminating in a point below. There were four complete decks, and the height between the upper and spar decks was 7 feet, between the others 8 feet. Abaft the foremast was a house, 23 feet long by 16 wide, for a work room, shelter for the watch, and hospital. Aft of the fore hatchway a house, 25 feet long by 16 wide, and 6½ feet high, contained the galley, blacksmith-shop, and

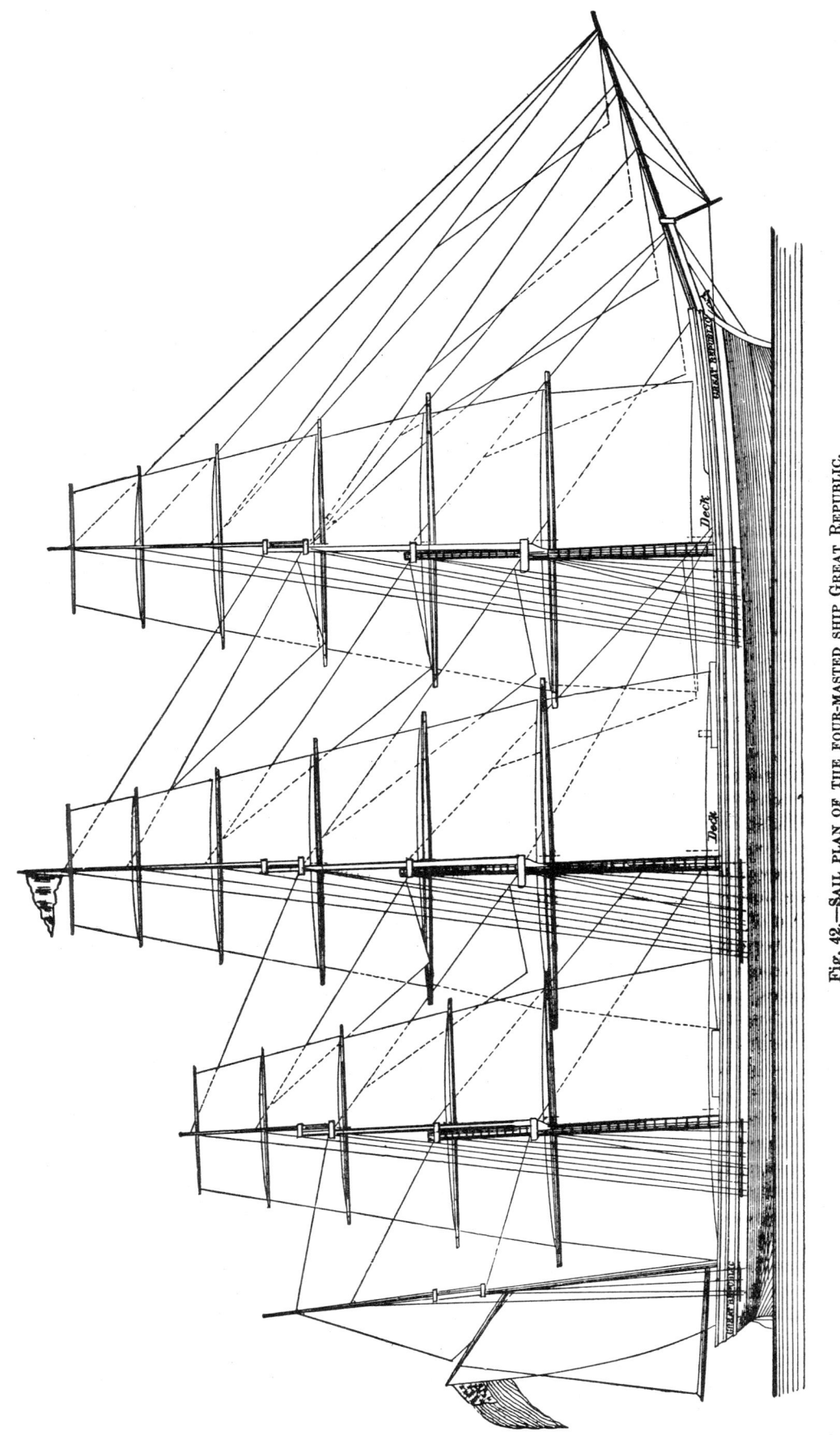

Fig. 42.—Sail plan of the four-masted ship Great Republic,

Showing the fashion now prevalent of dividing the topsail into upper and lower topsails.

engine-room for a donkey engine of 15 horse-power. Abaft the mainmast a house, 40 feet long by 12 wide and 6½ feet high, served as a mess-room for the officers, and had a staircase to the quarters of the petty officers and boys on the deck below, while farther aft a house, 17 feet long by 11½ wide, protected a staircase to the vestibule of the cabins below. Near the taffrail there was a small wheel-house. Under the spar-deck were accommodations for a crew of 100 forward, space for spare spars and rigging, a tonnage space aft of the foremast, a large sail-room aft, a store-room, rooms for 30 boys, state-rooms for the lower officers, and a dining-saloon 30 feet long by 14 feet wide, with four state-rooms on each side; and aft of that a vestibule, with stairs to the deck above and the cabins below, the captain's and chief officers' state-rooms, and an after cabin, 25 feet long by 14 wide, with six state-rooms. The chain lockers in the lower hold were ample. She had four chains of 120 fathoms each, two of 2½-inch iron, with 6,500- and 8,500-pound anchors, and two of 1½-inch iron, with 2,500- and 1,500-pound anchors, and two hemp stream cables and several hawsers. There were three hawse-holes. To build this vessel required 1,500,000 board feet of pitch-pine, 986,000 feet of white oak, 336½ tons of iron, and 56 tons of copper, besides her sheathing. There were about 50,000 days' work upon her hull.

There was little timber in the Great Republic longer than 50 and 60 feet, but the oak was in much shorter lengths. If ships of this size are to be built hereafter, the best timber in the United States for the purpose is the Puget Sound fir, on account of its length and other qualities. The Great Republic never sailed as a four-master except to New York city for a cargo. While loading she caught fire, her upper works being burned off, and she was cut down one deck and refitted as a three-master. She lived the usual life of a ship, but, with her shortened sail area, did not develop remarkable speed.

After 1857 there ceased to be a necessity for great speed and size. Too many ships had been built, and a reaction set in, which lasted for many years. The California excitement was over, the rush to the gold mines had slackened, and the settlers of the new territory had begun to produce for themselves the common necessaries of life, which had previously been sent to them from the East by clipper ships. Owing to the enormously high prices of food, agriculture had made rapid progress in California, and when it became so productive as to answer the requirement of the territory for food ships sailing around cape Horn experienced much difficulty in getting cargoes. By 1857 there were from 100 to 150 large ships in the California trade (more than were needed to transact the business), and rates of freight fell off one-half, and the ships were thrown into the general trade of the world. In the next place, steam vessels had been built to run on all the principal ocean routes. Steamers took all the passenger, mail, and express freight business at once, and in consequence, except in the case of a few scattered lines of packets sailing to Australia, South America, and Asiatic ports, there was no longer any need for sailing vessels to be fitted out with large cabins and roomy passenger accommodations. Three-deck sailing ships were useless for many years, and when those in existence had worn themselves out they were not replaced, the large sailing tonnage being reduced to two-deck ships. The reaction in American shipping circles that began in 1857 was helped by the extraordinary losses of vessel property in the winter of 1856 and the first part of 1857. There were several disastrous storms, the coast was strewn with wrecks, and more than 400 American vessels were lost, worth over $11,000,000. The loss of capital was itself a severe blow. The reaction was helped by the high prices of merchandise that prevailed in the world at large at that time, export trade being checked in various countries. In the general freighting business across the Atlantic there was also a reaction, owing to the falling off in immigration and to the importation of railroad iron to America which followed the financial panic of 1857. The Crimean war had come to an end, liberating a large amount of tonnage which had been in the service of the allied armies for the transportation of troops and munitions of war. To complete the list of depressing causes, the war of 1861 broke out in the United States, and the foreign and coasting trade of the southern states was completely cut off for four years. Cruisers from English ports were sent out to capture and burn American vessels. The rates of insurance rose so high on American vessels and cargoes that no one could afford to pay them, and the owners of American tonnage, finding themselves in a position where, to save themselves from bankruptcy, they were obliged to sell off all their ships, sold a large quantity of shipping to the United States government for war purposes and 800,000 tons to foreigners, our merchant marine declining heavily from 1861 to 1865 in consequence. All in all, that whole period of eight years from 1857 to 1865 was unfavorable to the production of ships of large tonnage; in fact, it almost put an end to American ship-building. The reaction on some coasts was painful. When, to use the expressive phrase of the Maine men, "the bottom dropped out of things" in 1857 there was great havoc among the ship-building firms of the whole country. Many towns in New England which had been building and launching large sailing vessels every year since the great expansion began, 30 years before, ceased entirely to build, and large ships then under way often lay idle a whole year at some wharf awaiting a purchaser in vain. In many of these towns there has not been another large ship built down to the present day. Numbers of builders were completely ruined, and in Maine the ship-yards of Bath and Thomaston were about the only ones that withstood the shock. From 1861 to 1865, in New York, Philadelphia, Baltimore, and Boston, the building of large sailing vessels ceased on account of the war; when the war ended the high prices of labor in those cities prevented the industry from reviving, and those who wanted ships went to the country towns to have them built, both labor and materials being cheaper in those places. No traces of the industry remained at the four great ports named, except the construction of vessels requiring the greatest mechanical skill and ingenuity, such as yachts and steam vessels, and excepting also the repair of old vessels—a class of work which is naturally required in ports frequented by large fleets of vessels, where repairs have to be made immediately.

Since 1865 there has been a change for the better, and sailing ships have again come into demand in spite of the great increase in the employment of steam in ocean navigation. One cause has been the fact that the eight years of reaction diminished the world's supply of shipping and made new vessels necessary. There was, however, an enormous expansion of the foreign trade of the United States, and that has been the main cause of the improvement. Railroad building had made a demand for iron beyond the power of the United States to meet. Nearly every species of iron and steel has been required, and those articles, with coffee, sugar, manila hemp, jute, tea, and European, South American, and Asiatic goods of every description, have been imported in immense quantity. On the other hand, the productiveness of the farms and forests of the United States has been greatly developed, and the exportation of grain, tobacco, cotton, provisions, kerosene, lumber, etc., has grown to five and six times what it was before 1865. A special feature of the export trade has been that from the Pacific coast. Before the war that coast had no export trade, and ships sailed thither from every part of the world with cargoes and departed in ballast, a few cargoes of lumber, canned salmon, and seal skins being all that were sent away from that 1,500 miles of coast.

After 1865 the wonderful fertility of California wrought a change. A good crop of wheat in the eastern states would average from 20 to 25 bushels to the acre, while on the wheat ranches of the Pacific 25 bushels per acre was a small crop. Forty bushels would be an average, and a production of 50 and 55 bushels to the acre was so common as to cause no particular comment, and wheat raising became as profitable as gold mining. In Oregon the soil was found to be equally productive, and one plowing and planting was often good for two crops. The first year's crop would be 40 bushels and more, and that of the second year, springing up from the seed shaken out naturally in gathering the first year's crop, would sometimes amount to 20 and 25 bushels per acre. As soon as the coast began to have wheat to export San Francisco became one of the most profitable ports in the United States for traffic, and American ships at first had the advantage in the trade. Sailing from the Atlantic states with miscellaneous cargoes of goods, they not only got the freight out, but had a good freight of wheat back to England. The general trade of the world having revived, tonnage was in demand, and wheat freights from San Francisco to Liverpool accordingly rose to a profitable figure. A complete revolution in the carrying trade of the Pacific coast was the result, and ships have ever since sought that coast from all parts of the world in ballast, coming even from England without a cargo to get one of wheat back. The coast now exports 850,000 gross tons of wheat annually, and supplies about 600 ships with outward cargoes. This business all accrues to sailing vessels. A very few steamers have taken cargoes of wheat from San Francisco to England, but, in the main, this was only because they had brought a cargo to the coast and could not afford to go away in ballast. The voyage of 13,600 miles from San Francisco to Liverpool is too long to make it profitable to employ steamers in the business, sailing ships paying better, on account of their large available capacity and smaller expenses, and it is this profitable trade chiefly which has caused the revival of ship-building in American yards since 1865, and is again leading to the production of large sailing merchantmen. The newest ships, those built in Maine within the last two years, are from 2,000 to 2,400 tons register, carrying from 3,000 to 3,600 tons of wheat; and they are again growing larger year by year.

The California vessel of to-day is no longer an extreme clipper, nor is it the bluff freighting ship of 1840, but it is a handsome, medium clipper, with towering masts and spars, full on the floor, with a good bow and fair run, capable of carrying a great cargo at an excellent rate of speed. The midship section is in the center of the length, the ship floats on an even keel, its carrying power is $1\frac{1}{2}$ times the register tonnage, and it draws from 20 to 24 feet of water. A few of those built at Thomaston and Bath, Maine, within the last five years out of the profits of the California wheat trade are of about 2,000 tons register and carry 3,000 gross tons of freight. Four-masters are now talked of, though none have as yet been built; there are a few British four-masters in the California trade.

Another class of sailing vessel which grew into great repute before 1861 was the schooner. It has been noted that the original coaster was the sloop, its broad beam, shallow draught, big fore-and-aft sail and one or two jibs, simplicity of rigging, and ease of management by about three men making it the right vessel for running along the coast and into and out of rivers. Ketches and brigantines were used for voyages as long as from Salem to Chesapeake bay, for instance, and the two-masted schooner followed. During the packet times trade and travel increased so fast that large vessels were required for coasting, the square rig being preferred. Brigs, barks, and ships were much in favor, but after 1840 they went out of use for coasters, their places being taken on the one hand by steamboats, which were built for the passenger and mail service between all the large Atlantic and Gulf ports, and on the other hand by two- and three-masted schooners, built for freighting. The fore-and-aft rig came to be preferred for coasting vessels for several reasons. Fewer sailors were required to handle the vessel, and a schooner could be worked into and out of harbors and rivers more easily than any square-rigged craft. Her trips could also, as a rule, be made in quicker time, as she could sail closer into the wind, and it was hardly necessary for her to sail from Maine to New York by way of the Bermudas, as some square-rigged vessels have done during baffling winds. The schooner rig became universal in the coasting trade about 1860, and there is probably not a bark or a ship left in this trade anywhere except on the Pacific coast, where the voyages are long and the winds blow in trades, and even there there are few purely square-rigged vessels in the trade. On the lakes the schooner is the popular rig, a few square topsails being sometimes added on the forward mast. Originally registering no more than 40 or 50 tons, the schooner has become in course of time a large vessel, the two-masters ranging from 100 to 250 tons, the three-masters from 300 to 750 tons. The popular size now for a three-masted coasting schooner on the Atlantic is about 550 or 600 tons, and it is probable that more vessels of the schooner rig are built in the United States every year than there are of all other rigs put together. With square sails on the foremast the vessel is called a barkentine, and many of this class are used for transoceanic service, for which they are well adapted. The hulls of American schooners are as strongly built as those of any other vessels of their size; in fact, the scantling is far heavier than it was in full-rigged ships 75 years ago. They are constructed with a view to class A 1 on the books of the American Shipmasters' Association, and no large ship can do better than that. The best materials and workmanship are put into them. For transoceanic trade, and on the Pacific coast, where the waters are deep, the schooners are keel vessels with some dead rise; but on the Atlantic coast, where the harbors are so frequently shallow and obstructed with sand-bars, the schooners are center-board vessels with flat bottoms. In all cases, however, the models are full, the beam large, the bow sharp and long, the run clean, and the sheer considerable forward. Above the water an American schooner has the jaunty air of a yacht. Schooners with sharp bottoms do not pay, and few are built.

In 1880 an advance was made in the building of the William L. White, of Taunton, Massachusetts, at a ship-yard in Bath, Maine. The hull of the vessel was large enough for a Californian. She was 205 feet long on deck, 40 feet beam, and 17 feet deep in the hold, being 309 feet in length over all from the end of the jib-boom to the end of the spanker boom. She registered 996 tons, and was able to carry 1,450 tons of anthracite coal. This vessel was rigged as a four-masted schooner. To have fitted her out with three masts would have required such large lower sails that the strain upon the masts would have been destructive, and she was therefore furnished with four, the after spar being called the spanker mast. This divided her 5,017 yards of canvas into smaller sails and made her a good schooner, sailing well, easily handled, and requiring a crew of only five men before the mast, besides her two mates and captain. This was the first four-masted schooner built for actual ocean service in America, and probably the first ever so employed in the world, although there is on record a case where a small one was built in England in 1800 for packet service to India. This was the Transit, a little vessel 98 feet long on deck, 22 feet beam, drawing 11½ feet of water. She was rigged with four fore-and-aft lower sails, and there were three square upper sails on the foremast and two fore-and-aft topsails on the after three masts. The lower topsail was spread by a gaff above, and the upper topsail was the usual triangular sail. There were three head sails. A few small vessels were built in imitation of the Transit, but it was left to the Americans to adopt a rig for heavy freighting on the Atlantic ocean. The same yard in Maine which produced the William L. White has since built two other four-masters. One launched in the fall of 1882 is of large size, being of 1,137 tons register. She is 192 feet long on deck to the after side of the stern-post, 40 feet beam, and 16 feet depth of hold, having two decks and 5,000 yards of canvas in her sails. The four-masted rig is a common one on the northern lakes.

Before leaving the subject of ships to describe the localities where they are built reference ought to be made to the ingenious invention of bending wooden frame timbers and hanging knees. This subject occupied attention for many years, especially about 1850, in New York, Boston, Philadelphia, and in the United States navy-yards, and it is probable that the invention would have come into extended use except for the decay of the American merchant marine and the introduction of iron hulls. It is well known that the outside planking of a wooden vessel must be well softened by steaming in a long steam box before being fastened to the vessel's side, especially on those parts of the hull where the surface is greatly curved, this process being necessary in order to allow the plank to be bent without breaking. In the construction of yawls and other small boats the frames are not generally cut from crooked timber, but are composed of slender pieces of white oak, steamed and bent to the proper curvature on molds and allowed to harden in shape by cooling. In iron vessels the frames are all gotten out of straight angle iron, cut to the proper length, heated in a furnace, and bent to the curvature required on a large slab made for the purpose, and it was considered one of the triumphs of the invention of the iron ship that the frames could be made in one continuous length. J. Scott Russell says: "A single tree never furnishes an entire frame. If trees could be found to grow to the right curves for complete frames, it would be glorious times for wooden ships." It has always been one of the disadvantages of wooden hulls that the frames can only be made of a large number of separate short pieces lapped together and given such heavy molding thickness as to compensate in part for the large number of joints. There is no doubt that frame timbers in one piece from keel to plank-sheer would impart greater strength to the ship and lessen the weight of wood, and lighter scantling could be employed. About 1850 it was the inspiration of several men at New York and Boston to experiment in this direction. Machines were made for the bending of straight pieces of white oak, steamed, into ship's knees, and afterward three or four were made of large size and at great cost for the production of bent frame timbers. J. W. Griffiths, of New York, and Thomas Blanchard and C. Allen Browne, of Boston, were prominently identified with this matter. In 1853 futtocks, steamed and bent by machinery, were introduced into the steamer Ocean Bird at New York. In July, 1856, a number of 10½-inch white-oak knees, steamed and bent, were tested at the Novelty iron works, in New York, by Lieutenant J. T. Worden and Naval Constructor B. F. Delano, and the same year a full set of bent hanging knees was put into the bark Lexington, built by Edward F. Williams, in

Brooklyn, New York, and another set for both decks into the bark Jane Daggett, built by Webb & Bell at Greenpoint. In consequence of the favor with which the new idea was regarded in naval circles, the steam sloop-of-war Pawnee, which was built in Philadelphia in 1858, was supplied with 60 machine-bent timbers from 20 to 24 feet in length. These were the longest futtocks which had been used up to that time, and were inserted in the difficult curvatures of the bilge amidships. In 1858 the ship Richard S. Ely, at East Boston, was supplied with bent hanging knees. New notions are proverbially and necessarily slow in winning general favor, and the pioneers of this new invention had the usual experience and expended and lost a great deal of time and money in their experiments. But having worked out their ideas on a small scale, the owners of the invention determined upon a bolder policy. In 1864 all the patents became concentrated in the hands of Mr. Browne, and Mr. Griffiths continued his indefatigable championship of the new idea. Bent knees continued to be occasionally used. In 1869–'70 a two-decked ship for the California and East India trade, with bent frames, was built for Glidden & Williams and M. D. Ross at East Boston. This vessel (called the New Era) was finished in May, 1870, and left for Liverpool (via Saint John's, New Brunswick) in June of that year on her first voyage. She was enthusiastically claimed by her owners to be the strongest built ship and the best carrier of her size in the world, and she certainly was a good ship. The details of her construction were as follows: Length at load-line, 183 feet; breadth, $38\frac{2}{12}$ feet; depth, $23\frac{4}{12}$ feet; height between decks, $7\frac{1}{12}$ feet; register, $1,146\frac{3}{4}$ tons. Two decks, half poop, trunk cabin; house on main deck; open topgallant forecastle. Keel, gum wood, 12 by 20 inches, in four pieces; stem and apron, white oak; stern-post the same. Every frame timber, floor, sharp rise, knee, breast-hook, rail forward and aft, and chocks thereon, was bent. Frames, white oak, in one length from keel to gunwale and rail, 11 by 13 inches over the keel, tapered to 6 inches molding at the plank-sheer and spaced 21 inches, the joint over the keel strengthened by a floor timber extending from bilge to bilge. Ceiling, pitch-pine, 6 inches, except on bilge, where it was 8 and 9 inches. Keelsons: main, pitch-pine, 15 by 30 inches; sister keelsons, each 12 by 13 inches. Planking, pitch-pine; garboards, 7 and 8 inches, thence to wales 5 inches; wales, 6 inches. Lower deck beams, 7½ by 10 inches, spaced 21 inches, with pitch-pine stringer 6 by 12 inches. Upper deck beams, 7 by 10 inches, spaced 21 inches, with strake 5 by 14 inches, bolted to the under side of beams, and a water-way above 12 by 13 inches. Two hanging knees of white oak, bent, at each end of all beams, sided 5 to 6 inches, with 4-foot arms, bolted to the sides of the beams and to the frame timbers. Besides the bent deck hooks forward and aft there were two pairs of pointers, with large bent hooks in the throat, at each end of the lower hold. Fastening, iron and copper. The ship was well salted. In model she was very full on the floor and otherwise adapted to large capacity. Draught, 20 feet. Anchors, 3,675, 3,500, and 1,000 pounds; standing rigging, wire rope. The New Era proved to be strong, dry, and satisfactory in every respect, and obtained high rates of freight and low rates of insurance, the final test of a good ship. Her actual cargoes were as much as 1,460 tons of coal and 1,555 tons of wheat. Her original rating was A 1* for 12 years, and after survey she was pronounced a model vessel in type of construction. She saw much general service in carrying ice, coal, grain, and mixed cargoes in all latitudes, and her bent frames showed remarkable freedom from decay.

The experiment with the New Era was sufficiently satisfactory to promise a more extended popularity of the principles on which she was built. But the times did not remain favorable to American shipping interests, the continual agitation for "free ships" and the general uncertainty as to the future checking enterprise in this as in many other directions. The machines were costly, and none except a few large contract yards could afford to own them; and finally their most energetic advocate, Mr. Griffiths, died. It is believed that the idea of bent frames has now been practically abandoned.

Chapter III.—SHIP-BUILDING ON THE OCEAN COASTS.

It is now proposed to note the present state of the wooden ship-building industry on the various ocean coasts of the United States, beginning with Maine and taking up the different localities in geographical order.

MAINE.

Maine has long been the largest builder of merchant sailing vessels, her ship-yards producing the most and the largest of this class in the United States. Cheap timber, low wages, and the nearness of the fisheries, gave her this precedence originally. Her timber is now almost entirely gone, and she only keeps the lead through her low wages and the enterprise of her builders. Ship-building and ship-owning are the only trades the people know in more than fifty towns on the sea-coast, but they practice both callings in dull times because they do not know what else to go into, and in good times they follow them because both are profitable. These fifty towns are composed mainly of ship-owners, ship-carpenters, calkers, riggers, sail-makers, anchor-makers, rope-makers, shipsmiths, painters, boat-builders, lumber dealers, fishermen, sailors, and other persons, who live by the various branches of the industry; in all there is a population of about 200,000 souls dependent on the prosperity of shipping for their support. In some of the smaller places the building, repair, and operation of fishing vessels are the specialties followed; in others the building is all of large class ships and coasting schooners. Since 1857 these towns have had a varying fortune. In some the old builders were ruined by the reaction of that year, and have never attempted an ambitious class of work since; in others, while ship-building is not what it was once, a large vessel or two is built every year, serving to keep the industry so far alive that if there should ever be a large demand for ships the men would be there to build them; but the tendency of late years has been toward a concentration of the business in Camden, Rockland, Thomaston, Bath, Yarmouth, Freeport, East Deering, Portland, and Kennebunkport, to the detriment of the smaller towns, the latter having experienced stagnation and loss of population in consequence.

In the following notes of the state of the industry in different localities no attempt at entire completeness is made, the intention being merely to present such general and important facts as could be gathered from the leading men of each place by necessarily brief personal visits or by correspondence.

At Eastport and Calais, on Passamaquoddy bay, there was formerly an extensive industry in the building of fishing vessels and coasting sloops and schooners, and from 1871 to 1876 every yard on the bay was busy. The people owned the vessels, and but few were sent away. In the five flush years every man who had anything to do with the industry in any way became loaded down with shares in vessels varying from one thirty-second to one-fourth part, and as long as freights were good and fishing paid this activity continued. Vessels cost from $24 to $43 per register ton; but freights declined in consequence of the steamboats that were built to run along the coast, and fishing, by reason of the fishery treaty with Canada, as well as the vessels, ceased to pay. The local taxation amounted to about $2\frac{1}{2}$ per cent. annually, and every one then wanted to sell, but no one to buy. Building virtually stopped, and has ever since been confined chiefly to fishing boats of from 16 to 25 feet in length; occasionally a brig or a small schooner of from 10 to 50 tons, with now and then a tug, is built. There has latterly been a change for the better, but it is a slight one, and vessels do not yet pay more than 4 or 5 per cent. clear of insurance and taxes. The woods used are beech, birch, and maple in the bottoms of vessels, with very little oak. Spruce and hackmatack frames and planking are popular; they cost less, and in most cases last as long. White pine is put into the decks. There are few professional builders of either boats or vessels on the bay, and those who build generally hire a master carpenter to superintend the job, who employs the men, while the owner pays the bills. On the islands there are a large number of men, half landsmen, half seamen, who farm, fish, and build boats by turns, and so much of the smaller class of work is done by them that little is left for the professional builders. During the census year wages varied from $1 50 to $2 per day of ten hours, according to the skill of the man. At Calais there was a marine railway for the repair of small vessels.

On the Aroostook river, in Maine, there is as yet no vessel building. During the census year there was one flat-bottom stern-wheel steamboat, carrying about 50 tons, and that was the only vessel in the whole region. The other craft employed was the batteau, a flat-bottom skiff with pointed ends and flaring sides, which was used in driving rafts of logs down the river. It is estimated that about 75 of these light and fragile boats are made every year for lumbermen. They are constructed of pine boards, at a cost of from $10 to $25 each, and will carry about half a ton.

East Machias formerly built many vessels of good size. There are four yards in the town, but they have been lying idle since 1876. In one of them the plant was quite complete and expensive, including a machine-shop, saw-mill, and carpenter-shop. At Machiasport the same state of facts existed, only one small schooner being built in the census year. Local taxation was complained of by the owners, who declared that assessments ought to be made on the net income of the vessel, and not on the cost.

At Cutler the principal builder was M. B. Stevens, who had built 28 brigs, schooners, and barks, during the census year; but none were built during the preceding four years, the losses of capital by armed cruisers during the war, the taxation of shipping, and the general decline of business having produced the result. Here, as elsewhere, there was much complaint that the national laws were not framed to protect the owners of shipping.

At Brookline coasting was once the life of the place. Fifteen years ago the town owned 40 or 50 good sized vessels, but there were not half a dozen left in the census year. There was no repairing, and a few small sloops and boats were all that were being built.

Harrington, once a prosperous village, is now becoming depopulated by the loss of its main industry, and there has been a heavy loss to the town by the decline in the value of vessel property in the coasting trade, some men having lost $50,000 each. The large ship-yard of H. W. Ramsdell has been sold for saw-mill purposes, and the inhabitants were moving to other parts of the country, as there was little other business they could follow to advantage at home.

At Millbridge there is still some building, but not much. This town has many skillful workmen, but ship-building is no longer depended upon for a livelihood. Wages, in consequence, were low, seldom exceeding $1 50 per day. The shareholders in vessels complained of the burdens of tonnage duties, local taxation, and compulsory pilotage at the principal harbors, while the captains of coasting vessels were so familiar with the different ports that they claimed to be able to get into and out of them all in safety without pilots, and the extravagant charges they had to pay, for no good purpose, were a source of constant complaint.

At Bluehill ship-building was the principal business 20 years ago. Several families were engaged in it extensively, owning parts of all the vessels they built, and the town was prosperous. The industry has since entirely died out, and only a few old vessels lingered in the possession of the town in the census year, the owners all hoping soon to be rid of the burden of repairing even those. There is still enough timber on that part of the coast to do considerable building if there was any call for it. A large number of the small towns on this part of the coast east of the Penobscot told the same story as Bluehill.

There is no ship-building at present at Ellsworth, and a gloomy view of the future of shipping was taken there. The cause of this dullness and the desirable remedies were given by builders to the following effect: Tonnage taxes should be abolished, especially in the coasting trade; duties should be remitted on all materials in American ships; a certain amount of the duty on goods imported in American bottoms should be remitted, and some of the heavy consular charges should be abolished.

At Bucksport there is still some work done, a bark of 568 tons and three schooners of 15, 17, and 86 tons each being built in the census year. There are two marine railways in the place, one capable of hauling vessels of 300 tons out of the water for repair, the other for vessels of 1,200 tons. The owner charges a fee of 10 cents per ton for hauling out, which he does with horse-power and windlass, and the vessel employs the carpenters, calkers, and painters to make the repairs. From thirty to fifty vessels are taken out per year; but the business is dull, the maritime interests of the town having greatly decayed. The woods used at Bucksport were: Frames, hard wood, oak, and hackmatack of local growth, worth $30 per thousand board feet; keelsons, beams, ceiling of hold, and outside planking, pitch-pine from the southern states, worth $35 per thousand feet; stem and stern posts, white oak; deck plank and cabins, white pine of local growth, worth $30 per thousand; knees, hackmatack; masts and spars, white pine and spruce. Spruce, being light, able to withstand the heat of warm climates, and costing only $15 per thousand, is somewhat used in frames. A deterioration in the hard wood now used is noticed, owing to its being from second-growth trees. Carpenters' wages were $1 75 per day; fasteners, $1 50; joiners, dubbers, calkers, and spar-makers, $2 and $2 25. The Bucksport vessels cost from $45 to $50 per register ton, but builders and owners said that taxation, consular charges, pilotage fees, the laws concerning seamen, etc., weighed heavily on shipping.

On both sides of Penobscot bay there are many ship-building communities, the principal ones being Rockland, Camden, Searsport, and Brewer. At Rockland there are several marine railways for hauling coasting schooners out of the water for coppering, repair, and rebuilding. The limestone quarries of this town have given a great deal of employment to coasters, and a great many of the shipping men own from ten to twenty vessels each, either wholly or in part. Repairing and coppering are, however, the principal work of the yards. Spruce from Isle au Haut and other parts of the coast is much used here; the local supply of timber is almost completely exhausted.

Searsport was formerly an active ship-building town. All the vessels built were owned there, and it is said that there never was a vessel built on contract at Searsport for outside owners. A few years ago, when coasters became unprofitable, builders and investors turned their attention to other forms of business, and the industry has nearly died out in consequence, two or three small schooners a year being about the only product of the town. Excellent ship-yards exist, but their value is not rated above one-third what it used to be.

At Camden three schooners of 383, 415, and 436 tons register, respectively (three-masters), were built in the census year, and there is always more or less work going on in the yards of the town, although nothing to compare with earlier years. Ten years ago and previously such wood as could be obtained in Maine was used in Camden vessels, especially in the smaller ones. Floor timbers were hewn from hard wood; that is to say, from beech, birch, or rock-maple, which is what is meant in Maine by "hard wood". Hackmatack and spruce tops were used with oak planking, and sometimes oak frames and oak planking; but of late years Virginia and Maryland white-oak frames have been obtained for large vessels, and southern pitch-pine has come into universal use for ceiling, planking, deck frames, stanchions, plank-sheer, etc. This southern lumber costs very little more than that of Maine; and as the importation of it makes business for the coasting vessels, it has become the favorite at Camden, as well as at many other building centers. The prices are: Hard wood, hewn, $29 per thousand board feet; hackmatack, $38 per thousand feet; pitch-pine, $26; southern white oak, $35. Pitch-pine has the advantage of coming in longer lengths than any other lumber; besides it is durable and strong. The Camden builders say that hard wood and hackmatack frames, or white oak frames planked and ceiled with yellow pine and well salted while building in the frame spaces above light water mark, are an improvement upon the old custom of white-oak frames with white-oak plank and ceiling, as oak in contact with oak is said to decay. The wages at Camden varied from $1 50 to $2 per day of 10 hours, according to the skill of the men, and the cost of building a vessel ranged from $45 to $55 per register ton. One firm, when asked about the prospects of sailing vessels as compared with steam, replied to the effect that they had less fear of steam vessels, except between large ports, than of bad laws in regard to taxation and the shipment and discharge of seamen and of inattention to shipping interests abroad by the consuls. Three months' extra pay and the discharge of the sailor are demanded abroad whenever a technical flaw can be found in the articles of agreement, and it was claimed that the consul too often looked after the interest of an unprincipled seaman rather than after that of an American ship. The seamen are mostly foreigners, and the consul aids them to take thousands of dollars out of the ship. A good seaman need never be without a good ship in any part of the world, as the ship is more often in need of good seamen. The law requiring ships to transfer wrecked or destitute seamen from Calcutta to New York for $10 was severely condemned, and tonnage dues and local taxation were also deemed hard burdens when a ship was earning little money. One member of the firm said:

I think we shall require sailing vessels, like those of the present model, wide and shoal, for the coasting trade, such as for coal and pitch-pine lumber, and also for lighter cargoes, as steam cannot take their place. A three-masted schooner of 600 tons will pay better for the amount invested than a steamer in the coal business. No one would think of carrying pitch-pine on a steamer. I think that to build up our commerce the burdens on shipping ought to be taken off, so that the man who invests either in a sailer or a steamer shall get back a return equal to that on other investments. There would then be little trouble about our having a commerce, both sail and steam, to compete with any other nation.

It should be explained that on Penobscot bay, as, indeed, throughout Maine generally, the majority of builders are also owners of vessels.

Belfast is one of the old ship-yard towns of Maine, but the industry is quiet at present. Some work was done in the census year, but not much, and very little had been done for the previous five years. The vessels of Belfast are generally coasters, and cost about $48 a ton. Hard wood (beech, birch, and maple), spruce, and hackmatack are somewhat used for floor timbers and keels; but oak is preferred, especially in large vessels. Oak and pitch-pine cost one-third more, and are now known to be more durable. Hard wood costs $28 a thousand at Belfast; hackmatack, $36.

At Brewer the work done is principally repairing, two large marine railways being employed there to haul out the steamboats of the bay and river and any other vessels needing repair. Steamboats and small vessels are occasionally built for the river.

Thomaston is famous for her large ships. The first vessel, so far as can be ascertained, was built in 1787. Some of the early vessels were partly owned by General Henry Knox (the friend of Washington), who lived on a fine estate in Thomaston. Sloops, schooners, and occasionally small ships were built in the early years; but not over three or four were built in any one year until 1825, when the business began to be more active. In 1845 came the first rush, but ships of no larger size than 565 tons were built until 1848. After that large vessels were in order, one of 991 tons being constructed in 1850 and one of 1,146 tons in 1851. Several vessels of about 1,200 tons and upward were launched yearly until after the crash of 1857. Thomaston has given birth to many of the finest builders of vessels and most proficient sea captains in the United States, one of the leading builders, Edward O'Brien, having built since 1850 the following full-rigged ships:

Year.	Name.	Register tonnage.	Register length.	Breadth.	Depth of hold.
			Feet.	Feet.	Feet.
1850	Edward O'Brien	797	158	33	16$\frac{7}{12}$
1854	S. Curling	1,697	205	40	29$\frac{1}{12}$
1855	Vesper	1,497	213$\frac{1}{12}$	38$\frac{9}{12}$	19$\frac{3}{12}$
1856	Mary O'Brien	1,297	191	38$\frac{5}{12}$	19$\frac{7}{12}$
1858	Mary A. Campbell	1,373	195	39	19$\frac{7}{12}$
1860	Ellen Creighton	1,287	193$\frac{7}{12}$	37$\frac{1}{12}$	18$\frac{5}{12}$
1863	Edward O'Brien	1,552	211$\frac{3}{12}$	39$\frac{9}{12}$	19$\frac{1}{2}$
1866	Wm. A. Campbell	1,535	209$\frac{10}{12}$	41$\frac{7}{12}$	24
1866	Andrew Johnson	2,006	215	41	30
1869	John Bryce	1,968	217$\frac{1}{2}$	42	21$\frac{5}{12}$
1870	A. McCullum	1,951	215	42	29$\frac{5}{12}$
1874	Alida	1,672	223	42	24$\frac{5}{12}$
1875	Belle O'Brien	1,903	237$\frac{5}{12}$	42	26$\frac{5}{12}$
1877	Alex. Gibson	2,194	247$\frac{5}{12}$	42$\frac{1}{12}$	37$\frac{1}{12}$
1877	Baring Brothers	2,167	243$\frac{9}{12}$	42$\frac{1}{12}$	29$\frac{5}{12}$
1878	Frank F. Curling	2,201	245$\frac{5}{12}$	42$\frac{1}{12}$	29$\frac{5}{12}$
1879	J. B. Walker	2,178	247	42$\frac{2}{12}$	27$\frac{7}{12}$
1881	Gen. Knox	2,218	251	42$\frac{1}{12}$	29$\frac{1}{12}$
1882	Edward O'Brien	2,157	259	42$\frac{9}{12}$	28$\frac{1}{2}$

The large ships are generally three-deckers, have billet heads and square sterns, and carry sky-sails on every mast. The frames are of white oak from the South; the planking and ceiling, keelsons, deck beams, deck plank, lower masts, and topmasts pitch-pine; the knees hackmatack, from Maine and Canada; the treenails locust; the light spars spruce; and the cabins white pine, oak, and walnut. In the new Edward O'Brien and the Andrew Johnson the lower masts and some of the yards are of boiler iron. When the former was launched an anchor of 4,200 pounds was dragged by her from the yard to the river, plowing a furrow 5 feet deep and pulling large trees from the ground.

There has been one other large builder in Thomaston, Captain Samuel Watts, who has built about thirty full-rigged ships for the merchant service, among them the Samuel Watts, of 2,035 tons; the Loretto Fish, of 1,945 tons; the Joseph B. Thomas, of 1,938 tons; the H. L. Gregory, of 2,020 tons; the Alfred D. Snow, of 2,075 tons; the Abner I. Benyon, of 2,044 tons; and the Cyrus Wakefield, of 2,013 tons. The size of these huge merchantmen will be better appreciated when it is understood that few ships under the English flag approach them in register tonnage. The largest iron clippers of England are in the grain trade from California to Liverpool, and seldom exceed 1,600 tons register; but it is not known that many of 1,600 tons ever visit San Francisco.

The large California ships of Chapman & Flint, of New York, until within a few years have also all come from Thomaston; but a few years ago their yard was spoiled by a new railroad running through it, and it was removed to Bath.

These three firms have always built for themselves, and belong to that class of old shipping families in New England which grew up after 1812 whose enterprise and family pride made the fortune of American shipping. The history of all is about the same. Beginning modestly with small vessels, they put smart young men in charge of them, were prudent in all their expenses, used good judgment and great energy in the management of their affairs, and made money. Every year or two these firms would build a new vessel out of the profits of the old ones and put it in trade along with the others; but as trade expanded they built larger and larger, and in time each came to have a fleet of from ten to fifteen of the finest and largest class of ocean carriers. They would never sell a new vessel, but would keep it until it was about twenty years old, when they would sell it at half price to Germans, Italians, or other foreigners and build a new ship to take its place. Their vessels were put into the trade that paid them best at the time, the cotton business of southern ports and the trade of California and China employing the most of them. Some of them went into the carrying of guano and nitrate from South America to Europe, bringing back iron, salt, and heavy goods; others traded to India; but of late years the grain trade of California has given them the best occupation. The problems of building good ships have all been solved, the cheap labor and fairly cheap materials at the command of the Maine men leaving them little to desire with regard to cost, and whenever they are asked what is needed to revive American ship-building they invariably reply from their point of view as owners. One reply at Thomaston was to the effect that—

One of the disadvantages under which we labor is double taxation, governmental and municipal. Another is the shipping commissioner act, which does not allow a ship to trade for its crew direct and to pay them off whenever desired. The three months' pay business is another. This weighs so hard on us that ship-owners have almost come to look on our consuls abroad as enemies to our shipping. The laws make sailors so independent that there is no inducement for them to try and save a ship from wreck when she is in trouble, as they get their pay whether there is anything saved or not.

Besides the three firms above named other persons have built vessels at Thomaston. The handsome ship Harvey Mills, of 2,186 tons, was built there by a gentleman of that name for himself, and is 231 feet long, 43 feet beam, and $29\frac{1}{2}$ feet deep in the hold.

Saint George's harbor is a little place near the mouth of the Penobscot for the repairing of fishing vessels, and considerable business is done at the marine railways there.

Bristol, Bremen, and Friendship, like a large number of other places on the coast of Maine, are fishing towns. Fishing schooners have been built from time to time at Friendship since 1830, and average about 40 tons in register. Most of the building has been of a class commonly called "shore boats". A few vessels have also been built at Bristol at irregular intervals, and some builders have sometimes employed as many as 25 men at one time. There are only two or three regular yards. Some of the building has been done by men who constructed one or two vessels and then no more. A. & M. Gammage & Co., at Bristol, have built about 55 schooner-smacks since 1854—8 of them ranging from 105 to 127 tons, the rest averaging about 40 tons—nearly all for owners at other places in Maine and Massachusetts. Most of the work in these towns, however, is on fishing boats, particularly in Bremen, which is noted for the number of its boat-builders and the excellent product of their labor. The boats are mostly sailing boats, from 18 to 26 feet long over all and from 6 to 9 feet wide, with center-boards, wash-boards along the gunwales, and with a cuddy forward, in which is placed a small stove. These boats are mostly used as lobster boats, and are largely employed in winter; and as they go out some distance from land a stove is necessary, both for the men and also to keep the lobsters from freezing until they can be transferred to live-cars and sent to market by sailing smacks. The house adapts them also for shore fishing, and in the right seasons they go out beyond the islands of Monhegan and Matinicus, take their fish, and then sail with them to the port which promises the best market. The boats are generally built during the winter. The keel of the boat is laid in the early part of the season, and the owner works on it at odd times, taking the entire season to complete it. One man working steadily could build a 16-foot lobster boat, worth $80, in about a month, and a 25-foot boat, worth $200, in two months. The builders are fishermen themselves, and usually have a small shop, in which the molds and tools are kept and the work is done. By long practice some of these fishermen have become expert boat-builders and have got orders for boats from other men, and with the aid of a lad or two it is not unusual for one of them to build from five to eight boats in a winter. Five Bremen builders have already built and sold from 20 to 100 boats each, ranging in length from 15 to 25 feet. In the yards where the smacks are built the workmen are often fishermen who have learned the art of carpentry, but a portion of them are small farmers. The rest consist of regular carpenters, who go to Bristol, Bremen, and Friendship in winter and roam for work elsewhere in summer.

Dennysville is little interested in shipping now, but there has been a great deal of work at this place in the last 15 years, and a large amount of money has been put into coasters. Losses and shrinkage of values being so heavy that it did not pay to repair the vessels, these have depreciated greatly, and the town is depressed in consequence. Complaint was made here of taxation and of the compulsory pilotage fees at New York and elsewhere.

Waldoboro' is a little town supported mainly by its shipping interests. Large vessels have been built for coasting and foreign trade here, and during the clipper-ship period the town was prosperous, carpenters earning high wages and bosses receiving from $5 to $7 a day each. Only a bark and a schooner were built at Waldoboro' in the census year, and the manner in which the bark was provided for illustrates the way in which a great many of the Maine vessels originate. One of the owners, having $7,000 of surplus cash on hand, proposed to build a bark and to pay the carpenters as his share in the vessel. The other shares were taken up by those who supplied lumber, iron work, sails, and other materials and work, each contribution being rated at $\frac{1}{4}$, $\frac{1}{8}$, $\frac{1}{16}$, or $\frac{1}{32}$, as the case might be. This vessel was built, sent out to sea, and had paid two dividends before application was made for the facts about her for the census. The owners had never had a settlement; no one knew what the shares of the others had cost them and what was the actual cost of the ship, and it had to be figured up especially for the census. Every one in Waldoboro' was discouraged. The ship-yards were idle, with little prospect of anything good ahead; the supply of local timber was exhausted; and to build a ship all the lumber, iron, etc., had to be brought by coasting vessels from other parts of the country. Complaint was made of taxation, pilotage fees at the great cities, and competition of steamboats in the coasting trade. Enterprise was almost at an end, and the town was losing its population. The Waldoboro' vessels cost about $55 per register ton.

Damariscotta and New Castle, two villages divided by a small stream, have carried on the building of large vessels for a long time, schooners, brigs, barks, and ships having been constructed extensively for local owners, and often by the owners for themselves. Before 1861 packets and clippers were built here, but the later ships have been for the California trade, and are of about 1,300 tons register. Wages are low, owing in part to the stagnation of business, and on that account ships can be advantageously built, as the cost would not exceed $45 or $46 per register ton. The death of some of the more enterprising men, and the general decay of the American carrying trade, have seriously affected the town. The ship-yards lie idle nearly the whole year round, and people are moving away.

Wiscasset was formerly engaged in building to a considerable extent, but the business is now virtually dead. In the latter part of 1880 a schooner was launched, however, and there are quite a number of persons who occasionally build scows and gondolas for river use; still they do not follow the business regularly, and what they do cannot properly be regarded as ship-building.

Boothbay was formerly an active town, and before the reaction of 1857 a great deal of large-class tonnage was produced there. At Boothbay and East Boothbay 100 sail of large brigs, barks, and ships had been launched, many of them being built on speculation for the general market; the demand was so great after 1845 that most of them were sold on the stocks long before completion. Boothbay vessels were famous for their excellence, the fruiters, all schooners, being very smart and able vessels, long and sharp, and carrying a great deal of sail. When the crash came building stopped at Boothbay, not to be resumed down to the present time, and many builders were ruined. The vessels on hand were unsalable at any price, and one that was sent to New York to find a purchaser lay there for 11 months before she was sold. Since that time only fishing craft have been built at these little towns, smacks and menhaden steamers being the product. At Boothbay, however, there is considerable repairing done, and the two railways are pretty constantly employed. Fishing vessels are generally hauled out twice a year, once for painting the bottom, and once for a general calking, repainting, and refitting, paint, oakum, pitch, iron, a little timber, cordage, and canvas being the materials consumed. In heavy weather Boothbay is often the resort of hundreds of vessels, which run in for shelter and bring considerable work to the railways.

At Georgetown the first builders were tempted into the business by the fine growth of native white oak and pine on the island. Vessels were built here long before the Revolution, and more than 150 sail in all have been launched from the different yards. The industry saw its best days, however, in the prosperous times before 1857. A great many ships and barks of from 1,100 to 1,454 tons were built in 1854, but the reaction of 1857 ended the business for Georgetown so far as anything except fishing vessels were concerned. A few fishing smacks of from 40 to 100 tons have since been built by the people on the island, but the business has been limited. Those

SHIP-BUILDING ON THE OCEAN COASTS.

who went into the construction of smacks did so at first because they owned farms with groves of white oak on them, and the work was generally done in the winter, when the men would otherwise have had nothing to do.

At Phippsburg there is one yard, at which the owner builds a schooner or a large ship every year or two for his own use. There has always been some work at this place.

At Richmond there are two yards, in one of which the owner has built for himself about 50 vessels. He never sold a new ship. His beginnings were small, but he now builds about one ship a year of large size. The Theo. W. Allen, finished in the census year, was of 1,537 tons, and the Eureka, in 1876, registered 2,101 tons. The timber for Richmond vessels is imported from the southern states, only the knees and a little hard wood being of Maine growth. The cost of building is about $48 per register ton.

At Bath, the principal ship-building town of the United States, the business dates back to 1745, sloops and small schooners having been built at that early date for the coasting trade. This town enjoyed the advantages of a broad, deep river, which seldom, if ever, froze over in winter, and of an abundant supply of the finest white-oak and white-pine timber, the banks of the river, as well as the whole of the surrounding country, being covered with dense forests of this valuable wood. The roads were bad, and traveling and trade were chiefly by water; but the town prospered more than any other on the coast. The first few experiments were successful, as the vessels made money, and the town went on building, increasing the size of its vessels and the field of their operations year by year. In 1762 Captain Swanton built the first ship-rigged vessel on the Kennebec, the Earl of Bute, for a merchant in Scotland. He afterward built a ship every year until the revolutionary war, and in 1776 built a privateer of 18 guns, which did good service in the war. After the Revolution quite a number of ship-yards were in existence in the town, launching sloops, brigs, and schooners of from 100 to 300 tons, an occasional bark and ship of from 200 to 400 tons, and now and then a privateer. Both in the building and in the management of vessels Bath men have been successful from the earliest times. About 1800 the cost of building was $30 a ton. The ship Reunion, of 281 tons, cleared her cost three times in as many successive voyages to England. After the war of 1812 this business grew considerably, from 7 to 15 vessels being launched yearly. By 1840 the capacity of the larger vessels had increased to 680 and 725 tons; they were owned on the river, were square-rigged vessels, and were used in the general trade to Europe, South America, and Asia. In 1841 the daring experiment of the Rappahannock, 1,133 tons, was made by Clark & Sewall, followed by the construction of other large craft; and the years from 1841 to 1857 constituted a period of great prosperity, in which several Bath families built up large fleets of vessels and accumulated much wealth. In 1851 the town launched 25 vessels, and in 1854 about 35, eleven of them being from 1,080 to 1,580 tons register each. It is remembered that in the latter years 25 large square-rigged vessels lay at the wharfs of Bath at one time receiving their sails and outfits, while a large number of ship-yards were busy along the river all the way up to Augusta. The crash of 1857 wiped out nearly all the ship-yards of the Kennebec, except at Bath, Richmond, and Phippsburg, and the bulk of the business has ever since been concentrated at Bath. The principal shipping families of this town have been the Houghtons, the Pattens, and the Sewalls, who owned large fleets of fine vessels. They and others have built an average of one and two large merchantmen every year. A few yards were owned by contractors. Bath finally became the principal building place of sailing tonnage in the United States; a distinction it has enjoyed to the present time. The building of large vessels has brought a great deal of business to Bath, and about 1,300 vessels, of a total of 720,000 register tons, have been built in this enterprising place down to 1882.

The production of fishing vessels never assumed important dimensions in Bath until after the late war. Before that time fishing schooners had been built at irregular intervals by the larger firms, chiefly as a means of keeping their men employed; but about 1865 several firms made a specialty of smacks and fruit schooners of from 50 to 200 tons burden. For ten years a great deal of this business was done, about 20 vessels being launched yearly, and the activity in this branch of the industry was the more appreciated because work in the larger yards was dull. The schooners were of a superior and much admired model, and orders came in for them so fast that there were often two or three building in each yard at the same time. Contracts were generally made in the fall, and the work was completed in the spring; but after 1877 this branch of the business fell off considerably. Bath has no fishing interests of any account, and the tendency of fishermen is to have their vessels built near their own homes, nothing except very low cost tempting them to go far for their craft. Besides, 1877 was a time of losses and shrinkage. Owners were not always willing and able to take what they had ordered and pay for it, and vessels built for sale found no buyers. One smack of 82 tons which cost $4,100 was left on the builders' hands for 18 months, and was finally sold for $2,800. At present few smacks are built in Bath; but the yards launch plenty of schooners, principally coasters and fruiters.

There are at present eleven ship-yards in Bath; the proprietors of six of them build only for themselves. One firm has been known for making remarkably good vessels, which always sailed in the cotton trade to Liverpool, bringing back salt and manufactured goods. This firm brought the first southern pitch-pine to Bath to use for planking. The lower deck beams would not always be planked, and pine lumber was taken on in the southern ports and laid in loose, to aid in storing cargo. On returning to Bath after a round trip the masters left the dunnage lumber behind, and it was used in ceiling new vessels. Yellow pine came in such long pieces that its value was appreciated as soon as it was necessary to build large sized vessels. This firm now builds full-rigged ships only of from 1,700 to 2,000 tons register, employing them in the California trade, and, to some extent, in the great ice business of the Kennebec to American ports. The durability of these vessels has been great, owing to care in the selection of materials and judicious salting. The ordinary mode of salting a ship is to fill the frame-spaces from the plank-sheer to the stops, put in at light-water mark, with mingled shavings and rock-salt, and sometimes with salt alone, from 50 to 70 tons of salt being required for a large vessel. This firm often bored auger holes in the top timbers, filling them with brine, which percolated through the heart of the timbers the whole length of the stick. Timbers thus treated were often as bright after 20 years' service as when first put in.

The Sewalls began just after the Revolution, being led into the business, in part, by the possession of a large farm, coming down to the bank of the river, heavily timbered with oak, hard wood, and pine. The regular building by the concern began in 1823, and the brig Diana and several other vessels were made from timbers cut from this farm. This house first engaged in the lumber trade to the West Indies and the cotton trade to Europe, some of their vessels also doing packet service. The list of vessels built by them and a description of the Rappahannock have been given elsewhere in the paragraphs speaking of the increase of size in shipping. The house is now extensively engaged in the California trade, building 1,900- and 2,000-ton ships at the rate of about one a year, besides a few schooners.

At two other yards the owners build vessels of the largest class for themselves. In clipper times their vessels were sharp, and were heavily strapped with iron. Iron knees 25 feet in length and weighing 1,700 pounds were used in some of them. The ships are all large class, and are of about 2,000 tons register.

The Pattens have built about sixty square-rigged vessels, all for themselves. They began small, but all the later vessels have been from 1,000 to 1,500 tons register. Adams & Hitchcock and the Morses also build only for their own use. Their product is all in large coasting schooners, principally for carrying ice and coal.

There are other concerns in Bath who build their own vessels from time to time, but the work, other than that of the houses named above, is chiefly contract work for the general public. William Rogers generally has two or three vessels under way at once; and Goss & Sawyer and Goss, Sawyer & Packard have seven or eight schooners, barks, and ships, with an occasional propeller or steamboat. At the two yards last named there were built, in 1881 and 1882, 44 vessels, registering 34,000 tons.

The workmen in these yards are mainly Americans, three-fourths of whom have houses and families in the town; some have bank accounts. Although working for day's wages, their regular employment and prudent habits enable them to lay up money. They are nearly all men of middle age and upward, as few young men have been learning the trade in Bath of late years, owing to the gloomy outlook for American shipping.

Bath vessels are famous for their excellent models and their handsome appearance, and are popular with captains on account of the pains which have been taken to fit up the cabins in style and comfort. Nearly all the New Bedford vessels are now built in Bath, and business has been brought here from all the principal shipping towns of the north Atlantic coast, as also from the Pacific coast. A great many lumber vessels owned in San Francisco and on Puget sound were built in Bath.

All the early Bath vessels were built of native oak and hard wood, with white-pine houses, decks, and masts. Oak and hard wood were put into the keels, elm rarely, and sometimes black gum from the South. The stem and stern-posts, as also the planking, were always of oak; and this fashion, even after the introduction of pitch-pine, was retained for a while for the bow. The knees were formerly of oak. But the local timber of any value has been all cleared away, a century and a half of active ship-building and a large export trade in lumber having destroyed the old forests of this region. A little hard wood is still hauled in for use, and is prized for the bottom of a ship. White oak, beech, yellow birch, and maple are used indiscriminately for keels. Beech, birch, and maple are good for floor timbers where they are covered with salt water, Goss & Sawyer considering them better than oak, as they are stiff woods, and, being free from the acid contained in oak, do not rust the fastening. Many of the frames, even of the smaller vessels, however, and nearly all of those for the larger ones, are cut in Delaware, Maryland, and Virginia in the winter time from the superior white oak of that region. Hackmatack (or tamarack, as it is sometimes called) is used now to a large extent for the top timbers of the frames, as it is lighter than oak and more durable, and holds the iron fastening as does no other wood, its resinous nature protecting the bolts from corrosion. Ships with "hack" tops carry more cargo and are a trifle more stable than those with oak tops. The keelsons and all the other parts of the vessel are of southern pitch-pine, save the decks, houses, and spars, which are of white pine and spruce, and the knees, which are of hackmatack, brought in by rail from the backwoods or from Canada; the white-pine masts come from Michigan. Two cargoes of Oregon pine (yellow fir) have been brought to Bath and utilized for decking, masts, and spars. It is a remarkable fact that while Bath builds the cheapest wooden vessels in the United States at present, nearly every ton of timber, iron, pitch, hemp, salt, canvas, etc., entering into their composition is imported into the town from places outside the state. As the cost of material is two-thirds the cost of the ship, the state of Maine has a smaller interest in her own vessel building than the rest of the country. The price now paid for ship timber delivered in Bath is as follows: Oak plank, $45 per thousand feet; oak timber, hewn to the molds, $33; pitch-pine, sawed, $28; hard wood in the round log, $20, for what can be squared out of the log; white pine, $35; hackmatack timber, $35. **Knees** cost about as follows, the prices being governed by the siding thickness and freedom from defects:

5-inch knees	$0 75 to $0 90
6-inch knees	1 25 to 1 30
7-inch knees	2 25 to 2 50
8-inch knees	3 50
9-inch knees	4 20 to 4 50
10-inch knees	7 00
11-inch knees	8 00
12-inch knees	9 00
13-inch knees	10 00

Prices vary somewhat with the season of the year and the demand for them. Knees are obtained from the root, and rarely more than one can be obtained from a tree. A two-deck ship of 2,000 tons requires about 650 knees; one of 1,600 tons, about 550 knees; a bark of 850 tons, two decks, 425 knees; a large single-deck schooner of 450 or 500 tons, 260 knees; and a schooner of 300 tons about 210 knees.

The cost of building vessels at Bath is kept low on account of the system of operation, the low rate of wages, and the great efficiency of the men. The system prevails of contracting for the frames, which are cut in the South by cheap hands and delivered in Bath ready for putting together. In the contract yards such of the local hard-wood timber as is utilized is sawed to the proper shape by a steam jig-saw which will tilt to any angle and cut the timber of any bevel, two men doing the work more rapidly than a dozen men would with axes. The fastening, blacksmith work, joinery, calking, spar-making, sail-making, and rigging are all done by contract. The system practically amounts to this: The labor is divided among men skilled in their respective branches, and is thus more quickly and efficiently performed; and the contractor makes $2 or $3 per day more than the men, and that is about all. The carpentry work is all done by the day, the men getting from $1 50 to $2, according to their efficiency. One system which prevails in Bath, as well as throughout the whole of the United States, is that carpenters, calkers, and joiners supply their own tools. The outfit of a carpenter or joiner costs from $50 to $75; of a calker, $15. The fastening requires a special outfit of augers, etc., which is supplied by the contractor, costing about $175. The blacksmith contractor's outfit costs him about $400, the rigger's $300, the sail-maker's $200, and the block-maker's $1,200. This system saves the builder a great deal of expense. During the census year the average cost of building large vessels in Bath was $45 per register ton. Schooners cost $55 and $60, but there was a difference between the cost of contract work and that which the large houses did for themselves. In the latter case a good ship, regardless of expense, was the object, and large ships ranged from $43 50 to $54 per register ton in consequence. By taking time, watching the market, and buying when materials were low, a first-class ship did not need to cost over $45 per register ton, and a large schooner not over $53.

The Houghton Brothers supplied the following data about the cost of materials and of building large ships in the following years:

	1825.	1835.	1845.	1855.	1865.	1880.
White oak, Maine............per thousand feet..	$21	$25	$27	$27	$33	$35
White oak, southern...................do......				35	33	35
Pitch pine................................do......			26	28	50	30
White pine..............................do......	10	24	26	30	40	35
Hard wood..............................do......	15	15	21	22		
Iron bolts.............................per ton..	85	80 to 90		45	90	60
Cost, per ton, to build............................	45	50	45	60	70	45

There was much complaint in Bath of excessive taxation of vessels and of governmental regulations which interfered with the freedom of a ship both at home and abroad, the payment of compulsory pilotage at such ports as New York and Boston being especially complained of. The code with regard to the shipment and discharge of seamen was also strongly condemned, and the consular service was much criticised. Bath is the home of not only a large circle of ship-builders and ship-owners, but of a large number of men who have followed the sea all their lives. They have visited every part of the world, have had every possible opportunity to study the workings of the American consular system from the shipping point of view, and are unanimous in declaring that a complete remodeling of the system is necessary.

As to taxation of vessels in Bath, I give the following letter from Captain George A. Preble, the surveyor for the Bureau Veritas, in Bath:

Taxation of shipping in Maine is the same as that on all other kinds of property—a state tax, a county tax, and a town or municipal tax. The state tax is assessed on the several towns on a valuation established for every ten years. This valuation includes all the property of the towns, shipping included, and the tax varies, from year to year, usually about ¼ per cent. The county tax is assessed, like that of the state, on the valuation of each decade. The municipal tax is levied each year by the towns, and is more or less, according to the expenses, indebtedness, etc., of the different municipalities. This tax is upon a valuation taken each year.

Take Bath for an example: Our state tax is $26,600; county tax, $8,550. To cover these and our municipal expenses, interest on debt, etc., requires a tax of 2¼ per cent. on all the property, real and personal, owned in the city.

Here you see we have a tax of 2¼ per cent. on the value of our shipping. In Portland the rate is the same. In other towns it ranges from 1 to 2½ per cent., and in some cases even higher.

April 1, 1879, there was owned in Bath 82,627 tons of vessels, valued by the assessors at $2,000,536; tax, at 2½ per cent., $50,013. At the same date, as returned by the assessors of the cities and towns, the valuation of all the tonnage of the state was $10,045,835, the taxation on which would probably average about 2 per cent., amounting to about $200,916.

Of course immunity from this load of taxation would be a great boon to our ship-owners, and the question is as to its practicability.

The constitution of the state of Maine provides that all property shall be taxed equally, a provision which I believe is in the constitution of nearly all the states. To exempt shipping from taxation would require amendment of the constitution, which can only be effected by a two-thirds vote of each house of the legislature, and must be ratified by a majority vote of the people.

As the shipping is owned in a few towns along the coast, and none of it in the interior of the state, it would be impossible to get the required vote in the legislature or by the people. Men never vote to exempt others from taxation if the amount exempted is to be laid upon themselves. It is in the power of the general government to relieve the shipping interest from federal taxation. The tonnage duties or tax ought to be taken off. Oppressive laws, such as the law requiring three months' pay to seamen discharged abroad, ought to be repealed.

The consular service ought to be overhauled and its many abuses corrected. All materials entering into the construction and equipment of vessels ought to be admitted free of duty.

All these measures of relief to the navigation interest are within the power of Congress.

Yours, very truly,

GEORGE A. PREBLE.

In Freeport there was once much building. In 1854 ten yards were actively employed, and 13 vessels were launched. It was the era of big freights, one Freeport vessel clearing $21,000 more than her first cost on one voyage of 21 months. After the reaction of 1857 building declined, and only two yards are left in Freeport, which produce one large vessel each per year for the owners of the yards. A good deal of local timber is used here: hard wood for floors, oak for center work, and hackmatack for tops. Yellow pine is used for the keelsons, beams, and planking in and out.

Brunswick, once extremely active, is now dull and depressed, one or two large vessels a year being the only product of the town.

Yarmouth, the next building point going down the coast, still has two yards and builds a few vessels every year. The experience of the town is the same as that of others on the coast, and what is left of building here is merely to keep up the fleets of local owners. The vessels are large, however, and engage principally in the California and the East India trade.

Portland is a large and ancient shipping town. Coasting and fishing vessels were employed here as long ago as 1700. Before the Revolution this was one of the principal lumber ports for the exportation of masts, spars, and ship timber, generally to England. The royal charters had always reserved to the crown the timber suitable for masts and spars, and a great many large vessels came to Portland to obtain cargoes. These vessels were of about 400 tons register, carrying crews of 25 men, and took away from 45 to 50 masts, with a large quantity of lighter spars and timber, at a time. Masts 36 inches in diameter were worth $750 each delivered in England. A ship was built at Portland as early as 1728, but the tonnage of the town was chiefly in large sloops and schooners for coasting and for the West India trade. Many privateers were sent out from this town during the Revolution, and a sloop of 10 guns is spoken of. After the war was over the shipping of Portland increased rapidly; there were several yards around the harbor, and the building industry was active; but of late years the business has fallen off, and while the several large commercial houses still own considerable fleets of coasters and some large vessels, the ship work at the port now consists chiefly of repairing and of ceiling large vessels for the carrying of cargoes of grain. A large number of ship carpenters here devote their whole time to repair work, while a great deal more of that kind of business is done by the owners themselves at their own wharves. Portland has one large fixed dry-dock, built with stone walls, the gateway closed with a heavy caisson and the dock emptied with powerful pumps. This dock is the resort of a large number of the new ships built in Maine to receive their copper sheathing, the vessels also obtaining their outfits of sails, rigging, anchors, chains, etc., in the city while there. There is one shop at which good engines are made for steamers. At Cape Elizabeth, across the bay, a small marine railway, worked by horse-power, is used in the service of coasters and fishermen for hauling out the vessels to calk, paint, and repair. There are two or three yards for new work in the town, and two good ones over at East Deering. A propeller of 18 tons, one of 286 tons, and a barkentine of 349 tons were built in the census year; the steamers, barks, and schooners of the port are chiefly produced at East Deering, the high prices, and consequent higher wages, of the city tending to keep the industry down at Portland. One drawback of late has been the decline of the fishing business. In 1878 and 1879 several menhaden steamers, worth about $20,000 each, were built at East Deering, but the fish ceased to come into those waters and the demand for steamers fell off. W. S. Jordan & Co. replied to a question in regard to the future of the sailing vessel and the burdens on American shipping as follows:

Although steam is driving sailing vessels from one trade after another, and although improvements are constantly being made in marine engines, and it is impossible to tell where these improvements will end, still, on account of the relative cheaper cost of sailing vessels as compared with steam, they will be used for the freighting of the less valuable cargoes, such as lumber, coal, iron, and also for cargoes not easily and quickly handled, for many years to come. Steam has superseded sailing vessels for these cargoes to a large extent in the Mediterranean, the Black sea, and the Red sea trade; but it has a peculiar advantage there on account of the narrowness of the seas. Congress, by the removal of several annoying laws and exactions, could assist the navigation interests largely. These exactions are: 1. The payment of three months' extra wages to a crew when discharged in a foreign port; 2. Consular charges and extortions; 3. Compulsory pilotage on coasting vessels; 4. Our laws for admeasurement should be amended so as to conform to the English law, which measures cargo space only.

Kennebunkport is an old ship-building town. It originally enjoyed the advantage of an abundance of local timber, and in the prosperous days before the war of 1861 large numbers of trading vessels of all classes were built both for Boston houses and for local owners, the cotton ships being reputed able to carry more cargo to the register ton than any except those built at Boston. Losses and shrinkage of values have borne heavily upon the town. Two years ago the principal builder built a bark and a ship, which, in consequence of the decline of vessel property, brought $20,000 less than they had cost. Two or three large vessels a year, a few smacks, and a few menhaden steamers are the average product of the town. Fishing steamers register from 70 to 130 tons, and cost from $20,000 to $30,000 each. The local timber supply is now exhausted, but in early years, about 1830 for instance, Kennebunkport could build vessels of 1,000 tons and upward for $23 a ton. The price rose to $70 after 1861, and has latterly been about $55.

At Saco ship-building is now a thing of the past, as there has been nothing built at that port for seven or eight years except a few fishing smacks of 10 or 12 tons. Formerly a great deal of large tonnage was built there, but the general causes affecting the interests of owners have made the Saco people cautious about investing in new shipping property. The same is true of the York district, and for fifteen years there has been little or nothing done in that region.

At Kittery, on the western boundary of the state, there is some building and a good deal of small repairing at a marine railway.

It will be seen from the foregoing notes that ship-building in Maine is now carried on chiefly by those who build only for their own use. Contract work for other parts of the country is done at Bath and Kennebunkport, and fishing and other schooners are occasionally ordered from a number of the smaller places for owners in Massachusetts, Connecticut, and New York; but nearly all of the large ships and coasting vessels constructed in Maine are owned in the towns, usually by the firms that built them, and if not wholly owned by one house the shares are all taken up in the town. The large majority of fishing boats and vessels are also built by their owners. This peculiarity of the industry in Maine will account for the fact that the state possesses so few well-equipped ship-yards. The contract yards at Bath have the modern appliances of bevel steam saw, bolt-cutters, planers, treenail machines, etc.; on the other hand, the proprietary yards of Maine are almost wholly without these things, the work being performed by hand, and the difference in cost between ships built by contract and those built by owners for themselves is due in part to this fact. Some of the ship-building towns are fast going to decay; the young men are going off to other parts of the country, while the old men linger idly in towns they dislike to leave, but which provide them with little work by which they can live. The eight ship-building counties of Maine have not gained in population in 10 years, while the rest of the United States has gained an average of 30 per cent. The population of those counties, as shown by the census, is as follows:

	1870.	1880.
Hancock	36,495	38,129
Knox	30,823	32,863
Lincoln	25,597	24,821
Penobscot	75,150	70,476
Sagadahoc	18,803	19,272
Waldo	34,522	32,463
Washington	43,343	44,484
York	60,174	62,257
Total	324,907	324,765

A slight development of general manufacturing interests in a few places in these counties and the rise of summer resorts on their sea-coast are all that have prevented a marked actual decline.

NEW HAMPSHIRE.

Ship-building was carried on extensively at Portsmouth, New Hampshire, in early years, as there was a large supply of superior white oak and white pine in the neighborhood of the town. Several cargoes of masts were shipped to the royal navy-yards in England every year, and agents were employed to go into the woods, mark the best trees, and procure them, roughly formed into spars. The shore fisheries gave the first impulse to the building business, shallops, sloops, and ketches being built in great numbers for local use. Afterward the people went into coasting, and did a great deal of building for foreign owners. Ships of 200 and 300 tons were built on speculation, and were loaded with fish, oil, provisions, lumber, etc., and sent to the West Indies. If they returned, they brought sugar, molasses, coffee, rum, etc.; but they were often either sold with their cargoes in the West Indies, or, going to England, were sold there, and with the proceeds the owners bought canvas, anchors, cordage, and outfits for new vessels. When the revolutionary war began a considerable balance was due to the people of Portsmouth from England, about a dozen ships having been sold every year. There was also considerable trade to the southern states, and West India goods, with fish and provisions, were sent, to be exchanged for rice, naval stores, corn, and flour. The Portsmouth builders made a great reputation, and in consequence large vessels and frigates were ordered from them. The Faulkland, a 54-gun ship, was built as early as 1690; the America, 50 guns, in 1740 for the British government; and one of the same name, of 74 guns, was begun for the American Congress toward the close of the revolutionary war, but was afterward presented to France. Portsmouth vessels whose ownership was retained at home have been used chiefly in the West India, coasting, and cotton trades, and since 1853 have ranged in size from 900 to 2,000 tons register. The course of the building of the port since 1800 has been as follows:

VESSELS BUILT IN THE DISTRICT OF PORTSMOUTH FROM THE YEAR 1800 TO 1881.

Years.	Vessels.	Ships.	Barks.	Snows.	Brigs.	Schooners.	Sloops.	Total tonnage.
1800	18	5	1		12			3,403
1801	14	9		1	4			2,925
1802	11	5			3	2	1	2,045
1803	14	9			3	2		2,796
1804	18	10			1	7		3,288
1805	16	11				5		3,258
1806	13	8			3	2		2,702
1807	10	4			2	4		1,608
1808	11	5				6		1,666
1809	9	3			2	2	2	1,514
1810	10	8			1	1		2,800
1811	15	10			5			4,375
1812	4	1			1	2		626
1813	1					1		21
1814	11	1			3	7		1,315
1815	13	2			3	8		2,057
1816	14	2			2	9	1	1,612
1817	7				2	5		594
1818	20	3			6	10	1	2,733
1819	13	3			1	9		1,626
1820	9	3			2	3	1	1,450
1821	7	3			2	2		1,379
1822	9	4			1	4		1,656
1823	10	4			4	2		2,429
1824	12	5			3	4		2,650
1825	15	5			3	7		2,874
1826	6	4	1		1			1,977
1827	11	4	2		1	4		2,402
1828	10	5			1	4		2,113
1829	10	1				9		916
1830	7	2				5		1,308
1831	3	2			1			993
1832	7	3			2	2		1,798
1833	8	5			1	2		2,630
1834	8	4			1	3		2,348
1835	9	4	2		1	2		2,813
1836	8	6			1	1		3,853
1837	5	5						2,982
1838	9	5				3	1	2,959
1839	5	4				1		2,603
1840	8	4	1			3		3,243
1841	5	4			1			2,667
1842	1	1						526
1843	3	1				2		841
1844	5	3			1	1		2,280

SHIP-BUILDING ON THE OCEAN COASTS.

VESSELS BUILT IN THE DISTRICT OF PORTSMOUTH FROM THE YEAR 1800 TO 1881—Continued.

Years.	Vessels.	Ships.	Barks.	Snows.	Brigs.	Schooners.	Sloops.	Total tonnage.
1845	7	3	1		2	1		2,720
1846	9	4	1		1	3		4,113
1847	12	7	3			2		6,822
1848	9	4	2			3		4,277
1849	10	5	2			3		6,010
1850	9	9						8,258
1851	12	7	1			4		8,778
1852	12	11				1		10,271
1853	10	9			1			10,809
1854	9	8			1			9,096
1855	13	10			1	2		12,039
1856	13	13						13,419
1857	7	6			1			6,246
1858	6	5				1		4,683
1859	7	4				3		4,017
1860	7	3	1			3		3,543
1861	3	2				1		2,042
1862	1					1		24
1863	6	3				3		3,815
1864	7	1		2		4		1,933
1865	8	1				7		2,005
1866	6		1			5		2,374
1867	7	1	2	1		3		2,816
1868	6	2	2			2		2,733
1869	5	1	2	1		1		1,993
1870	1		1					494
1871	3	1				2		1,208
1872, none.								
1873	3	2				1		3,283
1874	2	1				1		422
1875	3	2					1	2,780
1876	6					6		111
1877	5	2		1		1	1	2,984
1878	3			1		2		536
1879, none.								
1880, none.								

Until within ten or fifteen years New Hampshire vessels were built out of native white oak. Of the 30 vessels which have been launched by one builder only two or three have had southern frames. The quality of the local oak was remarkably good, and vessels were sometimes built of it almost wholly, frames, stems, keels, keelsons, planking, ceiling, and beams, although hard wood was used in the floors and keels. These vessels were not, of course, so buoyant as they might have been, but they were lasting, being good for at least 20 or 30 years, and the rate of insurance on them was so low that it gave them great celebrity. Of late years southern oak and pitch-pine have been used at Portsmouth; but this is not entirely on account of the destruction of native timber, as the timber for ships of 2,000 tons can still be obtained in the state.

Builders attribute the complete stoppage of building in New Hampshire to the burdens of taxation and the growth of steam navigation and in part to the building of railroads alongshore, limiting the business in coasting vessels. There is now almost no ship work done at Portsmouth. The yards are abandoned, except in one or two cases, where repair work is done, the boat-shops are going to decay, and the principal work is now done at Seabrook, where a number of dories and small fishing boats are made every year.

Vessels are taxed in New Hampshire the same as other property, without regard to whether they are employed or not. In Portsmouth the rate is about $1 75 per $100 of valuation.

MASSACHUSETTS.

The first place in Massachusetts, coming down the coast, where there are any ship-yards is Newburyport. The Merrimac is navigable for small vessels for about 20 miles from the sea, and on this short reach are situated Newbury, Newburyport, Amesbury, Salisbury, and Haverhill. These towns were all active building places after 1650. The vessels ranged in size from sloops of 20 and 30 tons to ships of 300 tons, and a multitude of small fishing vessels were also built. Good oak grew abundantly near the river, and was not only used for the Merrimac vessels, but was exported extensively to England. Before and after the Revolution vessels of the largest class were built in great numbers, a large proportion of them for English owners. The vessels on this river suffered great loss during this war; 22 of them, with more than a thousand men, sailed from Newburyport and were never heard of again, while there were other heavy losses by capture and wreck. On the other hand, the privateers of the Merrimac brought back fortunes for some of their owners. The famous frigate Alliance was built at Salisbury point in that war. After the Revolution building was a prosperous industry for more than 75 years, from 20 to 35 vessels being built yearly. At first the Merrimac river merchants owned the vessels in large part and sailed them to the East Indies, Europe, and the West Indies, but afterward the East India trade went to Salem. Building continued, however, for such trades as were open to the Merrimac owners. From 1783 to 1882 there have been constructed in this locality 1,600 vessels large enough to register, two of them steamers of 3,000 tons each, measuring 380,000 tons, besides a vast number of small fishing craft. John Currier, jr., built 95 vessels, aggregating 86,000 tons; and about 50 vessels of from 1,000 to 1,600 tons register have been built, but the owners are now merely looking after their old vessels. It is related at Newburyport that among the vessels built many years ago there were a few of the class popularly known as "Jew's rafts". These vessels were constructed of good timber and lightly calked, and were dispatched with cargoes of lumber to Europe, where they were taken to pieces and sold for lumber. The majority of these rafts were safely navigated across the Atlantic, but one, at any rate, was never heard from after leaving port. The following is a summary of vessels built on the Merrimac from 1781 down to 1880:

	Sloops.	Schooners.	Brigs.	Barks.	Ships.	Steamers.	Total.	Tonnage.
1781 to 1789	10	21	12		5		48	4,148
1790 to 1799	19	89	96	1	56		261	32,133
1800 to 1809	9	86	93	3	93		284	47,406
1810 to 1819	11	121	70	1	44		247	37,042
1820 to 1829	1	93	19		30		143	20,265
1830 to 1839		106	14	10	36		166	19,097
1840 to 1849		55	15	22	43	1	136	43,484
1850 to 1859		47	2	13	66		128	72,156
1860 to 1869		34	6	20	32	4	96	57,310
1870 to 1880		51	2	12	19	8	92	45,936

These vessels were built in the following places: Newbury, 473; Newburyport, 427; Salisbury, 291; Amesbury, 256; Haverhill, 120; Bradford, 30; Rowley, 2; Ipswich, 2.

At present, except at Newburyport, ship-building has been completely abandoned on the Merrimac, and that town in the census year presented a desolate array of abandoned ship-yards, boat-shops, and rope-walks. The reaction of 1857, the war of 1861, and the burdens on shipping had nearly killed the industry. There was a boat-shop in the town in which the decay of the business was forcibly illustrated. A firm which had been in business in that shop for 54 years, and had made 1,300 yawls, gigs, and other boats for vessel use, had on hand in the census year 3 yawls made two or three years before, for which they could not find a purchaser. The repairing of vessels, the launching of an occasional scow or schooner, and work on a few small fishing and pleasure boats were all there was of the industry in Newburyport in 1880. Owners have put considerable capital into government bonds, railroads, and factories, and the old carpenters have become scattered, many of them being in the factories of the town, where they like their new work and will not leave it. The timber is pretty much all gone, and all that is at command must come from a distance. However, gloomy as was the prospect in 1880, there has been a change for the better, and a ship of 1,800 tons has been launched, one of 1,600 tons is building, and a schooner or two have been built.

Marblehead was once famous for her large fishing vessels, and the town did much building; but Essex has drawn away her business, and the town is running down in population.

Essex has always lived by ship-building. Her Chebacco boats brought her into prominence at a very early period, and the little town grew into existence and thrived for 200 years on this one industry of building fishing and trading boats, aided by the occupation of fishing. It has had its ups and downs, but in the main was prosperous until the fishery treaty with Canada made trouble and the use of tug-boats on the coast robbed her of a part of her business. Nearly all the clipper fishing schooners of Gloucester are built at Essex, and trading vessels and pleasure boats, as well as fishing craft, have been produced there in goodly numbers. In former years Essex vessels were all rigged in the town, and sail-making and rigging work flourished actively; but the invention of the steam tug-boat has wrought a change, and nearly all the new vessels are now towed to Boston or Gloucester to be fitted out. Essex vessels were formerly built of oak that grew near the town, the material, except the pine boards for cabins, which came from Maine, being hauled in by teams from within 25 miles of the place. Vessels are still framed and planked with oak, maple being used for the keels. Pitch-pine is also somewhat used for planking, and the keelsons are of either pitch-pine or oak. The decks and houses are of white pine. Oregon pine has been used for decking one or two vessels, but it is too expensive to compete with white pine on this coast. The pine spars come largely from Pennsylvania. Hackmatack supplies all the knees. There are now five yards in Essex, and all of them had something to do in the census year. In one of them a yacht was built 90 feet long, decked with Oregon pine and planked with pitch-pine. The other yards built schooners, and one yard had a wooden coasting propeller in course of construction. The builders were all despondent, and their business was steadily declining; and every year they were doing less work, as they had to compete so for contracts that there was no chance left for profits. Besides that, work was irregular, and they had great difficulty to keep gangs of men together large enough to build a schooner when they had got a contract. The men were scattering away to other towns and getting work at house-building, and in boot and shoe factories, cotton-mills, and other establishments; sometimes these men came back to the ship-yard when called for, but were showing more and more reluctance to do so, preferring the regular work and sure pay of the factory, and the result was the same as along the whole coast north of them. There were fewer old carpenters than there used to be, and no young men were learning the business. One leading builder had not taken an apprentice for twelve years, and did not know of one in the town.

The most profitable vessels that are built at Essex are sharp two- and three-masted schooners of from 150 to 250 tons register, as the river is not large enough to launch and float out a large hull. The model for which the town is famous is described in the chapter on fishing vessels, and is sharp, broad, low, and fast, sacrificing capacity to speed. Essex vessels are the best that can be put into the fruit business and for trading round the West Indies, as they can beat to windward with remarkable speed, and when loaded with fruit, if there is any wind, blow which way it may, they will make their passage quicker than any other vessel except a steamer. The cost to build and equip for sea at Essex is about $60 or $65 per register ton, but it must be remembered that the smaller a vessel is the more it costs in proportion to size. The above figures are not excessive, considering the tonnage of Essex vessels. Wages here were from $1 50 to $2 a day in the census year. Spar-makers got $2 25 a day; riggers, on account of the irregularity of work, $3; the joiner work, calking, blacksmith work, cabins, and spars were usually sublet to contractors, who, however, made no money on their contracts except to get a little more wages than the men.

Gloucester was once a large building center. Notes of the early operations in this line here have already been given in the chapter on fishing vessels. This town is the center of the fishing business of New England, and of late years has devoted itself almost entirely to enterprise in that direction; but all the timber in the vicinity having been cleared away, the building industry has been gradually transferred to towns where it could be carried on to better advantage. Of the 475 vessels in the district in 1880 (tonnage, 27,456), more than 215 had been built in Essex, about 133 in Gloucester, and the rest principally in Maine. The town retains its repairing business, and perhaps is better off than it would be if it did all its own building and none of its repairing. At Gloucester there are three marine railways, upon which fishing schooners are hauled out twice a year regularly, once to paint the bottom, and once to calk, repair, and paint the whole vessel. A great deal of repairing of sails, refitting of rigging, blacksmith work, and the replacing of lost anchors, cables, boats, and fishing apparatus are also done every year. One large boat-shop in town, at which seine- and whale-boats, dories, and pleasure boats are made to the number of about 300 yearly, had produced 3,700 boats down to the date of the census. Gloucester is one of the most interesting ports in the United States, its harbor being crowded with hundreds of fishing vessels of every description known on the New England coast. There was much complaint among fishing firms of the operations of the Canada treaty.

There are several other towns on Cape Ann at which some small work is done, Beverly and Rockport being the principal. The work is all in the way of sloops and fishing boats; but some of the small craft are yachts, and are used for the pleasure of summer visitors

Salem, once the leading ship-building center of New England, does nothing in building now except to construct pleasure yachts and repair vessels of small tonnage on its one marine railway. The ship-yards of the town and the mercantile houses in the West India, East India, and South American trades were what made the place originally. Her people began with fishing and boat-building, but their maritime business gradually changed to the coasting and foreign trade. Salem sent the first vessel around cape Horn to the East Indies, and many of her ships were extremely profitable. The first marine railway in America was established here. It was necessary to provide facilities for taking large square-rigged ships out of the water for repair, and Endicott Peabody is said to have been sent to Europe about 1822 to get plans and designs, the railway being built on his return. A windlass was planted to haul the hulls on the ways and was worked by means of horse-power, and the gearing was so crude that the horse was driven around in a circle a distance of 17 miles in order to get the vessel up the bank a distance of 450 feet. The first experiment was with a large ship of 700 tons, which was successfully handled and repaired; but when the time came to let her go back into the water some men took hold of the capstan bars to ease her down, and the momentum of the vessel was too much for them. After she started the capstan began to revolve at great speed, and the men lost control of her, and one of them had some bones broken; they afterward learned to knock out a pin from the gearing and let the vessel go. From 1781 to 1834 the building at Salem amounted to 61 ships, 4 barks, 53 brigs, 3 ketches, and 16 schooners, measuring 30,557 tons; but since 1834 the building interest has run down, the East India trade has gone to Boston, New York, and Philadelphia, and with it has departed nearly all that had kept the ship-yards alive. Schooners, brigs, and sloops have since been built, but not to any great extent. The cost of new trading vessels of late years has ranged from $60 to $80 a ton, the yachts costing from $100 to $150 per ton, according to the style in which they are fitted up. Salem schooners of 160 tons have been sent on long voyages, one going as far as California, paying 100 per cent. on its cargo. There is no timber or any especial advantage enjoyed here, and the merchants and capitalists who once had to have vessels for their business have gone into other branches of enterprise.

BOSTON.—More than one-half of all the vessels other than fishing craft built north of Narragansett bay before the Revolution were owned in Boston, and the enterprise of that port naturally took the direction of the coasting and foreign trade. The people of other portions of the New England coast caught the valuable fish that swarmed in the ocean in that latitude, and the merchants of Boston took the large proportion of the catch and marketed it abroad, bringing back West India and other foreign goods for sale in the communities that did not trade direct. Boston had no particular advantage for building vessels except the deep water of her harbor, as timber was so scarce that a large fleet of sloops was employed every year in bringing to her wharves even the fire-wood needed for cooking and for heating the houses. However, indeed for a long period, Boston was the first of American cities in the amount of merchant tonnage owned by her merchants, and she has always ranked as one of the first four. Her merchants, devoting themselves to trade, rather neglected ship-building, and bought their vessels at Salem, Scituate, Medford, Duxbury, Charlestown, and other places having timber. Medford was more immediately the resort of the Boston ship-owners after 1812, as a number of smart builders had established large yards there, who did a flourishing business as long as vessels were not required of any larger size than could be floated down the little Mystic river. After 1840 the Mystic men became cramped for room. Large ships were the order of the day, and large yards were established by them and by others in East Boston, where there had previously been some little building, and the industry sprang up almost all at once to magnificent proportions. Samuel Hall came from Duxbury and Donald McKay from Newburyport, various of the builders of the Mystic river transferred their yards to the place, and the thriving community of East Boston came rapidly into being, deriving its chief importance from this one trade. The principal builders in the great period from 1845 to 1855 were Donald McKay, Samuel Hall, Paul Curtis, Robert E. Jackson, A. & G. T. Sampson, and D. D. Kelly, the vessels built by them being packets for the Liverpool, Havre, Mediterranean, East Indian, South American, and Australian trades, and afterward clippers for the California trade. One of the first jobs of work at East Boston was the construction by McKay, at the instance of Enoch Train, of four packets to sail to England; he built many ships for Mr. Train in after years. The building business reached large proportions about 1854 and 1855, there being in one year 30,000 tons of shipping in process of construction at one time in the port of Boston. The wharves were crowded with vessels receiving their spars, rigging, and sails, and every shop and loft was crowded with orders and driven to its utmost capacity.

Few of the Boston builders took shares in their vessels, but built on contract or on speculation. Studying closely the requirements of trade, they devoted themselves to the production of vessels especially suited for the various employments of the day, leaving to others the operation and management of the ships. They often made voyages to Europe and to the West Indies, and even to the Mediterranean, in order to study the behavior of vessels at sea and the various considerations that should govern form of hulls and arrangement of the spars and sails, and it is probable that the superior excellence of Boston vessels sprang from the particular fact that builders gave their whole attention to the art. Their success depended on the making of good ships. In order to employ the force of skillful and well-trained men which they had got together and the capital which they had accumulated they were often forced to set up a ship without waiting for a contract. In such cases, as it would not do to build anything except a good vessel, their ingenuity was taxed to devise improvements in models and rig, and they were compelled to exercise sleepless care in regard to materials and the manner of putting them together. In the yards north of them, where people built for themselves, there was not the same attention to fine points in construction; but in Boston building was differentiated from owning, and the result was the natural one of superiority in the work produced. The Boston yards launched the best, largest, and finest specimens of marine architecture in New England; their packets were unexcelled, their clippers were the finest in the world, and their cotton ships carried more than any other vessels. The building on contract and speculation also compelled Boston men to do everything in their power to save labor, and their yards adopted every appliance that could be thought of for that purpose—bolt-cutters, derricks for lifting, steam-saws, treenail machines, etc.; and while they had to contend with high wages, and often with dearer materials, their ability as builders enabled them to keep their business until some time after 1861.

The best era at Boston was from 1840 to 1860, and during that time there was an astonishing production of packets, clippers, cotton ships, and coasting schooners. Some of the shipping houses of the port owned large fleets in the foreign trade. One firm had more than 20 vessels sailing to Australia; another once owned 33 ships and barks, with several steamers; and besides there were numerous packet and clipper lines of from 6 to 12 vessels each. It was seldom that a contract to build was given out to other parts of the coast, and when steamers were required for the coasting trade, they, too, were built in East Boston. The business reached large proportions, and about 1855 gave employment to several thousand men. The reaction of 1857 was a hard blow to the place, the establishment of subsidized lines of British steamers a still worse one, and the war of 1861 was still another disaster. Few builders of the clipper period survived all these shocks, and nearly all of them failed. There was much work for the yards through the war in the way of government vessels; but after 1865 the industry was a struggling

SHIP-BUILDING ON THE OCEAN COASTS.

one, and steadily declined. High wages and strikes among the carpenters and calkers gave the finishing blow; nearly all the old builders went out of business so far as new work was concerned, and the few that kept their yards going have had a hard time of it. In the census year the only merchant vessels built at East Boston were three coasting schooners, a few barges and tugs, and two ferry-boats, and there was nothing else, except a number of small yachts, pleasure boats, and ship boats. At South Boston, where large vessels have often been made, there was nothing except sail-boat building; at Chelsea the same; and on the Boston side a little boat-building was all that was done.

The principal ship work at the port of Boston now is the repairing and coppering of vessels, the necessary incident of every great commercial port. The water front of East Boston and Boston is lined in places with long rows of shops of shipwrights, joiners, riggers, sailmakers, and blacksmiths, who live by repair work, and there are several marine railways and three large fixed and two floating dry-docks, at which the heavy work is chiefly done. The fixed dry-docks are of the following sizes: One is 165 feet long, 46 feet wide, 32 feet at the gate, and 13 feet depth of water. The second is 250 feet long, 75 feet wide, 45 feet at the gate, and 16 feet depth of water. The third is of large dimensions, namely: 365 feet in length, 86 feet wide, 68 feet at the gate, and 17 feet depth of water. The docks are built on solid foundations. Repairing can be as advantageously performed in Boston in respect to materials, workmanship, and dock fees as in any part of the country; like the other branch of the business, however, it is in a state of decay. The business saw its best days in the era of the clipper sailing ship. The Boston vessels never returned to port without giving a good job of work to all the trades, and often spent from $5,000 to $8,000 in repairs of various kinds; but the old clippers have been driven off by British steamers and by foreign sailing vessels, both wooden and iron, which now throng the port almost to the entire exclusion of American tonnage. The master of a foreign ship will go to extraordinary trouble to avoid spending money on this side of the water. Repairing has declined as well as building. One firm of shipwrights that used to do $120,000 worth of business yearly did only $40,000 worth in the census year; another that used to do $18,000 worth only did $3,500 worth in that year, while the business of another shipwright had fallen from $22,000 to $6,000. A firm of ship painters, who in 1849 were painting 32 vessels at one time, had work in the census year only occasionally. Four-fifths of the old-time rigging work, sail-making, and boat-building has gone, and so much has repair work fallen off in late years that the painters, joiners, carpenters, and blacksmiths are often compelled to take up other work to make a living. Nothing except the coasting trade keeps this branch of the business at all alive.

The vessels coppered at Boston in the census year numbered 128, consuming 625,830 pounds of metal and nails. Wages were from $2 25 to $2 50 per day for carpenters and calkers, $2 for fasteners, $2 50 for painters, blacksmiths, and spar-makers, and $3 for riggers.

The timber used by the Boston builders was originally oak and white pine, but Donald McKay and others used pitch-pine when the era of large ships came on. During the war of 1861 oak was again resorted to; but since then the builders have returned to pitch-pine for planking, keelsons, and beams, using southern oak for the frames and center work. The spars were of white pine and spruce from Canada and Maine. Here, as elsewhere, oak and hackmatack frames, with yellow pine for planking, ceiling, beams, and keelsons, were regarded as making the best ship, and that combination of timber was said often to be strong and staunch for 30 years. Nothing was so good for iron and metal as hackmatack and yellow pine.

At North Weymouth, on the lower side of Massachusetts bay, a little work is still done, either a bark or a schooner being built at the one yard there nearly every year. Massachusetts white oak is used for frames, although it costs a third more than southern oak, and yellow pine is used for planking, ceiling, beams, and decking. A bark of 858 tons, built there in 1879, cost $46,000 fitted for sea, or about $54 a ton. The builder at North Weymouth complained that there is little profit in a contract now, not enough to encourage a contractor to build on his own responsibility.

South of Boston ship-building, except at a few scattered points, has ceased entirely. At Scituate, Cohasset, and Duxbury there is nothing left of the ancient industry. It is said that in 1846 and 1847 Duxbury built as many large and small vessels as were built at Medford, and of about the same class. There is good timber left for frames at Duxbury, and every facility for building exists; but the industry is dead, and nothing has been built since 1876. At Provincetown, on cape Cod, a little repair work and the building of a few whale-boats were reported, and at Wellfleet and Mattapoisett, where once there was a large business, amounting to hundreds of thousands of dollars, there are now built a few boats and yachts for the sea-side summer resorts. At Hyannis there was a marine railway, but it was out of repair, with no prospect of ever being used again, while from Nantucket and Martha's Vineyard building has fled completely. At Edgartown, on the latter island, there is some repairing and metaling of whaling vessels owned on the island and of vessels wrecked and stranded, amounting to perhaps $40,000 a year. No new vessels have been built for 14 years.

At New Bedford, an ancient and active ship-building port, there is nothing left except whale-boat building and repair work. From 25 to 30 whaling vessels are repaired and refitted at the port every year, and a number of coasting schooners, fishing-smacks, sail boats, and steamboats are calked, painted, and kept in order. There are two marine railways employed; several firms are engaged in boat-building, and this trade at least is active and prosperous, though it does not compare with that of 30 years ago.

At Taunton there is now little or no building. This place once built a great many vessels for the coasting trade, now supplanted in great degree by barges towed by steamers. The first firm to come from New York past Point Judith with coal barges in tow of steam-tugs began business in 1872 with a steamer and three barges of 500, 600, and 800 tons, respectively. This firm was running two steamers and seven barges of from 800 to 1,100 tons in 1881, and other barges were being built. Other firms followed, running barges of from 1,500 to 1,800 tons. This business is growing every year, and there are now some 20 or 25 barges running on Long Island sound to points east of Point Judith with coal. The Taunton barges have each taken the place of as many as 15 or 20 vessels of from 400 to 500 tons.

It is in Massachusetts, taking the state as a whole, that the decay of American ship-building is most apparent. In 1850 the state built 121 vessels large enough to register a total of 36,000 tons; but in 1880, counting even the coal barges, yachts, and tug-boats, there was a total of only 39 vessels, measuring 5,600 tons. A part of the old business of the state has been transferred to Maine, but four-fifths of the decline is an actual loss to the United States, that much of the business having vanished completely. There are more and larger vessels than ever in the foreign commerce of the state, but they are built mostly in Scotland, on the Clyde, are owned in England, and are managed by foreign-born men. Massachusetts has just passed a law relieving vessels from taxation, except on their net income, and this has given general satisfaction.

RHODE ISLAND.

There is now no ship-building in Rhode Island save in the way of pleasure craft and small vessels, but repairing is carried on to some extent. Newport was once an active shipping port, and a gentleman of New York city has a letter, written over a hundred years ago, in which a Newport merchant says: "We must look out now, lest New York get ahead of us." The town had large interests in vessels and carried on an active trade. Sloops, schooners, and whaling and square-rigged vessels have been built at different places on Narragansett bay; but the business declined soon after 1812, and is now in a state of decay. The tonnage of the bay is small, and there is little left to the once busy ship-yards and boat-shops except small work. At Newport there are a few boat-shops and one large marine railway and yard for the repairing of steamboats. The port is a harbor of refuge in storms, and is much frequented by fleets of yachts from New York and elsewhere, each of which brings work to the town. At Bristol the Herreshoffs build steam yachts and vidette boats, and there is a marine railway for hauling out coasting vessels, and at East Providence there is a large marine railway for coasting vessels, on which about 480 vessels have been taken out of water for coppering, painting, and repair. There are boat-shops at Tiverton and at Providence. This comprises the interest in Rhode Island, even repairing, the chief feature of the business, being a dull trade in comparison with earlier years, a change in the coasting trade having produced this result. Coal in enormous quantities is consumed in the New England factories reached by the railroads which touch Narragansett bay. This was brought to the bay in former years by two- and three-masted schooners, of which there were probably 200 engaged in the business; and the building and the coming and going of this fleet, with the repair work, boat-building, and outfitting to which the business gave rise, gave active employment to the carpenters of the bay. But the schooners have been largely superseded by coal carriers of another class, the Reading railroad having built a fleet of 13 iron steam vessels exclusively for the coal trade. The first vessel, launched in 1869, was of 420 tons register; but the later vessels are of 1,280 tons each, carrying 1,650 tons of coal. Each steamer has a capacity equal to that of four schooners of medium size, and makes three voyages to a schooner's one, averaging about thirty-three voyages a year each to New England ports. Other firms have gone into the coal trade with large flat-boats and keel barges, which they make up into fleets of from 2 to 6 vessels, carrying from 2,000 to 4,000 tons of coal. These fleets will carry the freight of a dozen medium schooners, and at less expense, though they consume more time. The combined operation of the steam colliers and barges has been too much for the schooners, and they have been unable to withstand the competition. There are now from 100 to 200 schooners less in the trade of Narragansett bay than there were in 1861, and the general decline of all branches of ship work on the bay is the consequence. At Newport there were once 17 boat-shops on Long wharf engaged in making yawls for the trading vessels of the bay. The shops remain, but the occupants of most of them are gone; the doors are locked for weeks, and the few that remain live by work on pleasure boats, fishing, and stray orders for yawls. Some of the boat carpenters have gone to Maine to practice their art there. No vessels of over 20 tons register have been built in Newport district for several years.

The Herreshoff boats are built by a man who has been blind from boyhood; they will be more particularly referred to in the chapter on steam vessels. They are composite; that is, they have iron frames and wooden planking. The shop is a prosperous one, and could probably build large iron vessels if called on for that purpose. It is one of the small resources of the country in the way of iron building establishments.

The tonnage built in the state in the census year amounted to 17 vessels, registering 380 tons. The general industry of building and repairing both employed an average of 343 men ten months in a year, producing $518,000 worth of completed work.

SHIP-BUILDING ON THE OCEAN COASTS.

CONNECTICUT.

The shipping interests of Connecticut now center in fishing craft, steamboats for the trade of Long Island sound, and coal barges. The state owns some coasting tonnage, however, as also a few brigs and barks for the West India and the general trade. Originally there was a brisk building business all along the Sound and on the Connecticut river. Every little village had a ship-yard, and a great deal of capital was employed in operating sloops, brigs, schooners, and barks in whaling and fishing and in the coasting and foreign trade. In 1840 there were built 49 vessels large enough to register, measuring 4,100 tons; in 1850, 47 vessels, measuring 4,800 tons; and in 1860, 35 vessels, measuring 7,700 tons.

The best days of the industry in this state were just before and during the war of 1861, when so many gunboats were built; but at present there is almost nothing doing for the foreign trade, and no whalers are built, the only work being on vessels for local use in and near Long Island sound.

At Mystic there were before the war of 1861 five ship-yards in active operation, building two and three large vessels each every year. Many packets and clippers were built here. Native timber was used largely, the state being well stocked with oak and chestnut, but pitch-pine and southern oak were used when local timber gave out. No large vessels have been built for several years; the old ship-yards are deserted, the town has lost nearly all its carpenters, and its growth is arrested. Only two small yards did any work in the census year, one of which built a schooner yacht, the other a small screw steamer. The location of the town is far up the river, and lacks trade of any kind, so that no repairing is done, the only orders being for an occasional pleasure yacht or a fishing steamer. The decline of the shipping interest of Mystic is attributed, first, to the cruisers of the war of 1861, and next to the general increase of burdens and expenses from the high prices and taxes. The opinion was expressed that the government could reasonably aid in the revival of shipping by taking off burdens, and with that aid, and the decreasing interest on money and government bonds, the shipping trade would gradually reach a state of new prosperity.

Noank is a little fishing village situated in New London county. This place has received an impetus from the building of a large marine railway especially for taking out of the water, for repair, the large steamboats of Long Island sound running from New York to Stonington. The Narragansett, which was wrecked by a collision in the Sound, was rebuilt on this railway, and other large jobs have been done. This railway owes its origin to the high prices of New York city, which made it desirable to create facilities for heavy repairs in some locality where labor was less costly; it is the largest on the Atlantic coast outside of New York, and is operated by steam-power. The cradle holding the vessel is drawn up the ways by a 20 horse-power engine, geared so as to develop several hundred horse-power, and acting on a massive iron chain, attached to the cradle at one end and winding around a windlass at the other. The repair work which comes to this yard keeps a force of from 50 to 100 men steadily employed. This yard has been supplied with a complete equipment of steam saws, bolt-cutters, derricks, and other modern appliances, which puts it in a position to build new vessels to advantage. A large wooden propeller which had been partly built on Long Island was completed at the Noank yard in the census year, as also a schooner and some barges for carrying coal and freight cars in New York harbor. The yard is run chiefly on work ordered from New York. The freight-car floats cost $11,000 each; the barges, having an individual capacity of 400 tons of coal, $9,000 each.

New London, at the mouth of the Thames river, has a broad, deep harbor, into which coasting vessels run for refuge in heavy weather, and sometimes 300 schooners and brigs are lying at anchor in the deep and safe waters of this excellent port. The place is visited annually also by large numbers of pleasure yachts, these visiting vessels furnishing the principal part of the ship work that is done in New London. There are two yards here near the fort, one with two, the other with four small marine railways. The only vessels building in the census year were a sloop yacht of 25 tons and a small schooner of 70 tons, but over 300 coasting vessels and yachts were taken out of the water for painting, coppering, and repair. There used to be some ship-building in New London, and it had extensive whaling interests. Many schooners, brigs, and barks of good size were required, and large numbers of whale-boats were built annually; but the business suffered the decline which took place everywhere when petroleum came into use, and a heavy blow was dealt to the New London firms particularly by the burning of their whale ships in the north Pacific by confederate cruisers and from losses by wreck. The catching of sea-elephants and seals has kept a very few whalers employed, and a few whale-boats are built in the town yearly; but the trade is dull and fast declining.

Along the Connecticut river, from Saybrook as far as Hartford, there was formerly a great deal of ship-building. The valley of the river was covered with a luxuriant growth of excellent timber (principally chestnut and white oak), and large numbers of sloops and schooners for fishing and for the river and coasting trades were built. The Gildersleeves, the oldest firm on the river, beginning in 1821, and building sloops, brigs, and schooners only for 20 years, began in 1841 to send forth barks and ships, of which they built 15 in all. The keels, keelsons, stem and stern-posts, and frames were of oak and chestnut—the oak prized for its strength and elasticity, the chestnut for its lighter weight, ease in working, and durability; the ceiling and planking were of oak, both on account of elasticity and because the hard, tough fiber fitted it to resist chafing and cutting by ice; the deck frames were of oak at the hatchways, with chestnut elsewhere, and the decking was of white pine. Just before the war pitch-pine was introduced for keelsons, ceiling, and beams, and it has ever since been used. This firm has built many steamboats, and during the war constructed several gunboats; but since the war it has built about 17 sail vessels of small size, only one, however, in the last eight years. Of late years the Gildersleeves have built scarcely anything except coal barges. Their principal business is repairing; but they have a marine railway at their landing, and keep a force of 25 men steadily employed. In all they have built 125 vessels.

At Rocky Hill there is a yard for barge building.

At Goodspeed's landing, in the town of East Haddam, there was once much building; but there is none at all now, the only work at present being the repairing of the steamboats of the Hartford line. Ships, schooners, war vessels, and steamboats have been built at this yard, the pay-roll sometimes carrying as many as 400 men, and a year's transactions amounting to over a million dollars. The carpenters are scattered, and a year's work now scarcely supports 25 men.

Essex is a little fishing village lower down the river with a small railway and two boat-shops. There was once some ship-building here, but there has been none worth mentioning of late years. The small boats of the town have been sold extensively in the South, but there is little left of this business.

Middletown, Middle Haddam, and other places on the river once aspired to be ship-building towns, but now the business is entirely extinct.

On the headwaters of the Connecticut river about 20 pine board batteaux are built every year for driving rafts of logs.

At Madison there is a ship-yard where a bark or schooner is still built every year, the cost of which is about $75 per register ton. Chestnut is used in the frames to some extent, as it is in all Connecticut yards, but the main dependence is on southern oak and pitch-pine. The wages in this yard were a little higher than at the extreme east, owing to the proximity of New Haven and New York, and ranged from $2 25 to $3 a day of ten hours.

At New Haven the product of the census year was one sailing vessel of 450 tons, a few coal barges, a few small fishing boats not large enough to register, a few row-boats, and a little repairing at one marine railway in Fair Haven. The town can scarcely be said to have any ship-building other than in the building of coal barges, and what is done is an insignificant fraction of the general business of the town. The first two coal barges were built in 1876 for the Empire Transportation Company. They were almost square, 38 feet long on the bottom, 40 feet on top, 24 feet wide, and 11 feet deep, each with one cross bulkhead amidships and a narrow deck 2 feet wide around the gunwales. The rest of the top was open. The floor timbers were $2\frac{1}{2}$ by 10 inches square, spaced 24 inches; the top timbers 4 by 6 inches, both sets tenoning into a square bilge log; the outside planking $2\frac{1}{2}$ inches; and the grub strake, or what should be a grub strake, 5 by 12 inches. The whole boat was built of yellow pine and oak, the frames being of oak, and each boat weighed about 20 tons and carried 200 tons of coal. These boats had a square resistance against the water, but they have proved a success so far as profitable coal carrying is concerned, and a large fleet of them has been built. They are towed back and forth between New York and New Haven by tug-boats in fleets of from 10 to 20. Seventy-nine box barges were built for this company, including 27 of different shapes and dimensions, but with the same sizes of scantling; the bow and stern were given a rake, to lessen the resistance. The new boats are able to carry 325 tons of coal each. The company built 10 more last fall, carrying 300 tons each. In 1881, inspired by the success of the old company, a new one, which took the name of the New England Transportation Company, was formed in New Haven, and built barges, lighters, coal-hoisters, and all the apparatus required for coal handling and transportation. Mr. Langly built for this company 30 square barges, 30 feet wide, 40 feet long, 11 feet deep, and carrying 250 tons of coal each; also 35 boats 30 feet wide, 11 feet deep, and 55 feet long on the bottom, with ends raking 45°, making them 71 feet long over all, and carrying 450 tons each. The latter boats were partly decked and had two cross bulkheads, and the hatches were 21 feet wide and 50 feet long, with 30-inch coamings, protected with light hatch covers; they were planked with $2\frac{1}{2}$-inch yellow pine, ceiled with 2-inch spruce and decked with $2\frac{3}{4}$-inch spruce. These two fleets do an immense business in coal transportation from New York harbor to New Haven, as one of them can carry 27,000 tons and the other 24,000 tons of coal at one trip. The fleets are made up of square boats and those with raking ends. They are all lashed closely together, with the bevel-bowed boats ahead and behind, and when in tow of a strong propeller they make pretty fair time and have reduced the cost of coal carrying to a point where coasting schooners and colliers can no longer compete. The boats are often wrecked and sunk, and sometimes capsize. Their flimsy construction makes them unable to withstand much of a shock, and they are loaded down so far as to be in danger of foundering; but if one of them is occasionally lost, it only costs $300 to replace it. These barges are only adapted to the waters of Long Island sound, as they could not venture past Point Judith, nor into any waters where they would catch the heavy ocean swell. They have driven a whole fleet of schooners out of the coal trade of the Sound.

At the Fair Haven marine railway about 60 fishing vessels are taken out of the water yearly, and a few thousand dollars' worth of work is done on them.

At Bridgeport ship-building ended 16 years ago. There was a large ship-yard here, and another at Black Rock, a short distance west. One builder has built 25 or 30 vessels at Bridgeport, many of them square rigged, and one of his ships, now 33 years old, is still a good vessel. A builder at Black Rock used to build a bark or a ship once a year. The war of 1861, high wages, and foreign competition have destroyed the business of the two ship-yards referred to. The timber in that region has been pretty thoroughly cleared off, large quantities of it having been sent to New York before the war. Chestnut is yet cheap, not exceeding $12 a thousand in the round log, delivered at the saw-mill; but the low price comes from the lack of demand, and a little ship-building would send up the price at once and rapidly exhaust the supply. The only relic of the yard at Black Rock is a small marine railway, worked by horse-power, which lies idle most of the time.

After passing Bridgeport there is no trace of ship-building on the Connecticut coast except at South Norwalk, where there are a marine railway, one large boat-yard, and a few boat-shops, and at Cos Cob, where there are two small railways for the repair of fishing and coasting schooners. Sharpies and fishing boats are owned in large numbers all along the coast, and many are built every year, partly by amateurs and partly by regular builders.

NEW YORK.

The early vessels of New York consisted of yachts, ketches, brigantines, barks, fishing boats, and sloops, and quite a number were built by the Dutch under the auspices of the Dutch West India Company. A three-masted vessel is spoken of as early as 1650, the shares in her being twenty-five in number; but vessels did not exceed from 100 to 120 tons each. About 1683 New York owned 3 ships, 3 barks, 23 sloops, and 41 small boats; in 1696 there were 40 square-rigged vessels, 62 sloops, and 60 small boats; but after 1700 the business was neglected at New York for many years, probably owing to the superior activity of the people of New England. The sloop was the popular boat at that early period, and having been developed from the old Dutch yacht it kept the round full bottom and broad beam which characterized all Dutch vessels of the seventeenth century. Its light draught fitted it for floating over the shallows of the Hudson river, and it was the universal boat for traveling and freighting on the river to Albany. A sloop cost from $500 to $600 about the year 1650, a canoe $10 or $12. By 1771 the sloops of the Hudson river had become large, powerful boats, and there were 125 sailing between Albany and New York. When occasion required, deep ones were built to venture to places as far away as Barbadoes, Surinam, Santa Cruz, etc., whither many of them did actually trade, and for such small vessels they carried valuable cargoes. For instance, the Olive Branch went to the West Indies in 1770 with 7 tons of flour, $47\frac{1}{2}$ barrels of herring, 7,000 staves, 11 horses, 1 negro, and apples, poultry, onions, etc., to the total value of £591; the return cargo, mostly rum, was worth £448. In 1785 the Experiment, of 50 tons, was fitted out from Albany for China, being manned by 7 men and 2 boys, and carrying an assorted cargo. She left December 18 and was gone 18 months; the return trip, with tea, chinaware, etc., took 4 months and 12 days. These sloops ran out from the Hudson all along the coast, trading and carrying passengers, but were best fitted for the river trade and other local uses, such as fishing and pleasure sailing in the bay. A large fleet is now employed on the Hudson. The rise of New York in commercial activity was slow. The merchants traded to the West India islands and built many vessels to sell in those islands, but neglected the trade of Europe, and were far behind Boston in general-enterprise until after the revolutionary war. The best business between New York and Europe was in English hands. The packet lines which were started in 1756 to run to Falmouth with letters, passengers, and freights were all English, and it was not until after the Revolution that New York merchants began to show the energy which has ever since characterized them. Privateering was a marked feature of New York enterprise before the Revolution. During the French war and up to 1758 the port had sent out 48 privateers, 695 guns, and 5,660 men, and others continued to be sent out until the city was captured in the revolutionary war. The privateers were brigs and schooners, long, deep, and sharp on the floors, sitting low in the water, and sailing with a drag, built in defiance of the rules and prejudices of the age, and so fleet that they were seldom overtaken even by the best frigates. New York had a few vessels of the same class in the slave trade, and their forms came down to the years following 1812 in the brigs and fruiting schooners of New York, and are perpetuated in some respects in the pilot-boats and yachts of to-day.

A few large ship and brig rigged vessels were built after the Revolution, but the shipping interests of New York were so limited that when the Manhattan, of 600 tons, was built for the East India trade by Samuel Ackerly in 1799 the yard drained the city of its carpenters, and the ship, when launched, took off nearly every sailor left in the port.

The ship carpenters in New York after 1800 comprised many able men, among them being Samuel Ackerly, Henry Eckford, Christian Bergh, Forman Cheeseman, Sneadon & Lawrence, and Adam & Noah Brown. These men were smart in improving their ships, and constructed a great many vessels, both for local and foreign owners, including a number of war ships. The frigate President, built by Mr. Cheeseman, was so famous in the war of 1812 that strenuous efforts were made for her capture. She was fast and able, but was finally taken by three English vessels and sent to England, and by order of the admiralty was there dismantled and taken to pieces for the purpose of ascertaining the secrets of her construction and excellent qualities. This proceeding has often been resorted to in the history of shipping. To Christian Bergh is said to belong the credit of the invention of the close rudder. Rudders had previously been made with a straight stock, and swung on their pintles in such manner that a large opening in the counter was required. This opening was clumsily closed with a piece of tarred canvas nailed to the rudder-stock and the counter. Mr. Bergh fashioned the stock so that the whole apparatus turned on its center, instead of on the fore edge of the rudder. The wood-work around the rudder-head was then fitted close, and the water was thus effectually excluded without the aid of canvas. Ship-building was dull in the harbor of New York during the war of 1812, but privateers were built from time to time, and the art was kept alive. Many builders, including Mr. Eckford and Adam Brown, found employment during the war on the northern lakes, where they built the vessels that won the battles of lake Champlain and lake Erie. After the war of 1812 many large vessels were built in New York; but there was at first a lack of carpenters, which embarrassed the yards extremely, and it was at this period that the practice sprang up of taking a large number of apprentices to train in the yards. Regular work soon made an abundance of new shipwrights and attracted some from other towns, especially from New England, so that by the time New Yorkers began to go extensively into the building of packet ships there was no lack of good men.

Packet building was the best work of the New York yards after the war of 1812. Up to 1814 the best ships on the middle Atlantic coast had been produced at Philadelphia, the fashions of the day having nearly all been set there; but after 1814 building went ahead strong in New York, and the fashions were thereafter set by the builders on the East river. In the construction of packets the best talent of the day was employed; and these vessels and the river steamboats, which were then coming into prominence, gave work to a long row of ship-yards extending from Pike street, all along the East River front of the city, for a mile and a half. A few yards were also employed over in Brooklyn. The timber first used was New York state oak and white pine, oak and chestnut from New England, live oak from Florida, and locust from Long Island, strength, durability, and finish being the main requisites so far as the carpenter's art was concerned. When business had finally become brisk 20 ship-yards and 6,000 men were employed. In early years the majority of the Liverpool packets were built by Smith & Dimon, Isaac Webb & Co., and Brown & Bell, while the London and Havre ships were generally built by Christian Bergh, Thomas Carnely, Jacob H. Westervelt, and William H. Webb. The other builders worked on barks, brigs, schooners, sloops, and steamboats, among them being Fickett & Crockett, Westervelt & Mackey, Eckford Webb, Perrine, Patterson & Stack, and George Steers on sailing vessels, and Lawrence & Folkes, Devine Burtis, Bishop & Simonson, William Collyer, Thomas Collyer, and Capes & Allison on steamboats. After 1850 the New York yards went into clipper-ship building, and then began the greatest period of activity which the port had ever seen, from 50 to 100 vessels being built yearly, or from 30,000 to 60,000 tons. Twenty or thirty grand vessels were often building at one time, and the whole river side echoed with the ring of calking-irons. Bustle and excitement prevailed on every hand. Oak and pitch-pine timber began to be brought from the South, and the enormous quantities of all kinds of wood consumed gave busy employment to large numbers of coasting vessels and made the port the largest lumber-yard in America. The cost of building was about $55 per register ton, the vessel being fitted out at that price ready for sea. This was in ordinary years. The majority of the vessels built were for New York city owners, and every ship launched for a house in the packet, tea, or California trade meant not only the disbursement of from $20,000 to $30,000 for labor among the mechanics of New York city, with a further outlay of from $50,000 to $70,000 for materials, but it had still another significance; it meant the steady support of thousands of skillful men at high wages in the annual repair of the large fleet of wooden vessels produced. The packets and clippers were continually subject to heavy repairs. They were put in charge of men who would put on all sail and drive through all sorts of weather, and it is known that one American clipper, a well-built ship, had to have $15,000 worth of work done on the return from her first voyage. The repair bills of all of them were large, and as long as the bulk of the tonnage that crowded New York harbor flew the banner of America from the peak the repairing at the port was one of the largest and the most profitable of all the industries there carried on.

William H. Webb, the great builder of packets and clippers at New York, and afterward of wooden steam vessels, built more tonnage on foreign account than any other builder at this port (138 vessels). One of his ships was the Ocean Monarch, of 2,145 tons, and another the great iron-clad steam ram Dunderberg, considered in her day the most formidable fighting ship in the world. He probably trained more apprentices than any other builder, and gave an immense impulse to American ship-building thereby, his apprentice boys, now full-grown men, being at this day scattered all over the United States and doing good and honorable work wherever found.

The list of his ships will be useful, as illustrating the growth of the building industry in New York, the size and character of the vessels built in each year being about what was required from all leading builders at the different stages of the history of the port. The list is as follows, the data being obtained partly from the custom-house books at New York and partly from the records of the yard, and is as complete as can be made in the time allowed:

Year.		Register dimensions in feet. Length.	Breadth.	Depth of hold.	Tonnage.
1840	Brig Malek Adhel	80	21	7¾	120
	Ship James Edwards	122	31	20	500
1841	Ship Agnes	122	28	19	450
	Ship Helena	136	32½	20	650
1842	Ship Liberty	143	28½	20	750
	Ferry-boat Wallabout	94	23	8¾	199
	Ferry-boat New York	94	23	8¾	199
	Fishing smack Prouta	45	15	6½	36
	Fishing smack Viva	45	15	6½	36
	Fishing smack Ligera	58	19	8½	76
1843	Ship Montezuma	160	35⅔	21	916
	Ship Cohota	145	33	20	720
	Ship Yorkshire	174	36⅔	21½	1,165
	Schooner Vigilant	55	19	5	50
1844	Ship Zurich	136	35	20	680
	Ship Montauk	127	19½	14½	540
	Brig Ramon de Zaldo	90	22	8¾	160
	Ship Panama	136	33	20	670
1845	Ship Havre	160	36	21½	1,000
	Ship Silas Holmes	145	33	20	730
	Ship Fidelia	160	35	21	1,050
	Steamer Genil	161	28	10	174
1846	Ship Marmion	160	36	21½	1,080
	Ship Columbia	170	36½	21⅔	1,180
	Ferry-boat Williamsburg	115	26	10	315
	Ship Admiral	160	35½	21½	1,080
	Ship Sir Robert Peel	160	35½	21½	1,080
	Ship Splendid	130	33	22¾	750
	Ship Bavaria	160	35½	21	1,060
1847	Ship New York	164	37	22	1,165
	Ship Isaac Wright	170	38	22¼	1,130
	Ship Ivanhoe	170	38	22¼	1,130
	Ship Yorktown	170	38½	22¼	1,150
	Ship London	170	38½	22¼	1,145
	Steamer United States	244 7/12	40	30 10/12	1,857
1848	Ship Caleb Grimshaw	170	37⅔	22¼	1,160
	Steamer Ajax	140	24⅝	10½	370
	Steamer California	199⅛	33½	20	1,057
	Steamer Panama	200⅓	33 10/12	20⅙	1,087
	Steamer Cherokee	214	35	22	1,450
	Steamer Tennessee	214	35	22	1,450
1849	Schooner S. M. Fox	98	26½	11	250
	Tug Goliah	145	31½	10¾	411
	Ship Guy Mannering	190½	40⅕	28⅔	1,419
	Ship Gallia	171	39⅙	27¾	1,191
	Ship James Drake	130	28½	20¼	483
	Ship Albert Gallatin	192½	40¼	20⅛	1,435
	Ship Catherine	135 10/12	31½	19 5/12	611
	Ship Manhattan	182	39½	27⅔	1,299
	Ship Isaac Webb	188	39¾	28	1,359
1850	Ship Vanguard	176½	38½	22½	1,196
	Steamer Florida	214	35¼	22⅓	1,261
	Steamer Alabama	214	35½	22	1,300
	Ship Celestial	158	34½	19	860
	Ship Joseph Walker	181½	40	23	1,325
	Steamer Union	214	34	22	1,400
1851	Steamer Golden Gate	269½	40	30½	2,067
	Ship S. M. Fox	170¼	36 1/12	26½	1,062
	Ship Isaac Bell	171	37	26½	1,072
	Ship Challenge	230½	43⅛	27⅓	2,006
	Schooner Clifton	26¾	21	7½	106
	Ship Great Western	191⅓	40½	20¼	1,443
	Ship Gazelle	184	38½	22¾	1,244
	Ship Invincible	221½	41⅓	24⅚	1,769
	Ship Sword Fish	169½	36½	20 1/12	1,035
	Ship Comet	229	42	22¾	1,836
	Steamer Edgar	137	24½	9⅝	310
1852	Schooner Plandome	100	26½	11	250
	Schooner Manhasset	100	26½	11	250
	Ship Annawan	153	33	20	800

Year.		Register dimensions in feet. Length.	Breadth.	Depth of hold.	Tonnage.
1852	Bark Robert Mills	126½	30⅔	14	488
	Ship Australia	192	40½	27¾	1,448
	Steamer George Law	272	40	32	3,000
	Ship Flying Dutchman	187⅝	38½	24½	1,200
	Schooner Reemplaco	77	21⅓	7⅝	113
	Steamer Augusta	220	35½	22	1,600
	Steamer Knoxville	220	35½	22	1,600
1853	Brig Volante	113	26¾	11¼	307
	Brigantine Fanny	86¼	22⅓	9¼	158
	Ship John Bright	191 7/12	40½	28 7/12	1,444
	Ship Young America	236½	42	28¼	1,962
	Steamer San Francisco	281½	41	24⅚	2,272
	Steamer George Law	278¼	40	32	2,141
	Bark Snap Dragon	142⅙	30⅝	18⅙	619
	Ship Flyaway	190½	38	21½	1,275
	Bark Milton	134	31	14¼	536
1854	Ship Cultivator	192	40½	28½	1,448
	Ship Harvest Queen	188¼	40	28½	1,383
	Ship Thornton	191½	40⅛	28½	1,422
	Bark Houston	132½	30⅝	14	518
	Steamer Pelayo	198¾	30½	14	811
	Ship Aurora	201¾	42	29	1,639
	Ship James Foster, jr	191½	40	27½	1,410
1855	Ship New Orleans	160⅔	35½	21⅔	924
	Ship Neptune	191	40	28	1,406
	Bark Alamo	133	30½	13⅔	507
	Bark Texas	135	30⅚	14⅔	554
	Brig Josephine	129	23⅓	9⅙	259
	Brig Sabine	123	28¼	12⅔	399
	Side-wheeler America	170⅔	28	12	545
1856	Ship Silas Wright	191½	40½	28	1,443
	Bark Fanny Holmes	142	33	17½	700
	Ship John H. Elliott	173	36⅝	23	1,077
	Bark Alice Taintor	139½	32½	18	667
	Propeller Astoria	159½	23⅛	12	425
	Steamer Cuba	200	30⅔	14	821
	Steamer Gautemala	127	22	8⅓	218
	Ship Intrepid	179⅔	37⅔	23	1,173
	Ship Ocean Monarch	240	46	30¼	2,145
	Ship Uncowah	169	35⅔	22	988
	Side-wheeler William H. Webb	200	33½	12½	655
1857	Ship Black Hawk	180	36⅔	23	1,108
	Ship Roger A. Heirn	173⅓	37	23	1,089
	Bark Trieste	136	30	14⅔	550
	Steamer Moses Taylor	246	34	17	1,372
	Ship Resolute	190½	40⅛	28	1,413
	Revenue-cutter Harriet Lane	179	30½	13	750
1858	Steam-frigate General Admiral	302⅚	55	34	4,600
	Propeller Japanese	217	36⅔	17½	1,530
	Bark Martinho de Mella	138⅙	31½	18⅙	623
	Steamer Yorktown	250	37⅔	16¾	1,500
	Bark Harvest Queen	115	17	11¼	316
	Steamer Mississippi	251	38⅓	23½	1,500
	Steamer A. Marshall	178	38⅝	22½	1,450
1861	Steamer Constitution	342½	44⅔	22⅓	3,315
	Steam-frigate iron-clad Re d'Italia	275	54	33½	3,500
	Steamer Re Don Luigi de Portugallo.	273	54	33½	3,500
1863	Steamer Golden City	343	45	23	3,373
	Steamer Colorado	340	45	31½	3,728
	Iron-clad steam-propeller Dunderberg.	380	72⅚	22⅝	5,090
1864	Steamer Sacramento	304	42½	29⅙	2,647
	Steamer Henry Chauncey	320	43 7/12	27 4/12	....
	Steamer Montana	320	43 7/12	27 4/12	....
	Steamer Bristol	360	47½	22	2,692
	Steamer Providence	360	47½	22	2,692
	Steamer China	363	48	31½	....
	Bark James A. Borland	143	32	18⅝	637
1869	Ship Charles H. Marshall	188½	41⅔	28½	1,630

In addition to the above, Mr. Webb built, by subletting the contracts, the following: Schooners Mary C. Allen, Antonia, Cayatino, and Bonita, of from 80 to 107 tons, in 1851; the steamship James Adger, 215 feet long, 33 feet beam, and 21 feet hold, in 1852; the steamboat Pittston, 120 feet long, 19 feet beam, and 6 feet hold, in 1852; and the side-wheel tow-boat Leviathan, 175 feet long, $29\frac{5}{8}$ feet beam, and $11\frac{3}{4}$ feet deep. He also rebuilt the ship Elisha Dennison, $107\frac{1}{2}$ feet long, $27\frac{3}{4}$ feet beam, and $17\frac{1}{6}$ feet deep, only the stem and keel of the original ship remaining after the repairs were completed.

Since 1865 there has been a steady decline at New York. The running of foreign lines of subsidized steamers from Europe to New York resulted in a complete annihilation of the packet lines and of the few American steam lines to Europe, and, followed as it was by the war of 1861–'65, this competition gave a crushing blow to the industry. It is probable, however, that the building of ships would have ceased at the port in time, in consequence of the high prices for labor and plant, even had there been no other moving cause. Property became too valuable in both Brooklyn and New York for use as ship-yards, and the cost of living became so high that the workmen were repeatedly compelled to demand higher wages, and always gained the advance demanded until 1866, when a great strike occurred, in which they were beaten. Wages rose from $1 75 and $2 a day in 1861 to $3 25 and $3 50 in 1865. This advance was a serious embarrassment to the builders of New York, and the strike of 1866 permanently drove the construction of large sailing vessels away from the port. While the men were out a vast amount of work was sent to places farther east, and very little, except part of the repair work, came back; and it has not been possible to build ships of any size at this port since 1865 in competition with the eastern yards. In New York city proper the business is completely extinct. The old ship-yards have been converted to other uses, and are now occupied by wharves, factories, lumber yards, and blocks of buildings; and four floating dry-docks of various sizes, a row of scattered boat-shops and sail-lofts on South street, and a few pump- and block-shops and shipwrights' offices, are all that are left of the original industry. In Brooklyn there are ten yards devoted in part to the construction of small vessels, such as tug-boats, scows and lighters, pilot-boats and yachts, and small pleasure boats. Now and then a ferry-boat or a steamboat is built; but the yards do very little new work in the aggregate in the course of a year, and are all, in the main, supported by repairing. One or two of them are lumber yards, where scow-building is carried on as an incident of the business; but general ship-building appears to have come to a permanent end in this harbor.

Repair work, the coppering of wooden vessels, and the sheathing of grain ships are the principal branches now carried on, the port having immense and admirable facilities for this work. It appears from the returns of the shipwrights of Staten island, New York, and Brooklyn that about 7,000 vessels were repaired on the New York side of the harbor during the census year, the total cost of the work being $4,500,000, and an average of 2,500 men were employed during ten months of the year. The work consisted of carpentering, calking, painting, and metaling. A total of 297 vessels were entirely or in part coppered below water, the old metal being stripped off, the hulls tarred and felted or papered, and new yellow metal put on. In round numbers, the weight of sheathing metal consumed was 2,999,000 pounds, large sailing ships taking from 23,000 to 26,000 pounds each and small schooners from 5,000 to 8,000 pounds. The ship buys the metal, has the nail holes punched by a machine on South street, and then sends the sheets to the dry-dock in New York or Brooklyn, where the ship is being repaired. The average charge for the labor of cleaning the vessel and putting on the metal was 35 cents per sheet, but on a new vessel the charge was 23 cents, including tarring and felting. About half the copper used was foreign, and cost 13 cents a pound; the rest was American, at 16 or 17 cents a pound. On account of the preponderance of foreign tonnage in the port of New York the greatest number of jobs of coppering and of all other branches of repair work were for foreign vessels, which were chiefly Italian, Norwegian, German, and British, and it was the universal testimony that whatever a vessel required could be done here more promptly and substantially than in the majority of other large shipping ports of either America or Europe. As repairs were more costly, however, than in Europe, foreign vessels habitually avoided every possible dollar of expense, and ordered nothing done except that which was strictly required to obtain a fair rate of insurance after the vessels had secured a charter. The repairs to British vessels were very slight, the best and largest jobs being generally upon American vessels, namely, on ships in the California and the East Indian trade, coasting schooners, yachts, tugs, river steamboats, ferry-boats, and coasting steamers.

The ceiling of grain vessels is a special business. As about 2,900 cargoes of wheat, corn, and oats are exported by sail and steam every year, the insurance companies have made regulations for protecting grain from injury in transit and for preventing the cargo from shifting and throwing the ship over on her beam ends. It is required that the bottom of the hold shall be completely floored with two thicknesses of inch board, breaking joints, which is supported on scantling from 12 to 15 inches above the ceiling proper of the vessel. The sides of the hold are clapboarded grain tight, the stanchions are boarded up, so as to make a fore and aft bulkhead, and about four cross bulkheads are required, one away forward, one in the stern, and the other two between them. The pump well has to be cased up in such manner that a man can go to the bottom of it and work there, and the masts and tanks are also cased. A vessel thus fitted up is allowed to carry grain in bulk in the lower hold, with a little loose grain on the lower deck, which is allowed to run down into the hold as the grain settles to keep it constantly full. Between decks the grain is in bags. All grain vessels have to be ceiled; and as one ceiling lasts only about a year, the business gives steady employment to three large concerns. From 8,000,000 to 10,000,000 feet of spruce, pine, and hemlock are consumed yearly, worth from $250,000 to $300,000, the labor amounting to between $330,000 and $450,000. Ship ceiling began in New York 30 years ago, the Liverpool packets being fitted for bulk grain about that time, and the business has grown gradually ever since.

Another branch of business is that pursued by the Coast Wrecking Company. This company has a yard and a wharf at Staten island, and engages in the specialty of saving vessels that are stranded on the coast or have been sunk by collision or otherwise in and around New York harbor. It owns 2 steamers and 2 schooners, and employs from 60 to 110 men. An idea of the nature of the work may be gained from the report of its operations in the census year. The company's submarine divers examined the bottoms of 1 bark and 4 steamers, pumped out 1 ship and 3 steamers, and stripped the following vessels, which had been driven ashore or saved their cargoes: 7 schooners, 2 barks, 1 brig, and 2 steamers. It raised 1 steamer, 1 schooner, and 1 bark, which had sunk in the harbor, and rescued the following stranded property: 2 schooners; 3 brigs, 1 ship, 6 barks, and 3 steamers. The compensation of the company varied from 10 to 33 per cent. of the value of the property saved in the case of stranded vessels, but in vessels stripped it was about 50 per cent. Large as was the income, the expenses were larger yet, owing to the cost of maintaining the system, and the company made no profit during the census year.

On Staten island there used to be some activity. Oak and chestnut were plentiful, and workmen could live on the island for less than it cost to live in New York. A few vessels were built before 1861; but timber is now scarce and dear, and building is nearly gone. There are three yards on the northern part of the island, all kept alive by repair work, and at one of them, in Stapleton, a large marine railway was constructing in the census year for future use. On the southern end of the island, at Tottenville, there is a little community of 8 ship-yards, each of which does repairing and some building. There are 8 marine railways in these yards, all worked by horse-power, which take out from 400 to 500 small vessels yearly for painting, calking, and repair. Labor costs from $1 75 to $2 75 a day, being from 25 to 50 cents cheaper than in New York. This is a fishing locality, with coal depots in New Jersey, and the work is largely for smacks, tugs, and coal barges. The new work is in the way of steam tugs and propeller yachts chiefly.

Long Island, New York, was the scene of some of the earliest boat and sloop building in the country. The eastern end of the island was engaged in whaling by boats and sloops from shore as early as 1690, and the northern coast has been engaged from the time of the Revolution in sailing wood sloops to New York with lumber and fire-wood. Greenport and Sag Harbor once had large whaling interests. This island had the advantage of some good timber, the best and largest growth of locust on the Atlantic coast being found here, and there was besides some good oak. On the sea front the water is not deep enough for the building of large vessels, and the work has always been confined to fishing boats and to the small sail and row boats called for in the summer time by visitors at the summer hotels, which are scattered along the whole length of the island. In the census year there were built at Patchogue, Islip, Blue Point, Belle Port, and Bay Shore 17 cat-rigged boats and sloops, ranging from 5 to 24 tons register, and costing from $800 to $2,500 each. The builders have regular yards, and employ 3 or 4 men in building boats and from 6 to 8 on sloops, paying from $1 50 to $2 50 per day. A large sloop takes 8,000 feet of lumber. At Islip there is a marine railway; at Sayville, Blue Point, and Belle Port, each one; and at Patchogue three; all for small work, and each doing from $300 to $1.500 worth of business annually. At Sag Harbor there is now nothing except repair work.

At Greenport a barkentine of 667 tons was built of southern oak and pine in the census year for local ownership, at a cost of $49 per register ton—a cheap vessel. Labor here was from $1 50 to $2 per day. There is a marine railway for coasting vessels, which keeps about a dozen men busy during ten months of the year.

Port Jefferson is the principal locality on the Sound coast, and ship-building is of ancient date here. In early times large numbers of wood boats came to this little hill-locked harbor to load for the New York market. As the business grew up the young men wanted to go on the water themselves, first going as sailors, and then, after vessels were built for them, as captains. Oak, locust, and hickory grew densely over all the neighborhood, and in the busy years before 1857 there was a large industry, there being 10 or 12 yards and seventeen vessels on the stocks at once. One sail-maker employed 16 men and cut up 50,000 yards of canvas yearly. Since 1866 it has been the practice to build six or seven vessels a year, but within five years there has been a change. In the census year only 4 coasting schooners, aggregating 1,326 tons, were built; and the sail-maker above referred to employed only 3 men and cut up 14,000 yards of canvas. The local supply of timber being now exhausted, southern pitch-pine and oak, with some oak and chestnut from Connecticut, are used. A second or third growth of locust and oak covers the hills, but it is small, and is good only for stanchions and treenails. There are three yards in the harbor, employing from 75 to 100 men. Labor was from $1 50 to $2 a day, and the cost of building was from $50 to $60 per ton, according to the completeness and quality of the outfit. Good schooners are built here, the port being an excellent place for this work, and two of the yards have each two large railways. The nearness to New York brings work from that city; but the principal part of the business is on large yachts, sail and steam, the harbor being crowded with these handsome vessels. The active business in repairing keeps the workmen together and enables the builders to take an occasional building contract at low figures, but bitter complaints were heard about compulsory pilotage at New York.

At Setauket, before the war, five or six large schooners and square-rigged vessels were launched yearly. They had oak and chestnut frames, oak planking, chestnut beams, and white-pine decks, houses, and spars. Originally the timber was cut near the town; afterward it was bought in Connecticut, but now it comes from the South. The price for oak is now $30 per thousand feet; chestnut, $20; southern pine, $30. In 1870 the ship Adorna, of 1,460 tons, was built here for the cotton trade at a cost of $110,000. Her floors and lower futtocks were of oak and chestnut, the cant frames and top timbers of live oak and locust, the transoms, apron, and knightheads of live oak, the keel, stem, and stern, as also the planking, of white oak, and the keelson, ceiling, and beams of pitch-pine. The Adorna was a heavy vessel, but, being built full, was a good carrier. The owner was also a merchant, and made $50,000 profit on one voyage. This decided him to build a big ship. She was to be 234 feet long on the keel, 250 feet over, 48 feet beam, and 31 feet deep in the hold, of about 2,700 tons register, a three-decker, and the largest sailer afloat. She was built of live oak, locust, white oak, and pine, the same as the Adorna; but after $62,000 had been spent on her the owner failed. This vessel was sold to a coal company and cut down one deck, and was finished at Noank, Connecticut, as the steam-collier Wilkesbarre. This failure stopped the work at Setauket, and there was nothing doing in the census year.

Northport has been at times a busy place. A few years back a vessel of from 500 to 700 tons was built every season; sometimes two. A little repair work at 2 yards was all that was reported in the census year. There is a railway here for small vessels, and an unfinished schooner yacht had been standing a long time in the frame in 1880.

Huntingdon and one or two other small places on that coast do small jobs of building and repairing.

On the other side of Hell-Gate channel, at City island, New York, there are two large yards, with marine railways for building and repairing, which get much business from the coasting craft that throng the Sound. At one of them there were built in the census year two schooners of 156 and 212 tons, respectively, and a sloop of 14 tons, at a cost of $35,000, or $92 a ton, for the hulls and spars alone. Two barges of 500 and 700 tons respectively were built for $22,500.

At Rye, on the same side of Hell-Gate channel, is an establishment for the building and repair of yachts, the owner of which has a loft and a numerous collection of valuable models. In the census year this shop produced the following boats: Sail-boat, $22\frac{2}{3}$ feet long, costing $350; sail-boat, $22\frac{2}{3}$ feet, $373; sail-boat, 22 feet, $450; sail-boat, 25 feet, $510; hull of a steam catamaran, $600; yacht, 41 feet, $2,550. Oak, white pine, and cedar, with some yellow pine, were used in these boats.

On the Hudson river the yards are all on the west shore. There has been a great deal of building on the east side in times gone by, but the railroad which runs at the river's edge has cut off the good sites and the water is generally too shallow for large vessels. Yonkers, Peekskill, and Poughkeepsie do boat-building only. The first place going up the river is Nyack, where many sloops are built, and river vessels go there in large numbers for repairs. Three sloops, of 130 tons each, were built in the census year.

At Newburgh there are two marine railways for repairing tugs, barges, and sloops. The firm which owns them has a yard for building iron yachts and ferry-boats. Four tugs of 274 tons and a ferry-boat of 414 tons were built in the census year.

Rondout is the river port of the Delaware and Hudson canal. There are ten yards on both sides of the canal engaged principally in canal-boat and barge work, but one owner has a yard with large shops for the repair of his own fleet of 30 towing steamboats. Oak and pitch-pine from the South and chestnut from the river are the timber used at Rondout; some oak from the river is also used. In the flitch, oak costs $25 and $30 per thousand; good plank, $35 and $40; best, $60. Chestnut costs $25; southern pine about $30. Wages were from $1 50 to $2 50 per day.

Athens has long been the principal place for the building and repair of river vessels of the larger class on the Hudson. It is a little village on the western bank of the river, and has two large boat-yards, at which there is work for from 50 to 150 men. Several ice-barges, tugs, and steamboats are often drawn up on the bank at once for repair, and there are generally two or three new boats building at one time. In the census year the new work consisted of five screw tugs, a large ferry steamboat of 1,200 tons, and two ice-barges, at a total cost of $185,000. The ice-barges are keel-boats, broad and full, sharp at both ends, with deck-houses nearly their entire length, and are run from the ice-houses, which line the river all the way to Albany, to the city of New York in the summer time. Each of the two above referred to was 130 feet long, 32 feet broad, and 10 feet deep in the hull, cost $11,000, and consumed about 110,000 feet of oak, yellow pine, white pine, and chestnut. The prosperity of Athens is much retarded by the high cost of timber, frame oak costing $40 per thousand feet, planking $60, pitch-pine $30, and white pine $50. Wages are from $1 50 to $2 50 per day.

Malden, once an active building town, now does very little work.

The scarcity of timber along the Hudson is producing its inevitable result. When good oak plank costs $60 a thousand feet and frame timber anything like $40 the hulls of small vessels might as well be built of iron, as the small excess of first cost would be quickly compensated by the diminished cost of yearly repairs. The change from wood to iron is now rapidly going on on the Hudson, the new steamboats, tug-boats, and ferry-boats being frequently built of iron.

SHIP-BUILDING ON THE OCEAN COASTS.

New York state has always taxed her tonnage the same as other property. In 1881, at the strong suggestion of prominent men, a law was passed by the legislature exempting all vessels of the state engaged in foreign trade from state and local taxation of all kinds, with the expectation that this would benefit the port of New York materially, and, while not helping to restore its old building industry, would, at any rate, encourage its shipping houses and aid in the establishment of ocean-steamship lines.

New York has the first and most important requisites for maritime development, her deep harbor, her railroads, and her river and canal connecting with the great lakes having made her the gateway through which flows the bulk of the foreign commerce of the United States, besides a vast coastwise trade. Two-thirds of the value of the whole foreign trade of the country passes through New York harbor, and of the 21,000 vessels which arrive at American seaports every year 8,000 enter at the port of New York alone. In all, about 7,000,000 tons of shipping engaged in the foreign trade come to this busy harbor annually, being just half of the total tonnage arriving on our coasts from foreign ports. About 800 vessels are constantly in port at New York, among them a great number of the largest steamers afloat. If but one-half of the commerce of New York were transacted in American vessels, the tonnage of our merchant marine would be double what it is now, and the United States would have a larger shipping interest than ever before in her history; and if the bulk of it were done in American vessels, as it used to be before 1855, the United States would have a larger fleet than Great Britain. But the facts of the case are that the bulk of the trade is now transacted in foreign vessels. Of the 7,000,000 tons of shipping in the foreign trade which come to the harbor annually only 1,500,000 tons are American. There is no expectation in New York of a revival of ship-building in the harbor itself, as wages and prices are too high, and the work would be done in country places.

NEW JERSEY.

New Jersey was originally stocked with a heavy growth of white-oak and hard-wood timber, with a valuable variety of yellow pine and a great deal of cedar on the sand barrens and swamps along the coast and on the lower part of the peninsula. The early population did little in vessel building except at Salem and Burlington, where river sloops and fishing boats were built. At the time of the Revolution the state had no ships and no foreign commerce of any account. Since 1815 there has been some building at various localities, and of late years a large repairing business has grown up in Jersey City, on New York harbor, and at Perth Amboy, below Staten island, where there is a coal depot. In the lower part of the state many streams exist large enough to float coasting vessels, and on some of these ship-building is quietly carried on with the aid of such timber as remains available. On the Atlantic front sail-boats for fishing and pleasure sailing are built, and on the Delaware river repairing and small building go on at two or three places. At Camden, the principal building center of the state, there is a considerable industry.

The Jersey City yards are 18 in number, and have 2 railways and 10 floating dry-docks for hauling out vessels. They get their business from the various classes of vessels which throng New York harbor. The small dry-docks and railways make a specialty of barge and canal-boat work, but the large ones handle sailing vessels, tugs, and steamboats. About 250 men are employed during ten months of the year, the number of vessels repaired ranging from 1,500 to 2,000. If the year is a good one, repairs are freely made, and all the yards are crowded with work; but if profits are small, the vessels economize and the yards are dull. Jersey City is an important auxiliary to the resources of New York harbor; one of the largest yards is owned by a ship-owner who repairs his own fleet of excursion and passenger steamboats. Wages and prices are the same as in New York, but proprietors all speak of the fact that foreign vessels, especially steamers, avoid having work done here. Business was better when the bulk of the tonnage in port was owned by Americans.

At Elizabethport there is one railway for the repair of coal-boats and schooners.

At Pamrapo there is a little yacht-building from time to time, but the total is small.

Perth Amboy has 3 busy yards and 2 railways. The work here is for the coal trade, and is mostly repairing. The companies have had barges built here ever since 1860 for sending coal up to the city and points accessible from the harbor. Originally built for capacity only, the newer barges have been designed as well for small resistance. The Lehigh Valley Company ordered six new barges in 1880, and one was building at Perth Amboy when the place was visited. This barge was perfectly flat on the floor amidships and square on the bilge, the floor being carried well forward and aft. The bow and stern were sharp, the stem perpendicular, and the counter overhung the water about 5 feet. This boat was 125 feet long, 28 feet broad, and $11\frac{1}{4}$ deep amidships, with $2\frac{3}{4}$ feet sheer, and on 9 feet draught would carry 700 tons of coal. The floor timbers were of yellow pine, in one piece each, the top timbers 8-inch oak, and the bilge was strengthened by a pitch-pine log 12 inches square, fitted into the angle and well bolted to the timbers. A binding and a standing strake, each 6 by 12 inches, were fitted close to the bilge log, while a shelf, 12 by 12, supported the beam ends; amidships the beams rested on strong stanchions, heeling on a pitch-pine keelson 12 by 24 inches square. A long bar of iron ran down by the side of each stanchion and was bolted to the beam above and the keelson below; a light ceiling covered the whole interior of the boat. The deck was laid flush fore and aft, and was furnished with bitts, cleats, and a house for the boatman and his family.

New Brunswick, on the Raritan river, once built largely for the coasting and a little for the foreign trade. Oak was originally abundant; but the wood is now scarce, and frame timber costs $40 per thousand. Repairing is now the principal work.

In the region of Barnegat, Tuckerton, Greenbank, and West Creek there has been considerable building of coasting schooners for 40 or 50 years. Vessels of 400 tons have been built at Barnegat, and at Tuckerton one yard launched 17 vessels in all. About 300 men in Tuckerton once found a living in the different branches of this industry, but there has been no work done for several years, except upon small fishing boats, a dozen or twenty of the latter being built every year in door-yards by fishermen and half-professional builders. At Greenbank several large schooners, each carrying from 400 to 550 tons of coal, have been launched into the Mullica river, but there have been none launched since 1877. The timber used has been chiefly Jersey pine. It is resinous, though less so than Georgia pine, and is durable. The large main pieces of the frame, the stem, keel, and stern-post, and the outside planking were native white oak; all the rest of the vessel was Jersey pine. Thus built, Jersey schooners were good and lasting, and there are many in existence from 18 to 30 years old. They cost about $50 and $55 per register ton. Southern pine was used to some extent after the local timber grew scarce.

May's Landing, on the Great Egg Harbor river, lies buried in a pine wilderness, diversified with clumps of oak in the wet lands and on the river banks. Several hundred white-oak trees, from 12 to 30 inches in diameter, averaging 200 years old, grow in and about the village. Ship-building was once the life of this place. There were three yards, and from 2 to 5 vessels were launched every year, nearly all coasting schooners of from 200 to 750 tons actual burden. The work was done by contract for owners in New York, Philadelphia, Baltimore, and various parts of New Jersey. One vessel of 740 tons was named The Twenty-one Friends, from a peculiarity in her ownership. Two barkentines of 643 and 679 tons register respectively were built about six years ago, each for $45,000. One builder has built about 35 vessels here and at Somers Point, 12 miles away; another 20 vessels. Nothing had been built for four years when the town was visited in the census year; but a center-board schooner, with 130 feet keel, 35 feet beam, and 12 feet hold, was then under way, with a frame 21 by 10 inches, spaced 26 inches, and was to cost $25,000. The May's Landing yards have always built with Jersey pine in the frames, ceiling, keelson, deck beams, and decking; the planking and center pieces of the vessel only were of white oak. The pine is cheaper, costing only $25 a thousand feet, sided and delivered in the yard, but it is usual to buy from the saw-mill, hewing the frames from the flitch with axes. The May's Landing vessels have been durable, but clumsy. The ceiling and planking are not fitted on with edges faying so closely as in the eastern yards, and daylight can be seen through the side of the vessel sometimes before it is calked. The cant frames are arranged after a fashion which went out of use in eastern yards a long while ago. The space just aft of the stem is filled in with fore- and-aft cants heeling on a perpendicular frame, and sometimes the second frame is set more than one frame space aft of the first and the interval is filled in with cants heeling on the second frame. There are few labor-saving appliances in the May's Landing yards, everything being of the cheapest and simplest character. Wages, however, are low—from $1 25 to $2 a day. Business is depressed here, notwithstanding the abundance of good and cheap timber; good carpenters are lacking, and the spirit of enterprise is dormant.

There is very little else doing, going down the coast, except the construction of fishing boats and yachts at Atlantic City. Building was once active at Somers Point, Port Republic, and Tuckahoe, but the decay of coal carrying in schooners has depressed the business; besides, timber is scarce. Since the railroads have been opened through the pine wilderness to Atlantic City forest fires have repeatedly swept away large tracts of timber, causing a destruction equal to that of the ax, and the places named have been left without the original mainstay of the industry, the only work now done being of an occasional and purely local character.

Mauricetown and Leesburg, on the Maurice river, both close together, are the only places of any activity in the southern part of the state, the prosperity of the village first named being dependent on building and navigation. There are 50 or 60 sea captains living in the place, and almost everybody owns shares in vessels; it is the same with Leesburg, Dennisville, Millville, and Dorchester, all near by. The majority of the vessels owned on the river are for fishing and oystering, but there are many large coasters and barkentines. The three-masted schooners Harry B. Ritter, 643 tons; Thomas J. Lancaster, 653 tons; and Charles Platt, 632 tons, each carrying nearly 1,000 tons of cargo, have all crossed the Atlantic with grain cargoes from Philadelphia. They make triangular voyages—grain to Liverpool, coal to Cuba, and sugar to the United States. These vessels carry square canvas forward, and are really barkentines. The building on this river has been active for 50 years, the calculation being to launch a schooner or a barkentine from the yard at each of the several villages above named every year. Two schooners were under way in the census year. The wood used was formerly native pine and oak; but the home supply is now nearly exhausted, and the accessible large trees are gone. The frames, knees, and planking are wrought out from white oak; the rest of the vessel is yellow pine; and the outfit and top gear are usually bought in Philadelphia. The cost of building here is about $52 or $55 a ton. The builders claimed that the cost could be kept down to $45, but with a good outfit $55 was the standard cost. Small schooners of 60 tons and under cost as high as $150 per register ton. Wages are from $1 50 to $2 a day. Dorchester is the principal place for repairing river vessels, and two railways, worked by hand or by horse-power, exist there. The nearness of this river to the southern timber supply and the vicinity of the iron regions, with Philadelphia near at hand to provide outfits, are points of advantage for builders.

At Port Norris and Salem there are small railways for the repair of fishing vessels.

There is a good deal of small building here and there on the Delaware river, but it does not take the form of an active industry except at Camden. Its public importance consists entirely in its being a field in which ship-carpenters can be recruited in an emergency.

Camden has five large ship-yards, employing 300 men and a capital of $500,000, one being used for the construction of iron vessels. There is a large floating dry-dock, capable of taking out of water the largest steamers in the trade of Philadelphia, across the river, which is engaged mainly in repairing. The other yards chiefly thrive by the same branch of industry, but two have large marine railways, where calking, painting, coppering, carpentry, and blacksmith work are done. The large repair business gives them great advantages for the building of new vessels, as they have a force of skilled men employed and a complete equipment of labor-saving machinery. An occasional contract to build enables them to keep the men busy, and they can employ men for lower wages than they would have to pay if work were irregular. Large schooners of southern oak and yellow pine are built here nearly every year at from $52 to $55 per ton. The wages of the best men were $2 75 a day on new and $3 on old work. The building of the census year was 3 propellers, aggregating 457 tons; 1 schooner of 673 tons, and a sloop of 6 tons, valued in all at $80,000. The new iron vessels were 4 tugs, aggregating 382 tons, and worth $76,000. The yards of Camden all handle large vessels, and are of great value to the shipping interests of the river; but it is the testimony of all the yards that work is less active now than it was 25 years ago. The river was formerly thronged with coal schooners and American sailing vessels, but steam colliers have nearly superseded schooners, while the large sailing ships have been driven off by coasting and foreign steamers. The change is detrimental to Camden. The finest facilities in New Jersey for building wooden vessels exist in this town, as the yards have steam saws, bolt-cutters, derricks, and all the large and small tools which have been invented; but their proximity to a large city leaves little or no profit in building, wages and taxes being too high. Philadelphia is full of large lumber yards, but the timber for a ship cannot be bought sufficiently low to compensate for high wages and taxes.

PENNSYLVANIA.

Pennsylvania had a great wealth of forest growth at the time of its settlement, and one of the masts of the first European vessel that ascended the Delaware river caught in the branch of a tree standing on the shore where Philadelphia was subsequently founded. Oak and pine grew in profusion from the edge of the river to a vast distance inland. The early population were traders, and after they had fairly embarked in commercial enterprise their progress was rapid. Eighty-five vessels cleared from Philadelphia in 1723, 171 in 1730, 212 in 1735, and from 1749 to 1752 over 400 a year. Some of these were ships from the parent country, some were from the West Indies, and some belonged in New England, but a large proportion were of local build and ownership. It will be recollected that in 1730 the British West India islands asked that the continental colonies be required to buy West India produce from them alone. The request was resisted by Philadelphia, and the colony threatened to retaliate by developing her manufacturing interests at the expense of England, and the movement was beaten for the time. The imports in 1730 were £48,592, the exports £57,500. In 1763 and 1764 Mr. Grenville convened the colonial agents in London and explained his plan for drawing a revenue from America. His taxes promised to stop all trading with the French and Spanish colonies. The trade was even then unlawful, but it had been connived at, as it provided the continental population with gold and silver for their remittances to England. This time the plan to concentrate the trade in the ports of the British islands could not be defeated, and by making the officers of naval vessels officers of the customs nearly the whole colonial trade with the French and Spanish colonies was destroyed. This bore hard on Philadelphia, and the province was soon drained of specie, for in 1764 her imports were £700,000 and her exports only £300,000. Philadelphia did not submit quietly, but, like the other colonies, built fast vessels and evaded the English regulations when she could, and the commerce of the port grew to be so large that in 1773 a total of 426 square-rigged vessels and 370 sloops and schooners entered and cleared. Pennsylvania vessels carried grain, flour, flaxseed, timber, iron, pork, and beef to the West Indies, Portugal, Spain, and the Mediterranean, and were often sold abroad with their cargoes; they were cheaper than those of European build, and, owing to their having been built for a half-smuggling business, were fast and good vessels. Philadelphia was known long before the Revolution for what Gordon calls the "noble manufacture of ships".

During and after the Revolution ship-building was extensively carried on, and it is known that the city produced the finest craft in the New World; certainly many famous war vessels and large trading ships were built. After the war of 1812 building was again active. Philadelphia had a large East India trade, and was noted for her smart captains and big vessels. Her ship-yards were numerous, and the talent employed in them was good; but the business of the port declined after the Erie canal had given New York an impetus, and during the packet and clipper-ship periods the production of tonnage fell behind that of New York, although many excellent vessels were built. Since 1865 it has steadily declined so far as wooden sailing vessels are concerned, wages and all the cost of carrying on a ship-yard having risen too high. A schooner is occasionally built, but it costs $55 and $60 a ton, although oak is only $27 in the flitch delivered, and captains can do better by going to Maine. The tonnage of the river has gradually been converted into steam vessels, and, so far as new work is concerned, the yards have been devoting their attention for 20 years chiefly to tugs, steamboats, and coasting propellers. There are two great establishments in the city, with enormous capital, building iron vessels.

At Philadelphia facilities for repair work are good, and there are six yards devoted chiefly to this business. One firm has a fixed dry-dock capable of admitting the largest ocean steamer in the port and of taking in two of the smaller class at once, and the repair of iron vessels is made a specialty; another has two large railways, operated by a steam windlass, for steamboats and sailing vessels, the yard being equipped in the most modern manner. Another firm has a large floating sectional dry-dock, built in place of the old railway which was started in 1828; 49 vessels were coppered there in the census year. The yards all complain of a decline of repair work, owing to the change in the tonnage of the port from sail to steam and from wood to iron. The one thing which has affected the business most has been the construction of the Reading railroad iron steam colliers. The company used to give cargoes to several hundred coasting schooners yearly, but began in 1869 to buy vessels. The following iron steam propellers were built, at a total cost of $2,656,510:

Years.	Names.	Register tonnage.	Number of voyages up to May 11, 1881.	Tons of coal at a cargo.	Cost of vessels.
1869	Rattlesnake	417	389	500	$71,925
1870	Centipede	436	402	500	71,925
1870	Achilles	763	326	1,000	115,120
1870	Hercules	764	328	1,000	114,430
1870	Leopard	609	242	800	105,125
1870	Panther	699	338	800	104,925
1873	Reading	1,283	218	1,650	283,570
1874	Harrisburg	1,283	241	1,650	283,570
1874	Lancaster	1,283	207	1,650	283,570
1874	Perkiomen	1,035	235	1,200	224,660
1874	Berks	553	236	600	146,980
1874	Williamsport	1,283	207	1,650	283,570
1874	Allentown	1,283	216	1,650	283,570
1874	Pottsville	1,283	197	1,650	283,570

Each vessel makes from 30 to 35 trips a year. The fleet will now deliver to points along the Atlantic coast from 450,000 to 500,000 tons of coal yearly; they run mainly to Boston and nearer points this side, but often go as far as Portland, Maine. This traffic would employ from 150 to 250 schooners steadily. The public has been benefited by the reduction in the cost of freights, but the ship-yards of the Delaware have lost by it, as the schooners used to have a great deal of repair work done. Another cause of the decline of business is the care taken by foreign vessels to avoid every possible dollar of expense in an American port.

One branch of the business which is quite active yet in Philadelphia is the fitting out of vessels; nearly all the hulls built on streams flowing into Delaware bay are sent up to the city in tow of a tug and receive their masts and spars, sails, rigging, spar iron work, anchors, and chains there. Some are fitted out at the yards, but the outfits are bought in the city, several prosperous firms living by this outfitting business.

Chester is the only other building town in Pennsylvania. The work there is exclusively on iron vessels.

At Marcus Hook there is a small railway for painting and repairing fishing craft and small vessels.

As a state, Pennsylvania is devoting substantially its whole attention to the building of iron vessels, and a revival of the old wooden-ship industry is not now looked for.

DELAWARE.

There are many good points for building on the Delaware river and along the streams that flow through the lower part of the state. The supply of oak is large, and the quality of the wood is the best, Delaware white oak having long been regarded as the finest, toughest, and most durable on the whole Atlantic coast. Growing on lands never too dry and generally full of swamps, and near enough to the ocean to get the benefit of the salt air, the timber reached perfection. For the last fifty years at least its cost has been less in Delaware by from $6 to $10 a thousand than when delivered in New England, the freight alone by coasting vessel having been $5 and $6 per thousand feet. Labor-saving machinery has not been introduced, except at Wilmington, and all the ship-yard work in the lower part of the state is done in the old-fashioned way, by hand-power, requiring the expenditure of several hundred days more of manual labor in making the vessel than where machinery is fully used. Building has been restricted also by sand-bars at the mouths of streams; on some of the rivers a great industry could be developed if the channels were deepened so that vessels drawing 10 or 12 feet of water could float out to sea.

Wilmington has four large yards, two of them engaged exclusively in iron work. The other two build wooden boats, schooners, barges, tugs, and steamboats. One yard has two marine railways, the other one a railway for the repair of coasters. There is also one dry-dock. Wilmington vessels have been prized for their speed and durability. The bark Sarah S. Ridgeway, of 869 tons, built in 1877, once ran from Rio to New York, laden with coffee, in 26 days 14 hours, her time beating by two days that of two steamers which sailed with her. Wilmington orders come chiefly from Philadelphia, and wages are $2 and $2 50 per day. The present industry of the city in the way of building will be described in the chapter on iron vessels.

At Bethel, in Sussex county, there is a small marine railway for repair work.

At Milford, on the Mispillion river, there are four yards, all in active operation. One firm has built about one vessel a year, or 25 in all. They began with a river schooner of about 50 tons, 50 feet keel, 22 feet beam, and 5 feet deep, which traded to Philadelphia, but of late years they have built schooners of 200, 500, 600, and even 1,000 tons actual burden, the three-masted schooner Annie Miller, lately built, carrying 1,000 tons of coal. Originally vessels were mainly built of oak, deck frames and all. In the census year a schooner was nearly finished measuring 130 feet on the keel, 33 feet beam, and $11\frac{1}{2}$ feet hold, with center-board, flat on the floor, but with sharp bow and run; frames sided 15 inches and molded 12 inches over the keel, tapering to 10 by 7 at the plank-sheer; room and space, 22 inches; transoms, 12 inches; keelson, 27 by 14 inches; sister keelsons, 15 by 9 inches; keel, 14 by 18 inches; center-board, 20 feet long; ceiling, $3\frac{1}{2}$ inches on the floor and 6 on the bilge; outside planking, $3\frac{1}{2}$ inches; water-ways, $9\frac{1}{2}$ by 5 inches; deck-beams, 12 by 10 inches in the center; carlines, 9 by 6 inches; decking, 3 inches. The schooner is of oak throughout, except the deck frame, ceiling, water-ways, and stanchions. The decking and houses are of white pine. At another yard a barkentine (two-decker) finished in the census year was 140 feet on the keel, 35 feet beam, $16\frac{1}{2}$ feet deep in the hold, the between-deck space being $5\frac{1}{2}$ feet. Another firm began here about 12 years ago and built one coasting schooner of about 450 tons burden every year, but lately have launched about three a year. This firm build on contract for owners in the state and along the Delaware river chiefly. Their three-masted schooner, the Governor Hall, of 1,000 tons burden, was 130 feet on the keel, 34 feet beam, and $16\frac{2}{3}$ feet deep in the hold, the between-decks being 6 feet; frame, oak, 12 by 16 inches; room and space, 23 inches; keelson, oak, 28 by 15 inches; sister keelsons, 15 by 8 inches; center-board, 7-inch oak and 22 feet long; center-board keelson, 22 by 14 inches; clamps, 5-inch pitch-pine; bilge ceiling, 5-inch oak; lower deck and deck frame, pitch-pine; upper deck, 3-inch white pine; outside planking, $3\frac{1}{2}$-inch oak; wales, 5 inches; knees of oak roots. The fourth was also building in the census year. The four yards build from three to six vessels a year. They get their oak from the saw-mills of the surrounding country, paying from $18 to $22 a thousand for flitch delivered in the yard. Oak planking costs about $33 a thousand, the price in Philadelphia being $45, as in the eastern yards; pitch-pine, $28. The frames are all hewn by hand from the flitch, and, while a derrick is sometimes used to set them up, the carrying of the beams and timbers is generally on the shoulders of the men. Labor ranges from $1 25 to $1 75 a day, but sometimes $2 is paid for the best men. The carpenters are usually white men, but a few colored men have been trained to ship-yard work and make very fair mechanics. The cost of building varies from $50 to $55 per register ton for first-class vessels, the smaller ones costing from $70 to $100 per ton, according to the way in which they are fitted out. One firm had been offered twenty-four contracts, which they could not take owing to lack of facilities and of carpenters. The narrowness of the river here was once an embarrassment in launching vessels of any size, but this has been overcome by planting the ways so as to launch down-stream and by sapping away the opposite bank. The yard owners were all anxious for the removal of the sand-bar at the mouth of the river.

At Milton, 12 miles away, vessels have been built for 50 years or more. There are oak forests all around, and half the face of the country seems to be under timber. Originally the curved pieces of the frames were cut from trunks having a natural crook, and when none except straight oak trees were left it was thought that ship-building would be seriously embarrassed. However, it was found that good frames could be cut from straight-grained timber, and the industry has thrived in a quiet way at this woodland village down to the present time. There are now three yards at Milton. In the census year 4 schooners were built, aggregating 1,362 tons, costing $79,700, an average of $59 a ton; but larger vessels were built for $50 per register ton.

The yards at Milford are of the most primitive description, a shop to keep the tools in, the hand-tools themselves, and a steam-box comprising the outfit in each case. A builder hires about 15 men when he has a vessel under way, or just enough to handle the heavy timbers, beams, and plank, and when a large stick is to be placed in position or a plank brought from the steam-box all hands are called off. Building is accordingly a slow process, as each yard can only finish about one large schooner yearly. Although slow in building, both the Milton and the Milford vessels rank well with insurance companies. The length of time they stand on the stocks exposed to wind and weather is an advantage, as the timber becomes thoroughly seasoned; and they all are salted above light-water mark, and are good for 20 or 30 years. Originally the Milton vessels were entirely of oak; they are still mainly of oak, but yellow pine is used in the deck frames and clamps, and perhaps in the keelsons. The knees are all from oak roots or branches. Oak in the flitch, hauled in from local saw-mills, is $18 and $20 a thousand feet; oak plank, $28 and $30; yellow pine, $29; white-pine decking, from $35 to $37. Oak is so plentiful, that here, as elsewhere in Delaware, fine trees stand even in the ship-yards and cast their shade over the men at their work. Labor costs from 75 cents to $1 50 a day. Many colored men are employed, and they take to the trade willingly and make fair mechanics. Milton and Milford vessels both are generally sent up to Philadelphia by tug to receive their sails, rigging, and outfit.

Fréderica, Delaware, does some building, and Seaford used to do some; but at the latter place nothing is now done. Seaford is situated on the banks of the Nanticoke, a fine stream, penetrating dense forests, but a few bad years in coasting caused people to invest their money in other property. A bar at the mouth of the river has also been a source of injury to the business. A little repairing of small sailing vessels is all that is left to Seaford.

A Delaware schooner of 600 tons requires 190,000 feet of oak, 100,000 feet of yellow pine, 35,000 feet of white pine, and 30 tons of iron for fastenings, castings, spar work, etc., and in the purchase of the timber a saving of from $3,500 to $4,000 could be made over what the Maine men, for instance, have to pay. Wages are lower than in Maine, for a great deal of colored labor can be utilized. The state is close by the greatest iron-producing region of the country, and iron can be bought to advantage. Outfits can also be bought at a lower cost than in the east. With a proper equipment, such as derricks, steam-saws, etc., vessels could be built in Delaware, to class A 1, with a red star in Lloyds for 11 years, at $45 a ton.

MARYLAND.

Chesapeake bay has been known from the earliest times for the speed and beauty of its vessels. The peculiar form and rig of the fishing craft of this region have already been described. The rakish air of the boats has also been shared by the larger vessels of the bay. The schooner rig was popularized at an early day, and schooners and brigs were the principal trading vessels until long after the Revolution, though there was occasionally a larger vessel employed. Chesapeake bay vessels engaged in the trade to the West Indies, the same as did all the others of the continent, and were also built largely for the slave trade, both employments calling for speed and a handy rig. In its origin the slave trade was regarded as a proper mode of obtaining workmen for the West Indies and the continent of America, and was carried on mainly by the British, French, and Portuguese. In 1761 the British had 28 vessels (3,475 tons) in the trade, and in 1776 they had 192, measuring 22,296 tons. By a return to parliament in 1789 it appears that 38,000 slaves were carried annually in British vessels to America and its islands, 20,000 in French, 10,000 in Portuguese, 4,000 in Dutch, and 2,000 in Danish vessels, about 74,000 in all. Slaves cost from £8 to £22 in Africa, and sold for from £28 to £35 in the West Indies. It was a profitable business, and appears to have been engaged in to some extent by American vessels built on the Chesapeake and in New England. Those of the Chesapeake were the swiftest, and were all brigs and schooners. They were generally built especially for the trade, and were sold in the West Indies and elsewhere to those who carried on the business. The between-deck space of $5\frac{3}{8}$ or 6 feet was divided by bulkheads into rooms for the men, women, and boys, respectively, and in a large brig there was room for 600 people. The hold was about 10 feet deep, and carried from 30,000 to 40,000 gallons of water, stores for a cruise of about 100 days, and the ballast. The schooners and brigs of the Chesapeake, both merchantmen and slavers, were broad of beam before the center and above the water-line and sharp on the floor, often having about 20° of dead rise. The bow was sharp and flaring above the water, the front of the forecastle deck being often as round as the section of an apple. The hulls were lean aft, and thus sailed with considerable drag. They were long in proportion to breadth, had low bulwarks, looked low in the water, and carried raking masts, in order to bring the effort of the sails farther aft, where the lateral resistance of the vessel in the water was located. The topmasts were so slender that they sometimes bent to the wind like whips; a circumstance thought favorable to speed. These vessels were able to carry a heavy press of canvas, would go into the wind remarkably fast, were smart and handy, and had a world-wide fame. Cheap, good, and abundant timber made Chesapeake bay an active ship-building region even before the revolutionary war, and after the independence the shipwrights of Baltimore were among the first to petition Congress for legislation in behalf of the maritime interests of the country. The legislation that followed was a great benefit to Baltimore, and made her one of the principal ship-yard centers of the continent.

The history of the industry in Baltimore is about the same as that of the other large commercial ports, except that her tonnage was chiefly in fore-and-aft-rigged vessels and she would build 125 schooners in a year to 20 ships and brigs. The fisheries and local trading of the bay called for the production of large numbers of small schooners; and the same style of vessel was employed in coasting and in the large trade to the West Indies which sprang up in course of time. In the busy years after 1840 there were as many as 15 ship-yards in south Baltimore and elsewhere in the harbor actively engaged in building schooners, brigs, clipper ships, and steamboats. Some of the old builders, still living, remember the time when from 20 to 25 vessels were on the stocks at once and everybody was making money, and the industry was growing so fast that in the large yards there were anywhere from 15 to 20 apprentices at a time learning the trade. The clipper ships of Baltimore had many of the peculiarities of the schooners. They were as sharp on the floor, sailed with a drag, had flaring bows and raking masts, and were noted for their quick voyages, but carried high bulwarks to keep the ship dry. The extreme vessels ceased to be built after the California excitement was over, as their tendency to sag at the ends and get out of shape operated against them; but improvements were made in the model, and some of the best vessels in America were then launched from the Baltimore yards. The Cyane, a clipper bark built in Baltimore 35 years ago, is to-day a strong and good vessel. She is 132 feet long over all, 24 feet beam, and $12\frac{1}{4}$ feet hold, having one deck, but with a second and open tier of beams to strengthen her. The bulwarks are $5\frac{3}{4}$ feet high. She requires ballast when empty, being so sharp as to be top heavy; but when loaded to her draught of 13 or 14 feet she is a good carrier, easy at sea, and a fast sailer. The war of 1861, with the changes which took place in that period in favor of steam vessels and the strikes and high wages, put a virtual end to ship-building in Baltimore, few merchant vessels, other than side-wheel steamboats and propeller tugs, having been built since that time.

The principal business of Baltimore now is the repairing and outfitting of vessels, and the city is to Chesapeake bay what Philadelphia is to the Delaware river and bay and Boston is to Cape Ann. Sails and outfits are supplied by a few large firms, which operate on an extensive scale and are able to buy cheap and to undersell all their competitors on the bay. There are 17 ship-yards in the city, with 19 railways and 3 floating dry-docks. One yard, near the fort, is devoted to the building and repair of iron vessels, and has a full outfit of machine, boiler, and other shops, besides a large fixed dry-dock built of masonry. The length from the groove of the outer gate to the head of the dock is 470 feet; from the inner gate, 450 feet; greatest width on top, 113 feet; width on bottom, 45 feet; depth, 26 feet, leaving, with the blocks, 23 feet for a vessel. The dock is elliptical in plan, the sides descending in steps. Over 8,000 piles were driven to support the sides, in which about 2,000,000 feet of lumber were used. The width at the entrance is 123 feet; at the gate 83 feet. The gate is a caisson built like the hull of a vessel, to displace water enough to sustain its weight. It has two decks, the lower one for the machinery. The pumps are operated by steam on shore, and can empty the dock in two hours. Congress ceded the land for this structure on condition that government vessels should be docked free of charge. The other docks and railways of the city are large enough to accommodate wooden ships of the largest class. A large number of the smaller vessels of the Chesapeake are owned by colored men, and in order to secure prompt and inexpensive repairs of their vessels they organized a stock company a few years ago with a capital of $40,000 and established a yard with two marine railways. Originally there were 300 stockholders in this enterprise, but the number has been reduced to about 150. The yard employs 70 men, nearly all of them negroes, and pays them the current rate of wages in the city. They haul out about 460 vessels a year. The shipwrights of the port have formed an association, with rules, which bring a great deal of work on foreign vessels to them. The Italian, Norwegian, and British grain ships avoid expense where they can, and used to go upon the railways, paying hauling fees only, and doing as much as possible of the calking, painting, etc., themselves; but the association requires that the repair work shall be done by the yard hauling out the vessel, so that the system in vogue in New York of running a dry-dock merely for the hauling fees does not prevail here. These rules have, however, driven a great deal of the work on the bay vessels from this port to the country railways scattered along the bay. The fees for hauling in Baltimore were as follows: Side-wheel steamers, 15 cents per register ton, or 7½ cents a ton a day for 5 days, and 5 cents a ton a day thereafter; propellers of 800 tons and over, the same; of from 600 to 800 tons, 12 cents a ton, or 6 cents a ton a day for 5 days, and 5 cents a ton a day thereafter; tugs under 100 tons, $10, or $6 a day for 5 days, and $5 a day thereafter; from 100 to 150 tons, $15, or $8 a day; sailing vessels of 800 tons and over, 15 cents a ton, or 7½ cents a ton a day for 5 days, and 5 cents a ton a day thereafter; from 600 to 800 tons, 12 cents, or 6 cents a ton a day for 5 days, and 5 cents a ton a day thereafter; from 100 to 600 tons, 10 cents a ton, or 5 cents a ton a day; from 50 to 100 tons, $10, or $6 a day; from 25 to 50 tons, $8, or $5 a day; under 25 tons, $6, or $4 a day; scows of over 100 tons, 10 cents a ton, or 5 cents a ton a day; under 100 tons, $10, or $6 a day.

Builders also charge a regular commission on the labor bills and materials used. There are no spar-yards here, each yard making its own spars, nor is there any machine for punching the nail holes in sheathing metal, the work being all done by hand. A punching machine was once tried, but the workmen objected to its use. Wages were $2 50 and $2 75 a day. The timber used has always been Maryland and Virginia oak and pitch-pine and Pennsylvania white pine until late years, when Georgia pine has been imported, on account of having more heart and less sap-wood. Spruce spars come from West Virginia. Oak has always been cheap; but it used to range from $15 to $20 per thousand feet, though by watching for chances the yards at times have got it as low as $5. Oak in the flitch now costs $25, and planking and heavy pieces, for keelsons, $45. Georgia pine is $35 per thousand feet. One firm in Baltimore ceils ships for grain and fits them for cattle transportation, using about 4,500,000 feet of white and yellow pine yearly.

Havre de Grace has a marine railway and ship-yard. Scow schooners for duck shooting and coal barges are the principal new work, but the repairing of coal-boats and schooners is the main support of the yard. There was on the stocks in the census year a barge 170 feet long, 21 feet beam, and 13 feet deep, with 4 feet sheer. The floor was flat, the bilge square, the sides slightly flaring, the bow and stern sharp, stem straight, and the stern broad on deck and overhanging. The whole boat was built of oak, 140,000 feet being required. The frames were 98 in number; the top timbers 6 by 8 inches; side planking, 3 inches; ceiling of sides, 5 inches; bottom plank, 4 inches; ceiling of floor, 2 inches, and about 400 bushels of salt were used above light-water mark. Carpenters were hard to get.

At Annapolis, on the bay below Baltimore, there is a small marine railway, and a small fishing boat is occasionally built.

At Cambridge, on the eastern shore of the bay, there are 3 yards, including 2 railways, and a little community of sail-makers, riggers, and blacksmiths. The moving spirit of this town is one of William H. Webb's apprentices, a builder of long and varied experience, who has plied his art both on the Atlantic and Pacific coasts and in China. Several coal barges for the Lehigh Valley Company were built here of the same model as those at Perth Amboy. The building at Cambridge has been confined to sloops and schooners for the bay and tugs and barges;

but the place is favorably situated for an extensive business, as it is in a county which is clothed with fine oak and pine timber down to the coast and on the islands of the coast. Although this region has furnished frames for the New England ship-yards for fifty years, and although large quantities of planking and oak of all sizes for the construction of wharves, houses, etc., are exported annually, yet many tracts of first-growth oak and pine remain untouched. When Cambridge was visited a tract was passed at Airey's station, a few miles from the town, through which were strewn the frame timbers for a large vessel, hewn to the proper shapes and lying on the ground, ready for shipment to some New England yard. Probably building can be carried on to the best advantage here when the builder is also the owner of his own timber. His oak frames would not cost him over $15 per thousand feet; when bought from the saw-mills in the flitch the cost was only $25 per thousand, or $10 less than in New England. Three small schooners and a tug were built in the census year. Wages were from $1 25 to $2 a day, a few men getting $2 50.

At Pocomoke City there are 2 yards, which produce a few bay and river vessels of small size every year. In the census year these yards built 4 schooners, registering 162 tons, and costing $16,500. Much repair work is done. Wages range from $1 to $2 per day, the average being less than $2. There were no labor-saving appliances in the yards, but one yard was run in conjunction with a saw-mill. This county is heavily wooded with oak and pine, and the saw-mill was paying not to exceed $10 per thousand for large oak trees in the round, delivered in the yard, the cost for sawing being about $2 50 per thousand. A great deal of the heavy timber around here has been cut off and exported from the bay. South of Pocomoke there have been camps for several years employed in cutting timber for the ship-builders of Maine, their operations being now carried on nearer Accomack, and some of the forests have been culled for everything above 12 inches in diameter; still, much heavy timber remains in other places, and there is an abundance for a local ship-building industry. In the flitch oak is sold at Pocomoke for $22 and less per thousand.

Crisfield is also a building town. The work here has already been referred to in the chapter on fishing vessels.

Solomon's island, on the Patuxent river, has two yards and two railways. The fishing industry supports this place. Bug-eyes and pungies are the vessels built.

At several places on the bay, notably at Oxford, Saint Michael's, Broad Creek, Sharptown, Whitehaven, and Salisbury, there is a good deal of repairing of vessels at small railways.

What makes a ship is principally wood, iron, and men's labor. Large schooners, barks, and ships each consume from 280,000 feet of lumber, 18 tons of iron, and 4,300 days of labor, to 960,000 feet of lumber, 120 tons of iron, and 9,000 to 14,000 days of labor, according as steam saws, derricks, and other labor-saving appliances are used in the yard or not. If Maryland were to become an active ship-building state, it is probable that the cost of labor would rise to the scale paid in Maine; but in the purchase of oak and pitch-pine her builders would enjoy an advantage of from $10 to $15 a thousand feet for oak and about $3 to $5 a thousand for pine. With labor-saving machinery they could build the cheapest wooden vessels on the Atlantic coast.

VIRGINIA.

The ship-building of this state began in 1622. The home company, at great trouble and expense, sent out Captain Thomas Barwick with 25 carpenters in order to build the pinnaces, shallops, and large vessels needed for trade and transportation in the new province, and on their arrival they began to build small sail-boats for the river and bay trade. The magnificent extent and the excellence of the timber were noted in all reports on the colony's resources. Oak and pitch-pine covered the face of the country; but the population never took much interest in ship-building, as there were other occupations that paid them better, the best industry being agriculture, to which they devoted their whole attention, leaving to the inhabitants of the rugged and poor soils of New England the construction and management of ships. A number of small vessels and boats were made, but seldom in the whole history of the colony and state down to the present time has more than 2,000 tons of shipping been built in any one year. The town in which the industry has principally flourished is Norfolk, and from 1840 to 1855 barks and ships were occasionally built there for the West India and the Brazilian trade for local shareholders. In 1853–'54, at the Norfolk yards, 10 vessels were launched, registering a total of 3,600 tons; but since 1855 there has been no building of large vessels, except a few steamboats.

At Alexandria there are two ship-yards, with a marine railway. The principal concern, started in 1874, had built two large three-masted schooners and one tug and repaired a large number of Potomac river vessels when the yard was visited in the census year. Schooners cost $50 per ton. Vessels have been built here occasionally from the earliest days, and there was a public ship-yard during the Revolution for the construction of government vessels. Alexandria enjoys some advantages with reference to timber, and is a convenient point for the repairing of steamboats and sailing craft plying to and from Washington. A new yard has been started within two years, and is now building its second vessel. Squared oak costs from $20 to $22 a thousand at the yard, pitch-pine $23 and $25; but in the log oak can be delivered for about $15 a thousand for what can be squared out of it. The yard has a complete outfit of steam saws, and does its own squaring of the timber. A boat of a style peculiar to Chesapeake bay and the Potomac river was building here in 1881. It was a "long-boat"—an undecked center-board schooner with two fore-and-aft sails and a large jib—many of these vessels being employed in carrying cord-wood to Washington. A few years ago, owing to a scarcity of wood for fuel, the "long-boats" had a profitable season or two, and as a consequence many were built. These boats are shallow, flat on the floor, have round sides, straight bodies, and sharp bow, with quarter decks and cabins aft, draw only 18 inches of water light and 3 feet loaded, and will carry from 60 to 80 cords of wood each. A long-boat lying at the wharf at Alexandria measured 77 feet in length from stem to stern, $14\frac{1}{2}$ feet beam, and $2\frac{7}{12}$ feet in depth of hold below the gunwale. The frames were single, 5 by 3 inches, and extended from gunwale to gunwale. They were bent at the bilge, the ends being sawed in two longitudinally, to enable them to bend without breaking. The new boat was larger, and the frames were double. This boat was 82 feet over all, 77 feet keel, 23 feet beam, and $3\frac{5}{6}$ feet deep in the hold. The double frames were sided 7 inches and molded 6. In each one floor extended from bilge to bilge, having one curved top timber at either end, the other half of the frame being composed of one short floor, with a futtock to turn the bilge and a top timber. Room and space, 21 inches; keel, 15 by 6 inches, laid flat, narrowing to 7 by 6 inches at stem and stern; center-board keelson, 15 by 10 inches; center-board, 20 feet long; side keelsons, 7 by 7 inches; one bilge strake, 5 inches, with a clamp under the beams; no ceiling. The planking was of 2-inch oak, and the beams were spaced about 4 feet apart to support the sides. A washboard extended the whole length, with a short deck forward for working the jib and a small one aft for the helmsman, the latter surrounding the cabin. The vessel was all open amidships. These boats are loaded by laying the cord-wood fore and aft on the frames until the hold is full, and the gunwales are then piled with sticks laid transversely. The space within is then filled up with sticks, laid athwartships as high as convenient. They are fit only for river use, being too flimsy for rough water. Preparations are making in Alexandria for the cheap manufacture of rolled iron by a new process, with a view to iron-ship building; but so far the company has only been making blooms, not having put in the necessary machinery for rolling iron. Confidence is felt in the experiment, and an iron-ship yard is the ultimate object in view. Few places have better advantages than Alexandria for the manufacture of iron ships in materials, climate, labor, and cheap transportation.

Going down the Potomac and the Chesapeake one passes headlands, rivers, and bays in profusion which seem to have been qualified by nature for ship-building. The water is deep, and the shore is covered with oak and pine, and in spite of more than half a century of cutting there is a great deal of large timber left. Tracts can be bought where the stumpage, as it is called, does not exceed $1 a thousand feet; that is, the trees standing in the woods will sell for what can be squared out of them at the rate of $1 a thousand. There is no building in these beautiful bays of the Virginia coast, however, other than canoes and small fishing and trading schooners, the work being on canoes principally. There are few regular builders, except at Pocoson, Back Bay, and Hampton.

At Norfolk there are four yards, and, in addition, two or three in which something is occasionally built. In all, the yards have five marine railways for repairing, one of them sectional. The latter will hold two vessels at once, one of which can be launched without disturbing the other. Ship work here was originally on small vessels, but in the years of general maritime excitement the city ventured into full-rigged ships, four ships of a total of 2,900 tons register being built in 1853–'54, as well as a number of brigs and schooners. The yellow fever broke out in 1855, destroying this prosperity completely. There has been some small building since in different years, but the vessels have not exceeded 300 tons register, except the Rockaway, a steamboat of 1,950 tons, 275 feet long on the keel, 293 feet on deck, 38 feet wide in the hull, 66 feet over all, $11\frac{1}{2}$ feet deep, drawing 6 feet of water, which was built in 1876, and was calculated to make 20 miles an hour. The empty hull was sent off to New York in the spring of 1877 to receive her machinery, but she broke adrift in a storm, went ashore, and was dashed to pieces. The work of the city is now chiefly on tugs, barges, canal-boats, river steamers, and the large fleet of small produce schooners employed in this locality, and consists principally of repair work. The builders say that the presence of the navy-yard has the effect to keep up prices and wages, which is detrimental to the private yards. Wages were from $2 to $3 a day in the census year; laborers got $1 50; the average was about 50 cents a day higher than in Maryland and Delaware. Oak was $22 50 a thousand in the flitch, $30 for short plank, $40 for long plank; pitch-pine about $28, the price varying from $20 for short stuff to $40 for the finest, the fair average of a cargo being $28 a thousand. Black gum (*Nyssa multiflora*) has been much used here for keels, on account of the great lengths obtainable, its tenacity, and strength. The worms are thought to bite it quicker than oak, but by coppering this can be prevented. In 70- and 80-foot lengths gum costs $25 a thousand; in short lengths from $15 to $18. Vessels have been planked with gum at Norfolk, and the wood was found to be serviceable. A marine railway was built with gum in 1838, and when the ways were repaired two or three years ago the wood was sound and bright and the iron bolts in it were scarcely corroded.

The trading vessels peculiar to Norfolk were the little farming sloops and schooners, which flock into the harbor in large fleets in the summer time, bringing vegetables for the New York and Baltimore steamers. Often 150 of these little vessels enter the harbor about two hours before the departure of a steamer, racing at full speed, with everything set, and loaded high above the deck with a profusion of boxes and barrels packed with melons, cabbages, tomatoes, and vegetables of nearly every description. They dash straight in to get the best positions nearest the wharves, and often crowd in so thick that the steamer cannot make its berth. In consequence, a number of them are obliged to cast off and go swarming out into the bay, and cruise back and forth like a swarm of butterflies until they are allowed to return, when in they come again with a rush, jostling and crowding, the air being torn with the good-natured jabbering and arguing of the crews. There are a good many bug-eyes and canoes in this "trucking" fleet. These boats, large and small, are owned largely by negroes, and their crews are principally negroes. They are built on the vegetable farms all around Norfolk and across the James river on the peninsulas above. There are a few regular builders on the Nansemond, Chuckatuck, and Back rivers. A sloop 26 feet long, 11 feet broad, and 3 feet deep will cost about $300; a large sloop 45 feet long, $2,000. An average size, 9 tons, would be 35 feet in length, 13½ feet beam, and 3½ feet hold. Owners follow their own fancy in rig, some preferring the sloop rig, others the schooner. The majority of the boats are schooners, but they seldom have topmasts or topsails, and the space amidships is open. The boxes and barrels are stowed in this hatchway until the hold is full, and are then piled clear across the deck and as high as the sails will allow. Aft there is a little house. These boats have no bulwarks, but only a chock or low rail around on the plank-sheer. They are full and flat, partaking of the canoe model. Some of the sloops are of a flat-iron shape. The smart boats each make from $8 to $12 a day in the summer time. The charge for freighting vegetables is 3 cents for a box and 6 cents for a barrel, or from 4 to 10 cents, according to distance. Oysters are carried for from 3 to 5 cents a bushel, and sometimes the boats can make two trips in one day. The colored men make money with them, and when of a frugal disposition save money, and are often able to buy schooners of larger size.

SOUTHERN ATLANTIC AND GULF COASTS.

At various times since the Revolution vessels of good size have been built at the principal ports on the southern coast, a large number of flat-boats and small fishing vessels for local use having been built every year; but on the whole the industry has received no special development in this part of the country.

At Elizabeth City, North Carolina, there are two yards, one of which has a railway, and both do repairing. There are good facilities here for building, and before the war they were employed, but since the war business has been dull. A sloop and a small steamboat for shoal-water use were built in 1880.

Bell's Ferry, North Carolina, occasionally builds a small stern-wheel steamboat; Tarboro' the same.

Washington, North Carolina, could build large and good vessels. There are two yards in the town, but business is irregular. At one time these yards had 30 men employed, at another only 4 or 5, but since the war there has been little done here. A schooner of 175 tons and 3 barges were on the stocks in 1880, and a sloop of 29 tons and 2 steamboats of 69 and 97 tons were built.

Beaufort and New Berne, North Carolina, are both dull. At New Berne vessels of the largest class can be built at one yard, which, however, produces only 3 or 4 fishing and sail boats yearly. Some repairing is done.

Charleston, South Carolina, has a few repair shops and four yards. The building in 1880 was a sloop of 10 tons, 2 steamboats of 21 tons each, and 4 schooners averaging 16 tons each. The cotton and lumber vessels and steamboats that visit the harbor make quite a little industry in repairing, and that is the chief work done by the shipwrights of the city.

Coosaw, South Carolina, has a small private railway. Barges are built and repaired there for a local mining company.

At Georgetown, South Carolina, a clumsy steamboat of 69 tons was built in 1880 by house carpenters.

The state of Georgia does not build extensively. In 1880 the only new work was 2 steamboats of 243 and 296 tons respectively for river service, built at Wellborn's Mills and Lumber City. At Savannah a few shipwrights find some repair work to do.

Florida builds fishing boats in large numbers on the coast, with an occasional steamboat at Jacksonville. The state has been referred to at length in another chapter.

Along the Gulf coast there is now little ship work east of the Mississippi.

New Orleans has a number of boat-shops, repair shops, a few small yards, and four large repairing establishments with dry-docks. The new vessels of 1880 were 3 schooners, 60 tons; 1 lugger, 7 tons; and 1 steamboat, 149 tons, the steamboat being the largest vessel built in the whole state. An average of 173 men were employed in repairing, doing $222,000 worth of work. New Orleans might be a building port if yellow pine were sanctioned by the insurance companies for frame timber. Seventeen luggers, schooners, and steamboats were built in the state outside of the city in 1880, a total of 290 tons. There were besides numerous sail-boats too small to register on the lakes and bayous, but the yards where the latter are made are modest affairs. Information gathered from various sources shows that a considerable number of excellent carpenters are scattered all over Louisiana who could be collected into large yards and utilized for important work if there were great need for so doing. In order to encourage ship-building, Louisiana has a law on her statute-books, almost forgotten, that any vessel built in the state shall be free from tolls and wharfage dues.

Texas has a little ship-building at Lynchburg, in the Galveston district, and at Indianola and Matagorda. Two schooners of 248 tons each were built at Lynchburg in the census year; and in the whole Galveston district, 5 sloops, 68 tons; 6 schooners, 618 tons; 1 tug, 8 tons; and 2 steamboats, 51 tons. Vessels have to be built for shoal water in this region. They are full on the floor, with not over 4° of dead rise, and are nicely modeled fore and aft. Nearly all the schooners built now in Texas are from 65 to 95 feet on the keel, 20 to 28 feet beam, and from 5½ to 8½ in molded depth. The first question asked by an owner is, "How many tons will she carry on 5 and 7 feet draught of water?" The cargoes are lumber, wood, bricks, sugar, molasses, cotton, and oysters. Most of the vessels built are of from 10 to 20 tons.

ARIZONA.

In Arizona there is as yet no ship-building. The Southern Pacific Railroad Company has a yard, with ways, at Arizona City, on the Colorado river, for the repair of river boats, with ample facilities for construction, and it is thought that steamers and barges will be hereafter required to connect the navigable portions of the river with the railways that cross it when all the plans are perfected.

CALIFORNIA.

The ship-building industry would have sprung up quickly in California after the discovery of gold if there had been any timber available out of which vessels could be made; but the state was destitute of material near the coast, and lumber had to be brought from the eastern states, and so little available wood was there in California that wooden houses had to be gotten out in the East, frame and all, and brought around cape Horn for the people to live in. Up in the mountains there was some timber, but it was too far away. Down to 1865 the vessels used on this coast were nearly all built in the East; but lumber was finally brought from Humboldt bay and the Columbia river, and then ship-building began to be followed in California as a native industry. Carpenters were attracted to the coast at an early day. They came from Maine, Massachusetts, and New York, and built a few vessels here and elsewhere on the coast as experiments; but many of the men went off into other trades, and the majority in California settled down to the profitable business of repairing vessels at San Francisco. The high cost of labor was always a great drawback, and at a time when gold could be washed out of the sand of any mountain stream, and when fortunes were being made every day by lucky prospectors, there was no inducement which would keep mechanics at work at their trade except twice and thrice the pay they could get on the Atlantic coast. Wages have always been $4, $5, and $6 a day on the Pacific coast, as compared with $2 and $2 50 in the East, and this has always been a drawback to the industry. The shipwrights who came from the East comprised many men of talent and experience, who were both good mechanics and smart managers; but labor has been so high that for the higher class of vessels, such as steamboats, it has been almost impossible to build in competition with eastern men. A number of the California vessels have been set up in the East, knocked down, shipped to San Francisco, and then completed, while others have been built and sailed around cape Horn to the coast; in fact, as before stated, Pacific coast vessels were mainly of eastern build down to 1865, and the majority of them have been since. Within the last fifteen years, however, a large number of small vessels have been built on the Pacific coast.

The timber of the Pacific coast is the yellow fir, which grows in dense forests all the way from northern California to the boundary of British Columbia and beyond it for some distance, and covers the face of the whole country, except the Willamette valley, as far inland as the Cascade mountains. White cedar, sugar pine, and other useful varieties of wood are scattered through the forests, while south of the fir belt there stands a dense growth of redwood, with here and there on the banks of streams a light growth of white laurel, a low, crooked tree, suitable for stem and stern posts, for which it is popularly used. The early vessels of the coast were necessarily built of fir, there being no other suitable material. On the lowlands in various parts of California there is some live oak, but it is of poor quality. Twenty years of modest experiment and some tests at the Mare Island navy-yard showed that fir was a good timber, as it proved tough, strong, and durable, and was lighter than oak. The balsam with which it was impregnated preserved iron bolts from corrosion. It had one peculiarity, which especially endeared it to the ship-builder's heart. The trees grew from 150 to 300 feet in height, good commercial trees being an average of 200 feet high. Keel and keelson pieces and plank could be obtained of any length, and a vessel could be built with a far less number of butts and joints than in any other part of the United States. The immense supply made the timber cheap, which was another valuable point, and as soon as durability and strength were proved lumber schooners, steamboats, river barges, and grain ships were built with great success. Vessels were entirely built of fir except the stem, stern, and rudder posts, which were of laurel, and the cabins, which were of white cedar and redwood. The industry has now become a flourishing one, with every prospect of rapid development.

At San Francisco there are three yards devoted to new work. The Dickie Brothers have built 7 steamers for the trade of the Sandwich Islands, 3 government vessels, a large propeller of 2,000 tons for the trade to Mexico, and lumber schooners and barkentines to complete a total of 20. The propeller was launched in 1882, and had a flat floor with about 4° dead rise, straight sides, and a quick bilge, with a long sharp bow and good run, being, in fact, of the most approved propeller model. She was built of fir throughout, except the stem and stern posts, which were of oak and laurel, and the cabins, which were of white cedar finished with fine woods, was 288 feet long over all, 35 feet beam, and 28 feet in depth from the spar-deck, and was a three-deck vessel. Sticks of 76, 106, and 108 feet composed the keel, and the keelson was in length from 113 to 117 feet. The planking was from 40 to 100 feet in length. The fir for this vessel cost from $20 to $32 a thousand in San Francisco, according to length, but the average cost was not over $25. When visited, the yard was preparing to build a barkentine 165 feet long,

38 feet beam, and 14 feet hold, which was to carry 750,000 feet of lumber, and it was intended to complete her for $75 per register ton. This yard had a band-saw for getting out the frames, derricks for hoisting, bolt-cutters, and a complete equipment generally. For the large Mexican steamer they were able to saw out five frames a day with the labor of two men, but nine frames a day was the average for a barkentine. The members of this firm are of Scotch descent, and back to their great grandfather have all been in the business. One result of this long experience was the perfection of a set of books, in which the accounts of the yard were kept in a way seldom seen in the United States except in the iron-ship yards of the East and a few steamboat yards on the Ohio. Every detail of the labor and materials of their ships is classified, the labor in some cases being divided into thirty-three branches, and the utility of this system is found in close bidding for work, especially repair work, for the books show what it costs to do everything required on a ship, even to taking off and putting on a single streak of planking. Mr. Turner began in 1868, and had built 56 vessels, aggregating 5,115 tons, up to 1882. Of this number 44 were yachts and brick and lumber schooners; the others were brigs, barkentines, propellers, and sloops. Among his schooners were several fleet and famous yachts, but his largest vessels were a barkentine of 395 tons and a brig of 348 tons. He discarded the old plan of the broadest beam at two-fifths the length from the bow, made his models long and sharp forward and full aft, giving the stem more of a rake than is usual in the East, and by giving the masts a good rake and bringing the anchors, chains, and weights generally farther aft he produced a class of stiff, fast vessels which have won popularity on the coast and have been widely imitated. In several of his vessels he has put in the masts in one piece from heel to truck; the lower mast and topmast are in one stick, a top being added above the lower sails for convenience. Sticks of 106 and 108 feet have been used by him several times, but longer ones might be employed, for they are easily obtained. He has also introduced the Bermudan sail for the spanker of brigs and the mainsail of two-masted schooners. The boom is long, but at the head the sail tapers to a point, as in the Chesapeake bay boats. The topsail in such cases is a long stretch of canvas, passing down by the head of the mainsail and spread by a sheet running down to the outer end of the boom. This rig has been found useful in squalls, and as the Pacific ocean is one of sudden and violent winds it is there that the rig has been found of value. Turner's yard has a full equipment of modern machinery. At another yard in San Francisco yachts and small vessels are built.

There are a large number of firms of shipwrights, sailmakers, riggers, and boat-builders in San Francisco who do work for the whalers, grain and lumber vessels, and steamers which frequent the port. There are two floating dry-docks and one large fixed dry-dock, the latter intended for the Pacific Mail and other heavy steamers. The fixed dock was built at Hunter's point, up the bay a short distance, by a company organized in 1867, and is 421 feet long on the keel-blocks, 120 feet wide on top, and 60 feet in the clear on the bottom, 32 feet deep, with 22 feet of water on the miter-sill. It is quarried out of the serpentine rock, the sides being made of Puget sound fir, in beams 10 inches square, so arranged as to form a series of steps, and secured with 1½-inch bolts of California manufacture, sulphured into the rock. The keel-blocks are of laurel from Russian river. The gate is a caisson of Oregon fir, calked, coppered, and fastened with treenails and composition bolts and spikes, and is 92 feet long, 20 feet beam, 68 feet keel, and 24 feet hold. A double steam-engine, with pumps, is placed within the caisson. The two engines to pump out the dock, with cylinders 22 by 48 inches, are run on high pressure, and are supplied from 4 tubular boilers, each 16 feet long and 54 inches in diameter. Each pump lifts 30,000 gallons a minute. This dock cost $675,000, and is an important element in the shipping resources of the port. The floating-docks are of different sizes. One is 80 feet wide by 210 feet long, and takes out sailing vessels and steamboats; the other is for tugs and small craft. Repair work of more than $600,000 in value is done at these docks and at the wharves and sail-lofts of the city every year.

At Oakland, across the bay, there are two large yards owned by the Southern Pacific railroad and the ferry companies. Two wooden side-wheel steamboats were put together there in the census year, the materials having been gotten out in the East and shipped to California. The work at these yards, each of which has marine railways, is mainly in repairing the steamboats of the companies.

At various places on the bay of San Francisco and up the Sacramento river there is some building of vessels. Flat-boats and stern-wheel steamboats are required on the river, and short scow-schooners are required for the brick, wood, and hay trades of the city. There are few regular yards, the work being done by carpenters, who are hired to do the job, or by amateurs. Scow-schooners are about 50 feet long, 18 feet broad, and 5 feet deep, and on deck are about 9 feet broad at the ends, with the bow and stern raking considerably from the flat of the floor.

Humboldt bay ranks second in importance on the Pacific coast for ship-building, and is the center of the redwood lumber region. The bay is thronged with lumber schooners engaged in that trade to San Francisco, and excellent facilities exist for the building of vessels. In the years 1874, 1875, and 1876 the bay produced 31 schooners, registering 4,059 tons, but latterly the vessels built at Humboldt have been schooners of 250 and 300 tons register, which are smart and handsome, and are noted for their speed and good qualities. The yards are in close proximity to the saw-mills, and get their timber for $10 and $12 per thousand.

The general custom in building vessels on this coast, so far as payments are concerned, is that seldom anything is paid when the keel is laid. Sometimes the builder receives a small amount when the contract is signed, but the

SHIP-BUILDING ON THE OCEAN COASTS.

payments are usually divided into four parts; one quarter when the frames are all up, another when the vessel is ceiled and the deck-frame is in, another when it is planked and the decks are laid, and the last quarter when it is complete for sea, with the exception of provisions. Others only contract for hull, spars, and iron work, the owner furnishing the outfit. When a builder starts a vessel and has little money, the owner supplying him with materials and money, his claim is good after the vessel is launched.

OREGON.

Few sailing vessels are built in Oregon. There is an abundance of timber, but as the population of the state lives in the valleys of the rivers the production of the ship-yards is almost entirely in the line of vessels for river transportation. A small schooner was built in 1845 at Astoria, near the mouth of the Columbia river, by traders for their own imperative needs, and it is believed that this was the pioneer vessel of the Pacific coast. A few other small schooners have been built from time to time on the rivers, but the production has not been numerous. As it belongs properly to the chapter on steam vessels to describe the industry in this state, reference is made to that chapter.

At Coos bay, Oregon, on the sea-coast, one, two, or three schooners, ranging from 200 to 500 tons register, have been built annually for 20 years for the lumber trade. The yards are near the saw-mills. These schooners are flat, one-decked vessels, with long bows, handsome square sterns, and broad beam, and are excellent sea boats. The schooner Isabel, of 185 tons, was 103 feet in register length, 29 feet beam, and $9\frac{1}{2}$ feet depth of hold; the George C. Perkins, of 389 tons, 142 feet long, $33\frac{1}{2}$ feet beam, and $11\frac{3}{8}$ feet hold; the barkentine Klikitat, of 493 tons, one-decker, 163 feet long, 39 feet beam, and $12\frac{1}{2}$ feet hold; the schooner Trustee, of 281 tons, $133\frac{1}{2}$ feet long, $35\frac{1}{2}$ feet beam, and $9\frac{1}{2}$ feet hold; and these are the average sizes of vessels in the lumber trade of that bay. It was difficult to learn the cost of these schooners accurately, but they probably cost \$70 per register ton. Wages have been \$3 50 and \$4 a day, and fir costs not to exceed \$12 per thousand feet. A few large vessels have been built on the bay. The Western Shore was constructed there for a San Francisco firm, and it is said that this ship made the fastest three consecutive runs to Liverpool on record. Her best time was 97 days from the Columbia river to Liverpool.

WASHINGTON TERRITORY.

There are 11 ship-yards in Washington territory, all of them on Puget sound and its branches. Small sloops and schooners were built at various places more than 25 years ago. The names of some of the first of any size are:

		Tons.
1859.	Schooner General Harney, built at Whatcom	60
1863.	Steamboat J. B. Libby, built at Utsaladdy	119
1865.	Steamboat Colfax, built at Seabeck	83
1867.	Schooner Alaska, built at Port Townsend	139
	Schooner Cora, built at Port Orchard	155
	Steamer Chehalis, built at Turn Water	88
	Bark North West, built at Port Madison	515
1868.	Bark Tidal Wave, built at Port Madison	603
	Schooner Clara Light, built at Steilacoom	179
	Barkentine Grace Roberts, built at Port Orchard	269
1869.	Schooner Alice Haake, built at Port Blakeley	253
	Propeller S. L. Mastick, built at Port Discovery	194
	Bark Forest Queen, built at Port Ludlow	511
	Steamer Alida, built at Seattle	114
1870.	Steamer Favorite, built at Utsaladdy	257
	Steamer Etta White, built at Freeport	97
1871.	Steamer Zephyr, built at Seattle	161
	Ship Wild Wood, built at Port Madison	1,099
1872.	Steamer Blakeley, built at Port Blakeley	176
	Schooner Serena Thayer, built at Port Blakeley	206
1873.	Steamer Empire, built at Port Madison	732
	Barkentine Modoc, built at Utsaladdy	452
	Schooner Z. B. Haywood, built at Port Ludlow by Hall Brothers, their first on Puget sound.	

Since 1873 there has been a regular building business at Port Ludlow, Port Madison, Port Blakeley, Seabeck, and Seattle. The largest vessel was the ship Olympus, of 1,110 tons, built at Seabeck in 1880.

The vessels of Puget sound have been mainly schooners and barkentines for the exportation of lumber to the lower coast, the Sandwich Islands, and Australia, and steamboats (stern-wheelers) for the local trade and passenger traffic of the Sound and the rivers flowing into it. A few large sailing vessels, not exceeding half a dozen in number, have been built for the grain trade to Liverpool. All the tonnage of the Sound has been built from yellow-fir timber, with pine and cedar for the cabins and laurel and white oak for the stem and stern posts.

The leading and most profitable industry of Puget sound is lumbering. Fir forests completely cover the face of the land to the water's edge, and the view from the steamboats is an unbroken wilderness of dark-green trees as far as the eye can reach, with towering snow-clad mountains rising here and there from its surface. There are 15 or 20 saw-mills at different points from Port Discovery to Tacoma and Olympia at the head of the Sound, and lumber camps have been established near them, often within a stone's-throw of the water's edge. The ship-yards have all been established in the saw-mill towns, and as near as practicable to the mills. At Port Blakeley a lightly built railroad track has been made from the mill to the yard, to carry up what lumber is required. The nearness to the mills enables a builder to order the timber as fast as he needs and to save the cost of transportation.

Port Townsend is a small place on the edge of a bay near the entrance to the Sound. There has been some building and a good deal of trade here. All the coasting propellers from San Francisco call at this point, and extensive wharves have been built for their accommodation. All back of the town are fir forests, and the shore is lined with vast quantities of fir drift-wood. The only vessel building in 1881 was a small propeller, which a carpenter was making largely out of stuff he had picked up on the beach. There was no saw-mill here.

On Discovery bay, back of the town a few miles, is located a large saw-mill, at which a few vessels have been built. This beautiful bay is 10 miles long, the water deep and clear as crystal, and the shores are covered with dense woods. The bay is well fitted for ship-building. Two schooners of 475 tons, a propeller of 194 tons, and a barkentine of 450 tons have been built close by the saw-mill. It was stated here that fir is as good as hackmatack for its tenacious grip on an iron bolt and freedom from corrosive acids, but in spiking on the harpings and rib-bands to hold the frames in position builders have to use iron washers under the head of the spikes, otherwise it would be impossible to get the harpings off. The mill sells ship timber, taking the vessel right through, long and short together, for $12 a thousand; the frame stuff costs only $10 a thousand. The woods hereabout are full of gigantic white cedar trees, an excellent material for cabins and houses. Laurel trees were noticed growing on the banks of the bay often two feet in diameter, and all gnarled and crooked.

Port Ludlow has been a building town for 20 years. The village has the largest saw-mill on the Sound, and the only one that can cut a log which is 8 feet in diameter. It was idle in 1881, owing to the non-arrival of certain expected machinery, but a barkentine was being built then with lumber towed up from Port Gamble. The principal firm of builders in the territory established themselves here in 1873 and built a schooner or barkentine nearly every year down to 1880, when they moved to Port Blakeley, opposite Seattle. A few years ago labor could be had for $2 50 and $3 a day; now the men are paid $3 a day, and are supplied with cabins to live in and with food at a cook-house run by a Chinaman. Their pay thus amounts to $4 a day. A barkentine 160 feet long, 38 feet beam, and 14 feet hold, built when wages were low, cost $34,500; the same vessel would now cost $38,500. The saw-mill here supplies sawed timber for ship-building for $12, taking the ship right through. The ordinary pieces for frames and planking are sold for $10 a thousand; finishing lumber for $20 a thousand; but the price is sometimes $12 and $22 a thousand, respectively.

The barkentine building at Port Ludlow was 172 feet long on water and 182 feet on deck, molded; $39\frac{1}{2}$ feet beam molded, and $21\frac{1}{4}$ feet in molded depth amidships—a broad and full vessel, calculated to have great stability, and to carry 800,000 feet of fir, 350,000 feet of it on deck. Her scantling will show the best results of experience with the yellow fir. Keel, 166 feet long, in two lengths, one of them of 112 feet, the keel in two depths; total size, 16 by 30 inches; shoe, 8 inches. Frames, double, 22 by $15\frac{1}{4}$ inches, molded 12 inches at the bilge and $7\frac{1}{4}$ inches at the gunwale. Double floors amidships; room and space, 28 inches. Keelson, 16 by 56 inches; sister keelsons, 16 by 16 inches, with pieces 112 feet long in the keelsons. Ceiling, on the floor, 4 inches thick, 16 inches wide; 10 feet on the bilge, 10 inches thick; clamps, 8 inches. Planking of bottom, 4 inches, 16 inches wide; garboards, 7, 6, and 5 inches; wales, 5 inches thick, tapering to 4 inches at the hooding ends, and $7\frac{1}{2}$ inches wide. Beams, 14 by 16 inches, spaced 4 feet, with one lodging knee and a heavy hanging knee at each beam end. Water-way, 12 by 20 inches; plank-sheer and rail, each 6 by 18 inches; decking, 4 by 4 inches. Stanchions to beams, 10 by 16 inches, strapped to the beams and keelson with 3 by $\frac{1}{2}$-inch iron. Composition bolts were used under water, galvanized iron above. The vessel was square-fastened with 1 bolt and 3 locust treenails in every frame, as many of the latter as possible going clear through, and wedged. The whole vessel was of yellow fir, including the stem. The dead-eyes of the rigging were put on with an iron key, which could be quickly knocked out to clear away the shrouds, for convenience in loading and discharging heavy lumber. Amidship there were planted four short masts, or shifting posts, heeling on the keelson and projecting 12 feet above the deck, to keep the deck load of lumber from moving about in a seaway, and iron rods were to be carried over the top of the lumber from the posts to temporary stanchions lashed to the bulwarks of the vessel. It took 400,000 feet of lumber to build this barkentine, but her cost was not known when the yard was visited. The lumber for this vessel cost not to exceed $10 per thousand feet. Wages were equivalent to $4 a day.

Port Gamble is a large saw-mill town at the entrance to Hood's canal. A fleet of from 5 to 10 schooners, barkentines, and barks are constantly loading there with lumber, and the proprietors of the mill own most of them. Being Maine men by birth, their vessels have mostly been ordered from the Maine yards, but they are now beginning to build on Puget sound.

Port Madison built no vessels in the census year. The Wild Wood, a bark built there in 1871, was opened in 1882, and was found as sound and bright as when new.

SHIP-BUILDING ON THE OCEAN COASTS.

Seabeck, a saw-mill town on Hood's canal, is in the heart of a dense fir forest, and faces a magnificent range of snow-clad mountains, which lie across the country many miles away. The yard is a stone's-throw from the mill. The builder had built on Puget sound up to 1881 the bark Forest Queen, of 511 tons, at Port Ludlow, which carries 650,000 feet of lumber; the two-masted lumber schooner Leads; the bark Cassandra Adams, of 1,127 tons, now in the grain trade, which cost $72,000; the tug Holyoke; the ship Olympus, of 1,110 tons, at a cost of $80,000; and the barkentines Mary Winkle and Retriever. The Retriever was 161 feet long to the after-side of the stern post, 37 feet beam, and $13\frac{1}{2}$ feet depth of hold, and was of about 600 tons register. She had lumber ports in her bow and stern. Her greatest breadth was amidships. The bow was sharp, with hollow water-lines, and was cut away at the fore foot, as in all lumber vessels.

The Cassandra Adams is a two-decker, and carries 1,950 or 2,000 net tons of wheat as her cargo. She has made the trip from San Francisco to Liverpool in 114 days (good fair time), and has brought 1,500 gross tons of coal from England home in 110 days. Her register dimensions are: Length, $196\frac{1}{2}$ feet; breadth, $40\frac{1}{2}$ feet; depth of hold, 22 feet; total length from chock to taffrail, $210\frac{1}{2}$ feet; keel, 184 feet. The frames, double, are 24 by 18 inches over the keel, molded 10 inches at the lower deck and $7\frac{1}{2}$ at the upper deck; room and space, 30 inches; lower-deck beams, 15 by 18 inches; upper-deck beams, 12 by 18 inches, spaced $6\frac{1}{2}$ feet; ceiling for 13 feet on the bilge, 14 inches, tapering to 8 inches above; outer planking, 5 inches; decking, 4 inches. The vessel was over-sparred originally, the fore and main yards being 90 feet long and the lower topsail yards 80 feet; but she was altered after a few voyages, the long lower yards being removed and the 80-foot yards lowered to take their places. Other alterations were made to reduce the weight of the top gear. Her dead rise was about 13°.

The Olympus was the largest single-decked ship in the world. She was built for the lumber trade from Puget sound, and her ordinary cargo was 1,250,000 feet of fir; but on one trip she carried 1,450,000 feet, of which 700,000 feet was on deck. In her first 11 months this ship earned $40,000 in freights, which paid half her cost. She was burned at sea north of cape Flattery, a fire having started in some bales of hay in the hold, into which a spark had been accidentally dropped. The Olympus was built full, with about 28 inches dead rise, and over 1,400,000 feet of lumber and 65 tons of fastening were consumed in her construction. The stem raked considerably, as in all Pacific coast vessels. Her dimensions and scantling were: Keel, 210 feet long; $223\frac{1}{2}$ feet long on deck; beam, $43\frac{1}{2}$ feet; hold, $17\frac{1}{2}$ feet. Keel, 20 by 48 inches. Frames, double, 24 by 19 inches over the keel, molded 9 inches at the deck; room and space, 30 inches; keelson, 20 by 81 inches; sister keelsons, 20 by 40 inches; a strake next to them, 9 by 16 inches. The long keelson bolts were over 11 feet long, and were of $1\frac{1}{2}$-inch iron, a 250-pound hammer being used to drive them, pile-driver fashion. Ceiling on the floor, 5 inches; on bilge and up to the deck, 16 inches, the thick strakes edge-bolted in every space with $1\frac{1}{2}$-inch iron; garboards, 12 inches; bottom plank, 5 inches; from bilge to deck, 6 inches, plank square-fastened with through treenails; beams, 18 by 22 inches, spaced about $7\frac{1}{4}$ feet; 8-inch lodging knees, fir, and two 10- and 11-inch hanging knees at each beam end, the knees spreading diagonally below the beam; hanging knees molded 26 inches in the throat, with arms of 5 and 9 feet; water-way, 3 strakes of 12 by 14 inches; plank-sheer and main rail, 8 by 22 inches; decking, 4 by 4 inches; stanchions of bulwark, 8 by 12 inches; beam stanchions, 12 by 22 inches, strapped to beam and kneed to keelson, and 4 Sampson or shifting posts, projecting 13 feet above the deck. The yards on the fore and main masts were 80, 72, 63, 50, 41, and 34 feet, while those on the mizzen-mast were 62, 57, $50\frac{1}{2}$, $40\frac{1}{2}$, 34, and 30 feet, and the main rigging was susceptible of being cast loose when loading and discharging cargo. The ship spread about 5,200 yards of canvas, being sparred in accordance with long experience in the coasting trade of the Pacific. She carried a donkey-engine in a deck-house forward.

The yard at Seabeck has a jig-saw and works out all the frames by steam-power. The town presents great advantages for ship-building, as the water of Hood's canal, which is a broad lagoon, is deep and free from rocks, and never freezes in the winter time. Timber covers the whole country in almost inexhaustible supply. This territory is rapidly filling up with American, Swedish, and German labor, and there is no lack of good mechanics, and with a thoroughly systematic way of doing business large vessels ought to be built at Seabeck for $45 a ton.

At Port Blakeley there is one yard. The Halls built a few large ships in their earlier years at Cohasset, Massachusetts; but when the clipper era began they went to Boston and engaged in the general ship work of that port. In 1873 one of them came to Port Ludlow, whither the others followed him the next year, and in 1880 they came to Port Blakeley. Up to 1881 they had built a pilot-boat of 59 tons, a yacht of 52 tons, 15 lumber schooners, 3,348 tons; 8 Sandwich Island schooners, 853 tons; 4 barkentines, 1,578 tons; and 2 steamers, 475 tons; a total of 31 vessels and 6,365 tons. The average cost of these vessels has been about $70 per register ton, but in consequence of good management and the use of machinery this cost is being steadily reduced, and it is now not in excess of the cost of vessels of similar sizes on the Atlantic coast. The owners have fitted up the Port Blakeley yard at considerable expense, and have sent a delegate to Bath, Maine, to report on the labor-saving appliances there employed and to purchase steam saws, planers, and a full equipment for their yard. Their schooners are fast, handsome, and popular, and have long, sharp bows, with slightly hollow lines, the top sides having a faint curve home, and at the stern round in sharply over the arch-board in a strikingly graceful fashion. There is not a straight line on the surface of the hulls anywhere. Located near a large saw-mill, the Halls have run a light railroad track down to the mill and bring up their lumber on platform cars. For keelson pieces over 90 feet in length they pay $16 a thousand; for less than 90 feet, $11 a thousand; for bed logs for center-board schooners and rough, clear lumber for stanchions, $16; planking clear of heart and knots, $12; deck plank, planed, $22 50; for all the rest of the material in the ship, $11; but the average of the vessel does not exceed $12, and the average length of stuff is 20 feet more than that of eastern yards. In the mold-loft of the yard there are fir battens "for laying down" 90 feet in length.

A barkentine 180 feet in length, 162½ feet on the keel, 38 feet beam, and 15 feet hold was in frame in the winter of 1881. The keel was in two pieces, one of them 126 feet long and 26 by 15 inches wide, with a 6-inch shoe in addition; scarfs 15 feet. The frames were 22 by 16 inches, spaced 31 inches; filling pieces between the frames, 6 feet long, to receive the chain-plate bolts; keelson, 16 by 40 inches; sister keelsons, 14 by 14; beams, 13 by 15 inches, spaced 3 feet; decking, 4 inches; stern-post, 26 by 28 inches; stanchions, 8 by 15 inches, strapped to beams and keelson; stem, fir, with root at the heel; gripe piece, laurel. The planking was 5 inches thick. The rudder-post projects below the planking to avoid leaks—a practice now general on the coast.

At Seattle there are two small marine railways, besides one other small yard, and there are two or three persons in the town other than the owners of the above property who occasionally build small schooners and steamboats. The first steam mill on the Sound was set up at Seattle in 1853, and although it has been in operation for 30 years the only observable impression that has been made on the dense fir forests is the clearing of a space for the town to stand on. The town is a large collection of houses, spreading all over the side of a hill which rises at the head of a deep bay, and stumps of trees are scattered all through. The bay is the only considerable harbor on the Sound with an abundance of good anchorage ground for vessels. There are valuable deposits of coal a few miles inland which are being mined, and a large number of coal ships visit the wharves of the town every year. Four iron steam colliers have been recently built in Pennsylvania to carry this coal from Seattle to San Francisco. The owner of the marine railway has been in Seattle for 20 years, and has built many small vessels, schooners, and stern-wheel steamboats. Most of the stern-wheel boats of the Sound have been made on this bay. In 1881 the cost of fir, delivered in the ship-yards, was $10 a thousand feet for frame timber, $12 for timber over 45 feet in length, and $15 for pieces from 60 to 100 feet in length. The decking and finishing lumber cost $20 a thousand; for a 500-ton vessel the material could be bought for from $12 to $15 a thousand right through. Builders had noticed a difference in the lasting qualities of fir cut in winter and that cut in summer, as some of the early boats whose frames were hewed out in the woods in winter in the eastern fashion proved lasting and serviceable, while others built from timber taken from the saw-mill without regard to the season of cutting decayed rapidly. Fir vessels have been known to last from 27 to 35 years. There was a great deal of talk all along the Sound about this, and most of the builders intend to select their timber hereafter from winter-cut trees. The vessels built at Seattle in the census year were: 2 stern-wheel steamboats, 321 tons, 1 propeller and 1 side-wheel boat, 473 tons. The side-wheeler was for the navigation of the open Sound, for which stern-wheel boats are not suited in the winter time, as the wind catches in their high sterns and makes them hard to steer. They are therefore used for the rivers of the territory. Seattle has the only repairing business of the territory, and wages are $3 75 and $4 a day.

At Tacoma, New Dungeness, Utsaladdy, and a few other places on the Sound small vessels and boats were built in the census year for local use. When William H. Seward visited these towns he said: "Sooner or later the world's ship-yard will be located here."

The cost per ton of new vessels on Puget sound closely approximates that of the East, and, except for the cost of labor, the cost on Puget sound would be less than in any other part of the United States. The immense and growing grain trade of the Pacific coast seems to guarantee a cargo to a ship immediately after launching, and when the Northern Pacific railroad has completed its lines through to Tacoma and Seattle from the wheat-fields of Oregon and Washington the new ship can load before leaving the Sound. It was a Bath-built ship, the Dakota, which in 1881 carried away from Tacoma the first cargo of grain. The ships for this trade were built in a state 3,000 miles away, which is utterly destitute of local ship-building timber and pays an average of $35 a thousand feet for her timber, when on Puget sound timber can be bought for $12 a thousand feet—a saving of from $20,000 to $25,000 on a big ship. Puget sound has great advantage also in the length of the timber it can furnish.

ALASKA.

Portions of Alaska have plenty of timber. Its production is chiefly in the way of Indian canoes, of which there are estimated to be 3,000 in the territory, each made from a single spruce or cedar log and owned by natives. Some of the canoes will hold 60 persons. The records of the custom-house at Sitka show only the following vessels:

Date of papers.	Vessel.	Tonnage.
April 13, 1880	Schooner Lesnoy	9
September 7, 1880	Schooner Mary	11½
September 14, 1880	Schooner Mary Caton	8
September 25, 1880	Schooner F. F. Feeney	9
March 18, 1881	Scow-schooner L. L. Martin	32½
May 23, 1881	Schooner Onward	6½
June 11, 1881	Schooner Flying Scud	26

These, with the exception of the scow-schooner L. L. Martin, were all built at Kadiak and Oonalashka. In January, 1882, there were five small schooners of about 20 tons each constructing at Kadiak island. The yellow cedar of Alaska is admirably adapted to ship-building purposes, and in a report to the Treasury Department by Collector William Gouverneur Morris, dated November 25, 1878, this subject was alluded to.

NORTHERN LAKES.

The facts about the building of sailing vessels on the northern lakes are introduced in this chapter because the vessels built are of large size and resemble in character the sailing tonnage of the ocean coasts.

The northern lakes seem to have invited navigation as early as 1679, and it is supposed that the little 60-ton schooner Griffin, built on the Niagara river in that year for La Salle, the Catholic missionary, was the first vessel on the lakes. This schooner, carrying La Salle, and manned by a crew of six persons, set sail in August for Mackinaw, where she arrived safely, and was there loaded with furs for a return voyage, but was never heard from after her departure. In accordance with the fashion of the times, this schooner carried a square sail on the forward mast. Sloops and small schooners were occasionally seen on lakes Erie, Huron, and Michigan during the years of exploration and settlement of the country, but it was not until after the revolutionary war that any great number were constructed. It is believed that the first vessel on lake Ontario larger than an Indian batteau was the one built at Sodus Bay, New York, in 1789. During the 20 years preceding the war of 1812 a flourishing commerce sprang up between the principal towns and ports on the lakes, and quite a number of sloops and small schooners were required for the transportation of mails, freight, and passengers. The ship-building industry, however, had not reached any special development when that war broke out; and it will be remembered (as elsewhere stated) that in order to construct the vessels required for public defense it was necessary to bring master builders and carpenters from the city of New York. The first brig on the lakes is believed to have been the Union, of 96 tons, built in 1814.

It is hardly necessary to relate in detail the story of the growth of the merchant marine of the lakes, as in its general features it is the same as that of the shipping of the ocean coasts. As the country filled with people vessels increased in number and size; they were often built too large for the times, and there were several periods of reaction and depression. Builders originally followed sea-coast ideas, but as the special requirements of the lake trade became apparent they made experiments of their own with models and rigs, and finally departed entirely from the traditions of the sea-coast and developed a class of tonnage especially suited to the lakes and having its own peculiar character.

The first ship on the lakes was the Julia Palmer, of about 300 tons, built at Buffalo in 1836. Several other ships and a number of barks were employed after that date in trading to the upper lakes, but the experience of a few years demonstrated the entire unsuitability of the square rig for these waters.

The first clipper schooner was the Challenge, which was built at Manitowoc, Wisconsin, in 1851, by William W. Bates. She was 80 feet long on the load-line, 22 feet wide on the main beam, and $6\frac{1}{2}$ feet deep in the hold, and differed from the ordinary type of lake vessels in having greater proportionate breadth, lighter draught, a longer and sharper bow, and greater lifting power at the bow. The dead-flat section was located amidships. She carried a center-board, and a red stripe was painted on her side to show the light-draught water-line. During the construction of this little vessel a great controversy raged in the shipping circles of the lakes in regard to the innovation on established models. The Challenge reimbursed her owners in two years, and the Clipper City was then built in 1853 by the same constructor for the same owners. When the Clipper City was ready for sea there was put into her cabin, in a frame, a scale of displacement, showing her weight at any depth of immersion, the object being to supply the means for a close estimate of the tally of a lumber cargo. This scale of displacement was drawn by a man who was afterward governor of Wisconsin. These two schooners introduced the clipper idea.

It is reported that the first vessel on the lakes to have her load-line marked on her sides was the R. B. Hayes, built at Gibraltar, Michigan, by Linn & Craig. The rules for free-board and load-line on the lakes are to be found in the book of rules for construction of lake vessels, prepared for E. P. Dorr, of Buffalo, in 1876, free-board being slightly less than in deep-sea craft.

The clipper idea is suited for schooners on the lakes that draw less than 10 feet of water, as their greater proportionate breadth would give them a lower percentage of shell to gross displacement and help their capacity and burden. Nevertheless, it must be said that the ideas of 40 years ago govern the vast majority of owners and builders on the lakes, and the preference is for the full model. The big vessels are limited to a draught of 14 or 15 feet, there being only that depth of water over the reef known as the Lime-Kiln Crossing, in the short river leading from lake Huron into lake Erie. The larger sailing craft are all constructed with that fact in view, and, in consequence, are either perfectly flat on the floor or have not to exceed 18 inches of dead rise. The midship section is a rectangle with the lower corners rounded, the curves of the bilge amidship being swept in with a radius not to exceed 18 inches. With reference to passing through the Welland canal, and also to the navigation of the narrow channels of the rivers that constitute so many of the harbors of lake cities, the beam of sailing vessels is kept narrow, while the bows are full and the stem is perpendicular, or nearly so. The lake model, so called, is therefore characterized by great length and fullness, the body of the vessel being nearly straight. The broadest part is rather forward of amidship, and the sterns are square and very broad on deck. The visitor from the Atlantic coast, accustomed to the untrammeled models of deep-sea schooners, is greatly struck by the odd appearance of the lake hulls. Nevertheless, the lakers are admirable vessels, and are exactly adapted to the commerce in which they are employed, being fast, great carriers, cheap, and profitable. No more can be said of any vessels. The difference in dimensions between the lake and ocean models will appear from the following data, showing the approximate register measurements of fair average schooners of various sizes:

300 tons .... { Lake schooner: Length, 146 feet; beam, 26 feet; hold, 12 feet.
{ Ocean schooner: Length, 125 feet; beam, 32 feet; hold, $10\frac{1}{4}$ feet.

650 tons .... { Lake schooner: Length, 186 feet; beam, 34 feet; hold, 14 feet.
{ Ocean schooner: Length, 145 feet; beam, $34\frac{1}{4}$ feet; hold, $16\frac{3}{4}$ feet.

850 tons .... { Lake schooner: Length, 210 feet; beam, 36 feet; hold, 16 feet.
{ Ocean schooner: Length, 175 feet; beam, 40 feet; hold, $17\frac{1}{4}$ feet.

Four-masted schooner...................... { Lakes: Length, 278 feet; beam, 39 feet; hold, $21\frac{1}{4}$ feet.
{ Atlantic coast: Length, 205 feet; beam, 40 feet; hold, 22 feet.

The popular style of vessel on the lakes is the three-masted schooner with a center-board (Fig. 43), carrying at least one large lower yard on the foremast, although frequently having two or three. Its rig presents a very different appearance from that of the schooner of the Atlantic coast, owing to the square sails and the difference in the length of the masts. On Atlantic vessels the masts are usually nearly of the same length, but this is not the case on the lakes. A comparison will be interesting:

MASTS OF ATLANTIC COAST SCHOONERS.

500-ton schooner: Foremast, 89 feet; mainmast, 90 feet; mizzen-mast, 91 feet; all three topmasts, 52 feet.
600-ton schooner: Foremast, 91 feet; mainmast, 92 feet; mizzen-mast, 93 feet; all three topmasts, 56 feet.
750-ton schooner: Foremast, 93 feet; mainmast, 94 feet; mizzen-mast, 95 feet; all three topmasts, 58 feet.

MASTS OF NORTHERN LAKE SCHOONERS.

500-ton schooner: Foremast, 88 feet; fore-topmast, 65 feet; mainmast, 92 feet; main-topmast, 65 feet; mizzen-mast, 80 feet; mizzen topmast, 58 feet.
650-ton schooner: Foremast, 98 feet; fore-topmast, 74 feet; mainmast, 102 feet; main-topmast, 74 feet; mizzen-mast, 86 feet; mizzen-topmast, 57 feet.
850-ton schooner: Foremast, 100 feet; fore-topmast, 80 feet; mainmast, 106 feet; main-topmast, 80 feet; mizzen-mast, 94 feet; mizzen-topmast, 75 feet.

The rake of the masts varies from $\frac{5}{8}$, $\frac{3}{4}$, and 1 inch to the foot, going aft, to $\frac{3}{4}$, 1, and $1\frac{1}{4}$ inch to the foot.

The lake schooners spread so large an area of canvas that the spectacle they present while passing and repassing certain points in the summer time is a beautiful one. At Detroit, for instance, past which city they must nearly all go, and where the panorama of lake commerce is seen to the best advantage, the scene on a fair summer's day is always an interesting and sometimes an exciting one. A curious feature is the practice of collecting from three to six schooners, arranged tandem, in tow of a large freighting propeller or a large tug. The vessels are about 500 fathoms apart, and are each attached by a heavy tow-line of that length to the one ahead of it. Each vessel spreads all the sail it can profitably carry, the tug or propeller puts on every pound of steam, and the tow passes rapidly along to its destination. When out on any of the lakes, if a storm should arise, the tow-lines are all cast off and each vessel takes care of itself.

The shape of the hulls of the lake schooners permits the use of a great deal of straight timber in the frames. The floor timbers, and for a long distance amidship the top timbers also, are nearly straight. It is the practice, therefore, to cut the frames out of heavy plank (or flitch, as it is called), 5, 6, or 7-inch flitch being used, according to the size of the vessel, the spacing of frames being, as a rule, from 20 to 22 inches. The comparative thinness of the timbers rendering injudicious the use of treenails for fastening on the plank, iron bolts and spikes are used instead. The planking is usually square-fastened with two spikes and two iron bolts in each frame, but the practice varies, in some vessels three spikes and one bolt being used, in others four iron bolts. In the larger hulls the ceiling and sometimes the planking is edge-bolted. The main keelson is laid with two tiers of logs only. There is a sister keelson on each side of the main keelson, and the floor out to the bilge is strengthened with a number of floor keelsons, varying in depth from 10 to 16 inches, placed from 2 to $2\frac{1}{2}$ feet from center to center. The flooring of the hold is laid with two thicknesses of light pine or hemlock plank, and in order to save storage room the heavy wooden knees characteristic of ocean vessels are dispensed with, the purpose for which they are introduced being accomplished by employing a strong shelf of white oak, usually 5 inches thick and often 30 inches wide, edge-bolted to the frames and strongly bolted to the beams. This shelf is composed of either two or three streaks of plank, one streak being thicker than the others, the beam end being so grooved as to fit down over the thicker streak and bear firmly on the whole width. White oak is the material used throughout the vessel, except in the beams, which are often of white pine, and in the decking, houses, and spars, which are also of white pine, some of the lighter spars being of spruce. Further reference is made to the details of construction in the chapter on steam vessels; but it is believed that all the main points in which the carpentry of lake vessels differs from that of the sea-coasts are represented in the above data.

SHIP-BUILDING ON THE OCEAN COASTS.   139

The standing rigging of almost all the lake vessels is now of wire, and nearly all carry topmast shrouds. Poop decks are a regular feature, and there is a cabin aft on the poop deck, while a small house abaft the foremast shelters the crew. The vessels have topgallant forecastle decks and patent windlasses. All the fittings of lake vessels are of the most improved character.

Within a few years it has not been uncommon to build four-masted schooners for the lake trade. A handsome one was on the stocks at Huron, Ohio, in the census year. She was 278 feet long on the keel, 39 feet on the main

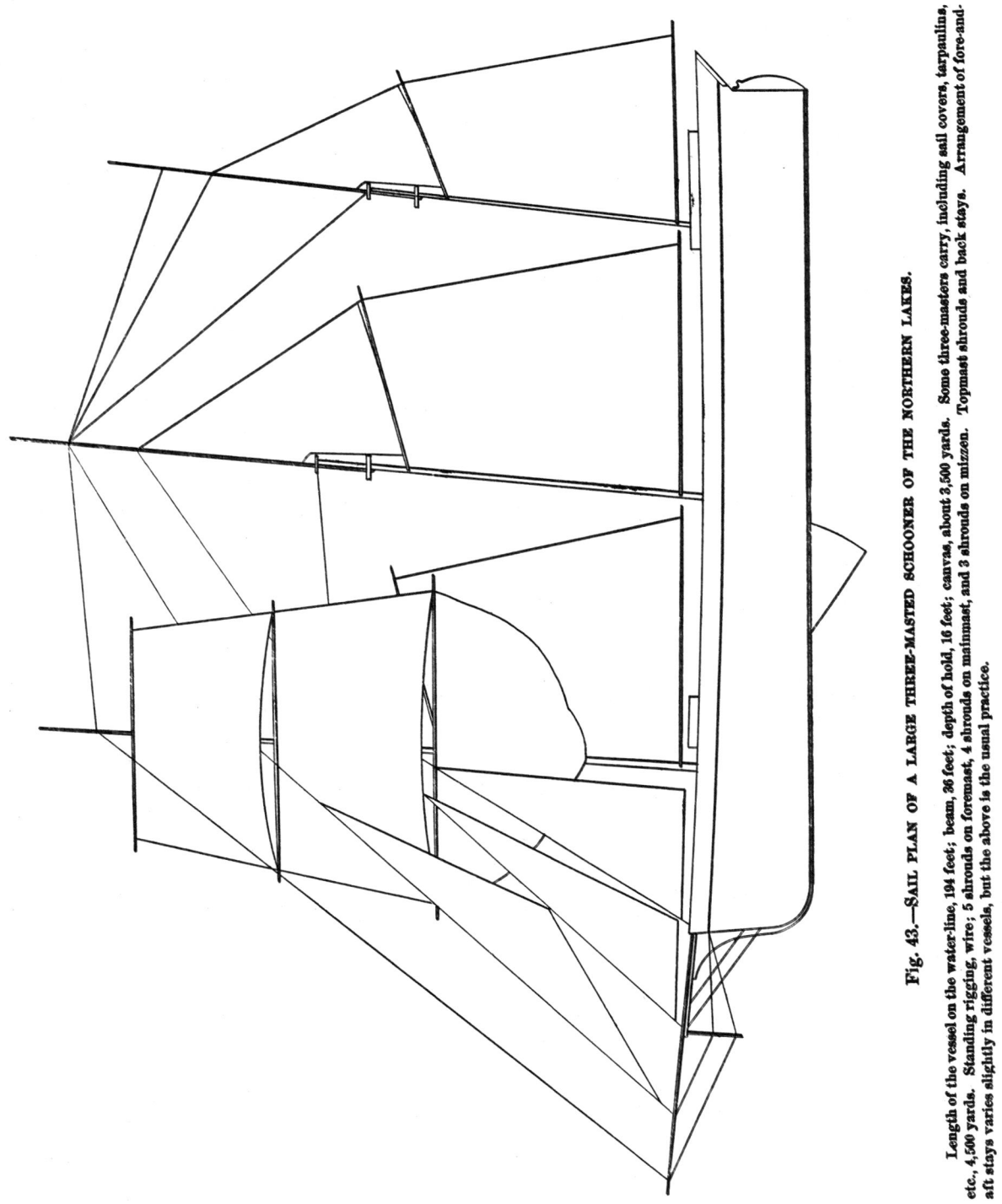

Fig. 43.—SAIL PLAN OF A LARGE THREE-MASTED SCHOONER OF THE NORTHERN LAKES.

Length of the vessel on the water-line, 194 feet; beam, 36 feet; depth of hold, 16 feet; canvas, about 3,500 yards. Some three-masters carry, including sail covers, tarpaulins, etc., 4,500 yards. Standing rigging, wire; 5 shrouds on foremast, 4 shrouds on mainmast, and 3 shrouds on mizzen. Topmast shrouds and back stays. Arrangement of fore-and-aft stays varies slightly in different vessels, but the above is the usual practice.

beam, and 21½ feet deep in the hold, and the overhang of the stern was about 9 feet. The frames were cut from 6-inch flitch; they were triple on the floor and double on the sides of the vessel, and were molded 16 inches over the keel, 15 inches at the bilge, 14 inches just above the turn, and 8 inches at the main rail. Room and space, 22 inches. The main keelson was 16 by 17 inches; the sister keelsons, 16 by 16 inches; the assistant sister keelsons, 14 by 14 inches. There were 7 floor keelsons on each side of the group in the center, the first one on each side sided 10 and molded 14 inches, and all the others sided 8 and molded 14 inches. Spacing, 30 inches from center to center. Flooring of the hold, 2-inch hemlock, two thicknesses; ceiling 8, 9, and 7 inches thick on the bilge, diminishing to 6 inches at the plank-sheer; outside planking, all 5 inches. The ceiling and planking are edge-bolted every 4 feet. There were about 300 tons of iron fastening in this vessel, and its capacity was expected to be from 3,300 to 3,500 tons of cargo dead weight.

One five-master has been built of such dimensions as to make her the largest schooner in the world. This vessel, the David Dows (Fig. 44), was constructed at Toledo, Ohio, and was finished in 1881. She is 275 feet long over all, 260 feet on the keel, 37½ feet on the beam, and 18 feet deep in the hold, and registers 1,419 tons, with a carrying capacity of about 2,500 tons. The frames of this vessel (double) were 14 by 18 inches over the keel, spaced 21 inches; the ceiling 7 and 9 inches on the bilge, 6 inches on the sides, tapering to 5 inches at the plank-sheer, and the planking 4 inches. The hull was strapped on the outside with iron. A middle row of deck beams was introduced, but were not decked. The masts, going aft, were respectively 93, 97, 97, 93, and 88 feet long; the topmasts, 65 feet, except the jigger-topmast, which was 55 feet; bowsprit, 37 feet; jib-boom, 65 feet; yards on the foremast, 75, 65, 55, and 45 feet long; booms, 50, 50, 46, 43, and 36 feet long; gaffs, 40, 40, 40, 38, and 30 feet. The David Dows carried five jibs and gaff topsails, and was a noble-looking vessel.

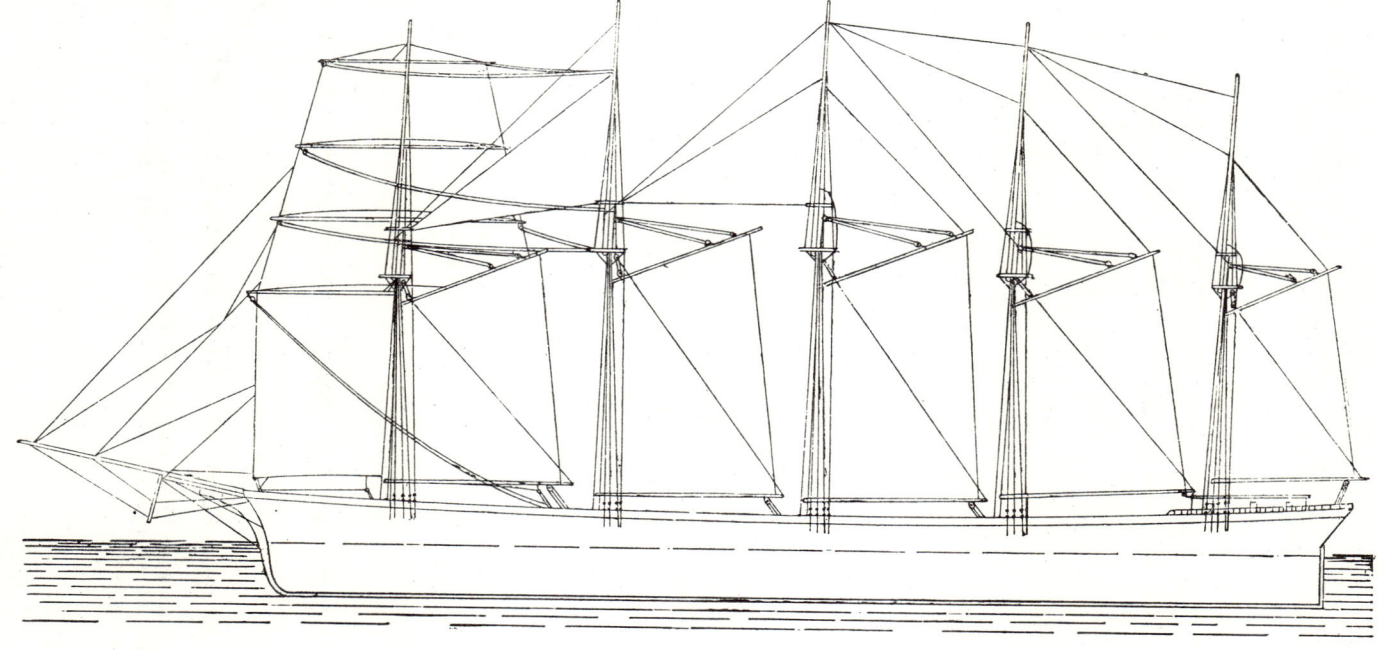

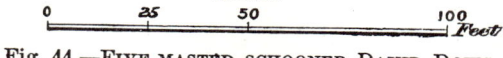

Fig. 44.—FIVE-MASTED SCHOONER DAVID DOWS.
Built at Toledo, Ohio, for the grain trade of the northern lakes.

The lake fleet finds its best employment in transporting the lumber, iron ore, and grain of the West to the lower ports, where the cargoes are transferred to the railroads for dispatch to inland cities or to Atlantic seaports. The vessels carry back large quantities of coal and some miscellaneous merchandise.

There are few places on the lakes where ship-yards are devoted exclusively to the construction of sailing craft. The tendency now is strongly in the direction of steam, and Toledo and Huron, Ohio, were perhaps the only places found in the census year at which propellers were not building. A description of the industry on the lakes can more appropriately be given in the chapter on steam vessels.

GENERAL REMARKS.

In large cities like Boston, New York, Philadelphia, and Baltimore, where the old sailing-packet and clipper-ship business has passed into the control of the foreign steamship lines, the common expression is, "The day of the sailing ship is past; hereafter nothing will do except steam." This is especially the opinion of old houses at New York, which have sold off their big sailing ships one by one. These houses depended almost entirely on the passenger, mail, and fast-freight traffic of the ports at which they were established, the very traffic for which the foreign lines of steamers especially competed. Having seen this traffic taken from them by the steamers, the proprietors of the old packet and clipper lines look upon steam vessels as the only carriers of the future.

On the other hand, there is a different feeling in the country towns, whose ships are built for the general trade, and seldom, if ever, sail in regular lines, but go hither and thither to every part of the world. On the Pacific coast particularly the current opinion is anything but a gloomy one. In many country localities the cost of building is reasonably low. The old shipping houses keep on constructing new sailing ships year after year, and though feeling the competition of steam to some extent, they have, as a rule, operated in trades in which it has not yet been successfully introduced, and have put their vessels into long voyages to California, China, Australia, and the East Indies, or in certain branches of the coasting trade, such as lumber and ice carrying, for which sailing vessels are better adapted than steamers. The causes which have affected the prosperity of ship-owners who do not live in large cities are not so much traceable to the development of steam navigation as to high taxes, unfavorable regulations, excessive port charges, and the unequal tonnage dues which tax a sailing ship as much as a steamer which does five times the business. The country ship-owners, therefore, believe that with favorable national legislation they can employ sailing tonnage profitably and successfully and for the good of the public.

Considering that steam has made such progress in the trade between large ocean ports, it is remarkable that, so far as the country at large is concerned, the bulk of the business is still done by sailing ships. On the 25th of January, 1882 (as shown by the *Maritime Register* of New York, which prints every week a list of all the vessels engaged in the foreign trade of the United States), there were 5,351 vessels actually so engaged that week, of which only 546 were steam vessels, as follows:

Nationality.	Sailing vessels.	Steamers.	Nationality.	Sailing vessels.	Steamers.
Total	4,805	546	Portuguese	21	
			Italian	386	5
American	837	24	Austrian	130	
British	1,974	387	Russian	59	
Norwegian	736		Greek	2	
Swedish	93		Haytian		1
German	355	39	Chilian	5	
Dutch	25	12	Mexican	2	3
Belgian	1	18	Costa Rican	3	1
Danish	18	4	Hawaiian	6	
French	55	20	Miscellaneous	6	
Spanish	91	32			

This is a fair average showing of the respective number of sailers and steamers now in our foreign trade at any one date. By reason of its larger size and its more frequent trips, a steamer is reckoned as equal to five sailing vessels; but even on that basis the sailing tonnage exceeds the steam in our foreign trade.

Looking now at the cargo carried rather than at the vessels, it will be found that the sailing ship still transacts by far the largest part of the foreign commerce of the United States. The statistics on this point are fragmentary, and no complete statement can at present be made, as no government report on this subject has heretofore been prepared; still, the general fact is well known. Inquiries have been made for this report at nearly all the principal custom-houses of the country, and the testimony is uniform on that point. The only exact data which can be given are those of 1880 at the port of New York, this being the one American port at which steam has gained the most upon the sailing vessel. The grain trade of that port in 1880 was as follows:

Nationality.	SAIL VESSELS.		STEAM VESSELS.	
	No. of cargoes.	Bushels.	No. of cargoes.	Bushels.
Total	1,760	62,621,000	1,148	44,117,000
American	29	1,176,000		
British	522	24,644,000	907	36,816,000
German	46	2,072,000	110	2,460,000
Belgian			52	2,308,000
Dutch	8	339,000	23	806,000
Danish	4	63,000	16	426,000
Norwegian	475	13,374,000		
Swedish	32	864,000		
French	24	548,000	19	457,000
Spanish	21	358,000	7	180,000
Portuguese	8	163,000		
Italian	369	12,370,000	14	664,000
Austrian	209	6,276,000		
Russian	12	370,000		
Haytian	1	4,000		

Besides exporting most of the grain from New York, the sailing vessels carry nearly all the petroleum, lumber, and coal and a vast quantity of provisions and general merchandise. Taking the whole business of the port, the sailing fleet does fully half the whole business, and probably more. The same state of facts exists at all other American ports, and on the Pacific coast the export trade is almost wholly in sailing vessels.

For general trading, especially for long voyages, there is every reason to believe that sailing ships will continue to be built, as they can carry a cargo at a lower rate of freight than steamers. A ship of 2,000 tons register, built in Maine, will cost close upon $100,000, carry from 3,000 to 3,200 gross tons of freight, and sail at an average rate of speed of 6 miles per hour, which can be increased to 8 miles by sharpening the bow of the vessel. If a propelling engine were now to be put into the same ship, so as to convert her into a cargo steamer, there would be added to her weight 225 tons of boilers and machinery and 600 tons of coal, and a large proportion of her cargo space would be rendered useless. This would increase her cost from $30,000 to $40,000, and she could carry only 2,200 or 2,500 tons of cargo. If the ship were built with an iron hull, as a steamer ought to be, there would be a further increase to the first cost of $20,000 if she were built in England, and perhaps $30,000 if she were built in America. In either case, whether wooden or iron, her running expenses would greatly exceed those of the sailing vessel, as she must have a large crew. She burns coal continually, interest must be paid on the large investment in her, and in spite of her more frequent trips and ability to live at a smaller margin of profit the steamer could not carry freight at the same low rate as the sailing ship. Both for the owner and for the public at large, therefore, the sailing ship is the more profitable vessel which can be employed.

In the coasting trade, especially in carrying lumber, ice, and some other classes of goods, the schooner is pre-eminently the best carrier. Steamers are expensive, and their draught is too great for the hundred shallow harbors and small places on the southern coasts.

There is as yet little demand for sailing ships in this country of any other material than wood. Three or four vessels have been built of iron, and several more which had been wrecked on our coast have been repaired and put under the American flag; but up to 1880 there has been no progress in the direction of iron sailing tonnage. The reason of this is the high cost of iron. England went into iron sailing tonnage because her forests had become exhausted and timber was so dear that it mattered little, so far as cost was concerned, whether a vessel was built of iron or of wood; and as an iron vessel was more durable, a strong preference grew up for it. In America there has, thus far in our history, been plenty of timber, the cost of which has been moderate, and in spite of the gradual destruction of the Atlantic-coast forests a wooden ship can still be built in this country for less money than it costs to produce an iron ship of the same capacity in the most favored locality. First-class oak and pine vessels are built in America at the present time for from $45 to $50 per register ton; in Glasgow the cost for iron sailing vessels is $60 per register ton. The difference in cost on a vessel of 2,000 tons is from $20,000 to $30,000 in favor of the oak and pine vessel, and when the fir of Puget sound is thoroughly utilized this difference will be more marked.

The following return, showing the cost of iron sailing vessels, angle iron, iron plating, and oak wood in Glasgow, has been furnished for this report by Hon. Bret Harte, United States consul at that port:

Year.	Iron ships, cost per register ton. (£ s.)	Angle iron, per gross ton. (£ s.)	Plate iron, per gross ton. (£ s.)	Oak wood, per thousand board feet. (£ s. £ s.)
1852				7 1 to 8 4
1853				8 4
1858				8 8 to 9 4
1859	14 5	7 7½	8 13½	
1860	14 13	7 12½	8 15	
1862	14 13	7 12½	8 15	
1863	14 16½	7 12½	8 15	9 8 to 11 9
1864	16 0	7 0	9 1¼	
1867	16 5	7 16¼	8 15	
1868	14 14	6 13¾	7 13¾	8 8 to 9
1870	14 5	6 15	7 13¾	
1873				13 6 to 14 7
1875	17 12½	9 10	10 0	
1876	15 14	7 10	8 1¼	
1877	14 16½	7 1¼	7 13¾	8 8 to 10 5
1878	13 12	6 12	7 2½	
1881				12 6 to 12 10
1882	12 17½	5 5	6 5	

A letter from John Lloyd, esq., Deptford yard, Sutherland, England, dated February 17, 1882, obtained for this report by Hon. E. A. Merritt, American consul-general in London, states that in 1857 the price of British oak per thousand board feet was from £6 5s. to £9 11s., according to the size of the ship. Plate iron was £9 15s. per gross ton in 1857, £8 5s. in 1861, £11 in 1865, £10 15s. in 1872, as high as £14 in 1873 for a short time, £9 10s. in 1875, and £5 in 1880.

Hon. S. B. Packard, American consul at Liverpool, has gathered for this report the prices of English oak. From various firms of old standing in different parts of England was learned the fact that the average price of English oak 15 or 20 years ago ranged from £12 10s. to £20 10s. per thousand board feet for navy timber and from £8 7s. to £12 10s. per thousand feet for merchant ship timber. About the end of the last century the price was £12 per thousand. The prices of Canadian oak, imported, have been, per thousand:

Years.	Price.				Remarks.
	£ s.		£ s.		
1823	13 2	to	15 12		With 16½ shillings duty in British vessels.
1824	11 16	to	13 17		Do.
1825	13 2	to	15 12		Do.
1830	6 12	to	9 14		Do.
1835	8 16	to	12 10		Do.
1840	10 12	to	12 10		Do.
1845	7 12	to	12 10		With 20 pence duty in British vessels.
1850	6 12	to	8 13		Do.
1855	9 7	to	13 2		Do.
1860	7 13	to	10 12		Do.
1865	9 14	to	10 12		Do.
1870	9 14	to	10 15		Do.
1875	11 2	to	12 3		Free of duty.
1880	7 12	to	11		Do.
1881	10 12	to	13 3		Do.
1882	9 7	to	13 3		Do.

An examination of these returns shows that oak has been too expensive in England for 30 years past for the building of cheap vessels. With oak at $45 and upward per thousand feet and iron at $40 per ton and less iron ships and wooden ships of the same tonnage cost about the same price, and with iron about $30 or $35 per ton and oak at $55 and $60 per thousand, as at present, the iron ship is much the cheaper vessel of the two. In America the conditions are reversed. Here the cost of materials always has been in favor of the wooden ship. For instance, to build a sailing vessel of 2,000 tons register about 950,000 feet of oak, pitch-pine, and white-pine lumber and 150 tons of iron and copper are required. These materials can be bought for $42,000. A vessel of the same capacity, built of iron, requires about 1,100 tons of that metal, rolled into plates and angles, and the material could not be bought for less than $70,000 or $80,000. The ship would cost from $85 to $100 per ton, against $45 to $60 per ton for the wooden ship, and with a difference in cost like that it would seem as if wooden tonnage would continue to be preferred in America for all trades in which the winds are the propelling power. The wooden ship, in fact, is the cheap ship of the age, and its low cost, with its buoyancy, stability, and general excellence as a carrier, makes it still the popular vessel in America.

It must be said, however, that a sentiment is growing among the larger owners of American sailing vessels in favor of iron, as it has been discovered that in the California grain trade, and in all the ports of the world where wooden and iron vessels come into competition, the insurance companies favor iron vessels, and the latter get cargoes quicker and earn higher rates of freight. A curious point in favor of iron is, that should a wooden vessel go ashore or be damaged by storm in transit the cargo must bear a part of the loss under the "general average" insurance rules. An iron vessel, if in serious trouble, is more apt than a wooden one to be a total loss, in which case the cargo bears no part of the loss; and if properly insured the whole value is recovered from the insurance companies. American owners now say that they will buy iron ships as soon as the cost of them is reduced to a point at which they can afford to buy.

Chapter IV.—STEAM VESSELS.

To England and America jointly is due the honor of applying steam practically to locomotion on the sea. There was a time when America led the world in the amount of steam tonnage employed, the vessels of the Mississippi River valley alone exceeding the whole steam tonnage of the British empire; but since that time England has surpassed her, especially in deep-sea navigation, and several other European countries have also become active in that branch of enterprise. America, however, remains the foremost country in the amount of native steam tonnage locally employed. She still builds vessels for transoceanic service, but the number of her vessels actually employed in foreign trade is at present small.

The steam tonnage of the United States comprises 5,139 tugs, yachts, paddle-wheel steamboats, and ocean and lake propellers, aggregating 1,221,206.93 tons register. Fully 2,900 of these vessels are each of less than 100 tons register, being yachts, passenger launches, fishing steamers, small ferry-boats, and tug-boats, the majority tug-boats, of which the enormous commerce of the sea-coasts and lakes has led to a remarkable multiplication. There are only 13 vessels in the whole fleet of more than 3,000 tons register, namely:

	Tons.
Ocean propellers to Liverpool:	
Ohio	3,101
Indiana	3,101
Illinois	3,101
Pennsylvania	3,101
Pacific mail steamers to China:	
City of Tokio	5,079
City of Pekin	5,079
Ocean propellers:	
City of Sidney	3,016
City of Para	3,532
City of Rio de Janeiro	3,448
City of New York	3,019
Alaska	4,011
China	3,836
Solano (paddle-wheel transfer boat)	3,547

About 45 vessels range from 2,000 to 3,000 tons register. They are coasting propellers and paddle-wheel steamboats on Long Island sound and the Hudson river, and comprise also about half a dozen of the larger Mississippi river steamboats. About 250 vessels range from 1,000 to 2,000 tons register, and include the majority of the coasting and lake propellers and the larger steamboats of the West. The remaining 1,900, ranging from 100 to 1,000 tons, are ferry-boats, river steamboats, excursion steamers, tug-boats, and freighting propellers. Of the whole fleet, about 175 are employed on the deep sea and not over 30 in foreign trade.

After the invention of the steam-engine in England the minds of men all over the world turned instinctively to the subject of steam locomotion on land and sea. This idea occurred to a large number of persons at the same time, and ingenious mechanics set their wits to work to devise the means of applying the new power; and it seems to have been the dream of them all eventually to propel heavy ships in calms at sea or against baffling winds, and even to regularly cross the ocean with steam vessels. The first thought of those who attempted to evolve something practical in steam navigation was to tow ships in and out of harbors and rivers, to tow boats on canals, and to propel boats against the current of rivers. Those were the needs of the times. A patent for a steamboat was obtained by Jonathan Hulls in England in 1736 for harbor towing, a small, stern paddle-wheel concern; and experimental boats were tried in England in 1788, 1789, and 1802, two of them for towing on the Forth and Clyde canal. In America a mechanical genius by the name of John Fitch experimented on the Delaware and the Schuylkill in 1786 and 1787 with small steamboats propelled by banks of vertical oars, with which he attained a speed of from 4 to 7 miles an hour, and James Rumsey, another American, tried the plan of forcing a current of water out from the stern of the boat by steam-power. In 1793 Fitch made the first experiment on record with a screw propeller. He built a long-boat, 18 feet in length, with 6 feet beam, and fitted it up with a crude sort of engine and a screw-wheel at the stern. The boiler was an iron pot with a wooden lid, the two cylinders wood, made like barrels, and hooped with iron, and the pistons were attached to each end of a horizontal walking-beam. The boat was tried on the old Collect pond in New York city, a body of water 60 feet deep, which has since been filled up and given place to solid ground, and on which now stand the Tombs and several blocks of business buildings. A speed of 6 miles an hour was attained with this boat. Various other experiments were made in America on the Hudson and the Delaware rivers, the results of which may be summed up by saying that they proved the impracticability of propelling boats by any appliances other than paddle-wheels and screw-propellers.

STEAM VESSELS.

The news of the invention of steam towing-boats on the Forth and Clyde canal was a great stimulus to American inventive talent, as it not only urged Rumsey and Fitch to great exertions, but brought out three men of great intelligence, who, after many years of experiment and the loss of a good deal of money, first made steam navigation a success. Robert Fulton, with his partner, Mr. Livingston, and John Cox Stevens, of Hoboken, New Jersey, were these men. Fulton and Livingston first experimented on the river Seine, at Paris, and built two small boats there in 1803, obtaining moderate results only, but fully establishing in their minds the practicability of steamboating. Mr. Stevens spent $20,000 and 13 years' labor in trying to perfect a screw-propeller driven with a rotary engine. In 1804 he constructed a boat 25 feet long and 5 feet wide, with a Watt engine and a screw-propeller, with which he tried to cross the Hudson from Hoboken to New York, and obtained a speed of 4 miles an hour, but the steam-pipe burst just as he was approaching the New York side. He persevered with his boat, however, and finally took it around by sea to the Delaware river, this being the first ocean voyage of a steam vessel on record. This boat was the Phœnix. It is not necessary to recount all the devices tried by Fitch, Rumsey, Evans, Morey, Stevens, Fulton, and other enterprising Americans in that period of evolution of the steamboat; but, it may be repeated, the sum of all their efforts was to prove that boats could not be driven with any mechanical appliances save those of the paddle-wheel and the screw-propeller; the paddle-wheel was preferred, as being simpler.

Fulton's first experiment on the Seine taught him a lesson which has governed the construction of river steamboats in America down to the present time. Vessels were built with light timbers and planking in those early days, and when laden with a general cargo the weights were distributed equally to all parts of the hull. Without foreseeing the consequences, Fulton put into his first boat a heavy engine, which concentrated the weight all at one point, and before the machinery was in working order it broke through the bottom of the boat and went down into the mud of the river. It was afterward raised and used in other experiments, but in later vessels the weights were better distributed. When steamboat building was at length fairly introduced a strong truss of pine braces and iron rods, called the hog-frame, was set up on each side of the long and narrow hulls of the boats, to stiffen and protect them against the weight of heavy machinery.

In 1806 Fulton bought a 20 horse-power engine from Boulton & Watt in England and set out for America to introduce steam navigation to his native land. His original idea was to engage in business on the Mississippi river, and the pioneer boat built by him on the Hudson was intended to be taken around to that great stream of the West. But the West was not yet settled, whereas the Hudson was thronged with a busy traffic, and Livingston and Fulton having secured exclusive rights on the Hudson for steam vessels from the state legislature, it was finally decided to concentrate all efforts on the navigation of the latter river. The Clermont was built by Charles Brown, on the East river, in 1807, and in the latter part of that year she made her first trip to Albany. This was the beginning of practical steam navigation.

"The North River Steamboat of Clermont," for that was her name, was 133 feet long, 16½ feet wide, and 7 feet deep. She was flat on the bottom, with almost perpendicular sides, a bow full, somewhat like that of a river sloop, and had a straight stem; but she was afterward enlarged by being sawed in two lengthwise and filled out, which made her 22 feet wide and 141 feet long. No mechanical drawing of the hull was ever made, but her shape and scantling have been preserved in written memoranda. The bottom was of yellow pine, 1½ inches thick, tongued and grooved, and set with white lead, and having been put together was laid on a platform and floors were laid across edgewise 4 by 8 inches square and 24 inches apart. Under the machinery the floors were of oak, 8 inches square, but at the ends they were of spruce, for lightness. The boat had a bilge log with spruce top timbers. At first there were no guards; consequently there was no support for the outer ends of the axle of the paddle-wheels, and as she was decked only at the bow and stern the boilers were open to view. The wheels were forward of the center of the boat, and were 15 feet in diameter; they had 8 arms, with buckets 4 feet long and 24 inches dip. The shaft was of cast iron, 4½ inches in diameter. The boat also carried a heavy fly-wheel 10 feet in diameter, hung outside of the boat and extending below it. This attachment was an inconvenience in shoal water, and was afterward discontinued. The boiler was 20 feet long, 7 feet deep, and 8 feet wide, and drove an engine whose cylinder had 24 inches diameter and 4 feet stroke. Afterward strong guards were built on the boat to support the wheels, and a house was put upon them to keep the spray from dashing on board the boat, which it did copiously at first, to the discomfort of all. This boat drew 28 inches of water.

The first trip of the Clermont made a great sensation at New York city and all along the river, and great crowds came to witness her departure and her voyage up the river. The boat made the first 110 miles in 24 hours, and ran the whole distance of 150 miles in 32 hours; but omitting the time spent in landings the voyage was made in 28½ hours, an average of 5 miles per hour. The Clermont was a success from the start, and immediately excited a feeling of intense hostility all along the river. The Hudson at this time was thronged with a multitude of sloops, packets, and freighting boats, by which the whole of the traffic between New York city and the interior of the state was transacted. The packets would clear from Albany one day, discharge and load at New York the next, set sail on the third, and arrive in Albany again on the fourth. Some of these boats were excellent vessels. For instance, in 1806 a stock company had been formed for the purpose of expediting travel on the river, and the sum of $6,000 having been subscribed, the sloop Experiment, of 110 tons, was built and superbly fitted with state-rooms and berths throughout her whole length below deck. In 1807 the company raised $6,000 for a second sloop.

These boats made the trip to Albany in 27 hours, at a cost to the passenger of $5. Similar vessels were engaged in the trade of the river, though no others were so large. Fulton's daring experiment of steam navigation was therefore, in substance, a bold attack on a vested interest, and there was intense feeling against him on the part of all the river men. Their hostility was practical, too, and put him to a good deal of trouble and expense, as sloops constantly got in the way, and frequently ran against the Clermont boldly, with the design of smashing the paddle-wheels. Fulton was not the man to be daunted by warfare like that, but persevered, and made his operations a triumphant success. During the winter of 1807 the boat was laid up, enlarged as before stated, and launched again, and in 1808 she was constantly engaged in making trips to and from Albany, and always went full of passengers.

In 1808 Charles Brown built the Raritan, of 120 tons, designed by Fulton's own hand, and the Car of Neptune, of 295 tons. The latter was 157 feet long on the bottom, 171½ feet on deck, 22 feet broad on the floor, and 26 feet on deck. The Paragon, of 331 tons, was built in 1811. In 1812 the Firefly, of New York, was built to run to Newburgh, and a ferry-boat of 118 tons was built to ply to the Jersey shore. It was Fulton who designed the double-end ferry-boat with dropping bow and stern, which has ever since remained in use.

The war of 1812, which broke out at this stage of the development of steam navigation, did not interfere with the progress of experiment. In fact, it was the cause of a step in advance on the part of America, as it suggested to the fertile mind of Fulton the idea of the first steam war vessel in the world. He proposed to the government a floating battery, with guns pointing in every direction, which would steam at the rate of 4 miles per hour and cost the sum of $320,000, about the amount a first-class frigate could be built for. The offer was accepted, and the vessel was built in 1814. She was 156 feet long, 56 feet broad, and 20 feet deep. The paddle-wheel was 16 feet in diameter, and was hung in the middle of the hull, as in some of the modern western river ferry-boats. The buckets were 14 feet long, with 4 feet dip; the boiler was 22 feet long, 12 feet broad, and 8 feet deep, and the cylinder 48 inches by 5 feet. Tonnage of the vessel, 2,475; draught of water, 10 feet. The walls of this steamer were 5 feet thick, and she was in every respect a formidable ship. Her speed was 5½ miles per hour. This powerful battery gave great satisfaction to the naval authorities, and had a surprising effect on the imagination of people abroad, who published the most extraordinary reports of her powers. It was declared in England that she could discharge 100 gallons of boiling water per minute, brandish 300 cutlasses by machinery over her gunwales, and dart out 300 iron spears from her side every quarter of a minute. She was destroyed by an explosion of her magazine in 1829.

The model of the original North River boats resembled that of a sloop or an immense skiff. They were at first decked only a short distance at the stem and stern, but afterward the whole length of the boat was decked. The engine was open to view. Away aft was a house very much like that of a modern Erie canal-boat, which was raised to cover the boiler and to serve as a shelter to the apartments for the officers, and it was in this part of the boat that the passengers were accommodated. As in the Clermont, the boiler was of the form usual in the Watt's engine, and was set in masonry. The wheels at first were without houses, and when the breeze was brisk the spray from them dashed aboard and made the boat wet. The cross-heads connected with the piston instead of the walking-beam now in general use. The fuel used was wood, some of it cut from the public commons; and a correspondent writes to an Albany paper of those early days complaining bitterly of the enormous consumption of wood by the two steamers Fulton was then running. He placed the value at $5 a cord, and stated that the boats consumed thousands of dollars' worth per annum. The cost of fuel was then the principal item in the cost of running boats. At first it was $150 per trip; but Lackawanna coal, used first on the Car of Neptune in 1816, reduced the expense to $30, and this was regarded as the commencement of a new era in steam navigation.

Fulton and Livingston had a monopoly of the river for a few years; but in a short time the traffic was thrown open to the competition of all, and boats were built by different persons as fast as the trade of the river would warrant it.

As speed was an important element in travel, the steamboats built by opposition lines began to race with each other as early as September, 1809, the first race on record taking place in the month referred to between Fulton's boat and one built by an Albany company. The Albany vessel had advertised to leave at the same hour with Fulton, and the coming race was the exciting topic of that year. The friends of Fulton were led by Professor Kemp, of Columbia College; those of the Albany boat by Jacob Stout. The boats raced down the river and victory was long in suspense, and it was not until after the thirtieth hour of the race that Fulton's boat fairly led.

For many years Charles Brown built nearly all the Hudson River boats, but when this new form of carrier became an assured success other builders devoted their attention to the same class of vessel. New York was the principal center of steamboat building, but vessels were also constructed at Newburgh, as well as at Philadelphia and Baltimore, for the navigation of the rivers of those regions. Very few of these boats were less than 100 feet long, and the great majority were from 120 to 180 feet.

The desire for speed and light draught on the Hudson led to many changes in the forms of boats, the most striking of which were in the proportions of breadth to length. The early boats had about 18 feet beam, and were from 6½ to 9 times as long as they were broad. In the Car of Neptune the proportion was 7.8. By giving the vessels greater beam, namely, from 20 to 24 feet, and occasionally 26 feet in place of 18, they secured lighter draught, which was of the first importance in navigating shallow rivers. At New York the proportion of length to breadth was from 5 to 7; at Philadelphia and Baltimore from 4 to $6\frac{3}{4}$. The depth of hold was from 7 to 9 feet, and the draught of water from $4\frac{1}{4}$ to 7 feet, but some of the fastest boats drew 6 feet. When light draught had been duly obtained by widening the beam speed was secured by again lengthening the hull and adopting a rounder midship section. A beam of from 22 to 24 feet was retained for the Hudson river service, but the length was increased until it was from 8 to $10\frac{1}{2}$ and occasionally 12 times the breadth. The Albany, built in 1832 at New York, was 272 feet long, $26\frac{1}{6}$ feet beam, and $8\frac{1}{3}$ feet deep in the hold, registering 588 tons; the Swallow, built in 1836 at New York, was 225 feet long, 23 feet beam, and $8\frac{1}{3}$ feet deep in the hold, and registered 426 tons; the Home, a New York boat, built in 1837, was 211 feet long by $22\frac{1}{2}$ feet beam and $11\frac{1}{2}$ feet depth of hold, and was of 537 tons register; and these were large and fast boats for their times. It is to Robert L. Stevens that the Hudson river is chiefly indebted for its clipper steamers. He paid much attention to the subject of speed, and secured the object by improving the steam-engine and by making the bow and run of the boats sharper and longer than ever before attempted. Some of the early steamers were lengthened by being hauled ashore, cut in two, and having 25 or 30 feet added to their middle. False bows 20 feet long were put on other boats, and after 1830 new boats were frequently built with solid ends so keen and sharp that they parted the water without raising a ripple or throwing scarcely any spray. In later years a speed has been attained of from 20 to 28 miles per hour.

The boats built to traverse Long Island sound were broader and deeper than those of the river, as they had to encounter boisterous winds and heavy swells. The following are the register dimensions of a few of them:

Year.	Name.	Where built.	Length.	Breadth.	Depth of hold.	Tonnage.
			Feet.	*Feet.*	*Feet.*	
1835	Benj. Franklin	New York	160	$31\frac{1}{2}$	10	468
1835	President	do	$183\frac{3}{4}$	$32\frac{1}{3}$	11	615
1836	Massachusetts	do	202	29	12	676
1836	Narragansett	do	$212\frac{1}{2}$	27	$10\frac{1}{3}$	576
1836	Rhode Island	do	212	$27\frac{5}{6}$	$10\frac{1}{3}$	588

The engines placed in the early boats were of small power proportionate to tonnage. In the Clermont the power was one-eighth of the tonnage, and this was about the proportion in all the early boats; but twenty years afterward it was one-fifth the tonnage, and still later the engines were more powerful yet.

It is surprising how quickly steamboats sprang into existence in different parts of the world after the building of the Clermont, one being built on the Saint Lawrence in 1809, and a second one in 1813. Abroad, the success of Fulton created great excitement, the English people being especially inspired by it. They built their first steamboat at Glasgow in 1811, and several others at various ports within a few years afterward, and then pushed forward in general navigation with energy. They directly encouraged the builders by large orders for the navy, and in 1839 England had 96 war steamers in use, America having only built one. Other countries followed. The first steamboat on the Mississippi was built in 1811.

Having no rivers of great length, the English were compelled to adapt their boats to deep-sea navigation. The Americans, on the other hand, devoted their talents chiefly to the problems of smooth-water navigation and to conquer the wilderness through which the rivers extended, as well as to build the boats required for inland trade. Besides, there was no impulse in that period to send out steam into the deep-sea trade, for the country had an abundance of the fleetest and finest sail shipping in the world.

Fulton employed the ordinary paddle-wheel from the start—a large, light, double wheel, carrying boards, fixed on the outer ends of the spokes, about 4 feet long and dipping 26 inches into the water. Builders were never quite satisfied with that wheel, because the buckets struck and left the water in such a way as to lose a great deal of power. An astonishing number of inventions were patented from 1807 for forty years afterward intended to introduce a better wheel. One object striven for was to make the buckets movable, so that they would enter, pass through, and leave the water in a vertical position. Theoretically, this would be a perfect paddle-wheel, but the device could never be made strong, light, and satisfactory. A great deal of money was lost from time to time by inventors in experimenting with the idea; several tried to feather the paddles. All sorts of shapes in buckets were also tried. They were patterned after fishes' tails, ducks' feet, and birds' wings, and were made of various triangular forms, with the pointed end outermost in some wheels and the base of the triangle out in others. Few of these multifarious devices were ever put to use, and none ever stood the test of more than a year or two. The ordinary paddle-wheel has not been superseded in river steamboats to the present day, and its defects were overcome as far as possible in the later boats, especially after 1835, by the introduction of narrower paddles and larger wheels, the diameter of some wheels being from 40 to 46 feet. Huge houses were built to shelter these enormous wheels, and were thereafter a feature of all American river boats. The popular diameter to-day in Hudson River and Long Island Sound boats is 40 feet. Large wheels enable the buckets to enter and leave the water in nearly a vertical position, so that there is less concussion when they strike and less water is lifted when they emerge. For the same reasons small buckets are better than wide ones; in many of the early boats the buckets were too wide and had to be changed.

While the paddle-wheel was developing in America the screw-propeller was coming into commercial use. Little attention had been paid to the subject of the screw here after the first experiments by Fitch and Stevens. In England they needed something better than paddle-wheels for a vessel, rolling and pitching on the open sea, and in 1825 a premium was offered for the best device for propelling a ship without paddles. In response a naval officer invented a screw with two blades projecting from an axis at an angle of 45°, and one or two boats were fitted with it. Engineers strongly advised the perfection of the screw, and in 1836 two practical inventions were brought out, one by F. P. Smith, of London, and one by Captain John Ericsson, of Sweden, then resident in London, that of Smith being on the principle of the Archimedean screw, a spiral wrapped around an axis. The propeller of Mr. Smith was 2 feet in diameter, with a pitch of 29 inches; the diameter of the shaft was 6 inches, and the length of stroke 15 inches. The screw consisted of two turns of a single blade on a long axis, and it was tried on a little 34-foot boat, having 6½ feet beam and 4-foot draught, which was taken out to sea, and made an average of 8 miles an hour. In the first experiment with this boat on a canal it is said that a part of the blade accidentally broke off, when she "immediately shot ahead at a sensibly greater speed". A stock company was formed to test this propeller, and in 1839 a vessel was built, called the Archimedes, which was 125 feet long, 106¾ feet long between perpendiculars, 21$\frac{10}{12}$ feet extreme breadth, and 13 feet in the hold. She drew 9½ feet of water, and was of 237 tons register. The stern was given an extra amount of overhang, so that the rudder might be fitted aft of the screw and the stern protect them both. Her propeller was at first a single-bladed screw 5 feet 9 inches in diameter, with 8 feet pitch, making one complete turn on the axis; but this was afterward taken off and replaced by one with two blades, each making a half turn around the axis. The trials with this boat in 1840 aided to bring screw propulsion into more general notice. The Archimedes sailed around England and Scotland, calling at many ports *en route*. Many subsequent experiments were made, both with this vessel and with Mr. Smith's double screw of two half-threads; but this special form of propeller never attained any commercial value, and a successful introduction of the new mode of propulsion was effected by Captain Ericsson.

The first practical screw vessel was the Francis B. Ogden, a wooden boat specially built to test the Ericsson propeller, which was first tried on the Thames in April, 1837, and was 45 feet long and 8 feet broad on the beam, drawing 2¼ feet of water. Mr. Ogden, the American consul at Liverpool, being among the first to perceive the advantages of the propeller as operated by Captain Ericsson, entered into an arrangement with the inventor to secure an interest in his patents in the United States, and in appreciation of his encouragement Captain Ericsson's first vessel was named after him. The boat was fitted with two propellers, each 5 feet 3 inches in diameter, consisting of a short hub or cylinder of iron, to the periphery of which were fitted several blades having a spiral twist. The performances of this vessel were remarkable, as a speed of 10 miles an hour was attained from the start and surprising power was developed. This little boat towed a schooner of 170 tons at a speed of 7 miles an hour, and an American packet ship, the Toronto, was towed up the Thames at the rate of more than 5 miles per hour. In spite of these successes, the engineers of London did not regard the screw with favor; and although one day, for the purposes of experiment, the little boat took in tow the admiralty barge with a distinguished company of lords and scientific men on board and drew it through the water at the rate of 10 miles per hour smoothly and noiselessly, the admiralty refused to encourage Captain Ericsson, on the ground that it would be impossible to steer vessels driven by his propeller. Ericsson wanted to build a war vessel for the English navy, but fortunately for America he failed to secure an order.

Captain Robert F. Stockton, of the American navy, was in London in 1837, and through Mr. Ogden became acquainted with Captain Ericsson. Having made an experimental trip in the Ogden on the Thames, he at once saw the importance of screw-propulsion, and immediately gave the Swedish engineer an order for two iron boats for the United States with steam machinery and propellers of Ericsson's own design. These vessels were ordered entirely on Captain Stockton's private account, so as to bring the subject of screw-propulsion before the attention of Americans. One of the boats built by his order was the Robert F. Stockton. She was built of iron by the Lairds of Birkenhead, and was launched in 1838. Her dimensions were: Length, 70 feet; beam, 10 feet; depth of hold, about 9 feet; draught, 6¾ feet. The two propellers, 6¼ feet in diameter, were placed directly aft of the stern-post and forward of the rudder, the two screws being in line. The Robert F. Stockton was tried first as a steamer, in which capacity she made 11 and 12 miles an hour; and afterward as a tow-boat, with four square coal barges in tow, she made 5½ miles per hour. The trials proving satisfactory, the vessel was rigged as a two-masted topsail schooner and sent to the United States under sail in charge of Captain Crane, an American, with a crew of four men and a boy, and was the first commercially successful screw-steamer and the first iron vessel to cross the Atlantic. In 1840 the Stockton was sold to the Delaware and Raritan Canal Company and her name changed to the New Jersey, and for many years she was employed on the canals and the Delaware and Schuylkill rivers as a tug-boat. The screw was thus practically introduced in America by Captain Stockton, and sprang into favor at once. A great many vessels were built with that form of wheel, and in less than ten years after 1839 there had been 150 vessels built in America and fitted with screw-propellers.

Captain Ericsson remained in London to push his invention into commercial use. The Novelty, a freight boat for the London and Manchester canal, and the Enterprise, a canal passenger boat, had been built and fitted with his propellers, and had established the practical utility of the screw before the Archimedes was constructed for Mr. Smith. The Enterprise was subsequently employed with success as a tug-boat on the rivers Mersey and Trent.

STEAM VESSELS.

Captain Stockton was so sanguine that he could induce the United States to adopt the screw for the navy, and Captain Ericsson was so confident that this would be done, that the latter resigned his professional engagements in London and in 1839 came to the United States. In spite of the experiments of Mr. Smith popular interest in screw-propulsion was very faint in England after 1839, and it was not until after the Americans had put the new idea into extensive use both on the ocean and on the northern lakes that England awakened to its advantages. The Archimedes was successful in 1840; but in 1841 only three English merchant vessels had been fitted with screw-propellers, and it was not until 1843 that the frigate Rattler was converted to a screw steamer. On the other hand, by December, 1843, forty-two vessels in America had been fitted with screws, including the Vandalia (1841) and nine other lake propellers, four for the Hudson river, four for Long Island sound, a number for the coasting service, and a number in Canada.

Captain Stockton had been finally successful in inducing the United States government to build one of three war-ships ordered in 1839 as an Ericsson propeller, and through his efforts the Princeton was fitted with a screw and with machinery placed below the water-line. She was the first war vessel of her class on the face of the earth. She was 164 feet long, 30½ feet in beam on deck, and 21½ feet deep in the hold, had two decks, and weighed, when launched, 418 tons gross. Her deepest draught with 200 tons of coal on board was 19¼ feet, her mean draught 17 feet, and her register capacity was 673 tons. The Princeton was built with a flat floor amidships, with a sharp bow and great leanness aft. The stern-post was given the unusual thickness of 26 inches at the propeller shaft, tapering above and below, and the stern overhung 15½ feet. Hanging from it was a wrought-iron rudder-post, so placed as to leave 6 feet in the clear between it and the stern-post, heeling on an oak extension of the keel. The rudder was framed of iron, filled in with oak plank, being in all 5¾ inches thick. The propeller was Ericsson's peculiar idea. It had a brass drum 8 feet in diameter, with 6 brass blades riveted to it, having a true helicoidal twist. The extreme diameter of screw was 14 feet, the pitch 35 feet, and the length in the direction of the axis 2 feet, and the whole wheel weighed 12,000 pounds. The Princeton cost $212,000, and was a successful steamer, making 13 miles an hour on her trial trip. She was full rigged as a ship, and saw a great deal of sea service, visiting the Mediterranean, taking part in the Mexican war, and sailing to other parts of the world.

It is not certainly known where the screw-propeller was first adopted in America for tug-boats, but it appears from the records that the iron tug R. B. Forbes, of Ericsson's design, was built at East Boston as early as 1845 and was supplied with twin screws, working in opposite directions. This tug was a large boat of about 300 tons burden, was especially adapted for outside work in rough water, and lived long enough to be bought by the government during the last war and to take part in the capture of Port Royal. The screw was adopted for towing at Philadelphia in 1849. Some one in that city who had two towing boats of the old paddle-wheel type saw the advantage of propeller tugs for harbor and canal use when he saw the Robert F. Stockton towing 4 coal barges at the rate of a mile in 11 minutes. The first propeller tug-boat built on the Delaware was constructed by William Cramp, of Philadelphia, and was fitted with engines made by Jacob Neafie. She had a wooden hull 80 feet long, 17 feet broad, and 8 feet deep. This boat did excellent service on the Delaware, and her success brought a great deal of business to her enterprising builders. It was thought at first that the entire screw should be below the hull of the vessel, in order to exert its full power; but Mr. Cramp departed from that idea and fitted the Sampson with a 6-foot wheel, only half of which was below the hull, and with a 3-foot keel to protect the screw. After a number of boats had been built of that style some one wanted a light-draught tug, and the broad keel was then removed and the wheel placed entirely above the bottom of the vessel. This boat proving to be as efficient as its predecessors and much more handy, a revolution was effected in the form of tugs. The screw has now superseded the side-wheel for towing purposes, and at the present time there are more than 1,800 of these admirable boats in use in different parts of the United States, chiefly in the sea-coast harbors and on the northern lakes. It is remarkable that in England paddle-wheel towing-boats have lingered in use down to the present time. The tug of our American harbors is a little propeller varying from 30 to 120 tons register. A few of large size range from 130 to 170 tons register, but the average tug is of about 80 tons, and is about 90 feet long, 18 feet wide on the beam, and 9½ feet deep in the hold. One of 170 tons would be 120 feet long, 22 feet beam, and 12 feet deep in the hold. The hulls of the tugs are sharp and deep, but not long, and float at about 8 feet draught, drawing a foot or two more aft than forward. Those that go out into rough water are given a good deal of sheer forward. The stems are perpendicular; the sterns are round and overhang from 6 to 10 feet. Although these little vessels sit low in the water, the deck being not more than 2 or 3 feet higher than the load-line, the bulwarks are always low. A house covers the machinery, which is placed amidships, and the pilot-house is either at the front of this cabin or on top of it at the forward end. Strong towing bitts are placed forward and aft of the house. A tug is simply framed and easily built, and it is a favorite boat for a rising master carpenter to undertake as his first effort at ship-building.

It has already been stated that it was the dream of Fitch, Fulton, Stevens, and other pioneers to cross the ocean with vessels propelled wholly by steam; they looked at the matter from the point of view of engineers and enthusiasts. While steam vessels were developing a speed of only 5 or 6 miles an hour the owners of deep-sea tonnage saw no advantage in steam except as a means of driving the vessel onward in calms or of enabling it to hold its course in protracted storms. In 1819 there was on the stocks in the yard of Crockett & Fickett, at New York, a staunch little ship of 380 tons, originally intended to run from that city to Savannah as a packet. Before her completion she was bought by a company, who finished her as a full-rigged ship and then put into her between decks a horizontal engine of 90 horse-power, with boilers in the hold, and fitted her with side paddle-wheels, unhoused, to make the crossing of the ocean. In May, 1819, Captain Moses Rogers took this ship to Savannah, and on the 26th of the month he set sail from that port for Liverpool, crossing the ocean in 25 days, during 18 of which she was under steam. The time made was not remarkable, but she was the first steam vessel to cross the Atlantic. In the summer she again set sail, and went around Scotland to the Baltic and to Cronstadt, where she anchored September 9. An effort was made to sell her in Sweden and then in Russia, but it was not successful. The king of Sweden offered $100,000, payable in hemp and iron, delivered at New York, but the offer was refused. The Savannah left October 6 for home, arriving at Savannah November 30. She made two voyages to Europe, and once went to Turkey, and excited much interest everywhere. The Savannah was naturally a slow sailer, and this probably was the cause of her failure as a steam vessel. After her second voyage her machinery was taken out, and the vessel ran as a coasting packet to Savannah for several years. Over $50,000 was lost in her career as a steam vessel, and she was finally wrecked on Long Island. This primitive experiment advertised to the world the enterprise and progressive spirit of American ship-builders; it startled the people of England into a determined development of their system of steam navigation. In 1823 English companies were formed with a view to establishing lines of steam vessels to the Mediterranean, with connections to India. In 1825 there was great excitement in England on the subject, and it is on record that 45 companies were formed in that year in Liverpool alone to trade with steam packets to every part of the world. Most of these projects were bubbles, which burst almost as soon as they were set afloat, but some of them were the germs of the later grand enterprise and success of the English people in steam navigation. The first steamboat was sent to India in the latter part of 1825, and others soon followed. Regular lines were established to France, Spain, and the Mediterranean, then to India and the West Indies, and finally, in 1839, to America. By 1857 there were regularly employed in the British steam mail service, under pay from the government, 121 large vessels, registering 140,000 tons, carrying 8,140 men as officers and crews, and receiving $5,335,000 a year as compensation for carrying the mails, while in her whole merchant service there were 1,670 steam vessels, registering 666,000 tons. Besides the liberal subsidies which were paid, the British government aided in the development of steam by ordering the construction of a multitude of war vessels—a policy which enabled the builders of machinery and vessels to prepare an expensive plant and train up a large force of competent engineers and mechanics. This was an advantage, as it created the facilities for building the heaviest class of steam shipping and solved many problems in regard to propelling power with which Americans afterward had to contend.

While England was pushing out to all parts of the world America was developing her river and lake boats. After the opening of the Erie canal the Hudson became the scene of the busiest internal traffic then ever seen. The West, which at the beginning of the century had been a trackless wilderness, was filling up with people. Trade was springing up rapidly on the lakes and on the western rivers, and a general increase in the size and the number of steamboats and lake propellers took place. On the lakes, where there was depth of water, the boats increased in all their dimensions; but on the rivers, where they could not venture on more than 6 to 8 feet draught, they were limited to extending the length and breadth. It is hardly necessary to follow the successive steps by which the river steamers attained the extraordinary dimensions which have been given them in the last 20 years. Suffice it to say, that the spirit of rivalry led to the production of vessel after vessel constructed to surpass everything which had preceded it in the power of its engines, the fleetness of its trips, the size and magnificence of the palace built upon its decks for the accommodation of passengers, and in its capacity for carrying deck-loads of freight. When the New World was finished for the Hudson river it was the longest and fastest vessel in the world, being 380 feet from stem to stern. The hull was 50 feet wide, the entire width over the wheels was 85 feet, and the wheel was 45 feet in diameter. The hog-frame of this boat rose 25 feet above the deck, and a row of masts from 40 to 50 feet in length, heeling on the keelson, capped with iron and rigged with iron rods or shrouds extending to the sides and ends of the boat, aided to impart rigidity to the light and shallow hull. Several strong longitudinal keelsons were put in to add to her strength and keep her broad, flat floor in shape. Her cabins were of immense size, and few hotels at that day could accommodate so many travelers. There were 347 state-rooms and 600 berths. The cabins contained elegant parlors, sumptuously decorated with carved work and gilding, rich carpets, and costly furniture. There was also a large dining-room for the entertainment of guests. Her speed was 20 miles an hour. Large as was this remarkable vessel, her length has since been eclipsed by the St. John, built for the same river in the year 1864, which was 407 feet from stem to stern. Her register dimensions were: Length, 393 feet; beam, 51 feet; depth of hold, $10\frac{8}{12}$ feet; gross tonnage, 2,645. She was built at Greenpoint. Nothing had been built since the historic galley of Ptolemy Philopater that approached her, that boat having been her superior in length by 13 feet, and the expensive steamers of the transoceanic service only now exceed her length. In speed these Hudson river boats have never been beaten. The Daniel Drew, the Mary Powell, and others have made from 25 to 28 miles an hour, and sustained that speed over long stretches of the river.

The steamboats of New York city have been admired by the builders of the whole world for the excellence of their construction. The cabins have been the most costly part of these vessels, owing to their size and the luxury

STEAM VESSELS.

of the joiner work, the carving, gilding, decoration, and furnishing. Nevertheless, the hulls have displayed the greatest ingenuity. Light, strong, and durable, they have never been excelled in the qualities that make them remarkable. They are modeled flat on the floor amidships to secure small draught, and are given long, sharp bows and long, narrow runs to secure speed. The form of the model entails weakness; but builders have found a way to give the boats the slender scantling that preserves their light draught, and yet to make them strong enough to withstand the action of powerful marine engines. Excellence of framing, thoroughness of fastening, and the use of none but the very best materials secure this result. A description of the scantling of two representative New York boats is here given:

A HUDSON RIVER BOAT.

The City of Troy, built by John Englis at Greenpoint (Brooklyn) for the passenger traffic of the river. Keel, 280 feet long; beam, 38 feet; depth from top of floor timbers to top of beam amidships, 10 feet. Side-wheel boat, with walking-beam condensing engine.

Keel.—White oak, 8 by 16 inches, with 8-foot scarfs, fastened with $\frac{7}{8}$-inch screw bolts.

Stem.—Perpendicular; white oak, 10 by 15 inches. Apron, same size.

Stern-post.—White oak, 12 by 15 inches at the keel, 12 by 12 at the head, fastened to the keel by composition dovetail plates. The stern square, above water.

Deadwood.—Yellow pine, at bow and stern.

Frames.—White oak amidships; white oak and chestnut at the ends of the boat; top timbers, oak, chestnut, and hackmatack; double frames, the timbers each 5 by 16 inches over the keel, molded $5\frac{1}{4}$ inches at the deck, with true diminish between. Spacing, 26 inches under the engines, 28 inches forward and aft. Frame timbers thoroughly fastened with 4-foot laps.

Keelsons.—Main, yellow pine, 12 by 20 inches; side, three each side of the main keelson, yellow pine, 10 by 20 inches, coming together at the bow and stern. Two $\frac{7}{8}$-inch bolts, clinched, in each frame. Engine keelsons, yellow pine, with screw bolts through each timber.

Ceiling.—Bilge, yellow pine, six strakes, 5 by 8 inches, bolted edgewise every 4 feet and square-fastened to frames. Clamps, yellow pine, two strakes, 4 by 12 inches, 8 foot scarfs, 2 bolts and 2 screw-bolts in each frame. Yellow pine braces, 4 by 8 inches between clamps and bilge strakes, crossing at 45°, strongly fastened and keyed. Flooring, light stuff.

Beams.—White pine, 6 by 6 inches, one to each frame. Wheel beams 14 by 14 inches, molded 10 inches at the gunwales, 8 inches at the edge of the guards. Every other beam under the boilers 10 by 12 inches, molded 8 inches at the gunwales, 6 inches at the guards. Beams supported by light stanchions on the keelsons. The beam ends secured by knees; 8-inch knees on the main beams.

Decking.—White pine, $2\frac{1}{4}$ by 5 inches.

Planking.—White oak, except the strings; two strakes 4 by 12 inches, yellow pine; all the rest oak, 3 inches thick; first six strakes under strings 6 inches wide, then to lower turn of bilge 8 inches wide. Fastening to 6-foot water-line, two 6-inch composition spikes and two $1\frac{1}{4}$-inch locust treenails, the latter driven through and wedged; above the 6-foot line, galvanized iron spikes and treenails. The butts bolted.

Plank-sheer.—White oak, $3\frac{1}{4}$ by 5 inches. Rail 3 feet from deck, yellow pine 3 by $6\frac{1}{4}$ inches.

Hog-frame.—White pine; the chord about 12 by 14 inches, and the heels of the braces resting on oak chocks (or shoes), placed on the edge of the hull and securely fastened to the frames. Suspension rods from the chord to the frames and cross rods.

Gallows frame.—Yellow pine, according to the designs of the engineers.

Masts.—Six in number, 55 feet long, heeling on the main keelson, diameter 15 inches, and of white pine, capped with iron and fitted with iron rods, with turnbuckles, as follows: The two after masts, two $1\frac{1}{4}$-inch rods to the after quarter of the boat and two 2-inch rods on each side to support the guards; the one next forward, two rods to the engine keelsons and two on each side to the guards, all three connected with a $1\frac{1}{4}$-inch rod. Forward mast, $1\frac{1}{4}$-inch rod to the bow, secured by a strap to the deadwood, two $1\frac{1}{4}$-inch rods each side to the guards; second mast, two $1\frac{1}{4}$ inch rods each side to the guards; third mast, two $1\frac{1}{4}$-inch rods each side to the guards, and two of the same size to the engine keelsons.

Materials.—All first class, free from check, spot, or blemish, and the hull thoroughly calked, pitched, scraped, and painted.

Miscellaneous.—Wheel-houses, guards, cabins, etc., as usual.

SIDE-WHEELER FOR LONG ISLAND SOUND.

The Old Colony, for the Newport line, built by John Englis in 1864. Length from forward side of stem to after side of stern-post, 310 feet; beam, molded, 42 feet; hold, from floor timbers to under side of deck, 14 feet.

Keel.—White oak, in 45-foot lengths, with $7\frac{1}{2}$-foot hook scarfs, the scarfs fastened with $\frac{7}{8}$-inch composition bolts, clinched.

Stem.—White oak, natural crook, 10 by 14 inches, extending 12 feet above deck. Apron, 10 by 12 inches.

Stern-post.—White oak, 14 by 14 inches, with a large inner stern-post, kneed and thoroughly bolted. The stern square, above water.

Deadwood.—Oak and hackmatack, bolted with $\frac{7}{8}$-inch bolts.

Frames.—Double, spaced 24 inches, white oak; timbers 8 by 17 inches under the engines, etc., 7 by 17 forward and aft. Molding diminishes in a true taper to 6 inches at the gunwales. Futtocks, white oak and chestnut, sided 7 inches. Top timbers, locust, chestnut, and hackmatack, sided 6 inches. Entire space between the floors the whole length of the vessel filled in with white pine to 17 inches above the base line.

Keelsons.—Main, white oak, 14 by 24 inches, lower tier fastened with one 1-inch composition bolt clinched on a ring under the keel and one bolt driven to within two inches of the bottom of the keel in each frame; upper tiers of main keelson, square-fastened. Sister keelsons, white pine, bolted transversely every 5 feet with 1-inch iron, and vertically to each frame with $\frac{7}{8}$-inch composition. Side keelsons, 3 each side of the main keelson, same height as latter. Keelsons all tied with cross-beams of oak, 10 by 12 inches, every 20 feet jogged over each keelson and strongly kneed to the sides of the boat. On each side of engine bed there are similar cross-beams kneed to the sides of the boat. Outboard tier of keelsons placed over the floor heads. The keelsons converge at the bow and stern.

Breast-hooks.—Two forward and two aft.

Ceiling.—Bilge strakes, 5 in number, 7 by 12 inches, white oak, square-fastened with $1\frac{1}{4}$-inch bolts and locust treenails. Ceiling, up to clamps, 5-inch white pine. Clamps, 3 strakes, 6 by 10 inches each, scarfed, keyed, bolted to frames, and bolted edgewise every four feet.

Beams.—White pine, 7 by 8 inches. Wheel beams, 16 by 20 inches; under the boilers, 12 by 14 inches. A beam on every frame. Knees under every beam alternately in and out, and where not kneed on the outside the beam is braced with an oak or locust brace. Wheel and boiler beams kneed inside and out.

Iron straps.—The hull is strapped diagonally on the inside of the frames with two sets of iron bands, 4 inches wide, ⅝-inch thick, crossing each other, and connecting at the top with a longitudinal band, 6 inches wide, ¾-inch thick, running clear around the boat close under the wheel beams. The straps are hot riveted to each other and the longitudinal chord; two blunt bolts into each frame. One set of straps is let into the frames, and the ceiling notches over the other.

Decking.—White pine, 3½ by 5 inches.

Planking.—Garboards, 5 and 4 inches; bottom plank out to bilge, 3½ inches; all the rest 4 inches, except that the wales, 3 strakes, are 6 inches thick and 12 inches wide. Wales jogged 1 inch over frames. All white oak, square-fastened with composition spikes and locust treenails to the 11-foot water-line, with iron spikes and treenails above. Butt bolted with ⅞-inch metal.

Bulkheads.—Four, water-tight.

Suspension frame.—White pine and oak, with cross rods, vertical rods, and straps, to hold and secure the hull in the best possible manner.

Masts.—Five in number, with iron rods and turnbuckles to the keelsons and guards.

Model.—The floor almost flat amidships; the bow sharp, but shorter than in river boats.

Miscellaneous.—Wheel-houses, guards, cabins, etc., as in eastern passenger steamboats. Engines, walking-beam, low pressure, condensing.

The engines of the eastern boats have always been worked at low pressure. In principle they are the same as the first one brought from England by Fulton in 1806, except that the steam is used expansively. Having little room in the hull to stow away the machinery, and perceiving no advantage in changing the form of the engine in order to make it more compact and get it all below deck (a matter of importance in ocean vessels), the eastern river builders have retained the old idea of a low-pressure condensing engine with a long walking-beam placed aloft, the steam working expansively and the stroke of the piston being long and rapid. The pressure in the boilers has been on an average about 15 pounds per square inch, seldom going higher than 30, and it has often been the complaint of the builders of hulls that more speed might have been obtained if the boats could only have carried more steam. Low pressure was found to be more economical in fuel, and has been preferred. The stroke in large eastern boats has been about 10 feet, the piston traveling from 300 to 500 feet per minute and the machinery smooth and free from vibration. In the Mississippi River boats a long and slower stroke has been preferred, and high pressure without condensation has been the rule.

The paddle-shaft in eastern boats has been variously placed from one-third to one-half the boat's length from the bow, but in the Mississippi River side-wheel boats it is about the middle of its length.

On the Mississippi river the paddle-wheel has been shifted from its place on the side of the hull to the stern in all vessels built for towing purposes and in many built for freight and passengers. This was necessary to enable large boats to pass safely through the narrow canal at Louisville; but it was also the result of experience with both classes of boats, which demonstrated clearly the greater handiness of stern-wheelers for towing loaded barges and for navigating crooked channels and swift currents.

Steamboats for trips along the coast outside of the rivers and sounds were built as early as 1832, and in the course of 15 years steam vessels were plying between all the principal ports on the Atlantic and Gulf coasts. At first these vessels were all side-wheelers. They had deep hulls, and were sharp on the bottom like sailing ships, while the bows and sterns were not much sharper. The engines were the same in principle as those of the river boats, except that the walking-beam was shifted from its place aloft to a position near the bottom of the vessel, by the side of the steam-cylinder, which gave it the name of "side lever". Other changes were made with a view of bringing the weight of the machinery nearer to the bottom of the hull than in the river boats; but it must be said that, on the whole, less attention was paid in America to making the engines compact and stowing them away in the hold than in the vessels of England. However, they were good engines, securing a speed of from 10 to 12 miles per hour with a comparatively small consumption of coal. The builders of these vessels at New York were fortunate enough to attract the notice of the representatives of foreign powers in this country, and the speed and strength of their coasting steamers brought a large number of orders from Europe for steam frigates and men-of-war. The Kamschatka, built in 1838 for Russia by William H. Brown, under a contract with R. & G. L. Schuyler, was one of these ships, and was a sharp and fast frigate. Her register dimensions were: Length, 227½ feet; beam on main deck, 45½ feet; beam over all, 66 feet; depth from main deck, 24½ feet; tonnage, 2,282. After 1845 there was a change in the forms of hulls, and in order to secure the light draught needed for boats plying to southern harbors a flat bottom was adopted, with the sides amidship rising straight from the bilge to the main rail. The United States, built in 1847 by William H. Webb for C. H. Marshall & Co. for a New Orleans packet, was one of the first vessels of this class, and was intended to beat any other Atlantic vessel in speed. Departing from the standard type, Mr. Webb gave her a floor with ½ inch of dead rise to the foot, about 2½°, the water-lines of the bow and stern being slightly concave. Her register dimensions were: Length, 256 feet; beam, 40 feet; depth, 30½ feet; tonnage, 1,857; length from taffrail to head, 277 feet. For 50 feet at each end her frame, deadwood, and keelsons were of live oak, locust, and cedar, the frames being spaced 32 inches at the extreme ends, while amidships the lower timbers were of southern white oak, spaced 25 inches, the top timbers being live oak, locust, and cedar. She had five rows of yellow-pine keelsons amidships, 3 feet deep and 4 rows 16 inches deep, the bilge strakes were 12 inches square, and throughout she was of similarly heavy build, being a strong, heavy boat. The United States was sold to the German confederation for war purposes, but in later years went into the merchant service, where she was noted for the large cargo she carried on a light draught of water. Her launching draught was 7 feet 1 inch forward and 8 feet 4 inches aft, with a 12-inch keel. The large steamers which were demanded immediately afterward by the California excitement, with their successors, were all of this general type, and had full, flat floors, straight sides, and sharp bows and runs. This model has governed the form of American deep-sea steamers to the present day, the only departure having been to lengthen the bow into a longer, sharper wedge; a change made practicable when they began to build hulls of iron.

On the 3d of March, 1847, Congress authorized the Secretary of the Navy to make contracts for mail-steamship service once in two months, or oftener, from New York to Chagres, on the isthmus of Panama, and from Panama to Astoria, in Oregon, touching at Monterey, San Diego, and San Francisco, the object being to aid in populating the Pacific coast and to shorten the 120-day voyage around cape Horn to 30 days. George Law secured the contract for the Atlantic branch of the service, and called his company the United States Mail, and Howland & Aspinwall, of New York, secured the other contract, and called their company the Pacific Mail. For the Pacific service three steamers were built in 1847 and 1848 at a cost of $600,000: the California and the Panama, of 1,058 and 1,087 tons respectively, 200 feet long from the plank on the stem to the after side of the stern-post, $33\frac{1}{2}$ feet beam, and 22 feet hold, by William H. Webb, and the Oregon, of 1,099 tons, by Smith & Dimon. For the Law line three steamers were also built, namely: the Georgia, 2,727 tons, 255 feet long, 49 feet beam, and $25\frac{1}{2}$ feet depth of hold; the Illinois, 2,123 tons, $267\frac{3}{4}$ feet long on deck, $40\frac{1}{4}$ feet beam, and 31 feet hold; and the Ohio, 2,432 tons, 248 feet long, $45\frac{1}{2}$ feet beam, and $24\frac{1}{2}$ feet depth of hold. These were all wooden paddle-wheel steamers with from 33- to 36-foot wheels, capable of carrying several hundred passengers and about 1,500 tons of freight each. The California was the first afloat, but in the latter part of 1848 the three Pacific Mail vessels were sent off one after the other to begin the service on the Pacific coast. A railway was meanwhile building across the Isthmus. It was while the three ships were *en route* from New York that the news of the discovery of gold arrived in the East; and when the California touched at the Isthmus on the way to the north her captain was astonished to find an excited crowd of thousands of people awaiting her arrival, anxious to reach San Francisco at the earliest possible moment. Each one of the three ships went northward crowded to its fullest capacity.

It has already been explained what an impetus the California excitement gave to the building of sailing vessels, developing the great clippers; it also stimulated the construction of large steamers in an equally wonderful manner. It came at a time when the mail, passenger, and express traffic on our coasts was small; when only a few steam vessels were building for a few modest coasting lines plying between the Atlantic and Gulf ports, and before they had attained any considerable size. As soon as gold was discovered in California a trade sprang into existence in one year of greater magnitude than would have been reached in twenty years of ordinary growth on the Pacific coast, and the steam fleet engaged in that trade needed to be enlarged immediately. Steamer after steamer was added, and in the course of the following ten years 29 fine vessels of 38,000 tons register had been built for the Law and the Howland & Aspinwall lines alone, at a cost of about $8,300,000. It is estimated that in the first ten years these steamers had carried 175,000 persons to California and brought back $200,000,000 in gold. The trade finally grew beyond the capacity of the 1,100- and 1,800-ton vessels, and the companies daringly built of wood up to 2,600 tons, and then in 1861 up to 3,315 tons. The Golden City, of 3,373 tons, was built in 1864, being a steamer 343 feet long to the after side of the stern-post, 45 feet beam, and $29\frac{3}{4}$ feet hold. The California and Aspinwall steamers were all built at New York; and as the majority of all the Atlantic coasting steamers were also built there, besides vast numbers of sailing vessels, it made New York the great center of vessel-building in the United States. In the ten or twelve busy years before the war 10,000 men went to work in the ship-yards of that city every day, and Webb and one or two others had each more than 1,000 men. The row of ship-yards on the East River side of New York city had at the same time 20 or 30 great vessels on the stocks in different stages of construction. Unlike the sailing-vessel industry, which was distributed along the coast, the production of steamers was concentrated at a few points in the large cities, where there were engine-shops and banks with heavy capital, of which New York, Philadelphia, Boston, and Baltimore were the principal. The work of the New York builders gave them great reputation, and they were able to obtain large and profitable orders for war steamers from Russia, France, Italy, Portugal, Turkey, and other foreign governments, bringing millions of money to that city, among them the propeller frigate General Admiral, of 4,500 tons, 325 feet long, 55 feet beam, 34 feet hold; the iron-clad frigates Re d'Italia and Re Don Luigi de Portugallo, each of 3,700 tons, and the iron-clad ram Dunderberg, of 5,090 tons, 380 feet long, $72\frac{5}{6}$ feet beam, and $22\frac{7}{12}$ feet hold, with a $7\frac{3}{4}$-foot casemate. Taking the whole period from 1830 to 1861, there were built in the four principal cities of the Atlantic coast about 80 sea-going steamers for the coasting and California trades and on foreign orders, aggregating 120,000 tons in register and costing about $29,000,000. Five-sixths of this tonnage was produced at New York city.

The screw-propeller made its first appearance in the coasting trade at New York in 1841, the Clarion, of about 250 tons, being built in that year for service between New York and Havana. This little vessel was the pioneer of the present splendid fleet of screw-steamers in the coasting trade, and was driven by a $6\frac{1}{2}$-foot Ericsson wheel. Philadelphia quickly followed the example of New York, and, in fact, was much more energetic in adopting screw-propulsion. In 1842 six screw-steamers were built at Philadelphia, two of 80 tons each for trading to Baltimore, and four of 200 tons each to run to Albany and Hartford, with $6\frac{1}{2}$- and 6-foot wheels, respectively, all of the Ericsson patent. Other vessels of the same class followed from time to time. After 1850 the larger class of coasting steamers began to adopt the screw, and paddle-wheels were gradually superseded; and since 1865 few paddle-wheel vessels have been built for the coasting trade, except for that part of it which flows through Long Island sound, and in the coasting lines whose service is entirely outside of the bays and sounds the paddle-wheel has now, in 1882, almost entirely disappeared. As vessels increased in size the screw increased in diameter to 8 feet, then to 10 feet, and it is now 14 and 16 feet. The Ericsson patent was in the ascendancy in the earlier years; but engineers were never quite satisfied with it. Woodcroft, in England, and, following him, various American inventors, including Loper, at Philadelphia, had experimented with screws based on the principle of an expanding pitch. In the original propeller the blades were set at right angles to the axis, and had the twist of the real Archimedean screw, while in the Woodcroft and later propellers the blades took somewhat the form of the three- and four-leaved clover, and had a second twist in them, the pitch expanding from the axis to the periphery. The blade has become elongated in the course of the experiments of the last twenty years, and its form has changed from time to time, but the general principle of an expanding pitch has been retained. This type of propeller, usually with three or four blades, but sometimes with two, is now in universal use in America, except on the Erie canal. The shaft for the screw is carried out directly through the deadwood aft and the stern-post, and the pistons of the engines, as a rule, act directly on cranks connected with the shaft. The old system of cog gearing on the shaft has been superseded, except in a few types of small vessels; but in tugs and large steamers, as a rule, the piston acts directly on the shaft. The screw continues to grow into popularity every year, and is gradually being introduced into all branches of steamboat service. On the Hudson it is now employed in many ferry-boats and river freighting steamers, and the ferry-boats at Detroit also are now screw vessels.

In 1838 attention was called to transoceanic navigation a second time by the enterprise of some merchants of England. Great Britain was meeting with much success in her commercial schemes, and a great advance had been made in the construction of hulls and machinery suited to steam navigation over the open sea. The speed of steamers had been increased to 10 miles per hour, and it was then believed that, by employing the best resources of the naval art, steamers could be produced which would successfully contest for the supremacy in trade to the American continent. The most profitable traffic of that day was the carrying of mails, express freight, and passengers between England and the United States, which was almost entirely in American hands. The average time of the packets was from 19 to 21 days from New York to Liverpool and 20 to 26 days back. The Sirius, of 700 tons, was built at Bristol, and the Great Western, of 1,340 tons, at London, both fast and handsome paddle-wheel steamers, and were dispatched to New York from Cork and Bristol in 1838, their voyages being successfully completed in 17½ and 15 days, respectively. The time made going home to Falmouth and Bristol was 17 and 14 days, respectively. This experiment gave great satisfaction in London, securing favorable influence from the government, and the Cunard line of steamers was, in 1840, the product of the agitation on that subject. Several companies were formed, but the plans of Samuel Cunard were the first that received the approval of the government. Cunard built four paddle-wheel steamers of about 1,140 tons each, and he was authorized to carry the mails to Halifax and Boston for a yearly compensation of £80,000. In a few years the line was extended to New York, with a yearly compensation of £145,000, afterward increased to £173,000 a year. The plans of Cunard were carried out in such a manner that they met the expectations of the owners of the line and of the English government perfectly, and seldom has a grand commercial scheme been crowned with such triumphant success. The Cunarders and the various other steamers sent out to trade to New York and Boston got the mails and passengers at once and gathered up all the best of the other business to Liverpool in the course of a very few years; and while sailing packets persevered in competition with them so far as the heavy freight and emigrant traffic was concerned, yet the American lines were compelled to send off their ships, one after another, into other departments of trade, and in ten years from 1838 it had only become a question of time when they should all be withdrawn. Although we had 20,000 vessels at sea, we were compelled to depend entirely on British steamers running to every part of the globe for the transmission of the letters and dispatches of our merchants and ship-owners.

The first large American ocean steamer seems to have been the ship Massachusetts, of 751 tons, owned in Boston, which was sent out in 1844, with steam machinery and screw-propeller to be used as auxiliary power.

In 1847 two American steamers built at New York for Edward Mills by Westervelt & Mackay began the competition from New York to Europe with the British line. Mr. Mills had the encouragement of Congress in this matter. In 1845 the postmaster-general was authorized to contract with him for 20 trips a year to Europe for the sum of $400,000, the theory on which this grant was made being that America could only hold her position on the sea by creating a fleet of steamers. This class of vessels was expensive to build and run, and at the rates of freight and fares then current each trip would net the ships a loss of from $15,000 to $25,000. England was paying her steamers a sum which would make up their losses and give them a profit on their investments, and unless America would do the same thing she would lose the carrying trade. Congress was almost unanimous on this subject, and the contract with Mr. Mills was made, a portion of the money due him on his first year's service being advanced to aid in building the ships. Their destination on the other side was Bremen, and they were to sail once a month in winter and twice a month in summer. The ships were constructed like large sailing packets, but longer, and were simply long square-sterned three-deckers, with one white streak along the sides, painted black at intervals, for ports. The paddle-wheels were placed on the sides in the middle of length, the funnel being slightly forward of them. They were bark-rigged, had a full complement of spars and sails, and were stoutly built, in accordance with the rules then prevalent for sailing ships, but with additional weight and fastenings, in order to withstand the action of the engines. Their specifications were as follows:

	Washington.	Hermann.
Length on main deck	230 feet	241 feet.
Length on spar deck	236 feet	235 feet.
Breadth of beam	39 feet	40 feet.
Depth of hold	31 feet	31 feet.
Average draught of water	$19\frac{1}{2}$ feet	$19\frac{1}{2}$ feet.
Custom-house tonnage	1,640 tons	1,734 tons.
Engines	Two side-lever	Two side-lever.
Diameter of cylinders	6 feet	6 feet.
Length of stroke	10 feet	10 feet.
Diameter of paddle-wheels	$34\frac{2}{3}$ feet	36 feet.
Length of paddles	$7\frac{1}{2}$ feet	8 feet.
Depth of paddles originally	$3\frac{1}{3}$ feet	3 feet.
Depth of paddles in 1851		$2\frac{1}{2}$ feet.
Depth of paddles in 1852	$2\frac{2}{3}$ feet	2 feet.
Number of paddles in each wheel	28	28.
Average dip of paddles	$6\frac{1}{4}$ feet	
Number of revolutions per minute	11	11 and 12.
Pressure of steam	14 pounds	12 pounds.
Cut-off	$\frac{1}{3}$ stroke	$\frac{1}{3}$ stroke at first. $3\frac{1}{2}$ feet after change.
Boilers	2 iron flue, side by side	2 iron flue, side by side.
Boilers changed in 1851		4 tubular.
Height of chimney above grate	75 feet	75 feet.
Consumption of soft coal per hour	3,360 pounds	3,920 before the change. 3,546 after change.
Average speed per hour	11 knots	
Trips from New York to Bremen made in	From $12\frac{1}{2}$ to 16 days	From $13\frac{1}{2}$ to 17 days.
Trips from Bremen to New York made in	From $11\frac{22}{24}$ to 17 days	From $13\frac{15}{24}$ to $19\frac{1}{2}$ days.

The original paddle-wheels of the Washington were $37\frac{2}{3}$ feet, but they were changed after the first voyage on account of their excessive dip. The paddles being too wide at first in both ships, and the boilers not having capacity enough, new furnaces were added, and various other expensive alterations were made. The ships were excellent sea boats, and as good carriers as ocean steamers were in that day of bulky machinery and large coal consumption; but they never showed great speed, being beaten regularly on their voyages two or three days by the Cunard steamers.

In 1850 the Franklin and the Humboldt were built by Westervelt & Mackay at New York. They were intended for the Bremen line, but were placed by Messrs. Fox & Livingston in the trade to Havre. The details of construction were:

	Franklin.	Humboldt.
Length on deck	263 feet	292 feet.
Breadth of beam	$41\frac{5}{8}$ feet	40 feet.
Depth of hold	26 feet	27 feet.
Average draught	18 feet	$19\frac{1}{2}$ feet.
Tonnage	2,184	2,181 feet.
Engines	2 side lever	2 side lever.
Cylinders, diameter	7 feet 9 inches	7 feet 11 inches.
Cylinders, stroke	8 feet	9 feet.
Paddle-wheels, diameter	$32\frac{1}{8}$ feet	35 feet.
Length of paddles	$11\frac{1}{2}$ feet	12 feet.
Depth of paddles	1 foot 8 inches	2 feet.
Average dip of paddles	$6\frac{1}{2}$ feet	$8\frac{1}{4}$ feet.
Number of paddles in each wheel	28	36.
Boilers	4 iron flue, back to back	4 iron flue, back to back.
Boilers—length, height, and breadth		27 feet, 11 feet, 14 feet.
Height of chimney above grate	63 feet	65 feet.
Consumption of soft coal per hour	6,150 pounds	6,500 pounds.
Average pressure of steam	15 pounds	15 pounds.
Number of revolutions	13	14.
Cut-off at	3 feet	4 feet.

The average run of these ships from New York to Cowes was $12\frac{17}{24}$ days, and on the return $12\frac{22}{24}$ days.

Simultaneously with these two projects was conceived the idea of a line to Liverpool. Never beaten in the size, speed, and beauty of their clippers and sailing packets, the ship-owners and capitalists of New York had faith that they could go to the front with steamers also if the government would put them on an equal footing with the English shipping men, as it had ever since independence in regard to other maritime matters. The Liverpool line originated with Edward K. Collins, a man of exceptional enthusiasm and energy of character, who was successful in winning the support of some of the strongest men in New York city for his plan. Mr. Collins went into the matter with the express purpose of producing a line of steamers which would excel the Cunarders in every desirable point and would re-establish the commercial superiority of the United States. In aiding the project Congress was governed by the same idea, and also by a secondary consideration of some weight. A number of expensive steam frigates had been built for the navy, among them, in 1840 and 1841, the Mississippi and the Missouri, which had cost respectively $550,000 and $598,000. In 1843 the Missouri had taken fire at Gibraltar and was totally consumed. Congress shrunk from this expense and loss, and it was conceived that if private citizens could be encouraged to build steam vessels suitable for war purposes great sums of money would be saved to the public treasury. Under the laws of 1845 a contract was accordingly made with Mr. Collins, whereby he was to build and run four steam vessels from New York to Liverpool, making twenty trips per annum, and carrying the mails for $385,000 annual compensation. The ships were to be of 2,000 tons register, of the most powerful character, and suitable for men-of-war in case of need. The Cunarders were then of 1,140 to 1,500 tons register. Mr. Collins was resolved upon unquestioned excellence, and he forthwith prepared to build four ships of 2,800 tons register each of the best materials and workmanship and fitted with machinery of unusual power. The Arctic, of 2,856 tons, the clipper of the fleet, and the Atlantic, of 2,845 tons, were built for him in 1849 by William H. Brown, at New York, under the superintendence of George Steers, a famous builder. The Baltic, of 2,723 tons, and the Pacific, of 2,707 tons, were built by Brown & Bell, of New York. The machinery for these vessels was supplied by the Novelty and Allaire works of New York city.

In selecting a model for his fleet Mr. Collins chose some of the peculiarities of the modern swift propellers. He adopted a straight though slightly raking stem, a long, sharp, wedge-like bow, and a long, easy run. The floor was full, but with easy lines everywhere. The hulls were carried up out of water high enough to inclose the houses and cabins, and gigantic four-deck structures were produced, with a full complement of masts and spars, that loomed up long and large above every other ship in the port of New York and won the unqualified admiration of all who saw them.

The following are the details of construction of the Arctic and the Baltic: Length of keel, 277 feet; length on main deck, 282 feet; depth under spar deck, 32 feet; under main deck, 24 feet; beam, molded, 45 feet; round stern; 4 decks; 3 masts. Frame, white oak and chestnut, with tops of locust, live oak, and cedar; stanchions and timber-heads, white oak; apron, lower and main deck breast-hooks, and inner stern-posts, live oak; keel, white oak, 17 by 20 inches; frames, double, sided 24 inches, molded 21 inches over the keel; lower futtocks sided 12 inches each; all the other timbers 10 inches each. Spacing 30 inches amidships, increasing to 36 inches at bow and stern; floors filled in solid to the turn of the bilge. Ceiling, clamps, and water-way of lower decks, yellow pine; bilge streaks, five in number, 12 inches square, bolted edgewise every 4 feet; clamps of the lower deck, 8 inches; upper deck, 7 inches; all other ceiling under the main deck, 7 inches. Outside planking yellow pine, except the garboards, which were white oak, 15 inches wide and 9 inches thick, copper-bolted edgewise with 1-inch metal every 3 feet, and with two bolts through each timber; all the rest of the planking 5 to 7 inches thick and 6 to 8 inches wide to 3 feet above the main deck. Main keelson, white oak, 32 by 34 inches; side keelsons, yellow pine, except under the engines, where white oak, 22 by 42 inches, was employed; under the boilers, 22 by 27 inches. Lower and main deck beams, sided 12 to 14 inches, molded 13 inches in center, and 10 inches at the ends; spar-deck beams, $6\frac{1}{2}$ by 8 inches in the middle; beams, yellow pine, except that some white pine was used in the orlop and spar decks. Decking, white pine; orlop deck, 3 inches; lower, $3\frac{1}{2}$; main, 4; spar deck, 3 inches. Knees, white oak and hackmatack; bulwarks, 3-inch white pine. The hulls were square-fastened with two $\frac{7}{8}$-inch copper bolts and two locust treenails to 20 feet draught of water; above that galvanized iron and treenails were used. The frame was strapped with iron, crossing amidships like a lattice work, the spacing being 4 feet. The engines were two in number, large and powerful, of the side-lever type, having cylinders 95 inches in diameter, with 10 feet stroke. There were 4 tubular boilers, 22 feet long, $14\frac{1}{4}$ feet high, two 14 feet wide and two 15 feet wide. The smoke-pipe projected 45 feet above the spar deck. There were double furnaces. With 13 pounds pressure the engines had 800 horse-power. The launching draught of the Arctic aft was 10 feet. The hull weighed 1,525 gross tons; spar and top gear, 34 tons. With an ordinary cargo she drew 20 feet of water aft and about 6 inches less forward, and would carry 250 passengers and 2,000 tons of freight.

The best engineering talent of the day was consulted with regard to every point about the hulls and machinery of these four noble vessels, and in every detail they were of excellent design and workmanship and in appearance imposing. Service began with these ships in 1851.

The Cunard steamers were making the voyage from New York to Liverpool in from 10 days 6 hours to 14 days 3 hours, averaging in the year $11\frac{1}{2}$ days. From Liverpool to New York their time varied from 10 days 2 hours to 16 days 20 hours, averaging 12 days 9 hours. The Collins vessels beat this time from the start by an average

STEAM VESSELS. 157

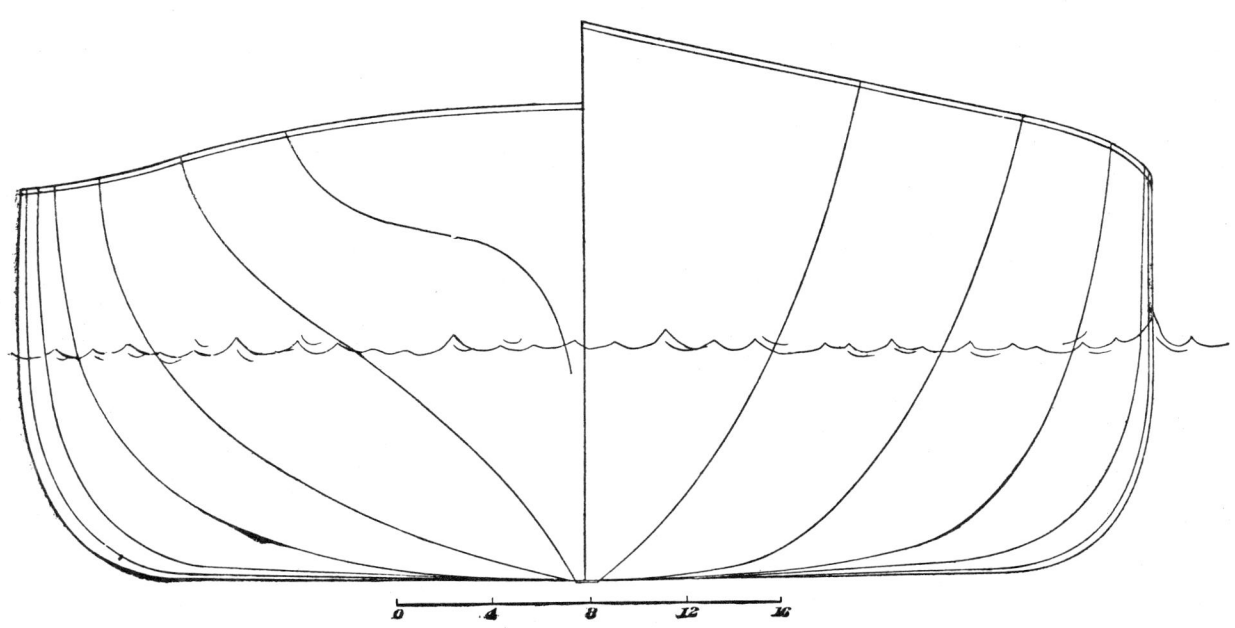

Fig. 45.—LINES OF EASTERN RIVER STEAMBOAT.

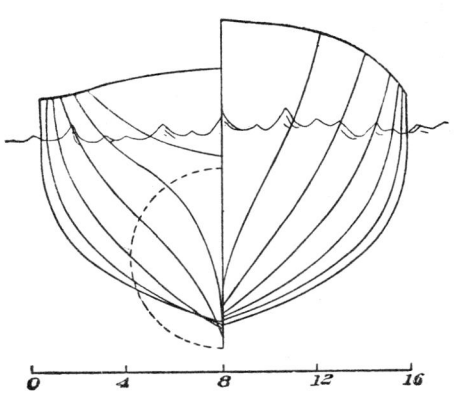

Fig. 46.—LINES OF HARBOR TUG.

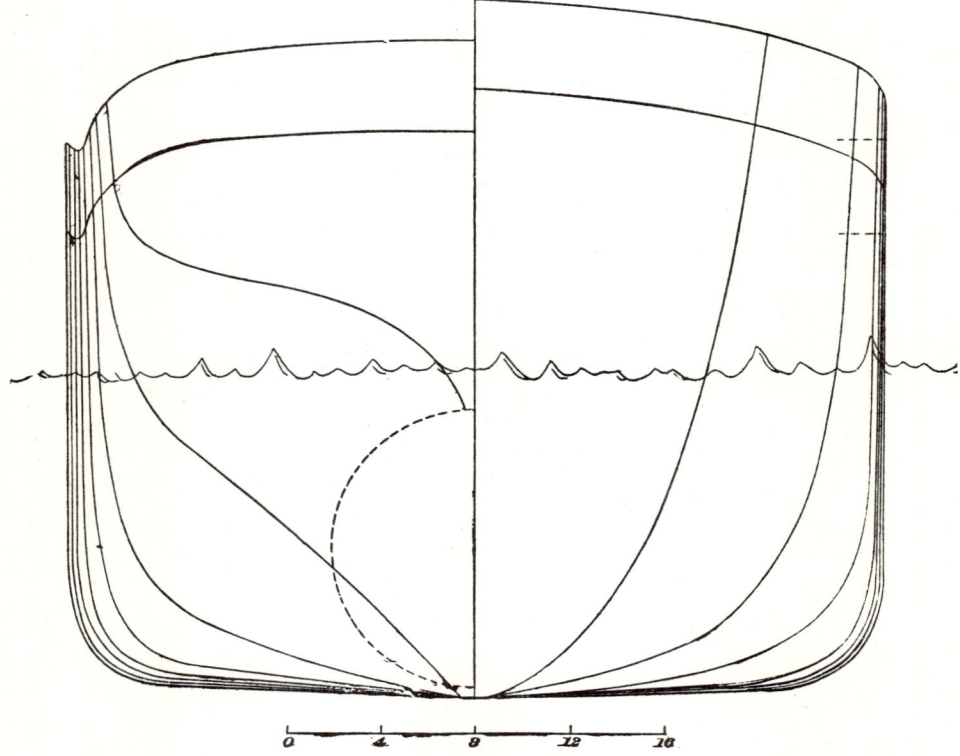

Fig. 47.—Lines of northern lakes propeller.

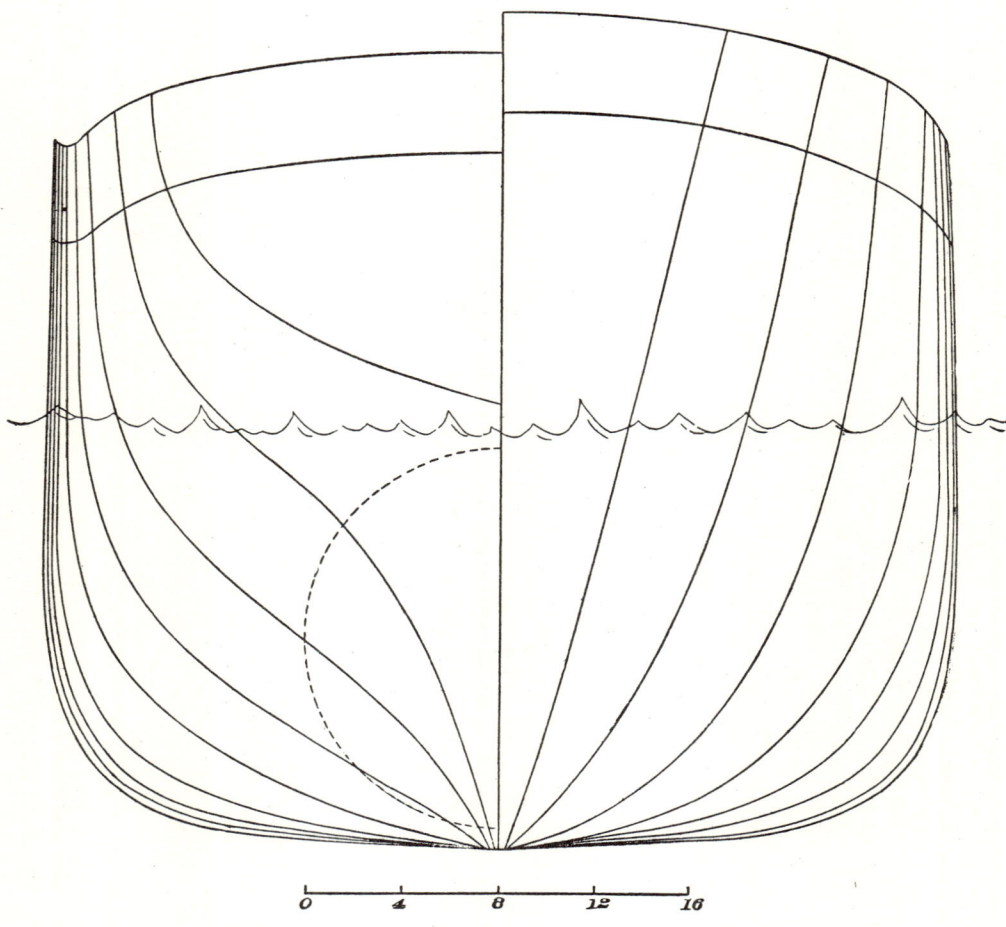

Fig. 48.—Lines of fast coasting propeller (iron).

of about one day, their voyages to Liverpool being made in from 9 days 17 hours to 12 days 9 hours, an average in a year of 10 days 21 hours; the return trip was accomplished in from 9 days 13 hours to 13 days 17 hours, the average being 11 days 3 hours. The ships had the confidence of the public, and were liberally patronized. From January to November, 1852, inclusive, for instance, they carried 4,306 passengers, as against 2,969 who went by the Cunarders. Their competition for freights brought the rates to Liverpool down from £7 10s. per ton to £4; a great public benefit, because the United States were importing enormous quantities of European manufactures and paying the cost of freighting to this country. The voyage to Europe was shortened by these ships and travel was promoted, and in eight years from the time they began the passenger traffic had increased fivefold.

The Cunard line began to build new and large steamers of greater power the moment the Collins line was undertaken. Collins' mail pay was increased to $858,000 a year, and greater speed was required of him. He fulfilled the requirement, and the company that backed him spent large sums of money in perfecting their engines and machinery and maintaining their boats in full efficiency. In 1854 the Arctic was lost at sea by a collision in a fog with the French steamer Vesta, only 45 out of the 368 people on board ever reaching land. The Pacific was lost in 1856 with all on board, numbering 186 persons, and a valuable cargo. The ship with her contents was insured for that trip for $2,000,000, and nothing was ever heard of her after leaving Liverpool, in January, 1856. Neither was built with bulkheads. Collins acted with energy in replacing the Arctic. In 1855 he built the colossal Adriatic, of 4,144 tons register, 345 feet long, 50 feet beam, and 33 feet hold, at a cost of $1,100,000. The ship cost more than was expected, owing to alterations in her machinery and her long detention in port while the changes were being made; but she was a good vessel, fast and capacious, and once in 1861 made a trip from Saint John's to Galway in the unprecedented time of 5 days 19¾ hours.

Beginning in 1853, a movement had sprung into existence for canceling Collins' subsidy. This agitation went on, until in 1856 the pay of Collins was reduced to $385,000 a year, and in 1857 it was withdrawn altogether by the refusal of the government to renew the contract; the contract with Mr. Mills also expired. Meanwhile the English people had been organizing new lines to America, and Collins and Mills could not contend with them single handed, as their round trips cost from $40,000 to $65,000 each, and ordinary receipts were from $10,000 to $16,000 less per trip. The Cunard line had a subsidy of $866,700 a year and the other English lines a generous compensation, though not so large. The odds being too great, the Collins and Mills ships were withdrawn and sold, and competition for the mail, express freight, and passenger business to the northern ports of America was deliberately abandoned to English, French, and German steamers. The war of 1861 broke out in the United States four years afterward. During and after that war the English steam companies extended their operations, and have since been gaining steadily in the trade of the whole Atlantic coast of North America. Beginning in 1856, Mr. Vanderbilt, of New York, ran a steamship bearing his name and two others to Havre for a short time, but afterward sold the vessel to the United States government. In 1866 an American company was formed in Boston, and two large oak-built wooden screw steamers, the Erie and the Ontario, were constructed at Essex and put into the business from Boston to Liverpool; but the English steamers instantly lowered their rates of freight, and after a very few voyages the two vessels had to be withdrawn.

A line was afterward started from Baltimore in connection with the Baltimore and Ohio railroad. This also had a brief existence.

The only other American steamship line to Europe was that which is still running from Philadelphia to Liverpool and has four iron propellers of American build. It was started in 1873. The ships run in connection with the Pennsylvania railroad, which owns the principal part of the stock of the company. The ships will be described in the chapter on iron-ship building.

The steam vessels of the United States were confessedly superior for transatlantic service to those of European build as much as the American sailing clippers were to their foreign rivals. Owing, however, to the artificial manner in which the steam shipping of Europe was brought into existence and maintained and the want of government compensation American owners of ocean steam tonnage were forced to withdraw from the traffic to Europe, and our builders were compelled to rely entirely on coasting trade for business.

Very few other attempts have been made to put American steamers into foreign trade. The coasting lines to the South have called at Havana in Cuba and have pushed their voyages to Mexico. Two or three attempts have been made to trade to Brazil. Commodore Garrison, of New York, ran some wooden steamers after the war from New York to Brazil for a few years with the aid of a subsidy, and John Roach ran a line of iron steamers during the years from 1878 to 1881.

The Pacific Mail has sent steamers to the Sandwich islands, Japan and China, and Australia. These ships will be more particularly referred to under the heading of iron vessels. No other attempts to run steamers in foreign trade have been made, except to Mexico and the West Indies.

As has already been seen, the steam craft of the United States were all built of wood in the earlier years. The frames were of white oak, chestnut, live oak, and locust; the planking was at first oak, but in time yellow pine came to be employed extensively at the ocean ports for the same purpose, as also for keelsons, beams, ceiling, etc. White pine has always been used for decking, houses, keelsons, and beams. On the western rivers white pine and poplar have been the light woods employed, nearly all the rest of the boat, outside and in, being of oak.

On the northern lakes the boats have been framed, planked, and ceiled with oak, beams, decking, and houses being of white pine. Of late iron has come into use extensively for hulls on the sea-coast and the northern lakes, and for many years past all the coasting steamers have been built of it; but this material is, as yet, little used on the western rivers, owing to the abundance of wood and the smoothness of the waters navigated. For the rough waters of the sea, and even for the smooth waters of deep rivers, iron is far superior to wood for steam vessels; and although its cost is high, it is now coming rapidly into use on the coast in all classes of boats, large and small. Tugs, ferry-boats, yachts, excursion steamers, Sound boats, and Hudson River boats, as well as coasting propellers, are now built indiscriminately of iron.

The localities in which steamers are now built in America, and the extent of the industry, are given below.

OCEAN COASTS.

In Maine steamboat building is limited. Small fishing steamers are constructed at Boothbay, Eastport, Portland, and Kennebunk as they are needed from time to time, and a few tugs are produced every year. Both classes of boats are propellers. Occasionally a river or coasting steamboat of the ordinary type, with side paddle-wheels and walking-beam engine, is required, and a number of small propeller launches have been made for summer travel between local points among the islands of the coast. Latterly in Bath whale-ships have been supplied with engines of small power, with a propeller wheel capable of driving the ships about 6 miles per hour. In 1882 a freighting sail ship was supplied with the same power as an experiment, for use in the latitude of equatorial calms. So far as Maine is concerned, steamers are only a small item in the product of the ship-yards.

Essex is the principal place for building steamers in Massachusetts. Wooden propellers and tugs are frequently produced in that town, chiefly on Boston account. At Boston the work in this line is now entirely confined to ferry-boats and pleasure boats.

In Rhode Island there is an establishment at Bristol, called the Herreshoff Manufacturing Company, which builds a special class of small swift propellers to serve as vidette boats and pleasure yachts. These boats are modeled, constructed, and fitted out with a view of getting the highest possible speed, while at the same time leaving room for large and comfortable cabins for the guests. Two vidette boats built for the English government were 48 feet long, 9 feet beam, and 5 feet deep from the gunwales, and were framed with oak; the planking was fastened with brass screws. The engines were of 125 horse-power, and in each case the whole boat with machinery aboard weighed only 7 tons. With a pressure of 140 pounds of steam and the propeller making 550 revolutions per minute the boats ran at a speed of $17\frac{2}{3}$ miles per hour. On their arrival in England they were each supplied with one Gatling gun, and were employed for the torpedo service. The late Herreshoff boats have been built with iron frames and wooden planking, and one of them has attained a speed of 25 miles an hour.

In model the Herreshoff boats have been varied, first one way, then another, as in regulating a watch, until the exact result has been attained at which the designer aimed. The hulls are long, low, and sharp from keel to gunwale, increasing in beam above the water. The water-lines are as sharp as practicable, and the draught of the hull forward is 2 or 3 feet less than it is aft. The hulls are built as lightly as possible, in order to obtain light draught, and the workmanship is correspondingly careful in order to obtain strength.

A description of the steam-yacht Leila (Fig. 49), built in 1878, will illustrate the Herreshoff idea. The boat is 100 feet long over all, and 95 feet 5 inches long from the forward edge of the stem to the after side of the stern-post on the water-line. Extreme breadth on deck, $15\frac{1}{3}$ feet; on the water-line, $11\frac{3}{4}$ feet; depth of hull amidships from lower edge of planking to top of deck beams, 5 feet 10 inches; draught forward, 2 feet $7\frac{1}{2}$ inches; aft, 5 feet $1\frac{1}{2}$ inches. Midship section, $54\frac{1}{2}$ feet from the forward edge of the stem. Coefficient of water-line, 62 per cent.; of midship section, 56 per cent.; displacement, 37 per cent.; dead rise, $21\frac{1}{2}°$. Angle of entrance at bow, $17°$; of run, $28°$. Frames, iron, $1\frac{1}{2}$ by $2\frac{1}{4}$ inches, $\frac{1}{4}$-inch thick; deck beams, 2 by $3\frac{1}{2}$ inches. Stem, oak, 6 inches thick; stern-post, oak, 7 inches thick. Planking, pitch-pine, $1\frac{1}{4}$ inches; keel, oak, 7 by 10 inches; deck plank, $1\frac{3}{16}$ inches. Bulwarks, very light, 30 inches high. The total weight of the boat, with machinery, water, and coal aboard, was $37\frac{1}{2}$ tons net. A brass propeller wheel was put in, 4 feet 7 inches in diameter, four-bladed, $9\frac{3}{4}$ inches long, with a pitch of 8 feet. The draught of water of the hull proper was so small that in order to bury the screw sufficiently the shaft was fitted very near to the top of the keel. The blades projected below the keel, which required the addition of a skag to protect the screw and support the metallic shoe underneath. The skag was $15\frac{1}{2}$ inches deep below the bottom of the keel at the stern-post and 5 feet long on the keel, being sided 7 inches. In some Herreshoff boats the skag is replaced by a bent brass arm, which is riveted to the keel and extends downward and under the screw and then up again to receive the heel of the rudder-post. The rudder was of metal, counterbalanced, the axis being placed at one-quarter the breadth from the forward edge. The engine was compound condensing, and had 2 vertical cylinders, placed side by side, one of them 9 inches in diameter, with 18 inches stroke, the other 16 inches in diameter, with 18 inches stroke. The pistons were connected with cranks on the shaft at right angles to each other. A surface condenser was employed, consisting of a single copper pipe running outside of the vessel under water around the stern-post. The boiler is a peculiarity of all the Herreshoff boats. It has a circular furnace, into which descends a double coil of continuous wrought iron pipe $1\frac{1}{3}$ inches in diameter and $\frac{3}{16}$ of an inch thick, arranged

STEAM VESSELS.

as if it had been wrapped around two cones, one fitting beneath the other. The flames play about these coils; all the water in the boiler is in this pipe, entering at one end as water and going out at the other as steam. The advantages of this boiler are light weight, economy of fuel, quick raising of steam, and security against explosions. In the Leila the combustion was 2¼ pounds of coal per hour per horse-power. A pressure of 125 pounds was maintained in the boiler with 350 pounds of coal per hour, the speed of the boat being 14 miles an hour, and it required only from 3 to 5 minutes after starting the fire to make steam from cold water to work the engine. A small house was built upon the Leila to cover the machinery. The pilot-house was in front of it, and the cabin aft.

The invention of the safety-coil boiler has led to a wonderful multiplication of steam yachts throughout the whole of the United States within the last ten years. On all the small inland lakes, especially in New York state, where rowing and sail boats have been owned by young men for years in great numbers, the steam yacht has sprung into great popularity. The boats seldom exceed 25 feet in length, and would not be large enough to register in the custom-house, even if they were subject to it, under the laws of the United States. They are usually open boats, carry from 10 to 20 persons each, and are the popular luxury of prosperous men who live near romantic lakes. The hulls of these boats are always built entirely of wood, after the fashion of large rowing barges, and sometimes have cabins, but usually have awnings only.

The steamboat building of Connecticut now consists only of an occasional vessel at Noank, a few river boats on the Connecticut river, and a small fishing steamer now and then at South Norwalk. A large number of river boats and war vessels have been built in times past upon the Connecticut, but the industry is nearly at an end.

On the Hudson river small boats of the ordinary side-wheel pattern are built at Newburgh, Rondout, and Athens from time to time as they are needed for local traffic. Many of them are for towing only, having no houses, except simply to protect the machinery and wheels and accommodate the officers and crew. The hull is low in the water, the deck is open, and the cabin is supported aloft by a bridge between the wheel-houses. Iron hulls have latterly been made at Newburgh for these boats. The large passenger boats are now nearly all made with iron hulls at the yards on the Delaware, and as the tendency is strongly in this direction at present the wooden steamboat building of the river is expected steadily to decline. Oak and pine are so costly upon the upper Hudson that iron will now make advances.

Since the adoption of iron for the hulls of the Long Island Sound boats and the coasting propellers steamboat building has steadily declined at New York city, and all the large business has been transferred to the Delaware river. Several large engine and boiler shops still exist, and an immense amount of work, both new and old, is done by them every year. Many of the Delaware river hulls receive their machinery in New York city, while the Morgan iron works supply nearly all the engines required by the iron propellers built at Chester. Excursion and river steamers for New York use, wherever built, also buy their machinery largely in the city; but so far as the building of the boats themselves is concerned the business has nearly disappeared, all that remains being the production of wooden tugs, small propeller yachts, wooden ferry-boats for local use, and an occasional excursion steamer of the river type for carrying passengers to and from the summer resorts in the immediate vicinity of the city. These vessels are seldom built within New York city itself, but are made in the ship-yards scattered along the water front of Brooklyn all the way from Hell Gate to the lower part of Gowanus bay. A few tugs are made at Tottenville, at the lower end of Staten island.

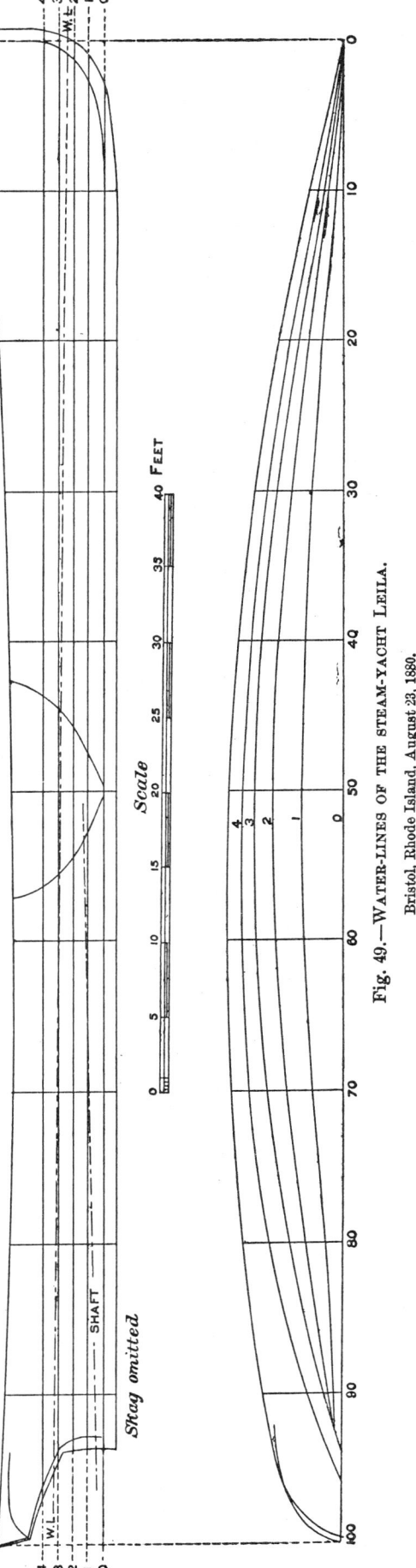

Fig. 49.—WATER-LINES OF THE STEAM-YACHT LEILA.
Bristol, Rhode Island, August 23, 1880.

The ferry-boats of New York are double-enders, sharp and swift, with side wheels, the deck highest amidships and dropping about 2 feet at the ends in a gradual curve. They are all of one general type, varying only in size. The machinery is stowed away in the hull as much as possible. The engine is low-pressure condensing, is often built with horizontal cylinder and piston, has a long stroke, and acts quickly. A narrow house rises in the center of the deck to shelter the machinery and cover the stairways to the hold, and on each side of this the deck is open for 10 feet, in order to allow horses and wagons to pass from end to end of the boat. The cabins for passengers are outside of the two gangways, one on each side of the boat, and extend two-thirds of the length, each cabin being in turn divided nearly in two by the wheel-house, which rises through it and leaves only a hallway 3 feet wide between the forward and after halves of each cabin. A roof covers the whole of the cabin, engine-house, and spaces between for teams, and the pilot-houses are on this roof, one at each end of the boat. A portion of the deck at each end is clear of structures of any kind, except the posts and chains needed to prevent the passengers and teams from crowding each other overboard while in the stream. These boats are an important feature of the business life of New York city. They run across the North and East rivers at numerous points, and from the city to Staten island, day and night, at intervals of from 5 to 30 minutes, according to the magnitude of the travel on each particular route. A large boat will carry 400 passengers and about 50 teams with wagons on a single trip. In the construction of this class of boats the New York builders have attained special excellence. The hulls are strongly but lightly framed with oak and chestnut and planked with oak, yellow pine being used for the rest of the vessel except the houses and the decking, which are of white pine and spruce, with cherry, black walnut, etc., in the joiner work of the cabins. They cost from $50,000 to $90,000 each, according to the size of the hull and the luxury of the cabins. The Jersey ferry-boat Princeton, of 888 tons, built in the census year, was one of the large class. She was 192 feet long, $36\frac{1}{2}$ feet beam, and $12\frac{1}{2}$ feet deep in the hold, and to build her it required 52,000 feet of oak, 10,000 feet of chestnut, 103,000 feet of white pine and spruce, and about 10,000 feet of yellow pine. Her machinery weighed 130 tons. Complete, the boat cost $85,000.

Steamboat building has taken the same course at the cities south of New York as it has at the latter port since the introduction of iron hulls, and the business has been absorbed in large measure by the iron ship-yards. Wooden boats are less in demand, and are only built for those whose capital is small and who need them for some special service. The yearly production is about as follows: At Camden, New Jersey, a few tugs, not to exceed five or six; at Philadelphia, two or three tugs, a yacht or two, and an occasional coasting propeller and small side-wheel steamboat; at Wilmington, an occasional tug and steamboat, some years none; at Baltimore, a steamboat every year or two for the Chesapeake bay business and three or four tugs; at Norfolk, sometimes nothing, sometimes a tug or a side-wheel steamer; at Elizabeth City and Washington, North Carolina, Charleston, South Carolina, and other points on the southern coast, an occasional light-draught stern-wheel boat, like a steam scow, for some local river service; at New Orleans, stern-wheel boats for the river and bayou trade. The whole wooden steam tonnage annually built at all these ports combined does not now equal the amount which was produced at either New York or Philadelphia alone in a single busy year before 1861.

On the Pacific coast steamboat building has developed slowly, owing to the lack of white-oak timber, which was long considered by builders the only wood fit for the hulls of the vessels. The practice has prevailed at San Francisco of ordering the finest of tugs and side-wheel boats in the East, where there has been a supply of oak timber, and where the art of constructing strong and light hulls has been thoroughly understood. Boats thus ordered have proved costly. In 1879 two side-wheel ferry-boats were completed at Oakland, on San Francisco bay, the hulls of which were gotten out in the East from oak and shipped by sailing vessels around cape Horn. These were the Garden City, of 1,080 tons, 210 feet long, 37 feet beam, and $13\frac{1}{2}$ feet hold, and the Bay City, of 1,283 tons, 230 feet long, $36\frac{2}{3}$ feet beam, and $13\frac{1}{2}$ feet hold. The boats were put together in Oakland, the houses being built on them from Pacific coast woods, and the expenditure for labor, at $3 and $4 a day, was $33,000 on each boat. The iron was bought from a rolling-mill in San Francisco, and the engines for one of the boats from the Risdon iron works. When completed they cost $130,000 and $150,000 respectively, or one-third more than they could have been built for in New York city. The expense of this plan has led to the building of local vessels at home. A great variety of steam craft—tugs, ferry-boats, transfer steamers, propellers, and launches—have been made from Pacific coast fir within the last five or six years, one of the largest of them being the Transit car-ferry, built at the Central Pacific ship-yard in Oakland. This large vessel is 338 feet long over all, $316\frac{1}{3}$ feet between perpendiculars, 40 feet beam, 75 feet wide over the guards, and $17\frac{1}{2}$ feet deep from the beams to the keel, and is supplied with vertical condensing engines with 60-inch cylinders and 11 feet stroke. The wheels are 29 feet in diameter, carrying 20 paddles 12 feet long and 20 inches wide. A still larger one is the Solano, of 3,549 tons, a side-wheel transfer boat employed to ferry the overland railroad trains across the river. She is the largest transfer boat in the United States. Her dimensions are: Length, 407 feet; beam of hull, $65\frac{1}{2}$ feet; hold, $17\frac{1}{2}$ feet. Four tracks are laid upon her decks, capable of receiving 48 cars and engines. In the Solano sticks of fir were used for keelsons 150 feet long and 24 inches square. The engines are placed amidships, one behind the other, and the wheels, instead of being placed at the ends of one long paddle shaft reaching across the boat, are situated opposite the engines that drive them. The boats built of native fir have done so well that there is now no probability of further orders being sent to the East, except, possibly, for engines. There are many handsome oak

STEAM VESSELS. 163

and pine tug-boats in San Francisco bay, the Monarch, of 195 tons, standing at their head. She was built on the Delaware in 1873, and is about 95 feet long, 20 feet wide, and 16 feet deep, drawing 14½ feet of water. Fir has been found latterly to answer as well for this class of vessel as any other timber, and as iron and machinery are now produced in San Francisco at moderate cost the city appears to be nearly independent of the eastern ship-yards.

A large wooden propeller was building in the upper part of San Francisco in the census year, and has since been launched. She is the most ambitious steamer built on the coast, and as she appears to be a complete success her construction is expected to give an impetus to the building of coasting vessels. The Mexico (Fig. 50) is a three-decker, 288 feet in extreme length, 275 feet between perpendiculars, 36 feet beam, and 28 feet deep below the spar deck, and is constructed entirely of Puget Sound fir with the exception of a few scattered pieces, which are of eastern white oak and Pacific Coast laurel. A statement of her scantling will allow a comparison to be made with oak and pine propellers in the East. The keel is in three lengths, 76, 106, and 108 feet, 16 by 22 inches square, with 11-foot scarfs and a 4-inch shoe. The keelsons are in pieces, some of them from 113 to 117 feet long. The main keelson is 16 by 23 inches, in three depths, with two 1⅜-inch bolts clear through each frame and the keel; the sister keelsons are single logs of 16 by 23 inches, fastened with 1¼-inch iron bolts. The frames are spaced 27 inches, floors and futtocks sided 10 inches and top timbers 9 inches, and are molded 18 inches over the keel, 15 inches at the bilge, and 6 inches at the upper deck. There are two floors to each frame amidships, filled in solid under the engines, and at each end there are at least 8 frames with floors cut from natural crooks. The frames are bolted to the keel with two 1⅛-inch iron bolts. The stem and apron are of white oak and laurel; the stern-post is of oak, molded 22 inches, and sided 16 inches at the keel and 28 inches at the center of the propeller shaft. The rudder-post is sided 13 inches at the keel and 16 inches at the counter, and is molded 18 inches. Both posts are secured to the keel with composition braces, one on each side, and one is fitted on top of the keel within the propeller space, each brace cast in one solid piece. The after deadwood and shaft box each have a heavy knee on the stern-post. Ceiling of the floor, 5 inches, fastened with 9½-inch spikes; on the bilge 12 inches thick, in four streaks, each 14 inches wide; thence to the lower deck, 10 inches; the 10- and 12-inch stuff edge-bolted with 1⅛-inch square iron in every frame space; from the lower to the main deck, 6-inch ceiling, edge-bolted with 1-inch square iron, with two ¾-inch bolts through each frame; from the main deck to the rail, 3-inch ceiling, spiked on. Clamps of the lower deck, 14 by 16 inches, in long lengths; main deck, 12 by 16 inches; upper deck, 8 by 12 inches. Water-ways of the lower two decks, 14 by 16 inches, in long pieces; plank-sheer, 4 by 14 inches. Planking: garboards, 10 by 16 inches and 7 by 14 inches; 5-inch planking to the main deck; 3 inches above that, all in lengths of from 40 to 100 feet, fastened with copper and locust treenails below the 14-foot water-line and with galvanized-iron spikes above. Beams of the lower deck, spaced 4½ feet, 12 by 14 inches square in the middle and 12 by 9 at the ends. Main deck beams, 12 by 12 inches square, tapering to 8 by 12 at the ends; spaced 4½ feet; upper deck beams 7 by 10 inches square, tapering to 5 by 10 at the ends. Knees of the lower deck, one hanging at each beam end, sided 10 inches, and 9-inch knees for the main deck. Two 11-inch hooks and pointers in the lower hold forward, with an 11-inch hook under each deck. The frame is single-strapped with 4½- by ¾-inch iron, set 6 feet apart, running from the main deck to the lower turn of the bilge, and riveted into a 5- by ¾-inch iron band running clear around the ship at the main deck. Amidships, four sets of straps cross each other at right angles. The decking is 4½, 4, and 1¼ inches, coming up from below. Three iron bulkheads of ¼-inch plates are fitted into the ship abaft the chain locker, forward of the coal bunkers and aft of the engines respectively. There were used in this vessel 70 tons of salt, 300 tons of bolts and straps, and about 900,000 feet of fir timber, and she cost $250,000 ready for sea. Her model is a good specimen of the coasting propeller of the present day.

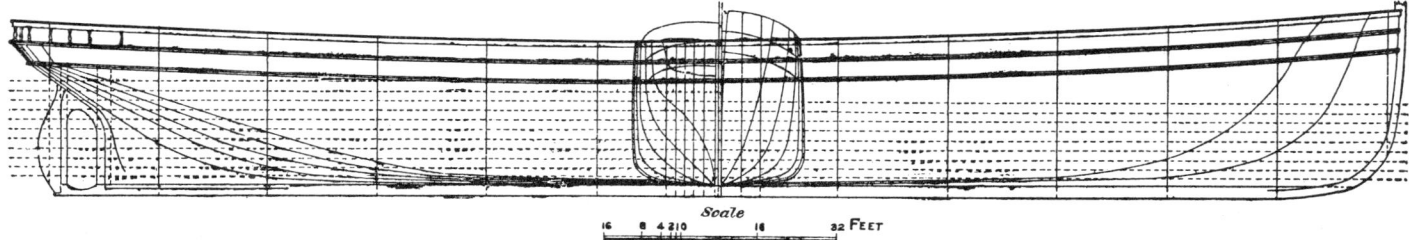

Fig. 50.—STEAMSHIP MEXICO.
Designed and built by Dickie Bros., San Francisco.

ON THE COLUMBIA RIVER.

From the Cascade mountains to the sea-coast Oregon is covered with an almost unbroken and impenetrable forest of yellow fir, cedar, pine, hemlock, and hard wood; but in the valley of the Willamette, and along the Columbia and the Snake rivers, eastward of the mountains, the country is open and is suited to agriculture. Population has followed the coast and the rivers. The first settlements were made at Astoria, near the mouth of the Columbia, by fur traders, and agriculture in the valleys and lumbering both on lands adjoining the rivers and at a few points on the sea-coast have been the occupations of the people.

The great highways of travel and trade in Oregon have been the noble Columbia river and its branches. Ocean steamers from San Francisco ascend the river to Astoria and Portland, and the merchandise and passengers which they bring have been distributed to other towns by a numerous fleet of local steamboats. The same boats, seconded by river barges, have brought back the grain and other produce destined for export, either to San Francisco by steamer or to Europe by sailing vessel. There is a small industry in building ocean vessels at Coos bay, on the coast, which has already been described in the chapter on sailing vessels. It now remains to describe the steamboat and barge building of the Columbia and its branches.

It is reported that the first steamboat building on the rivers was in 1850; since that date Portland has built many steamboats, and others have been built at Oregon City, Salem, The Dalles, Celilo, and Wallula. There has also been some work at Astoria. The excellence of yellow fir was first exemplified by experience at Portland. Among the early vessels was the side-wheel steamer Eliza Anderson, built in 1858 in that city. Winter-cut timber was used in her frame, and the boat stood on the sandy beach of the river, exposed to the sun and weather, one whole summer before she was planked; thus she became thoroughly seasoned, and proved an excellent and durable boat. About five years ago she was taken out of the water at Seattle, Washington territory, for repair, and her copper taken off, and it is said that after the vessel stood on the ways long enough for the bottom to dry the planking began to drop off, the fastening having become corroded by the galvanic action of the copper and salt water. The plank and the frame, however, were both bright and sound, and even aft of the wheels, where decay is most likely to take place, the fir was almost as good as new. A number of the other early boats showed the same longevity even when not salted; some did not, but the decay of the timbers has been traced to the fact that the wood was cut at the wrong season of the year and was not properly seasoned. The builders of the Columbia have had to learn by experience what they might have learned from the yards on the Atlantic coast, that timber proves lasting only when cut in the months when the sap had ceased running and when properly seasoned after being cut. When experiment had shown that the fir was a good material, steamboats, barges, and schooners were built as fast as they were required by the local trade of the state. In 1850 there were built 2 schooners, of 122 tons; in 1870, 1 schooner, 5 sloops and barges, and 11 steamboats, a total of 988 tons; in 1879, 11 steamboats, aggregating 5,383 tons; in 1880, 1 schooner, 2 sloops, and 13 steamers, a total of 2,466 tons; but since 1880 there has been an advance.

The first steamboats on the rivers were side-wheelers; but they were not the best for the business of these shallow rivers, and the later ones have been stern-wheelers. The Portland builders have been successful in producing a class of boats which vie with those of the Ohio in light draught, carrying power, and speed combined. It will be noticed elsewhere in this chapter that Ohio river boats have a rounded bow, with a long rake to the stem, which fits them for making landings alongshore, as the nose of the boat can be pushed up to the bank almost anywhere. The bottom is straight clear aft to the stern-post, and the run is formed by fitting two stern-posts, each carrying a rudder, into the stern 20 feet apart, and then modeling the stern as in ocean vessels, but suiting the requirements of two stern-posts. On the Columbia the boats are built differently. Forward, the keel begins to rise 15 or 20 feet from the bow and joins a rocker-stem; aft, the stern is not molded, but the bottom begins to rise 20 or 30 feet from the rudder and nearly reaches the surface of the water at the stern, which, above water, is cut off square. The boat is prevented from sagging by iron rods hooking into the keelsons away forward and aft and running up through decks and cabins to the top of central masts, and when they are in place they are screwed up until they take the weight off the bow and stern, and the vessel then keeps her shape perfectly.

Fig. 51.—O. R. & N. Co.'s STEAMER WIDE WEST.

One steamer built in the census year was the D. S. Baker, which was 165 feet long, 36 feet beam, and 5 feet hold, with a sharp bow and a square stern. The house covers the vessel from the stern forward to within 20 feet of the bow. The engines and the cargo space are on deck, and the cabins for passengers are built above the main house. The hull measures 302 register tons and the houses 408, a total of 710 tons. The stern-wheeler Hassaloe is 160 feet long, 31 broad, and about 5 feet deep. She has smaller houses, and registers 461 tons. The Frederick Billings is 199 feet long, 37 broad, and 7 feet deep in the hold, has towering cabins, and registers 1,236 tons. The smaller Columbia river boats range from 60 to 75 feet in length and 15 to 18 feet beam, and are each from 4 to 5 feet deep in the hold, the register being from 40 to 60 tons. The handsomest vessel on the river at present is the stern-wheeler Wide West (Fig. 51), built for passenger service. She is 215 feet long in the hull, 12 feet deep, molded, just aft of the bow, 10 feet deep amidships, the stern rising until the molded depth is only $7\frac{1}{2}$ feet. She is of 1,201 tons register. The guards are $3\frac{1}{2}$ feet wide, and she has a long, sharp bow, the fore part keeping on an even line with the keel and the boat sitting up forward well out of the water. The lower house covers the whole of the deck to within about 25 feet of the bow, and shelters the boilers, engines, and cargo. On the deck of this house is built a long, handsomely-furnished cabin and dining-room, with state-rooms on each side. As on the Long Island Sound steamers, there is a promenade around the cabin and out to the bow; above the cabin there is a short texas, and on top of that is the pilot-house. The Wide West is a fast, comfortable boat, and her speed has not been beaten on the Columbia river. The hulls of the river boats are made of yellow fir; the houses of white cedar and fir. The boats all have fore-and-aft bulkheads, side keelsons, and hog-chains, as in the Ohio river boats, the main hog-chains, however, generally running up to a tall mast in the center of the vessel. There are no bridges across the Columbia to interfere with the freedom of the builder in choosing the best arrangement of hog-chains and braces.

The barges built for river service are of considerable size, and are used for bringing down grain in bags to Portland, Kalama, and Astoria for shipment to Europe. Several are each 150 feet long, 35 feet beam, and 4½ feet deep, square at both ends, and registering 260 tons, while others are 185 feet long, 36 feet beam, and 7½ feet deep, measuring 360 tons each. The Wyetchie belongs to a larger class. She is 200 feet long, 44½ feet beam, and 10 feet deep, with a house on deck 18 feet long, 9 feet broad, and 7½ feet high. She is sharp at both ends, and registers 621 tons. The barges nearly all have small houses on deck, as they carry deck loads of grain in bags; they are towed by stern-wheel steamboats. The grain business of the Columbia is rapidly increasing.

Some of the little schooners of the river are fitted with small propeller engines, for use when going against the tide and the current of the river. They trade from point to point on their own account, dealing in butter, eggs, and produce.

At Portland, on the Willamette river, near the Columbia, there are five boat-yards. The largest is owned by the Oregon Railway and Navigation Company, and is employed for the building of steamboats and barges. A large barge was building in the census year. The yard is well equipped. This company is now making a large fixed dry-dock in East Portland, in which the iron coasting steamers of the line to San Francisco can be docked and repaired. E. Sorenson, formerly of Manitowoc, Wisconsin, was building a propeller for river service 130 feet long on deck, 28 feet beam, and 10½ feet hold, to cost $40,000. The frame of this vessel was cut out with a band-saw, at a cost of $300 for labor and use of the saw. A frame of the same size was hewn out by him on lake Michigan, where wages are one-half what they are here, at a cost of $980. The butts of the planking were secured in this propeller by through bolts, the rest of the fastening being spikes and treenails, and the ceiling was put on with treenails. This vessel was built entirely of yellow fir, which cost $12 per thousand for frame flitch and $20 per thousand for decking, planking, etc., dressed on four sides, and these were the ruling prices for ship timber in Portland. In one yard there was building a government stern-wheeler 150 feet long and 28 feet beam. This boat had a rocker stem and keel forward, and the bottom rose several feet aft, the height of the sheer from the base line being 10 feet at the bow, 6 feet amidships, and 8 feet aft. Wages were $2 50 and $3 a day for laborers, $3 50 a day for young carpenters, and $4 a day for the majority of men in the yards. There is some repairing of boats at Portland, and one of the yards has a small railway.

At Oregon City and at Celilo there are marine railways for the Oregon Railway and Navigation Company's boats. The yards at The Dalles, Wallula, and Salem occasionally build small vessels.

At Astoria there is one regular yard, but some small building is done from time to time by various persons there and at Oneatta and Columbia City in the district. The work is of a scattered and fragmentary character, but it is enough to train in ship-yard work many persons whose services may become available at any day when there is a demand for ship-building. Ships of the largest class could be built at Astoria, Portland, and other good points in the Columbia River valley. This valley is exporting 200 or 300 cargoes of wheat to Europe annually, and the trade promises to expand rapidly. British ships get this business. They are iron vessels, while sound yellow fir vessels, which would carry grain as safely and as well, could be built on the Columbia for two-thirds their cost. Timber is abundant and cheap, and yellow fir, cut at the proper time of year and put into a vessel in the summer time, when it can dry and season, is as lasting as white oak, and being lighter than oak, will make a more buoyant vessel, and thus a better carrier. There was building at Astoria in 1881 only one vessel—a large propeller tug, 110 feet long, 21 feet beam, and 9½ feet hold, to draw 9 feet aft and 7½ feet forward. The frames are 12 by 16 inches, 10 inches at the bilge, 7 at the plank-sheer, spaced 22 inches; garboards, 5 inches; bottom plank, 3½ inches; wales, 4 inches; ceiling on the bilge, 6 inches; clamps, 5 inches; beams, 10 by 10 inches, spaced 38 inches. In the floor timbers some tide-land spruce, taken from the roots, was used on account of its crooked shape. The stern-post and rudder-posts were white oak; the arch knee over the propeller was spruce; while all the rest of the tug was yellow fir, including the knees and hooks, which were fir roots. Mr. Whelan, the builder, bought his material for $12 a thousand right through. The knees cost 75 cents per inch of siding, and wages were $4 a day. The tug-boats of Astoria are powerful and handsome vessels. Each carries one mast, with a yard for the sail forward of the pilot-house; but some of them have second masts aft of the cabins, carrying schooner sails. Scow sloops are built to some extent for fishing and river cruising about Astoria.

NORTHERN LAKES.

When Fulton began his experiments on the Hudson river, on the shores of lakes Ontario and Erie only was there any white population. The pioneer of lake steamers was the Ontario, of 232 tons, built at Sackett's Harbor, New York, in 1816. She was 110 feet long, and was a side-wheeler. One followed at Kingston, Canada, of 700 tons. The second on the American side was at Black Rock, New York, in 1818—the Walk-in-the-Water, of 342 tons. In the next ten years there were twenty steamboats built on the two lakes, the most of them on the American side, and all side-wheel boats, for the local service of the towns on the lakes. Unlike the Hudson river boats, those of the lakes had to encounter rough water and stormy winds, and were accordingly built with strong, deep hulls, like sailing vessels. Each generally bore at least one mast, for spreading sail in case of the breakage of the machinery; in size they ranged from 50 to 892 tons, the majority being from 250 to 400 tons register.

In 1829 an event occurred which stamped a special character on all the vessels trading between the lakes, steamboats included. The Welland canal was opened to enable the tonnage of one lake to pass through to the other. The smallest locks were 110 feet in length and 22 feet wide, with 8 feet draught of water—a size which permitted the passage of a boat carrying 400 tons. After the opening of this canal hulls of sailing vessels took the bluff, full form ever since peculiar to the lakes. The bows were made round, the bottoms flat, and the bodies straight, in order to reach the greatest capacity that could go through the locks of the canal; all steamboats that were intended to pass from one lake to the other approximated that form of hull, but they were not very numerous. Those intended for the local passenger traffic of each lake kept a sharp form; but they were never so sharp and shallow as those on the Hudson river.

The building towns on the American side were Sackett's Harbor, Oswego, Rochester, and Black Rock, New York; Erie, Pennsylvania; Cleveland, Huron, Black River, Sandusky, and Toledo, Ohio; and Detroit and Monroe, Michigan, oak, chestnut, and pine being abundant in all these localities. Afterward steamers were built wherever there was a ship-yard of any size. Many were side-wheelers, ranging in size from 250 to 600 tons, with an occasional big steamer of 700 tons; they had low-pressure engines, with walking-beams oscillating in the air above the cabins, and were in every important respect, save that of depth and strength of hull and their one or two masts, like the eastern river steamers.

As early as 1818 the Walk-in-the-Water had run to Detroit, and as fast as the country along the lakes filled up with settlers the steamboats followed, carrying fresh legions of immigrants, and supplying them with the manufactured goods and general supplies which the necessities of a new country required. About 1830 steamboats were running regularly to Chicago, and this added 650 miles to the 270 miles of navigation from Buffalo to Detroit. After the Welland canal opened, in 1831, the first increase of the lake steamboats was in the direction of the number of boats. The increase in size came later.

The era of large boats began in 1844 with the construction of the Empire, of 1,136 tons, at Cleveland, Ohio, and the Niagara, of 1,084 tons, at Buffalo, in 1845. These boats were too large for the Welland canal route, and were expressly intended for the passenger traffic from lake Erie ports to those on lake Michigan; but three years afterward, in view of the rush of travel, others were undertaken. In 1848 there were built the Globe, of 1,200 tons, at Trugo, Michigan; the Queen City, of 1,000 tons, at Buffalo, New York; the Bay State, of 1,100 tons, at Clayton, New York; and the Empire State, of 1,700 tons, at Saint Clair, Michigan. These were long, sharp, and fast boats, with towering cabins, handsome and elegantly furnished, and were the pride of the lakes. They were oak built throughout, save that the decks, some of the beams, the houses, and spars were of white pine, were well salted, and, like most of this class, were long lived. Vessels increased in magnitude and cost year after year until the Plymouth Rock was built in 1854 at Buffalo. This vessel was of 1,991 tons register, and was 310 feet long, 42 feet beam, and 12 feet hold, being 60 feet wide over the guards. In 1857 a similar steamer, named the City of Buffalo, was built at Buffalo. This was the culmination of side-wheel steamboat building on the lakes, and since that period this class of boats has steadily declined in size, popularity, and importance. The railroads along shore began as early as 1857 to draw away the flourishing passenger traffic, and no boats of the size of the Plymouth Rock were afterward built with side wheels on the lakes. The City of Buffalo was converted into a propeller; the Western Metropolis, of 1,860 tons, was changed into a bark; the Mississippi, of 1,829 tons, and the Western World, of 1,000 tons, were dismantled, and the hulls converted into floating dry-docks at Cleveland; a large hull was converted to the same use at Buffalo, and another at Erie, Pennsylvania; others were changed into barges; and in one way and another all the large passenger boats went out of use, and their places have not since been filled. Most of them were relegated to freighting during their active existence; and while a few of this type of vessels have continued to carry passengers, yet that branch of their business is now merely nominal, as travel exists only on few routes. Paddle-wheel steamers are now rarely built of greater size than 600 or 800 tons. From first to last, over 300 side-wheel boats have been constructed on the American side of the lakes, including lake Saint Clair, and, in addition, about one-third of that number are known to have been built on the Canada side. Not more than three or four a year are now produced.

One cause of disappearance of side-wheel boats has been the growing preference for the screw-propeller. It was better fitted to the Welland canal traffic than the paddle-wheel, the greater width of the latter class of boats completely excluding large side-wheel craft from that trade. Boats fitted with propellers could keep their narrow beam and make the trip through the canal with ease and safety. The screw is now almost the only wheel used on the northern lakes. The principal reason, other than the above, which has caused the preference in its favor is the fact that the harbors of Oswego, Buffalo, Cleveland, Chicago, and Milwaukee are rivers and canals, and consequently demand a narrow class of steam-vessels. Large numbers of the old side-wheel boats were changed and the new style of wheel put into them.

The first propeller on the lakes was the Vandalia, of 138 tons, built at Oswego, New York, in 1841, a bluff-bowed boat, with cutwater, bowsprit, and foremast and a sloop sail. She had a long cabin aft of the mast. Her machinery was well aft, and her smoke-stack was very nearly in the stern. She made a trip to the upper lakes in 1842. In ten years 53 propellers had been built at Oswego, Clayton, Dexter, New York, Buffalo, Cleveland, Maumee, Huron, Black River, Detroit, Saint Clair, Grand Haven, and Milwaukee, a total of 17,000 tons; they ranged in size from 150 to 700 tons, all except 10 of them being under 400 tons, so as to make the passage through the Welland canal. The popular size was 350 tons, and they bore a strong resemblance to fast Erie canal boats fitted up for lake navigation. The boats were all strongly framed, planked, and ceiled with white oak, were well salted and proved durable, and usually did good service for 30 years unless they met with some casualty. The Canadians enlarged the Welland locks to 150 feet in length, $26\frac{1}{2}$ feet in breadth, and 10 feet depth of water, completing the work in 1853, and the change allowed vessels of 600 tons to pass from lake to lake. A few propellers for the canal were built, but the freighting of the lakes required large boats. An immense business had sprung up in carrying iron ore from the Michigan mines to Cleveland and other ports and grain and lumber from places on lakes Michigan, Huron, and Erie to the easternmost cities they could reach. Coal and merchandise were going back in large quantities from points on lakes Ontario and Erie, and Canada turned as large a share as possible of the eastward-bound grain and lumber destined for export to Europe to the lake Ontario and the river Saint Lawrence route. The facilities she created for the purpose would have led also to the building up of Oswego, New York, as well as of Kingston and Montreal; but she did not go far enough. Trade grew so fast that larger boats were demanded than could go down even to lake Ontario, certainly larger than could go to Montreal, and after 1855 a large number of screw-propellers of from 650 to 950 tons register were built, nearly all of them at Cleveland and Buffalo. In 1856 12 were built at Cleveland, aggregating 6,823 tons, and 14 at Buffalo, aggregating 8,633 tons, with 1 at Detroit of 862 tons and 1 at Milwaukee of 583 tons, as against only 2 side-wheel boats built in that year. This represents the actual building of the year. Some of the vessels were not documented at the custom-houses in the year they were launched. The boats were employed in trading from points above Detroit to Cleveland, Erie, and Buffalo.

In 1862 the B. F. Wade, of 1,120 tons, was built at Newport. Other large propellers followed, among them the Idaho, of 915 tons, and the Winslow, of 919 tons, at Cleveland in 1863; the D. Richmond, of 1,083 tons, at Cleveland in 1864; the Colorado, of 1,118 tons, at Buffalo, and the Roanoke, of 1,069 tons, at Cleveland in 1867; and after them vessels of from 1,200 to 2,000 register tons at all those places and at Detroit. With a view still to direct the export business of the lakes to Montreal, Canada has been enlarging the Welland and Lachine canals again, increasing the locks to 270 feet in length, 45 feet in width, and 14 feet depth of water. The work is now, in 1882, about completed, but again trade has grown fully up to the capacity of the canals. The most profitable propellers and schooners of the upper lakes are now from 1,600 to 2,000 register tons. They are from 270 to 280 feet in length, and draw 14 feet of water, and only by close squeezing and by lightening the boats at the entrance to the canals (reloading them at the port below) can they be employed in the canal traffic. Those longer than 270 feet, of which the number is large, cannot go into the canal. It must be said, however, that a medium class of iron steamers, drawing not over 14 feet of water, to which they are limited by a ledge of rocks in the Saint Clair river, and carrying up to 2,500 tons of grain, could be safely and perhaps profitably put into the through trade of the lakes, and preparations are making in Canada for trying the experiment. The distance from Chicago to Montreal is 1,261 miles, 1,005 miles of the route being lake navigation; from Chicago to New York, by way of Buffalo, the distance is 1,419 miles, of which only 865 miles are lake navigation.

Owing to the panic and the stop put to railroad building the freighting of iron ore and of coal fell off immensely, and building on the lakes was considerably depressed after 1873 for a few years. Since 1878 the business has revived, and is now brisk. New vessels have again come into demand, and at present about 25 propellers are required every year by the commerce of the lakes.

From 1841 to 1882 there have been built on the northern lakes more than 600 propellers varying from 50 to 200 tons for tugs and 130 to 2,000 tons for the passenger and freight business. The majority have been and are now employed exclusively in freighting, and are called "steam barges", in distinction from the class of boats which have houses from end to end for the accommodation of passengers. A barge has a small house aft, two stories high, to cover the machinery and to serve as quarters for some of the officers, and a small house forward, in the extreme bow, serving as a top-gallant forecastle, with a pilot-house atop. Between the two houses the spar deck is clear. It has one, two, three, and sometimes four masts, according to the fancy of the owners. The mizzen-mast seldom spreads a sail, as it is planted in close proximity to the smoke-pipe, and is used simply as a derrick for handling cargo. The propellers carry coal, grain, iron ore, and lumber.

The placing of the machinery away aft is a peculiarity of lake propellers. When light, the boats present a strange appearance, the bow being high up out of water and the hull down by the stern, and it is only when loaded that they sail on anything like an even keel. The practice of stowing the machinery aft is a convenient one with regard to the handling of cargo, and has only one disadvantage, that of tending to strain the hull when making trips in an unloaded condition. The lakes experience much heavy weather, and a hull working up and down in the waves with the stern as a fulcrum weakens rapidly amidships. To strengthen the hulls against this peculiar stress the builders of the lakes adopted the hog-frames of the side-wheel steamers for use in propellers. As soon as they began to build up to 175 and 200 feet in length some device of that sort was absolutely necessary, and as the hog-frame was the simplest means of gaining longitudinal rigidity, it was universally adopted, although undergoing some modifications in form. Instead of making the frame out of long, straight beams, united with iron rods, and giving it the angular appearance of a bridge-truss, the practice grew up of giving it the form of an arch, sweeping in a long, low, unbroken curve from end to end of the ship. The top chord was made out of several thicknesses of 4- or 6-inch oak plank, fitted so as to break joints, and strongly bolted together throughout the whole length, and was united to the hull with wooden braces, iron rods, and straps, the same as the ordinary hog-frame. It passed down through the deck and along the ceiling to the apron forward, the inner part aft being fastened to the hull in the strongest manner and secured with breast-hooks and braces. This was called the Bishop arch, from the name of the inventor. In the late propellers, say within the last five years, the hog-frame and the Bishop arch have both been discontinued, because they are both in the way, especially in handling lumber. The builders gain rigidity now by strapping the hulls with iron on the outside of the frames, by ceiling them heavily with oak, often bolting a broad arch strongly to the inner side of the timbers in the hold, and by augmenting the size and number of the keelsons. The propellers thus built strongly resemble ocean vessels in outward appearance, and are excellent boats in every respect.

Like the sailing vessels of the lakes, the propellers have to be built with flat bottoms, in order to carry full cargoes on a draught not exceeding 14 feet. The bottom being almost flat amidships and carried well forward and aft, the bilge is necessarily quick, being often described with a radius of not more than 18 to 24 inches. To strengthen this flat bottom the frames have double floors carried nearly from bilge to bilge, and a large number of keelsons are introduced. The central line of keelsons is usually composed of a main keelson about 16 by 32 inches, with a sister keelson each side about 14 by 26 inches. In some of the more recent large vessels the backbone is composed of three keelsons, side by side, 16 inches deep and 14, 16, and 14 inches wide respectively, with two rider keelsons atop, side by side, each 14 inches square. Floor keelsons parallel to the main are then put in, varying in size from 10 by 13 inches to 12 by 13 inches, according to the fancy of the builder, and from 12 to 20 inches apart. In all there are from 10 to 12 strakes of keelsons on the floor of the vessel in large propellers; in small propellers there is a great mass of keelsons in the center, with none at the sides. The bilge is strengthened with a few heavy strakes from 8 to 10 inches thick, molded to suit the curvature of that part of the vessel. The ceiling is then carried up in heavy strakes clear to the beams, being edge-bolted all the way up in the frame spaces. The spaces between the frames on the floor, and sometimes away forward, are generally filled in solid with white oak under the machinery, the filling extending a few feet up the bilge. Three methods are in vogue for flooring the hold. A usual method is to lay a course of 1½- or 2-inch pine or hemlock lumber athwartships across the floor keelsons, and on top of that another course of pine or oak planking about 2 inches thick, running fore and aft, trimming off all irregularities of the surface with an adze. A smooth floor is necessary, on account of carrying grain cargoes in bulk, the hold being cleared out, in discharging, with a steam shovel. A third method, a favorite one with the line propellers, which carry grain almost exclusively on the down trip, is to fit in a large number of chocks between the floor keelsons, their tops 3 inches below the tops of the keelsons. Three-inch oak plank is then laid on the chock flush with the top of the floor keelsons, the latter themselves forming a part of the floor. When the keelsons are massed in the center the flooring is laid on the frames, as in ocean vessels.

The beams of these vessels rest at each end on a broad shelf of oak plank from 4 to 6 inches thick and 2½ feet wide, to which they are firmly bolted; they are not kneed to the ceiling as in ocean vessels. The strake of the shelf next the side of the vessel is thicker than the one inside, and if there are three strakes the outer one is the thickest. The beam is cut to fit closely over the shelf-strakes and fays snugly to the ceiling. A heavy water-way is laid on top of the beam ends, and the beams are bolted strongly both to the shelf and the water-way. This arrangement of timber and iron makes the deck-frame a source of great lateral strength to the vessel. The beams are light, but are of white oak, and the manner in which they are secured protects the hull against racking stresses.

The sterns of lake steamers may be square, round, or elliptical, but the preference is for the elliptical stern, the old-fashioned square stern being now confined to sailing vessels. The overhang in propellers is from 12 to 18 feet, and the most convenient manner of framing it is to place in position a long and heavy "fan-tail" timber, resting on the deadwood and the head of the stern-post, and projecting the whole length of the overhang. The stern frames, or cants, heel on this timber.

It has become the fixed custom to supply propellers with masts and fore-and-aft sails, the sails being used almost constantly as auxiliary to steam; even when under a full head of steam every yard of canvas is spread if

STEAM VESSELS.

the wind favors. This practice has led to the introduction of center-boards to propellers. The freighting craft now have every requisite both of a good sailing vessel and a good steamer, and in this respect the propellers of the lakes are unique. The popular wheel on the lakes is the Philadelphia propeller, so called.

In the insurance rules for the characterization of lake vessels, drawn in 1875 pursuant to the action of a convention held in Buffalo in September, 1874, considerable stress was laid on the importance of adapting large vessels thereafter for transatlantic service. The Welland canal was soon to be completed, and the ocean service would permit of no looseness in construction; and rules were adopted for scantling, fastening, and freeboard suited to the broader field in which lake tonnage might thereafter possibly be employed. Builders have not been governed to any great extent by these rules, but owners have paid attention to them, and the result has been a decided improvement in the strength and excellence of hulls. Copper fastening has not as yet been introduced; but in all other respects the large lake vessels of the last six years have been so constructed as to adapt them to ocean service, and when the Canadian canals are completed more than a hundred staunch steamers could go at once into the carrying trade of the salt water.

LOCALITIES WHERE STEAMERS ARE BUILT.—On lake Ontario few steam vessels are now built. The railroads alongshore have deprived the water of a part of its carrying business, and tugs and canal-boats are now made to transact another part of it. The great side-wheelers and the numerous propellers of former times having nearly all disappeared, it is only now and then a steamboat or a tug is built on the American side of the lake, and then generally for some purely local use. Clayton, Ogdensburg, Oswego, and Irondequoit bay occasionally produce steamers, but the total production would not amount to more than three or four boats of small size annually. The scarcity of oak has had something to do with the change. The timber once grew in magnificent abundance, and ranged from $6 to $12 per thousand board feet, according to length and quality, but it is now scarce at $25.

A number of ship- and boat-yards flourish at Buffalo on the banks of the canals, and among them there are four or five which build and repair lake tonnage. This city has been a leading center of the industry from an early day, and since 1860 has produced steam tonnage actively. The grain trade began in that year to assume immense proportions, springing from 30,000,000 to 50,000,000 bushels in one year, since which time it has been steadily growing. Buffalo has a large lake trade, and the expansion of business gave rise to the employment of a fleet of propellers of the heaviest class, a large proportion of which have been produced locally. The city has had the advantage of engine-building works and the possession of large insurance capital, and has also until recently been able to buy oak at reasonable prices. The large repair business of the port has also been an advantage. Three yards had large dry-docks and railways, with steady work for several hundred competent workmen, and so were equipped to do new work cheaply. In 1873 the panic in financial circles made ship-building dull for several years, but since 1878 the yards at Buffalo have all been quite active. In 1879 and 1880 a good deal of tonnage, large and small, was produced, among the rest the propellers Rochester and New York, of 2,000 and 1,920 tons, respectively. The New York was 269 feet long, custom-house measurement, 37 feet beam, and $16\frac{1}{3}$ feet hold, with upper works, and was able to carry about 1,800 tons of cargo. The Rochester is a representative of the largest class now engaged in the lake trades. She is 287 feet long over all, 40 feet beam, 28 feet total depth of hold, with a carrying power of 2,200 tons. The keel of this vessel is 10 by 14 inches square, the frame 17 by 18 inches over the keel, the main keelson 16 inches square, sister keelsons 14 by 16 inches, and the floor keelsons 12 by 16 inches. The ceiling varies from 6 to 9 inches, and the planking is 4 and 6 inches. She is oak built throughout, except that the decking, houses, and some of the beams of the upper decks are of white pine. Following the late fashion, the hull is strapped with $\frac{1}{2}$ by 5-inch iron, 4 feet apart. Two compound engines, with 2 steel boilers, comprise the machinery, which will develop 1,000 horse-power and drive the vessel at a speed of 12 knots an hour. To build vessels of this size almost a million feet of lumber have to be bought, and as oak in Buffalo cannot now be bought to advantage, the builders are beginning to feel the severe competition of the yards farther west, which are nearer the oak supply.

The next point is Cleveland, Ohio, where three yards are devoted to the production of large propellers. A builder who has been in business more than 33 years had built a few small vessels, when, in 1878, he went into the construction of large propellers. He built in 1878 the John N. Glidden, of 1,323 tons, 222 feet keel, 35 feet beam, and 20 feet hold; in 1880 the A. Everett, of 1,200 tons, 210 feet keel, 35 feet beam, $18\frac{1}{2}$ feet hold; and in 1881 a propeller of 1,393 tons, 248 feet keel, $36\frac{1}{2}$ feet beam, $19\frac{1}{2}$ feet hold. These vessels were all two-decked and oak built, the frames, beams, ceiling, planking, keels, and keelsons being of that timber, while the deckings, houses, spars, and a few beams were of white pine. The frames were cut from 6- and 8-inch flitch and spaced about 22 inches from center to center. They were molded 16 inches over the keel, 14 inches at the bilge, and 7 or 8 inches at the plank-sheer, and as the timbers were not large enough to take treenails the planking was spiked on with bolts at the butts. Salt was freely used, a large quantity being placed between the frames in the usual manner, and the upper side of the beams was channeled and filled with salt and the keelsons thoroughly pickled. Hackmatack knees were used. The stem of a lake propeller is perpendicular, and the rule for the overhang of the stern is to extend it a little more than far enough to shelter the screw-wheel and the rudder. The three vessels of Mr. Radcliff consumed about 750,000 feet of white oak and 60,000 feet of white pine each, and cost about $75,000 apiece.

A firm which began to build in 1850 have launched a great deal of heavy tonnage for the trade of Cleveland and the lakes generally, making a specialty of steam craft. In 1880 and 1881 they built two oak propellers, costing $100,000 and $125,000 respectively. The steam barge Columbia, of about 1,300 tons, was on the stocks in the census year. She was 236 feet long on the keel, 250 feet over all, 35⅔ feet beam, 19⅔ feet hold, and drew 6 feet 5 inches when launched. It required 750,000 feet of oak, 50,000 feet of white pine, and 125 tons of iron to build her, and the total cost was $120,000. The frame was molded 16 inches at the keel, 14 inches at the bilge, and 6 inches at the head, and the double frame sided 12 inches. A main keelson was put in 16 inches square, with a sister keelson on each side 14 inches square. Floor keelsons, 12 inches square and a foot apart, were laid away out to the bilge on both sides. In a sharp ship these logs could have been placed amidships, and would have made a center keelson 2 feet thick and 11 feet high, but the flatness of the floor made the distribution of the keelsons preferable. There were only 8 inches dead rise. The ceiling of the bilge was heavy, to match with the keelson, but tapered to 6 inches, which thickness it carried to the upper deck, and was edge-bolted from the bilge to the rail. The bottom plank was 5 inches thick; that of the sides 4 inches, square-fastened with iron spikes and butt-bolted clear through. No hog-frame was used in the boat, but an arch of oak 4 inches thick and 6 feet in depth was strongly bolted to the ceiling and frame on each side of the vessel, extending from the bilge within 20 feet of stem and stern and rising to the upper deck amidships. The beams were spaced 2 feet apart below and 3 feet above, and rested on strong shelves, which in turn were strongly supported by heavy hackmatack knees. The ceiling, arch planks, and beams were grooved for brine. The machinery was placed away aft, within 20 feet of the stern-post, and was composed of two low-pressure engines 3 feet in diameter, with 3 feet stroke, and a boiler 12 feet in diameter and 18 feet long. The latter, which was between decks, rested in a wrought-iron pan, sustained by 16 double T-iron beams, 17 inches apart. The screw was 11 feet in diameter—a fair type of the ordinary lake propeller.

Another firm at Cleveland (T. Quayle's Sons) builds oak propellers of the largest size engaged in the trade of the lakes. Among the product of their yards are the following:

Years.	Propellers.	Keel.	Beam.	Hold.	Tonnage.
		Feet.	*Feet.*	*Feet.*	
1878	Delaware	250	36	16	1,732
1878	Conestoga	250	36	16	1,726
1878	Buffalo	260	36	16	1,763
1879	Milwaukee	265	36	16	1,771
1879	Chicago	265	36	16	1,847
1880	Wococken	250	37	19	1,800
1880	Henry Chisholm				1,775
1881	John B. Lyon	255	38	20	1,710
1881	City of Rome	268	40	21	1,908
1881	Cumberland	250	37	16	1,601

For the length over all from 16 to 18 feet must be added to the length of keel, according to the size of the vessel. The first five of these boats were fitted with Bishop arches, or hog-frames, and had each one spar, a foremast. The others had no hog-frames, but were strapped diagonally with iron on the outside of the frame timbers and belted with iron at the top of the straps. Arches of iron plate a foot wide were bolted outside and inside of the frames. Each carried 4 masts, the forward ones about 95 feet long, with short topmasts, the jigger having no topmast and ending in a pole and ball. The large propellers each consumed about 950,000 feet of oak, 90,000 feet of white pine, and 130 tons of iron, exclusive of machinery and outfits. The firm had a new oak 1,800-ton propeller on the stocks in the census year 261½ feet long on the keel, 278 feet long over all, 38¼ feet beam, and 22¼ feet hold, a four-master, designed to carry 1,900 tons of grain, which was being fitted with a center-board, for use when under sail. These lake propellers are always under sail when the wind favors, as well as under steam.

Wages in Cleveland ranged from $1 25 to $2 25 per day, the most of the men in the yard getting $2 and $2 25. It requires about 50 men, working nine months, to set a large propeller afloat, the labor bill being about $20,000. Oak costs about $25 per thousand board feet. In the round log, in rafts, it is delivered at the yard for $21 and $22 per thousand, and to saw it costs about $3 50 a thousand. The price of plank varies from $25 to $28. Before the war oak was bought in Cleveland for from $12 to $15, but the timber is now growing scarce. Cleveland has its own engine-building works, and thus possesses every facility for ship-building on a large scale. The yards here are all equipped in a thorough manner. The bevel saw is used for getting out the frames, and bolt-cutters, derricks worked by teams of horses, planers, steam-hauling apparatus, and every device known to man for simplifying and saving labor is employed. The large repair business of a port with an extensive lake commerce enables the proprietors of yards to keep their men together in the intervals of building, and thus they are always ready to take a new contract and perform the work promptly.

There are various places on the Ohio shore where fishing boats, schooners, tugs, and other vessels are built, but it is only at Cleveland that steamers are made a specialty. On the two rivers and the lake which connect lake

STEAM VESSELS. 171

Erie with lake Huron there are a number of places dependent on Detroit for machinery which produce a great deal of steam tonnage. They are, in order, Gibraltar, Wyandotte, below Detroit, Marine City, Mount Clemens, and Port Huron, all in the state of Michigan.

At Gibraltar there is one large yard, fitted up in first-class manner, capable of constructing the largest sized wooden propellers. The builders undertake about one a year. They employ from 30 to 50 men, pay them fair wages (about $2 a day), do a quiet but prosperous business, and build from 1,200 up to 1,500 tons, at a cost of $70 or $75 a ton equipped ready for sea. Their steamer in the census year was 246 feet long, 36 feet beam, 19¾ feet hold, a two-decker with 4 masts, registering 1,399 tons.

The yard at Wyandotte is exclusively employed in the construction of iron vessels.

Detroit has three large ship-yards, at which is done a mixed business of building and repairing. The repair business of the city is extensive. Engine and boiler shops exist here in abundance, and in the city is owned an immense amount of tonnage, which naturally seeks the home port for carpentry, iron work, and refitting generally. Detroit is one of the old and prominent building places of the upper lakes. The panic of 1873 was felt here severely, and little was done during the four years of depression save the keeping of old boats in repair. The yards were almost idle, and the workmen became very much scattered. In 1877 the country had recovered from the shock, and a new demand for iron and lumber sprang up. Michigan was the state which chiefly supplied the East with these products, and the thrill of new life in trade quickly set in motion every ax and hammer in the ship-yards of Detroit. Since that time business has been brisk and growing; in fact, the demand for ship-carpenters has been so great that about 250 Frenchmen have been brought from Quebec and Montreal to supply the deficiency at the yards, and though not so efficient as Americans, they are docile and are now being rapidly trained, and will add materially to the resources of Detroit for ship-building. Two of the yards here are owned by an organization of large capital, which also owns the iron ship-yard at Wyandotte and employs the best available engineering talent. Its contracts for sail or steam or wooden or iron vessels are executed in whichever one of its three yards can best perform the work. In the yards of this concern in Detroit every form of labor-saving device is employed. The hauling of timbers, the fashioning of them for ship's use, and the handling and lifting are all done by steam- or horse-power; nothing is done by human muscle that can be avoided. The operations of this large concern are thought to indicate the strong tendency in the commerce of the lakes to concentrate enterprise in the hands of a few large firms having heavy capital. Men of smaller capital find it difficult to withstand this competition, because the big concerns can build and repair at a lower rate of compensation, just as they can operate the vessels when built at a lower charge for freighting. There were built two schooners of 528 and 859 tons respectively in the census year, and the following wooden steamers: propeller Iron Age, of 859 tons, 175 feet long, 34 feet beam, and 20 feet hold, molded, and the screw ferry- and river-boat Garland, of 248 tons, 110 feet long, 29 feet beam, and 10 feet hold, molded—all oak built. Wages were $1 and $1 25 a day for laborers, and $2 and $2 25 for carpenters and other skilled men. Oak was formerly $10 and $15 per thousand feet, according to length and quality; it is now $20 in the flitch, $25 in the squared timber, and $30 for first-rate plank. The growing scarcity of good oak was complained of, and the shortness of the stuff put into the frames, keels, and keelsons of vessels was noticeable. One builder was building a screw ferry- and river-boat with a long raking stem, for ice-breaking in the winter, 107 feet long over all, the keel and stem of which were composed of six pieces, only one of which was more than 28 feet long, and that not over 40 feet. In the frame there was not a stick over 12 feet long. In the yard of the Dry-Dock Company a steam barge was building 250 feet long and 37 feet beam, to register about 1,600 tons. The bottom amidships was almost flat, and the sides were straight from the very quick bilge to the rail. The form was well adapted to the use of long timber, and on Puget sound the frames would have been made of not more than ten pieces each, six of them from 20 to 33 feet in length, with four short ones at the bilge. In this vessel there were fourteen pieces in each square body frame, two of them not over 30 feet, and ten pieces under 14 feet each. Longer stuff would have been hard to get, and consequently was too expensive. The tendency in Detroit is now strongly in favor of iron steamers.

Mount Clemens is a pretty little village strung out along a bluff on a tributary of lake Saint Clair, a community of saw-mills, lumber yards, and stave factories. There are three ship-yards in the place. The town is surrounded with woods, which formerly yielded large oak in abundance. A few big trees are still cut now and then not far from the town, and some fine specimens of the old growth were to be seen at the saw-mills when visited, one log being seen which was 35 inches in diameter and 360 years old. At one mill they told of sawing a white-oak log 4¼ feet in diameter and squaring 1,700 feet out of the tree, and a few years ago one was cut that was 6¼ feet through at the butt and 3¾ feet through 60 feet from the ground, furnishing five 16-foot logs. That gigantic specimen grew in a favored locality, and was probably not less than 350 years old. One oak tree was still standing near Mount Clemens 5 feet through at the butt. These giants of primitive growth are now rare, and in fact nearly all the large timber of this locality has been culled from the woods. Much of it has been squared up and rafted off to the markets on the lower lakes, and what is left is either small or grows on the uplands, where it fails to reach the perfection of the oak found in swamp lands. The best stuff put into Mount Clemens vessels now comes from swamps in Canada. It is a common practice here to buy the common stuff for a vessel in the woods, paying from $9 to $12 per thousand feet in the round log, delivered in the yard, getting the plank and better pieces in Canada. Plank costs from $20 to $26 per thousand, according to length; white pine $40 per thousand finished. Two or three small vessels for the freighting of coal, lumber, and grain are built at Mount Clemens every year. In the census year three steam barges were built, one of 325 tons for $30,000, the others smaller. Wages were $2 a day for the best men, but the majority of ship-yard hands got from $1 25 to $1 50. There was a large mingling of the lately imported Canadian French element among the men. Two medium-sized steam barges were on the stocks in the census year, and in one of them the builders were employing an original arrangement of the keelsons to gain longitudinal strength while economizing space. In most lake propellers the keelsons are spaced across the whole width of the floor and the ceiling laid atop of them, a plan whereby a foot in the depth of hold is lost. In this propeller they were assembled in the center. Five logs 12 inches square were laid side by side and strongly bolted to the frames and keel and to each other, and two riders were placed atop of them, each 14 by 16 inches and about 6 inches apart. In the forward hold an additional log, 10 by 12 inches, was placed on each rider; but for about half the length of the vessel forward of the machinery, where the stress chiefly comes, the 10 by 12 logs were replaced with 14 by 16 inch logs, which were sprung up 12 inches in the middle by oak blocks, placed at intervals. These two top strakes of the keelson took the form of an arch, and two strong bolts were driven through each arching log clear down through keelson, frame, and keel, imparting great strength to the structure. The vessel measured 160 feet on the keel, with 11 feet overhang of stern, 31 feet beam, and 11 feet hold. In general respects she was like other lake propellers.

Marine City is a small town on the Saint Clair river, and has about the same characteristics as Mount Clemens.

Port Huron, at the gateway into the lake of the same name, was formerly an active building locality. It is favorably situated at the entrance to the Saint Clair river, through which flows the whole current of the upper lake traffic, and there is an abundance of oak timber in its own county and all along the lake above. There are three large and well-equipped yards in Port Huron, but they do little except repair work. The panic of 1873 put a sudden end to the building of new vessels here.

East Saginaw and Bay City, both on the Saginaw river, and in the center of an immense salt and lumber business, build many fine wooden propellers for freighting. There are three yards in the former and four large yards in the latter. Schooners and tugs are also built, but the principal and the best product of both towns is in the line of large propellers. The industry has flourished for 20 years and more. The Saginaw river felt the effects of the panic of 1873 as much as the other lake towns, and a memento of that disastrous revulsion existed at East Saginaw in 1881 in the form of a center-board vessel in frame which had been begun in 1873. The panic came just as the frame had been set up. The payment of money stopped, and as the builder could find no one to aid him to complete the job the vessel was abandoned, the weather-beaten frames sagging and tumbling down into the grass that had grown all over the bank. This depression lasted about five years on the Saginaw river, and then there sprang up a new demand for lumber, which put life into every lumber-yard and ship-yard on the stream. In the census year business was brisk. Oak has always been cheap here, and the local builders still enjoy the advantage of buying at a slightly lower price than at any other point on the lakes. The peculiarities of the yards are the admirable manner in which steam has been utilized for as many purposes as possible and the thorough system employed in all branches of the work. The finest ship-yards for wooden ship-building in the United States are on the Saginaw river. Those at Bay City are four in number, of which one may be taken as a type of a northern lakes yard. A railroad runs past the yard, by means of which a great deal of the heavy oak is brought to the spot. The logs are rolled from the platform cars and lie upon the ground until called for, and a long rope from within the shops is attached to each log as it lies on the ground, or the end of the trunk is lifted up and supported by a pair of wheels and the rope is then attached. Steam-power is then applied, and the log is drawn across the railroad track down to the yard, through the gate, and along the beaten path to the saw-mill. It is there cut into flitch or square timber, as the case may be, planed, and passed on, all the while by steam-power, to a place in the yard where it can lie and season. The stick never changes end, and no steps are wasted in handling it. Whether designed to go through the bevel saw for fashioning into a frame or intended for the steam box to be softened for planking it passes on and on until it is finally lifted to its place in the vessel by a steam derrick. The yard has a complete equipment of bevel, jig, and joiner's saws, bolt-cutters, steam boxes, planers, treenail machines, and small tools. These arrangements were originally made necessary by the scarcity of labor; but they especially fulfill the purpose of saving expense in constructing the ship, and it is claimed that one-half of the labor formerly required is now saved. Nearly all the best yards on the lakes are organized on this plan. The Saginaw and some other lake builders launch their vessels sideways, a safer method than launching endways, owing to the great length of the vessels now required in the lake trade.

The Saginaw river vessels are built both for local owners and for others. A great deal of business comes from places even as far distant as Buffalo. Every new vessel can be immediately loaded with lumber and salt without leaving the stream. Oak is now brought from the interior by river and by railroad. Standing in the woods, it can be bought for $5 and $6 per thousand feet for short stuff and not exceeding $11 and $12 per thousand for long, and is cut, rolled to the water's edge, and rafted down, or is hauled to the railroad and placed on cars. At one yard in Bay City 1,500,000 feet of oak were floating in the river alongside of the wharf at one time in the census year. The cost of sawing in the yard is small, from $2 50 to $3 50 a thousand feet, and the slabs nearly or quite pay the expense, as a great deal of thin plank can be got out of them. Oak flitch can be bought from the sawmills, delivered, for $17 and $18 per thousand; white-pine decking and finishing stuff costs from $35 to $40 per thousand. It is a singular fact that the builders of the lake Huron region buy their decking generally in Toledo and other lake Erie ports. The long white-pine logs are rafted thither from the Saginaw river, and the finished lumber is freighted back; but the local mills do not handle that kind of stuff, owing to its length. Wages at Bay City and East Saginaw are low. Carpenters get an average of $2, and seldom more than $2 25; laborers $1 and $1 25 per day. Cheap lumber and low wages guarantee the production of cheap ships.

The Oceanica, launched early in 1881 for a Buffalo owner, is a good specimen of the Bay City propeller. She measures 1,490 tons, was built for ocean service, if required, and is 250 feet keel, $265\frac{1}{2}$ feet in length over all, $38\frac{3}{4}$ feet beam, $19\frac{1}{2}$ feet hold, with two decks and three masts. She had the usual full-bottomed model, and was oak built and strongly strapped. The frames were cut from 6-inch flitch, and the floors were trebled to 4 feet up the bilge; they were molded 16 and sided 18 inches over the keel, and spaced 22 inches. The main keelson was 16 by 17 inches; the two sister keelsons were 14 by 13 inches. Six floor keelsons on each side of the main keelson were 13 by 12 inches, all securely bolted through the frames with $1\frac{1}{8}$- and $1\frac{1}{4}$-inch iron. The thick stuff on the bilge was 11, 9, and 8 inches thick, with 6-inch ceiling above and 4 streaks of clamps 14 inches wide and 7 thick, all edge-bolted with 1-inch round iron. The shelf of the lower deck was 3 feet wide, 6 inches thick; of the upper deck, 3 feet wide; the middle streak 7 inches thick, the other two 6 inches. The outside plank is 5 inches thick, square-fastened with two bolts and two 10-inch spikes in every frame. Lower deck beams, 9 by 14 inches; upper deck beams, 7 by 10 inches, with 8-inch hanging knees under the shelves. The main strap, running around the vessel near the plank-sheer, is 10 inches wide and $\frac{7}{8}$ inch thick, while the diagonal straps are 5 inches wide and $\frac{1}{2}$ inch thick, and are riveted to the main strap and bolted through frames and ceiling. Amidships a few of the diagonal straps cross each other at right angles and are riveted to each other. The houses are away forward and aft, after the fashion of lake propellers, and the deck between is clear of everything and is very spacious. Five long hatches (long athwartships) are employed in handling cargo. The machinery for this vessel was prepared in Detroit, as is usual for the Saginaw river yards. The engines were compound, having a high-pressure cylinder of 30-inch bore and 40-inch stroke and a low-pressure cylinder of 50-inch bore and 40-inch stroke. The shaft was 11 inches in diameter, and carried a 12-foot wheel. Two steel boilers 9 feet in diameter and 16 feet long were put in. The lower masts were tall, the topmasts light; they were wire rigged, in accordance with the practice of the lakes. A Providence windlass was placed in the forecastle, with $1\frac{1}{2}$- and $1\frac{3}{4}$-inch iron cables. It cost $125,000 to build and fit this vessel out. Her capacity was 2,000 tons of heavy cargo on 14 feet draught of water, and she was manned with 16 men.

There are a number of small towns on the lake Michigan shore where vessel building is carried on from time to time, but at only two were there any steamers built in the census year, namely, Saint Joseph and Grand Haven. There is plenty of oak in the shore counties yet; but the panic of 1873 made business dull until within two or three years, and it was not until 1881 that the ship-yards of Grand Haven and Saint Joseph had fairly got to work again. The production of the latter town in the census year was the propeller Sky Lark, of 260 tons, 123 feet long, 23 feet beam, and $8\frac{1}{2}$ feet hold; the steamer Mary Graham, of 91 tons, a 96-foot boat; and the sloop J. C. King, of 14 tons, 35 feet long, 15 feet beam, and 5 feet hold. Facilities exist in the town for large work. Machinery is bought in Chicago. At Grand Haven, a large propeller was finished in 1881, after the close of the census year, 245 feet long over all, 35 feet beam, and $18\frac{2}{3}$ feet hold, registering 1,187 tons—a fine specimen of the lake steamer. Statistics were obtained in regard to 5 tugs, 226 tons, costing $43,000, a propeller of 335 tons, costing $35,000, and a schooner of 152 tons, worth $15,000; all built in one year. There are two yards in Grand Haven with every facility for large work. Wages are the same as in other parts of Michigan, viz: $2 25 for best carpenters, $1 25 and $1 50 for cheap hands. Short oak can be bought for $6 a thousand standing in the woods and $8 and $10 a thousand for long. To cut, haul, and saw brings the price up to $16 and $17 a thousand for flitch and from $20 to $25 for plank. White pine is $30 for decking, and from $20 to $40 for the houses. Some Norway pine is used, but not much. It is cheap, but the Michigan men use very little inferior stuff in their vessels.

At Muskegon a few tugs are built yearly.

On the Wisconsin shore there are three places where steamers are built, Milwaukee, Manitowoc, and Green Bay, and these towns complete the list of localities on the northern lakes producing steam tonnage—fifteen in all. The two yards at Milwaukee are both equipped in the finest manner. Each has facilities for docking and repairing vessels; each has built a large number of tugs, schooners, and freighting propellers, and at one of them since 1868 more than 35 vessels have been set afloat. Milwaukee felt the hard times following 1873 severely, and not until the census year had the construction of new tonnage again become active. Each yard began a propeller of medium size, and the prospect was that the general revival of trade and freighting would keep the yards busy with new work. Three hundred ship-carpenters could be employed at each yard in repairing and building, but business had not in 1880 revived to an extent sufficient to employ more than that number in all the ship-work of the city. The chief disadvantage at Milwaukee is the lack of local timber, as the oak has been cut off and the yards have to resort to places farther down the lake, or over in Michigan, for all their supplies of oak and pine, and, in consequence, have to pay $5 or $6 more per thousand feet; but their superior equipment of labor-saving machinery has thus far enabled them to overcome this disadvantage in competing for contracts.

Manitowoc, situated in the midst of forests and reached by railroad only within a few years, thrives chiefly on the work of its three large ship-yards. The tonnage produced at this place was formerly in the line of schooners and tugs, but since the revival of business, three years ago, a number of steamers have been built, the preference of owners now being for that class of vessels. In 15 years one yard built 30 sailing vessels and 3 or 4 tugs. Another yard, founded in 1855, has in late years built 15 sailing vessels, 6 tugs, and 7 or 8 propellers, and in 1881 had under way a propeller and a large tug for the lumber business. The third yard has not as yet done much. A large tug was ordered by three firms which had a large number of sailing vessels in the lumber business and expected to use the tug jointly. In the chapter on sailing vessels it has already been stated how popular is the practice on the lakes of collecting a string of from four to eight schooners, loaded to deep-water line with lumber, salt, or grain, hoisting all sail, and aiding them on the voyage with a powerful tug or propeller, sailing far ahead and attached to the foremost vessel of the tow with a long cable. The new tug at Manitowoc was designed for this purpose. Her dimensions and scantling are as follows: Keel, 150 feet; beam, molded, 28 feet; depth, molded, 13 feet; keel, 13 by 15 inches square; keelson, 14 by 14 inches, with a rider 6 by 8 inches on each side of the stanchions; sister keelsons, 12 inches square. As the boat was sharp on the floor, no side keelsons were required. Frames, 10 by $12\frac{1}{2}$ inches over the keel, molded $10\frac{1}{2}$ inches on the bilge and $6\frac{1}{4}$ inches at the head; spacing, 21 inches. Double floors were used, so as to avoid butts over the keel, and the frames were solid under the engine and bearings. Ceiling on flat of floor, 3 inches; bilge-streaks, 6 in number, $5\frac{1}{2}$ inches thick and 9 inches wide, edge-bolted; above that to the clamps, 5 inches, square-fastened with 2 bolts and 2 spikes. Planking: Garboards, 6 inches; all the rest 4 inches, being 10 to 13 inches wide on the bottom, 8 inches on the bilge, 7 and $6\frac{1}{2}$ inches on the wales, and 6 inches near the plank-sheer, square-fastened with 1 bolt and 3 spikes. Shelf, 30 inches wide, 5 inches thick, edge-bolted. Beams: Oak, 9 inches square, molded 8 inches at the end, notched over the thick streak of the shelf and dovetailed into the clamps; spacing, 30 inches; upper-deck beams, one of oak, 4 by 5 inches every 7 feet; the rest of white pine, 3 by 4 inches. Deck plank, 3 by 5 inches; upper deck, $2\frac{1}{2}$ by 4 inches. There are two hooks with pointers at each end of the boat, with braces between those forward. Plank-sheer, 5 inches; main rail, two pieces, 4 by 6 inches, with two stringer pieces of the same size; hanging knees under each deck, 7-inch siding in the hold, tow-posts going through both decks, capped with iron and kneed and braced below. The bow of this powerful boat was covered with $\frac{1}{4}$-inch sheet-iron, to resist the action of ice, and the stem was ironed with a piece 4 inches wide and 3 inches thick, which hooded the edges of the plating.

The yards at Green Bay occasionally build steam craft. The locality is a favorite one with contractors who have no fixed habitation and with some who have offices in Chicago, who get their contracts in that city and go to Green Bay to build the vessel. Oak is abundant and cheap, and expenses of all kinds are low.

Steamer building on the lakes is prosperous, successful, and profitable. Builders have fitted up their yards admirably, producing vessels that have satisfied the requirements of trade at each stage of western development, and their business has flourished peacefully under the protection of the navigation laws of the United States, which reserves to American vessels the trade between different parts of our coast. Their vessels are cheap, staunch, and durable. The center of their industry has moved westward with the disappearance of the oak forests of the East; but this, as well as all other changes, has been strictly in the line of adapting themselves to the circumstances under which their operations are carried on. Steamer building is the growing branch of the industry, as competition with railroads is gradually converting the lake tonnage into vessels propelled wholly or in part by machinery. The supply of oak is giving out, but building does not slacken on that account, and yards are being established for the construction of vessels of iron.

ON THE WESTERN RIVERS.

The Mississippi river and its tributaries drain a region a million and a quarter square miles in area. Nineteen populous states and several growing territories use these streams as commercial highways. The total length of route available for steamboat navigation is about 12,000 miles, besides portions of streams available only at high water, which would swell the aggregate to some 14,000 miles.

These rivers, while having some features in common, have special characteristics. The Ohio, the scene of the busiest traffic and most active boat-building, runs through a country that was covered originally by a great hard-wood forest, and even as late as 1850 the banks on both sides were covered with dense woods, with scarce a break except where towns were planted. The upper part of the river, from Pittsburgh to Cincinnati, flows between hills from 200 to 300 feet high, but below Cincinnati the high banks recede, and the country is more level. The Ohio is subject to great fluctuations in the depth of water. In August and September the river is so low that sand-bars and ledges of rocks show up from the river bed with not more than 18 inches of water over them, and hundreds of steamboats have to be laid up at Pittsburgh and Cincinnati in consequence. Three times in the year the river rises, namely, in February, in May or June, and in November, the spring rise being the highest. At Cincinnati in 1832 the river rose 63 feet (a) above low-water mark. The commercial activity of this river is intimately connected with the periods of deep water. In preparation for a rise, thousands of flat boats and barges are loaded with coal and other goods in the upper tributaries of the Ohio, towing steamers for moving them being held in

---

a It has reached $65\frac{1}{4}$ feet in 1883.

STEAM VESSELS. 175

readiness to take quick advantage of the flood, and when the water deepens to 6 feet it liberates the imprisoned fleets, and one after another they dart out from the Monongahela, Allegheny, Kanawha, and other streams and speed down the Ohio in rapid succession to their various destinations below. Intermingled with the tows of barges are large numbers of passenger and freight steamers, brought out to resume the traffic between the different river cities, and throughout its whole length the river is in a state of intense activity. The Ohio always has a rapid current; that is to say, from 2 to 3½ miles per hour in deep places and 7 or 8 miles over the shallows and in floods. There is one obstacle to the navigation of the Ohio, namely, the rapids at Louisville; but a canal has been built around them at a cost of $3,500,000.

The Mississippi river above Saint Louis is liable to fluctuations in the depth of water, but not to such an extent as the Ohio. There is seldom less than 4 feet of water all the way to Saint Paul, recent improvements having given that depth, and the river is available for navigation during seven months of the year. For five months the upper river is closed by ice, but below Cairo the river is never closed either by ice or low water. The whole stream is the route of a great commerce.

The Missouri river is not much navigated above Saint Joseph, although in times of deep water steamboats can run to Fort Benton, 2,600 miles from its mouth. The upper river is closed by ice five months in the year.

The southern rivers are seldom closed by ice or low water. At some points on the Tennessee wing-dams are used to deepen the channel, and at certain places windlasses have been established on the bank to assist boats against the current; that noble river affords passage to steamboats drawing 4 feet and less for a distance of 800 miles above and below the works in progress at the Mussel shoals, which interrupt navigation. Most of the other southern rivers are subject to variations in depth, but they are all good highways.

The traffic of the rivers is largely of a general character, such as would naturally be expected to grow up between a number of cities having means of easy communication with each other. In addition, however, it has strong special features. Saint Louis and the Ohio river towns, Pittsburgh, Cincinnati, and Louisville especially, have long enjoyed a large trade in supplying the South with agricultural implements, wagons, and manufactured goods generally. Coal is also sent in immense quantities from the upper tributaries of the Ohio to the towns farther down the river and all along the Mississippi, and grain is sent in increasing bulk from Saint Louis for export. On the other hand, New Orleans supplies the upper towns with groceries, railroad iron, and a large variety of other imported goods. In the varying nature of the products of the different parts of the region permeated by the rivers, and in their varying needs, all the elements exist of a large internal trade and a busy river traffic. The navigation laws of the United States reserve the navigation of these rivers to American vessels exclusively, and foreign vessels are not permitted to trade above New Orleans.

Steamboating in the West is carried on under very different circumstances from that in the East, as will have been already seen. The system of intercommunication is of enormous extent; the rivers are swift and fluctuate in depth; and steamboating has been compelled to adapt itself to these peculiarities of the situation. The imperative necessity has been laid upon builders, in the first place, of obtaining the smallest possible draught. In the early days, while under the influence of deep-sea ideas, and while building boats with double frames and heavy scantling generally, the only resource for light draught was to give the boats a perfectly flat bottom; but in later years, especially after 1840, builders learned to add to the flat bottom a system of building with single frames and light scantling, which greatly lessened the weight of their vessels and made them marvels of naval construction. Light-draught construction has finally reached the perfection of a fine art, and nowhere else are vessels built which can carry such heavy cargoes on so small a depth of water, steamboats existing to-day which float at the 6-foot water-mark with 2,000 tons of goods aboard. Next in order, builders have been compelled to study how to supply their boats with machinery of great power without increasing their weight. To breast the flood of the rivers, and especially to guide tows of loaded barges through intricate channels, boats must have engine power nearly equal to that of ocean steamers. Originally the ordinary type of condensing engines was used, with walking-beam oscillating in the air aloft; but these were soon given up for a lighter type with stronger action. Condensation was dispensed with first, and the walking-beam next. The engines were brought up from the hold and laid horizontally on deck, one on each side of the boat, with pistons and long connecting-rods directly attached to the paddle-wheel shaft, and were worked with a pressure of from 50 to 150 pounds of steam, and with a long, slow, powerful stroke. Though consuming an excessive amount of fuel, this type of engine had the advantage of being stronger and lighter and of occupying less room than that of the eastern boats. A third peculiarity of the western boats has arisen from the ever-changing depth of water, and the consequent impossibility of employing fixed wharves for landings. On inland lakes and the coast rivers no country landing is without its little cheaply built pier. On the western rivers, wherever any structure is employed at all, it can only be of the character of a floating wharf, or wharf-boat—a broad, flat-bottomed, strongly built barge with square ends, having an overhanging platform and a large deck-house to protect the accumulations of freight and shelter the officers of the steamboat companies. These floats are employed at all towns having a regular traffic, and are moored by strong cables to iron rings, bolted into the heads of piles driven into the river bank, there being rows of these rings all the way up the bank, for use at different stages of the water. But wharf-boats are expensive structures, and cannot be employed in country places, where steamers only call occasionally. There are thousands of localities all along the rivers where small lots of goods and a few people must be put off or taken on from time to time. At these points the steamer must shove her bow slowly up on the sloping sandy beach, keep her wheel slowly moving, throw a plank ashore quickly, carry a line up to a tree to steady her, and effect the transfer of packages and passengers before the current of the river swings her off again. To qualify steamers for landings of this description they have to be built with full bows, having a long rounding rake, the forward deck being carried out on them as broad as possible, often, though not always, overhanging at the sides like a platform, and framed square across on a line with the stem. The great passenger boats usually have bows as sharp at least as those on Long Island sound, but the great majority of western steamers have the full raking bow. So far as the fourth point above alluded to is concerned—the vast extent of the river navigation of the West—its influence is chiefly in the large size of the boats and the great multitude of them. At the present time the fleet includes 1,198 vessels, measuring 251,792.85 tons register, and even this large fleet cannot move the traffic of the western rivers. Auxiliary to the steamboats there is an immense fleet of flat-boats and barges, towed by steamers, for the carriage of grain, coal, iron, building-stone, and general merchandise. So extended has been the production of these barges of late years that the city of Pittsburgh, Pennsylvania, now owns the most vessel tonnage of any port in the United States, having about 3,800 vessels of all kinds, measuring in all 850,000 tons. On all the western rivers tributary to the Mississippi there are now 5,397 flat-boats and barges, measuring 1,251,528.74 tons. The grand total of the tonnage of the rivers is 6,595 vessels; capacity, 1,503,321.59 tons. The barges are now exempt by law from registration.

The steamers of the West in the early times were mainly side-wheelers, though stern-wheel boats were built to a certain extent; but the preference until after 1850 was for vessels of the class first named. Up to about that date stern-wheel boats were not sanctioned by the insurance companies for the Missouri, Red, and some other western rivers, though for towing they were far superior. Since 1850 they have come into common use, and outnumber the side-wheelers about three to one.

Steamboating was introduced to the West by the same men who were the pioneers on the Hudson. Fulton and Livingston, having secured what they hoped would be a monopoly of the Ohio and Mississippi rivers, in 1811 built at Pittsburgh the little stern-wheel boat Orleans, of about 200 tons burden, rigged with masts and sails, the latter to be spread when the rivers were broad and the wind fair. Wood was used for fuel. The boat was regularly and strongly framed, but had no guards or upper works, and, like all the early boats, only one chimney. January 10, 1812, she arrived at New Orleans for the first time, her speed being about 3 miles per hour. This pioneer of the rivers ran for two years between New Orleans and Natchez as a packet, and was sunk by a snag near Baton Rouge in 1814. When the Orleans made this first trip down the Ohio the river was navigated only by small sailing craft and flat-boats, the latter pushed along with poles or rowed with long sweeps, like oars; but the superiority and success of steam was so instantly demonstrated that new steamboats followed as fast as the capital could be secured to build them. The Comet, a stern-wheeler with vibrating engines, was built at Pittsburgh in 1813, and also ran down to New Orleans, her machinery being sold there for a cotton factory. The Vesuvius followed, built at Pittsburgh in 1813 by R. W. Fulton, and sent, like the others, to the great river below. A small steamer of 50 tons was built at Brownsville, on the Monongahela, in 1814, and the same year the Etna, of 300 tons, was launched at Pittsburgh for the trade between Natchez and Louisville. Wheeling next caught the fever; some one there built the Washington, the first boat with two decks. The machinery, which in previous boats had been placed in the hold, was set up on the deck of the hull—a position it has since retained in all western river boats. The low power of the engines had made it practicable to employ her predecessors only on the lower Ohio and the Mississippi when the current was less than 3 miles per hour, and they could never ascend the swifter parts of the river after having once gone down. The Washington was, on the other hand, a powerful boat for her size. After she had gone over the falls of the Ohio at Louisville, she made two trips to New Orleans and back to Shippingport, (a) performing one round trip in 45 days. Her success was the signal for the construction of a great many small steamboats at different points on the Ohio river, on which stream all the early building took place, and which to-day still produces five-sixths of all the new tonnage of the West. By 1818 there were half a dozen yards around the falls of the Ohio river near Louisville. Engines were often put in at New Orleans. In 1818, at Cincinnati, was built the General Pike, famous in her day, intended for passenger traffic exclusively. This boat had a 100-foot keel and 25 feet beam, and a handsome cabin was erected on her deck between the engines. The central hall measured 40 by 18 feet, and at one end there were 6 and at the other 8 state-rooms for travelers. She ran as a packet between Louisville, Cincinnati, and Maysville. These early boats were all strong and durable, as they were built from the native oak of the Ohio and were framed and planked on the same plan as boats for the deep sea. The East at one time aspired to build vessels for the West, and in 1818 the Maid of Orleans, of 100 tons, was sent from the Philadelphia yards. She was a two-masted schooner, with steam-power, for use on the river. She ascended as far as Saint Louis in 1818, and was the first craft that reached that city from an Atlantic port. There were few ventures of that sort, however. The early steamboats were all small and of low speed; traffic was light in those days, and little was expected of the boats except to carry comfortably and safely the mails, a little general merchandise, and the few travelers who were compelled by political or mercantile errands to pass from point to point in the sparsely settled regions of the West, and if they could breast the current of the rivers and make any sort of speed at all they fulfilled the needs of the

---

a At the lower end of the falls, now included in Louisville.

times. After 1820 the country grew rapidly in population. Manufacturing developed along the Ohio, and special attention was paid to the needs of the South. New Orleans was building up a thriving foreign trade, and the basis was established for a large exchange of products between the lower and the upper portions of the river. Travel and trade increased; rival steamboats came into existence, which strove to excel each other in speed, size, comfort, carrying power, and general adaptability to the special requirements of the river trade; boat-yards were established all along the banks of the Ohio, at Saint Louis, and at New Orleans; and for more than 50 years steamboat building flourished in the West, reaching large proportions. The yards were scattered principally along the Monongahela and Ohio. Active work was done at Brownsville, Pittsburgh, Allegheny City, Sewickley, and Freedom, Pennsylvania; Steubenville, Marietta, Ironton, and Cincinnati, Ohio; Wheeling, Virginia; Newport, Louisville, and Portland, Kentucky; Madison, New Albany, and Jeffersonville, Indiana; Cairo and Mound City, Illinois; Saint Louis, Missouri; Dubuque, Iowa; Stillwater, Minnesota, and New Orleans. Besides yards at these places, a large number grew into existence at intermediate points for the repairing of vessels or for the building of barges and flat-boats, or for both repairing and building.

The early boats were all of low speed, as has been before noted, and up to 1818 no faster trip had been made from New Orleans to Louisville than 19 days. The Shelby had made the trip in that time with 51 passengers and a cargo of groceries, dry goods, etc., having stopped at ten places *en route*. Her running time was 15 days and 5 hours, but the usual time up the river was from 25 to 30 days. The fast steamer Cincinnati made round trips from Cincinnati to New Orleans in about 40 days, but once consumed nearly 100 days on the upward trip alone, having broken down *en route*, finding no place where repairs could be made until she reached Louisville. Efforts were finally made to improve the time of passenger boats, especially after 1830, and with such success that in 1838 the Diana made the run from New Orleans to Louisville in less than 6 days, winning a premium of $500 from the Post-Office Department for so doing. The passenger boats were side-wheelers, with pretty sharp bows and flat floors amidships, drawing from 4 to 6 feet of water, and were from 400 to 600 tons register. In the smaller boats the cabin was on the main deck aft between the engines. In 1838 upper cabins were rare, but they came into popularity later; cabins are now never placed on the main deck, except in a few ferry-boats. When the era of fast boats began, in 1830, the speed of every new-comer from the ship-yard was tested, and the course selected for this purpose was the lower Mississippi, which was deep and comparatively free from bars. Racing over this course from New Orleans to the cities north became the fashion after 1830, and has remained a feature of western boating to the present day. Rivalry reached such a point at times that both before and after the late war boats were sent over the course, stripped of every pound of cargo, baggage, and incumbrance, including even a part of the wood work of the vessel, and were driven with the full power of the engines and sent along without making stops, merely to beat the record of all previous trips and establish a reputation for speed. The passion for fast time and the carrying of steam at high pressure led to immense loss of life and property by explosions until legislation interfered and regulated the pressure of steam and the strength of the boilers. The speed of later boats has been secured not so much by an increase of steam pressure as by enlarging the cylinders of the engines. From 1830 to 1840 cylinders varied from 18 to 24 inches diameter in passenger boats, and occasionally they were larger, though not often; but in later steamers the diameter was increased to 30 inches, and since the war it has increased to 42 inches in many boats. The stroke has been 5 and 6 feet in small boats and from 8 to 11 feet in the large and fast ones.

Without following the development of steamboating in the West step by step through all its history, it will answer the purpose of this report to give a few data about particular vessels and then pass on to the facts about the boats and boat-yards of to-day.

From 1830 to 1840 the popular size was from 100 to 300 tons register; a few smaller craft were used as ferry-boats at local points, and there were a few large ones of from 400 to 600 tons engaged on the long routes. The following were fair specimens of the dimensions popularly used:

Length from bow to stern.	Beam.	Depth of hold.	Register tonnage.	BOILERS.			ENGINES.	
				Length.	Diameter.	Number of boilers.	Diameter of cylinder.	Length of stroke.
Feet.	*Feet.*	*Feet.*		*Feet.*	*Inches.*		*Inches.*	*Feet.*
175	27	8½	440	24	42	8	25	8½
150	20	6½	166	20	40	4	22	8
165	28	7¼	295	26	42	6	22½	10
230	28	8	600	30	42	6	25	10
130	21	4	112	20	38	2	14½	6
134	18	5	130	18	39	4	27	5½
130	18½	5½	130	18	36	3	18	5
130	19½	5½	129	18	34	4	20½	5
158	26	8	307	21	42	7	30	6½
153	28½	10	435	21	40	9	30	6
137	21	6½	200	23	36	6	24	5
169	27	10	440	21	40	7	32	6½

These boats had sometimes one, but generally two smoke-pipes, and the cabin was sometimes aft between the engines and sometimes aloft. They all had ample deck room for cargo.

After 1840 larger boats made their appearance for passenger service on the Ohio below Cincinnati, and on the Mississippi from Saint Louis to New Orleans. These boats were all side-wheelers, and were all built on the Ohio. One of the first was the fleet Sultana, built in 1843, which was 250 feet long, 35 feet beam, and 8 feet hold. Her boilers were 7 in number, 32 feet long, 42 inches in diameter, the engines 30 inches in diameter and 10 feet stroke, and the paddle-wheels 30 feet in diameter, with 14-foot buckets. This boat developed a speed of $15\frac{1}{2}$ miles per hour going up stream, and made one trip from New Orleans to Louisville in 4 days 22 hours.

The Peytona was built in 1846 on the same measurements, except that she was 10 feet longer and had 6 boilers 32 feet by 42 inches; engines, $30\frac{1}{2}$ inches in diameter and 10 feet stroke, and wheels 33 feet in diameter, with 16-foot buckets. She beat the time of the Sultana to Louisville by 2 hours. This boat once ran from Evansville to Louisville, a distance of 200 miles, with 300 tons of freight, in 13 hours, the fastest time ever made on that river, (a) the ordinary trip between those two points being 24 hours.

In 1852 the Eclipse was built at New Albany, just below the falls, and was one of the largest boats ever built in the West, being 363 feet long, 36 feet beam, and 9 feet deep in the hold. She was sumptuously fitted up with a richly furnished saloon-cabin and a texas or steerage cabin atop, had 8 boilers 42 inches in diameter and $32\frac{1}{2}$ feet long and 2 engines 36 inches in diameter, and was the only boat of the day with 11-foot stroke. The wheels were 41 feet in diameter, with 15-foot buckets. How lightly built her hull was may be seen from the following data: Her frames were single, and were cut from 4- and $4\frac{1}{2}$-inch flitch oak, molded 13 inches on the floor, 10 inches at the bilge, and $5\frac{1}{2}$ inches at the heads. The main keelson was 12 by 16 inches, the bilge log 7 by $11\frac{1}{2}$ inches, and there were 18 floor keelsons, varying from $3\frac{1}{2}$ by 10 to 4 by 11 inches square. Fore and aft bulkheads of wood were put in to strengthen her. She was planked with $3\frac{1}{2}$- to $4\frac{1}{4}$-inch oak. The Eclipse was finished at a cost of $300,000, and for many years was the most fashionable and popular boat of the West. Her exploits were the pride of the people. In 1852 she ran from New Orleans to Louisville in 4 days 18 hours, and in the next year made the same trip in 4 days 9 hours 30 minutes, an average of $13\frac{1}{8}$ miles per hour, having lost 35 minutes *en route* by the blowing out of the packing of a piston. Her highest speed was 16 miles an hour. It must be remembered that this was up stream, as down stream it was not unusual for the Eclipse to make 25 miles an hour.

The A. L. Shotwell, built the same year as the Eclipse, was 310 feet long, 36 feet beam, and 8 feet deep in the hold. She had six 32-foot by 42-inch boilers, and two engines 30 inches in diameter with 10 feet stroke. The wheels were 37 feet in diameter, and had 15-foot buckets. The Shotwell was built sharp, with a view to speed, and was the only vessel that dared challenge the Eclipse. These two boats were racing when the latter made her celebrated record of 1853. Both were stripped for the effort, and carried neither passengers nor freight. Furniture, landing stages, and fenders were sent ashore, the bulkheads in the wheel-houses and part of the deck were removed, and everything was done that could be thought of to lighten the two boats and qualify them for the contest. The Shotwell, being the shorter boat, had the advantage in turning bends of the river, but she once ventured in too close, got aground, and lost $2\frac{1}{2}$ hours, and thereby lost the race. Her running time, however, was very nearly the same as that of the Eclipse, and her record made her one of the most popular boats of that day.

Following these two famous steamers came a number of large and swift boats for the packet service from principal points to the South and back. These ranged from 250 to 300 feet in length, and were sumptuously fitted up with upper and top-gallant cabins. They were, in the main, side-wheel boats, this type having always been preferred for passenger traffic on the grand routes; some were, however, stern-wheelers. They were all usually owned in Pittsburgh, Cincinnati, and Saint Louis.

The war interrupted the river traffic for a period of four years, and during its progress a great deal of the old tonnage disappeared. After that traffic was resumed, slowly at first, but with increasing activity, and a fleet of new boats came out fully the equals of the earlier steamers, some of them of great size and speed. Two of them were the R. E. Lee, built in 1866, and the Natchez, built in 1869. The Lee was 300 feet long, 44 feet beam, and 10 feet deep, with engines 40 inches in diameter and 10-foot stroke, and wheels 38 feet in diameter, having $16\frac{1}{2}$-foot paddles. The Natchez was very nearly of the same size, being $301\frac{1}{2}$ feet long, $42\frac{1}{2}$ feet beam, and $9\frac{1}{2}$ feet in the hold, her engines, however, being 34 inches in diameter, with 10-foot stroke, and wheels 42 feet in diameter, with 16-foot paddles. In 1870 these two boats raced from New Orleans to Saint Louis, a distance of 1,200 miles. Both boats stripped for the race, and left about 5 p. m. of June 30, 1870. They kept each other in sight a large part of the way, made about 17 miles an hour on the lower river, and were only an hour apart at Memphis and at Cairo. The R. E. Lee reached Saint Louis in the unprecedented time of 3 days 18 hours and 14 minutes, the Natchez arriving 6 hours and 33 minutes later.

Among the large boats the Great Republic was built at Pittsburgh in 1867. She was 296 feet long, $50\frac{1}{2}$ feet broad, and $9\frac{1}{2}$ feet deep; not a fast steamer, but a capacious one, and a large carrier. In 1872 she was enlarged at Saint Louis, and then became 350 feet long, with a register of 2,441 tons. She was dismantled in 1879 and converted into a barge for towing.

---

a Henry Clay was on board.

STEAM VESSELS.

In 1876 a steamer was built at Saint Louis called the Grand Republic, intended to be a monster passenger and cotton boat. She was 338⅔ feet long, 56⅔ feet broad on the beam, and 103 feet wide over the paddle-wheel guards, with a depth of hold ranging from 10½ to 17 feet. Her boilers were steel, 7 in number, 28 feet long and 42 inches in diameter. Two engines were 55 inches in diameter and 10 feet stroke, and were taken from the Great Republic, and two others were 26 inches in diameter, with 10 feet stroke. The power was immense. The wheels were 37 feet. State-rooms were supplied for 280 passengers, and the boat was so admirably built that she floated light at 32 inches draught forward and 48 inches aft, and on 10 feet draught could carry 4,000 tons of freight. Her cost was $190,000; her register, 2,600 tons. The boat was burned at her wharf in Saint Louis in 1877 while undergoing repairs.

Several large side-wheel boats came out in 1878, among them the Ed. Richardson, of 2,048 tons, and the J. M. White, of 2,028 tons, both remarkably handsome vessels, and good specimens of the side-wheel steamer of the West of the present time. The Ed. Richardson cost $125,000, and was 303 feet long, 48½ feet broad on the beam, and 10 feet deep in the hold. She had 9 boilers, 42 inches in diameter and 32 feet long, and the cylinders were 38 inches by 10 feet. The cabin was 140 feet long, from 26 to 45 feet wide, and 17½ feet high.

While many 300-foot boats have been built since 1878, that being a favorite length for the great Saint Louis packets, none have been built so large as the J. M. White. As a representative of her class she may be described in detail, and this description will answer for all the side-wheel boats, because others differ from her only in dimensions and the slight changes in scantling and size of engines due to the difference in tonnage. The hull of the J. M. White is 321 feet long, 48 feet broad on the main beam, 10½ feet deep in the hold in the shoalest place, the plank-sheer rising to 16½ feet at the bow and stern. This 6 feet of sheer is peculiar to boats built for the lower Mississippi, the river being too smooth above to require more than a faint rise of the deck forward. The floor amidships is nearly flat. The bilge is rounding and the sides are slightly flaring, and more than one-half the length of the hull amidships is straight, with only a faint taper in that part of its length. The bow is about 80 feet long, long and tapering, with hollow water-lines below, but flaring above, so that the deck may be carried forward as broad as possible, with 2 or 3 feet of guards. The after part of the boat is fuller. The hull is framed as follows: Keel, broad and flat; frames, molded, 11 inches, and sided 4½ and 5 inches amidships, increasing to 6 inches in the bow, with some of 4 inches aft; side timbers, molded 10 inches at the bilge and 5 inches at the head. The spacing varies from 14 inches amidships to 12 at the bow, with flitch side futtocks at the bilge. Main keelson, 11 by 18 inches; bilge or knuckle keelsons, 9 by 13 inches. Twelve floor keelsons parallel to the main, as follows: two, 4½ by 12 inches; four, 4 by 10; two, 6 by 10; two, 7½ by 9; two, 9 by 10½—this last pair supporting bulkheads and the heels of wooden masts or braces, over which the hog-chains of the boat pass. Ceiling, none, except that a light floor is laid on the bottom of the boat; three side streaks, or stringers, are fastened to the top timbers on each side for rigidity, one of them being 3½ by 12, the other two 4 by 12 inches. Clamps, 4 by 15 and 3½ by 13 inches. The beams, 4½ and 4 by 9 inches, are supported by several long rows of slender stanchions resting on the floor keelsons, and by three fore-and-aft bulkheads, made by nailing light poplar planks to the stanchions. The planking is, like the rest of the boat, white oak, 4½ inches thick on the bottom, diminishing to 4 inches aft, 5 at the bilge, and 4½ tapering to 4 inches on the sides. Decking, 2½-inch white pine. The bow for 25 feet is solid oak and iron, with strong breast-hooks and braces, and the guards amidships are 22½ feet wide. A strong iron band weighing 2,500 pounds is placed upon the fore edge of the stem, running under the boat and ending on the keel. Fore-and-aft rigidity is not left to depend on the keelsons and bulkheads, but is gained chiefly by an elaborate system of hog-chains, so called; that is to say, of long iron rods stretching from end to end and from side to side of the boat. These rods fasten under the main and heavy floor keelsons and run up over the end of long rows of square pine masts and braces, which are set up on the keelsons perpendicularly amidships, but are inclined forward in the fore body and backward in the after body. The rods vary from 1½ to 2 inches in diameter, and contain about 58 tons of iron; by their agency the weight, both of the ends of the boat and of the guards, rests in part on the central portion of the boat. This system is universal in all the steamers of the West, and a hog-frame is never seen. The great width of the J. M. White, 95 feet, affords spacious deck-room for the boilers and engines and the stowage of cargo. The lower deck is covered with a roof or deck, supported on light stanchions, and the sides are all open forward, being closed at times against the weather by canvas awnings only. The wheel-houses and a part of the lower deck aft are inclosed; the cabin is built upon the upper deck. The main cabin is 233 feet in length, 13 feet high in the clear, and 19 feet wide, exclusive of state-rooms. The office is in the forward part of the cabin on one side, the bar-room on the other. Twenty-three state-rooms, 10 feet deep, line each side of the central hall, and there are two state-rooms 13 by 14 feet. Aft of the main cabin is a hall 17 feet deep and 46 feet wide, exclusively for ladies. Tables are spread in the main cabin, at which 250 guests can sit at dinner. The pantry, cupboard, barber-shop, etc., are on the upper deck, forward of the wheel-houses. A promenade deck 30 feet wide by 64 feet long extends in front of the cabin, which is reached from below by an ash and black walnut stairway. On top of the main cabin is the texas, or upper cabin, 180 feet long by 28 feet wide, with 50 state-rooms, including accommodations for the officers, the cabin-boys, a few first-class passengers, and the colored passengers. A bell weighing 2,500 pounds hangs in front of the texas. The pilot-house is on the roof, and is 15½ feet square and 17½ feet high. These upper works are of the very lightest and frailest description, the stuff being white pine and poplar ¼ and ½ inch thick, supported by a very light framing of pine and fastened with small nails. Steam-power is supplied by a battery of ten steel boilers, each 42 inches in diameter and 34 feet long, containing two flues 16 inches in diameter. The smoke-pipes are two in number, reaching to a height of about 75 feet from the main deck, showily ornamented at the top, their mouths flaring like enormous sunflowers with coarse petals. The boilers are allowed to carry 173 pounds of steam. The stowage space for coal is provided in front of and around the boilers. The engines are placed horizontally amidships, one on each side of the boat, having 43-inch cylinders with 11 feet stroke. They are of the regular lever, puppet-valve type, and are each placed on two massive parallel timbers built up of solid oak logs, called cylinder timbers, scarped and keyed together. These cylinder timbers are a feature of all western boats. Heavy oak stanchions are placed in the hold to support their weight, and strong iron rods run down to the keelsons, securing them in position. The cross-head of each piston runs on iron ways on top of the cylinder timbers, and a pitman 44 feet long connects the cross-head with the crank of the paddle-wheel shaft. The escape steam finds its way into the open air, in slow, strong puffs, from pipes that rise through the roof of the texas like small smoke-stacks. No racing steamer has ever had larger wheels than the J. M. White, as they are 44 feet in diameter, and carry paddles 19 feet long by 3 wide, and are driven at a speed of 18 revolutions a minute. With 100 pounds of steam the engines develop 2,800 horse-power and drive the boat at a velocity of 20 miles per hour. The cargo is stowed on the ample lower deck, and also in the hold, and there is room for 10,000 bales of cotton. Small engines are provided for raising freight from the hold and for working the capstans and the landing stages. The landing stages are two in number, about 50 feet long and 8 feet wide, being strong but lightly built platforms, and, owing to the lack of room for them on the deck and the frequency with which they have to be used, they are carried suspended in the air over the forward deck, projecting diagonally upward, like horns. There are 290 tons of iron in the fastenings, hog-chains, boilers, engines, and outfit of this steamer, and with this load and about 60 tons of water and 400 tons of coal aboard she draws 6½ feet, and on a draught of 10 feet will carry 250 passengers and 2,600 tons of freight. This boat was built expressly for the cotton-carrying and passenger traffic of the lower Mississippi, and cost about $220,000.

The following are the main data of size, etc., of a number of the leading side-wheel boats of the West, including those above enumerated:

Year.	Boats.	HULL.			BOILERS.			ENGINES.		WHEELS.	
		Length.	Beam.	Hold.	Number.	Length.	Diameter.	Diameter.	Stroke.	Diameter.	Length of paddles.
		Feet.	*Feet.*	*Feet.*		*Feet*	*Inches.*	*Inches.*	*Feet.*	*Feet.*	*Feet.*
1843	Sultana	250	35	8	7	32	42	30	10	30	14
1844	J. M. White	250	31	8⅓	7	32	42	30	10	32	15
1846	Peytona	260	35	8	6	32	42	30½	10	33	16
1848	Aleck Scott	285	84	7⅔	5	32	42	30½	10	....	....
1852	Eclipse	363	36	9	8	32½	42	36	11	41	15
1852	A. L. Shotwell	310	36	8	6	32	42	30	10	37	15
1855	Princess	280	38	9⅓	6	34	42	34	9	40	....
1866	R. E. Lee	300	44	10	8	32	42	40	10	38	16½
1867	Great Republic	349½	50½	8⅓	....	....	....	....	....	....	....
1868	Frank Pargoud	250	41	9⅓	7	28	38	32½	9	36½	15½
1869	Natchez	301½	42½	9½	8	34	40	34	10	42	16
1876	R. E. Lee	315	48½	10½	9	32	42	40	10	39	17
1876	Grand Republic	338⅔	56⅔	10⅓	7	28	42	55	10	37	....
1878	John W. Cannon	250	43	9½	7	34	42	34	9	37½	16
1878	J. M. White	321	50	11½	10	34	42	43	11	44	19
1878	Ed. Richardson	303	48½	10	9	32	42	38	10	....	....
1880	Natchez	304	46½	9⅔	....	....	....	34	10	....	....
1881	City of New Orleans	300	48	9	5	30	44	26	10	35	15
1881	City of Baton Rouge	300	48	9	5	30	44	26	10	35	15
	Belle Lee	300	43	9	....	....	....	....	....	....	....
1881	Edward J. Gay	250	40½	8½	6	32	42	27	48	....	....
	Annie P. Silver	300	41	8⅔	....	....	....	....	....	....	....
	John A. Scudder	300	50	8⅓	....	....	....	....	....	....	....

These boats draw an average of between 36 and 48 inches light and from 6 to 10 feet loaded, carrying from 1,000 to 2,600 tons of cargo. On the upper Mississippi the packets are smaller, varying now from 180 to 230 feet in length and from 35 to 40 feet beam, drawing from 4 to 6 feet loaded. They are of the same type exactly as those of the lower river. The use of side-wheel boats is now confined almost exclusively to the Mississippi river and the lower portion of the Ohio.

On the upper part of the Ohio, the Missouri, the Arkansas, and all the other tributary streams of the West, the passenger and freight boats, as well as the towing boats, are almost exclusively stern-wheelers (Fig. 52). Experience has demonstrated the superiority of the stern-wheelers for handling fleets of barges, and the peculiarities of navigation on the Ohio have given them the preference for the passenger and freight traffic of that stream. The canal at Louisville is only 82 feet wide, and the largest stern-wheelers can slip through this channel with perfect ease, while on the other hand side-wheel boats usually measure from 83 to 95 feet over the guards, and are therefore shut out from the trade to points above Louisville. For another reason the river captains of the Ohio find it convenient to place the paddle-wheel aft. When the river is low the large boats bound for New Orleans cannot carry a full cargo without danger of grounding, and find it useful, therefore, to lay freight barges alongside of the steamer, one on each side (Fig. 53), loading one with goods and the other with coal and running in this manner to Cairo. At that point the whole of the cargo is transferred to the steamer. This is what they call "a light-water trip" on the Ohio, and for such purposes the stern-wheel boat is superior to all others. The placing of the wheel aft works a few changes in the build of the steamers. The wheel-houses and guards at the sides are dispensed with, the cylinder timbers are carried away aft and are made to project about

Fig. 52.—BUCKEYE STATE.
Built at Pittsburgh, Pennsylvania. Stern-wheel passenger and freight boat.

25 feet behind the hull, with a slight sheer upward; the paddle-wheel shaft rests on these timbers, and the system of hog-chains is extended aft, so as to support the weight of the large wheel and transmit the stress of it to the forward part of the boat. The only other important change is in the form of the hull. The model does not taper aft; it has to keep its full breadth on deck and on the bottom clear to the stern, so that there is no taper at all to the after body of the boat except for a few feet. The body is carried back square; the floor of the boat rises in the middle at the stern, however, so as to allow the water to clear easily, giving the stern the appearance of two hulls joined by arching timbers planked over. This form of stern permits the use of three or four rudders, those at the sides being hung on the upright stern-post, while those in the middle are hung on stout rudder-posts and project partly under the boat, being shaped on the balance-rudder principle. The bows of the stern-wheelers are all full and raking. The cylinder timbers in some of the stern-wheelers of recent construction are made of plate-iron, as are also the paddle-wheels, both being lighter in consequence.

The passenger and freight boats of this class are handsome vessels of from 200 to 265 feet in length and from 35 to 42 feet beam, and have from 6 to 10 feet depth of hold amidships, with ample cabins and upper works. Those that go down the Mississippi are given a good deal of sheer. They carry from 1,200 to 2,200 tons of cargo on 7 to 10 feet draught, their hulls being immersed to within a foot of the plank-sheer when loaded. The towing boats are not so large in the hull, and have small cabins, but they have stronger bows. They are now from 150 to 250 feet in length, and draw from 6 to 8 feet forward and not over 4 feet aft, the smaller sizes being used on the upper Ohio and in towing barges on the Mississippi. The great tow-boats make up large fleets of coal barges at Louisville below the canal and take them to New Orleans. The Ajax and the Harry Brown will take from 20 to 35 loaded coal barges at one time.

The average length of life of the western steamers is 7 years.

BARGES.—There are four classes of barges at present in use. The smallest is the flat-boat (Fig. 54), square and box-like, with a raking bow and stern, about 90 feet long, 16 feet wide, and 5½ to 7 feet deep, undecked, registering about 75 tons. Its use is always local on small streams for short trips for carrying about 115 tons of coal, stone, or other coarse cargo. Next is the coal barge, an open boat, strongly built, with raking ends, about 130 feet long,

24 feet wide, and 7½ feet deep, registering about 225 tons, and carrying from 400 to 500 net tons of coal. The later boats are 135 by 25 by 8 feet. The majority of the barges are employed between the coal mines in Pennsylvania and West Virginia and the markets below all the way to New Orleans. They are valuable boats, and are almost always brought back after the down trip. The coal boat, or broad-horn (Fig. 55), is about 170 feet long, 25 feet wide, and 9½ feet deep, registering about 375 tons, and carrying about 950 net tons of coal. The coal boat has a strong hemlock, pine, or oak bottom, but the sides are flimsy. It was formerly customary to leave coal-boats at New Orleans to be broken up for lumber, for the same reason that the immense multitude of grain barges which float

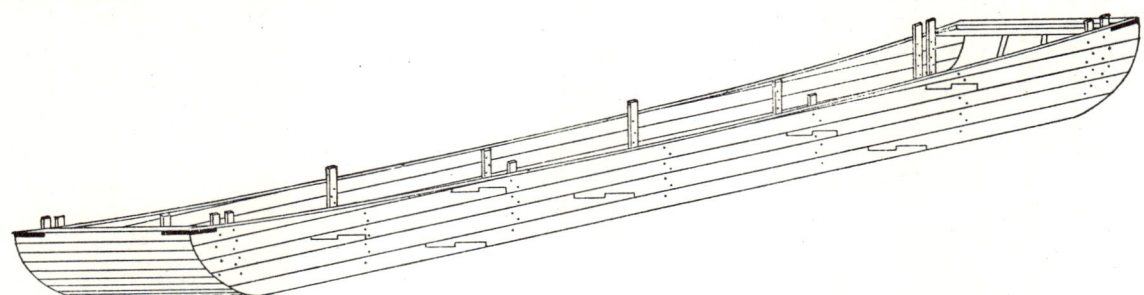

Fig. 54.—FLAT-BOAT.

90 feet long, 16 feet beam, 6 feet depth of side; capacity, 115 tons. Coal barge; same model exactly, except that there is a bulkhead in each end.

down the rivers of Russia every year are not taken back. To tow them to Pittsburgh again, a distance of 1,900 miles, in the face of the current did not pay. Latterly, however, since the boats have reached a large size and have been better built, it has been cheaper to bring them back than to sell them, and the majority are now built for more than one trip. Next in order is the model barge. These boats have hulls built like steamboats, sharp at both ends, decked, and covered with a house or "cargo box" when used for package freights. The smaller ones are used on the Mississippi above Saint Louis for carrying iron-ore, ice, building-stone, and other coarse freight, of which each carries about 500 tons on 5 feet draught, while the larger ones, 235 feet long, are employed in the bulk grain trade of the Mississippi to New Orleans, and carry up to 1,800 tons of cargo on about 8 feet draught.

Flat-boats are built as follows: They are put together on a long row of stout wooden horses or building ways. The sides are built up of four, or, in deep boats, five tiers of solid white-pine logs, 8, 7, and 6 inches thick, laid one above the other, and strongly bolted together edgewise with square iron spikes. In another part of the country where boats are also built with "gunwale" sides, namely, on the Erie canal, the bolts go clear through from top to bottom, being driven with great effort by a heavy swinging hammer; but on the western rivers each set of gunwales is fastened on separately, the bolts through one tier being driven in the intervals between those of the tier below. The lowest gunwale is made of three logs, 8 inches thick and 18 inches deep, fitted together with 5- or 6-foot scarfs. The tier above is 7 by 18 inches, fastened with 11 spikes 28 inches long by ¾-inch square. A third tier of logs in two lengths, scarfed, is then laid on and fastened with 12 spikes 44 inches long and ¾-inch square, the spikes thus going down into the lower gunwales. The fourth or top gunwale is 6 by 14 inches square, in three lengths, fastened with 14 spikes 40 inches long by ¾-inch square. On top of this gunwale sheer pieces are placed at each end 30 feet long, 15 inches high at one end, tapering to 2 inches at the inner end. This is spiked on with light iron, generally with 24-inch spikes. Each side of the boat is made in this manner, each being laid flat on the row of wooden horses until bolted. The sides are then raised to a perpendicular position. The floor is constructed by laying a number of floor timbers of pine or hemlock, 6 by 12 inches in 5-foot boats and 7 by 14 inches in deeper boats, athwart a number of fore-and-aft floor streaks; they are put in about 12 feet apart, the ends tenoning into the lower gunwale, which is always heavier than those above. The floor streaks or "streamers" are four in number, of 3 by 9 inch oak, laid from end to end of the boat, being fastened under the floors with strong spikes. The bottom is then planked across with 2- or 3-inch hemlock, when it can be had; otherwise, with white pine or oak; sometimes the bottom is built wrong-side up and then turned over. The plank of the raking ends is supported by rake timbers, heeling into a floor timber below and capped at the top by a transom or fender of oak about 9 by 13 inches square, this log being connected to the sheer pieces at the corners of the boat by short straps of iron 6 inches wide and ½ or ¾ inch thick. One strap is placed outside and another inside the corners of the boat, and the two are joined by screw-bolts through the wood. Oak or hemlock stanchions are set up on the ends of the floor timbers and bolted to the sides of the boat, and about 30 feet from each end of the boat one strong stanchion on each side is carried up above the top gunwale and shaped into a timber-head for towing purposes. A pair of stout oak bitts, 6 by 12 inches square, is put in at each end of the boat and fastened with strong screw-bolts, and usually a light bulkhead cuts off the raking ends of the boat from the rest of the hull, it being considered undesirable to allow the weight of the coal to rest there. Such a flat can be built with from 13,000 to 18,000 feet of lumber, according to depth, and 1,450 pounds of iron, and weighs from 18 to 22 tons, floating light at 4 from to 6 inches draught. These flats are well calked, but are not painted, and last six or seven years. The cost is from $500 to $650, depending on the size of the boat. The smallest item in the cost is labor, which, with wages averaging $2 a day, does not exceed from $85 to $100.

The coal barge is merely a larger and better flat-boat. The average size has been given, but the trade now calls for barges 135 feet long, 25 feet wide, and 8 feet deep. About 150 coal barges are built every year on the Monongahela alone. Owing to their size the several tiers of gunwales are laid in three and four pieces each, the logs varying from 20 to 50 feet in length. There are about 6 tiers of gunwales, 8 inches thick below and 7 and 6 inches above. It requires 34,000 feet of lumber and 3,000 pounds of iron to build a barge, and the expense is from $1,000 to $1,200, from $150 to $190 being for labor. They weigh about 45 net tons each, and, like the flats, draw only from 4 to 6 inches of water light. A few have been built at Pittsburgh 160 feet long, 24 feet wide, and 8 feet deep.

For coal boats, or broad-horns (Fig. 55), the standard size is now 170 feet in length, 25 feet beam, and 9 or 9½ feet in depth of side; but they vary in dimensions, sometimes being a foot wider, and sometimes 2 or 3 feet shallower. One large firm on the Monongahela builds them 165 feet in length, 28 feet beam, and 8½ feet in depth, the capacity and cost in all cases being about the same. The coal boat has a barge bottom, with one bilge-log or gunwale about 9 by 16 inches square, strengthened at the scarfs by a piece inside 18 feet long, 4 by 16 inches square, fastened on with 10 large treenails, 7 or 8 screw bolts, and a number of spikes. This bottom is generally built of hemlock or of hard wood, whichever can be most cheaply bought in the locality. A sheer piece is put on top of the gunwale at each end. The ends of the bottom overhang as in a flat, and the tops are flimsily built. A long row of studs, about 6 by 2½ inches square, is set up perpendicularly on the bilge-log and sheer pieces, clear around the boat, from 32 to 36 inches apart, and these are simply and lightly planked over, generally with broad 1½-inch hemlock boards, though sometimes with white pine. A thread or two of oakum is driven into the seams, so as to make the boat water-tight for

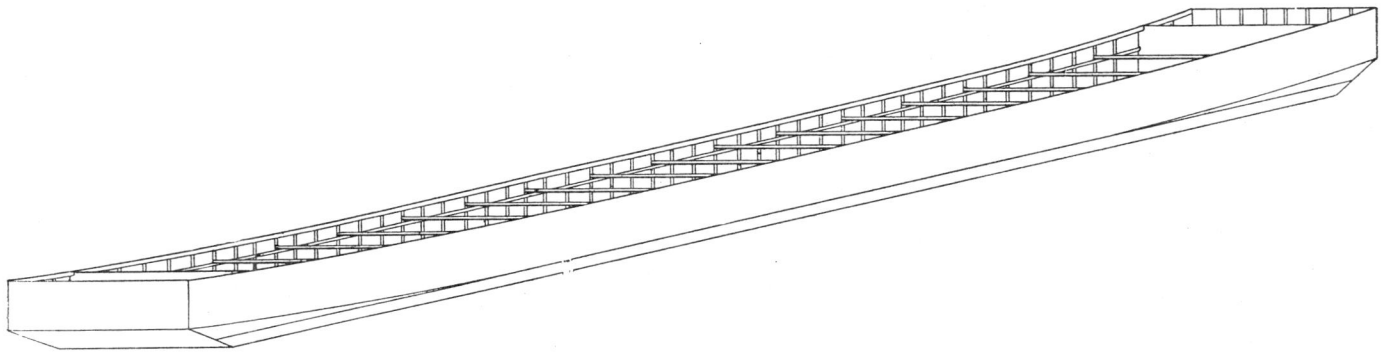

Fig. 55.—COAL BOAT, OR BROAD-HORN.

170 feet long, 25 feet wide, 9½ feet deep on the side; capacity, 950 tons.

one trip at any rate. Two-inch boards are used in boats which are to make several trips. This kind of a top needs to be braced, and accordingly carlines or light beams of 4 by 4 inch hemlock are put in about 8 feet apart, the ends supported by a light clamp, nailed to the studs. A light stringer is nailed to the head of the studs inside for additional strength. Coal boats are built on the Monongahela, upper Ohio, and Great Kanawha. The bottoms are usually built away up in the woods on the small tributaries, where hemlock and hard wood are cheap, and are floated down to the saw-mills below, where they are "sided up", as it is called. Bottoms vary in cost from $300 to $375. With wages at about $2, the labor of "siding up" costs about $95 and the materials $255, and the finished boat sells for from $800 to $900. Although this class of boat has nearly twice the capacity of a barge, it contains no more lumber—only about 35,000 feet in all. It draws only about 4 inches of water light, and stands up so high out of water after discharging cargo that it catches the wind and is hard to handle where the rivers are broad. The raking overhang of the bottom alone makes it possible to tow them up stream.

On the lower Ohio what are called "produce boats" are built from time to time on the same principle as the broad-horns. They are each about 122 feet long, 22 feet wide, and 7 feet deep, and cost from $800 to $900. After carrying a load of produce to New Orleans the boats are sold to the boat brokers for about $200 each, as it would cost nearly $300 to tow them back.

These three classes of barges were originally poled down the rivers or were rowed with sweeps, consisting of long poles with a short board nailed on the end at the proper angle for a paddle blade; for a great many years after the coal trade from the upper Ohio began the cargoes of coal were floated down the river in barges thus propelled. They generally went in pairs, and the crews were divided into watches and labored at the sweeps by turns; but that practice has been entirely discontinued so far as freighting is concerned. A certain number of flats are still owned by private persons, however, who deck and paint the boats, build houses on them, and employ them as traveling tin-shops, blacksmith-shops, and small trading vessels. They visit the bayous and sluggish rivers of the South at regular seasons of the year very much as peddlers travel about in wagons in northern communities, doing odd jobs of work, and are propelled in the old-fashioned way.

The pride of the western boatman is the model barge (Figs. 56 and 57). When painted, decked, housed, and well modeled these boats excite in a remarkable manner the enthusiasm of the river men, and the clippers of the ocean, with their fine proportions and towering clouds of snow-white canvas, do not stir a Jack Tar to more extravagant eulogy than the model barges receive from the western boatman. There are four sizes of these boats, carrying 600, 800, 1,000, and 1,200 or 1,300 tons of cargo respectively; and to say that the hulls are all modeled with a "pinkie" stern, that is to say, are sharp at both ends, and that they are framed on the same principle as steamboat hulls, is to describe the general points of their construction. Each has, however, only one hog-chain. This is placed in the center line of the boat, hooking under the main keelson at the bow and stern, and supported amidships by four or five pine posts or braces. A light collision bulkhead is built in the bow and also in the stern; when the hold is destined for grain in bulk or package freights it is ceiled up in such manner as to create a great cargo box, with an air-space of about 2 feet between it and the sides of the hull all around. This manner of ceiling up the hold diminishes the register tonnage without affecting the carrying power. The bodies of the boats are straight, the modeled portion of the ends being in length equal to about 1½ the breadth of beam.

The following are some of the sizes of model barges recently built:

Where built.	Dimensions.			Cargo box.		Register tonnage (tons of 100 cubic feet).	Carrying capacity in net tons.
	Length.	Width.	Depth.	Length.	Height.		
	Feet.	*Feet.*	*Feet.*	*Feet.*	*Feet.*		
Pittsburgh, Pa	183	30½	6	147	9	670	560
Do	186	34½	6⅔	153	8½	741	775
Do	186	34½	6⅘	153	10½	832	775
Do	200	35	7	....	....	399	840
Do	200	36	6½	169	10	908	825
Do	235	38½	7	210	10	1,298	1,200
Freedom, Pa	230	38	6½	200	9½	....	....
Cincinnati, Ohio	225	36	9	210	9½	1,250	1,300
Do	214	35	8	190	9½	975	1,050
Do	175	30	6½	....	....	250	525
Jeffersonville, Ind	220	34⅔	7½	200	10	1,050	1,000
Do	225	36⅓	7½	210	10	1,248	1,175
Do	226	36⅓	5⅔	210	10	1,107	1,000
Registered at Saint Louis, Mo., and built at various points on the Ohio.	160	32	6	....	....	215	625
Do	166	32	6	....	....	225	650
Do	180	31½	5⅔	150	10	674	600
Do	183	30½	6	150	10	670	600
Do	183	31	7	150	10	733	675
Do	200	36	7⅔	180	10	1,016	1,000
Do	200	36	8	165	10	996	1,000
Do	200	35⅘	6½	170	9½	836	850
Do	226	34⅔	8⅘	200	10	1,158	1,250
Do	226	36⅔	6⅔	200	10	1,164	1,100
Do	238	36⅓	8⅘	210	10	1,237	1,350

The use of model barges is continually growing between the principal trading points on the Ohio and Mississippi. The barges carry iron ore, railroad iron, tile, grain in bulk, and general merchandise. More than 120 are owned in Saint Louis, and are employed for the transportation of grain down the river and of imported iron and other goods back. The barges Monongahela and Allegheny were built at Belle Vernon, on the Monongahela, in 1880, at a cost of $9,000 each. They were 200 feet long, 36 feet beam, and 6½ feet hold, with cargo boxes 169 feet long, 11 feet in height to the top of the roof, and 33 feet wide. Their scantling were: Frames, single, 4 by 8 inches, spaced 14 inches; keel, 4 by 16 inches, laid flat; main keelson, two pieces, 1½ inches apart, so as to receive the heels of the stanchions, 5 by 9½ inches each; bilge keelson, 11 by 6 inches; three light floor keelsons each side; beams, 3½ and 4 inches by 5, the heaviest ones at the hatches, 28 inches apart; nine stanchions, 4 inches square, under every beam, there being about 600 in each boat; three hatches on each side of the main keelson bulkhead. On the floor light planking of 1½-inch pine is laid, with a railroad track and push-car upon it. Planking of the bottom, 4 inches; sides, 3 inches; top streak of sides, 4½ by 11 inches; decking, 2-inch pine. Cargo box, lightly framed and sided up. The hulls had 2 feet sheer, the cargo box 4. The whole boat was of oak, except the beams between the hatches, the bulkheads, floor, deck, and house, which were of pine or poplar. This is a good sample of the scantling of a model barge. The measurements of the keelsons are often varied, but their cross-sections have about the same area in boats of the same size.

One of the new large 1,200-ton barges was as follows: Length, 225 feet; beam, 36 feet; depth, 9½ feet, all oak, except where specified. Frames, 4 by 8 inches on the floor, single; spaced 14 inches in the body of the hull, 12 inches at the bow and stern. Keelsons: main, 6 by 8 inches; six stanchion keelsons, 6 by 6 inches; six intermediate floor keelsons, or footlings, 3 by 6 inches; bilge, 5 by 12 inches. Four clamps, one 3 by 10 inches,

STEAM VESSELS.

the others 2½ by 10 inches. Stringers on the top timbers, 3¼ by 6 inches. Poplar stanchions 5½ inches square under every beam on the main keelsons, sided up on each side with 1-inch poplar as a bulkhead. Stanchions on the six large side keelsons under every other beam. Beams, 3½ by 6 inches, in part pine; decking, 2-inch pine. Planking on the bottom, 4 inches; sides, 4, 3½, and 2½, with two upper streaks of 3 inches. Sides of the cargo box, 1½-inch

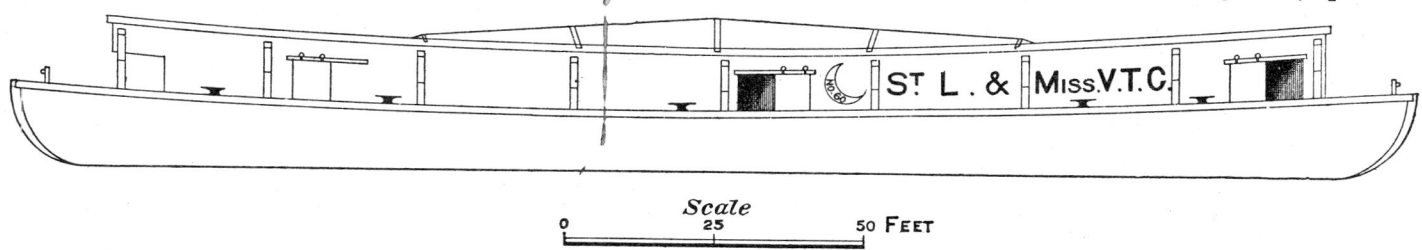

pine. Two heavy breast-hooks and a deck hook at each end, braced. Stem band at each end, 25 feet long, of 3½- by 2½-inch half-round iron, flattened out below and made flush with the planking of the bottom. Hog-chain, 1¾-inch iron; a strong plank-sheer of oak, pierced in nine places with strong oak snubbing posts, bolted to the sides below and rising above to within a foot or two of the top of the house to protect it. A strong beam across the boat on top of each pair of posts; about six 10-inch cavils or mooring cleats on each gunwale, and 12-inch bitts in the bow or stern. The barge has two 5½-inch pumps, with 3-inch gas-pipe waste. The weight of hull is about 200 tons. The boat floats light at 12 inches draught, increasing to 16 inches with age, and carries 1,200 tons on 6 feet draught.

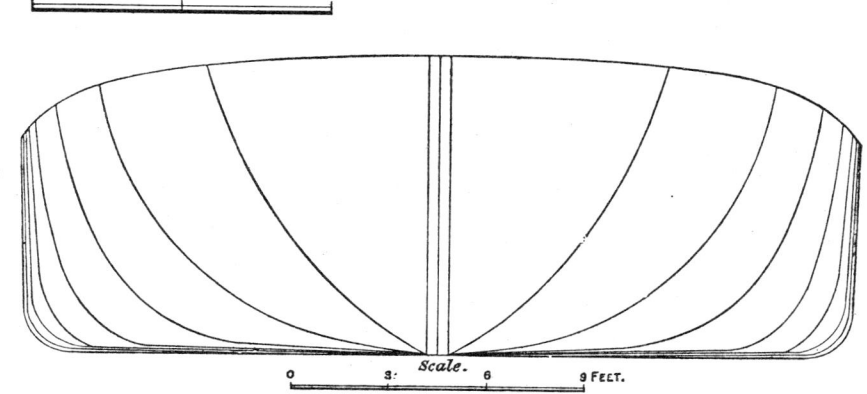

Figs. 56 and 57.—MODEL BARGE.
235 feet long, 36 feet beam, 9½ feet deep, registering 1,200 tons; carrying capacity, 1,200 tons.

The method of towing barges in the West differs from that of the East. On the Hudson river, Long Island sound, and elsewhere the tug steams ahead of the barges, drawing them with a long cable; but on the western rivers the barges are pushed. They are made up into a group, in files, often eight boats wide and four boats long (Fig. 58), strongly lashed together, and arranged ahead and alongside of the bow of the steamer. About one-fourth

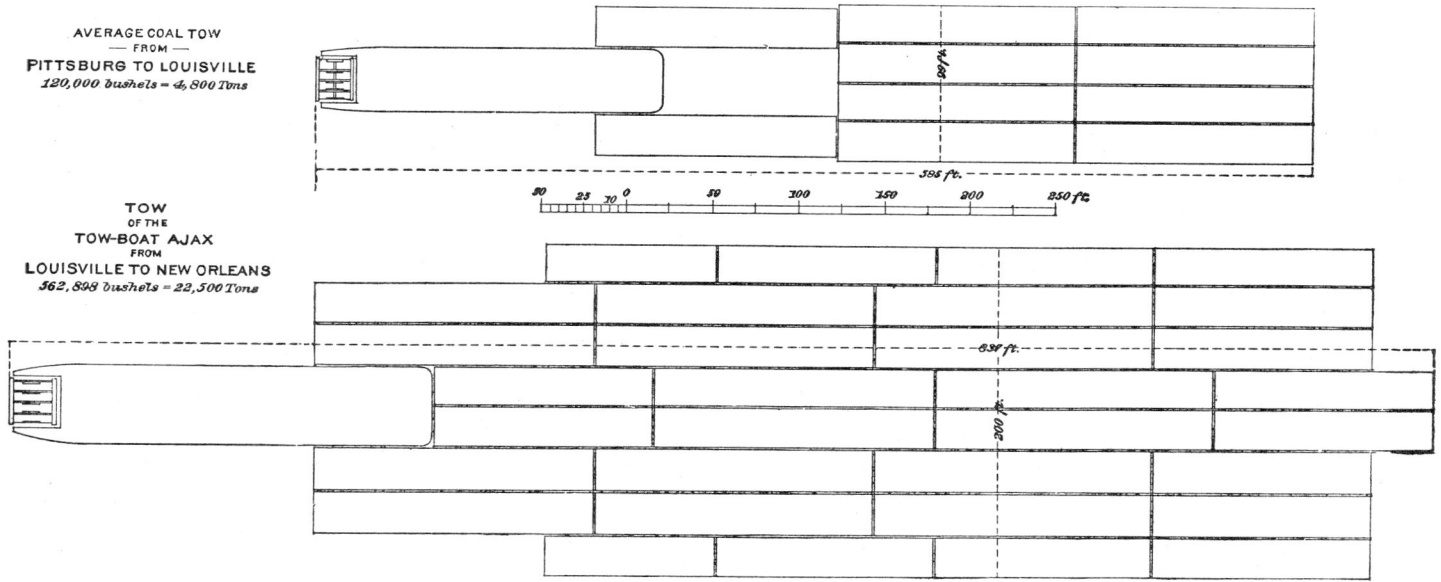

Fig. 58.—DIAGRAMS OF COAL TOWS.

of the length of the steamer is buried in the group. The deck is carried out square to the bow, ending in a strong transom or fender for pushing, and, being just two coal barges wide, allows the two central files of the tow to rest their whole weight against the steamer. A fleet thus made up is often 200 feet wide and 640 feet long, counting the tow-boat, and transports from 15,000 to 23,000 tons of coal. To steer such a fleet around the sharp bends of a rapidly running river is a delicate matter, and is accomplished by trusting largely to the current. When nearing a turn in the channel the steamer slackens speed and then begins to back strongly, the object being to check the headway and allow the tow to drift with the stream. The rudders are turned so as to throw the steamer over toward the convex shore, keeping the coal boats in the swiftest and deepest water. The tow floats down half sideways until a clear course opens up ahead, when the wheel is started forward strongly and the tow is pushed straight on again. Owing to the flat bottoms of coal barges it is comparatively easy to handle them in fleets of from 20 to 30. The model barges give the towing captains the most trouble, as they are long and have sharp ends, and five of the larger ones are all that any one cares to pilot down the river and back again.

The principal seat of the barge-building industry is around the head of the Ohio river; that is to say, on the Allegheny, Monongahela, and Great Kanawha rivers, and on the Ohio between Wheeling and Pittsburgh. On the Allegheny the industry is confined to the making of bottoms for coal boats. Hemlock is plentiful at various points all along the stream, and the conversion of the lumber to the purpose stated keeps a great many men busy in a small way in the winter time. The yards are generally in the vicinity of saw-mills. When built, the bottoms are set afloat, loaded with any coarse freight like hay, fire-clay, lumber, etc., that is on hand, and floated down the shallow river to its junction with the Monongahela. They are then towed to the yards in Pittsburgh or on the Monongahela for "siding up". The oak on the Allegheny is worthless, but the pine and hemlock are good.

The Monongahela for 35 miles above Pittsburgh is an active boat-building region, its industry thriving by virtue of the liberal supply of native oak and pine and the existence of an immense coal traffic. The river flows between high wood-covered hills which are full of soft coal, and every mile or two there is a hole in the hillside away above the river, running in often a mile or two, and sometimes away inland into a second range of hills. The coal is quarried underground and brought in small iron cars to the mouth of the mine, whence it is run out on a trestle-work until it is over the water's edge and dumped into chutes running down to within a few feet of the surface of the river. The flats, barges, and broad-horns lying in the stream are brought underneath, loaded with coal, and then moved aside and moored in large fleets, awaiting the months of deep water. The coal trade is active three times a year. Six or eight feet of water in the river bring a swarm of tow-boats up from Pittsburgh. Each steamer takes as many barges as it can handle down stream to Pittsburgh, Wheeling, Ironton, Cincinnati, and all the lower markets, the fleets intended for points on the Mississippi being doubled up after passing the canal at Louisville. Business is done with a rush in times of deep water, and a million tons of coal will often go out of the Monongahela in four weeks' time after a rise of water.

VESSEL-BUILDING LOCALITIES.—There are 31 boat and barge yards on the Monongahela, but such a large part of their product is destroyed every year by being broken up, by wreck, and by natural decay, that the yards are continually at work.

At Rice's landing, about 35 miles from Pittsburgh, coal-boat bottoms are made and barges built, about 20 or 30 of the latter every year. The bottoms are made from hard wood, at a cost of about $300.

At Brownsville there are three yards, two on one side of the river devoted to siding up coal boats with pine and hemlock, and the third, on the other side of the river, an old yard, where the smaller class of steamboats are built in considerable number. Almost without exception the boat-builders of the Monongahela have each a saw-mill in their yards, and the three at Brownsville are not exceptions. At the steamboat yard the mill is employed in general business to some extent, but its main use is to manufacture material for the boats. The oak comes down the river in rafts from points in West Virginia, and costs from $10 to $14 a thousand feet in the rough log, while the pine and hemlock come principally in the round log from the Allegheny river. While enjoying cheap timber, the Brownsville men labor under the disadvantage of having several dams across the river below them. Of steamboats, therefore, they can make nothing except the hulls for the medium class of boats, for they have to send them down over the dams. Hulls 250 feet long have to be built below the dams, and the majority at Brownsville do not exceed 180 feet in length. They cost from $2,000 to $4,000 each, one-third of which is for labor, and there are from 50,000 to 150,000 feet of lumber consumed in making each hull. Tow-boats are of heavier scantling, and, for their size, consume more material. The main yard at Brownsville built 10 hulls and many coal boats in the census year. Wages were low, ranging from $1 25 to $2 25 per day, but nearer Pittsburgh they were 50 cents or more higher. The coal boats at Brownsville were each 170 feet long, 26 feet broad, and 9 feet deep, costing $900.

At Greenfield 15 or 20 flats and about 25 broad-horns are built yearly. The size of flat in the census year was 90 feet long, 16 feet broad, and 5½ feet deep. Each cost $600, of which $100 was for labor. Hemlock and oak were the woods used.

California, below Greenfield, formerly had a yard or two.

At Belle Vernon there is a yard whose owners have built more than 40 model barges and numerous steamboat hulls. Oak costs from $13 to $15 a thousand feet in the squared log at this point. Three hulls and 2 model barges were built in the census year. The hull of the Plow Boy, 150 feet long, 28½ beam, and 3 feet hold, cost $2,000, while those of the Dacotah and the Montana, stern-wheelers, 252 feet long, 48⅔ feet beam, 5½ feet deep, and register capacity of the hull 575 tons, cost $8,000 each. A model barge 200 feet long, with deck-houses, costs $9,000. These river boat-yards used few heavy pieces of machinery, as the scantling of the boats is light. Bevel saws are not required, nor are bolt-cutters required to any extent.

At Monongahela City there are two yards, one of them devoted chiefly to repair work. At the main yard a large saw-mill is employed, and an active business is done in building and siding up coal barges and boats for the mines in the vicinity. The barges are 130 feet long. The repair yard is provided with a marine railway having five tracks, and vessels are taken out sideways, this being the fashion in the West. The windlass is worked by hand-power. Repairs consist of calking and carpentry work.

Three yards at Elizabeth are devoted to work for the coal trade. From 60 to 80 barges and flats are built yearly. A larger number of broad-horns are sided up; sometimes more than 150 bottoms are bought on the Allegheny. One firm had contracts out for 100 bottoms in the census year, to cost from $350 to $400 each, and in each of the yards a master carpenter was employed to build and side the boats for a certain sum per vessel, materials being supplied. This is a common practice on the Monongahela, where the yards are frequently owned, as at Elizabeth, by coal dealers. Contract prices for labor vary with the times. The following facts were obtained:

Flats.—Value of the boats in 1880, $500 to $690; labor, $90; lumber in each boat, 20,000 feet; iron, about 2,000 pounds.

Barges.—Value, from $1,000 to $1,300; labor, from $155 to $195; lumber in each boat, 34,000 feet; iron, 2 tons.

Coal boats (165 feet long, 28 feet beam, 8½ feet deep).—Bottoms, from $350 to $400; cost of docking and calking, each $70; siding up, $350, of which $95 was for labor; lumber in the top, 9,000 feet; iron, 750 pounds.

One of the Elizabeth concerns was busy in 1880 with a government contract, and it was building for the Mississippi river improvement commission two decked barges 211 feet long, 35 feet wide, and 5 feet deep, two of the same size but only 25 feet wide, and ten 100 feet long, 25 feet wide, and 5 feet deep. Near Elizabeth three small sectional dry-docks were stationed for repairing.

At Dravosburg a coal firm builds its own boats, consisting largely of strong barges, each 130 feet long, 25 feet wide, and 7½ feet deep, with six gunwales on a side, made of white pine, with the exception of the streamers and bitts. One consumes 31,000 feet of white pine, 3,500 feet of oak, and 2 tons of iron, the cost being about $1,000.

A few miles below this place is a new yard. Very little work was done in the census year, but some 135-foot barges were building in 1881, and four small sectional docks were employed in repairing.

At McKeesport, a manufacturing town, there are four yards, two of them devoted to repair work, the others to coal-boat building.

A large saw-mill is located at Six-Mile Ferry, at which from 50 to 75 coal barges of different classes are produced yearly. At this yard some barges of unusual size have been built. Each is 160 feet long, 24 feet wide, and 8 feet deep, consuming 36,000 feet of lumber, and cost $1,200 each, $265 of it for labor.

In Clare township, just above Pittsburgh and below the place last named, there are three yards which come under the influence of the high wages of the city. They were paying $2, $2 50, and $3 50 a day in 1881, and at one of them a mixed business of repairing and building was carried on. The proprietors said that work was leaving them for places further up the river, and for Freedom and Sewickley, below Pittsburgh.

Within the limits of Pittsburgh and Allegheny City there are three firms which build and side up boats, three firms which thrive by cabin building, one firm which is now building steel hulls for river vessels, and several firms which make engines and boilers. The joiner work of the cabins is generally ¼-inch white pine or poplar. About 45,000 superficial feet are required for the cabins of a steamer of moderate size, and about 95,000 for those of a 250-foot boat. Altogether on the two rivers there are built every year about 600 completed barges and hulls, employing an average of 420 men at steady work.

At Freedom, Pennsylvania, there is one yard, long established, where for 30 years river steamers of all sizes used on the upper Ohio have been built. Here were built the fast packets that ran to Cincinnati. One boat, the Messenger No. 2, 250 feet long and 60 feet beam, once made a famous trip from Cincinnati to Pittsburgh. She was stripped for the race, and "carried only her machinery and Jenny Lind". The voyage was usually made in 30 hours, but this time it was accomplished in 18. The proprietors submitted for inspection a great mass of specifications and contracts for hulls, almost all for stern-wheelers. One of them was for a 290-foot side-wheel boat, several were for 250-foot, and the rest for from 100- to 235-foot stern-wheel boats. The building price has been from $30 to $35 per register ton for strong-built hulls. The cabins and machinery are put in at Pittsburgh, where the vessels are usually owned. The lumber used at Freedom is white oak and poplar from the upper part of the Monongahela and white pine. The poplar comes down with the oak, being incorporated in the rafts as floats. The wood is light and durable, and is the best material for fore-and-aft bulkheads, cabins, etc. Oak costs in the log from $13 to $15 and pine about $10 per thousand feet, and the yard saws its own lumber. It was stated here that oak wastes extremely in working up, owing to the large quantity of defective pieces. A worm hole, a shake, or a stain in the wood causes its instant rejection, as no vessel owner will accept a stick or a plank having the slightest flaw. Were it not for this fact, nearly every cubic foot in the logs after they are squared could be used, for these western boats require little crooked timber in the frames and almost none anywhere else. The bilge is turned with flitch knees, nailed to the side of the frames, and only in the extreme bow and stern are crooked frame timbers used. The hulls of seven steamboats were built at Freedom in the census year, at a cost of from $30 to $35 per register ton of capacity. Two towing-boats were each 177 feet long, and one was 132 feet long. The Harry Brown, a towing-boat of 772 tons, was 210 feet long, 49½ feet beam, and 6 feet deep, and has proved to be a powerful boat. Her total cost was about $75,000, the machinery costing $22,000. One of the new boats was the passenger steamer Carrier, 250 feet long, 40 feet beam, and 5½ feet hold, registering 815 tons, built for the Missouri river trade. About 35 men find steady occupation at this yard.

At Sewickley, Pennsylvania, there is one yard, a new one, which, like the one at Freedom, is devoted entirely to steamboat and model-barge work. It has its saw-mill, bevel saw, and general outfit of tools. Four steamers were in course of construction when the yard was visited in the census year, of which two were afloat and two on the ways, all stern-wheelers. In 1881 the river was so low that there was not over 3 inches of water on the sand-bars above, and as at least 3 feet of water were required in order to send the hulls up to Pittsburgh the proprietors were compelled to put the tops of the new boats on at Sewickley, the joiners going down from the city every day for that purpose. The new boats were all for towing (Fig. 59), and were accordingly strongly framed. The two on the stocks were 192 feet long, 35 feet beam, 34 feet wide on the floor amidships, and were molded 6 feet deep. One of those afloat was 200 feet long, $38\frac{7}{12}$ feet beam, 46 feet wide over all, 6 feet deep, with 38 inches sheer forward and 18 inches aft. A description of this boat will show about how the towing steamers are made. Frames: floors single, 4 by $7\frac{1}{2}$ inches, extending from bilge to bilge in the square body; in the bow and molded part of the stern the floor reaches only half across the boat, and there are futtocks abutting over the keel; top timbers, 4 by $6\frac{1}{2}$ inches; spacing 13 inches. Stem sided 11 inches, molded about 30 inches in the thickest part; no apron, but a sort of stemson. Two stern-posts 11 inches thick. Keelsons: main, 7 by 18 inches; one wing keelson each side, 5 by 14 inches; two floor streaks each side, 3 by 8; bilge keelson, 5 by 10. Two clamps, 3 by 12, and $2\frac{1}{2}$ by 12 inches. No ceiling. Beams, 4 by 7 inches, with 9 inches spring; aft, $3\frac{1}{2}$ by 7. Head piece at bow, 8 by 16 inches, being 46 feet long. Stanchions on main keelson, 3 by 4 inches, sided up with 2-inch poplar to form a double bulkhead. Stanchions on wing keelsons, $3\frac{1}{2}$ by 4 inches, sided up with $2\frac{1}{2}$-inch poplar, forming a single bulkhead. Stanchions, 4 inches square on each floor streak. Plank of bottom, 4 inches; grub streak on the bilge, 5 inches; sides $3\frac{1}{2}$, tapering to 3 inches. Short flitch knees or futtocks at the bilge. The bilge secured at each frame by bolts of $\frac{1}{2}$-inch iron, driven clear through the streak of bilge planking, the frame timber, and the bilge keelson. Decking, $2\frac{1}{2}$-inch white pine. Top plank-sheer, 3 by 14 inches; under one, 2 by 12 inches; nosing, $3\frac{1}{2}$ by 11 inches. Cylinder timbers, oak, sided 13 inches, 4 feet deep in the thickest place. Heel pieces on the floors for the main hog-chain braces, each side, 13 by 22 inches. Four main hog-chain braces on each side of the boat from 42 to 46 feet long, white pine, 13 inches square below, 11 inches above, carrying on their top a $1\frac{3}{4}$ bar-iron rod, or, as they call it in the West, a chain, which descends at the ends to the keelson and supports the ends of the boat. In line with these braces is another set, called relief braces, 8 inches square, carrying a $1\frac{7}{8}$ chain, which supports the hull at different points from the others. On the main keelson there is a row of posts, or braces, 11 inches square, over which runs the main center chain of 2-inch iron, descending to the main keelson at each end. The bilges are supported by 8 thwartship $1\frac{1}{2}$-inch chains, supported by as many sets of light braces. The weight of the boilers and of the wheel is supported by other sets of chains and braces. Four rudders with 14-foot blades, the middle two to have 9-foot balance blades; rudder stocks 17 inches square. Stem band, $3\frac{1}{2}$-inch half-round iron for 9 feet; the rest of the way of flat iron 1 by 6 inches. Calking of bottom, 5 threads; of sides, 3 or 4; the oakum to be driven through flush with the inside of the plank, this being the universal practice in the West. Two spars, to stand on the forward deck at the fore edge of the upper works, 14 inches in diameter, 38 feet long. Two derricks, 9 inches in diameter, 34 feet long, and four 6 inches by 20 feet. Six boilers, each 47 inches in diameter and 28 feet long, having 6 flues 10 inches in diameter. Boilers set 40 feet from the bow. Chimneys, rising to 54 feet from the deck, 58 inches in diameter. Two engines, each $24\frac{1}{2}$ inches in diameter, 12 feet stroke, set 34 feet from the stern. Wheel, 28 feet in diameter; buckets, 28 feet long and 3 feet wide. Launching draught of hull, 20 inches aft and 24 inches forward; with machinery, water, and 285 tons of coal aboard, 42 inches even draught, the displacement being 785 tons.

There were seven steamers built at Sewickley in the census year, all towing and freight boats, the most of them stern-wheelers. One, the Florida, was a side-wheeler, 180 feet long, destined for coast service. The cost of the hull was from $30 to $35 per register ton. One tow-boat was 122 feet long; the others ranged from 180 to 260 feet, consuming from 100,000 to 225,000 feet of oak, pine, and poplar. The yard gives employment to 65 men in busy times at $1 25 a day for laborers and $2 25 for good carpenters.

Freedom and Sewickley are now the main dependence of Pittsburgh for her steamboats, as are the two rivers above the city for her coal barges. The whole tonnage of the city has to be renewed every six or seven years; as Pittsburgh owns the most of any port in the Union, the basis exists for a prosperous business. An effort is now being made to extend the use of iron hulls for steamers. During the last fifteen years the district about Pittsburgh has produced 340 steamers.

At Steubenville, Ohio, there is a small yard, where much work is done in busy years.

Wheeling, West Virginia, once did a flourishing business in making steamers and the machinery for them, and from 5 to 10 vessels were launched every year, as well as many barges. The principal firm owned a tract of 1,500 acres of timber in Marshall county, the trees of which they cleared off and put into boats. They built a class of vessels adapted for the small rivers and bayous of the South, both side- and stern-wheel, but when the war broke out lost heavily from inability to collect what was due. The industry in Wheeling was greatly affected by the war, and of late the yards have done nothing except to make a few barges from time to time. Two firms of joiners do a little business, however, in putting cabins on boats built at various points in that region on the Ohio and on the West Virginia streams, and one firm builds machinery for the same boats, from eight to ten boats a year being so fitted out.

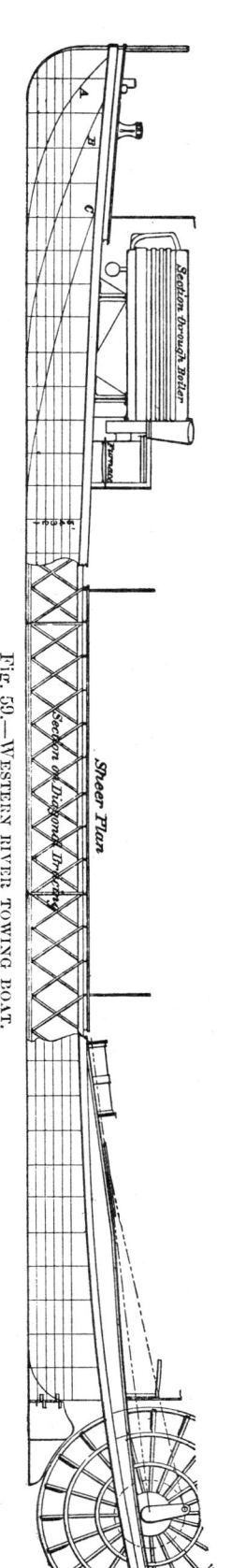
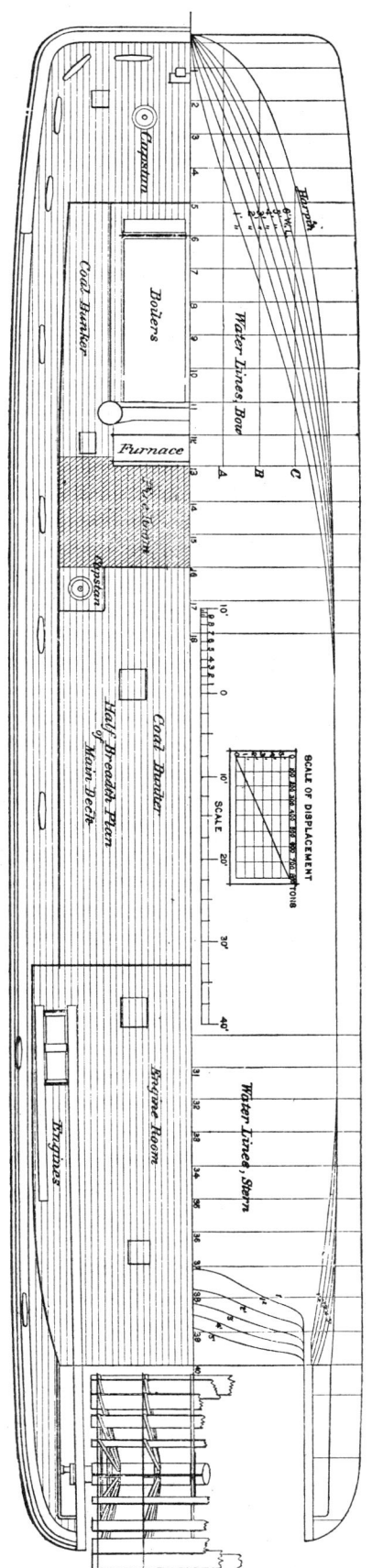
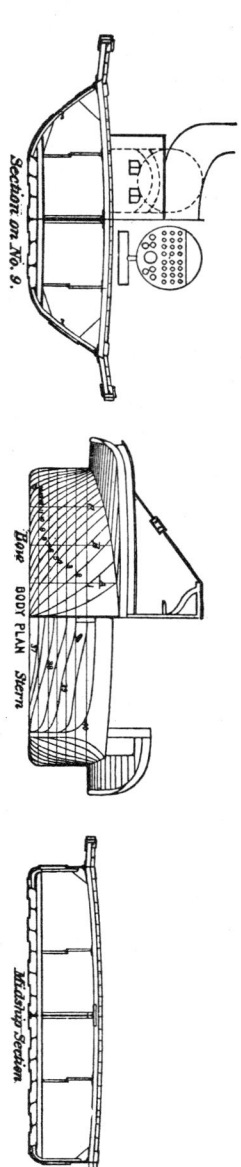

Fig. 59.—WESTERN RIVER TOWING BOAT.

This illustration is a good representation of the model of the stern-wheel steamboat of the West. The plan is intended for an iron hull.

A rising coal trade on the Great Kanawha river calls for local barge building, its commencement appearing at a number of points. From 30 to 50 boat bottoms are made on the Elk river every year, and are floated down to Charleston on the main stream and there sided up. At Coalburg, up the Kanawha, from 10 to 20 barges are built yearly by the coal company, and a dozen or more are made at Charleston. There is an abundance of timber in this region, and time will bring the capital and the enterprise; but saw-mills and railroads are needed. The one yard at Charleston could have built 100 barges in the census year if the lumber had been obtainable. Owing to low water in the river pine could not be brought in, and a lumber famine often occurs, during which oak will rise to $25 per thousand feet. The barges built at Charleston range from 100 feet in length, 18 feet beam, and 5 feet depth, to 130 feet in length, 24 feet beam, and 7 feet in depth. A little steamboat work is done here, and there is a float for repairing. Coal-boat bottoms cost from $150 to $250 at Charleston; the labor of siding up costs $45, and the boats, when finished, were worth $450. Wages were from $1 25 to $1 75 a day. The Kanawha is already one dependence of the cities on the Ohio for coal, every flood bringing out of the river a considerable rush of steamers and barges.

The points where small work is done in West Virginia are Point Pleasant, Murrayville, and Mason City; they enjoy the advantage of abundant timber.

A little yard at Marietta, Ohio, employs about 35 men in building small steamers. There is another at Ironton, Ohio, on the side of a steep bank, where many vessels have been launched, including more than 25 model barges; also a yard at Portsmouth, Ohio. At Middleport there is a dry-dock for repairing, and a small yard at Ashland, Kentucky, builds ferry and passenger boats and does repair work.

Cincinnati has two large yards. The Marine Railway and Dry Dock Company's yard is one of the largest and best equipped in the West, and has its own saw-mill and a complete outfit of machinery and tools, lumber being bought in rafts, hauled up on the bank by steam-power, and sawed to suit the vessels under construction. Few concerns in any part of the United States, excepting only the iron-ship builders, keep so elaborate a set of books as this company. A faithful account being kept of every foot of lumber of the various kinds, of every pound of iron, paint, and oakum, of the days of labor, and of every other detail of the cost of the several boats and jobs of repairing, the exact cost of each vessel is thus ascertained, and the various items tabulated for future reference. This process enables the firm to bid accurately and successfully for contracts. Bookkeeping is not as a rule minutely carried on by the ship-builders of the United States, and in a large number of yards the accounts are kept roughly, often on loose sheets of paper or in little pocket note-books, and sometimes on shingles. More than one large yard was visited (not on the Ohio river) where the proprietors did not know what a vessel had actually cost them when finished, the data about the various jobs of work not being thoroughly sifted out and kept apart. At the Cincinnati yard thorough system was observed, at no appreciable increase of running expense; and the facts obtained about river vessels in general were of the most satisfactory character. Seven steamers and three model barges were built by the Marine Railway and Dry Dock Company in the census year, viz:

	Tonnage.	Length.	Beam.	Width of floor amidships.	Depth of hold.	Cargo-carrying power.
		Feet.	*Feet.*	*Feet.*	*Feet.*	*Tons.*
Side-wheeler Natchez	1,477	303½	46½	38½	10	2,000
Stern-wheeler Granite State	531	223	35½	34½	5½	800
Side-wheeler Bostona	993	302½	43½	42	10	1,000
Stern-wheeler Will Kyle	1,017	260½	45⅔	43⅔	6⅓	1,350
Stern-wheeler Hettie	176	....	....	....	....	....
Stern-wheeler Pittsburgh	722	252	39	38	6	900
Stern-wheeler Clifton	716	152	39	37	6	900
Model barges 3 in number	236	160	28	27	5½	350
	270	180	32	31	6½	650
	270	180	32	31	6½	650

Although dependent on the tributaries of the upper Ohio for oak and poplar, and always embarrassed when the rivers are so low as to prohibit the rafting of logs, the Cincinnati yards are able to build as cheaply as their competitors up stream, hulls being made for from $20 to $30 per register ton. In Cincinnati, as in Pittsburgh and Wheeling, cabin building is a separate occupation; the contract is usually sublet to some joiner, who owns a large saw-mill and manufactures his own lumber. Poplar, the cheapest and best wood for cabins, is extensively used, and ranges in price from $16 to $30, but is usually nearer to $20 per thousand feet when finished. Oak, white pine, and poplar are the building woods. As a novelty, yellow pine and cypress from the South were put into the beams of the Natchez. This boat was sharp built and intended for speed. She was strongly framed, her floors being 4 by 11 inches square amidships and 5 and 6 by 11 forward, spaced 14 and 15 inches. Her main keelson was 9 by 18 inches, bilge 8 by 14 inches, ten floor streaks 6 by 10 inches, and stringers 3 and 3½ by 12 inches; clamps 3, 3½, and 4 by 40 inches. The central bulkhead of this boat was made of 5-inch poplar, edge-bolted with ½-inch iron 3 feet apart. The waste of wood in making these boats is nearly one-half. The Natchez consumed 390,000 feet of oak,

120,000 feet of pine and poplar, and 29,000 pounds of iron in the hull, and 200,000 feet of wood in her cabins. Her machinery weighed 200 tons, the cylinders being 34 inches, with 10-foot stroke. She was a strong, fast, handsome side-wheel boat, with broad guards for cotton carrying.

The other yard at Cincinnati made 3 steamboats, 4 model barges, and a wharf-boat in the census year. The barges were for the grain trade of the Mississippi. Contracts for more than 20 of those boats had been given out in the census year, distributed all along the Ohio. They were of two sizes: 200 feet long, 35 feet beam, and 8 feet hold, and 225 feet long, 36 feet beam, 9 feet hold, all with cargo boxes, and carrying about 50,000 bushels of grain. The cost of the barges was $9,000 and $10,000 each, according to size.

A yard at Covington, Kentucky, thrives chiefly by repair work. The shops are located on the high bank of the river, out of the reach of ordinary floods, and the vessels are drawn out by steam-power, sideways, upon the railway. A few small steamboats and 15 or 20 coal barges are produced in good years.

In Indiana there are large yards at Madison, Jeffersonville, and New Albany, all old building places. Four or five steamers and a few barges are launched yearly at Madison, and repair work is there done on a large set of ways.

Jeffersonville has two large and flourishing yards. It is remarkable that on the Ohio the yards are located chiefly on the northern bank. Those at Jeffersonville employ jointly about 400 men in good years, the majority of them men with families, who are prosperous. At least as early as 1819 boats were built here out of the oak that clothed the region in dense forests. The side-wheeler United States, of 700 tons, was launched in 1819 and sent to New Orleans to receive her machinery, which was imported from England and was modeled after that put into Fulton's steam frigate, then lately built at New York. The popular boats of that day were smaller than 700 tons, but quite a number of them were required, from five to ten being launched in this vicinity every year. The war of 1861 interrupted the business; but since that time it has grown to larger proportions than ever, and in no locality in the West have there been more large and famous boats built than at Jeffersonville and around the falls of the Ohio, a mile or two below. In 1866 the owner of the older yard put in a planer for fairing the planking, beams, etc. All the lumber of these western boats is planed. The diminish in the thickness of the plank at various points in the hull is put in by means of the planer, and the success of this machine led to its general adoption in the boat-yards of the West. In the census year the product of this yard was 12 model barges, several flats, and 6 steamboats. Eight of the barges were for the Mississippi Valley Transportation Company for grain carrying, and registered from 1,150 to 1,250 tons, being 200 and 225-foot boats, with cargo boxes. A little repair work is done. The bottoms of the freight boats here are given 3 or 4 inches of dead rise only; the passenger boats about 14 inches.

The other establishment at Jeffersonville was started in 1834, since which time it had built 318 steamboats up to the census year of 1879-'80, mostly stern-wheelers, but also including a great many of the fast and famous side-wheelers in the trade to New Orleans. Among their recent boats have been the J. M. White, the Ed. Richardson, the City of Baton Rouge, the City of New Orleans, City of Yazoo, Rainbow, and Jesse K. Bell. In the census year the product of this yard was eight steamboats, a two-wheeled propeller tug-boat, a barge, and a wharf-boat, besides considerable repair work. The barge was the Victor, of 168 tons, 115 feet long, 27 feet beam, and 7½ feet depth of hold. This boat was strongly built, and was sent to Galveston, where she was rigged as a two-masted schooner for shoal-water service, in which employment she has done very well. In waters where there is no current schooners of this class can successfully be employed. The model is in reality about the same as that of the Chesapeake bay bug-eyes, flat floored, sharp at both ends, with slightly hollow water-lines below; the broad beam fits it for a fore-and-aft rig. The tug-boat above referred to was the Wash. Gray, of 46 tons. She had a bow, deck plan, and house like an eastern harbor tug, but was modeled amidships and aft like a western boat, except that the floor was narrower. Her dimensions were: Length, 78 feet; beam, 18 feet; floor, 10 feet; hold, 6½ feet. This little boat, with her machinery, etc., weighs 110 net tons and floats at 7 feet draught. She is oak built with single frames, with short futtocks added at the bilge. The keelson is 7 by 12 inches square; side keelsons, 3½ by 9 inches. There are two fire-box boilers 64 inches in diameter and 14 feet long, and two double high-pressure engines 12 inches in diameter and 14-inch stroke. The screw wheels are 5½ feet in diameter, each weighing 3,300 pounds. This boat was well suited for harbor use, and was the first of her class seen on the Ohio, although it was not the first propeller. A few small propellers used here and there farther up the stream are supplied with wheels from Chillicothe, Ohio. At Saint Louis the propeller tug is a popular boat.

The oak for the Jeffersonville yards now comes from West Virginia, 550 miles away, as the local supply is very nearly exhausted. A little first-growth timber, large and fine, remains in the swamps of the river counties, and is sought for cylinder timbers; but the most of it stands so far away from the streams and railroads as to be practically inaccessible.

In Louisville little is done except occasional jobs of cabin building and the making of machinery and boilers, in which there is a flourishing business. One of the new boats from Jeffersonville lay alongshore in the fall of 1881 receiving her outfit, namely, the City of New Orleans, 300 feet long, 48 feet beam, 83 feet wide over the guards, and 9 feet hold. She was just one foot too wide to go through the canal, and the intention was to take her down the rapids, like many of her predecessors, when the water should be deep enough. Her draught with

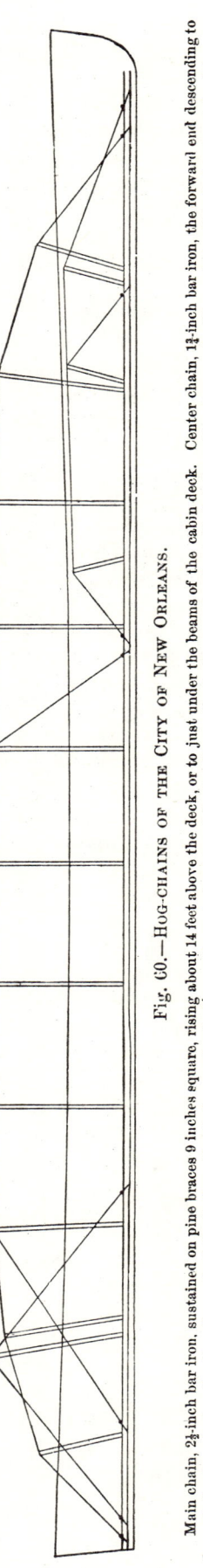

Fig. 60.—HOG-CHAINS OF THE CITY OF NEW ORLEANS.

Main chain, 2½-inch bar iron, sustained on pine braces 9 inches square, rising about 14 feet above the deck, or to just under the beams of the cabin deck. Center chain, 1¼-inch bar iron, the forward end descending to the main keelson just under the after end of the boilers, the chain running back over the main braces and descending to the keelson again, about 15 feet from the stern-post. Stern chain, 1¼-inch iron, sustained by one brace. Boiler deck and bow chain, 1⅛-inch iron, the braces rising to just under the deck beams.

machinery, coal, and water aboard was 42 inches aft and 30 inches forward. Her scantling were: Frames, single, 9 by 4 inches, spaced 15 inches; main keelson, 21 by 9 inches; eight floor keelsons, 9 by 4 inches; four wing keelsons, 7 by 12 inches, to receive the heels of stanchions and hog-chain braces; bilge keelson, 6 by 12 inches; planking, 4 inches on the bottom, 4, 3½, and 3 inches on the sides. Beams, 4 by 6 inches, spaced 21 inches; heavy beams, 12 by 12 inches at the end of the boiler deck. Stanchions, every other beam, 6 inches square, there being seven rows of them fore and aft, with about 30 extra oak stanchions, 10 by 3½ inches, under the cylinder timbers and paddle-wheel shaft. There were three stringers on the top timbers, each side, 9 by 2½ inches. Clamps, 13 by 3½ inches, and 12 by 3. As in all western boats, the boilers, five in number, were on the deck of the hull forward, each 30 feet long, 44 inches in diameter, with four flues, and were made of steel. Engines, one on each side, amidships, 26 inches in diameter, 10 feet stroke; wheels, 35 feet in diameter, with 15-foot paddles. While the hull sat low in the water, the cabins towered aloft to a height of 38 feet to the roof of the main cabin and 67½ feet to the top of the pilot-house. The halls of the main cabin were 220 feet long, 17 feet wide, and 13 feet high. The state-rooms, forty-five in number, were each 12 feet long by 10 feet wide, and were furnished in hotel style. This boat was intended for the passenger and cotton trade of the Mississippi. Her capacity was 250 passengers and 2,300 tons of freight on about 9 feet draught. Builders say that the greatest trouble they have in producing this class of boat is to hold up the sterns, bows, bilges, and guards, as well as to give proper support to the hull when it feels the weight of the boilers, and an elaborate system of hog-chains and braces is required. The fore-and-aft arrangement of the City of New Orleans was as follows (Fig. 60):

Forward of the wheel-houses there are thirteen cross-chains of 1½-inch iron, with braces 6 inches square heeling on the plank-sheer, as in the illustration on page 193 (Fig. 61), supporting the guard. The wheel-houses are supported by two chains of 2-inch iron at each end, running across the boat; braces, 9½ inches square. Aft of the houses are five cross-chains of 1¼-inch iron to support the guards, braces heeling on the plank-sheer.

There are also seven cross-chains of 1½-inch iron on the engine deck, sustained by seven of the main braces, with struts as in the illustration, the chains giving lateral support to the bilge of the boat. Under the boiler deck and forward are located nine other cross-chains of 1¼-inch iron, performing the same service. The total weight of wrought-iron consumed in this light and admirable system of chains was 48,000 pounds. By means of this system the guards were enabled to carry all the cotton bales that could be stowed upon them, the hull was kept from sagging or breaking down in any direction, and it was possible to give the whole boat the light scantling peculiar to the West. Were the same strength gained by heavier timbers, the boat would have weighed two or three hundred tons more. The New Orleans and the Baton Rouge have proved to be fast boats, the latter having run from New Orleans to Saint Louis, loaded, in 4 days 14 hours and 25 minutes, making fourteen stops.

New Albany, below the rapids, has a large yard, owned by a Saint Louis firm, and one other, at which several model barges were built in the census year; but since the completion of the canal to its full width the active business of New Albany has been transferred to the yards above the falls.

Evansville, Indiana, enjoys the advantage of abundant oak timber, and the finished lumber is said to cost no more here than the squared logs do at Jeffersonville and points above. Oak grows plentifully in this part of Indiana, but is cut close to the railroads and the main streams. Back in the country the growth is heavy and large, and a great deal of it is now cut for shipment by car and boat to other points. The builders can also draw on the rivers of Kentucky for ample supplies. Oak is cheaper at Evansville than white pine, and as a consequence many coal barges and flats are either built wholly of oak or bottomed with oak and finished with white pine, the pine timber having latterly been brought from Chicago by rail. While there are no regular boat-yards at Evansville, there are several master carpenters who build small steamboats, coal barges, and flats, as they are required, going down to the foot of the river bank and constructing their vessels there. A coal firm has a small set of ways on which repairing is done, and there is work enough to keep 15 or 20 men pretty busy; but nearly all have other trades to fall back upon when boat work is dull. A saw-mill boat was being finished in 1881 when the place was visited, and there were several barges on the bank. The saw-mill boat had a flat-boat hull, square on deck at both ends, with raking bow and stern. Her dimensions were: Length, 114 feet; width of hull, 22 feet; width on deck, 32 feet; depth of hold, 4 feet. A roof or upper deck was built over the deck of the hull, supported by light stanchions, the sides below being entirely open. On the upper deck were small cabins for the crew and a pilot-house. There were two boilers under the forward end of the sheltering roof 45 inches in diameter and 14 feet long, carrying 80 pounds of steam, and having about 40-horse power. There was a light engine aft to drive the paddle-wheel at the stern. The rest of the deck was taken up with saw-mill machinery, so arranged that logs could be hauled up over the bow of the boat, run aft, sawed, and discharged over the side amidships upon barges, each carrying from 150,000 to 200,000 feet of lumber. There were eight or nine of this class of boats in the South. They go about in the rivers and bayous and saw for the New Orleans and other markets, and their cost complete is from $8,000 to $11,000 each.

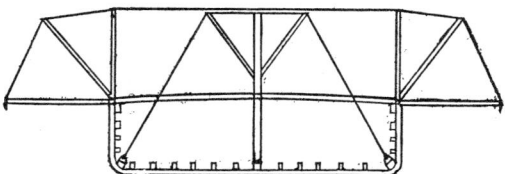

Fig. 61.—CROSS-CHAINS ON THE CITY OF NEW ORLEANS.

A number of traveling flat-boats, housed over for blacksmith and other shop work, lay in the river at Evansville. These boats were all fitted out with four or five long sweeps, and displayed hen-coops, clothes-lines, and all the paraphernalia of the simple housekeeping of the occupants.

At Evansville there are registered every year a number of small vessels built on the streams of Indiana, Illinois, and Kentucky. These vessels are not the product of regular ship-yards, but are made by men who are employed by the owner for the special job, just as a carpenter is employed to build a house. These boats are intended for local service, generally for river ferries, and do not require much knowledge of ship-building, and their construction is a small incident in the industries of their several localities. The places where boats have been latterly built at odd times are Pageville, Frankfort, and Caseyville, Kentucky; Shoals, La Fayette, Vevay, and Bridgeport, Indiana; Peoria, Grafton, Washington, and Newburg, Illinois.

Metropolis and Mound City, Illinois, on the Ohio, each has a ship-yard where barges and steamboats are built. At the latter place there are large marine ways. At Cairo there is always a large amount of tonnage loading and unloading, but only one small yard, which is devoted to the repair work of the Cairo City Coal Company. At Paducah, Kentucky, there are large and flourishing marine railways.

The western marine railways are unique. They have to be wide enough to take out vessels sideways, and are furnished with a sufficient number of tracks and cradles running on them to support the vessels at every point in their length. The Mound City ways, for instance, have 8 sets of tracks, each about 8 feet wide and 30 feet apart, so as to make the entire width of the railway about 275 feet; the pitch down the bank is nearly 2 inches to the foot. Each track carries a low car, or cradle. A broad, flat platform is built at the top of the bank, and an array of eight powerful iron windlasses, worked by a line of shafting laid along the surface of the ground, is set up under the fore edge of the platform. The slope to the river is 160 feet long in low water. The cradles, each held by two 1¾-inch chains, are allowed to run down the ways into deep water until they are under the boat which is to be hauled out, the windlasses are set in motion, the chains coil around the drums, and the cradles come up the bank slowly, the boat settling down upon them gradually. The windlasses each consist of a horizontal iron drum 30 inches in diameter, with a large cogged wheel at each end 7 feet in diameter. Power is communicated from the 6-inch main driving shaft to each end of the windlass by a cogged wheel on the shaft 3 feet in diameter, which gears into another of the same size, set on a small horizontal shaft at right angles to the main, planted on proper journals near the ground. Nearly under the windlass this small shaft carries a strong screw, which gears into a cogged-wheel, again 3 feet in diameter, mounted on a perpendicular iron shaft. On this latter shaft there is another strong screw, which slowly turns the large wheel of the windlass. All the iron work of this machinery, and all the wooden framing which carries it, are heavy and substantial. Ways of this size being necessarily expensive, costing usually about $100,000, few men have the capital to own them, and therefore the repair work of steamboats is necessarily concentrated at a few points.

The lower stretch of the Ohio, on account of deep water and the abundance of white oak, is well adapted both for repair work and for the building of large vessels. Alongshore, on both sides of the river, trees of large size can be had, and away up in the interior of Kentucky, accessible from the rivers, there is so much tall and fine timber that barge gunwales, keelson pieces, and plank can be got from 60 to 75 feet in length. Oak can be delivered in rafts at the several building points on this part of the Ohio for $10 to $13 per thousand in the round log, counting what can be squared from the log; for squared lumber the price was $16 and $18 per thousand in 1881. Other kinds of valuable timber exist in large supply, and poplar logs of 6 feet diameter are often rafted to Mound City, Metropolis, Paducah, and Cairo from the rivers in Kentucky. Black gum and cypress grow profusely, and an eastern sewing-machine factory has recently established a branch at Cairo to utilize the former for the cases of the machines. These great advantages for building have not yet been utilized; but when the oak disappears from the upper Ohio, and it certainly is going fast, the lower Ohio can be made the center of a great and prosperous industry. Cairo is one of the best places in the West to study the character of western tonnage. As the water is deep and the current swift and there is a large trade, this town is a busy shipping point the year round. There has been for some time a grain elevator here, and the Illinois Central railroad has lately erected another of large size. When the Mississippi above Cairo is closed by ice, therefore, the grain trade of Saint Louis is directed by rail to Cairo, and barges are loaded there with the shipments to New Orleans. The town has also a coal trade, the railroads giving access to the great Illinois coal-fields. Cairo is a port of call for all the steamers of the two rivers, and vessels of every class float by its doors and lie up at its wharf-boats. There have been 70 and 80 steamers in port at Cairo at one time, together with large fleets of model and coal barges. From 25 to 30 model barges lay near the elevator at the time the town was visited in 1881, hundreds of empty coal barges were moored below the town waiting for a rise of water to go up the Ohio, and many traveling shop-boats were pulled up on the bank. A number of propeller tugs built on the lakes, having been brought down to Cairo by the Illinois canal route, are owned at this place.

On the Mississippi river there is very little ship work of any class done except at Stillwater, Minnesota, Dubuque, Iowa, Saint Louis, and New Orleans, and at those places it is chiefly repairing. At the first two places facilities exist for work on river steamers and barges, and from time to time there is some building done. At Saint Louis there are six yards, and the work is almost wholly in the way of alterations and repairs. The 250,000 tons of vessel property owned in that city, with insignificant exceptions, have been built on the Ohio. Four of the six yards in the city do no building at all. Two of them have floating dry-docks, one a large marine railway, and at the fourth, which is owned by a steamboat company, there are machine-shops and floats solely for keeping the boats of the company in good order. The sectional docks can take out of the water vessels 300 feet long and 84 feet wide over the guards; that is to say, steamers of the largest size now employed in the trade of Saint Louis; but at the other dry-dock vessels of the smaller class are handled.

The marine railway is owned by the Sectional Docks Company, and is located in the southern suburbs of the city. It was started by Primus Emerson and his associates in 1856 or 1857. The original railway was made in seven sections of two rails each, each section carrying a cradle, the rails being 340 feet long from the gearing above to the lower ends in the river. A pitch of $1\frac{7}{8}$ inches to the foot was given to the ways, and heavy chains of $1\frac{3}{4}$-inch iron ran from the cradles to a long line of shafting placed under a rough shed on top of the bank. Emerson found that in hauling out long vessels an unequal strain was imparted to the several chains, as the cradles directly under the boilers and engines took the most weight, and that one chain often broke and it was impossible to equalize the pull. To remedy this in part he conceived the idea of detaching the chains from the front corners of the cradles and of carrying each set down through and around the cradles over friction sheaves, so that each cradle lay in the bight of the chain. The original railway cost \$120,000; but it was afterward enlarged, by the addition of two more sections, so as to be able to take out 360-foot vessels, and its value was then rated at \$250,000, its capacity being such that five steamboats and barges have been out at once on the bank undergoing alteration and repair. In the East, where vessels are pulled up endways on the bank, only one hauling machine or set of gearing is required; but here there are nine machines located on the top of the bank, arranged in a long row under the shed, each machine placed opposite a section of the railway. Power is communicated to the several sets of gearing by a main driving-shaft 390 feet long and $7\frac{1}{2}$ inches in diameter. This shaft runs out from the boiler and engine house along the surface of the ground at the top of the bank parallel to the river, and rests on journals strongly secured to wooden logs and piles. Opposite each set of gearing there is a strong cog-wheel on the shaft 50 inches in diameter, with cogs 2 inches thick, $2\frac{1}{2}$ inches high, and 6 inches from center to center, which drives that set of hauling machinery, and as the machines are driven by a common shaft they work in unison. The machines are strong, but simple in their arrangement. There is, first, near the ground, and resting on heavy oak logs, a shaft 10 feet long and 9 inches diameter at right angles to the main shaft, with a cog-wheel at one end gearing into the one first mentioned and a screw about the middle of its length gearing into a large wheel hung above it on another shaft parallel to the main one. The cog-wheel is 64 inches in diameter. The screw has four threads, and is 23 inches long and 30 inches in diameter. As before stated, the cog-wheel slowly turns a large wheel (hung above it on a shaft 20 feet long, just the width of one section of the railway) 12 feet in diameter, with a rim 3 inches thick, carrying 60 cogs 3 inches high. The shaft on which it is mounted is 15 inches in diameter at the wheel, but tapers to 10 inches at the ends, and hangs about 8 feet from the ground, being supported at the ends by a heavy framing of oak timber, which is a continuation of the wooden ways of that section of the railway. Close by the journals of this shaft are the strong little toothed wheels around which pass the cradle chains. Each set of hauling machinery can be worked independently, as on the main shaft there is a clutch which throws the cog-wheel in and out of gear at pleasure. By this means steamers can be taken up on any part of the railway. On top of the eighteen wooden ways running down into the water there are iron rails, on which the cradles run. About 300 tons of iron were consumed in this railway, exclusive of the engines and boilers.

There are two yards at Saint Louis devoted to new vessels, both started within five years. One is managed by United States engineers, who employ a few men in making flats, lodging-boats, snag-scows, etc., for the Mississippi river improvements; the other makes iron tug-boats, launches, snag-boats, and steamers, and has done something in the way of altering various iron gun-boats of the late war into merchant steamers. This yard will be referred to more fully under the title of iron vessels.

The tonnage of Saint Louis consists of about 170 steamboats (including a few propeller tugs), registering 61,000 tons; 250 model barges, registering 181,000 tons; about 25 flats, 2,600 tons; and from 16 to 20 wharf-boats. Her fleet includes few coal barges, and all her tonnage is of the finest class. Several companies here have been engaged in the shipment of grain to New Orleans, and by a recent consolidation and the giving out of new contracts they have created a fleet of 23 tow-boats and about 150 model barges, by means of which 9,000,000

Fig. 62.—United States Iron Snag-Boat Horatio G. Wright.

137 feet long, 28 foot beam, 90 feet wide across the guards, 8 feet hold.

bushels of grain can be shipped on a single trip. The present fleet of Saint Louis, of all classes, will wear itself out in six years, requiring the building of 40,000 tons of vessel property yearly to maintain it up to the present capacity, and there is a yearly increase in the grain trade. At present the ship-building talent, the skill, and the capital of western boat-building are mainly on the Ohio. On the other rivers, especially those westward of the Mississippi, there is at this time for the most part only the raw material; but this exists so abundantly, and is so cheap and good, that it would seem to afford a valuable opportunity to the people of Kentucky, Missouri, and Arkansas, the three states named being full of valuable oak, poplar, cypress, and black gum. The price of oak now ranges from $12 to $15 per thousand in the round log, delivered in the rivers. In other parts of the country suitable lumber is rapidly disappearing. There is water all the way from New Orleans deep enough to float out merchant sailing vessels and wooden propellers of any size now required in the coasting and the transoceanic trade, and the weather would permit work to go on twelve months in every year, whereas three months are lost on the Ohio on account of snow and ice.

There is some work at points below and west of Saint Louis. This work consists usually of the construction of small craft for local use, generally as ferry-boats or for short river routes. There are few or no regular yards, and the work is generally performed by house carpenters or amateur mechanics under the supervision of some competent shipwright. The points where small vessels are thus constructed from time to time are Lisbon, Glasgow, Missouri City, Kansas City, Leavenworth, Saint Joseph, Plattsmouth, Little Rock, Fort Smith, Poplar Bluff, and perhaps other places. At Memphis only repairing is done, but New Orleans occasionally builds small river steamers.

There is no building of vessels on speculation in the West, as there has been on the sea-coasts, nor do owners practice building for themselves. Keeping the management of their tonnage in the hands of their families is entirely unknown, the only thing approximating the latter feature of the Atlantic coast being the construction of their own flats and barges by a few of the Pennsylvania and West Virginia coal companies. Steamboat building is done entirely by contract with professional shipwrights, and barges are generally built in the same way. The rule for payments on contracts varies somewhat in different localities. The old rule before the war was half cash during the progress of the work, a payment being made at the beginning of the work and other payments at intervals; the other half of the stipulated price was paid in 4 and 8 months, or 3, 6, and 9 months after completion, security being required where the responsibility of the owners was not clear. On account of the credit system Ohio river men lost a good deal of money when the war of 1861 broke out. Since the war an effort has been made to bring the business nearer to a cash basis, but the custom still prevails of reserving one-third or one-half of the contract price until the completion of the boat. Builders buy their materials in about the same way, partly on time.

SNAGS.—While the danger of wreck from running against snags is now the chief peril to which boats are exposed builders have made little or no attempt to fortify their vessels against it, and there appears to be no way of doing it except by adding excessively to the weight of the hulls. The scantling of all boats is indeed made a trifle heavier forward, and the frames there are put in nearer together; but this is as much for helping the boat when it runs against the bank or upon a sand bar as for any other reason, and the light hulls are virtually left unprotected against snags. The lower part of the Mississippi below Cairo has always been dangerous on account of these destructive obstacles to free navigation. Wherever a bank washes away, full-grown trees fall into the water and float down stream until their roots become lodged on the bottom. The current swings the top of the trees down stream, and in time the action of ice and floating *débris* wears away the branches and even sharpens the points of the trunks. About one-half of all the losses of steamers are due to running against these formidable stationary rams, and the only way to remove the danger is to take out the snags. Organized work to that end goes on yearly under the supervision of the United States government, and boats are built especially for this service. They are stern-wheelers, with houses large enough to shelter the machinery and provide accommodations for the working force. The bow is broad, square across the boat, and plated with iron. The snag is felt for and caught with an iron chain hanging in a loop from the bow. It is then raised with a powerful derrick and windlass worked by steam, and is either dragged upon the deck of the steamer itself or hoisted out upon a flat-boat lashed alongside. The trunks are often 5 feet through and 60 feet long, and their average weight 17 tons, from which it will be seen how powerful is the machinery required to dislodge them from their anchorage in the soft bottom of the river and to lift them out upon the boats. Major Suter, of Saint Louis, has supplied the following memorandum of the operations of the snag-boat H. G. Wright (Fig. 62) in the one year of 1881 during eight months of work: Total number of snags destroyed, 1,909; number of trees cut on banks liable to cave into the rivers, 5,005; number of drift piles removed, 15. The following is a statement of the work done on the Mississippi, Missouri, and Arkansas rivers from March 28, 1868, to June 30, 1881, also supplied by Major Suter:

Rivers.	No. of snags pulled.	No. of trees cut.	No. of drift piles removed.
Mississippi	14,582	54,605	107
Missouri	13,309	47,042	335
Arkansas	5,083	8,059	76
Total	32,974	109,706	518

The removal of these trunks has probably saved a loss of from $500,000 to $750,000 of vessel property a year.

Chapter V.—IRON VESSELS.

Not more than eighty years have elapsed since iron was first employed in place of wood in the frames and outer planking of vessels. There are some men still living in England who remember the very first boat of this material, which was a little canal-boat with a wooden frame and bottom and sides of boiler iron. The lightness and buoyancy of the hull were the points that attracted attention at the time and led to the construction of other boats of the same class. It was at first supposed that iron hulls, on account of their light draught, would be best adapted for canals and rivers, and all the first vessels were intended for use on one or the other of those two classes of water routes. The first steamboat, a small affair, was manufactured at Horsley in 1821, put together in London, and then sent to France. A boat for the river Seine was shortly afterward exported in pieces from England and put together at Charenton, and in the course of the ten years following 1821 quite a number of small river steamboats were built for companies in England and on the Continent. There then followed a few packets for use on the coast. Finally, in 1838, sailing vessels of from 200 to 300 tons register were built at Liverpool and elsewhere for voyages to foreign lands. After 1840 the building of iron vessels for all trades became a permanent and prosperous industry. What tended to bring them into favor first was their lighter weight and longer life; a decisive victory was won for them when, in 1840, it was finally determined that for all large tonnage it was cheaper to build of iron than of wood. Timber had grown scarce and dear in England; on the other hand, iron and coal were cheap. As soon as builders had acquired sufficient confidence to make iron vessels a specialty it was found that they could build at a considerable saving on the first cost of a wooden ship, as when they learned to distribute materials properly they decreased the weight of the iron ships, built them at a lower cost, and saved from $10 to $20 per ton on the cost of a wooden vessel. This was an important point, and the result was seen in the rapid development of the industry in localities favorably situated with respect to the iron and coal mines. After 1840 a great deal of capital was invested in iron tonnage in England, and the production of wooden tonnage steadily declined year by year until, in 1882, it has virtually come to an end.

In America timber has always been cheap and abundant. The wooden ship has always been the cheap ship, and it remains so to-day. A strong motive for the production of iron tonnage never came to our people until after they had been for some time employing long and large steam vessels in the deep-sea trades. It is true that several small revenue-cutters, tugs, and steamboats had been built of iron in this country prior to 1840, and the subject of iron hulls for large-class tonnage had received a great deal of attention in the principal commercial cities. The superior buoyancy and durability of iron hulls were recognized, but their cost was a serious disadvantage; and Americans saw no reason for abandoning oak and pine for iron until experience had taught them that for large steamers strength and rigidity of structure were considerations of far greater importance than first cost. They then took up the question of the new material seriously, and the result was that after 1850 there began a movement which has finally led to the almost entire disappearance of wooden hulls in American steamers in the deep-sea trades and the universal adoption of iron hulls. For sailing vessels oak and pine retained their popularity; and although it is nearly 60 years since the first iron vessel was launched in America, not more than a dozen sailing vessels and half that number of barges are known to have been built in this country of any material except timber. The iron ship lasts longer; but the wooden ship is far cheaper, is practically as good a carrier, and, all things considered, is about as profitable. There is not much inducement for making sailing tonnage of iron, and there apparently will not be until the first cost of the two is more nearly equal than it is now. On the other hand, at least 590 iron steamers in all have been constructed, and the production has now reached a total of from 20 to 40 a year, and is steadily growing.

There is no record of the building of an iron vessel in the United States until 1825, when the little light-draught steamboat Codorus was launched in Pennsylvania for service on the Susquehanna river. This was four years only after the advent of the first iron steamboat in England. The Codorus may possibly have been one of several which were exported from England in pieces to America and put together here during that early period, but on that point nothing can be definitely stated. The boat was employed on the Susquehanna for a while, and was then sent south for river service there. In 1835 there were five iron steamers already on the Savannah river which appear to have been built in the north. New York was foremost in the matter of iron steamboat building in that early time. In 1836 a steam vessel of 600 tons was launched, originally with a view to trading to Europe. She was put into the mail service to New Orleans first, however, but subsequently abandoned the transatlantic branch of her career. In 1838 a pioneer iron steamboat was built in the West at Pittsburgh. There was next, in 1841, a revenue-cutter built at Boston. As early as 1842 Philadelphia had produced a line of small iron steamboats to trade to Hartford, Connecticut. That year was, relatively, a favorable one for the rise of an iron ship-building industry in the United States, for iron had just touched the lowest prices ever known on this side of the Atlantic. Pig metal had been as high as $55 per gross ton after the

IRON VESSELS.

war of 1812, and again as high as $52 50 just before the panic of 1837, while the average price had been $35, and it had never fallen as low as $27 50 until 1842. Anthracite iron went as low as $25 per gross ton in that year, and in 1844 it dropped to $24. Nothing like it had been known. The drop had a favorable effect on iron-vessel building, but only for a short time, because railroad building caused a rise in value of $8 per ton within a very few years. While iron ranged low a number of boats, all of moderate size, were built in New York and Philadelphia, and a now famous yard was started at Wilmington, Delaware; the most work appears to have been done in New York, the industry being fostered in that city by the great marine-engine shops, four iron revenue-cutters being built there in 1843, and a number of small merchant steamers about the same time. Then came the rise in iron. In 1850 iron had dropped again, pig metal going to $20 per ton, and a new yard was started in Boston. At New York there was some production, but again iron rose in value; and in 1854 prices had gone to $38 per ton, almost double what they were four years before. Few vessels were built, therefore, and these chiefly on foreign account, until 1858, when the general dullness in trade had brought the price of pig metal down again to $21 50. There was then every prospect of a prosperous growth in the industry. Materials and labor were both low, as they generally are at the same time in iron-ship building, for the raw materials of this industry are in reality the highly finished products of skilled labor, and the cost of materials is directly dependent upon the current rates of wages. American builders were learning to handle iron, and their workmen were becoming trained in the routine of the ship-yard. In addition to these things was the fact that the superiority of American iron had been discovered; an important matter, because it enabled American builders to construct hulls as light and strong as any in the world with a smaller quantity of material than would be put into similar vessels in England.

After the war of 1861 had broken out the value of every form of cast and rolled iron sprang up in a remarkable manner. In 1864 pig metal had touched $73 50 per ton, the highest figure in the history of the United States, and the average of that extraordinary year was $59 25, something entirely unprecedented. Wages also rose to the highest point perhaps ever known, for the army drew off an immense number of workmen. Other circumstances remaining as they were before the war, these events would have closed the gates of every iron-ship yard in America; but the period was exceptional, and those four years were, in fact, years of intense activity in all the yards. It was necessary to construct a large number of iron-clad war vessels immediately, and in the emergency the reliance of the government was almost wholly upon private ship-yards. Foreseeing that this would be the case, the proprietors in Boston, New York, Philadelphia, and Wilmington fitted up their yards in anticipation, putting in expensive machinery for the bending of iron frames and plates, the punching of rivet holes, and the forging and handling of iron bars and shafts. The contracts which they afterward received enabled them to go on and improve their plant, and several firms invested from $250,000 to $1,000,000 each in shops and machinery of the most massive description. The liberal expenditures for armored vessels during the war gave the iron-ship building interest the most powerful impetus it has ever received. The government was compelled from necessity to do that which had been done in England in times of peace from public policy, and was obliged to supply private ship-yards with so large a volume of business that they were thereby placed upon a solid basis of large capital and improved plant. This result has since proved of immense value to that part of the commercial community which is compelled to own and employ steam vessels in deep-sea trade, and has firmly established the art in the United States, improved the quality, and decreased the cost of American iron-built ships. The yards were dull immediately after the war, that is to say, from 1864 to 1870, because the government orders ceased, and there was an era of high prices, during which iron and labor were costly; but after 1870 iron went down rapidly, reaching $16 50 per ton in 1878, the lowest point in American history, and the price has ever since remained at a moderate figure. Steamer building became active in 1870 for the coasting trade, for companies in South America, and to a limited extent for our own foreign trade, and it has ever since gone on steadily and profitably. New yards were opened after 1870 on the coast, on the northern lakes, and on the western rivers.

No official separate record was kept of the iron-ship building of the United States until about 1868. In order to show the full extent of what has been done an attempt has been made to prepare a table of the production for this report; (a) but the only statement that can be made is one prepared by the Register of the Treasury, which, however, does not include about 100 vessels built on foreign orders and a number of coast survey, revenue marine, and other government vessels. It is as follows:

Year.	No.	Tonnage.	Year.	No.	Tonnage.
1868		2,801	1875	20	21,632
1869		4,584	1876	25	21,346
1870		8,281	1877	7	5,927
1871		15,479	1878	32	26,960
1872	20	12,766	1879	24	22,008
1873	26	26,548	1880	31	25,582
1874	23	33,097	1881	42	28,536

---

a Data have been gathered showing that almost exactly 600 iron vessels (not including war ships) have been constructed in the United States down to the year 1883; but the years when the ships were built and their register tonnage cannot be accurately tabulated without first incurring an amount of labor entirely out of proportion to the value of the figures when obtained.

Iron ships are constructed on the same general principle as wooden ones. They have a strong backbone or keelson of vertical iron plates, and at right angles thereto ribs or frames, running from the keelson to the gunwale of the vessel and giving to the hull its shape. The frames are strengthened across the floor of the vessel by having riveted to them vertical floor-plates extending from bilge to bilge. There is no ceiling in an iron ship other than a light plank flooring in the bottom of the hold and narrow strips or battens up the sides to keep the cargo from the iron work; but the lack of a heavy ceiling, such as is put into a wooden ship, is made up by greater thickness of outside plating. The outside of the frames is covered with strong iron plates, 6 to 8 frame spaces long and about 2 wide; the edges of each strake lap, and are fastened by a double row of rivets; the butts of the plates are fastened to each other by a strap inside, riveted to each plate by a triple row of rivets. The laps and butts are tightly sealed and made water-tight with hammer and chisel, and the plating makes a perfectly rigid outside shell, which gives the principal strength to the ship. The decks are supported by beams of iron, put in the same as the beams of a wooden ship and kneed to the sides of the vessel with iron knees, which, in this case, however, are part and parcel of the beams themselves. In its whole design the iron ship follows closely the structure of its wooden prototype, the only variations in construction being those which spring from assembling bars and plates in the one case and beams and planks in the other to produce a finished vessel. It is a much simpler process to build an iron ship than it is to build a wooden one. For instance, a frame, while composed of two angle-irons riveted back to back, extends in one length from the keel to the plank-sheer, whereas in the wooden hull the frame is made up of a large number of short pieces, which must be arranged with much care and ingenuity and be properly fastened together before the frame can fulfill the object of its existence. The plating of an iron vessel is also a simpler and easier affair than the planking of a wooden hull. The same simplicity prevails throughout the whole structure. It is only required that the work of the ship shall be done accurately. If frames are a little out of the true curvature they cannot be dubbed off with an adze after they are in position; they must be bent to exactly the right curvature in the first place. A bad seam cannot be closed with oakum, nor will iron, like wood, swell in water and close up the seams. In the iron ship all the parts must be made of the true shape before they are fitted into the vessel, and must match each other exactly, perfect accuracy being the requirement. Under the circumstances the iron-ship builder is put to one expense which the man who works in timber does not incur. He is compelled to employ fine engineering talent in his draughting room and mold-loft; with a good man in charge of that department of his business there is no trouble in building the ship. The value set upon accuracy is shown by the fact that good draughtsmen get $10 a day in the iron-ship yards, while the best mechanics receive no more than $3.

The art of building iron vessels is now well understood in the United States, and, whatever the class of vessel desired, it can be strongly and satisfactorily built, whether it be a river steamboat, a tug, a mud-scow, a steam-yacht, a sailing-yacht, a great paddle-wheel vessel for Long Island sound, a railroad car ferry, a coasting propeller, a steamship for the foreign trade, a large sailing ship, or an iron-clad man-of-war. American builders seem to have learned their art by intuition. The workmen are recruited principally from the machine and boiler shops, but a number have also been obtained from the old wooden-ship yards. A ship-carpenter makes as good a man for the iron-ship yard as does the boiler-maker, and with the aid of a very few machinists any wooden-ship builder could transfer his whole working force from wood to iron and in six months' time have as competent a set of men as he would require.

As the material for an iron ship is ordered in exactly the lengths and sizes required, angle-irons for the frames, beams, keelson pieces, stringers, etc., seldom have to be trimmed, as their lengths can be accurately ascertained from the draughts of the vessel and the mold-loft floor. The stem- and stern-posts are forged in accordance with measurements furnished, aided by a flat wooden mold. The outside plating is ordered from a wooden model of the vessel, which is made for the purpose, on whose surface the strakes of plates are accurately drawn with a lead-pencil. A small fraction of an inch is allowed in the length, so that they will not be too short, and the surplus is taken off by shearing and planing the edges; and while there is some other shearing, planing, and trimming of iron in the various parts of the vessel, the waste of material is so small as to form no appreciable item in the cost—a fact in striking contrast to the situation in a wooden-ship yard, where not less than one-fourth and often fully one-half of the timber is wasted in making the vessel. As the weight of iron is definitely known, great accuracy of estimate is possible in calculating the quantity and cost of materials. In ordering plating, for instance, the convenient rule is followed that a square foot of rolled iron one inch thick weighs 40 pounds. The real average weight is 40.28 pounds; but the rule of 40 pounds to the square foot is so close, that in buying the plating for a large vessel the weight may be previously known to within about one-fiftieth of the whole amount. The total weight of the angle-irons is closely calculated from the sizes, and can be approximated at any rate to within about one-fiftieth; the rule of ordering by width of flanges, so many pounds to the foot, allows of a perfectly accurate calculation, and this is the method preferred. The following are the sizes and weights of angle-iron rolled by the Phœnix Iron Company at Phœnixville, Pennsylvania:

Width of flanges and thickness of the iron.	Range of weight per running foot.	Width of flanges and thickness of the iron.	Range of weight per running foot.
Inches.	*Pounds.*	*Inches.*	*Pounds.*
1 x 1 x ⅛	0.83 to 1.13	3½ x 3½ x 5/16	8⅓ to 12
1¼ x 1¼ x ⅛	1 to 1⅓	3½ x 4 x ⅜	9 to 13
1¼ x 1½ x 3/16	1½ to 2⅓	3 x 4½ x ⅜	9 to 13
1½ x 1½ x 3/16	2	3 x 5 x 7/16	10 to 14
1¾ x 1¾ x 5/32	2 to 3½	3½ x 5 x ⅜	11⅔ to 15
2 x 2 x ¼	3 to 4	3½ x 6 x ⅜	11⅓ to 16⅔
2 x 3 x ¼	4 to 5	4 x 4 x 7/16	11 to 15⅓
2¼ x 2¼ x ¼	4⅓ to 5⅔	4 x 5 x ⅜	12⅓ to 17
2½ x 2½ x 7/32	5 to 7	4 x 6 x ⅜	14 to 17⅓
2½ x 3 x 5/16	5⅓ to 8⅓	4 x 6½ x ⅜	14⅔ to 20⅔
2¾ x 2¾ x ¼	6⅓ to 8⅓	4½ x 4½ x ½	14⅓ to 18⅓
3 x 3 x 11/32	7⅓ to 9⅔	5 x 5 x ½	16 to 20
3 x 3½ x ⅜	7⅔ to 11	6 x 6 x ½	19⅓ to 25

BULB T-IRON BEAMS.

Width clear across the upper flange, depth of vertical flange, thickness of the same, and diameter of bulb.	Weight per running foot.	Width clear across the upper flange, depth of vertical flange, thickness of the same, and diameter of bulb.	Weight per running foot.
Inches.	*Pounds.*	*Inches.*	*Pounds.*
3 x 5 x ⅜ x 1 5/16	12 to 33⅓	4½ x 8 x 7/16 x 1⅝	22 to 27
3½ x 6 x ⅜ x 1⅜	14 to 16	4⅜ x 9 x 7/16 x 1½	23 to 27
4 x 7 x 7/16 x 1⅜	17 to 21	5 x 10 x 7/16 x 1⅝	28 to 35
5 x 7 x 7/16 x 1¾	21 to 24	5 x 11½ x 7/16 x 1⅝	32 to 37

The raw material for iron-ship building is the finished product of the skilled labor of a rolling-mill, and this explains why the materials entering into an iron ship make about 60 per cent. of its cost; the labor bill is about 40 per cent. In a 1,200-ton sailing ship about 650 tons of finished iron would be used, in one of 2,000 tons about 850 tons, while in large ocean steamers of from 3,000 to 5,000 tons register from 1,300 to 2,000 tons of iron would be required for the hull and from 300 to 400 tons for machinery. In addition to iron, considerable coal and a certain amount of timber are consumed in the ship-yard. When a sailing vessel is built, the top gear is exactly the same as that of a wooden ship, except that hollow iron masts and yards are sometimes used. Allowing for all exceptions, even in sailing vessels the weight of iron used still constitutes almost the whole cost of the raw materials of the ship. It is difficult to state with exactness the price at which ship iron was sold to the builders in the census year. The supply came principally from the different rolling-mills in Pennsylvania, and the varying charges for freight to destinations in different states and the changing price of pig-iron affected the prices at which the several builders bought. Perhaps as fair an average as any are the following figures: Deck beams, curved to the crown of the deck, in 1880, 3.15 cents per pound; 1881, 3.1 cents per pound. Angle-iron, cut to length, 1880, 2.65 cents per pound; 1881, 2.55 cents. Plate iron, 1880 and 1881, average price 2.95 cents per pound.

Iron-ship building differs from the sister industry in the important respect that larger capital is required to carry it on. In the wooden-ship yard nearly all the workmen, to begin with, supply their own hand tools, and after the outfit of broad-axes, adzes, saws, bevels, chisels, calking-irons, mallets, rules, etc., is thus provided, little remains for the builder to purchase except a bolt-cutter, a few planking screws, a few large augers for boring bolt and treenail holes, a derrick, and a large cross-cut saw. Even if he supplies the yard with steam-power, a bevel saw, and a planer, it is hard for him to spend more than $15,000 or $20,000 on his plant, and he can build the largest wooden ships without them. There are plenty of builders of large wooden vessels in the country whose outfit of tools does not exceed $500 in value. On the other hand, an iron-ship yard cannot be established for a smaller investment than about $60,000, and for a large business the investment is anywhere from $200,000 to $1,000,000. The following is a careful estimate of the plant required for a yard having a capacity of one ship of from 2,000 to 2,500 tons a year:

One pair of rolls	$4,000	Hand tools	$2,500
Three punching machines	3,000	Engine, boiler, pumps, etc	4,000
One pair of shears	1,200	Shafting and pulleys	5,000
One planer	2,000	Blacksmith-shop and fittings	3,000
Two countersinks	1,500	Cranes and railways	3,000
One drill	800	Buildings, wood	10,000
One lathe	700	Foundations	4,000
One furnace	2,500	Sundries	5,000
One frame-bending slab	1,500		
Small tools	2,500	Total	57,200
Steam hammer	1,000		

This circumstance of the greater cost of plant limits the number of iron-ship yards which can exist in a country.

With reference to model, it should be stated that the change from wood to iron produces the effect of narrowing the beam of ships. The one weak place of the iron hull is the flat of the floor, which, on account of the thinness of the material, tends to buckle and collapse. This is offset to some extent by the use of vertical plates from 15 to 30 inches deep, according to the tonnage of the vessel, extending across the floor on each frame from bilge to bilge. These floor plates are strongly riveted to the upper edge of the frame angle-iron; the reverse angle-iron, which is riveted to the back of each frame, leaves the frame at the bilge and runs across the upper edge of the floor plate, being strongly riveted thereto. The floor plate, the angle-iron, and the reverse angle-iron united constitute the frame, which, while of narrow molding on the sides of the vessel, is thus of considerable depth across the floor. But even this is not enough. It has been considered safer by all builders of iron vessels, especially of sailing craft, to make the floor sharper, so as to give it a little more vertical stiffness, and then to narrow the beam a few feet. In order to gain the same register tonnage the hull is made longer. This narrowing of the beam makes the vessel swifter, both in the case of sailers and of propellers, which is an advantage, and its only drawback is that in sailing vessels it makes the ship crank. The center of gravity of an iron hull is always higher than in a wooden one, and the model aggravates the evil. The beam of an iron sailing ship is from 2 to 5 feet narrower than in a wooden one. The following comparison between average craft of the same tonnage will show the difference:

Tonnage.	IRON SAILING SHIPS (ENGLISH).			WOODEN SAILING SHIPS (AMERICAN).		
	Length on deck.	Broadest beam.	Depth of hold.	Length on deck.	Broadest beam.	Depth of hold.
	Feet.	Feet.	Feet.	Feet.	Feet.	Feet.
1,000	220	34	21	177	36	23
1,200	229	35½	21	186	37	23
1,300	230	36½	23	194	38	24
1,400	245	37	22	200	39	24
1,500	248	37⅝	23	215	40	24
1,600	253	38	23	220	40½	24
2,000	270	38	32	235	43	27

A description will now be given of the various localities in the United States where iron-ship building is or has been carried on and of the classes of vessels built. Any extended reference to the war ships built from 1861 to 1865 will, however, be omitted, as foreign to the purposes of this report.

North of Massachusetts, on the Atlantic coast, no production of iron merchant vessels has yet been reported.

An iron vessel was built in Boston as early as 1841. Jabez Coney, an iron manufacturer, paid some attention to ship-building, and obtained a contract for the revenue-cutter Saranac. It is believed that this was the first iron vessel in New England. Probably others were constructed in the following ten years, but none of large size. In 1853 the Atlantic works were incorporated by a special charter, and shops were established in East Boston with all the facilities required for engine- and ship-building. In their early history these works built almost entirely on foreign orders. They made engines for the Russian corvette Mandjoor, Le Voyageur de la Mer, a steamer for the Pacha of Egypt, and the Paraguayan steamer Argentina, and also built several steamers complete for the Russians and Chinese, one for the Sandwich Islands, and for American owners the composite steamer Niphon and the iron steamer Pembroke, the latter being afterward sold to go to the East Indies. In 1861 the works devoted their whole attention to United States government business, and built the iron-turret monitors Nantucket and Casco, the turrets for the Monadnock, Agamenticus, Passaconaway, and Shackamaxon, and the engines for five naval steamers. Since the war these works have built much machinery on government orders, two iron revenue-cutters complete, the Richard Rush and the Samuel Dexter, and the noted United States dredge-boat Essayons, which did service at the mouth of the Mississippi river. One of their vessels was the steamer William Lawrence, of 1,049 tons, for the trade between Boston and Baltimore, in which she is still running. An iron sailing vessel, the brig Novelty, was also built by them after the war for the transportation of molasses in bulk; the hold of the little vessel was completely lined with cement for the purpose. The works occupy four acres of ground, and the equipment is complete. Iron vessels could be undertaken at any time; but of late years little has been done except the construction of machinery for ferry-boats, yachts, excursion boats, etc., and the repair of iron vessels, and it must be said that, so far as the latter branch of the work is concerned, the port of Boston now supplies the yard with very little to do. Iron steamers throng the port, but they are all of foreign build and ownership, and display an indisposition to having work of any kind done on this side of the ocean that can possibly be avoided.

Le Voyageur de la Mer was built under a contract with George A. Stone, a young man who had been for several years a resident of Syria as a representative of a Boston commercial house. He was something of an engineer, and in an interview with the Pacha of Egypt he obtained a contract from him to build a ship. The steamer was 216 feet long, 37 feet on the beam, and 22 feet deep in the hold, and registered 1,300 tons. The plates and frames were rolled in Norristown and Philadelphia, Pennsylvania, machinery being put up in Boston for cutting, punching, and molding them. The hull required 3,000 plates and 300,000 rivets, a total weight of 881,000 pounds of iron. The steamer had an inner wooden frame of great solidity ceiled with pitch-pine, two flush decks, and five water-tight iron bulkheads, two extending to the upper deck. The boilers were four in number, and oscillating engines of 800 horse-power were put in, which were 54 inches in diameter, with 3 feet stroke. The propeller shaft was 13 inches in diameter, and carried a $15\frac{1}{2}$-foot wheel. This was one of the very first large iron boats in the United States.

In South Boston there is a yard in which 850 men can be employed, and there is a rolling-mill in the immediate vicinity. There are two large ship-houses on the grounds, a machine-shop of granite 300 feet long, various other buildings, and a derrick which will handle a weight of 60 tons. About $200,000 are invested in the property. The yard was established in 1857 by Harrison Loring, a young man who had had experience in making stationary and marine engines and industrial machinery, and who in 1841 had worked in the ship-yard of Jabez Coney on the iron revenue-cutter Saranac. Mr. Loring's first boat was the Sestos, for the East Indies, a small steamer, the plans for which were prepared in England. The owners were pleased, and Mr. Loring built for them a sister-boat. In 1860 he built two iron steamers of 1,150 tons each for the trade between Boston and New Orleans, but they were afterward sold to the government for employment in the blockading fleet. The iron propellers Mississippi and Merrimac, each of about 2,000 tons, were built in 1861, and afterward the monitor Nahant, the ram Canonicus, and the side-wheeler Winnipee, of 1,500 tons. Since the war the works have been devoted to machinery for sugar and paper factories. All the facilities exist for the construction of vessels. Mr. Loring regards American iron as the best for ship-building, on account of its superior tensile strength, and has repaired English-built vessels whose plates were so weak as not to have over one-half the tenacity of common cast iron. He states that Mr. Martell, the surveyor for Lloyds at Liverpool, admitted to him the necessity in England for something better than their rolled iron for plates, and the consequent adoption by them of steel for ship-building. The South Boston yard labored under the disadvantage of city rates of wages.

In a city like New York iron-ship building naturally began early. An immense amount of every kind of tonnage was built and owned there, and everything which related in any way to ships was eagerly studied by both builders and owners. Builders were enterprising, and watched with especial interest what was going on in England. After iron vessels began to be built in Liverpool and Glasgow the subject was considered in New York. In the years from 1830 to 1850 quite a number of iron steamboats, revenue-cutters, and tugs were constructed, and builders became familiarized with the idea of iron frames and iron shells for ships. In 1839, as already noted, the little iron propeller New Jersey, 70 feet long, 10 broad, and $6\frac{3}{4}$ feet deep in the water, arrived from England, on Commodore Stockton's order, to go on the Delaware and Raritan canal and the rivers Delaware and Schuylkill as a tug.

In 1858 there was quite a movement toward building iron vessels. The steamer Suchil, a side-wheeler, was launched from Bell's yard, on the East river, with 200 people on board. She was 140 feet long, 35 feet beam, and $5\frac{1}{2}$ feet deep in the hold, with three bulkheads and two 120 horse-power engines, and was launched in 43 days from the laying out of the iron plates for the keel on the building-ways. There were 250 tons of iron in her hull. She drew 12 inches light after launching and 16 inches with everything on board, and was ordered by the Tehuantepec Company to run on the California route from New Orleans via the Coatzacoalcos river. Her hull was modeled at the ends for a speed of from 10 to 12 miles per hour. In the same year the Novelty iron works built a steamboat 168 feet long and 30 feet on the beam, while the Morgan iron works began on a contract for four iron propellers to go to Siam. It was in this period that New York was building so many large and handsome wooden steamers for the coasting and California trades. The cost of iron vessels of that size was estimated with a view to competing for the orders of the companies, but the excessive expense and the lack of large plant defeated all efforts to introduce them.

In 1861 William H. Webb built the iron-clad propeller frigates Re d'Italia and Re Don Luigi de Portugallo for the Italian government. The contract for them had been entered into before 1861, and some trouble was experienced in completing them, but the work was finally accomplished, and the ships were sent across the ocean and delivered. The Re d'Italia was $282\frac{1}{4}$ feet long on the upper deck from the after side of the rudder-post to the forward edge of the hawse-pipes. The breadth of beam on the load-line was 54 feet, and the total depth of hold $33\frac{1}{2}$ feet. The Re Don Luigi de Portugallo was 3 feet shorter. The armor of these vessels was mounted on a frame of oak and locust of the most massive description, and the weight of each ship with everything on board, including armament, was 6,150 tons. Each was capable of a speed of from 15 to 17 knots per hour. The Re d'Italia made 14 knots on her first trip with steam up in only four of her six boilers.

A monster iron-clad was soon afterward built by Webb and sold to the French government. Originally ordered by Secretary Welles for the United States service, she was not completed until the war was over. Her builder then obtained permission to sell her abroad, and she was sold to France. This ship was called the Dunderberg, but was rechristened the Rochambeau after her sale. She was a long and powerful ram, lying low in the water, but with a high shot-proof casemate amidships for the working of the guns. The extreme length was 380 feet, the beam of the hull on the plank-sheer $59\frac{1}{2}$ feet, the beam over all above $72\frac{5}{6}$ feet, and the depth of hold amidships $22\frac{5}{6}$ feet, with a casemate $7\frac{3}{4}$ feet high inside, superimposed. The portion of the bow which formed the ram was 50 feet in length. Mr. Webb gave this ship an almost perfectly flat floor, so as to gain the largest possible displacement. The dead rise was only 4 inches. The hull was massively built of wood, with armor above of $4\frac{1}{2}$-inch iron. The frames were spaced 3 feet, and molded over the keel 17 inches, at the floor-heads 14 inches, above the bilge 13 inches, and at the plank-sheer 9 inches. The sides of the casemate were 3 feet thick, and were set at a slope of 35°, to compel the glancing of shot. A thousand tons of iron were used in the armor, and the displacement was about 6,900 tons. This weight was carried on 21 feet draught. The ship's engines (two in number) were built by John Roach & Son, and developed 5,000 horse-power, giving a speed of $15\frac{3}{4}$ miles per hour. This ship registered 5,090 tons, and was the fastest armed steamer in the world at that time.

Since the war it has not been practicable to carry on iron-ship building in New York city. There are four large engine-shops which are devoted almost entirely to marine work, one of them, the Morgan iron works, belonging to Messrs. John Roach & Son, who build at Chester, Pennsylvania; but the building of hulls in New York has ceased, prices, wages, and taxes being too high for that class of work.

The only place on the Hudson which has an iron-ship yard is Newburgh, where Ward, Stanton & Co. have lately added the construction of iron vessels to their old business of building and repairing wooden river boats. In the census year the river propeller ferry-boat City of Catskill, of 414 tons, and a tug of 115 tons were built. Another ferry-boat, the Hoboken, about 190 feet long and 40 feet beam, a double-ender with side-wheels, and a screw yacht for James Gordon Bennett, 246 feet long over all, 225 feet on the keel, 26 feet beam, and 18 feet deep, were in process of construction. The cost of tugs at this yard is about $200 per ton.

At Camden, New Jersey, on the Delaware river, there is one well equipped yard devoted to the construction of tugs and pilot-boats with compound engines and vertical keels. This yard has been established for many years, and has had its ups and downs; but it has now proved the superior excellence of iron hulls for tugs, and builds four or five of that class of boat every year, there being usually two or three under way at once. Two of the boats built here were the Brazil, of 120 tons, 105 feet long, 20 feet beam, and 11 feet deep in the hold, with compound engines having 18- and 30-inch cylinders and 22-inch stroke, and the Juno, of 84 tons, 85 feet long, 18 feet beam, and 9 feet hold, with compound engines 15 and 26 inches in diameter and 20-inch stroke. These boats were sent to Brazil and encountered rough weather on the passage, but behaved so well as to prove their fitness for any ocean voyage. The Inca, another of their tugs, was also a seaworthy boat. The first iron pilot-boat in the United States was built here for service at New Orleans. She was named the Jennie Wilson, and registered 77 tons. In 1880 another of the same class was ordered, also for New Orleans, and was sent to her destination the next winter. The second boat was the Underwriter, of 170 tons, $120\frac{2}{3}$ feet long, 22 feet beam, and 12 feet deep, sharp on the floor, keen in the bow, with a good deal of sheer, and handsome in her whole bearing. The engines were compound, with 20- and 36-inch cylinders and 28-inch stroke, driven by a boiler 11 feet long and 11 feet in diameter, and the wheel was 9 feet in diameter, weighing 3,847 pounds. In an ordinary tug the only house that is needed is one amidships to shelter the boiler and engines and make room for the stowage of spare cables, etc. There must also be a little pilot-house either atop or forward. In the pilot-boat, however, more cabin space is necessary. The arrangement on the Underwriter was as follows: Forward there was a pilot's cabin; next aft was the engine-room, large and airy; then a dining-room, with kitchen and pantry adjoining; and finally, farthest aft, the lodgings of the pilots, having 16 berths. The forward hold was fitted up with 10 bunks for the crew. The plating was of $\frac{7}{16}$-inch iron. Weight of boat, with all on board except coal and water, about 175 tons. In the census year this yard built four iron tugs—the Inca, 103 tons; the Phœnix, 95 tons; the Kate Jones (Fig. 63), 123 tons; and the Nellie, 61 tons—consuming 385 tons of iron in the four hulls and machinery. They were completed at a cost of $76,000, about $200 per register ton, or not much more than the cost of the same class of vessel well built of oak and pine. Wages in the yard were $10 and $12 per week for all the iron-work hands and $15 for carpenters. A tug 120 feet long was building, at the time the yard was visited, with plating of $\frac{6}{16}$-inch iron, rolled 10 feet long, 3 and $3\frac{1}{2}$ feet wide; frames, $3\frac{1}{2}$- by $3\frac{1}{2}$- by $\frac{3}{8}$-inch angle-iron, spaced 20 inches; beams, angle-iron; and rudder- and stern-posts of $2\frac{1}{2}$- by 6-inch iron. An average of 50 men find employment in the yard, but it could employ 200.

Philadelphia, from its nearness to the iron and coal mines and from the remarkable development of the iron-manufacturing industry in the towns lying back of and around her, has always enjoyed a great advantage in iron-ship building. The city has a large number of engine-building works, and is exceptional in the cheapness of her iron and coal. It was natural that she should take a lead in iron-ship building the moment the industry had reached a point where the price of materials and convenience of access to rolling-mills near by should begin to tell. It has already been noted that the first iron vessel in America was a light-draught river boat which was launched in 1825 for use upon the Susquehanna. One of the earliest iron boats of which there is any record in Philadelphia was a small barge, which was built by Jesse Starr four squares from the river and was hauled down to the water by horses. In the thirty years following 1825 quite a number of small iron vessels were built in the city—steamboats, revenue-cutters, etc.—I. P. Morris, James T. Sutton & Co., and Neafie & Levy building from time to time, the hulls being designed and laid down on the mold-loft floor by practical ship-carpenters. It does not appear, however, that the product of the industry was so large and important as that at New York until after the beginning of the war of 1861. The outbreak of hostilities being a signal for preparations in Philadelphia for large ships, William Cramp fitted up at once his wooden-ship yard (where since 1830 he had built 106 vessels of different kinds)

Fig. 63.—Tug Kate Jones.

Large cylinder, 30 inches; small cylinder, 18 inches; length, 109 feet; breadth, 20 feet; depth, 10 feet.

with machinery for the handling of iron plates and frames. His first vessel was the United States man-of-war New Ironsides, of 3,250 tons, 230 feet long and 56 feet beam, which was a strong wooden ship iron-clad above the water. She was built before the yard had been fully fitted up with machinery, and the armor plates were purchased from another concern. When the contract was made the timber for her frame was still growing in the woods; yet in six months' time she was launched and on her way to Charleston. Mr. Cramp afterward built the monitor Yazoo, the steamer Chattanooga, and a number of transports, and did a large amount of other government work. Meanwhile he was steadily improving the plant of the yard, and after the war it became one of the great iron-ship building concerns of the United States. When the building of war vessels ceased attention was turned to the subject of merchant steamers. Philadelphia had lines of coasting steamers to every port on the Atlantic and Gulf seaboard. They were old wooden boats, with a capacity seldom, if ever, exceeding 1,000 register tons, and were in part side-wheelers; as fast as they wore out they could be replaced by iron vessels, provided good ones could be built at not too great an increase of cost. The needs of the coasting trade were carefully considered, and a number of small iron steamers and tugs were built at the yard. Two propellers were built for the Clyde lines, and then, in 1872,

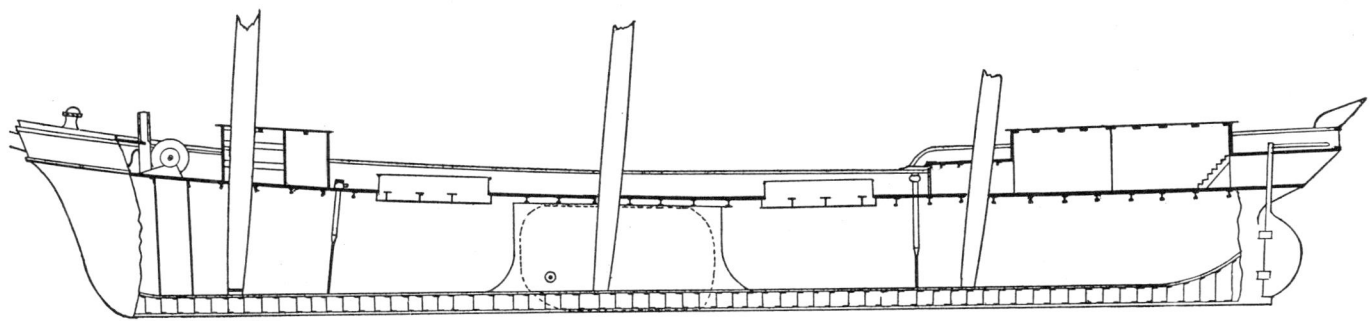

Fig. 64.—LONGITUDINAL SECTION OF THE THREE-MASTED SCHOONER JOSEPHINE.

Built by William Cramp & Sons, Philadelphia. Length on deck, 132 feet 3 inches; length on load water-line, 126 feet; breadth, molded, 34 feet; depth, molded, 12 feet; depth of hold in the clear, 9 feet 10 inches.

Mr. Cramp obtained the contract to build four steamers for the new American line to Liverpool of 3,016 tons each, at a total cost of $2,400,000. These boats made the reputation of the yard, and there being then no American steamers in the trade from the United States to Europe (and indeed there have been none since) it was deemed important to construct them in good style as specimens of American workmanship. They were modeled long and narrow, with fine bows and runs and slightly hollow water-lines. The dimensions of each were: Length over all, 355 feet; breadth of beam, 43 feet; depth of hold, 35 feet. Decks, 3 in number; 2 masts. Each ship was supplied with two compound 1,800 horse-power engines, with 57- and 90-inch cylinders, having 4 feet stroke, and a 16-foot wheel. The ships were completed in 1873, and proved fast, smart, and strong vessels; their speed was 13 miles an hour. They have now been running nine years, and are insured by English companies at the most favorable rates given to any iron vessels afloat. As passenger boats they fully answered all expectations; their average time from cape Henlopen to Queenstown is $9\frac{1}{2}$ days, and on the return 10 days 2 hours. Each carries 100 cabin and 800 steerage passengers, 1,740 tons of cargo, and 720 tons of coal on $20\frac{1}{2}$ feet draught of water. The export trade to Europe now requires steamers which can carry 3,000 tons of cargo, but in the day when they were built the American boats did all that was demanded of them.

After the American line was built this yard gave its attention wholly to the production of iron tonnage. Down to the present year the yard has constructed in all more than 50 vessels (the majority of them for the coasting trade), including a few yachts and the conversion of four fast steamers into men-of-war for the Russian navy. When the Russian contracts were being fulfilled the yard was so busy that it was compelled to employ a number of shops outside to aid in the work. The propellers made by the Cramps are characterized by long, keen, wedge-like bows, rising floors, good speed, and strong workmanship. The yachts Corsair and Stranger, which were finished in 1880, were sisters, 165 feet long, 23 feet beam, and 13 feet deep in the hold, and weighed complete, with all on board except coal and water, about 270 tons each. One of the vessels finished in 1880 was the coaster Chalmette, for the New Orleans trade, 338 feet long, 42 feet beam, and 31 feet hold, and of 2,983 tons register—a fast and handsome vessel. Three steamers were on the stocks in 1880, and there were contracts for others. The Cramps do a large business in repairing, a branch of work which is valued by all iron-ship builders as being the most profitable. In new vessels the proportion of labor to materials is as 40 to 60 per cent., whereas in repairing the proportion is as 65 to 35 per cent.

The Cramps have two establishments. At one of them, at the foot of Norris street, the ships are built. It is a large yard 600 feet wide by 700 deep, with a number of shops for the bending, shearing, and punching of frames and plates, the forging of bars and shafts, and the making of boilers and engines, and with five building ways and ample wharf and dock room. Plates and frames are ordered from rolling-mills at Johnstown and Phœnixville, Pennsylvania. The other establishment is at the foot of Palmer street, fronting 230 feet on the river, and extending back 620 feet. It has a machine- and blacksmith-shop for repair work and a basin dry-dock 462 feet long, 111 feet wide on top, and 23 feet draught of water. In making this dock 4,200 piles were driven. The pumps are

204 SHIP-BUILDING INDUSTRY.

centrifugal, four in number, with a joint capacity of 30,000 gallons per minute, and empty the dock in 45 minutes. The regular force of the company is 1,200 men, but in busy years 3,000 men can be employed. The working force of 20 wooden-ship yards is concentrated in these two establishments.

Only one iron sailing vessel has ever been built by the Cramps. This was the center-board schooner Josephine (Figs. 64 and 65), of 365 tons, 126 feet long on the load-line, 132¼ feet over all, 34 feet beam, and 12 feet molded depth,

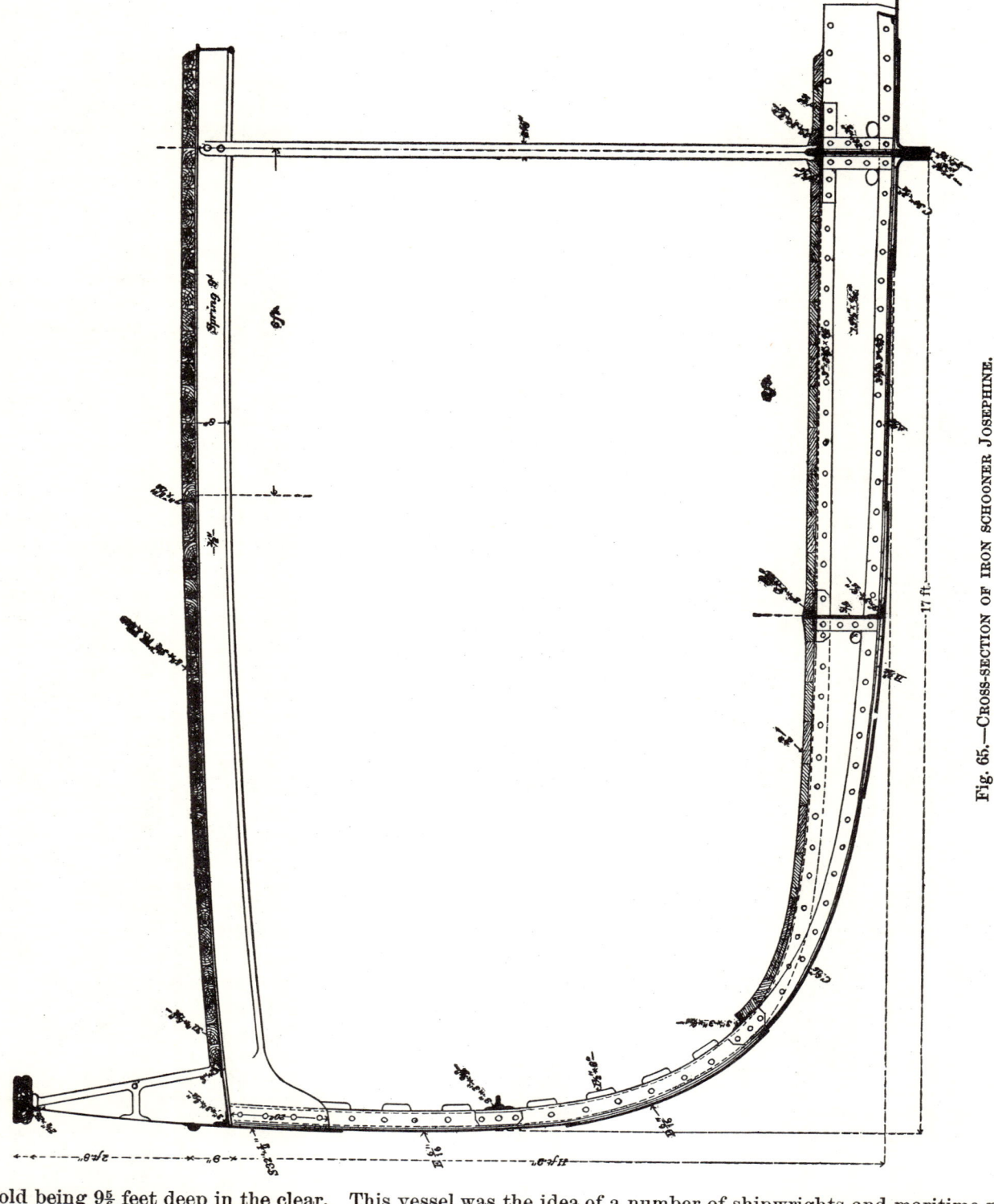

Fig. 65.—Cross-section of Iron Schooner Josephine.

the hold being 9⅚ feet deep in the clear. This vessel was the idea of a number of shipwrights and maritime people in Philadelphia, the most of them owners in other craft. John Main had had a small iron steamboat built by the Cramps, and thought that if a sailing vessel could be built with a hull something like that it would be a success. He enlisted the interest of several associates; the vessel was ordered, and was completed at a cost of $96 per register ton, or about $8,000 more than a wooden center-board schooner of the same capacity. She ranked as

A 1 for 16 years, however, and the owners expect to save that $8,000 more than once during her existence in escaping from the necessity of the continual calking and repair to which wooden vessels are subject. The scantling of the schooner is as follows: Keel, vertical center plate, 26 inches wide, $\frac{1}{2}$ inch thick; vertical side plates, below the frames, 7 inches wide, $\frac{5}{8}$ inch thick; frames, angle-iron, $3\frac{1}{2}$ by 3 inches by $\frac{6}{16}$ inch; reverse angle-iron frames, 3 by $2\frac{1}{2}$ inches, $\frac{5}{16}$ inch thick; spacing, 20 inches; floor plates, 15 inches deep over the keel, $\frac{1}{2}$ inch thick, extending from bilge to bilge, riveted to the vertical center plate by short angle-irons; on top of the frames, at each side of the center plate, there is riveted a continuous flat plate, fore and aft, 10 inches wide, $\frac{3}{8}$ inch thick, which is tied to the keel plate by continuous angle-irons, 3 by 3 inches by $\frac{6}{16}$-inch thick. This arrangement constitutes the main keelson. Eight feet each side of the main keelson is placed an intercostal side keelson, made of $\frac{5}{16}$-inch plates, rising 3 inches above the floors, and secured by fore-and-aft angle-irons, 3 by 3 inches and $\frac{3}{8}$ inch thick. There is a bilge keelson each side, composed of two angle-irons, same as the above, laid on the frames, and riveted back to back. Half way up the sides of the hold there is a stringer of two angle-irons, similarly arranged, and of the same size. Beams of bulb T-iron, 7 inches wide on top, 8 inches deep, and $\frac{1}{2}$ inch thick, spaced every other frame. A stringer plate over the ends of the beams is 31 inches wide and $\frac{3}{8}$ inch thick. The tie plate is 7 inches by $\frac{3}{8}$ inch thick. There are 7 streaks of outer plating. The garboards lap 7 inches on the keel, are riveted clear through, and are of $\frac{7}{16}$-inch iron. The next strake is $\frac{6}{16}$ iron; the next, $\frac{7}{16}$; and all the rest $\frac{6}{16}$, except that the sheer strake is $\frac{1}{2}$ inch. The bulwark plating is $\frac{1}{4}$ inch. The hold is floored with 2-inch yellow pine, the deck with $3\frac{1}{2}$-inch white pine, and there is one bulkhead in the bow. The total weight of metal in the hull was 225 tons. On the whole, the scantling of this schooner would be considered a little light, but this is due to the superior quality of American iron. On deck the arrangement was the one which is customary in schooners. Forward there is a house $6\frac{1}{4}$ feet high and 11 feet long, through which rises the foremast. There is also a small top-gallant forecastle for the windlass. Aft there is a poop-deck, on which there is a house 23 feet long, with quarters for the officers. The schooner spreads 3,150 running yards of canvas. She is a good carrier, taking 550 tons of cargo at a trip, and is regarded as a successful vessel. She would be followed by others of the same class except for the first cost. (a)

The firm of Neafie & Levy, in Philadelphia, has been engaged in the construction of iron vessels of small size since 1844. This firm came into existence in 1838, and built its first vessels in 1844. The product of this establishment has been principally engines and propeller wheels. Up to the fall of 1882 it had built and put into vessels no less than 737 engines. Its propeller wheel is a specialty, the manufacture of which has grown into a large business. About 350 per year are now produced, varying from $2\frac{1}{4}$ to 15 feet in diameter, and are sent out all over the country. The firm takes contracts for both wooden and iron hulls. The latter are built upon its own grounds, but the wooden craft are generally constructed by a subcontractor. The following is the list of iron vessels built by this firm:

Name.	Year.	Length.	Breadth.	Depth.	Name.	Year.	Length.	Breadth.	Depth.
		Ft. In.	Ft. In.	Ft. In.			Ft. In.	Ft. In.	Ft. In.
Conestoga	1844	80 0	16 0	6 0	General Scott	1860	225 0	32 0	10 0
Barclay	1844	125 0	20 0	6 0	Union	1860	225 0	32 0	10 0
Tecumseh	1844	35 0	8 0	3 6	Russia	1860	75 0	15 6	7 0
Apure	1844	160 0	23 6	6 0	Siberia	1860	75 0	15 6	7 0
San Juan	1844	110 0	14 0	3 6	Amoor	1860	75 0	15 6	7 0
Rancocas	1844	125 0	16 6	6 6	Van Vliet	1862	75 0	15 6	6 6
Montezuma	1852	60 0	10 6	3 6	Joseph Thompson	1862	158 0	23 0	8 6
Gov. Moorhead	1852	100 0	17 6	3 0	General Meigs	1862	158 0	23 0	9 6
Orinoco	1852	115 0	23 0	8 0	Pocahontas	1862	160 0	30 0	9 0
Decatur	1855	65 0	15 0	5 6	Charles Pearson	1863	130 0	26 0	14 0
Bordman, No. 1	1855	125 0	19 6	7 0	Havana	1863	230 0	34 0	24 0
Bordman, No. 2	1855	100 0	19 0	6 0	Dashing Wave	1863	60 0	18 0	4 3
Jacob G. Neafie	1856	80 0	19 6	7 0	Julia Saint Clair	1866	129 0	37 0	4 0
Major Brewerton	1856	91 0	19 6	7 6	Bandy Moore	1866	129 0	37 0	4 0
Fanny Cadwallader	1856	158 0	23 8	8 0	Ida	1870	65 0	15 0	6 0
Elizabeth	1856	158 0	23 8	8 0	Seminole	1871	80 0	18 0	8 0
James Gray	1857	85 0	18 0	8 0	Cynthia	1871	95 0	18 0	8 0
Sagua	1859	120 0	24 0	6 0	Mary Louisa	1871	86 3	18 0	8 0
Octarara	1859	158 0	23 8	8 0	W. E. Gladwish	1873	118 0	24 0	9 0
Philadelphia	1859	200 0	29 0	9 0	Sallie	1872	60 0	13 0	6 0
Pacific	1859	75 0	15 3	6 6	Tisdale	1872	98 0	18 0	8 0
William Woodward	1860	158 0	23 8	8 0	Alfred and Edwin	1872	100 0	21 0	7 0
Ounalaska	1860	75 0	15 6	7 0	J. G. Witterbee	1872	108 0	20 0	9 0
Arasapha	1860	120 0	25 0	8 6	Ethel	1872	60 0	14 0	6 0
Oriental	1860	210 0	32 0	20 8	Convoy	1873	85 0	19 0	9 3

a During the winter of 1882–'83 there has been established in Philadelphia one new yard. Some repair shops in the northern part of the city, owned by the Reading railroad and originally intended for iron-ship building, but never used for that purpose, have been bought by a company of New York men. They are to be placed under the management of Lieutenant Gorringe, late of the United States navy, and a contract has been taken for a sailing ship, which it is at present proposed to construct during 1883.

Name.	Year.	Length.	Breadth.	Depth.	Name.	Year.	Length.	Breadth.	Depth.
		Ft. In.	Ft. In.	Ft. In.			Ft. In.	Ft. In.	Ft. In.
Dahlia	1874	141 6	25 0	10 6	Conoho	1881	170 0	23 6	9 0
William S. Stokeley	1874	100 0	18 0	8 6	W. M. Wood	1881	80 0	17 0	8 0
Ivanhoe	1874	67 6	14 6	6 6	William T. Hart	1881	294 6	42 0	13 0
Startle	1876	60 0	14 0	6 6	Battler	1881	110 0	22 0	11 0
Transfer, No. 1	1877	100 0	21 0	10 0	William A. Marburg	1881	105 0	21 0	9 6
Cuba	1878	211 0	32 6	21 6	Nat Wales	1881	85 0	18 6	9 0
Ella Andrews	1878	80 0	17 0	8 0	Storm King	1882	118 0	21 0	13 0
John E. Tygert	1879	115 0	22 0	6 0	City of Philadelphia	1882	100 0	19 6	11 0
Neptune	1879	115 0	20 0	6 0	Leo	1882	90 0	19 0	9 0
Rattler	1879	110 0	22 0	11 0	City of Alma	1882	110 0	20 0	5 0
Atlantic	1879	159 3	30 0	11 9	Rushing	1882	100 0	19 6	10 6
Transfer, No. 2	1880	100 0	21 0	10 0	Tyson	1882	176 0	23 6	10 0
George H. Watrous	1880	100 0	21 0	10 0					

At Chester, Pennsylvania, there is one large yard, the property of John Roach & Son, of New York. In 1868 the founder of this business, after a long experience as a boiler and machine builder in New York, had bought the Morgan iron works of that city, a large establishment at the foot of Ninth street, on the East river, in which most of his machinery has since been built. In 1872 Mr. Roach bought a large property at Chester and developed there a great iron-ship yard, his first vessel being launched in 1873. It has always been a busy yard, producing regularly not less than four and sometimes as many as ten large class steamers a year. The largest American steamships afloat came from these works. The yard itself is the most important one in the United States.

The plant at Chester is elaborate, complete, and of the very first order, and represents an investment of about $1,000,000. The works cover about seventy acres of ground, and have a front of 2,500 feet on the Delaware river. The river is over a mile wide at this point, with depth enough to float the largest steamer of the present day. Building slips have been substantially constructed on heavy piling, making accommodations for the building of ten large vessels at once, and the docks and wharves have been furnished with shears and hoisting engines for masting vessels and putting aboard the boilers and machinery. A short distance below the ship-yard proper, and located on the river bank, are the Chester rolling and steel mills and a blast furnace, the latter with a capacity of 700 tons per week. The furnace alone cost $250,000. These works are owned by the proprietors of the ship-yard, cover about thirty acres, and employ 800 men; and it is not too much to say that they constitute the best plant in the United States for making plates and armor of iron and steel and steel castings. It is an interesting fact that at these two establishments, owned by one firm, iron and steel ships can be created, beginning with the ore itself and ending with the finished steamer, completely equipped for sea. Every part of the work is done by the one firm, and it is believed that this is the only establishment in the world possessing such complete facilities.

In the ten years from 1873 to 1882, both inclusive, the total tonnage built by John Roach & Son aggregated about 148,000 tons, the average being 14,800 tons per year; the largest product in any one year 28,190 tons. The ollowing are some of the details concerning the vessels built:

Names.	Year when built.	Side-wheel or screw.	Length.	Breadth.	Depth.	Tonnage.	BOILERS.			ENGINE.	Wheel diameter.
							Number.	Diameter.	Length.	Diameter and stroke.	
			Ft. In.	Ft. In.	Ft. In.			Ft. In.	Ft. In.		Ft. In.
City of Waco	1873	Screw	244 0	36 0	19 9	1,549	4	10 0	9 6	30 and 56 x 54	13 0
Erie	1873	Side-wheel	192 0	36 0	14 0	750	1	10 0	30 0	46 x 11	22 0
Colima	1873	Screw	312 0	40 0	29 3	2,906	4	13 0	9 9	51 and 88 x 42	16 3
Colon	1873	....do	300 0	40 0	29 3	2,714	4	13 0	9 9	51 and 88 x 42	16 3
Garden City	1873	Side-wheel	184 10	33 6	14 0	840	1	10 10	34 0	48 x 120	22 0
City of San Antonio	1873	Screw	232 8	36 0	22 0	1,450	2	14 9 / 13 9	10 6	48 x 48	13 0
George W. Elder	1874	....do	258 0	38 0	21 4	1,569	4	10 0	9 6	30 and 56 x 54	13 0
City of Guatemala	1874	....do	258 0	36 0	20 1	1,490	4	13 0	9 6	30 and 56 x 54	13 0
City of Panama	1874	....do	258 0	36 0	20 1	1,490	4	13 0	9 6	30 and 56 x 54	13 0
State of Texas	1874	....do	248 0	36 0	19 9	1,549	4	13 0	9 6	30 and 56 x 54	13 0
Berks	1874	....do	196 6	28 6	12 9	553	1	12 0 / 10 0	8 9	20 and 34 x 30	....
Perkiomen	1874	Screw	219 5	37 0	15 9	1,035	2	10 3 / 11 2½	8 8	27 and 45 x 36	11 0
City of Peking	1874	....do	419 0	47 4	36 1½	5,080	10	13 0	10 6	51 and 88 x 54	20 3
City of Tokio	1874	....do	419 0	47 4	36 1½	5,080	10	13 0	10 6	51 and 88 x 54	20 3
City of Chester	1875	....do	206 6	33 6	15 10½	1,106	2	9 0 / 12 6	11 6	24 and 44 x 45	10 0
City of Sidney	1875	....do	352 0	40 0	29 0	3,017	6	13 2	10 6	51 and 88 x 60	20 0
City of San Francisco	1875	....do	352 0	40 0	29 0	3,019	6	13 2	10 6	51 and 88 x 60	20 0
City of New York	1875	....do	352 0	40 0	29 0	3,019	6	13 2	10 6	51 and 88 x 60	20 0

IRON VESSELS.

Names.	Year when built.	Side-wheel or screw.	Length.		Breadth.		Depth.		Tonnage.	BOILERS.				ENGINE.	Wheel diameter
										Number.	Diameter.		Length.	Diameter and stroke.	
			Ft.	In.	Ft.	In.	Ft.	In.			Ft.	In.	Ft. In.		Ft. In.
Rio Grande	1876	Screw	308	0	39	0	21	0	2,566	4	11	10	10 0	34 and 60 x 54	14 0
Newbern	1876	...do	162	9	24	3¼	9	0	846					24 and 36	8 0
Alert	1876	...do	190	9	32	0	15	0	1,246	5	8	0	8 1	28 and 42 x 42	12 0
Alliance	1876	...do	190	9	32	0	15	0	1,246	5	8	0	8 1	28 and 42 x 42	12 0
City of Savannah	1877	...do	272	0	38	6	24	6	2,029	4	12	8	10 6	38 and 68 x 54	15 0
City of Macon	1877	...do	272	0	38	6	24	6	2,093	4	12	8	10 6	38 and 68 x 54	15 0
City of Washington	1877	...do	320	0	38	0	27	7	2,618		18 0 / 20 7		18 0	40 and 74 x 72	16 0
Western Texas	1877	...do	239	7	34	0	16	0	1,121	2	10 3 / 8 6		10 0	24 and 44 x 44	11 6
Panama Railroad Tug	1877	...do	98	3	18	1¼	6	0	75	1	10 3 / 8 6		9 11	20 x 24	6 9
Niagara	1877	...do	292	0	38	1	23	6	2,265	4	11	10	10 0	34 and 60 x 54	14 3
Saratoga	1877	...do	292	0	38	1	23	6	2,265	4	11	10	10 0	34 and 60 x 54	14 3
Gate City	1878	...do	272	0	38	6	24	6	1,997	4	12	8	10 6	38 and 68 x 54	15 0
City of Columbus	1878	...do	272	0	38	6	24	6	1,992	4	12	8	10 6	38 and 68 x 54	15 0
Saratoga	1878	...do	318	6	38	1	21	3½	2,426	4	13	6	10 6	40 and 74 x 54	15 6
City of Para	1878	...do	368	6	38	4¾	28	7½	3,532	6	13	0	10 6	42½ and 74⅜ x 60	16 0
City of Rio de Janeiro	1878	...do	368	6	38	4¾	28	7½	3,548	6	13	0	10 6	42½ and 74⅜ x 60	16 0
Oregon	1878	...do	300	0	38	1	23	6	2,335	4	12	8	10 6	36 and 60 x 54	15 0
Manhattan	1879	...do	246	9	35	3¼	20	0	1,575	2	11 6 / 10 5		22 0	28 and 53 x 48	13 0
City of Alexandria	1879	...do	332	6	38	6	24	7	2,480	4	14	6	11 0	42½ and 78 x 54	16 0
Elias	1879	Side-wheel	173	4	27	3	8	2	240	2	7 4 / 9 0		13 2	26 x 72	19 SW
Santiago	1879	Screw	290	9	38	10½	22	0	2,359	4	13	3	11 0	38 and 68 x 54	15 0
Colorado	1879	...do	329	1	39	1½	21	0	2,765	4	13	3	11 0	38 and 68 x 54	15 0
Juan Mir	1879	Side-wheel	165	0	28	1¾	11	0	425	1	10 6 / 9 2		11 0	28 x 36	9 9
City of Augusta	1880	Screw							2,870					42½ and 82 x 54	
Yosemite	1880	...do	182	0	23	6	18	7	450	2				28½ and 40 x 33	
Breakwater	1880	...do	225	0	35	0	20	0	1,045					38 and x 48	
Newport	1880	...do	325	0	38	6	23	0	2,735					48 and 90 x 54	
Columbia	1880	...do	310	0	38	0	23	0	2,722	6				42½ and 82 x 54	16¼
Louisiana	1880	...do	348	0	39	0	28	5	2,840					28 and 56 x 72	
Guadalupe	1881	...do	317	8	39	5	21	4	2,839					38 and 70 x 54	
Cygnus	1881	Side-wheel	212	6	31	4	11	3	857					53 x 144	
Cepheus	1881	...do	213	6	32	4	11	5	857					53 x 144	
Sirius	1881	...do	229	0	32	5	11	1	993					53 x 144	
Walla Walla	1881	Screw	310	0	40	6	22	2	2,131					40 and 74 x 54	
Umatilla	1881	...do	310	0	40	6	22	3	2,131					40 and 74 x 54	
Willamette	1881	...do	335	9	39	1	24	0	2,264					38 and 70 x 54	
San Marcos	1882	...do	317	8	39	5	21	4	2,839					38 and 74 x 54	
Guyandotte	1882	...do	267	0	40	5	24	4	2,140					38 and 74 x 54	
Roanoke	1882	...do	265	0	40	0	26	9	2,140	(a)	(a)		(a)	38 and 74 x 54	(a)
San Jose	1882	...do	283	0	37	0	21	0	2,010					34 and 62 x 54	
San Juan	1882	...do	283	0	36	4	22	3	2,010					34 and 62 x 54	
San Blas	1882	...do	283	0	37	0	21	0	2,010					34 and 62 x 54	
Tallahassee	1882	...do	280	0	40	7	24	1	2,700					38 and 74 x 54	
Chattahoochee	1882	...do	280	0	40	7	24	1	2,700					38 and 74 x 54	
Nacoochee	1882	...do	280	0	40	7	24	1	2,700					38 and 74 x 54	
Pilgrim	1882	Side-wheel	378	0	50	0	17	6	3,500					110 x 168	
Finance		Screw	300	0	38	0	22	0	2,000					36 and 66 x 54	
Advance		...do	300	0	38	0	22	0	2,000					36 and 66 x 54	
Reliance		...do	300	0	38	0	22	0	2,000					36 and 66 x 54	

a Figures correspond to those of steamers of the same size above.

The success of this yard has been due to qualities on the part of its founder which have characterized the leading ship-builders of America in a marked degree—energy, a fertile mind, and remarkable ingenuity in adapting vessels to the trade in which they were to be employed. A special study would be made of the kinds of cargoes carried by the vessels in a particular coasting route, and an idea would be formed of a ship which would carry more of the given varieties of goods on a lighter draught of water and at a faster rate of speed than the vessels already in the trade. This idea would be worked out in a ship, in which the builder would take perhaps a quarter interest, in order to show his confidence in it. His operations have been in the main successful, and the two establishments have at times been employed to their full capacity. Fifteen hundred men can be employed in the works at New York, and about 3,000 at Chester. It is one feature of the operations of the firm that measures are taken to secure willing work from the men. They are encouraged to be inventive and faithful by a system of rewards and promotion. Furthermore, the *personnel* of the ship-yard is kept at a high grade of character by the constant recruiting of young men of mechanical education who are fresh from school and are given a chance to go into the yard and rise.

The vessels built at Chester include many of note. The City of Peking and the City of Tokio ran for a long time from San Francisco to China, and were large carriers of cargo and small burners of coal. The Para and the Rio de Janeiro were the builder's own venture in the way of a line of steamships to Brazil, in which trade they ran for three years, being then withdrawn and sold to the Pacific Mail Company. All of the coasting steamers have long, sharp, wedge-like bows, good runs, and easy lines, and have been remarkable for their speed, light draught, and cargo-carrying power. The City of Washington, built in 1877, made in 1879 the run from Havana to New York, 1,230 miles, in 75 hours 21 minutes, the fastest ocean time then recorded for a consecutive period of 75 hours. Her average speed was $16\frac{3}{4}$ nautical miles per hour. The steamer Newport, built afterward by this firm, made the same run in 72 hours 15 minutes. Mr. Roach is now building a sailing vessel of about 2,040 tons, besides many steamers.

A yard was established in 1880 at Marcus Hook, Pennsylvania, for the building of vessels, engines, and boilers, under the title of the Pioneer iron works. A foundery, machine-shop, and blacksmith-shop were put up and fitted with machinery, at a total cost of about $75,000, and eight or ten vessels were built in that and the next two years, consisting of tugs, yachts, and small passenger and freight boats; but the concern did not prosper, and has since gone out of existence.

At Wilmington, on the Delaware, besides the two yards devoted to the construction of wooden vessels, there are two large yards engaged in iron- and steel-ship building. The industry was established here at an early date. The city is practically as near to cheap coal and iron as though it were planted upon the Schuylkill, and the same freight rates govern deliveries there from all parts of the country as at Philadelphia; in fact, iron-ship yards can be located advantageously anywhere upon the western bank of the Delaware for a distance of 90 miles so far as cheap materials are concerned. The two yards in Wilmington devoted to this industry are those of The Harlan & Hollingsworth Company and The Pusey & Jones Company. Both concerns build railway cars, but both have extensive ship-building plant, and rank among the four leading establishments in the United States devoted to the industry now under consideration.

The Harlan & Hollingsworth Company began business in 1836 and built the first iron coasting steamer constructed in the United States. In 1843 they turned their attention to the needs of the merchant marine, and after having turned out two small iron vessels began the construction of the steamer Bangor, which was completed and launched in the following spring, and was, as stated, the pioneer of the great fleet of American-built iron steamers that has sprung into existence in the last forty years to take the place of the old-time heavy wooden coasting craft. The success of the Bangor brought Wilmington at once into active competition with New York as well as with the eastern wooden-ship yards in the construction of the large number of iron steamers which the coasting and inland trades began to demand. Wilmington had skilled labor and cheap materials, and a low scale of wages prevailed, because operatives could afford to accept them on account of cheap rents and moderate living expenses. In the early years of the struggle to establish an American iron-ship building industry The Harlan & Hollingsworth Company stood practically alone, for there were then few, if any, concerns in the country sufficiently well equipped to execute contracts regularly for the large class of iron vessels. The success of their yard was due to the fact that each vessel produced was built with as much care in design and construction as though it were being made by an owner for himself, and the behavior of the vessels afterward was, in consequence, a standing advertisement of the good qualities both of iron ships and American work. The yard received many orders, and it has been busily engaged from the first in building iron vessels of every description, its product being the most varied of that of any American establishment. The concern covers 43 acres of ground, on which there are about fifty different shops and buildings. Those employed in ship work are supplied with machinery modern in type and massive in build. The plant includes, among other things, shears for trimming heavy plates, planers, rolls for bending plates to the proper curvature on the sides of the ship, machines for punching rivet holes in frames and plates, hydraulic riveting apparatus, by means of which rivets can be clinched solidly with one thrust by steam-power, frame-heating furnaces, bed-plates for bending the angle-iron frames to the proper outline, steam-hammers, mold-lofts and pattern shops, and the proper apparatus for constructing engines and boilers. On the wharf there is a set of masting shears that can handle a weight of 100 tons, and engines and boilers are lifted almost bodily into the air and deposited gently in their places in the hulls floating alongside. The secret of the success of iron-ship building in America is, in large part, the use of labor-saving machinery of this description. The water-front is 1,350 feet long, and the yard has a large dry-dock. About 3,000 men can be employed by this establishment. As in the case of the other iron-ship yards with large plant, this constitutes a valuable resource of public importance to the United States; and it is safe to say that if the four large yards on the Delaware did not exist the government would be compelled to maintain several establishments of similar magnitude for naval purposes, with their consequent great expense for the repairs necessary to keep them in order.

The Harlan & Hollingsworth Company is now building vessels of steel in response to the demand for the employment of that material. One iron sailing vessel, the bark Iron Age, built at this yard, was finished in 1869, and had the following dimensions: Length, 142 feet; beam, 30 feet; depth, $18\frac{1}{2}$ feet. During the war there

IRON VESSELS.

were constructed the following vessels for the government: The iron-clad double-turreted monitor Amphitrite, the iron sloop-of-war Ranger, and the iron-clad monitors Patapsco, Saugus, and Napa. Charles Morgan, of New York, was one of the first merchants to understand the advantage of iron hulls in the coasting trade, and up to 1882 this yard had built for his coasting lines no fewer than 31 iron steamers. Propellers of the largest and finest class have been the favorite product of the yard, but orders have also been taken for steam craft of almost every description, and during late years a study has been made of side-wheel bay and river steamboats. The following is a list of the vessels built at this yard:

VESSELS BUILT BY THE HARLAN & HOLLINGSWORTH COMPANY, WILMINGTON, DELAWARE.

Class.	Name.	For whom.	Tonnage.	Kind.	Type.	Year built.	Remarks.
Steam propeller	Bangor	Parties in Maine	450	Iron	Propeller	1844	Twin-screw engines. Burned at sea; repaired and sold to United States government.
Do	Ashland	George W. Aspinwall	300	..do	....do	1844	Lost during the war.
Do	Ocean	do	300	..do	....do	1844	Do.
Do	W. Whilden	Anthony Reybold	450	..do	....do	1845	Altered into a propeller; running between Baltimore and Philadelphia. Engine, 28 inches diameter by 26 inches stroke.
Steam ferry-boat	Delaware	Winnissimmet Ferry Company	270	..do	Side wheel	1846	Of Boston, Mass.
Steamship	Willamette	George W. Aspinwall	450	..do	Propeller	1849	
Steam ferry-boat	Winnissimmet	Winnissimmet Ferry Company	270	..do	....do	1850	Of Boston, Mass.
Steamer	Victoria	Island of Trinidad	750	..do	....do	1850	For Freeman Rawdon.
Steam ferry-boat	Dido	Camden and Philadelphia Ferry Company.	220	..do	....do	1850	Inclined low-pressure engine, 31 inches diameter by 7 feet stroke.
Hull for dredge		Delaware and Chesapeake Canal Company.	100	..do	Propeller	1851	
Steamer	Clayton	Cornelius Vanderbilt	150	..do	Stern wheel	1851	For service on Chagres river. High-pressure engine, 9¼ inches diameter by 3 feet stroke.
Do	Bulwer	do	150	..do	....do	1851	For service on Chagres river. High-pressure engine, 9¼ inches diameter by 3 feet stroke.
Steamboat	Richard Stockton	Camden and Amboy Railroad Company.	700	..do	Side wheel	1851	Running on North river as an excursion boat. Vertical beam-engine, 48 inches diameter by 12 feet stroke.
Do	Wyoming	Philadelphia and Havre de Grace Steamboat Company.	520	..do	....do	1851	2 low-pressure vertical condensing beam-engines, 29 inches diameter by 8 feet stroke.
	Zephyr	Joint account, Cape Fear River.	150	..do		1851	2 inclined engines, 14 inches diameter by 4 feet stroke.
Steamboat	Major Reybold	Reybold Bros	450	..do	....do	1852	Running on Delaware river. Low-pressure vertical condensing beam-engine, 40 inches diameter by 12 feet stroke.
Steam ferry-boat	Maryland	Philadelphia, Wilmington and Baltimore Railroad Company.	1,150	..do	....do	1852	Still in use as a transfer steamer in service of New England Transfer Company between Jersey City and Harlem; thoroughly overhauled in 1883. Two horizontal low-pressure condensing engines, 40 inches diameter by 8 feet stroke.
Steamboat	Thomas A. Morgan	Rockhill, Burdon, Cone, and others.	520	..do	....do	1853	Low-pressure vertical condensing beam-engine, 44 inches diameter by 10 feet stroke.
Steam ferry-boat	Tri-Mountain	Winnissimmet Ferry Company.	280	..do	....do	1853	Low-pressure vertical condensing beam-engine, 36 inches diameter by 8 feet stroke.
Steamboat	Ogden	Accessory Transit Company of Nicaragua.	160	..do	Side wheel	1853	2 inclined engines, 16 inches diameter by 5 feet stroke.
Do	Isaac C. Lea	do	160	..do	....do	1853	Do.
Steam propeller	Thomas Sparks	Philadelphia Steam Propeller Company.	600	..do	Propeller	1853	High-pressure engine, 32 inches diameter by 28 inches stroke.
	San Carlos	Accessory Transit Company of Nicaragua.	650	..do		1854	Low-pressure engine, 44 inches diameter by 11 feet stroke.
Steam propeller	Richard Willing	Baltimore and Philadelphia Steamboat Company.	450	..do	Propeller	1854	High-pressure engine, 28 inches diameter by 26 inches stroke.
Iron barge	Planet	Philadelphia Steam Propeller Company.	390	..do		1854	
Steam propeller	Sophia	do	390	..do		1854	
		Delaware and Raritan Canal Company.	100	..do		1855	
Steam ferry-boat	W. W. Harllee	Wilmington and Raleigh and Wilmington and Manchester Railroad Company.	220	..do		1855	Low-pressure engine, 26 inches diameter by 6 feet stroke.
Bell beacon		United States government	40	..do		1855	
Do		do	40	..do		1855	
Do		do	40	..do		1855	
Do		do	40	..do		1855	
Do		do	40	..do		1855	
Steam propeller	Kahukee	D. Clark, Scotland Neck, N. C.	150	..do	Propeller	1855	Engine 24 inches diameter by 20 inches stroke.
Steamboat	Logan	W. Whilldon and others	320	..do	Side wheel	1855	
Do	James A. Requa	New Granada Canal and Navigation Company of New York.		..do	....do	1855	Two high-pressure engines, 24 inches diameter by 8 feet stroke.
Steam ferry-boat	Hunter Woodis	City of Norfolk	750	..do	....do	1856	
Steamboat	Curlew	Dr. Thomas Warren, Edenton, N. C.	350	..do	....do	1856	Low-pressure engine, 29 inches diameter by 9 feet stroke.
Do	Swan	John Richardson, Savannah	220	..do	....do	1856	2 high-pressure engines, 14 inches diameter by 5 feet stroke
	Amazon	John A. Moore, Augusta	450	..do	Stern wheel	1856	2 high-pressure engines, 22 inches diameter by 6 feet stroke.
	Saint Mary's	Claghorn and Cunningham, Augusta.	450	..do	Side wheel	1856	2 low-pressure engines, 30 inches diameter by 8 feet stroke.
	General Rusk	Harris, Morgan & Co., New Orleans, La.	750	..do	....do	1856	Low-pressure engine, 44 inches diameter by 11 feet stroke.

VESSELS BUILT BY THE HARLAN & HOLLINGSWORTH COMPANY, WILMINGTON, DELAWARE—Continued.

Class.	Name.	For whom.	Tonnage.	Kind.	Type.	Year built.	Remarks.
Steamboat	John A. Warner	J. Cone and others	650	Iron	Side wheel	1856	Low-pressure engine, 44 inches diameter by 11 feet stroke.
Do	Antioquia	Everett & Brown, New York	600	..do	....do	1857	2 high-pressure engines, 24 inches diameter by 8 feet stroke.
Do	Cecile	Fenn, Peck, and others	460	..do	....do	1857	Low-pressure engine, 38 inches diameter by 10 feet stroke.
Steam propeller	J. S. Shriver	Baltimore and Philadelphia Steamboat Company.	450	..do	Steam propeller.	1857	High-pressure engine, 28 inches diameter by 26 inches stroke.
Steamboat	Pilot Boy	Captain Whillden	375	..do	Side wheel	1857	Machinery taken from the steamer Napoleon.
Barge	Faith	David Clark, N. C.	150	..do		1857	
Do	Hope	......do	150	..do		1857	
Steam propeller	Ellen S. Terry	O. G. Terry, Hartford, Conn	460	..do	Propeller	1857	High-pressure engine, 28 inches diameter by 26 inches stroke.
Steamship	Matagorda	C. Vanderbilt	1,250	..do	Side wheel	1858	Running in the Gulf of Mexico. Beam engine, 44 inches diameter by 11 feet stroke.
Steamboat	Ariel	Philadelphia, Wilmington and Baltimore Railroad Company.	360	..do	....do	1858	Engines out of steamer W. Whillden, 28 inches diameter by 26 inches stroke.
Steam tug	Flamenco	Panama Railroad Company	100	..do	Propeller	1858	Engine 18 inches diameter by 18 inches stroke.
Bungo		R. A. Joy, S. A	30	..do		1858	
Steamship	Arizona	Charles Morgan	1,100	..do	Side wheel	1858	Running in the Gulf of Mexico. Beam engine, 44 inches diameter by 11 feet stroke.
Barge	Enterprise	J. H. Anthony	160	..do		1858	
Steamboat	Georgianna	G. R. H. Leffler	750	..do	Side wheel	1858	Machinery taken from the steamer Gladiator.
Steamship	Champion	C. Vanderbilt	2,000	..do	....do	1858	Lost at sea; 2 engines, 42 inches diameter by 10 feet stroke.
Steam propeller	Indianola	C. de Goicoarea	450	..do	Propeller	1858	Engine 32 inches diameter by 10 feet stroke.
Steam tug	Indio	Fernando J. L. Calvo, Cuba	100	..do	..do	1859	Engine 26 inches diameter by 24 inches stroke.
Steamship	Benj. Deford	Merchants' and Miners' Transportation Company.	1,500	..do	Side wheel	1859	Low-pressure engine, 56 inches diameter by 11 feet stroke. Running now among the West India islands; name afterward changed to the San Jacinto.
Do	S. R. Spaulding	......do	1,500	..do	....do	1859	Lost at sea in a cyclone. Low-pressure engine, 56 inches diameter by 11 feet stroke; name changed afterward to San Salvador.
Do	Austin	Charles Morgan	1,150	..do	....do	1859	Now in the Gulf of Mexico. Beam engine, 44 inches diameter by 11 feet stroke.
Steam tug	Adriatic	S. & J. M. Flanagan	120	..do	Propeller	1860	High-pressure engine, 18 inches diameter by 18 inches stroke.
Do	Champion	......do	120	..do	....do	1860	Do.
Steam propeller	F. W. Brune	New York and Baltimore Transportation Company.	450	..do	....do	1860	Engine 28 inches diameter by 26 inches stroke.
Do	Fairfield	D. D. Simmons & Bro	190	..do	....do	1860	Engine 18 inches diameter by 18 inches stroke.
Steamship	W. G. Hewes	Charles Morgan	2,250	..do	Side wheel	1860	Now in the Gulf of Mexico.
Steam propeller	Louisiana	S. & J. M. Flanagan	750	..do	Propeller	1860	Engine 32 inches diameter by 28 inches stroke.
	Honduras	James Bishop & Co	150	..do	Stern wheel	1860	Engine 9 inches diameter by 4 feet stroke.
Lighter		Panama Railroad Company	260	..do		1860	
Steamboat	Virginia Dare	Albemarle Steam Packet Company.	400	..do	Side wheel	1861	Sold to government and called Delaware. Engine 38 inches diameter by 10 feet stroke.
Steamship	Hatteras	Charles Morgan	1,450	..do	...do	1861	Now in the Gulf of Mexico. Engine 50 inches diameter by 11 feet stroke. Called St. Mary when built.
Do	Salvador	Panama Railroad Company	1,600	..do	Propeller	1861	Burned and wrecked. Engine 48 inches diameter by 54 inches stroke.
Steamboat	Tequendama	United Magdalena Steamboat Company.	250	..do		1861	Two engines, 21 inches diameter by 6 feet stroke.
Steam propeller	General Burnside	R. F. Loper	650	..do	Propeller	1861	Engine 30 inches diameter by 28 inches stroke.
Do	Martha Stevens	New York and Baltimore Transportation Company.	460	..do	....do	1861	High-pressure engine, 28 inches diameter by 26 inches stroke.
Steamship	Saint Mary's	Charles Morgan	1,400	..do	Side wheel	1862	Now in Gulf of Mexico. Engine 50 inches diameter by 11 feet stroke.
Steam tug	S. F. Du Pont	S. and J. M. Flanagan	160	..do	Propeller	1862	Low-pressure engine, 26 inches diameter by 24 inches stroke.
Do	Rescue	Our own account	160	..do	....do	1861	Sold to United States government. Low-pressure engine, 26 inches diameter by 24 inches stroke.
Steamship	Crescent	Charles Morgan	1,400	..do	Side wheel	1862	Now in Gulf of Mexico. Engine 50 inches diameter by 11 feet stroke.
Iron-clad monitor	Patapsco	United States government	1,200	..do	Propeller	1862	Two Ericsson engines, 40 inches diameter by 22 inches stroke.
Steamship	Vineland	R. D. Wood & Co	450	..do	....do	1862	High-pressure engine, 24 inches diameter by 24 inches stroke.
Do	Alliance	J. B. Bloodgood	650	..do	....do	1862	Engine 34 inches diameter by 34 inches stroke.
Iron-clad monitor	Saugus	United States government	1,500	..do	..do	1863	Engine 48 inches diameter by 24 inches stroke.
Steamship	Clinton	Charles Morgan	1,450	..do	Side wheel	1863	Now in Gulf of Mexico. Engine 50 inches diameter by 11 feet stroke.
Iron-clad monitor	Napa	United States government	850	..do	Propeller	1863	Low-pressure engine, 22 inches diameter by 30 inches stroke.
Steamer	Frances No. 1	Charles Morgan	850	..do	Side wheel	1863	In the West Indies. Engine 50 inches diameter by 11 feet stroke.
Do	Louise	......do	850	..do	....do	1863	Running on Chesapeake bay. Engine 50 inches diameter by 11 feet stroke.
Lighter		Panama Railroad Company	220	..do		1863	

IRON VESSELS.

VESSELS BUILT BY THE HARLAN & HOLLINGSWORTH COMPANY, WILMINGTON, DELAWARE—Continued.

Class.	Name.	For whom.	Tonnage.	Kind.	Type.	Year built.	Remarks.
	Vergoechea	United Magdalena Steamboat Company.	300	Iron	Side wheel	1864	Two engines (high-pressure), 21 inches diameter by 6 feet stroke.
Steam propeller	Wilmington	Williams & Guion	750	..do	Propeller	1864	Engine 44 inches diameter by 6 feet stroke.
Steamer	Frances No. 2	Charles Morgan	850	..do	Side wheel	1864	Engine 50 inches diameter by 11 feet stroke.
Steamship	Morgan	....do	1,450	..do	....do	1865	Gulf of Mexico. Engine 50 inches diameter by 11 feet stroke.
Do	Harris	....do	1,450	..do	....do	1865	Do.
Do	Harlan	....do	1,450	..do	....do	1865	Do.
Steamboat	Lady of the Lake	....do	800	..do	....do	1865	Washington and Norfolk. Engine 50 inches diameter by 11 feet stroke.
Do	Mary	....do	850	..do	....do	1865	Gulf of Mexico. Engine 50 inches diameter by 11 feet stroke.
Steamer	City of Norfolk	....do	900	..do	....do	1866	Do.
Do	City of Lawrence	Norwich and New York Transportation Company.	1,400	..do	....do	1866	On Long Island sound. Engine 65 inches diameter by 11 feet stroke.
Steamboat	Laura	Charles Morgan	850	..do	....do	1866	On Long Island sound. Machinery from the steamer Magnolia.
Launch		Panama Railroad Company	220	..do		1867	
Do		....do	220	..do		1867	
Steamship	J. W. Garrett	New York and Baltimore Transportation Company.	450	..do	Propeller	1867	
Do	Josephine	Charles Morgan	1,500	..do	Side wheel	1867	Lost at sea. Engine 50 inches diameter by 11 feet stroke.
	Sue	Our account	600	..do	....do	1867	Engine 32 inches diameter by 9 feet stroke.
	Carrie	P. L. Willingham and others	250	..do	....do	1867	Engine 16 inches diameter by 6 feet stroke.
Barge	Ianthe	New York and Baltimore Transportation Company.	350	..do	....do	1868	
	Twilight	Captain Crawford and others	420	..do	....do	1868	Engine 38 inches diameter by 10 feet stroke.
Steamship	Costa Rica	Panama Railroad Company	600	..do	Propeller	1868	Running on the Pacific ocean. Engine 48 inches diameter by 66 inches stroke.
Barge		....do	220	..do		1868	
Do		....do	220	..do		1868	
Do		....do	220	..do		1868	
Do		....do	220	..do		1868	
Do		....do	220	..do		1868	
Do		....do	220	..do		1868	
Steam ferry-boat	Southampton	East River Ferry Company	500	..do	Side wheel	1868	Engine 48 inches diameter by 10 feet stroke.
	Maggie	Eastern Shore Steamboat Company.	375	..do	....do	1869	Engine 32 inches diameter by 6 feet stroke.
Bark	Iron Age	Tupper & Beattie	650	..do		1869	
Ice-boat		Chesapeake and Delaware Canal Company.	50	..do		1856	
Do		....do	50	..do		1856	
Steam collier	Leopard	Philadelphia and Reading Railroad Company.	609	..do	Propeller	1870	Engine 40 inches diameter by 30 inches stroke.
Steamship	Wyanoke	Old Dominion Steamship Company.	2,067	..do	Side wheel	1870	New York to Richmond. Engine 70 inches diameter by 11 feet stroke.
Do	Hutchinson	Chas. Morgan	1,435	..do	....do	1870	Gulf of Mexico. Engine taken from the steamer Mary Roberts.
Do	Whitney	....do	1,338	..do	....do	1871	Gulf of Mexico. Engine 56 inches diameter by 11 inches stroke.
Steam propellor	Roanoke	Baltimore Steam Packet Company.	531	..do	Propeller	1871	Chesapeake bay. Engine 34 inches diameter by 34 inches stroke.
Steamship	William Crane	Merchants' and Miners' Transportation Company.	1,418	..do	....do	1871	Baltimore to Boston. Engine 60 inches diameter by 44 inches stroke.
	Helen	Eastern Shore Steamboat Company.	350	..do	Side wheel	1871	Engine 30 inches diameter by 6 feet stroke.
Steam tug	Transfer	Baltimore and Ohio Railroad Company.	101	..do	Propeller	1872	Engine 28 inches diameter by 28 inches stroke.
Steamship	Old Dominion	Old Dominion Steamship Company.	2,223	..do	Side wheel	1872	New York to Richmond. Engine 75 inches diameter by 11 feet stroke.
Do	Acapulco	Pacific Mail Steamship Company.	3,000	..do	Propeller	1872	New York to Aspinwall.
Do	Granada	....do	3,000	..do	....do	1872	San Francisco to China.
Steam ferry-boat	Peerless	Gloucester Ferry Company	299	..do	Side wheel	1872	Engine 38 inches diameter by 8 feet stroke.
Steamer	Gussie	Charles Morgan	998	..do	....do	1872	Gulf of Mexico. Engine from steamship Matagorda.
Launch		Panama Railroad Company	260	..do		1873	
Do		....do	260	..do		1873	
Steamship	General Whitney	Metropolitan Steamship Company.	1,849	..do	Propeller	1873	New York to Boston. Engine 36 inches diameter by 60 inches stroke.
Do	Johns Hopkins	Merchants' and Miners' Transportation Company.	1,471	..do	....do	1873	Baltimore to Boston. Engine 60 inches diameter by 44 inches stroke.
Steam propeller	Westover	Baltimore Steam Packet Company.	577	..do	....do	1873	Chesapeake bay. Engine 34 inches diameter by 34 inches stroke.
Steam ferry-boat	Pennsylvania	Camden and Philadelphia Steam Ferry Company.	220	..do	Side wheel	1873	Engine 38 inches diameter by 9 feet stroke.
	Richmond	Old Dominion Steamship Company.	1,438	..do	Propeller	1873	Engine 50 inches diameter by 60 inches stroke.
	Hampton	....do	624	..do	Side wheel	1874	Engine 38 inches diameter by 9 feet stroke; sold to Mexican waters, and name changed to Tlacotalpan. Now running in Gulf of Mexico.

SHIP-BUILDING INDUSTRY.

VESSELS BUILT BY THE HARLAN & HOLLINGSWORTH COMPANY, WILMINGTON, DELAWARE—Continued.

Class.	Name.	For whom.	Tonnage.	Kind.	Type.	Year built.	Remarks.
Steam ferry-boat	City of Chelsea	Winnissimmet Ferry Company	273	Iron	Side wheel	1874	Engine 38 inches diameter by 9 feet stroke.
Steam propeller	Shirly	Baltimore Steam Packet Company.	576	..do	Propeller	1874	Chesapeake bay. Engine 34 inches diameter by 34 inches stroke.
Steam sloop	Ranger	United States government	1,100	..do	....do	1874	In the United States service. Compound engines, 22 and 48½ inches diameter by 42 inches stroke.
Steam propeller	Seaboard	Baltimore Steam Packet Company.	662	..do	....do	1874	Chesapeake bay. Engine 34 inches diameter by 42 inches stroke.
	Chowan	Albemarle Steam Navigation Company.	459	..do	Side wheel	1875	Machinery from the steamboat Ella.
	Tangier	Eastern Shore Steamboat Company.	589	..do	....do	1875	Engine 32 inches diameter by 9 feet stroke.
Steamship	Lone Star	Charles Morgan	2,255	..do	Propeller	1875	New York to New Orleans. Engine 50 inches diameter by 60 inches stroke.
Do	New York	..... do	2,255	..do	....do	1875	Do.
Steam ferry-boat	Dauntless	Gloucester Ferry Company	301	..do	Side wheel	1875	Engine 38 inches diameter by 9 feet stroke.
Do	Delaware	Camden and Philadelphia Steamboat Ferry Company.	371	..do	....do	1875	Machinery from the old steamer Delaware.
Fire-boat	Protector	New Harbor Protection Company.	158	..do	Propeller	1875	Engine 26 inches diameter by 28 inches stroke.
Steamship	Algiers	Charles Morgan	2,270	..do	....do	1876	New York to New Orleans. Engine 50 inches diameter by 60 inches stroke.
Do	Morgan City	......do	2,271	..do	....do	1876	Do.
	Columbia	Delaware River Steamboat Company.	664	..do	Side wheel	1876	Engine 50 inches diameter by 11 feet stroke. Now on the Delaware river.
Steam yacht	Meteor	Carson Lumber Company	20	..do	Propeller	1876	Engine 10 inches diameter by 12 inches stroke. Now running on lake Tahoe, in the Rocky mountains.
Steam ferry-boat	Flushing	East River Ferry Company	581	..do	Side wheel	1876	Engine 44 inches diameter by 9 feet stroke.
Steamboat	Carolina	Baltimore Steam Packet Company.	984	..do	....do	1877	Baltimore to Norfolk. Engine 60 inches diameter by 11 feet stroke.
Do	B. S. Ford	Chester River Steamboat Company.	379	..do	....do	1877	Chesapeake bay. Engine 38 inches diameter by 9 feet stroke.
Steam ferry-boat	Columbia	West Jersey Ferry Company	389	..do	....do	1877	Engine 38 inches diameter by 10 feet stroke.
Steamship	Aransas	Charles Morgan	1,157	..do	Twin propeller.	1877	Gulf of Mexico. Twin screws; engine 30 inches diameter by 36 inches stroke.
Steam ferry-boat	Jas. M. Waterbury	Nassau Ferry Company	413	..do	Side wheel	1877	Engine 38 inches diameter by 9 feet stroke.
Dredge	Hull	American Dredging Company	69	..do		1877	
Steamer	Republic	J. Cone and associates	1,285	..do	....do	1878	Now running on the Delaware river. Engine 66 inches diameter by 12 feet stroke.
Steam tug	Jose Gonzales	Lyles & Gilson	30	..do	Propeller	1878	Engine 14 inches diameter by 14 inches stroke.
	Mary Morgan	Charles Morgan	370	..do	Side wheel	1878	Engine 38 inches diameter by 9 feet stroke.
Steamer	Saint John's	Commercial Navigation Company.	1,098	..do	....do	1878	Engine 66 inches diameter by 12 feet stroke. Ran on the route between Charleston and Jacksonville.
Steam yacht	Victor	J. T. Gause	14	..do	Propeller	1878	Engine 6 inches diameter by 8 inches stroke.
Steamer	Virginia	Baltimore Steam Packet Company.	990	..do	Side wheel	1879	Baltimore to Norfolk. Engine 50 inches diameter by 11 feet stroke.
Steam yacht	Dione	E. A. Harvey	7	..do	Propeller	1879	Engine 18 inches diameter by 10 inches stroke.
Steam ferry-boat	Cooper's Point	Camden and Atlantic Railroad Company.	389	..do	Side wheel	1879	Engine 38 inches diameter by 10 feet stroke.
Do	Rockaway	East River Ferry Company	521	..do	....do	1879	Engine 44 inches diameter by 9 feet stroke.
Do	No name given	Oregon and California Railroad Company.	440	..do	....do	1879	Engine 20 inches diameter by 60 inches stroke.
Steamship	Decatur H. Miller	Merchants' and Miners' Transportation Company.	2,296	..do	Propeller	1879	Baltimore to Boston. Compound engine, 24 and 54 inches diameter by 48 inches stroke.
Steam ferry-boat	Newtown	Nassau Ferry Company	450	..do	Side wheel	1879	Engine 38 inches diameter by 9 feet stroke.
Do	Arctic	West Jersey Ferry Company	394	..do	....do	1879	Engine 40 inches diameter by 10 feet stroke.
Sailing yacht	Mischief	J. R. Busk	111	..do		1879	
Transfer boat	Canton	Philadelphia, Wilmington and Baltimore and Baltimore and Ohio Railroad Companies.	1,178	..do	Side wheel	1880	2 independent engines, 36 inches diameter by 9 feet stroke. Transfer steamer in Baltimore harbor.
Steamer	Albany	A. Vansantvoord	1,380	..do	....do	1880	On Hudson river.
Steam ferry-boat	Long Beach	East River Ferry Company	520	..do	....do	1880	Engine 44 inches diameter by 9 feet stroke.
Steamboat	Excelsior	Potomac Steamboat Company	774	Wood	....do	1880	Engine 40 inches diameter by 9 feet stroke.
Steam yacht	Falcon	Norris Peters	120	Iron	Propeller	1880	Engine 16 inches diameter by 16 inches stroke.
Pilot boat	Pilot	Board of Maryland Pilots	190	..do	....do	1880	Compound engine, 22 and 36 inches diameter by 26 inches stroke.
Steamer	City of Worcester	Norwich and New York Transportation Company.	2,490	..do	Side wheel	1881	New York to New London. Engine 90 inches diameter by 12 feet stroke.
Steamboat	Ida	Maryland Steamboat Company	589	..do	....do	1881	Chesapeake bay. Engine 40 inches diameter by 10 feet stroke.
	Gaston	Baltimore Steam Packet Company.	847	..do	Propeller	1881	Compound engine, 26 and 44 inches diameter by 36 inches stroke.
Steam ferry-boat	Baltic	West Jersey Ferry Company	399	..do	Side wheel	1881	Engine 42 inches diameter by 10 feet stroke.
Do	Wenonah	Camden and Philadelphia Steamboat Ferry Company.	439	..do	....do	1881	Engine 44 inches diameter by 10 feet stroke.
Do	Beverly	......do	439	..do	....do	1881	Do.
Do	Jamaica	Nassau Ferry Company	435	..do	....do	1881	Engine (inclined) 38 inches diameter by 9 feet stroke.
Do	Baltimore	Pennsylvania Railroad Company	730	..do	....do	1882	Engine 46 inches diameter by 11 feet stroke.
Do	Chicago	......do	730	..do	....do	1882	Do.

IRON VESSELS.

VESSELS BUILT BY THE HARLAN & HOLLINGSWORTH COMPANY, WILMINGTON, DELAWARE—Continued.

Class.	Name.	For whom.	Tonnage.	Kind.	Type.	Year built.	Remarks.
Steamboat	Avalon	Maryland Steamboat Company	589	Iron	Side wheel	1882	Chesapeake bay. Engine 40 inches diameter by 10 feet stroke.
	Corsica	Chester River Steamboat Company	368	..do	Propeller	1882	Engine 26 inches diameter by 24 inches stroke.
Steamship	Excelsior	Morgan's Louisiana and Texas Railroad and Steamship Company	3,264	..do	....do	1882	New York and New Orleans. Compound engine, 36 and 76 inches diameter by 54 inches stroke.
	City of Jacksonville	De Bary Merchants' Line	481	..do	Side wheel	1882	Two inclined engines, 30 inches diameter by 6 feet stroke.
Total tonnage			132,606				

The Pusey & Jones Company has built about 100 iron vessels, 80 of them for foreign owners, chiefly in South America. A few of the above have been built of steel, on foreign account also. The yard has especially studied the requirements of the river trade of South America, and has made a large number of stern-wheel and side-wheel paddle boats.

One of the large vessels of this concern is the Hudson, built in 1874 for the Cromwell line to New Orleans with engines on a new principle. The steamer is a two-decker, with cabins on the upper deck, and is schooner rigged. Her dimensions are: Register, 1,872 tons; length on the load-line to the afterside of the stern-post, 280 feet; beam, molded, 34 feet; depth from upper deck to keel, 26 feet. Her scantling were as follows:

Keel.—Bar-iron, 10 by $2\frac{1}{4}$ inches, scarfed 24 inches.

Stem.—Bar-iron, 10 by $2\frac{1}{4}$ inches.

Stern-posts.—Forward or propeller post, 11 by 5 inches; rudder-post, 10 by 5 inches; bottom part, 7 by 7 inches, the foot extending forward 7 feet, so as to form that much of the keel.

Frames.—Angle-iron, 5 by 3 inches; $\frac{1}{2}$ inch thick for 160 feet amidships; 5 by 3 by $\frac{7}{16}$ inches forward and aft of that; spacing, 24 inches. The frames are double under the engines; the frame runs to the main deck, and the forward cants to the forecastle deck. Reverse angle-irons, $3\frac{1}{2}$ by 3 by $\frac{7}{16}$ inches for 180 feet amidships, then $3\frac{1}{2}$ by 3 by $\frac{6}{16}$, running to the main deck and lower deck on alternate frames.

Floor plates.—Over the keel, 22 inches deep, $\frac{9}{16}$ inch thick for 170 feet amidships; forward and aft, $\frac{1}{2}$ inch thick, and not less than 11 inches deep at the bilge—all carried to the upper part of the bilge. In the ends of the vessel the plates increase in depth, as is usual in all iron vessels, tying the sides together like partial bulkheads.

Beams.—Lower deck: Bulb, T-iron, 9 inches deep, $\frac{1}{2}$ inch thick for 160 feet amidships; fore and aft, 8 inches deep by $\frac{1}{2}$ inch thick. Main deck: Same kind of iron, 8 inches deep by $\frac{1}{2}$ inch thick for 180 feet amidships, and then $\frac{7}{16}$ inch thick. Angle-irons, $3\frac{1}{4}$ by 3 by $\frac{7}{16}$ inch, form the top of the T in both sets of beams. Fifteen orlop beams of double T-iron in the hold, 10 inches deep; top and bottom flanges 5 inches wide, $\frac{9}{16}$ inch thick; forward of the forward bulkhead, angle-irons, $4\frac{1}{2}$ by 4 by $\frac{7}{16}$; forecastle beams, 5 inches deep, $\frac{7}{16}$ thick.

Stanchions.—Lower hold, $3\frac{1}{2}$ inches in diameter; between decks, 3 inches.

Plating.—Garboards: $\frac{5}{8}$ inch thick amidships, $\frac{9}{16}$ forward and aft. Bilge and bottom strakes, $\frac{5}{8}$ inch, tapering to $\frac{9}{16}$ at the bow and stern; from the bilge to the sheer strake, $\frac{9}{16}$ inch for 175 feet amidships, tapering then to $\frac{1}{2}$ inch. Sheer strake, $\frac{11}{16}$ inch for 180 feet amidships; then for 22 feet, $\frac{5}{8}$ inch; then, $\frac{9}{16}$ inch. Forecastle bulwark plates, $\frac{7}{16}$ inch. The sides are double riveted, except in the heavy plates and the butts, which are treble riveted, and in the plates which are not more than $\frac{7}{16}$ thick, where the seams are single riveted.

Keelsons.—Main: intercostal, rising the full depth of the floor plates and 10 inches above them of $\frac{11}{16}$-inch iron, each intercostal plate being secured to the floors by two angle-irons at each end $3\frac{1}{2}$ by 3 by $\frac{7}{16}$ inch. A plate 10 inches wide, $\frac{5}{8}$ inch thick, is laid flat on top of the floors each side of the intercostal plates, and is secured to the latter by an angle-iron 5 by 4 by $\frac{9}{16}$ inch. Two angle-irons of the same size, continuous fore and aft, are riveted to the upper edge of the intercostal plates, and on top of them again is a flat plate, 8 inches wide and $\frac{11}{16}$ inch thick. This collection of plates and angles is riveted at every point. Side keelsons are put in half way to the bilge for about 200 feet amidships. They are intercostal, $\frac{9}{16}$ inch thick, rising 5 inches above the floors, secured to the floors by angle-irons at the ends $3\frac{1}{2}$ by 3 by $\frac{7}{16}$ inch, and by a continuous angle-iron fore and aft, each side on top of the floors 5 by 4 by $\frac{9}{16}$ inch. The bilge keelsons at the upper and lower turn of the bilge are composed of two angle-irons, each 5 by 4 by $\frac{7}{16}$ inch, riveted back to back.

Stringers.—On the ends of the deck beams, all three tiers, around the ship. Lower deck, 30 inches wide and $\frac{9}{16}$ inch thick for 140 feet, tapering to 20 by $\frac{1}{2}$ inch at ends. Main deck, 46 by $\frac{9}{16}$ inch amidships, tapering to 26 by $\frac{1}{2}$ inch at the ends, riveted to the shell by pieces of angle-iron and to frames by a continuous angle-iron 5 by 4 by $\frac{9}{16}$ inch thick. On hold beams, 8 by $\frac{3}{4}$ inch, with angle-irons on top of and below the beam ends $4\frac{1}{2}$ by 4 by $\frac{9}{16}$ inch.

Tie plates.—Fore and aft on the beams, on each side of the hatches, on lower deck, 12 by $\frac{1}{2}$ inch; on main deck, 18 by $\frac{1}{2}$ inch.

Bulkheads.—Four transverse, $\frac{5}{8}$ inch thick, stiffened with angle-irons 5 by 3 by $\frac{1}{2}$ inch, spaced 2 feet apart. The bulkheads run to the main deck, and are water tight. There are bulkheads on each side of the engine and boiler rooms, forming, with the sides of the ship, bunkers for coal. Shaft tunnel of $\frac{5}{8}$-inch iron.

Rudder.—Wrought iron, $7\frac{1}{2}$ inches in diameter at the head, the frame all forged, and plated with $\frac{5}{8}$-inch iron.

Bulwarks.—Height, $3\frac{3}{4}$ feet; light iron, with white oak rail, $7\frac{1}{2}$ by $2\frac{1}{2}$ inches.

Wood work.—Ceiling of the floor of the hold, $2\frac{1}{2}$-inch pitch-pine; sides of the hold, 2-inch pine; decking, 4-inch yellow pine; foremast, 72 feet in height above the main deck, white pine, 22 inches in diameter; mainmast, 80 feet by 21 inches.

Boilers.—Four in number, return tubular, 9 feet in diameter, 14 feet long, of $\frac{1}{2}$-inch iron, with 140 tubes, $3\frac{1}{2}$ inches each; safety-valves set at 77 pounds; allowed to carry 75 pounds of steam; working pressure, 65 pounds.

Engines.—Vertical; surface-condensing poppet-valve. Cylinder, 48 inches in diameter, 6-foot stroke; steam cut-off at 7 inches from beginning of the stroke; revolutions, 65 per minute.

Wheel.—Screw; 15 feet in diameter; 22 feet pitch; gun-metal blades.

Class.—A 1 for 20 years.

The engines of the majority of propellers are of the compound surface-condensing type, in which steam is expanded at a low pressure. In the Hudson, however, the working pressure is 65 pounds. The ship has been driven at an average of $12\frac{1}{2}$ knots on a consumption of 20 tons of coal per day, and her speed often averages 14 knots for the whole trip to New Orleans.

At Baltimore there was some iron-ship building before the war, in a fragmentary way, however. One of the vessels launched by Ross and Thomas Winans in 1858, designed to be a new type of express steamer and to carry only passengers and a small quantity of valuable freight, was 180 feet long, with 16 feet beam, without keel or cutwater, but was provided with four high-pressure engines. The hull was arched on deck in such way that no sea that came aboard could be retained, and the boat was large enough to accommodate about 20 passengers, the mails, and a limited amount of express matter. Baltimore is favorably situated for the construction of iron vessels. The war interrupted the growth of the business, but another beginning was made in 1872 by the construction of two composite vessels for the government by William E. Woodall & Co., the small sailing vessels Speedwell and Bibb. The following year the little schooners Palinurus and Research, each of 76 tons, were built by the the same firm, and in 1876 the Earnest of 80 tons, the Ready of 80 tons, and the Drift of 87 tons, all schooners, and, like the others, all for the coast survey. The timbers and deck frames of these boats were of angle-iron, all the rest oak and pine. Woodall & Co. also designed the composite single-deck propeller Thomas G. Gedney, of 133 tons, for the coast survey, which was built by Delamater, of New York, in 1875. This vessel was 130 feet long on deck, $24\frac{1}{2}$ feet beam, molded, and 8 feet deep in the hold. The stem, apron, knight-heads, keel, stern-post, and deadwood were of oak and locust, and the planking yellow pine, 6 inches thick on the garboards, $4\frac{1}{2}$ on the wales, and 3 on the bulwarks. Yellow pine, 12 by 5 inches, was used for the plank-sheer and rail, and white pine, $3\frac{3}{4}$ inches square, for the decking. The frames were of angle-iron, 3 by $2\frac{1}{2}$ by $\frac{3}{8}$ inches, spaced 18 inches; the reverse angles $2\frac{1}{4}$ by $2\frac{1}{4}$ by $\frac{5}{16}$, extended on alternate frames to 6 inches above the bilge keelson and to the deck. The floor plates were 12 inches deep over the keel, $\frac{3}{8}$ inch thick, and diminished to a molding of 3 inches on the bilge. Although the vessel had a wooden keel 10 inches square, an iron keel plate was laid on top of it 18 inches wide and $\frac{3}{8}$ inch thick, which ran clear fore and aft and lapped on the stem and the stern-post. The keelson was intercostal, of $\frac{3}{8}$-inch iron, with flat plates on each side of it, same thickness and 18 inches wide, and with an angle-iron on each side, uniting the vertical to the flat plates, $2\frac{1}{4}$ by $2\frac{1}{4}$ by $\frac{5}{16}$ inches. A double angle-iron side keelson each side was composed of 5 by 3 by $\frac{7}{16}$-inch iron. Bilge keelsons, double, of angle-iron, 3 inches by $3\frac{1}{2}$ by $\frac{3}{8}$. The deck beams were 5 inch bulb T-iron. One narrow strip of $\frac{3}{8}$-inch plating about 9 inches wide was riveted to the frames just below the floor head, and another 18 inches wide was riveted on the timbers as a sheer streak. There were 3 bulkheads of $\frac{1}{4}$-inch iron. The planking was put on with screw bolts, the heads countersunk, cemented, and plugged with wood, and five streaks on the bilge were edge-bolted amidships for 90 feet with $\frac{5}{8}$-inch iron. This vessel was coppered over the planking. The hull thus made was light and strong, and the vessel did good service.

In 1876 a regular iron-ship yard was established in Baltimore on the point near the fort by the firm of Malster & Reaney. Shops were put up for the various operations of the ship-yard, including boiler and blacksmith, machine, joiner, and boat shops; also a foundery and mold-loft, with a wareroom 500 feet long, and office and store-room. A large basin dry-dock was also made on the grounds 450 feet long and 113 feet wide on top, measured inside the basin gates. A fair equipment of machinery was purchased, including a steam riveter. The work of the yard has been chiefly boiler building and repair work, but vessels have been built from time to time, and the business appears to be on a substantial foundation. The following was the production up to the census year:

Description.	Name.	Kind of wheel.	When built.	Length between perpendiculars.	Beam molded.	Depth of hold.
				Ft. In.	Ft. In.	Ft. In.
Tug	Alexander Jones	Screw	1876–'77	97 0	22 0	10 0½
Do	Camilla	....do	1877–'78	62 0	16 0	7 0
Ice-boat	F. C. Latrobe	Side wheel	1877–'78	200 0	34 0	14 0
Yacht	Chronometer	Screw	1877–'78	42 6	6 9	4 10
Steamer	Enoch Pratt	Side wheel	1878	155 0	29 0	8 6
Tug	Canton	Screw	1879	70 0	16 6	7 9
Ferry-boat	Robert Garrett	Side wheel	1880–'81	125 0	25 0	11 0
United States light-house tender	Holly	....do	1880–'81	146 3	23 8	9 6
Do	Jessamine	....do	1880–'81	146 3	23 8	9 6

A beginning has been made in iron-ship building in San Francisco in spite of the high cost of iron and of labor in that city. The first appears to have been repair work on two large Pacific mail steamers, the City of Peking and the City of Tokio, by men sent out from the East; but in 1879 the iron propeller Bolivar, 13 years old, was taken out of water and enlarged by the Risdon iron works and the Dickie Brothers, wooden-ship builders. She was built in Hull, England, and sold here for $20,000. Registering 1,083 tons, she was cut in two, lengthened 68 feet, and enlarged to 1,462 tons register at an expense of $120,000.

The port of San Francisco is visited yearly by two or three hundred iron sailing vessels from England, and whenever an accident happens to any of them, impairing their seaworthiness, they must have their repairs made there. The Risdon iron works have had several large pieces of work to do on ships driven ashore and damaged. In the bottom of one 33 plates were put, in another almost an entire new bottom was necessary, and there have

IRON VESSELS.

been a number of similar jobs. In 1879 the ship Jessie Osborne, of Dumbarton, Scotland, of 1,079 tons, only two years old, was wrecked a few miles north of the city, and had a large hole knocked through her hull. She was bought by San Francisco shipping men, raised by tightening the decks and forcing air into the hull under great pressure, towed into port, and there repaired, and when finished cost the new owner about $60,000. Another job of work was on an English iron ship, oil laden, which took fire off the coast of South America. She was towed to the Sandwich islands and then to San Francisco, when the beams which were warped by the heat were either straightened or replaced and the whole ship was repaired and made as good as new.

In the course of these operations the Risdon works and the Dickie Brothers have acquired a considerable acquaintance with iron vessels, and have lately built two small propellers, one for a local water boat, the other of 30 tons for owners in Ecuador. The water boat was finished in the winter of 1881–'82, and is 65 feet long, 13 feet beam, and 7 feet deep, modeled like a tug, weighing about 25 tons with everything aboard except water. The tank holds 10,000 gallons. She has two high-pressure engines, with 8 by 8 inch cylinders, and two boilers 6 by 6 feet, and with a pressure of 100 pounds of steam develops 35 horse-power. The plating is $\frac{1}{4}$ and $\frac{5}{16}$ inch thick; the deck is of corded iron plates $\frac{5}{16}$ inch thick. The rivets of the shell were driven cold.

While the skill has been acquired necessary for iron-ship building, the future of the industry in California is in doubt. Timber is too cheap to encourage a demand for iron sailing ships, and propellers can be built in the East at much lower prices than in San Francisco; but it is of great value to the maritime community to have on the Pacific coast the present means of repairing disabled iron vessels.

Iron boats were first introduced on a river in the South about 1830, the pioneer iron boat of the United States, the Codorus, having been sent to that part of the country about that year. Information in regard to the matter is not very definite, but it is known that the Savannah river had a number of iron boats at an early period. Five were running in 1835. They had all the experiences to which river boats are subject. One of them, built in 1834, was hauled out in 1843 for examination; her bottom had not been perceptibly worn in nine years' service, and there was no trace of her repeated encounters with snags, except an indentation here and there in the hull.

Iron boats were first introduced in the West in 1839. The experiments in Georgia had shown their desirability for service on shallow rivers. Light draught is a *sine qua non* in boats navigating streams where the water dwindles in dry months to 5 feet draught and less, and toughness and strength of hull are important where snags and sunken logs abound in the river bed. The experience of early navigators in the West taught them the value of strong, light, safe boats, and led them to a few attempts at the production of something better than wooden hulls. As before stated, the beginning was in the year 1839, at Pittsburgh; and although comparatively few boats have been built, yet the experience of late years has fully confirmed the lessons of the earlier time. Light hulls are just as desirable as ever; indeed, they become more desirable, now that trade has reached such large proportions and steamers must carry from 2,000 to 3,000 tons of cargo, instead of 400 and 500 tons, as in 1839; and strength and durability also continue to be qualities of the highest importance. About one-half the losses in the West are due to the snagging of wooden boats, their hulls being necessarily of such flimsy construction that the first strong thrust from a sunken tree sends them to the bottom of the river. Vessels that survive the danger of snags and the peril of fire perish, in any event, from natural decay alone in six or seven years. Ocean vessels, with their heavy frames and planking, live for fifteen and twenty years, often longer. In the West the whole tonnage of the rivers must be renewed every six or seven years. In a fleet so perishable the cost of maintenance is excessive. Natural depreciation goes on at the rate of 16 per cent. a year; insurance ranges from 8 to 12 per cent.; interest is not less than 6 per cent., and annual cost of painting and repair amounts to as much more. The cost of maintenance of tonnage in the West is therefore from 30 to 35 per cent., or twice that of the ocean fleet. Steamboat men, therefore, thoroughly understand the value of a safer and more durable class of tonnage than that which they now own, and nothing except the cost of iron boats has stood in the way of their universal adoption.

The pioneer iron boat at Pittsburgh was the Valley Forge, which was built at the iron works of Robinson, Minnis & Miller, on the south side of the Monongahela, a short distance above the bridge. She was 165 feet long, 25 feet beam, and 5½ feet deep, and was a side-wheeler. This first experiment was regarded as the inauguration of a new and great industry. In 1841 the boat was lengthened 15 feet, making her 180 feet long, and over the paddle-wheel guards she was 50 feet wide. She was then as large as the locks at Louisville would admit. A cabin covered her whole deck, with accommodations for 200 passengers. The frames were of angle-iron, the beams of T-iron. The plating of the hull was ¼ inch thick, and the lower deck was laid with $\frac{3}{16}$-inch iron plates. Her keel was of flat plate iron, 12 inches wide, dished. The cylinder timbers and frames of the wheels were also of iron. Owing to the lightness of the hull she could carry 400 tons on about 4½ feet draught. The Valley Forge cost, however, twice the amount for which a wooden steamer of the same size could have been built. She ran successfully on the Ohio, Cumberland, Tennessee, and Mississippi rivers until 1845, a part of the time as a packet between Nashville and New Orleans, and was sunk once in the Mississippi, but was raised, and did good service thereafter. In 1845 she was dismantled and broken up. Trade had increased in the West, and boats of twice her size were being built and run at small additional expense. Her machinery was transferred to another vessel, and the iron of the hull was sold to the government for 2½ cents per pound and sent to Harper's Ferry, where most of it was used in the manufacture of musket barrels. Experience with this vessel taught the need of thicker plates on the bottom of the hull, and also threw some doubt for a time on the utility of iron boats on the upper Ohio, where the bed of the river is generally composed of rock and gravel and the stage of water is so scant that boats rub on the bars. Some of her bottom plates had been worn down to $\frac{1}{16}$ inch in thickness. In 1845 the iron revenue-cutter George M. Bibb was built at the Fort Pitt works, on the Allegheny, at Pittsburgh, and was dispatched to the Gulf of Mexico. She was at first propelled by a screw, but the wheel did not work well, and it was taken out at Cincinnati and side paddle-wheels substituted. She was then sent on to the Gulf. Soon after two other iron revenue-cutters were built at Pittsburgh, the Lake Erie and the Lake Michigan, which were sent through to the lakes via the Lake Erie canal.

In 1847 the Allegheny was built at Pittsburgh, also for the government, and was a larger boat than her predecessors. Her dimensions were: Length on deck, 185 feet; on the keel, 171 feet; beam on deck, $33\frac{1}{3}$ feet; beam at the wheels, 25 feet; depth of hold, 19 feet; mean draught, $13\frac{1}{2}$ feet; register, 1,200 tons. The total weight of the hull was 425 net tons; her total displacement, 1,050 tons. The machinery, with coal-bunkers and chimney, weighed 573,000 pounds. Her engines cost $61,000; the whole boat $292,000. Captain Hunter, of the United States navy, under whose direction the Allegheny was built, supplied her with two wheels amidships $14\frac{2}{3}$ feet in diameter, with paddles $3\frac{1}{2}$ feet wide and $2\frac{1}{6}$ feet long, the intention being to place them where they would be protected from cannon shot; but in service these wheels failed to give satisfaction, and were taken out and the boat provided with common paddle-wheels. An extended cruise was taken by the Allegheny, and from New Orleans she went to Norfolk, and thence to the Mediterranean. It was at first thought that she would answer for a war steamer, but she proved too light for the purpose, and was strengthened afterward by putting in new frames between the old ones. The Hunter, 100 feet long, was also built at Pittsburgh on the same principle as the last-named boat.

This was a good beginning in iron steamboat building in the West, but the high cost of the vessels deterred transportation companies from ordering the new class of tonnage. During the war several other government vessels were constructed at the iron works in Pittsburgh, among others the monitors Manayunk and Umpqua and the light-draught gunboats Sandusky and Marietta. The war having come to an end before any of these vessels were finished, they did not reach the lower waters, but with the exception of the Manayunk were detained at Cairo and sold. The hulls were broken up and a great deal of the iron found its way back to Pittsburgh, to be worked over into new forms. Since the war about 15 other iron boats, mostly of small size, have been built, all for private owners, a number of them tugs. Three light-draught boats were made by Hartupee & Co. on South American orders. They were sent to New York and shipped thence to their destination, and were, respectively, 135 feet long, 26 feet beam, $4\frac{1}{2}$ feet hold, 85 feet long, 15 feet beam, and 3 feet hold, and 50 feet long, 12 feet beam, and $2\frac{1}{2}$ feet hold. None of the seven or eight concerns which built iron boats at Pittsburgh had regular ship-yards, but they were all proprietors of iron works. The largest vessel of the period since the war is the steel dredge boat made by G. W. R. Bayley for use at the mouth of the Mississippi, 200 feet long, $32\frac{7}{12}$ feet broad, and 10 feet hold, with 28-foot paddle-wheels, and engines 21 inches in diameter by 7 feet stroke. The Bayley was admirably adapted to the purposes for which she was built, being light, strong, and serviceable.

At Pittsburgh coal is abundant and cheap. The whole region is full of excellent iron, and there has been no lack of fine engineering talent or of workmen of the highest skill. But in spite of all these advantages and the conceded utility of iron boats there has been one obstacle to overcome which the iron men have found insuperable. Oak has been as abundant as iron, and far cheaper. From the beginning down to the present day the wooden hull has cost only about one-half the expense of an iron hull, and it has been in vain to compete for orders from steamboat owners. At present there is only one yard building iron vessels in Pittsburgh, the property of James Rees & Sons, which is employed chiefly on foreign orders. The specialty of this firm was originally the construction of steamboat engines, but in 1878 they went into vessel building, the firm being then known as Rees & Thorn. The yard is on the Allegheny side of the city. Down to 1882 the following vessels had been built:

1878. Stern-wheel steamboat Francisco Montayer, 150 feet long, 28 feet beam, 4 feet hold, for South America.
1879. Stern-wheel steamboat Victoria, 155 feet long, $32\frac{1}{4}$ feet beam, 5 feet hold, for South America.
1879. Stern-wheel steamboat Venezuela, 120 feet long, 24 feet beam, 3 feet hold, for South America.
1879. United States medical boat Benner, 118 feet long, 19 feet beam, $3\frac{1}{2}$ feet hold.
1879. Steam catamaran for Saratoga lake, New York, each hull 146 feet long, 14 feet beam, 5 feet hold; the hulls of steel.
1880. Three small tugs for the government, 37 feet long, $7\frac{1}{2}$ feet beam, $3\frac{1}{2}$ feet hold; hull of steel.
1881. Stern-wheeler Roberto Carlistor, 112 feet long, 22 feet beam, 3 feet hold, for South America.
1881. Stern-wheeler De Castro, 112 feet long, 22 feet beam, 3 feet hold, for South America.
1881. Stern-wheeler Chattahoochee, 155 feet long, $31\frac{1}{4}$ feet beam, 5 feet hold, for the Chattahoochee river, Alabama.

The Chattahoochee was building in the census year, and was of Siemens-Anderson steel throughout, very light and strong. She was perfectly flat on the bottom, the bilge quick, and the sides flaring 6 inches, as in other river steamers. The frames were 2 by 2 inches by $\frac{1}{4}$ inch, and every other one carried a reverse angle-iron; spacing 14 inches. The hull was provided with five transverse bulkheads and three running fore and aft, the latter being principally depended upon for strength, especially when in contact with snags. Plating, $\frac{1}{4}$, $\frac{3}{16}$, and $\frac{1}{8}$ inch steel, fastened with double rows of $\frac{3}{8}$ and $\frac{5}{8}$ inch rivets, driven cold. The deck frame was of steel, but planked with pine. The Chattahoochee was built for the cotton trade of the Chattahoochee river, and was expected to carry nearly 400 tons of freight.

IRON VESSELS.

Only a few iron boats have been built at Cincinnati. One was an excursion steamer, for use in the vicinity of New Orleans, 130 feet long, 36 feet beam, and 4 feet hold; but she was too shallow for the waters navigated, and by mismanagement was sunk in deep water. Another boat of larger size, built about ten years ago, is running yet. She is 200 feet long, and draws only 30 inches of water, light. The lack of demand for such expensive craft prevents the development of the industry in Cincinnati.

The work done at Dubuque has been of a fragmentary character, and nothing is doing now.

At Saint Louis, in the Carondelet suburbs, there is one large yard owned by the Western Iron Boat Building Company. It was established in 1874 by Charles P. Chouteau, one of a firm owning a large rolling-mill in that locality, under the superintendency of Theodore Allen, of New York, who, with a partner, A. H. Blaisdell, is the present owner.

This yard had produced the following boats down to the year 1882:

1874. Snag-boat O. G. Wagner, for the United States government.
1875. Stern-wheel tow-boat A. Humphries, 125 feet long, 24 feet beam, and 6 feet hold.
1876. Stern-wheel tow-boat W. J. Florence, 120 feet long, 20 feet beam, and 5 feet hold.
1877. Stern-wheel tow-boat Bessie, 120 feet long, 20 feet beam, and 4½ feet hold, for rafting.
1877. Stern-wheel freight-boat Charles P. Chouteau, of 1,304 tons (being the monitor Winnebago altered and lengthened 72 feet), 296 feet long, 54 feet beam, and 8 feet hold. This steamer carried 8,866 bales of cotton and 15,000 sacks of cottonseed into New Orleans on one trip in 1880.
1877. Twin-screw propeller Indianola, United States mail dispatch boat, 90 feet long, 15 feet beam, and 6 feet hold.
1878. Side-wheel United States survey-boats Iris, Doris, Clytie, and Thetis, each 54 feet long, 10 feet beam, and 4½ feet hold. The bows of these boats were peculiar, the stem being inclined backward; a style which did not prove desirable, and which was afterward altered.
1879. Side-wheel United States launch Hebe, 78 feet long over all, 75 feet on the water-line, 15 feet beam, 27 feet over all, 4 feet hold; two engines, 12 inches in diameter, 2 feet stroke; wheels 12 feet in diameter and 5 feet across.
1879. United States snag-boat Horatio G. Wright, side-wheeler, 187 feet long, 62 feet beam, 90 feet over all, 8 feet hold; weight of iron in the hull, 534 tons; total weight of boat, 885 tons; cost, $130,000.
1879. Propeller barge Electra, 66 feet long, 11 feet beam, 4½ feet hold; a tender to the snag-boat.
1879. Two side-wheel United States survey-boats, 82 feet long, 13 feet beam, and 4½ feet hold.
1879. Two stern-wheel United States snag-boats, John R. Meigs and Chauncey B. Reese, 170 feet long, 36 feet beam, and 6 feet hold.
1880. Stern-wheel freight-boat No. 19, 130 feet long, 26 feet beam, and 7½ feet hold.
1880. Screw-tug Susie Hazard, for Saint Louis owners, 95 feet long, 19 feet beam, 9 feet hold; draught of water, 8 feet.
1880. Stern-wheel snag-boat C. W. Howell, 145 feet long, 36 feet beam, and 6 feet hold.
1881. Side-wheel transfer steamer, for the Texas Pacific railroad, being the monitor Chickasaw altered; under construction.
1881. Two tow-boats for the Mississippi River Improvement Commission, under construction, 175 feet long, 32 feet beam, and 6 feet hold.

This company introduces into its new boats the longitudinal system of framing, and it would do the same if it were to construct model barges of iron. Up to the present time no orders have been received for model barges, as the cost of vessels of the new 225-foot size would not be less than $25,000, exclusive of the house on deck, which is more than twice the contract price of wooden barges complete. It is estimated that an iron boat would last from 30 to 40 years, and thus outlive five of the other kind, besides being 15 per cent. lighter, and not grow heavier with age, as do wooden boats. Nevertheless, excess of first cost proves a serious drawback to their introduction. It will illustrate the character of the new Saint Louis steamers to describe the scantling of the tow-boat built in 1881. The data are as follows:

Model.—175 feet long, 32 feet beam, 6 feet depth of hold; the bottom perfectly flat; bilge turned in the square body with 12 inches radius; bow modeled for 75 feet, with entrance long and fine for a western boat. Sheer forward, 5 feet; aft, 2 feet.

Frames.—Longitudinal, 3 feet apart, 2 by 2 inches, with a vertical floor plate 6 inches high, $\frac{3}{16}$ inch thick, with a 2-inch angle-iron along the upper edge. These floor frames draw together in the bow, and when 18 inches apart the outer ones stop short. Between the longitudinal frame irons 2- by 2-inch transverse irons are worked intercostally 3 feet apart. Every other transverse floor frame carries a vertical plate 8 inches high, $\frac{3}{16}$ inch thick, with a continuous angle-iron from bilge to bilge 2 by 2 by $\frac{5}{16}$ inches. The bow is framed on the transverse system with 2½-inch angle-iron. Side frames of the square body, 18 inches apart, 2 by 2 by $\frac{5}{16}$-inch angle-iron, running from the gunwale to the first longitudinal frame on the floor of the boat; every other side frame carries an 8-inch plate, with an angle-iron along the outer edge of it. The transverse floor plates deepen as the bow grows finer, the foremost one being 3 feet in depth.

Bulkheads.—Two longitudinal, 12 feet apart, running from away aft to about 30 feet from the bow, where they are 6 feet apart and end on a transverse bulkhead. They are of $\frac{3}{16}$-inch iron, secured to the skin with 2½ by 2½ by $\frac{5}{16}$ angle-irons; at top, two 2 by $\frac{3}{8}$ angle-irons. Four transverse bulkheads, of $\frac{3}{16}$-inch iron, worked between the sides of the vessel and the other bulkheads, and made water-tight.

Stem.—A plate, with cheek pieces for the apron, and broad enough to land the outside plating on and hold it securely.

Keelson.—Depth 18 inches, of $\frac{3}{8}$-inch plate, secured below to the skin with a 2 by 2½ by $\frac{5}{16}$ angle-iron on each side of the plate, stiffened with two similar irons at the upper edge. The keelson deepens to 36 inches at the stern of the boat.

Stern.—Framed transversely, and raking so as to allow the use of balance rudder; a floor plate on each frame. Fan-tail of $\frac{3}{16}$-inch plate iron.

Beams.—Spaced 18 inches, of 2½ by 2½ by $\frac{5}{16}$ angle-iron. Every other beam has gusset knees of $\frac{3}{16}$ iron, connecting it with the side frames and fore-and-aft bulkheads. In the center line of the boat and parallel to it, 8 feet each way, 3 by 3 by $\frac{3}{8}$ angle-irons are fastened to the under side of the beams with clips, with stanchions of 2¼ angle-iron on each plate floor, except that on the main keelson they are of 2½-inch iron. There is a 12-inch girder on the keelson stanchions.

Stringers.—Three on the top timbers on each side of 2½ by 2½ by $\frac{5}{16}$ angle-iron, fastened to clips. They are continued to the stem with a 6-inch plate of ¼ iron, and when the inboard edges of the plate approach to within 2 feet the plate is made in one piece across the boat to form a breast-hook. Stringer plate on the beams 24 inches wide, $\frac{3}{8}$ inch thick, with butt straps treble riveted. Gunwale stringer plate 20 inches wide, with 8 inches worked outboard, $\frac{3}{8}$-inch iron. An angle-iron is riveted on this plate 2 inches from the inside edge to abut the planking of the deck against.

Outside plating.—All $\frac{3}{8}$, $\frac{5}{16}$, and $\frac{1}{4}$ inch thick, rivets $\frac{3}{8}$ inch, 4 diameters apart.

Guards.—Four feet wide amidships, broad at the bow, sustained by outriggers of $2\frac{1}{2}$-inch angle-iron 2 feet apart, turned down 8 inches on the plating and riveted. Over plank-sheer, 12 inches wide, $\frac{5}{8}$ inch thick; under plank-sheer, 12 inches wide, $\frac{1}{4}$ inch thick. Facing, 8-inch channel iron.

Rudders.—Three in number, one a balance rudder. The wing rudders hang on skegs of $\frac{3}{16}$ iron plate made independently and riveted on with angle-iron.

Cylinder timbers.—Iron, 46 inches deep at the transom.

Machinery.—Three steel boilers, made of $\frac{26}{100}$-inch plates; diameter, 42 inches; length, 28 feet, with five 10-inch flues. Two engines, 20 inches in diameter, 6 feet stroke.

Houses.—As usual on tow-boats.

Weight of iron.—Gross weight of iron purchased for hull, 394,640 pounds; waste about 6 per cent., leaving net weight of iron in hull 370,960 pounds.

It is the belief of those in the West most competent to judge that iron or steel is destined finally to take the place of wood in all the larger vessels used for transportation on the rivers. The experience already had on the deeper rivers proves conclusively the durability of iron boats and the small cost of their repairs. Bottom plates on recent boats after eight years' service have shown a reduction of only 2 per cent. in weight, and the framing and interior work have shown no perceptible deterioration. The business of the rivers is at present largely in the hands of persons with limited capital, who cannot afford the expense of iron or steel hulls, and there has therefore been no competition between rival lines of wooden and iron vessels to elicit information as to the commercial superiority of the latter. It is, however, well known that the river traffic of the West would be greatly promoted if freight rates could be lowered; but they cannot be materially lowered at present, owing to the high cost of maintenance and replacement of wooden tonnage. It is the opinion of many in the West that this state of affairs will continue to interest the more observing and intelligent men engaged in transportation until they realize that freight can be carried profitably at lower rates by employing more efficient and more durable hulls, and they will then build boats of either iron or steel, or with iron frames and wooden planking.

On the northern lakes iron ships are of recent introduction, but the new idea is making rapid progress. Since the war the trade of the lakes has grown to large proportions, the cargoes moved by the best paying class of lake vessels being not less than 1,500 tons in dead weight, and often ranging as high as 2,500 tons and more. The peculiarities of the channel between lakes Huron and Saint Clair and of the harbors of the principal cities, and the expectation that laden vessels will before long run direct from Chicago to Montreal through the Canadian canals and perhaps on to Europe, govern the forms of ships. The lake model is, and necessarily must be, long rather than narrow, and limited to about 14 feet draught. In order to give wooden vessels of this model proper strength the hulls must be built with heavy scantling, a great deal of extra fastening and strapping, and with a quantity of timber in the keelsons not seen in any other class of vessels. Wooden hulls are heavy, and there is need on that account alone of the lighter hulls of iron, even if no other considerations came into play. It will be remembered also that the machinery in lake steamers is placed far aft, and that the tendency of its vibration is to rack and strain the hull. Besides, the timber of the lakes is disappearing, and the cost of wooden ships is rising. These are all cogent reasons for building iron ships.

The rise of iron works and boiler and engine shops and the existence of large wooden-ship yards in Buffalo made that city the natural center for first attempting the construction of iron boats on the lakes. The proprietors of large shops turned their attention to iron hulls more than twenty years ago, and from time to time built tugs, yachts, and freight boats of small size until a familiarity with the principles of construction had been obtained. About 1870 an interest in iron propellers was awakened, and the Anchor line contracted for four new vessels of large size to go into their trade to the upper lakes. These propellers were completed in Buffalo in 1871. At various times from 1870 to 1873 there were also built in Buffalo for the various transportation companies five others, all by Gibson & Craig, as subcontractors under the King iron works. They were as follows:

Year.	Name.	Length.	Beam.	Hold.	Tonnage.
		Feet.	*Feet.*	*Feet.*	
1871	India	210	$32\frac{1}{2}$	14	1,239
	China	210	$32\frac{1}{2}$	14	1,239
	Japan	210	$32\frac{1}{2}$	14	1,239
	Alaska	$212\frac{1}{2}$	32	$13\frac{3}{4}$	1,288
1872	Cuba	$231\frac{2}{3}$	$35\frac{2}{3}$	$13\frac{5}{12}$	1,526
	Russia	$231\frac{2}{3}$	$35\frac{2}{3}$	$13\frac{5}{12}$	1,502
	Java (since lost)	$231\frac{2}{3}$	$35\frac{2}{3}$	$13\frac{5}{12}$	1,502
1873	Scotia	$231\frac{2}{3}$	$35\frac{2}{3}$	$13\frac{5}{12}$	1,502
	Arabia	224	34	15	1,203

IRON VESSELS.

The only other man that ever built of iron in Buffalo (besides those now in the business) is believed to be George H. Notter, a tug- and canal-boat builder, who in 1875 constructed an iron steam yacht 100 feet long.

There are now two yards in the city, that of David Bell and the one belonging to the Union Dry Dock Company. Mr. Bell was originally a builder of boilers and engines, and machinery still constitutes the largest part of his yearly product. In 1861 he ventured to build the screw steamer Merchant, of 720 tons, 200 feet long, 29 feet beam, and 14 feet hold, and has since taken such contracts as could be secured for yachts, tugs, and small propellers. Three of his vessels, launched in 1871 and 1873, were the revenue-cutters Albert Gallatin, of 250 tons; Alexander Hamilton, of 250 tons; and G. S. Boutwell, of 198 tons—all propellers, and all afterward sent to stations on the Atlantic coast, where they have remained in service. Up to 1882, 26 iron vessels had been built at this yard, all steamers, and two yachts and a tug included in the number were being completed in the fall of 1881. Ten of the whole number were yachts, and some of these boats were plated with steel $\frac{3}{16}$, $\frac{1}{4}$, and $\frac{5}{16}$ inch thick, in order to lessen their weight, the cost of steel at Buffalo being only slightly in excess of iron. Mr. Bell has built of both wood and iron, and says that he has been able to construct tugs of the two materials which scarcely varied in cost. For instance, a wooden tug built in 1876, 70 feet long, 16 feet beam, and 8 feet hold, cost $12,500 to build and equip, whereas he was able to build one iron tug of 64 tons, 76 feet long, 16 feet beam, and 8 feet hold, at a cost of $13,000 only; and he believes that the development of the iron industry of the lakes will in time reduce the cost of materials for large vessels to a point where iron steamers can be built at so nearly the price of wooden ones as to supersede entirely the latter style of boats. He paid 4 cents a pound for angle-iron in 1875 and $2\frac{9}{10}$ cents in 1881; for plating he paid $3\frac{1}{2}$ cents in 1875 and $2\frac{7}{10}$ cents in 1881.

The tug on the stocks in the fall of 1881 was 90 feet long, 18 feet beam, and 10 feet deep in the hold, $11\frac{1}{2}$ feet molded, and was built with 37 tons of iron in the hull. Like all of his small boats, she has a bar-iron keel and stem $4\frac{1}{2}$ by $1\frac{1}{2}$ inches. The stern-post is 6 by 2 inches, tapered in the fan-tail to $1\frac{1}{2}$ inches. The frames are 3 by $2\frac{1}{2}$ by $\frac{3}{8}$ inch, spaced 18 inches; floor plates, $\frac{1}{4}$-inch iron. The deck beams are of white oak, 4 by 4 inches, the short ones near the boiler and engines being 3 by 4. The plating is all $\frac{3}{8}$-inch iron. Two iron bulkheads cross the boat of $\frac{3}{16}$-inch plate, stiffened with $2\frac{1}{2}$- by $2\frac{1}{2}$-inch angle-iron. The plank-sheer and bulwarks are of heavy white oak, while the deck and house are of white pine. There is only one boiler, 8 feet in diameter and 16 feet long, and one engine, with 24-inch cylinder and 26-inch stroke. Steam is used at high pressure, 120 pounds being allowed. An 8-foot screw wheel is fitted at the stern with 13 feet pitch, the shaft being of steel $6\frac{7}{8}$ inches in diameter. In model the tug was fuller than those used in Atlantic coast harbors, and cost complete about $19,000. In order to fit her for ice breaking in the harbor of Toledo the stem was not given the usual curvature, but, while perpendicular above the water, raked sharply below at an angle.

One of the new yachts was 106 feet long on deck, 17 feet beam, and 11 feet deep, frames spaced 18 inches, scantling light throughout, with white-pine beams resting on an iron shelf, wooden deck, and 4 transverse water-tight bulkheads.

The Union Dry Dock Company has long been a builder of wooden propellers of the largest class, but its managers in 1881 put into their large yard the plant for making iron vessels. The first boat, finished in 1882, was the propeller H. J. Jewett, a two-decker of 1,953 tons, 285 feet long over all, $265\frac{1}{2}$ feet on deck, $39\frac{8}{12}$ feet beam, and $25\frac{1}{2}$ feet hold, with houses on the upper deck. She was built of the ordinary lake model, and was given a double bottom, in order to carry water ballast when returning to the upper lakes light, and also in order to save the vessel from sinking in case she should strike a rock in making the Lime Kiln crossing above Detroit. Seven water-tight bulkheads were put in across the ship. She was furnished with two steel boilers and two compound engines of 1,000 horse-power, capable of driving her at a speed of 15 knots. Her carrying capacity is 2,400 tons. The iron plating of her bottom is $\frac{5}{8}$ and $\frac{9}{16}$ inch thick on her bottom, $\frac{1}{2}$ inch on the sides, and $\frac{6}{16}$ inch between decks. The frames are 3 by 4 inch angle-iron, spaced 21 inches; reverse bars, 3 by 3 inch. The floor plates are $\frac{7}{16}$ inch. The company has now on hand two iron vessels. The revenue-cutter Fessenden has been hauled out on the stocks, and an entirely new iron hull of substantially the same model is being constructed in place of the old wooden one. The boat is 188 feet long, 28 feet beam, and 12 feet hold. A new boiler will be put in, and the engine repaired. The other vessel is a new tug, 65 feet long, 15 feet beam, and 8 feet hold.

Cleveland is one of the most noted wooden-ship yard centers on the lakes; but here, as at Buffalo, attention has lately been turned strongly to the advantages of iron tonnage. The Globe iron works have been for many years making machinery and boilers for lake boats on a large scale, and in 1880 the owners prepared to extend their plant sufficiently to undertake the building of iron hulls. The main works are situated in the city, near the lake, close by Presley's dry-dock. Having bought a half interest in the dock, the company located a ship-yard in the western edge of the city and put in an outfit of shops, planers, punching machines, frame-bending apparatus, rolls, etc. In 1881 they raised the frames of their first vessel, a large lake propeller (Fig. 67). The ship was completed in the spring of 1882, and launched at the opening of navigation. The following are points of interest in her construction:

The vessel: screw propeller, $302\frac{1}{2}$ feet long on the spar deck, 288 feet between perpendiculars, 39 feet beam, 25 feet from spar deck to base line, with double bottom for water ballast. Fall home of the topsides at plank-sheer, 8 inches. Weight of vessel with all on board, 950 tons; cargo on 14 feet draught, 2,770 tons; coefficient of displacement, 80 per cent.

Keel.—Flat plate, 2 feet wide, $\frac{11}{16}$ inch thick.

Frames.—Angle-iron on the floor, 3 by 3½ by $\frac{6}{16}$ inches, weighing about 8 pounds to the foot; top timbers from the bilge upward, 3 by 4 by $\frac{6}{16}$, weighing about 9 pounds to the foot. Reverse angles, 3 by 3 by $\frac{3}{8}$ inches. Floor plates of $\frac{5}{16}$ iron, 16 inches deep on the keel, 14 inches at the lower turn of the bilge, increasing to 20 inches in the molding near the upper turn of the bilge; the floor plate ends at a point 40 inches above the base line of the keel. Partial bulkhead plates are carried on a certain number of top timbers, 23 inches wide at the foot, 12 inches wide at the upper deck, and $\frac{5}{16}$ inch thick, with reverse angle riveted to the outer edge of the plate. The deck of the double bottom is stiffened by single 3 by 3½ inch angle-iron floor frames, which are connected to the top timbers and reverse angle-irons of the partial bulkhead by curved angle-iron futtocks.

Keelsons.—One main keelson of $\frac{10}{16}$-inch iron, 3¾ feet high, continuous fore and aft, cutting through all floor plates, riveted to the latter with 3 by 4 by $\frac{6}{16}$ angle-iron clips, and stayed to them on each side by channel-iron struts, riveted to the floor plate and the vertical clip. The foot of the main keelson is fastened to the keel and gutter plate by angle-irons 4 by 4 by $\frac{7}{16}$ inches; the upper edge is stiffened by reverse angle-irons 3 by 4 inches, riveted on each side, flat flanges uppermost. There are three side keelsons on each side of the main keelson, spaced 4½ feet apart, and corresponding in height to the main keelson. They support the deck of the double bottom, and allow of

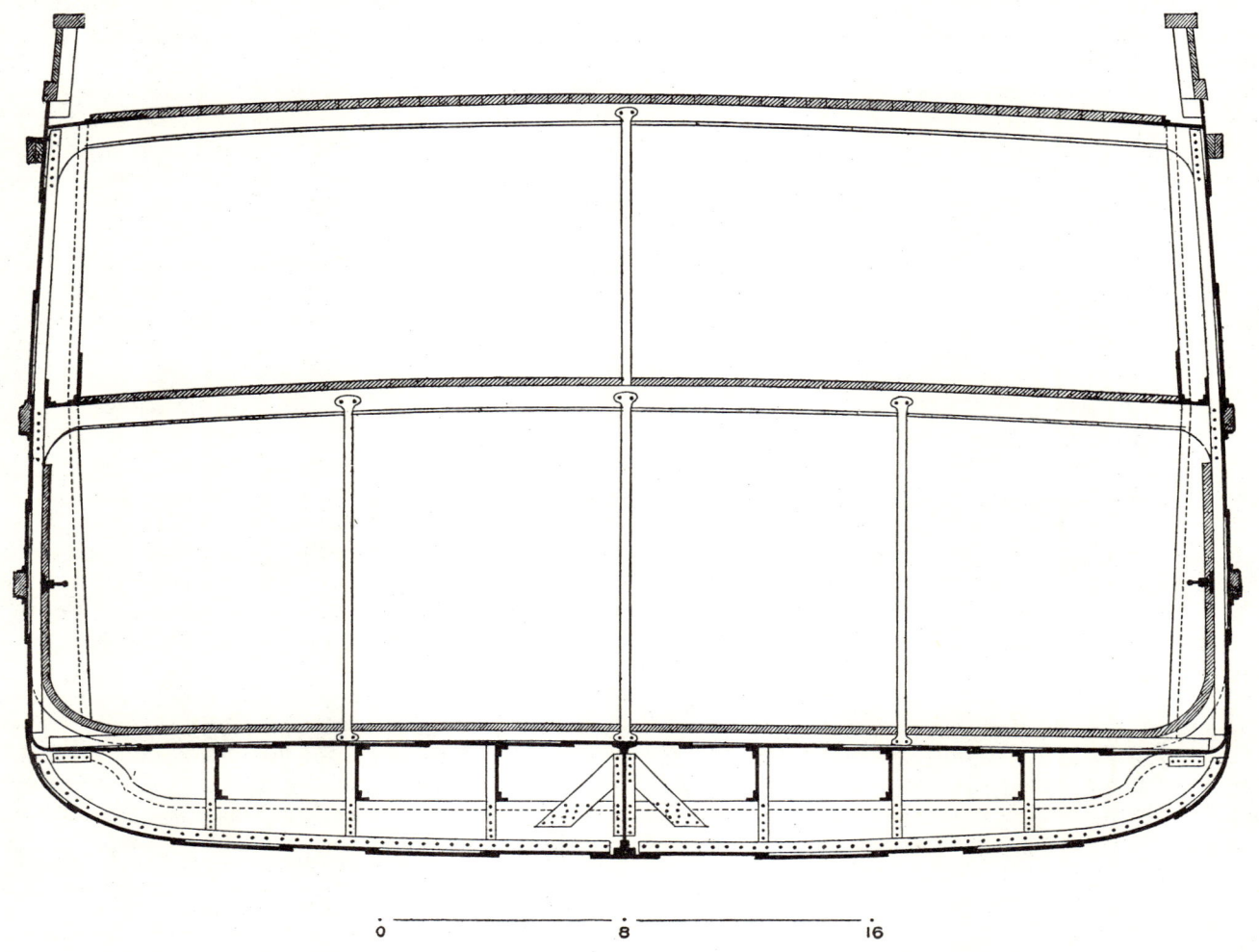

Fig. 67.—MIDSHIP SECTION OF AN IRON PROPELLER, NORTHERN LAKES.

Built by the Globe iron works at Cleveland, Ohio, in 1881–'82. Length over all, 302½ feet; breadth, 39 feet; molded depth, 25 feet; displacement on 14 feet draught, 3,714 tons.

a crown of about 3 inches in the double bottom. Side keelsons of $\frac{6}{16}$-inch plate, fitted intercostally riveted to a vertical angle-iron 3 by 3 inches at each floor plate, the angle-iron reaching to the top of the keelson, and also to a continuous horizontal angle-iron, same size, which is laid upon and fastened to the top edges of the floor plates. One angle-iron, 3 by 3 inches, along the upper edges of the side keelsons.

The double bottom, or water-ballast deck, extends from the collision bulkhead to the engine bulkhead, with a capacity for 700 tons of water. It is divided into 6 compartments by transverse bulkheads. The deck of this bottom is of ¼-inch iron plates, 4½ feet wide, laid in fore-and-aft streaks, the center of each streak laid on one of the keelsons, and the edges riveted and water-tight. The edges of the plates next the sides of the vessel cut through the frames, curl upward, and lap 6 inches between the edges of two streaks of outer plating, the rivets of that seam going through the three thicknesses of plate. By this device and the angle-iron futtocks within the double bottom is firmly united to the rest of the ship. Angle-iron floor frames are laid across this deck of the double bottom, and upon them is laid a floor of 1-inch white pine, and on that a floor of 2-inch oak plank, breaking joints with the pine. The lower hold is ceiled on the sides also in this manner.

Plating—Out and in; $\frac{9}{16}$ of an inch from keel to the lower deck; then ½ inch; sheer streak, $\frac{5}{8}$ inch, rising one foot above the upper deck beams.

Beams.—Lower deck, bulb **T**-iron, 10 inches deep, with angle-irons 3½ by 6 forming the flanges. Upper deck, bulb **T**-iron, 8 inches deep. Stanchions to lower deck, 3¼ inches in diameter; upper deck, 2¾ inches.

IRON VESSELS.

Stringers.—Hold stringer on frames half-way between bilge and deck beams, bulb ⊥-iron, 10 inches deep, with angle-irons 3½ by 6 for the upper flanges. Flat stringer plate on ends of lower deck beams, 18 inches wide, $\frac{7}{16}$ inch thick; vertical plate 12 inches wide, $\frac{7}{16}$ thick on frames, the two plates united with 3 by 3 iron in the angle. Broad stringer plate of $\frac{5}{8}$-inch iron on the upper deck beam ends. Tie plates on lower deck beams, $\frac{7}{16}$ by 12 inches.

Decking.—White pine, 4 by 6 inches on the lower deck, 3½ by 6 on the upper.

Fenders.—Three in number, one at the 9-foot water line, oak, 5 by 8 inches square, held between 3- by 3-inch angle-irons, one opposite the lower deck, oak, 5 by 8 inches, held between 3- by 4-inch angle-irons, and one, 8 by 10 inches, at the upper deck, fastened to the sheer streak.

Boilers.—Two, 8¾ feet in diameter, 18 feet long, tested to carry 100 pounds of steam.

Engines.—Compound, with 30- and 56-inch cylinders and 4 feet stroke, acting on cranks at right angles to each other, placed away aft. Two double hoisting engines on the spar deck to handle freight. Duplex steam-pump for water ballast, double-cylinder steam steering apparatus, and steam windlass.

Miscellaneous.—Transverse bulkheads, iron coal bunkers, iron house on deck over the boilers. A wooden cabin aft for crew, and another cabin in the bow for the captain and mates, with pilot-house above. Three masts.

From 150 to 175 tons weight are added to the vessel by the double bottom.

In Chicago there has never been much of anything done in the way of iron-ship building, or, indeed, in any other branch of the general industry, except repairing. In 1881, however, an iron tug was constructed at the yard of the Dredging and Dock Company, the first in the city. A Norwegian who had had some experience in iron-ship yards in his own country was employed to superintend, and a few mechanics were brought from Norway to do the work. The boat was 77 feet long on the keel, 88 feet over all, 18 feet beam, and 11 feet deep, and the model was that of the ordinary keel tug-boat. The ship-yard plant was very simple, and comprised only a rough shed, a furnace or two, a steam-engine, a frame-bending plate, and a few drills. The lack of a punching machine was supplied by hand-work and a steam reamer and drill. This handy tool, not yet generally used in American yards, was worked by a light wire rope running out from the shed, and was taken from place to place in the tug wherever rivet holes had to be bored and countersunk. The tug cost complete about $22,000. While the dredging company built the boat for its own use, the intention is to develop a business in iron-vessel building when the times warrant an effort in that direction.

The principal iron-ship yard of the lakes is at Wyandotte, Michigan, a short distance below Detroit. This yard was established in 1870 by Frank E. Kirby, C. E., formerly of the Allaire works, in New York city, for Captain E. B. Ward, who had been making Bessemer steel at Wyandotte ten or twelve years before, and who had on hand a lot of the old steel ingots when the yard was started. Three vessels were built, and the business was then interrupted by the panic of 1873. In 1877 the yard passed into the ownership of the Detroit Dry Dock Company, and it has ever since been actively engaged in the production of iron tonnage under Mr. Kirby's superintendency, 13 vessels having been built down to 1882, all steamers. The following is a list of the boats built:

1871. Propeller E. B. Ward, jr., iron, of 388 tons, 150 feet long, 26 feet beam, and 14 feet deep; now owned at New Orleans and employed for towing.

1873. Tug Sport, steel, of 45 tons, 65 feet long, 14 feet beam, 9½ feet deep, molded; worth $10,000, and owned at Grand Haven, Michigan.

1873. Side-wheel steamboat Queen of the Lakes, iron, now owned on some inland lake.

1878. Side-wheel steamer City of Detroit, composite, of 1,094 tons and 600 nominal horse-power, 240 feet long, 36 feet beam, 14 feet deep-molded; worth $145,000, and owned at Detroit.

1879. Side-wheeler Idlewild, iron, of 312 tons, 140 feet long, 26 feet beam, 10 feet deep, molded; worth $40,000.

1880. Propeller City of Cleveland, iron, of 1,221 tons and 1,800 horse-power, 225 feet long, 32 feet beam, 14 feet deep, molded; worth $155,000, owned in Detroit.

1880. Side-wheel car-ferry Transport, iron, of 1,595 tons and 2,000 nominal horse-power, 265 feet long, 46 feet beam, 79 feet wide over all 17 feet deep, molded, with three railroad tracks on deck. About 120 feet of the boat amidships had a straight body. Boat worth $180,000. Experience with a previous wooden transfer boat, 280 feet long, that cost $230,000, led the Michigan Central Railroad Company to decide in favor of iron for future boats. The Transport was plated with ¾-inch iron all over.

1880. Propeller Boston, iron, of 1,829 tons and 750 nominal horse-power, 280 feet long over all, 265 feet long molded, 36 feet beam, and 17 feet deep, molded; worth $170,000.

1880. Propeller Lehigh, of the Anchor Line, iron, of 1,704 tons, 255 feet long over all, 36 feet beam, 17 feet deep, molded; worth $155,000.

1880. Propeller Brunswick, iron, of 1,120 tons, 5 feet shorter than the Lehigh.

1881. Propeller Clarion, iron, of 1,712 tons, 255 feet long over all, 36 feet beam, 17 feet deep, molded; worth $155,000.

1881. Propeller City of Milwaukee, iron, of 1,148 tons; worth $150,000.

1881–'82. Propellers Michigan and Wisconsin, iron, with double bottoms 3 feet deep (the first of their class at this yard), 230 feet long over all, 34 feet beam, and 14 feet deep, molded, and housed on the upper deck the whole length of the vessel.

A representative laker is the Boston, a fine steamer, carrying 83,000 bushels of wheat or about 2,600 tons of cargo on 15 feet draught of water at a speed of 12 miles per hour. The principal data of her scantling are:

Keel.—Flat plate, 33 inches wide, ¾ inch thick for 200 feet amidships, tapering to ½ inch at the ends.

Stem.—Hammered scrap iron in one length, size at top 2¼ by 6 inches, increasing to 2¼ by 8 at the load water-line, and tapering thence away to 2½ by 4.

Frames.—Angle-iron 3 by 4 inches, 9 pounds to the foot, spaced 20 inches. Reverse angles 3 by 3, 8 pounds to the foot, lapping on the floor plates 3 inches and on the frame angle-irons 2½ inches, going on alternate frames to the top height and to the lower deck. A doubling piece of 3 by 3 inch angle, 8 pounds to the foot, on the top edge of the floor plates opposite the reverse angle-irons, going through a score in the keelson plate, and riveted through the floor plate and reverse angle-iron.

Center keelson.—Vertical plate, 21 inches deep over the keel, ½ inch thick.

Floor plates.—Molded at the thwart 21 inches, at the ends 13 inches, ½ inch thick amidships, $\frac{7}{16}$ inch at the ends of the vessel, connected to the keelson plate by 3 by 3 inch angle-iron.

Main keelson.—Vertical plate, 10 inches deep, ½ inch thick, connected to a 26 by $\frac{9}{16}$ inch gutter plate by double angle-irons 3½ by 3½ inch, 10 pounds to the foot, with 3 by 3 inch double angle-irons on the top edge.

Sister keelsons.—Intercostal of $\frac{9}{16}$-inch plates, connected to the floors, and with double angle-irons 3½ by 6 inches, 12 pounds, on the floors the entire length of the vessel.

Bilge keelsons.—Double angle-irons 3½ by 6 inches, 12 pounds, placed back to back.

Beams.—T-bulb iron 9 inches deep, 25 pounds to the foot, on alternate frames; hold beams, channel iron, 8 inches deep, 25 pounds.

Stringers.—Main deck 48 inches wide, $\frac{9}{16}$ inch thick, tapered in width and thickness toward the ends. Hold 16 inches wide, $\frac{9}{16}$ inch thick amidships. Ties on main deck 12 by ⅝ inches amidships, with plate of the same athwartships on each side of the hatches.

Plating.—Worked in fair lines, in and out strakes, garboards ¾ inch; bottom, the same; bilge plates, ⅝ inch; sides of the vessel, ½ inch; sheer streak, $\frac{9}{16}$, then $\frac{8}{16}$, at the ends ½ inch; width amidships, 54 inches, worked 12 inches above the beams of the deck. Butts and laps double riveted; sheer streak amidships triple rivets.

Bulkheads.—Five in number, of ⅜-inch iron below the 14-foot water-line, $\frac{5}{16}$ inch above, stayed vertically on one side by 3 by 4 inch 8 pound angle-iron, spaced 3 feet, and horizontally on the other side by angle-irons every 5 feet. Coal-bunkers of 5 pound plate, stiffened with T-iron.

Wood work.—The main deck is housed by means of 5 by 6 inch oak stanchions fastened to the sheer streak, set 30 inches from center to center, and passing through a white-oak main rail 5 by 16 inches. Pine carlines are thrown across, the sides are boarded up with white pine, and the top or spar-deck is planked with 2¼ inch decking. Main-deck plank, white pine, 3⅞ inches thick; hatch coamings, white oak. Three white-oak fenders on each side of the vessel. Flooring of hold, two thicknesses of 1-inch pine boards, the bilge covered with 2-inch pine and the sides of the hold with 1-inch pine. One pine mast forward.

On the whole, it can be reported that the building of iron and steel vessels has made sufficient progress in the United States to have created the plant and trained the labor for producing sailing and steam craft for the merchant service of every description and of any size. No facilities exist for rolling and shaping armor-plates of the great thickness now required for iron-clads, but the merchant service is well provided for, and the industry is growing in spite of the high cost of American labor and materials. New yards are continually coming into existence, the general development of American industry is reducing the cost of materials, and the use of machinery is reducing the expenditures for labor upon vessels. The competition in rival yards is lessening the margin of profit for which their proprietors are willing to build, and the tendency is all in the direction of favoring the substitution of iron or steel tonnage in place of wooden. The total quantity of iron yearly consumed by the industry is not large, and should Congress provide the way for placing the American builder on a par with the European builder so far as the cost of iron and steel is concerned it seems probable that the tendency toward the more modern class of tonnage would be greatly accelerated. This industry is a valuable one, nationally, in many important particulars. It robs the country of none of its resources. The exportation of grain, cotton, and tobacco is the shipping away of so many thousand tons of the best constituents of American soil, and the construction of wooden tonnage destroys the forests. There are other industries which effect changes for the benefit of this generation for which future generations will have to pay. Iron-ship building appears to inflict no injury so far as consumption of materials is concerned, and it is a department of activity which employs a greater proportion of human labor to the value of material used than almost any other which can be named.

Chapter VI.—CANAL-BOATS.

Government classification of merchant tonnage is determined by the motive power of the vessels. There are three classes in all—sailing, steam, and unrigged vessels. The latter forms a large and important element in all statistical reports as well as in the ship-building industry, and includes canal-boats, flat-boats, and river barges. The total register capacity of the present fleet of these vessels is larger than is commonly known (because barges and canal-boats are exempt from registration now), and the following is an approximate statement for the year 1880:

Class of vessel.	No. owned in the United States.	Register tonnage.	Value.
Steam	5,139	1,221,207	$80,192,495
Sail	16,820	2,366,133	59,152,950
Unrigged	16,697	2,899,970	16,439,264

It has been convenient to speak of barges and flat-boats in connection with river steamboats, and it only remains to speak of canal-boats, which comprise about one-half of the whole unrigged tonnage. Owing to the rapid growth of railroads the canal system of the country has been somewhat overshadowed in late years. In New England the canals have been superseded, and in one or two cases have been used as the bed of the railroads that took their place. In the middle states a few small and a few branch canals have been given up. However, many important routes still remain in existence in New York, Pennsylvania, New Jersey, Ohio, Illinois, Maryland, and Virginia; some have been enlarged and supplied with a new and superior class of boats, and their resources have been thoroughly utilized. The cheapness of transportation has rendered them valuable to the commercial world, and there has been a great deal of legislation looking toward their preservation, maintenance, and extension.

The population supported by the barges of the United States is not known, but those that live by canal-boat navigation now number about 40,000. Counting those who attend to the locks and keep the canals in order, the number is about 60,000, which is equal to that of the persons engaged in the coasting trade of the United States. The boats numbered 8,771 in 1880, having a register capacity of 1,253,688 tons, and being worth $8,273,255.

NEW YORK STATE CANALS.

The Delaware and Hudson canal, belonging to a company of that name, extends 108 miles from Honesdale, Pennsylvania, to Rondout, New York, on the Hudson river, coming down to the river via Esopus creek, and averages 48 feet wide at the top and 32 feet on the bottom, with 6 feet of water. In 1870 there were 879 boats on this canal, all employed in the transportation of coal from the mines to the river. About a million tons are moved yearly. Coming down from the mines, the boats lie alongside of a wharf in the middle of the creek at Rondout, where the coal is taken out by steam-hoisting apparatus and dumped in immense mounds on the wharf. There are 45 derricks for hoisting coal on the wharf, all operated by one line of shafting, which supplies the power. More than 240 boats are often lying at or near this wharf at one time. The boats all rendezvous at Rondout. There are eight yards at Rondout devoted to canal work, having among them one dry-dock and nine sets of canal railways of four rails each for taking boats out of water. The company has its own yard here, at which it both builds and repairs, and in the census year 42 boats were constructed. The other yards do not often make canal-boats, but prefer to contract for the various classes of barges used in freighting on the Hudson river and Long Island sound, such as coal-barges, ice-barges, boats for cement and brick, and tugs. The barges are either scows or double-end framed boats from 90 to 130 feet in length and 26 to 34 feet on the beam, and the ice-boats have deckhouses the entire length. When not engaged in building the private yards in Rondout are busy repairing; in fact, this latter occupation forms the bulk of their business. New boats are built at the company's yard and at private yards in the country, chiefly at Ellenville, Phillipsport, Port Benjamin, and Alligerville, New York, and Honesdale and Hawley, Pennsylvania. In ordinary years there are from 50 to 70 boats built at these country yards.

The Delaware and Hudson model is what would be called sharp at both ends, and though rather full, it is sharp for a canal-boat. The floor is flat clear fore and aft. There is a deck in the bow and one in the stern of the boat, with a little cabin, 6 feet fore and aft, in the stern. The body of the boat is not decked, but is covered, when necessary, with hatches. The details of construction are prescribed by the company. The boats are 91 feet long from face of stem to outside of stern, $14\frac{1}{6}$ feet beam, and 6 feet deep; sheer, 15 inches forward, 8 inches aft. The scantling is as follows:

Bilge log.—Hard wood, 10 by 10 inches, with 4½ foot scarf, bolted with ⅝-inch screw bolts. Under the stem- and stern-posts the logs are connected with a strong knee.

Keel.—None; only a heavy garboard.

Floor timbers.—Hard wood, 4 by 5 inches square, spaced 18 inches, let into the bilge log 4 inches. Side timbers white oak, 4 by 5 inches, let into the bilge log 4 inches, spaced 18 inches, but set in the center of the floor-frame spaces; spaced 13 inches in the bow and 15 inches in the stern; side timbers straight.

Keelson.—Oak or yellow pine, 7 by 10 inches square, bolted with ⅝-inch iron.

Stem- and stern-posts.—White oak 8 by 16 and 13 inches, each with a knee on the keelson, and each with 3-inch knight-heads. The stem rises 10 inches above deck.

Clamps.—Oak, white pine, or yellow pine, 3 by 14 inches, in long lengths, three spikes and one ⅝-inch bolt riveted on a ring in each timber.

Braces.—Main, oak or pine, 4 by 12 inches, 32 feet long, butting under the midship beam under the clamps, the lower ends resting on the bilge log fore and aft; reverse braces, oak or yellow pine, 4 by 9 inches, two each of the following lengths, 18, 17, 15, 12, and 9 feet, and a brace 5 by 7 inches and 12 feet long, to fit the stem and upper breast-hook, heeling on the keelson.

Beams.—Eight of them white oak, 5 by 8 inches; forward beam, 7 feet from stem; forward cabin beam, 11 feet from stem-post; after-cabin beam, 6 feet from stern-post, the other five beams equally spaced amidships; hanging knees sided 5 inches; carlines of oak 3 by 8 inches.

Decks.—Two-inch white pine.

Plank-sheer.—Oak or yellow pine, 2 by 11 inches

Ceiling of floor.—Two-inch hemlock.

Planking.—Bottom, 2-inch hard wood, with 4½- by $\frac{5}{16}$-inch spikes in each timber; sides, 2-inch oak or yellow pine, 7 inches wide, increasing to 2½ and 3 inches in thickness on the walls.

Breast-hooks.—Oak, sided 6 inches, with braces, two forward, two aft.

Narrow wash-board deck along the gunwales, with white-oak coaming 4 by 9 inches square, and a high coaming of oak or yellow pine bolted on top of that 3 by 8 inches. Hatches made of 1-inch white pine.

Bitts.—Oak windlass bitts forward, and three oak timber heads, 5 by 10 inches, on each side of the boat, fastened to the sides with ⅝-inch bolts.

Railings.—Aft, oak, 3 by 4 inches, placed edgewise, and resting on 2- by 3-inch chocks, 8 inches long; forward, 14 feet long, 2 by 3 at bow, 2 by 2 at after end, bent round to the curve of the bow and bolted.

Rudder.—Stock, oak, 8 by 12 inches, with 5 iron bands; blade, 6½ feet long, 5 feet wide, 2 inches thick, with batten 2 inches thick and 8 inches wide from after upper corner to heel of stock; batten a foot wide on inboard end; blade cut so as to allow 10 inches drop to rudder.

Guards at stern.—White oak, 5 inches thick, 20 inches wide at stern-post near plank-sheer, supported with 6 knees or chocks, strongly bolted around the curve of the stern with ⅝-inch iron; stern plank, 6 feet long, 5 by 10 inches, to be let into stern-post and run over and fastened to guard; bumper, 8 by 14 inch oak, to butt the stern plank and guard, strongly bolted; a bar of iron, 4 inches wide, to extend around the guard and bumper, 5 feet each side, and to be continued around to the sides of the boat, with bars 2½ inches wide.

Fenders.—Forward, four on each side, oak, 3 by 4 inches, 14 feet long, bent around the curve of the bow and fastened through the planking into the timbers by 7-inch spikes; irons, 2½ inches wide, ½ inch thick on the fenders, and 14 feet long, fastened with spikes with countersunk heads.

Bilge irons.—Three on each side, both forward and aft, 3 inches by ½ inch, not less than 14 feet long, fastened with spikes with countersunk heads.

Stem iron.—Four inches wide, ¾ inch thick, extending from the after side of the stem at the head over the head and down the fore side of the stem, and under the bottom of the boat 2 feet, fastened with 6-inch round spikes, with countersunk heads, 8 inches apart.

Cabin.—White pine, with berths under the stern deck, and roofed with 2-inch white-pine decking.

Paint.—Two coats on the top sides, and over beams, decks, cabins, coamings, etc. Below water, graved with hot tar.

It requires about 21,000 feet of timber to build a boat, viz: 10,500 feet of oak or yellow pine, 5,800 feet of hard wood, 3,200 feet of hemlock, and 1,600 feet of white pine; also 3,800 pounds of iron, 100 pounds of oakum, and 2¼ barrels of pitch and tar. Each boat carries 130 tons of coal. The cost of one in 1880 was about $1,200. The company encourages the building of boats by accepting those built at private yards, assigning them to boatmen at a rating of $1,500 apiece and then employing them on the canal. About $20 is deducted from the freight money earned on each trip; from the remainder the boatman pays interest, running expenses, and living. He can pay for his boat in about six years, meanwhile having earned his support, and then has a boat which is good for from four to six years longer as his own property. A good feeling exists between the men and the company. Both parties make money, and between them they maintain a building and repairing industry which is of considerable local value. In all there are about 25 yards on the canal, producing yearly about 50 or 60 boats and doing about $100,000 of repair work. In 1880 the company had $540,000 invested in boats and barges, ten of the latter carrying 560 tons each.

In the northern part of the state of New York the yards build boats suitable only for the Erie canal, save those on the Black River canal, which is one of the branches of the Erie, and is the one of least capacity. The Erie canal is 365½ miles in length, extending from Albany, on the Hudson river, to Buffalo, on lake Erie. The average prism is 70 feet wide across the top and 52½ feet across the bottom, with 7 feet depth of water, allowing a draught of 6 feet for loaded boats. The locks are 110 feet long and 18 feet wide. The canal, completed in October, 1825, and opened for business in 1826, now gives employment to 4,350 canal-boats, 18,000 horses and mules, and about 20,000 men. The speed of the boats is limited to 4 miles per hour, but with horses moving at a walk, and with the detentions at the numerous locks of the canal, boatmen think they do well if they average 2 miles. The large boats each carry from 7,600 to 7,800 bushels of wheat, or 240 tons of coal, on one trip, or from 160,000 to 170,000 feet of lumber. To the length of the main line of the Erie canal must be added the 155 miles of Hudson River navigation to New York city and the length of the branches of the Erie which still remain in use. Some of these branches have been abandoned within the last five years as being of small capacity and having a commerce insufficient to warrant the expense of maintaining them; but there are still in operation the Champlain canal, connecting Albany with lake Champlain, 66 miles long; the Black River branch from the Erie at Rome, 78 miles long; the Cayuga and Seneca canal, 25 miles; the Oswego canal, 38 miles; the Oneida River improvement, 20 miles; also a part of the Chemung canal, 23 miles, although officially abandoned. There are several lakes in central New York, each about 40 miles long, which are navigated by canal-boats, and are virtually branches of the canal, namely, Oneida, Cayuga, and Seneca. The total of canal navigation of the Erie system thus amounts to about 860 miles. Before the war there were navigating these waters from 2,200 to 3,500 horse-boats, the number fluctuating with the activity of trade, the clearances varying from 80,000 to 104,000 a year. New boats were built in different years as follows:

	Tons.
1844	378
1846	477
1847	1,466
1848	457
1849	215
1850	152
1851	213
1853	590
1854	760
1858	255

During and since the war trade between the West and the East has grown enormously in volume, owing to the large exportation of grain and provisions which has been developed, and in consequence all the transportation lines from the West to the sea-coast have been crowded with traffic and the business of the Erie canal has about doubled. The number of boats built yearly is about 600. Owing to the large size of the modern boats the number of clearances is not so large as formerly, although the traffic has doubled. In 1880 the clearances were about 70,000.

The Black River canal was originally little more than a feeder upon which the Erie depended for a supply of water; but of late years the lumbermen, who are busily at work in the outskirts of the Adirondack region cutting spruce, hemlock, and hard wood, have found this branch a valuable route for getting their product down to market, and it has grown in importance. Every year during the warm months large rafts of lumber in the log are towed down by teams of horses, and some of the stuff is shipped by boat. The boats are small, bluff-bowed, carrying 90 tons each on 4 feet of water, and cost about $1,100 each. Not more than 10 or 15 are made yearly. There is no oak or white pine of any consequence in the region, and what is used of that kind of timber comes by way of the Erie canal from the West. Builders use the native lumber, hemlock and hard wood, as much as possible. Hemlock costs no more than $7 and $8 per thousand feet; spruce, $9 or $10, sawed.

In the lake Champlain region a large tonnage of canal-boats is employed in the business of the lake, and the principal freighting is done in carriers of that class. Iron ore comes down from Port Henry and lumber from the Canadian markets, both going to Troy, Albany, New York, and other points along the Hudson river and westward on the Erie canal. Steam tugs bring the boats down the lake, and they are then sent through the canal to the Hudson river by teams of mules and horses and forwarded on down the river in fleets drawn by tugs and side-wheel tow-boats. June 1, 1880, the following tonnage was enrolled and licensed in the district, every boat liable to trade to Canada being documented:

	No.	Tonnage.
Canal-boats	510	40,175
Schooners	27	1,730
Wooden steamboats and tugs	10	912
Iron steamboats and tugs	2	137
Barges	5	353
Total	554	43,307

The building points are Fort Ann, Ticonderoga, Whitehall, Essex, Crown Point, and Champlain, and there is one yard at each place, about 90 men being employed in all. The yearly product is about 90 boats, worth from $2,500 to $3,000 each, and registering from 110 to 125 tons. They are of the regular Erie canal pattern. At the Ticonderoga yard the owners build for themselves. In 1880 they had from $50,000 to $75,000 invested in canal-boats. They were preparing to put about $30,000 more into 15 new boats in 1881. Their craft are each 98 feet long, $17\frac{1}{4}$ feet wide on the floor, $17\frac{2}{3}$ feet on the beam, and 8 feet deep, decked, and carry 150 tons on 4 feet and 250 tons on 6 feet draught.

On the Oswego Branch canal, running from the Erie canal to lake Ontario at Oswego, there are 10 yards, employing about 60 men, building a few boats every year, and doing a good business in repairing. These boats are of the largest sizes, and the harbor at Oswego is always full of them. They take part in the grain, the coal, and the lumber trade, and a large number of them, being engaged in the foreign trade, are enrolled and licensed at the Oswego custom-house. The fee for measurement is about $12 per boat.

On the Erie canal proper there are 80 yards scattered all along the way from Albany to Buffalo, employing an average of about 1,200 men for ten months in the year and producing from 300 to 400 boats yearly, while also enjoying a large business in repairing the 4,350 boats owned on the canal and its branches. In the early years from 1825 to 1860 timber was abundant in all the counties through which the route ran, and building and repairing were both well diffused along the course of the canal; but the land has now been cleared off and brought under a high state of cultivation, oak, pine, and hard wood are scarce and dear in many counties, and the result is, that while all the yards do a certain amount of repairing business the building of new boats is tending to concentrate in Rochester, Lockport, Tonawanda, and Buffalo, where timber can be obtained from the West at relatively lower prices than on the eastern portions of the canal.

The little old-time shapely boats with good bows, carrying 30 tons of cargo on about 3 feet draught of water and moving along briskly in tow of two or three horses, are now no longer seen on the Erie canal. The smallest of the horse-boats are the few that come down from the Black River branch, or those which occasionally stray up into this part of the state from Rondout, each carrying from 90 to 130 tons of freight; but where there is one of these boats there are a hundred of the class belonging to the Erie canal proper, large, heavy, almost box-shaped craft, bearing from 200 to 250 tons of goods on 6 feet of water and moving slowly along in tow of two horses. One of the old fashions was to build canal-boats with square, raking ends, and it was only abandoned in 1855 upon the peremptory command of the state authorities, issued to prevent them from injuring each other with their sharp corners. A regulation was adopted in May of that year forbidding any new boat to navigate the canals of the state unless it should have a round or elliptical bow, described with a radius of not less than $8\tfrac{2}{3}$ feet. In order to give a boat all the capacity the law will allow, builders sweep in the curve of the bow with just about that radius, cutting off the sterns abruptly, so that the cubical contents come within 10 per cent. of that of a perfectly square box. It is only since steam has been introduced into canal-boats that bows and sterns have been given a better shape, but the sharper form is still confined to steam craft entirely.

A good canal-boat (Fig. 68) ought to last fifteen years, but it must be taken care of; the majority disappear in about ten years. On the other hand, there are plenty of boats running that are from twenty to thirty-four years old, well built of choice materials in the first place, and well taken care of by their owners since.

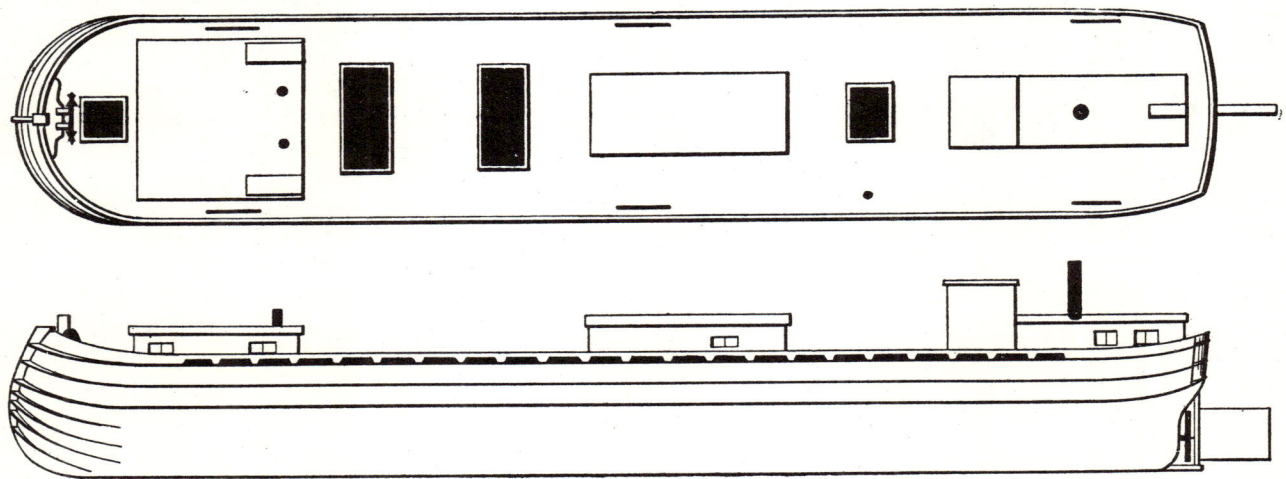

Fig. 68.—Steam canal-boat, Erie canal.

98 feet long, $17\tfrac{3}{8}$ feet wide, and 10 feet deep. The hull is that of a laker, and represents the general style of the decked boats of the Erie canal.

A great many different varieties of boats are run on the Erie canal, all of them being specimens of four principal types, namely, the scow, the laker, the bull-head, and the steam canal-boat.

The scow is a straight, open boat, sometimes framed, but usually with solid sides, built up of white-pine logs 5 inches thick and from 12 to 14 inches wide, scarfed, closely fitted together and fastened by long iron rods or bolts $\tfrac{1}{2}$, $\tfrac{3}{4}$, or 1 inch in diameter, spaced from 16 to 19 inches, according to the fancy of the builder, driven clear through from the topmost "gunwale" to the bottom of the bilge log. The sides are made on wooden horses and fastened, and are then raised to a perpendicular position with a derrick, and the sheer is given by a log properly trimmed. The floor is made by placing single frame timbers across the boat 4 by 6 inches square, spaced about 12 inches, perfectly straight, letting the ends into the bilge log, and planking the bottom with oak or hard wood. About six stout oak beams are fitted in at equal distances apart to strengthen the top of the boat. A short, round, smooth bow is put on by setting up 4-inch frame timbers, molded to the proper curvature, and planking them horizontally from side to side. Four iron bands or straps are spiked upon the fore foot, connecting the bow with the bottom. The stern is short, round, and regularly framed. There are usually a small deck forward, a narrow wash-board along the gunwales, and a small cabin with steering deck aft. Windlass bitts are fitted into the extreme bow, and a small house is built there for the stable, a necessary feature of a horse canal-boat; for while one team of horses is towing the boat, another team must be quartered on board feeding and resting. Three light strips of iron are fastened to each side above water for fenders. Scows are now 98 feet long over all, 17⅔ feet beam, and 9 or 10 feet deep on the side, and weigh from 40 to 45 tons, and will carry 240 tons of cargo each, or from 160,000 to 180,000 feet of lumber, on 6 feet draught of water. They register from 102 to 118 tons. Originally small and built like flatboats, they have grown in size with every enlargement of the locks of the canal and depth of the channel until they have reached the dimensions given. Scows are best adapted for carrying coal, lumber, barrels of apples, and goods not easily damaged by the weather. They are sometimes framed, and when so built are usually ceiled on a plan calculated to give longitudinal strength. The ceiling is put on in curved lines, the foot of each curve touching the bilge log and the arc rising in the center. Over this ceiling is another, about four streaks of plank wide, the center of the arc touching the bilge log amidships and the ends rising to the gunwale at the bow and stern. But few of this style of boats are now built, the "scow side" of solid logs being the preference. It requires from 325 to 400 days of labor to build a scow, and about 18,000 feet of white pine and 10,000 feet of oak, and 3,500 pounds of round iron, 2,000 pounds of flat bar iron, 1,500 pounds of spikes, and 600 pounds of castings, or nearly 4 tons of iron; but some builders fasten more strongly and use from 4½ to 5 tons. The cost of a scow is from $2,600 to $2,800, varying with the times; it varies also with the extent to which it is decked over. The scow proper is an open boat, but is sometimes one-quarter decked over and sometimes half decked.

The laker is a regularly-framed boat, with perfectly flat bottom, square bilge, perpendicular sides, straight body, round bow and stern, and decked entirely over. It is made of oak and white pine, but if hard wood can be obtained in the locality the latter is used in the bottom planking, as it wears smoother. Sometimes the laker is made with scow sides, but molded at bow and stern, a boat thus built being four or five hundred dollars cheaper. Nevertheless the preference is for a framed boat. The lake boat has about the same dimensions as the other boats of the Erie canal, but is deeper than the scow, and it is 97 or 98 feet long, 17½ or 17⅔ feet beam, and 10 or 10½ feet in depth of side. The scantling varies slightly with the fancy of the builder or the stuff which he can buy to advantage, but a fair description of the laker as built in large yards is as follows:

Stem- and stern-posts.—Oak, with 2-inch oak plank aprons; stem, 13 by 14 inches at the head.

Keel.—None, only a heavy garboard plank.

Frames.—Floor timbers oak, single, 3 by 8 inches, 17 feet long, or clear across the boat, spaced 15 inches; side timbers, 3 by 5 inches, 10 feet long, joined to the floors by two sawed knees or futtocks, which are about 2 feet long, a foot wide, and 2 inches thick; bow and stern frames heavier, about 4 by 10 inches.

Keelsons.—Main, oak, 10 by 12 inches square, bolted into every floor; bilge keelson, 2 by 12 inches. It is not uncommon to use sticks from 75 to 80 feet in length.

Beams.—Chestnut, when practicable, 5 inches square, with carlines 2¼ by 5 inches.

Planking.—Oak, 2 inches thick.

Ceiling.—On floor, 1¼-inch white pine; clamps, 2- and 3-inch white oak.

Decking.—White pine, 2 inches thick.

Rail.—A narrow strip of 3-inch oak, resting on thin chocks, in all about 6 inches high. In the bow there is a strong oak chock, 15 inches high and 10 inches thick, running around on the gunwale to the straight body and tapering to 6 inches high, and the same in the stern.

Houses.—One forward for horses, with hatch on top and on side to the deck; one away aft for boatman and his family, rising about 2 feet above the deck-way to allow for windows; all of white pine.

Breast-hooks.—Two in bow and 2 in stern, strongly braced.

Fenders.—Oak, about 7 in number, butting on the stem- and stern-posts, and running around the curve of the bow and stern to the flat of the sides, spiked on, and ironed on the outer surface with 3- by ⅜-inch straps. The fenders are spread apart as they go around the curve, so that the lower ones protect the bilge. There are three wearing streaks along the top sides, being thick streaks of planking, ironed with half-round bars the whole length, 1½ or 1¾ inches wide. Two other straps of light iron are placed on the rail, on the outer and inner edges respectively.

Stern.—Overhang about 2 feet, enough to house the rudder-stock. There are two strong fenders or guards of oak across the overhang at the upper and lower edges of the perpendicular face, being a continuation of wearing pieces around the stern of the boat. They are about 15 inches wide and faced with iron. Between them the stern is usually pierced with a window. A strong chock above the upper guard, on which is painted the name of the boat.

Rudder.—Stock, about 10 inches in diameter; blade, 7 or 8 by 5 feet.

A lake boat, or laker, requires the following materials: 18,000 feet of oak and hard wood, from 20,000 to 22,000 feet of white pine and chestnut, 5,800 pounds of bolts, spikes, and nails, from 1,500 to 2,000 pounds of flat iron, 600 pounds of castings, 10 or 12 barrels of salt, $90 worth of paints and oils, and $50 worth of oakum. From 450 to 500 days of labor are required to complete a boat, and, as labor was $1 75 and $2 a day in 1880, the labor bill on a laker amounted to from $900 to $1,025. These boats are well salted in the bow and stern, on the floor timbers and top sides, register from 125 to 139 tons, weigh from 65 to 72 tons, and carry from 225 to 240 tons of cargo. They are usually painted white, and the stern is often profusely ornamented by a sign-painter, the name and home port being conspicuously painted in gilt and red and blue letters. About one-half of the boats on the Erie canal are of this type. Being good for almost any service, these boats are dispatched with cargoes to points on the small lakes in central New York, and often across lake Ontario and on long voyages on lake Champlain, and are popularly used in forwarding grain from Buffalo and Oswego to New York city via the canal and the Hudson river. Their tight decks and high hatch coamings, covered with tightly fitted hatch covers, protect their cargoes from the wash of an occasional wave. The boats cost an average of about $3,800, varying from $3,700 to $4,200.

The bull-head is either a framed or a scow-sided boat with molded bow and stern, completely housed from end to end. The house rises from 2 to 3 feet above the gunwales, and is decked over on top, there being no deck below, as in the laker. It is considered that this type of boat most perfectly protects grain and other valuable cargoes. It is most in demand when grain freights are high; when coal, lumber, and other coarse freights pay the best scows are in demand, while in other years every one builds a laker or a bull-head.

It is rare that a man builds his own boat on the Erie canal. A few have a number of boats built for themselves, but instances of this sort are not common. The great majority of yards build on contract or speculation, and most of the boats are sold on credit. The canalmen are expected to pay a certain sum down in cash, from $300 to $1,000, as they are able to gain the confidence of the builder, a certain other sum being then paid annually. Women can usually get good credit, a great many boats being owned and run by them; they do not spend their money in dissipation, are good managers, and have the name of being sure pay. Owing to the prevalence of the credit system the large builders always have a great deal of money afloat, as they express it, and run a certain amount of risk, because if the year should be a bad one the boatmen make little more than running expenses and are unable to pay their installments, the boats meanwhile depreciating in value. Good years, however, enable the boatmen to liquidate all arrears and save their investments.

As before stated, the horse packet is no longer seen on the Erie canal. Just before railroads were made through the state of New York travelers journeyed to and fro between the Hudson and the West by way of the canal. Boats were built for this traffic with sharp bows and good sterns, being well fitted up on board with berths and cabins. The horses drawing them were able to go along steadily at a trot, in strong contrast with those of the freighting boats, which toiled along painfully at a walk. Packets still exist on the canal, but they are steamers.

The steam craft of the canal are of three classes: First, the freighting propellers, patterned like lakers, each carrying a little boiler and engine away aft in the stern, leaving the hold amidships and forward entirely clear for cargo, and usually taking a consort, or regular canal-boat, which is pushed straight ahead. Next, the cable-towing boats, employed on the level of the canal between Tonawanda and Buffalo, a distance of 42 miles, the boat carrying only the towing machinery and a supply of coal. Lastly, the packets, which are either propeller launches or small steamboats.

The idea of using steam for freighting on the canal was started long ago, but the first practical boats were built in 1871. The state offered a bounty for a successful steam canal-boat which should be built at small expense and would run alone and without washing a swell over the tow-path of the canal. The prize was a large one, and resulted in the perfection of the Baxter boats, seven of which were built by a company having $100,000 capital. The original idea was to propel these boats with twin screws at the stern; but this plan was abandoned, and the later boats were each propelled by a single screw, having four blades mounted on a large central drum or hub. The state paid $35,000 for the building of the first seven boats, and seven more were constructed soon afterward by the company. The mistake was made of running the boats independently at first. Owing to the competition with the railroads horse-boats were hardly paying expenses, and, as steamers were more costly to operate, they lost money. The result was that the company failed and was sold out, and the boats passed into other hands. It was then found that by taking in tow an ordinary boat, lashing the two together in a direct line, one ahead of the other, the steamer in the rear, the average expense was greatly reduced; and the cost of towing on the Hudson being entirely avoided, the boats have since been operated with profit. The Baxter boats were 96 feet long, 17 feet beam, and 9 feet deep in the hold, and had fairly sharp bows. With 6 feet of water one was able to carry 215 tons of freight, and with $5\frac{1}{2}$ feet 200 tons, making a round trip from New York to Buffalo and return in 16 days, as against 25 to 30 days on the part of a horse-boat. Cost of the trip, about $650. The machinery cost $3,000 and weighed 6 tons.

Another style of propeller is that of the Rapid, a steamer invented in 1876 by Gordon W. Hall at Havana, New York, a little town located a mile from the head of Seneca lake on an old and now abandoned canal. One peculiarity of the Rapid was that the furnace of the boiler was arranged like a base-burner stove. Once filled with coal, the furnace needed no more fuel for eight hours; and it was supplied with contrivances for shaking the grate and controlling the steam, so that the man at the helm could both steer the boat and attend to the engine without leaving his place. The Rapid was 98 feet long, $17\frac{2}{3}$ feet beam, and $9\frac{1}{2}$ feet deep in the hold, the engine, of 35-horse power, occupying with the boiler a horizontal space of 5 by 7 feet only. The coal consumption was 1,600 pounds a day, and the boat and consort were worked by 4 men. The Rapid carried 100 tons of coal from Havana by way of the lake and canal to Buffalo. She then took 8,000 bushels of wheat to Rochester, and then made several trips to New York with 7,700 bushels at a time. The time of the trip from Buffalo to New York and back again, towing two boats from Troy to New York, was from 16 to 19 days, and the total expense of the whole round trip, including tolls, insurance, and port charges, was $310. She made round trips with a consort from Buffalo for $600. The machinery of the Rapid was designed for fitting into any canal-boat by a slight alteration of the stern, and cost $1,800. Mr. Hall built several boats at Havana carrying his machinery, each one costing $6,000 complete, and then in 1880 introduced the idea into Lockport. No alteration is caused in the construction of canal-boats by putting in the propeller machinery except to give the stern a few feet of overhang and to change the location of the captain's cabin. The space in the stern occupied by the cabin in horse-boats is consumed by

CANAL-BOATS.

the machinery in the propeller and by the little house built to shelter it and the steersman. The stable being abolished, the captain's cabin is moved forward to the bow. The boats may be framed or built with scow sides. Three were built at Havana in the year 1879–'80 with $4\frac{1}{2}$-inch scow sides of white pine, hard-wood bottoms, and framed bows and sterns planked with 2-inch white oak. Each took 12,000 feet of hard wood, besides 5,500 feet of oak, and 19,000 feet of white pine, with 4 tons of iron and 5 tons of machinery, and cost $6,000.

The cable boats carry no freight, but are exclusively employed in towing horse-boats between Tonawanda and Buffalo. They are each 80 feet long, $15\frac{1}{2}$ and 16 feet on the beam, and 8 feet deep, drawing 5 feet of water. The principle on which they act is a novel one in America, but is in use on rivers and canals in Europe under the name of the Belgian system of cable towing. A steel wire cable, an inch in diameter, weighing 9,000 pounds to the mile, is laid on the bottom of the canal, with no anchorage except that given by its own weight. On one side of the towing-boat, outside the hull, a series of wheels, five in number, are hung on horizontal axles. The first wheel, near the bow, is 20 inches in diameter; it underruns the wire cable and lifts it from the canal bottom. Three others are amidships, and the cable passes under the first one, a tension wheel 6 feet in diameter, then over the center one, a grooved wheel 5 feet in diameter, and then under the third, another tension wheel 6 feet in diameter. The cable then runs over a 20-inch pulley at the stern of the boat corresponding to that in the bow and falls back to the bottom of the canal again. All the wheels play loosely on their axles except the grooved one amidships, which is rotated slowly by the power inside the boat, and by its grip on the cable hauls the tug, with its tow of six boats, along at a speed of about 3 miles an hour. The tug is supplied with two engines, one of 20-horse power to haul on the cable, and another of 10-horse power, driving a small screw-wheel at the stern of the boat, for use in emergencies only. Eight of these boats built at Lockport in the census year cost $8,500 each.

Business was dull in the boat-yards of the Erie canal in 1879 and 1880, as they had not escaped the general depression following the panic of 1873, and had in addition been subjected to the effects of the severe competition of the railroads. Boatmen, in consequence, felt poor in 1879 and 1880. They starved their boats during the period of low freights, avoiding every expense, and went right by the boat-yards continually, pumping water out of their leaking boats, instead of putting them into some dry-dock and having them repaired. They have had better years since.

On the eastern part of the canal there was not much building of new boats in the census year, and indeed there is not much in any year now, the chief reliance of buyers in that region being on the lake Champlain yards. The places that still do some building on the canal are Albany, West Troy, Crescent, and a few little yards around Oneida lake. In good years from 30 to 50 boats are launched among them. The other yards from Albany to Syracuse did little except repairing. Between these two cities ordinarily no boat need journey more than half a day without coming in sight of some little dry-dock or a yard where it can be taken out of water and have damages repaired, the principal places being West Troy, Crescent, Schenectady, Port Jackson, Little Falls, Constantia, West Vienna, Bernhardt's Bay, North Bay, Utica, New London, Rome, Fayetteville, Canajoharie, Liverpool, and Chittenango. The canal dry-dock is a simple structure, and is placed alongside of the tow-path, or perhaps adjoining the berm bank of the canal. It is often cut out of the solid rock, and is usually nothing more nor less than a lock large enough to hold one or two boats. Any vessel needing repairs is floated in, the upper gate is closed, the water is drawn off, as from a lock, the boat is left high and dry, and the carpenters go to work on it.

Little Falls has two dry-docks, and at each of them there has been in times past much building. In good years from 400 to 500 vessels are docked for repairs. From the books at these yards some data were obtained of the earlier times. Twenty years ago boats were 75 and 80 feet long, $14\frac{1}{2}$ feet beam, and 6 feet deep, drawing $3\frac{1}{2}$ and 4 feet of water, and scows were built with 3- and 4-inch sides. The hills around the town were originally well covered with valuable timber, and supplied the boat-yards with all the oak, hard wood, and pine required. At present there is no timber in the locality. During the war materials ranged high, white pine costing $70 per thousand feet, oak $50 per thousand, and the best $60 and $70. Pitch was 10 cents a pound, once rising to $50 a barrel (it was about a cent per pound, or $2 50 per barrel in 1880). Iron rods were $12\frac{1}{2}$ cents a pound in war times; cut spikes, 10, 12, 15, and 17 cents; wrought spikes, 18 cents; oakum, 15 cents, $10\frac{1}{2}$ cents in 1880. The prices of all materials have declined from 30 to 50 per cent. since the war, and pitch has declined more.

Going westward from Syracuse, there are dry docks at Jordan, Port Byron, Montezuma, Seneca Falls, Rochester, Lockport, Madison, Middleport, Tonawanda, and Buffalo, with small yards here and there at other places. Although 40 miles away from the canal, there are 6 yards at Ithaca, 1 at Trumansburgh, at the head of Cayuga lake, and 2 at Havana, a mile above the head of Seneca lake. The Ithaca yards buy timber to advantage, and build from 25 to 30 large-class boats every year. They are now paying some attention to fitting up their craft with machinery.

At Havana, where a number of steam canal-boats have been made, Gordon W. Hall has a machine-shop as well as a boat-yard. A steamer similar to the Rapid had just been finished when the town was visited in 1880 and lay in the canal drying its paint. It was a full-sized laker, 93 feet long on the keel, $98\frac{2}{3}$ feet over all, $17\frac{2}{3}$ feet beam, and $9\frac{1}{2}$ feet in the depth of side, scow sided. The forward cabin was 8 feet from the bow, and was 13 feet wide, 14 feet long, and 7 feet high in the clear, extending 28 inches above the deck, containing 5 rooms, and rested partly on the lower breast-hook braces and partly on stanchions, there being a clear space of $4\frac{2}{3}$ feet under it available for grain cargo. Amidships there was another house 16 feet wide, 8½ feet fore and aft, rising 3 feet above the deck. In the extreme stern was the engine-house, with a companion-way in the after end. It was 20 feet long fore and aft, 6 feet wide, and 3 feet high above the deck, with a steersman's house in the forward part rising 3 feet higher, a feature peculiar to steam canal-boats, as in horse-boats the man at the tiller stands out exposed to all weathers. The boat was completely decked, and had three hatches.

Nearly all the yards on the main line of the canal from Syracuse to Rochester complained of dull times. In place of from $15,000 to $25,000 worth of repair work yearly, as in old times, each was not doing more than a third or a quarter of that business, and building had virtually ceased, having all been monopolized by Rochester, Lockport, Tonawanda, and Buffalo.

The following yards were found at the places named: Rochester, 5, employing 90 men and building from 40 to 50 boats yearly; Lockport, 4 yards, 160 men, product 60 to 80 boats yearly; Tonawanda, 7 yards, 90 men, from 50 to 100 boats yearly; and Buffalo, 10 yards, 150 men, from 50 to 80 boats yearly. The banks of the canal in the parts of these towns where the yards are present a busy spectacle—new boats under construction, with piles of lumber, and often with sheds, shops, and saw-mills around them; newly painted vessels floating in the canal; dry-docks, with boats going in and out and some high and dry receiving repairs, and a constant stream of traffic moving by in both directions in unending procession. The lumber for the building yards comes almost wholly from the upper lakes, arriving in rafts and ship-loads at the ports of Buffalo and Tonawanda. Oak and white pine, sawed, each cost from $30 to $35 per thousand feet. About one-fourth of the wood is wasted in building a boat. Lakers and bull-heads consume 38,000 and 40,000 feet each; scows, 28,000 or 30,000 feet each.

In Rochester the yards mostly do new work. They sold lakers and bull-heads in 1880 for from $3,700 to $4,200 each, the bull-head being the cheaper boat. Scows were sold for about $2,600.

In Lockport a large repairing business is added to the other branch of the industry. Two firms have each 3 dry-docks, built of masonry like canal locks. Timber is bought at Tonawanda in rafts. The builder who has a saw-mill saves a few dollars per thousand feet by doing his own sawing. Mr. Morgan had been in business for sixteen years, but in 1879 he began anew with a partner and built a large fleet of boats the first year, launching 14 in one day. Morgan & Benedict reported for the census year 22 new canal-boats, worth $3,500 each, and 8 cable-towing boats, worth $8,500 each. In 1880 attention began to be paid to steam on the canal by the Lockport builders, and Mr. Hall, of Havana, came to the city and began the manufacture of his engines, wheels, and boilers, the prospect being fair for the rise of a large fleet of new propellers.

Tonawanda being a lumber market, has great advantages for boat-building, and the yards were all rushing work in 1880. Scows were popular that year, as the port was shipping immense quantities of lumber to the East. One firm, owning a large saw-mill, built 22 open coal barges in the census year, 92 feet long, 17¾ feet beam, and 10 feet sides, at a cost of $2,500 each. A ship-chandlery firm which fits out hundreds of boats yearly with tow-lines reported that a new canal-boat requires 160 pounds of manila rope; those that go out on the lakes or the Hudson river must each have in addition another line 6 inches in circumference and 25 fathoms long, weighing 180 pounds.

At Buffalo there is work for both the canal and the lake; a fact which inures to the benefit of the builders to some extent, as it keeps up the supply of good carpenters, but is probably of greater advantage to the men themselves. The canal yards are strung out along the canal, and are principally engaged in building. Wages are higher in Buffalo than in the country yards, and the owner of an old boat is pretty sure to send it to the place where its repairs can be most cheaply made. Lumber comes entirely from the upper lakes.

CANALS IN THE WEST.

There are two canals in Ohio, the Ohio and the Miami and Erie, both of small capacity, and now falling into disuse. Both are still used for a great deal of small local traffic, and are capable of being converted into valuable routes of transportation by the deepening of their channels. The draught of water available for boats is 3½ and 4 feet, but 6 feet of water in each canal would work a great improvement in their traffic. The Ohio canal runs from Cleveland to Portsmouth, on the Ohio river, a distance of 323 miles. There are 19 miles of feeders and 67 miles of branches. The Miami and Erie canal runs from Toledo to Cincinnati, on the Ohio, a distance of 246 miles, and has 25 miles of feeders. In addition to these two works there is an improvement on the Muskingum river by which 91 miles of that stream above its junction with the Ohio at Marietta are made available for steamers and steam canal-boats. On the two canals the boats freight lumber and ice southward and coal northward, besides doing some general business in the transportation of paper stock, provisions, and general merchandise.

The old-time boats of Ohio were able to carry only about 45 tons of cargo each. They were then, as now, 80 feet long, 14 feet wide, and 4 or 4½ feet deep, drawing 3 feet of water, and were rather sharp and fast boats; but in late years they have been built fuller and given 4 feet draught, so that their capacity has been increased to 80 or 90 tons. They are neat boats, but are not large enough; and, considering that the large 240-ton boats in the state of New York find it hard to hold their own against railroad competition, it is not surprising that the smaller craft of Ohio have been hard pressed since the war, the discouragement among the boatmen being so great that very few new boats have been built for ten or twelve years. About 1870 the old Philadelphia and Erie canal was abandoned, and about 40 canal-boats were taken over to the Ohio canal. There has been almost no building on the latter since, not to exceed 5 or 6 boats being built in any one year.

Steam canal-boats have been tried in Ohio for 20 years. There is a firm at Chillicothe which in 1860 began making engines and propeller wheels for canal and river navigation. Their first boat was a small packet to run on the river to Portsmouth. During the war this boat was employed in carrying cotton from the South, and was finally destroyed. The firm had in 1881 built 50 or 60 canal-boat engines in all, 15 of them at one time, about 1865. So far as the engines are concerned, their boats have been successful. The machinery is light, weighing from 4 to 6 tons only, including boiler and wheel. The Chillicothe wheel has a special reputation in the West, and is much used. It consists of a cast-iron hub, with three short and narrow arms; to these arms are riveted the blades of the wheel, three in number, made of wrought iron, 1 inch thick nearest the hub and $\frac{1}{4}$ or $\frac{3}{8}$ inch at the outer edge. The blades are shaped like truncated triangles, bases outward, and twisted to give them the pitch. The object in putting on wrought-iron blades is to allow of their being promptly detached and straightened or replaced in case of accident. The engines do not act always directly on the shaft, but drive the propeller by means of gearing. Chillicothe machinery, owing to its light weight, is well adapted for river steamers. In 1881 the shops were building a double upright engine to drive twin screws. The cylinders were 11 by 15 inches; the boiler 3 by $16\frac{1}{2}$ feet, made of $\frac{3}{8}$-inch steel, with about 70 flues, and intended to carry 100 pounds of steam. The whole weight, including wheels, was 14,000 pounds, and the cost \$5,000. A set of engines for a 100-foot boat weighed 21,000 pounds, and nine or ten have been made weighing 30,000 pounds each. The cylinders were 11 by 15, 12 by 16, and 15 by 17 inches; boilers about $3\frac{1}{3}$ by 18 feet, steel. While the engines for the canal have done well enough, the boats themselves have not, owing to the small draught of water and the heavy summer growth of grass in the canals. The wheel draws the water away from the after part of the boat and the stern drags on the bottom. With 6 feet of water in the canals these boats would do well; but as they cannot get it, they have all left the canals and gone into river service, what transportation there is being done entirely by horse-boats.

The Ohio boats are all framed, the object being to secure as light a hull as possible. The model is the same as that of the bull-head of the Erie canal. The house is not continuous from stem to stern, but consists of three small houses, one in the bow, one amidships for a stable, and one away aft for the captain, with a little roof or gangway 3 feet wide running from one to another. A few are completely housed, and are called two-deckers. The frames are sawed out of $1\frac{3}{4}$-inch oak, molded 11 or 12 inches over the keel, 9 near the bilge, $4\frac{1}{2}$ on the bilge, and 3 at the gunwale, spaced about 14 inches. There is a light ceiling of 1- or $1\frac{1}{2}$-inch oak or 2-inch white pine. The outside is planked with $1\frac{3}{4}$-inch oak. There are three fenders on the bow, one at the plank-sheer height, the other two a foot apart below, extending around the curve of the bow and ironed with 2- by $\frac{3}{4}$-inch straps. The stem is oak, 12 by 4 inches, ironed on the face with a 3- by 1-inch strap. Houses, white pine. The stern overhangs just enough to house the rudder-stock. About 13,000 feet of wood, a ton of iron, and 80 pounds of manila line are required for one of these boats, and they cost \$1,100 and \$1,200 each.

There are about 15 small yards scattered along the Ohio canal, and less than that number on the Miami and Erie. An old builder is C. H. Payne, of Akron, who spent 30 years in Pennsylvania, and has been 18 years at Akron. He had built 128 boats in all up to 1881, but only one boat in the latter year.

The Illinois and Michigan canal extends from Bridgeport, on the outskirts of Chicago, to La Salle, on the Illinois river, a distance of 96 miles, exclusive of feeders. The channel is 48 feet wide at the bottom and 60 feet at the top, and has 6 feet of water, the available draught for boats being $4\frac{2}{3}$ or 5 feet. There are 15 locks on the canal, each 110 feet long and 18 feet wide. They permit the construction of longer boats than are used anywhere else in the United States. The boats that go through to the Illinois river are 103 feet long, 14 feet wide on the floor, $17\frac{7}{12}$ feet wide on the beam, and 6 feet deep. Of late years a few larger ones have been built for use exclusively on the summit level, extending from Chicago to Lockport, a distance of about 20 miles. These are 120 and 128 feet long, and cannot pass through the locks. In order to assist the dispatch of boats from Chicago through to Saint Louis the state of Illinois and the United States have built two dams with locks in the Illinois river, one at Henry, the other at Copperas creek, making 90 miles of good river navigation with 7 feet of water. Navigation also extends to the Kankakee feeder, 4 miles in length, and on the Kankakee river for a distance of 12 miles. A good farming country extends along the Illinois canal, and considerable grain is shipped to market, and lumber is shipped from Chicago. The trade consists principally of grain, lumber, and stone, but it is the stone business that gives rise to the large boats of the summit level, as extensive quarries are situated along that level and beyond it to a distance of 33 miles from Chicago. Another feature of the freighting is the bringing of ice to the city of Chicago in the summer-time. The largest number of boats run on the canal in a year was 240, in 1863, the number of clearances issued being 7,044; there has been a steady decline in the number of boats from that year to this, the total number in 1881 being 138 boats and the clearances 4,459. This falling off has been counterbalanced, however, by the increase in size of the boats and the faster time made by them. In 1863 there were only 619,000 tons of freight transported on the canal, whereas in 1881 there were 826,000 tons, making the freighting of the year the largest on record with one exception. In 1873 there were 173 boats, and 849,000 tons were carried. Steam canal-boats are now taking the place of the older fashioned craft, as being better suited to the navigation of the river and the summit level. In

1881 there were 24 boats; 7 tugs were also employed. The steamers are 120 and 128 feet long, about 20 feet wide, are strong and handsome, and are oak built, with pine decks and houses. Each is provided with two pretty large engines and twin screws as a rule; the machinery weighs about 10 tons, and has power enough to push one consort and tow one other behind. The stone is carried on deck, the boat having strong bulwarks about 3 feet high to aid in stowing and securing it. Steamers are built every year at a cost of $5,500 and $6,000, and are so efficient that they replace more than their own number of the old horse-boats. In other words, while the change to steam is taking place new boats are not built as fast as the old ones are worn out. There are only three yards on the canal, namely, at Bridgeport, Lockport, and Peru, (a) respectively, but the work done is chiefly repairing. Among the ideas tried on this canal was the building of boats with a peculiar stern, to serve as consorts to steamers, the stern being recessed 10 feet or so, so that the bow of the steamer might just fit into it. The idea served no useful purpose.

IN THE MIDDLE STATES.

In New Jersey there are two old and useful canals: the Delaware and Raritan, from New Brunswick to Bordentown, 44 miles, 80 feet wide on top, with 7 feet of water, and the Morris, from Jersey City to Phillipsburg, 103 miles, 45 feet wide on top, with 5 feet depth of water. The traffic in coal is large, and both canals are thronged with boats in the warmer months of the year. Formerly they were supplied with boats by local builders, but the oak and pine have been entirely cut off in the counties traversed by the canals and little is left for the local yards to do except to repair the old boats. The building is done almost entirely in Pennsylvania, in the upper Schuylkill region, where pine and oak still abound among the hills. The New Jersey yards are located as follows: Perth Amboy, 2; New Brunswick, 4; Bordentown, 2; Trenton, 1; Washington, 1.

In Pennsylvania there was originally a large network of canals having a total length of 920 miles. Some of the routes have fallen into disuse, but a few are still in operation, and are important factors in coal and iron transportation, the principal ones being as follows: Schuylkill, from Philadelphia to Pottsville, 108 miles, navigable by boats carrying from 180 to 200 tons; Union, from Middletown to Reading, 85 miles, traversed by 100-ton boats; Tide Water canal, from Columbia to Havre de Grace, 45 miles, 30 miles in Pennsylvania, navigable by 150-ton boats; Pennsylvania, from Clark's Mills to Northumberland, 85 miles, and a line to Huntingdon, 90 miles, 150-ton boats; the north and west branches of the Susquehanna, 50 and 70 miles respectively, 100-ton boats; and Lehigh, from Easton to Mauch Chunk, 50 miles, 120-ton boats; in all, about 620 miles of navigation. It is believed by the state authorities that the time will come when cheapness and not rapidity of transportation will be the great desideratum and the canal system of the state will be reconstructed on a large scale, but at present the tendency is toward a discontinuance of canal navigation. Though millions of tons of the products of the state have been moved to market economically by these valuable water-ways, it is nevertheless true that they would all fall into prompt disuse except that the Pennsylvania, Reading, and Lehigh railroads find them useful auxiliaries in the transportation of iron and coal. On the north branch of the Susquehanna there is one yard at Espy where the Pennsylvania company builds its own boats, and where small steam craft are occasionally launched. At Lewisburg, on the west branch, there is one yard. Other important building places have been Chester, Schuylkill Haven, Landingville, Philadelphia, Hamburg, Reading, Port Providence, Middletown, and Highspire. At Chester the yard has disappeared, and the industry appears to be declining at all the other places named. From 50 to 60 canal-boats are now built annually, whereas in 1871 there were about 150. Previous to 1870 the canal-boats of Pennsylvania were in the main framed boats. Those for the Schuylkill canal were 101 feet long over all, $17\frac{1}{2}$ feet broad, and 9 feet deep amidships, with a draught of 16 inches when light and of $5\frac{1}{2}$ feet when loaded with 180 tons. The bows and sterns were moderately full, but would be regarded as sharp on the Erie canal. The frames, planking, and keelson were of white oak; the ceiling, bridging, deck, and houses of white pine. The cost was from $1,800 to $2,000 per boat. After 1870 the majority of the boats were of the "log bilge" pattern. Those employed on the Schuylkill canal were $102\frac{1}{2}$ feet long over all, 17 feet broad, and $8\frac{1}{2}$ feet deep; capacity on $5\frac{1}{2}$ feet draught, 195 tons of coal; cost, $2,250 each, new framed boats being worth $2,400 each. This was the price in 1873, but in 1879 the price of "log bilge" boats had fallen to $1,750. At Middletown, in 1873, boats of a smaller class were built, 86 feet long and $16\frac{1}{2}$ feet wide, carrying 150 tons, for about $1,650 each, prices varying from year to year according to the times. There is, of course, much repairing of the boats on all the canals; like the other branch of the industry it is declining, but should the long-cherished plans of the state authorities ever be carried out for an enlargement of the canal system, especially for the opening of a first-class route through to the Ohio river, boat building and repairing would awaken to a new activity.

In Maryland there is a canal route $184\frac{1}{2}$ miles long extending from Georgetown to Cumberland, along the valley of the Potomac river. The prism is from 50 to 60 feet wide on top and 40 feet, wide on the bottom, with 6 feet depth of water. The locks are 100 feet long by 16 wide, large enough to pass 120-ton boats. The greater portion of the boats now running on the Chesapeake and Ohio canal, as it is called, are 92 feet in length, $14\frac{1}{2}$ feet wide, 6 and $6\frac{1}{2}$ feet deep, and draw 5 feet of water when loaded. Nine-tenths of all the building and repairing of these boats takes place at Cumberland, where there are six firms actively engaged the year around; the rest of the

---

a Peru is not strictly on the canal, but on the Illinois river just below the outlet of the canal, which is at La Salle.

work is done at Hancock and Williamsport. Timber is cheap in this region, particularly oak and white pine. Labor is also low, the best men getting $1 50 per day. The boats cost about the same as those on the Delaware and Hudson canal, namely, from $1,100 to $1,300, a few going as high as $1,450, and the labor bill varies from $350 to $450. At Hancock there are two canal dry-docks. Repair work is necessarily a large business on a canal so steadily employed in freighting coal, and contrary to the general rule in these cases labor is only about one-fifth or one-quarter of the expense in boat repairs on this canal. About 60 or 70 boats of the shape usual in Maryland are built at the three places named above in fairly good years, and a certain number of them are apt to be steamers, for the tendency toward steam locomotion has been felt on this canal within the last ten years, and several of the new class of boats are in operation. Their cost is $3,000 each, twice that of a first-class horse-boat; this makes their introduction slow, but their number appears to be growing. Three or four years ago this canal claimed to have the best type of steamers in the country. It certainly is one well adapted to a trade where a heavy cargo is carried in one direction and no cargo is carried on the return trip. To make the boat run on an even keel when light the boiler is placed a little forward of amidships and the steam is carried in covered pipes to the engine in the stern. The engine acts directly on the propeller shaft, and is so arranged that it can be raised or lowered so as to throw the wheel, outside the boat, up or down, adapting its immersion to the loaded or light condition of the boat. The levers for controlling the steam and changing the immersion of the wheel are all within reach of the steersman, who is thus the engineer as well. A fireman is required to attend to the boilers and "bow" the boat through the locks. The propeller is a Neafie & Levy wheel. Such a steamer made the round trip from Cumberland to Georgetown and back, a distance of 369 miles, with 75 locks to pass each way, in 4 days and 20 hours, consuming from $4\frac{1}{2}$ to 5 tons of coal. The machinery complete costs about $2,000. The canal has never been a very profitable investment for the state of Maryland or the stockholders so far as dividends on its traffic are concerned, but it has been of service to the public in bringing down coal and iron from the interior at low rates of freight.

In Virginia a canal extends from Richmond to Buchanan, on the James river. It is $196\frac{1}{2}$ miles in length, and is 40 feet wide, with 4 feet depth of water. This canal was begun as a route for through traffic between the Ohio river and the sea-coast, but it is now virtually abandoned.

The Dismal Swamp caonal is about 30 miles long, but is not much used for canal-boats. Its importance is due to the fact that it is part of the long interior water route along the middle Atlantic coast, and allows of the passage of vessels through from Norfolk harbor to the sounds of North Carolina.

Chapter VII.—UNITED STATES NAVY-YARDS.

In a report upon the ship-building resources of the United States it seems appropriate to refer briefly to the establishments under the exclusive control of the government.

In the Revolution our fighting ships were built in private yards, and were mainly privateers for local owners, but included a few frigates for the government.

After the disbanding of the navy of the Revolution very few ships of war were required for a number of years, but in 1794 the necessity of protecting American commerce against pirates in the Mediterranean led to the construction of new vessels. The ships were built, as before, in private yards. The subject of establishing governmental navy-yards then came up, and was much discussed by public men; but no action was taken until 1801, when the President, on his own responsibility, bought sites for the establishments which were afterward created at Portsmouth, Boston, New York, Philadelphia, Washington, and Norfolk. Congress acceded to this action and appropriated the money to erect buildings and establish the plant for the construction, equipment, and repair of vessels. After that date for 60 years all the regular fighting ships of the United States were built by the government itself. The first achievement of the navy-yards was to send out a number of the frigates which gained so brilliant a fame in the war of 1812 and immortalized the navy of the United States. At the close of the war of 1812 naval stations were established at Whitehall, Sackett's Harbor, and Erie, on the northern lakes, and at Newport, Baltimore, Charleston, and New Orleans, on the coast, and the depredations by pirates in the West Indies led in 1821 to the location of a naval station at Key West and a navy-yard at Pensacola. A yard was established at Mare island, on the Napa river, in California, at a later date, and a naval station near New London, Connecticut.

No settled policy was ever followed by the government in building up the plant of its navy-yards. Expediency, and the sudden emergencies which have arisen from time to time, governed appropriations. Immense sums of money have been expended; nevertheless, nothing except the resources of the private ship-yards of the country has saved the national government from humiliation in naval operations in times of public peril. Incomplete as the navy-yards have been, however, they have been of great utility to the country. During their development in the years from 1812 to 1861 their ability to produce good ships was proved, and they reacted beneficially on the private ship-building interests of the country. There had grown up in them a race of constructors and engineers (in part recruited from the ranks of private life) whose investigations, experiments, and teachings were of vast service to the builders, outfitters, and owners of our merchant tonnage. In the years from 1860 to 1865 the government was suddenly called upon to improvise a navy, and the emergency was so great that 137 vessels were bought outright from the owners of ships, schooners, and steamers, 59 more being bought to load with stone and sink as obstructions to harbors. There also had to be built in 1861 14 screw sloops-of-war of 2,200 tons each, 23 gunboats of 500 tons each, a few western river gunboats, and a few iron-clads. The sloops were built mainly at the navy-yards, but the rest of the vessels could only be constructed at private yards. The contracts were given out all along the coast from Baltimore to Belfast, Maine. The 23 gunboats were built as follows: 1 at Baltimore; 1 at Wilmington; 3 at Philadelphia; 6 at New York; 1 each at East Haddam and Mystic river; 3 at Boston; 2 at Portland; and 1 each at Newburyport, Kennebunk, Bath, Thomaston, and Belfast; the cost varying from $52,000 to $56,500 for the hulls, and $31,500 to $47,500 for the machinery. From 10,000 to 12,000 men were employed in the four northern navy-yards at Philadelphia, New York, Boston, and Kittery, but even then the resources of the government were utterly inadequate to the emergency and the private ship-yards were the main dependence. The iron-clads and other armed vessels which were afterward built were made almost wholly by private establishments. From first to last in the four years of war the following ships of war were finished and sent into the service:

    60 screw sloops, 845 guns in all, registering 116,303 tons.
    47 paddle-wheel steamers, 452 guns, 44,532 tons.
    23 gunboats, 123 guns, 11,661 tons.
    11 tugs, propellers, 22 guns, 3,390 tons.
    62 iron-clad monitors and steamers, 189 guns, 73,988 tons.

The navy-yards were much improved during the war, and did all the work of which they were capable. They proved to be valuable aids in building the sloops-of-war and in repairing the disabled and damaged vessels, but were overwhelmed by the demands upon them, and it was fortunate for the government that extensive private facilities existed. The material obtained regarding public yards is not complete, but it is such as could be gathered in the time allowed.

UNITED STATES NAVY-YARDS.

KITTERY, MAINE.

The establishment here is called the Portsmouth yard, as it is located across the harbor from the city of that name in New Hampshire. The equipment is all that is required for the building and repair of wooden vessels. The shops and buildings are now old and dilapidated, however. The sectional marine railway is one of the largest in the country, as two large ships can be repaired upon it at the same time. In this yard some of the sloops-of-war were built, and much valuable work was done from 1861 to 1865. Six large vessels are now laid up here in ordinary, and the Massachusetts, now useless, is on the stocks. The yard is at present occupied with an occasional task of rebuilding some old ship and repairing the government vessels which cruise on that part of the coast. Two or three wooden ships could be undertaken at once at this yard in case of need. There is at least 24 feet of water here at low tide.

BOSTON, MASSACHUSETTS.

At Charlestown, in Boston harbor, the government has about $10,000,000 invested in grounds, shops, machinery, and general ship-yard plant. In ordinarily busy years about 500 men are employed in building and repair work and in the manufacture of ordnance stores, cordage, blocks, iron work, boilers, and whatever happens to be required for the maintenance of ships of war. The sum of $383,000 was expended for labor in the yard in 1879–'80, and the further sum of $1,597,000 for materials. In this yard all the hemp and wire rope used in the navy is manufactured. The following statement has been prepared by Commodore Badger:

UNITED STATES NAVY-YARD,
Boston, Massachusetts, September 19, 1882.

The Census Agent on Ship-building, Department of the Interior, Washington, D. C.

SIR: In compliance with your request, I hereby forward the required data for the completion of your report on the capacity of the navy-yard under my command relative to the building and repairing of ships of all kinds.

The various shops in this navy-yard are all in good condition, and are as follows:

1. *The principal machine-shop.*—This is among the largest and best fitted in the country, and is capable of doing the work necessary for iron- or steel-ship building. It contains all the most improved tools and machinery, and is two stories high, the upper floor being used for light work.
2. *A smaller machine-shop.*—Especially adapted for separate light work in iron and steel.
3. *Boiler-shop.*—Fitted with machinery and tools for building stationary, portable, and heavy marine boilers.
4. *Heavy forge-shop.*—Especially fitted for rolling iron from scraps and making heavy forgings.
5. *Two iron and brass founderies.*—Fitted for heavy and light work, all the machinery and tools in prime order.
6. *Smithery.*—For engine forgings and other work.
7. *Two copper-shops.*—One for making copper and brasses for heavy marine engines, while the other is fitted for lighter work.
8. *Pattern-shop.*—For making patterns for any size of marine engines. In these shops, that is, the pattern-shop, machine-shop, etc., a number of large engines have been made and numerous extensive repairs conducted on others.
9. *Rope-walk.*—The best in this country, and contains all the newest machinery for making rope of hemp, manila, hide, or wire.
10. *Sail-loft.*—Very large, and equal to every emergency.
11. *Boat-shop*, which has always been capable of carrying on its proportion of the work.
12. *Mold-loft.*—With all necessary tools and machinery for work under that head.
13. *Spar-shed.*—Of sufficient size and capability, with a large number of mast spars on hand.
14. *Saw-mill.*—With bevel and other saws, the best of any at our navy-yards, and capable of doing, with its machinery, all the necessary work to carry on wooden-ship building.
15. *Block-shop and rigging lofts.*—Both of sufficient size and equal to any demands.
16. *Joiner-shop.*—Most complete, with all the machinery and room necessary.
17. *Plumber-, tin-, and small cooper-shop*, also *paint-shop*, each of which is capable of performing the work coming under its head.

For convenience of carrying on work all the shops enumerated from 1 to 8, inclusive, are close together; and there is sufficient steam-power at hand to carry on the most extensive business, three of the engines having 100 horse-power each. There are, besides, provision and other store-houses in the yard for stowage of ship materials, all well supplied, and two wet-timber docks for seasoning purposes.

As to docks, slips, and sheds for the building and repair of ships, there is but one dry-dock, built of granite at a total cost of $993,915. This dock is capable of receiving any ship not over 379 feet long, 60 feet beam, or 27 feet draught of water. There are three ship-houses with building-ways and three building-slips, making in all six sites for the building of ships. Four of these sites are at present occupied by old-style ships, which will not be completed. With all of the ways clear six vessels might be built at this yard at one time, all the ways being now in good condition.

For constructing the largest iron or steel ships sheds adjacent to the ship-houses could with ease be erected in six weeks, at a cost of not more than $30,000, containing furnaces for heating plates and all the necessary appliances for completing the work.

There were during the late war about 5,000 men employed to advantage in this navy-yard, and this I consider as many as would be necessary to work the yard to its full capacity.

Since its establishment in 1800 there have been launched at this yard 39 ships-of-war, of which the most important or conspicuous were:

The Independence, ship-of-the-line, launched in 1814.
The Marion, sloop-of-war, launched in 1839.
The Bainbridge, brig, launched in 1842.
The Cumberland, frigate, launched in 1842.
The Plymouth, sloop, launched in 1843.
The Vermont, ship-of-the-line, launched in 1848.

The Princeton, frigate, launched in 1851.
The Merrimac, frigate, launched in 1855.
The Hartford, frigate, launched in 1858.
The Monadnock, double-turret monitor, launched in 1864.
The Guerriere, frigate, launched in 1865.
The Worcester, frigate, launched in 1866.
The Alaska, sloop-of-war, launched in 1868.
The Intrepid, iron torpedo-boat, launched in 1874.
The Vandalia, sloop-of-war, launched in 1874.

Several vessels were also built for the Treasury Department at this yard for duty in the light-house service, coast survey, and revenue marine, and most extensive repairs have been made to vessels of all classes.

I am, respectfully,

O. C. BADGER,
Commodore United States navy, commanding United States navy-yard, Boston, Massachusetts.

Captain C. C. Carpenter, equipment officer, reports the following materials used in outfits in the year ending June 30, 1880:

Pounds of iron and steel	891
Pounds of hemp rope	21,619
Pounds of manila rope	41,023
Pounds of hemp rope shipped to other stations	186,882
Pounds of manila rope shipped to other stations	297,086
Yards cotton canvas used for sails	9,579
Yards flax canvas used for sails	8,881

It is in this yard that some experiments have been made with a machine for bending the oaken frame timbers of ships so as to make them in one piece from keel to gunwale. The machine cost $160,000, and bent a large number of knees and timbers in a satisfactory manner. The yard is much resorted to for tests of the strength of timber growing in different parts of the United States. This establishment is highly valued by officers of the navy, as its location is an excellent one. The water is deep, the approaches are capable of defense from attack, and the harbor is easy of access but difficult to blockade. No embarrassment is likely to arise on account of ice, and the proximity of the ship-yards, engine-shops, and general mechanical facilities of the city of Boston adds materially to its resources.

NEW LONDON, CONNECTICUT.

The yard at this point is located on the eastern bank of the Thames river. It enjoys deep water and a fine climate, and was established in 1868. The grounds have been graded and a large building erected, but at present the place is mainly a depot for the laying up of old navy vessels.

BROOKLYN, NEW YORK.

This is the most important of the navy-yards. There are 245 acres within the inclosure, and the plant represents an investment of about $15,000,000. Located on the water-front of Brooklyn opposite the heart of the city, and directly across the East river from the business portion of New York, the land alone which it covers is estimated as worth $25,000,000. Its equipment is complete, and the important iron works and engine-shops in the great communities bordering on the East river can be depended upon for assistance in fitting out navy vessels when required. The New York shops made the best and cheapest machinery that was built during the war. There are laid up at this yard a number of old war ships, some of them of the type of frigates of 60 years ago. On the stocks are 3 wooden vessels in frame, the Java, the New York, and the Colossus, which have been there since the close of the late war, and of which the New York alone is said to be worth finishing. The yard has done little or no building of late years, but repairing and outfitting are carried on to a considerable extent, and experiments and investigations of various kinds are continually undertaken. The aid to the commodore commanding the yard has prepared the following data for this report:

NAVY-YARD, NEW YORK, *November 24, 1882.*

The Census Agent on Ship-building, New York City.

SIR: In reply to your request, I take pleasure in furnishing the following information:

The yard comprises some 245 acres, with a water-front of nearly 2¼ miles. In addition to the shops and appliances for the construction, repair, and outfit of ships, the yard contains a complete naval hospital, a laboratory, extensive marine barracks, and receiving quarters for 6,000 men. The sewer which empties much of Brooklyn's refuse into the Wallabout bay and constantly shoals the water-way is about to be removed, an appropriation for that purpose having been made by the last Congress. Among the buildings are:

1 iron-plating shop.
1 smithery.
1 steam-engine machine-shop.
1 ordnance machine-shop.
1 boiler-maker shop.
1 plumber-shop.
1 cooper-shop.
1 joiner-shop.
1 block-shop.
1 foundery.
1 shipwright's shop.
1 saw-mill.
1 oakum mill, with drying platform.
1 wheelwright's shop.

UNITED STATES NAVY-YARDS.

3 buildings for the reception, preparation, and distribution of provisions and clothing, all fitted with boilers and machinery for their respective purposes.
1 mold-loft.
1 sail-loft.
1 rigging-loft.
1 yards and docks storehouse.
1 steam-engineering receiving storehouse and offices.
1 ordnance and navigation storehouse and offices.
1 chain-cable storehouse.
1 construction storehouse and offices.
1 equipment storehouse and offices.
2 steam iron derricks.
1 steam floating derrick.
1 tar shed.
6 timber sheds.
2 cart sheds.
7 sheds for general purposes.
1 spar shed.
1 boatbuilder's shed.
1 gun-carriage shed.
1 tank shed.
1 shipwright's shed.
1 foundery shed.
2 ship-houses.
2 pitch-houses.
1 gate-house.
7 officers' houses.
2 coal-houses.
2 guard-houses.
1 lyceum and offices.
1 civil engineer's office.
2 reservoir houses.
1 engine-house (steam-fire).
2 music-stands.
1 chapel.
2 oil and paint-shops.

ON ORDNANCE DOCK.

1 gunner's house.
1 howitzer shed.
4 shell, shot, etc., houses.
1 ordnance storehouse.
1 boiler-house.

HOSPITAL GROUNDS.

1 hospital.
1 laboratory.
1 chapel.
2 officers' houses.
2 stables.
2 boiler-houses.
1 coal-house.
1 gate-house.
1 cart shed.

MARINE BARRACKS.

1 marine barrack.
1 commandant of marines' house.
1 general quarters for marine officers.
1 gate-house.
1 boiler-house, with sheds.

There is one stone dry-dock, with boiler and attached engine. There are no marine railways, but there are slips already built where railways could be readily added.

Iron ships can be built. There is no other yard in the country that could be so easily prepared for the demands of present iron ships. With the addition to the present plant of a furnace for the bending of angle-iron any iron ship could be constructed to meet the present demands.

More than sixty ships of war have been built at this yard, including the following:

President (frigate).	Medina.	Maumee.	Mercury.
Erie (sloop-of-war).	Albany.	Shamrock.	Quinnebaug.
Savannah (44-gun ship).	San Jacinto.	Mackinaw.	Shawmut.
Sabine (44-gun ship).	Dolphin.	Peoria.	Severn.
Vincennes.	Iroquois.	Tallahassee.	Java.
Peacock.	Oneida.	Algonquin.	New York.
Enterprise.	Adirondack.	Colossus (iron-clad monitor).	Plymouth.
Relief.	Octarora.	Florida.	Swatara.
Fulton.	Miantonomoh (iron-clad monitor).	Tennessee.	Alarm (iron torpedo-boat).
Levant.	Ticonderoga.	Nyack.	Trenton.
Missouri.	Lackawanna.		

The highest number of ships building at one time was seven. In an emergency, with the present condition of the water-front, ten ships could easily be built at once, and with projected extension and deepening twice that number.

Over 7,000 men have been employed at the same time in this yard, 4,000 of them in the construction department alone. The number of men that could be employed would depend entirely upon the appropriation Congress might give, the possibilities of the yard exceeding any possible appropriation.

Very truly, yours,

W. H. JAQUES,
Lieutenant United States Navy.

The land occupied by this yard is in demand for commercial purposes; but the location is one of the best in the United States, and it so nearly fulfills all the conditions of a good site for a navy-yard that the officers of the navy do not advise its sale. With the completion of proper forts at the entrances to the harbor and around the city of Brooklyn the yard could not be captured. The water is deep, the plant is in excellent condition, and the lines of communication with the interior are held to be of the highest value. The chief drawbacks here are the floating ice in the river, occasional fogs, and the lack of proper facilities at the yard for docking vessels.

PHILADELPHIA, PENNSYLVANIA.

The League Island yard, in the lower edge of the city of Philadelphia, is of recent date. The old yard was farther up the Delaware and nearer the heart of the city, but it was too small, and was removed to the island in 1868. The equipment is not yet complete. Repair work occupies the men employed here chiefly, and is all work on the topsides and top-gear and on the inside of vessels, because the facilities do not yet exist for taking the ships out of water. For calking and coppering recourse is had either to the private docks in Philadelphia or to the navy-yard at New York. A number of iron vessels are laid up at the island awaiting repairs or completion. It will require several years of dredging and filling in before there is enough solid ground at this yard for the necessary accommodation of the establishment. The following official data have been obtained from Commodore Simpson, commandant of the yard:

NAVAL CONSTRUCTOR'S OFFICE,
UNITED STATES NAVY-YARD, LEAGUE ISLAND, PENNSYLVANIA,
September 21, 1882.

SIR: Referring to the communication from the census agent on ship-building, dated 16th instant, requesting information relative to the facilities of this yard, I have to state that there is no plant for iron-ship building, no building-shop for building a ship of either wood or iron, no dry-dock or railway, and no derricks or other means of raising heavy weights by steam-power.

The shops devoted to the repair of vessels consist of two machine-shops, a smithery, spar shed, boat- and block-shop, paint-shop, saw-mill, mold-loft, and brass foundery, together with accommodations for plumbers, etc. There is no iron foundery or furnaces for heavy forging.

The shops are amply provided with steam-power, and the tools are sufficient for repairing two or three vessels at one time; but the machinery for a ship of large size could not be manufactured here at present, owing to the lack of tools sufficiently powerful, such as trip-hammers, boring-mills, etc.

From 800 to 1,000 workmen can be employed with the present facilities.

No vessels have been entirely constructed here, though the Juniata was quite extensively repaired.

Very respectfully, your obedient servant,

F. L. FERNALD,
Naval Constructor, United States Navy.

Commodore EDWARD SIMPSON, U. S. N.,
Commandant Navy-Yard, League Island, Pennsylvania.

WASHINGTON, DISTRICT OF COLUMBIA.

The yard at Washington is an important one, and though covering 42 acres of ground is crowded with buildings. The establishment is one of the first class. It is embarrassed at times by the shoaling of the water in the eastern branch of the Potomac, arising from the wash of earth from the neighboring hills, but the trouble is easily corrected by dredging. The following data have been obtained through the agency of Commodore Pattison, commandant at the yard, from Chief Engineer Henderson, Commander Howell, Commander Casey, Chief Engineer Menocal, Constructor Pook, and Master Carpenter Collins:

STATEMENT OF THE AREA, BUILDINGS, EQUIPMENTS, EMPLOYÉS, WATER-FRONT, ETC., OF THE UNITED STATES NAVY-YARD AT WASHINGTON, DISTRICT OF COLUMBIA, OCTOBER 1, 1882.

The yard covers 42 acres of ground, and is filled with the shops and storehouses necessary for building, fitting, and repairing the largest vessels. It is capable of employing 4,000 men upon such work. The water-front is 1,250 feet in length. The shops cover an area of 261,246 square feet, and the storehouses 49,281 square feet. The following is a description of the different shops, ship-houses, etc., with their equipments, and the number of employés in each:

DEPARTMENT OF CONSTRUCTION AND REPAIR.

Brass foundery and finishing shop.—Area, 5,418 square feet. Employment for 60 men. Contains 1 furnace, 1 drying oven, 3 brass furnaces, 4 cranes, 22 lathes, 4 planers, 4 drill-presses, 1 boring-machine.

Blacksmith and coppersmith shop.—Area, 4,535 square feet. Employment for 60 men. The first contains 14 forges and 1 steam-hammer; the second 3 forges and complete outfit for all coppersmiths' work.

Copper-rolling mill.—Area, 24,047 square feet. Employment for 43 men. Fitted with 5 nail-machines, 4 sets sheet-rolls, 1 set rough rolls, 1 set finishing rolls, 6 furnaces, 3 shears. The daily capacity of the mill is 2,500 pounds sheathing and 3,000 pounds bolts.

East saw-mill.—Employment for 10 men. Contains 1 circular saw, 1 futtock saw, 1 bench saw, and 1 planer. It is situated in the ship-house, covering the marine railway.

West saw-mill.—Area, 15,978 square feet. Employment for 10 men. Contains 1 sash saw, 1 futtock-mill, and 1 spindle-planer.

Mold-loft.—Area, 11,820 square feet, over timber shed. Employment for 10 men. The largest vessels can be laid down. A draughting-room is attached.

Ship-house.—Area, 18,672 square feet. It is 306 feet long, and a first-class frigate can be built in it.

Marine railway.—Length of track, 495 feet, width 20 feet; can take a vessel of 52 feet beam. There is a hydraulic pump with 2 engines of 25 horse-power each for raising and lowering the cradle.

Joiners' shop.—Area, 10,111 square feet. Employment for 75 men. It contains 2 planers, 3 lathes, 1 band, 1 gig and 1 circular saw, 1 saw gummer, 1 molding-machine, 1 grating cutter, 1 mortising and 1 tenoning machine, 1 gouging-machine, 1 boring-machine, and 1 drill press.

UNITED STATES NAVY-YARDS.

Boat shed, employing 18 men.
Paint-shop, employing 75 men.
Calkers' shop, employing 150 men.
Iron-platers' shop, small and incomplete.

Besides the two engines for the marine railway there are two in the rolling-mill of 1½ horse-power each, one of 40 horse-power in the iron-platers' shop, 1 of 60 horse-power in the east saw-mill, and 1 in the joiners' shop and west saw-mill.

Five vessels could be built at one time, employing 1,000 men, and about 20 vessels could lie at the wharves for repairs. This department could thus employ 1,800 men.

There is no plant for building iron vessels.

DEPARTMENT OF STEAM ENGINEERING.

Machine- and erecting-shop.—Area, 52,749 square feet. Employment for 620 men, including an outside gang of 200 men employed on board the ships. There are the following tools in these shops, viz: 32 vises, 17 planers, largest 36½ by 20 by 20 feet, 15 shaping machines, largest 7½ by 1½ by 4⅔ feet, 61 lathes, 7 boring machines, largest 100 inches by 20 feet, 9 slotting-machines, 20 drill-presses, 2 facing-machines, 5 screw-cutting machines, 20 other machines (various), 7 wood and 6 iron cranes.

Boiler-shop.—Area, 12,720 square feet. Employment for 250 men. It contains the following: 2 riveting machines, largest can rivet to center of 13-foot plate, 1 set plate rolls, 2 trip hammers, 1 punching and shearing and 6 punching machines, 2 shears, 4 iron cranes.

Foundery for iron and brass.—Area, 14,904 square feet. Employment for 100 men. Contains 4 cupolas, 2 of 30 tons, 1 of 12 and 1 of 5 tons, 4 blowers, 2 reverberatory furnaces, 1 for iron, of 15 tons capacity, and 1 for brass, of 4 tons, 12 brass furnaces, of 200 pounds capacity, 4 iron and 5 wooden cranes.

Pattern-shop.—Over machine-shop. Employment for 30 men. Area, 20,000 square feet. Contains 12 benches, 2 circular, 2 gig, and 1 band saw, 4 lathes, 3 face lathes, 3 planers, 3 molding-machines, 1 rod machine, 1 boring and 1 mortising-machine.

Two steam-engines are employed, one a Corliss engine, the other a vertical engine built in the yard.

Total area of shops is 100,373 square feet, and the total number of employés 1,000.

The shops of this department are the largest in the yard and the most complete in their outfit. The machinery is large, and the most powerful engines and largest boilers can be constructed. The machine-shop is second to none in the United States, either public or private.

DEPARTMENT OF YARDS AND DOCKS.

In addition to the plant already referred to are the following: 2 iron cranes, one of 15 tons and the other of 20 tons; 1 masting shears of 65 tons; 1 platform scales of 10 tons.

Complete system of gas throughout the yard, buildings, etc.

Car-tracks connecting all the principal shops with wharves, cranes, scales, etc.

Store-houses and buildings for the care and protection of all public property.

DEPARTMENT OF ORDNANCE AND GUNNERY.

Brass foundery and blacksmith-shop.—Area, 6,251 square feet. Employment for 50 men. They contain the following, viz: 1 cupola of 10 tons capacity; 6 brass furnaces of 200 pounds; 4 reverberatory furnaces for bronze, capacity of each 10,000 pounds; 1 wooden crane and 1 blower; 2 forges.

Machine-shop.—Area 16,551 square feet. Employment for 425 men. It contains 69 lathes, largest swings 4 feet 3¼ inches and 56 feet 7 inches long; 7 planers, largest 21 by 7 feet; 2 slotting-machines; 5 shaping-machines; 1 machine for boring the trunnion bearings of gun-carriages; 4 drill-presses; 1 large testing-machine for metals, limit 100,000 pounds per square inch; 2 round-ball turning-machines.

Pattern-shop.—Area, 5,484 square feet. Employment for 20 men. Contains 1 band, 1 scroll, and 1 circular saw; 3 planers; 1 spoke planer; 1 boring-machine; 5 lathes; 9 benches.

Shell-house.—Area, 7,847 square feet. Employment for 150 men. Has a complete outfit for strapping shells, fitting gun-gear, etc., with a large storage capacity for shells and gear.

Laboratory.—Area, 4,420 square feet.

A new gun foundery has been built, covering 19,185 square feet, but never fitted.

There are two steam engines attached to this department, one for the machine-shop and a small one for the pattern-shop.

Total area of shops, 59,738 square feet, with employment for 645 men.

EQUIPMENT DEPARTMENT.

Forge-shop, anchor-shop, iron-rolling mill, and fagoting-shop.—These shops are all in the same building, covering an area of 35,268 square feet, and can employ about 90 men. The forge-shop contains 3 furnaces, one capable of heating 8 tons, and two with capacity of 5 tons each; 1 large steam-hammer, weight 16,500 pounds; 4 wooden cranes, and 1 forge for heavy work. The anchor-shop contains 4 forges for heavy work and 3 furnaces for light work; 2 Dudgeon steam-hammers, one with a cylinder of 16 inches and one with a cylinder of 20 inches diameter. The rolling-mill contains 1 train of rolls 19 inches in diameter for 4 to ½-inch round iron, angle, square, and flat iron, trim to 4 feet in width by 14 feet length, and ⅜ inch thick; 1 proof-shears. The fagoting shop contains 3 scrap furnaces, capable of heating 1,600 pounds each; 2 Dudgeon steam-hammers, diameter of cylinders, 12 inches. These shops are fitted with 1 engine of 78 horse-power, 1 engine of 60 horse-power, and 1 engine of 18 horse-power, 2 blowers, 10 large wooden cranes, and 1 small iron crane.

Blacksmith-shop, chain-cable shop, and galley-shop.—These shops are in the same building with those of department of steam engineering. They cover an area of 20,753 square feet, and employ 220 men. The blacksmith- and chain-cable shop contains 40 forges, 1 steam-hammer of 3¼ tons, 1 chain-proving machine, 1 furnace, 2 link-benders, 1 large fan (used also by department of steam engineering), 6 iron cranes. In attached machine-shop are 1 lathe, 2 drill-presses, and 4 vises. The galley-shop contains 2 lathes, 4 drill-presses, 1 planer, 1 shaper, 1 bolt-cutter, 20 vises, 1 outfit of tinner and coppersmith tools, 5 forges, 3 wooden cranes, 1 iron crane, 1 small steam-hammer, and one combined punch and shears. In attached pattern-shop are 1 small lathe and 2 benches.

Rigging-loft (over iron store).—Employs 50 men, and is fitted complete for rigging largest vessels.

Sail-loft (over timber shed).—Employs 35 men, and is fitted for all canvas work for fitting first-class frigates. The buildings of this department cover 56,021 square feet, and employ 395 men.

This department is supplied with the necessary implements, etc., for making anchors, chains, and galleys for the entire navy.

MEMORANDA OF VESSELS BUILT AT THE NAVY-YARD, WASHINGTON, D. C.

Name.	Class.	Tonnage.	Date of building.
		Old measure.	
Columbus	Line-of-battle ship	2,480	1819
Potomac	First-class frigate	1,726	1821
Brandywine	do	1,726	1825
Saint Louis	Second-class sloop	700	1828
Columbia	First-class frigate	1,726	1836
Saint Mary's	First-class sloop	958	1844
Water Witch 1	Side-wheel steamer		1844
Water Witch 3	do		1846
Water Witch 4	do		1852
		New measure.	
Minnesota	Steam frigate	3,000	1854
Nipsic	Steam sloop	615	1874

MEMORANDA OF STEAM MACHINERY BUILT IN THE ENGINEERING DEPARTMENT OF THE UNITED STATES NAVY-YARD, WASHINGTON, DISTRICT OF COLUMBIA.

Names of vessels.	When built.	Description of engines.	Displacement, in tons.	Indicated horse-power.	CYLINDERS. No.	CYLINDERS. Diameter.	Stroke.
						Inches.	Inches.
Water Witch	1852	Inclined	578	180	1	37½	72
Union	1846	Horizontal, vertical shaft		400	2	40	48
Hancock	1853	Vertical, oscillating		80	2	20	21
Minnesota	1854	Horizontal trunk	4,700	1,200	2	79½	36
Swatara	1863	Horizontal, back-acting	900	600	2	36	36
Resaca	1863	do	900	600	2	36	36
Naval Academy	1863	do		600	2	36	36
Saco	1863	do	900	450	2	27	30
Richmond	1863	do	2,700	1,400	2	60	36
Bon-Homme Richard	1865	Horizontal, direct-acting		4,400	2	100	48
Epervier	1867	Horizontal, back-acting		600	2	36	48
Swatara	1872	Horizontal, compound back-acting	1,900	1,200	2	42 and 64	42
Quinnebaug	1872	do	1,900	1,200	2	42 and 64	42
Marion	1872	do	1,900	1,200	2	42 and 64	42
Vandalia	1872	do	2,200	1,200	2	42 and 64	42
Galena	1874	do	1,900	1,200	2	42 and 64	42
Mohican	1875	do	1,900	1,200	2	42 and 64	42
Steam cutters, first class	About 100 to date	Vertical, direct-acting	8	25	1	8	8 and 10
Steam cutters, second class			5	15	1	6	6

NORFOLK, VIRGINIA.

This yard is one of the most conveniently situated on the coast for the building and repairing of vessels, and is much employed by the department for that purpose. Many of our ships of war have been rebuilt here. The yard was of great service to the confederate navy after 1861, although much of the property it contained was destroyed by fire. Several wooden vessels could be undertaken at once here, and the situation is the most favorable in the country for obtaining cheap white oak of the best quality. The yard is deficient in plant for iron-ship building, but the shops and tools exist for making engines and boilers of the largest class. One of the strong points of the location is that the harbor is never obstructed by ice, and the mildness of the climate, the ease of access to the harbor, and the ample anchorage for a large fleet make the place the most valuable rendezvous for war vessels on the whole Atlantic coast.

PENSACOLA, FLORIDA.

The navy-yard at Pensacola is the only one on the Gulf, and on that account it is an important station. The lack of proper facilities prevents any work being done at present, except in the way of repairing tugs and small vessels. Before the war the yard was well equipped, and the department is now making every effort to have it restored to its former condition. A large dry-dock is in process of construction, a timber shed has recently been built, and machinery is also being bought. The yard was formerly in good condition, but at the close of the war of 1861 it was in a state of complete dilapidation. So far as the construction of wooden vessels is concerned Pensacola is favorably situated, live oak and yellow pine of the best quality growing in abundance in the surrounding country

UNITED STATES NAVY-YARDS.

MARE ISLAND, CALIFORNIA.

This is a large and important yard, the only one on the Pacific coast, and is situated on an island at the junction of the Napa river with the Sacramento opposite Vallejo. Appropriations for its equipment have been liberal. The grounds are large, the buildings are numerous and strong, and the machinery equipment is already extensive. A floating dry-dock is employed for examining the bottoms of vessels, but a large stone dry-dock is being built to take its place. It has long been considered desirable to create the means here for building iron vessels, and steps have been taken with that object in view, an iron-plating shop having recently been completed. The wooden war-ship Mohican, propeller, is in frame on the stocks, and is covered with a shed. The yellow fir of the Oregon region has been used in its timbers, and the ship is considered by the department as worth completion. One of the four unfinished iron monitors of the government, the Monadnock, lies upon the stocks at Vallejo, opposite and below the navy-yard. Like its sisters, the Terror at Philadelphia, the Puritan at Chester, and the Amphitrite at Wilmington, it is awaiting the appropriation necessary to put it in launching condition. This yard is held to possess many great advantages. The depth of water is from 24 to 26 feet, which is ample for any war ship of the present day, and the fresh water of the Napa river preserves the hulls of wooden vessels laid up here from the attacks of the teredo. There is an abundant supply of good timber, which can be brought down by interior routes from the north. The climate is mild, the yard almost inaccessible to attack, and the present value of the buildings is over $4,000,000.

16 S B

Chapter VIII.—SHIP-BUILDING TIMBER.

At the time of the settlement of her American colonies the forests of England had begun to be severely taxed for a supply of good ship-building timber. During the early part of the seventeenth century the British navy had increased rapidly in importance, and the trade to the East Indies and other distant parts of the world was leading to the production of an immense number of ships. Not only was the consumption of oak for the building of new vessels large, but the warfare continually waged by England upon the sea required the incessant repair of ships and made a demand upon the oak forests of the country for that purpose almost as large as for the building of new vessels. The cultivation of young timber was totally neglected in England, and as the local consumption was large and the forest area small the supply of navy timber grew continually less. As early as 1660 naval officers had already become apprehensive that there would soon be a deficiency of oak timber in England. The price of the wood had nearly doubled in fifty years. The contract price paid for straight timber about 1663 varied from £2 to £2 15s. per load of 50 cubic feet, and for knee timber the prices varied from £2 15s. to £3 3s. per load.

The scarcity of proper timber for the construction of the best class of vessels was a serious matter to a country whose safety in defense depended almost entirely on the possession of a strong navy, and the Fellows of the Royal Society were appealed to for suggestions as to the proper manner to increase the timber supply. The subject was taken up by Mr. Evelyn, one of the Fellows, who recommended "that a universal plantation of all sorts of trees should be encouraged, as the only way of insuring a sufficient supply in the future". Mr. Evelyn agitated the subject of the growing deficiency of timber for forty years, and the facts he presented to the British public so alarmed them that timber trees were planted on private property in almost every part of England, especially in the royal forests, England having in this matter heeded the profitable example of Portugal.

Oak trees large enough for the construction of vessels of considerable size are from 100 to 250 years old, so that these young plantations were not available for several generations after the time of Evelyn. The trees became large enough to cut about the time of the American revolution. A report made by Lord Melville in 1810 states "that the vast quantities of great timber consumed by our navy during the present reign were chiefly the produce of the plantations made between the Restoration and the end of the 17th century".

A fresh demand was made upon the timber resources of England shortly after the Restoration by the celebrated "navigation act", which compelled Englishmen to employ British built vessels only, and a still greater demand sprang up after the independence of the American colonies, from the fact that English merchants could then no longer own a vessel built in the colonies, and had to build their vessels at home. The destruction of British oak increased largely, therefore, year by year, reaching in 1811 about 260,000 loads annually, and although the quantity of timber required diminished somewhat after that date, owing to the fewer losses of ships by war, yet the timber supply continued to decrease also and the price of oak rose steadily. During the war of 1812 English oak brought £7 5s. per load, and for thirty years after that it still brought an average of about £6 per load. From the necessities of the case England soon became obliged to rely on foreign countries for a large part of the ship timber she required. The first importations were of white oak from the Canadian provinces; a further quantity was imported directly from America; in fact, every country in the world producing timber of any value was resorted to by the English builders. Many vessels were built after the war of 1812 out of European larch, and a great many others were built out of fir from the Baltic. Pitch-pine was also imported from the United States, and other kinds of timber were brought from the cape of Good Hope and from the East Indies.

After the war of 1812 there were several periods of great stagnation in the maritime enterprise of England. Several investigations into the causes were ordered by parliament, and in 1833 and 1847 the subject was inquired into exhaustively. One of the principal topics discussed by the parliamentary committees on all these occasions was the high price of ship timber and its effect upon the cost of English-built ships. It was shown that vessels built in London cost £28 per ton, and those on the other coasts of the country from £15 to £18 per ton, while vessels built on the Baltic could be constructed for £8 to £10 per ton, the cost in America being from £10 to £12. These differences were almost entirely due to varying cost and abundance of timber. The most serious feature of the high prices and scarcity in England was the fact that the causes were such that there was no room for hope for the future. With the increase in population and progress in refinement the general consumption of timber in the useful arts and the heating of houses had been increasing. More wood was required annually than could be produced by the natural growth of the forests. The high price of food had rendered the land valuable for cultivation, the fields had been cleared and plowed, and there had been an utter neglect of the planting of young trees on land that could not be tilled. Besides that, under the protecting legislation of England, the requirements of the merchant navy were constantly increasing, and the manner in which estates are owned in England soon interposed an obstacle to the cutting of timber even where forests still existed. At the time that the building of iron vessels became an industry the English oak was virtually all gone, and the difference in cost between the ship built of timber and the one built of iron was hardly worthy of mention. The invention of the iron ship was the salvation of the naval art in England, and probably of her merchant marine.

As the English forests were already giving out when colonies began to be planted in the New World, it will be seen that the emigrants enjoyed a decided advantage over their brethren at home in the manufacture of ships—an advantage improved, however, substantially only for the local needs of the colonists themselves. The multiplication of vessels in the colonies during the early part of their history was remarkable.

The country was covered with large, tall trees, suitable for ship-building, and the excellence of the timber was repeatedly mentioned in the reports and narratives of the early discoverers. Foremost were the white-oak trees, growing in dense and almost continuous forests along the whole north Atlantic coast and extending in a scattered way down even into the heart of the yellow-pine region in Georgia. The trees existed in enormous supply, generally had straight trunks, though yielding a great deal of crooked timber, grew from 60 to 80 feet in height, and averaged $3\frac{1}{2}$ to 4 feet in diameter at a man's height from the ground, while sometimes found as large as 8 feet in diameter. Tough, strong, elastic, and, if cut in the right season of the year, durable, this valuable timber has proved the mainstay of American ship-building from the earliest days to the present time. It is especially suited for the frames and vertebral pieces of vessels, and in spite of its weight is the best wood for the planking of the vessels of every size. Such as grows near the sea-coast and in the swamps is remarkably free from defects of every kind, and so abundant was the timber once that early builders used nothing except the heart of oak in their vessels, sawing off the outer or sap-wood and selecting nothing except the durable inner portion. The fastidiousness of the builders led to an unnecessary destruction of the tree, for of timber thus handled at least one-half becomes waste. So cheap was American oak that vessels built of it for the first hundred years cost only about one-half the price of oak vessels in Europe. It was at first supposed that no timber should be put into a vessel's frame except that which had a natural curvature, and when the crooked timber had been culled from the forests there was some doubt whether its place could be supplied. A practice soon became general, however, of hewing the frames out of straight timber; a practice due to necessity, but found to answer nearly as well. The discovery led again to a great destruction of timber. It is estimated that frames cut from the log or from flitch waste at least one-third and often one-half of the original tree.

The causes which led to the disappearance of the oak in England also came into operation here, and within the recollection of persons now living the white oak has almost entirely disappeared as a ship-building timber in the states in which that industry has been the most actively carried on. In Maine virtually all of the oak accessible from the coast is gone, and only a few small and scattered bodies of it now exist. It is thought that in the western part of the state, in the vicinity of Wells, there is oak enough still left to supply the frames of about 200 vessels; but it grows largely on property where it is valued for its effect in the landscape, and cannot be utilized commercially. The white oak was not indigenous to the valley of the Kennebec to the north of Waterville, nor on the Penobscot north of Bangor, but it did grow inland as far as those points. Many of the more inland bodies of it were not reached for many years; but the construction of railroads finally brought them all into market, and the urgent demand for timber has led to their destruction. There are oak trees of the red and other species (very good timber) found in the mountainous and broken parts of Maine; but they are not at present accessible, nor do they exist in quantities sufficiently large to add materially to the resources of that state for ship-building timber. Owing to the great scarcity of oak on the coast people have lately been compelled to use trees of second growth and all the poorer varieties which, fifty years ago, no Maine man would have introduced into his vessel. It is not to be supposed that the gradual wasting of the forest wealth of Maine has been allowed to go on without remonstrance from the state government. In 1868 the board of agriculture of that state aroused the attention of the landholders to what was going on, the facts coming to many minds with the force of a new revelation; and in consequence of the alarm then existing the people of Maine began to cherish their forest trees as never before. It is believed at Augusta that in the older and better settled portion of the state the amount of growing wood and timber is now suffering no material diminution, and it is thought by some that the area in the state devoted to forestry is now larger than it was twenty years ago. It is to be borne in mind, however, that this is chiefly due to the fact that ship-builders have been driven to other states for the material for their vessels, especially for those of a large class, and having found in the southern states a sufficient and cheap supply, they have for the last twenty years been importing into the state all the timber they needed. This circumstance is giving the forests of the state a chance to rest and recuperate; meanwhile, the state is left without a local supply of oak, and is entirely dependent on the resources of other parts of the coast.

The southern part of New Hampshire was once densely covered with oak, and the Portsmouth vessels were always constructed from local timber. Both on account of the excellence of the wood and the good workmanship of the builders there was a time when New Hampshire vessels got the best rates of insurance in the country, but all of the timber within easy distance of the coast has now disappeared. The northern part of the state is stocked with red oak, intermingled with other timber, and when railroads are built in sufficient number to cover that region a great deal of timber will come into market; but there is no prospect at present of this being done in time to benefit the decaying ship-building industry of the state.

In Vermont white oak is still in fair supply, and is scattered over a large part of the state, more especially in the counties bordering on lake Champlain. The woods have been much culled near the rivers and lakes, but what is left is small and of good quality. Vermont has enough oak for her own limited use for a long time, with some to spare. Owing to the lack of cheap transportation much of it will not be called for until the supply elsewhere becomes so reduced that the increased price will pay the cost of hauling long distances, and by that time the supply will probably be much lessened by local consumption.

In Massachusetts nearly all the oak is gone. It is stated that, while a certain amount is still to be found in the state, much of it is preserved as a feature of patriarchal estates, and little ever comes into market except by reason of the division of estates and the necessity of paying off legacies, when the oak is cut and sent into the market as a means of raising ready money. Massachusetts oak is of excellent quality.

A small supply of oak is still to be found in the state of Connecticut; but ship-building has almost ceased in that state, and were the industry ever to reach considerable proportions again the supply would not last more than a few years.

A large part of New Jersey was originally covered with the finest white oak, but the clearing of the land for cultivation and the use of oak in the general arts has nearly removed the timber from the state. For a long period forests of this timber flourished almost untouched in the southern part of the state, but the railroads have made it accessible, and it is disappearing at a rapid rate. There are only a few places left where oak timber of any size can be cut. A little of it can be found in the vicinity of May's Landing, there being several hundred trees of large size in and around that village from 12 to 25 inches in diameter and ranging in age from 80 to 200 years. There is also a good deal of the timber in the vicinity of Maurice river, where for the last thirty-five years a considerable number of fishing and coasting vessels have been built every year; but practically the white oak is so nearly extinct in New Jersey that, except on Maurice river, the builders do not depend upon it for the frames of their vessels. The sloops, schooners, and brigantines built in eastern New Jersey are nearly all framed with Jersey yellow pine; the planking and center work only are of oak.

The largest oak forest now existing, growing close upon the Atlantic coast, is on the peninsula of Delaware and in the states of Maryland and Virginia. This region has been resorted to by the ship-builders of Maine, Massachusetts, and New York for more than fifty years. The timber originally covered the whole face of the country from the Delaware river to Chesapeake bay and beyond, and the trees were so tall that the majority of them would yield logs 2½ feet square and 60 feet in length without a spot or defect, the moist lands in which they grew and the exposure to the breezes of the sea being particularly favorable to the production of durable timber. Delaware and Maryland white oak became famous more than fifty years ago for its lasting quality and its general excellence. The possession of this abundant supply of cheap timber led to no great development of the ship-building industry of the states in which it grew; nine-tenths of all the oak felled upon the peninsulas has been cut for exportation to northern markets or to Europe. Serious inroads had already been made into the supply at the time of the war of 1861, and during that war, to supply the demands of the navy, an immense quantity of it was cut. At one time there was serious apprehension of the entire failure of the supply of large timber, and large quantities of it were cut and transported to the north for storage in the navy-yards, so that at least the government should not be without material for building vessels. At least one-half of the face of the country on the Delaware, Maryland, and Virginia peninsulas is still covered with a thick growth of oak trees, but nearly all the first growth near navigable water has now been removed. It is supposed that Worcester county, Maryland, has more oak than any other locality at present, as there was very little cut in that county before the railroad was built through it a few years ago; but since a way of transportation has been opened wood-cutters have been operating there vigorously. There is now very little good ship-timber left in eastern Maryland, except in that county, and it is estimated that in twenty years' time, at the present rate of consumption, the whole supply of large pieces for ships' frames will have been destroyed. The growing scarcity of large trees is illustrated in part by the rise in price of timber standing upon the stump. In times past it has been bought for $1 a thousand feet, standing in the tree, and even at the present time, in counties having a great deal of it, the price is sometimes as low as that; but the usual price at present is seldom lower than $3, even in places where it is difficult to get it out, the average from $4 to $10 a thousand, and before the trees have been felled, hewed into frame timber, and transported by water to Maine the value has risen to $35 a thousand feet. If the second growth of oak in this region were as good as the first, and if the demand for the timber were limited to the requirements of the United States alone, it is probable that several generations would elapse before the price would rise much higher. But it is found, in the first place, that the second growth of oak is not so good as the first. Owing to the gradual clearing up of the country the soil has grown drier, or some other change has taken place which seems to affect the quality of the timber, and many of the local builders in Delaware and Maryland who are familiar with the timber resources of their states believe that the first growth of white oak can never be replaced and that the destruction of timber now going on is permanent. In the next place, the demand is not limited to the United States, Delaware and Maryland white oak being now sent to the Canadian provinces and to Europe in large quantities. The finest pieces, intended for keels, stems, stern-posts, rudder-posts, etc., are cut expressly for the Saint John's market, and this trade has grown so large as to hasten materially the disappearance of the timber.

There is good oak in the Alleghany region south of Pennsylvania extending nearly to Georgia, but it is too far away from the sea to be cut for ship-building while any considerable quantity remains in the coast counties of Delaware, Maryland, and Virginia, and, though cheap where it stands, the expense of bringing it down for shipment would be considerable.

Along the northern lakes the white oak has disappeared with the same rapidity as on the sea-coast. Originally the country was covered with almost one unbroken forest containing oak, pine, hemlock, and hard-wood from lake Champlain to the head of lake Superior; but in the place of this grand growth of timber there now exists an almost unbroken series of cleared and cultivated fields and thriving cities for a distance of more than a thousand miles. A few small forests remain, as in the Adirondack region in New York and on the peninsulas of Michigan and Wisconsin, and some oak remains scattered in small quantities all along through the tier of states bordering on the lakes, but nine-tenths of all the timber is gone. Professor Sargent predicts that what is left of some varieties will be cut off in twenty years, and one need only go into the ship-yards on the lakes to learn that an oak famine is impending. Even in Michigan, where the best white oak in the West is found, people are now importing timber to some extent from Canada in order to eke out the local supply, and more than one large owner of tonnage on the lakes has told me that on account of the diminution of the oak supply he expects to convert his property into iron vessels in the course of a few years. The western forests have been the more severely taxed for oak because that is the only good timber the builders of the lakes have had. They are too far from the southern market to buy pitch-pine, and their white pine is too soft and perishable for use in vessels except for decking, beams, houses, and spars. Lake vessels are framed, planked, and ceiled with oak. This fact, and the general demand for oak timber for houses, cars, and other local purposes, its exportation to the East and to Europe, the clearing up of the country, and the disastrous losses by forest fires, have caused the trees to disappear with remarkable rapidity. The wood has become so scarce that the price of flitch oak has risen from $10 per thousand board feet to $20 in the last twenty years, while squared oak has risen from $15 to $25 per thousand feet, and plank to $30 and $35 per thousand.

While speaking of oak, mention should be made of the forests of the Ohio River valley. The greatest hardwood forest in the country originally grew over the face of the territory extending from Arkansas and Missouri eastward all along both sides of the Ohio river, and up the Cumberland, Tennessee, Kanawha, and other great branches of the Ohio to the mountains of Virginia, and over the mountains down to the coast. On the northern side of the Ohio the oak has been pretty well cut off, except in scattered lowlands; but on the southern side of the river, in West Virginia, Kentucky, Tennessee, and western North Carolina, and away west in Missouri and Arkansas, there is an abundance of white-oak timber. Now that coal is the popular fuel used on river steamboats and in railroad locomotives the felling of timber is going on more slowly, and some of the forests are practically uninvaded. There is probably more white oak in that region than in all the rest of the country put together, and there are immense tracts of trees of large size. The quality is not always so good as that of the coast oak, but there is enough timber growing in moist land to make the wood sufficiently sound for ship-building purposes. The unfortunate feature of the situation is that there is no practicable way of getting it down to market, as the only route to the sea-coast is by way of the Ohio and Mississippi rivers to New Orleans. It could be floated thither in rafts, as it now is to all points along the Ohio river, by felling a certain number of poplar trees, to float the rafts; but the distance is great, and the rafts would continually be lost in the swift current of the river or by getting aground on sand-bars. The scheme is financially too perilous to be attempted, and the cost of freight from New Orleans to the northern yards would in any event be a serious drawback. It is doubtful whether this timber can ever be much used for deep-sea ship-building unless the vessels are built upon the Mississippi river, for by the time that prices on the coast are so high as to warrant the rafting of it to New Orleans or the freighting of it overland by railroad it will probably be as cheap to build ships of iron as of white oak. A good deal of oak is indeed being sent in cars to the sea-board at the present time, but not for ship-building.

From this review it will be seen that the ship-building of the United States cannot probably depend upon the oak supply of the country for many years longer. Were shipping and trade what they were two hundred years ago, the supply might last a long time; but there has been a great change since America was first settled, and timber is now being consumed in a more rapid ratio than formerly. In old times vessels were small. A 400-ton ship was a monster, and a thousand small vessels were a great fleet, worthy of national pride. Less than 200,000 feet of timber would build a large vessel of the days of the pilgrims; on the other hand, at the present time, the coasting schooners of ordinary size require from 300,000 to 400,000 feet of lumber, and the barks and deep-sea ships from 700,000 to 950,000 and even 1,100,000 feet each. That is to say, every large ship requires the felling of from 160 to 250 trees which are from 100 to 250 years old, a growth which could not be replaced in the life-time of less than four generations. Not only are vessels larger, but there are more of them than there were two centuries ago; and the larger the vessels the heavier the scantling in proportion, and more timber is used in repairing and rebuilding them. Besides the wood consumed by the vessels themselves, a great quantity is cut annually for the building and repairing of wharves and piers in the harbors in which shipping is employed, and the trees cut for those objects are unfortunately the younger ones. The forests are thus being stripped of both large and small trees. No opportunity is given them to recuperate, so that while the consumption of white oak is far greater in proportion to the number of vessels built than it was 200 years ago, the circumstances are also such that it is almost impossible to entertain the slightest hope of ever replacing the timber when it has finally been cut off.

Second only to white oak in importance in ship-building on the Atlantic coast is the yellow pine of the southern states. This tree is properly the yellow or long-leaf pine, and all from Virginia southward is of this variety. In the ship-yards it is called indiscriminately "pitch-pine" and "yellow pine"; but the yellow or pitch-pine of New Jersey is another variety. The southern pine is a tree from 60 to 80 feet in height, with a trunk from 2 to 4 feet in diameter and the grain coarse, but compact and straight, and having far less sap-wood than the northern varieties, such as the pines of Virginia and New Jersey. The wood is heavy, strong, and rigid, is full of turpentine, and holds iron tenaciously, being also free from the acids which destroy an iron bolt. It does not grow much more than 100 miles inland from the sea-coast, but for at least that distance it forms almost an unbroken belt of timber from the southern boundary of Virginia all the way to Texas, skipping, however, the lower part of Louisiana. It has been cut off only along the course of the railroads and the rivers of the several states in which it is found. In Mississippi and Alabama the trees do not stand so thickly as in the other states, and are consequently larger and finer. The supply of this valuable timber is very great. It is used principally in the planking, ceiling, keelsons, water-ways, rails, and beams of vessels, and occasionally for decking and spars. Lower masts, with a core of oak and an outside of yellow pine, bolted and hooped together, are now commonly made for the large ships, and topmasts are frequently made of a single pitch-pine stick. The timber is cheap in the states in which it grows, and it is surprising that it is not utilized there for a great local ship-building industry. In a 2,000-ton ship, consuming 900,000 or 1,000,000 feet of timber, as now built in Maine, there is from 150,000 to 200,000 feet of oak, white pine, and hackmatack, and 750,000 or 800,000 feet of southern pitch-pine. It would be cheaper to freight the oak, white pine, and hackmatack to the south than to freight the vastly larger quantity of pitch-pine north. If the straight-grained pitch-pine can be used for frame timber, the whole ship could be built in the South at a large saving on northern prices, probably to from $35 to $40 per register ton. Builders and insurance companies seem afraid of pitch-pine frames, but possibly this is because the experiment has not been tried.

Next after pitch-pine the timber most valued by shipbuilders in this country is white pine. This valuable tree occupies common territory with other timber in the region extending from the valley of the Saint Lawrence to beyond the great lakes, and southward along the Alleghany Mountain system to the high ridges of Georgia. In old times the supply was immense. The trees are from 80 to 150 feet in height, those full grown being from 3 to 4 feet in diameter near the butt. The wood is soft, clear, free from knots, susceptible of a beautiful polish when worked, and extremely buoyant when placed in the water; but it is not strong enough for frame timber, and there is no record of its ever having been used for that purpose in this country. A few ships were built in England of white pine during the period of the greatest alarm there about the failure of the oak supply; but as these vessels lasted on an average only three years, the experiment with that timber was not repeated.

White pine is largely valued for decking and the construction of cabins, as also for masts and spars. Its value for the latter use has always been so great that in the early patents granted to the colonies the trunks suitable for masts were reserved to the crown. A surveyor of the woods was appointed, who was given a license to go into the woods and mark such trees as were suitable for naval use. In a general way, trees of a diameter of 24 inches and upward just above the butt were reserved for the king, and persons who should fell one of them without permission were liable to a fine of £100. It is noted by Hutchinson that a pine, which when felled and made into lumber would be worth scarce twenty shillings, would bring £20 when sold for a mast. The cost of all kinds of naval stores in England in that period was high. The following were the prices of American pine delivered at the yards in England in 1770, obtained from an old history:

			BOWSPRITS.			YARDS.		
			Diameter.	Length.	Value.	Diameter.	Length.	Value.
			Inches.	Feet.	£ s.	Inches.	Feet.	£ s.
			38	75	48 0	25	105	25 12
			37	75	42 0	24	102	25 12
			36	73½	36 0	23	96	20 8
			35	70½	34 0	22	93	16 16
			34	69	32 0	21	88½	14 8
			33	67½	24 16	20	84	11 12
			32	64½	23 4	19	81	9 4
			31	63	20 16	18	76½	7 4
			30	61½	16 0	17	73½	5 4
			29	58½	12 0			
			28	57	6 16			
			27	55½	5 7			
			26	52½	4 16			

In 1768, 36-inch masts were worth £153 each delivered at the king's yards in England. In 1789 the lower masts of a 90- or 74-gun war ship, made from spindles of hard wood hooped and bolted together, cost from £500 to £525 each, the topmast, single sticks, £50 each, and the maintop-gallant masts from £8 to £9. From these figures it will be understood what a boon to England was the discovery of the magnificent white-pine timber of the American coasts.

In order to encourage the importation of spars liberal bounties were granted by act of parliament, and there were annually shipped from Portland, Maine, Portsmouth, New Hampshire, and a few other New England ports an average of about fifty ship-loads of spar-timber per year until after the revolutionary war.

The white pine was one of the first trees to disappear from the New England coast, and it is now so nearly extinct that builders are obliged to depend upon sources of supply hundreds and even thousands of miles away. New Hampshire, Vermont, New York, Pennsylvania, Ohio, and Michigan have been successively resorted to, and within the last five years two cargoes of spars have been brought from Oregon. Pitch-pine spars are now being brought to New England from Georgia. There is no prospect that trees large enough for masts will ever again be raised in Maine. In New Hampshire, Vermont, and other northern states, and as far west as Michigan, the white pine is also practically exhausted, while in Michigan, Wisconsin, and Minnesota, where there are many very large pine trees in the mixed hard-wood forests, timber-cutting is going on so fast by means of saw-mills and other steam apparatus that the extinction of the big timber is now expected within the present generation. Professor C. S. Sargent, census expert in charge of the forestry investigation, reports that it is probable that the large specimens of white pine in Michigan, Wisconsin, and Minnesota will be totally exterminated within the next ten or twelve years. It has already become cheaper for the Maine men to make their masts from strips of yellow pine and oak, bound securely together with iron hoops, than it is to bring white-pine trees from the distant parts of the country in which alone they are at present found. Lower yards on large ships are now often made of two sticks spliced, and topmasts are made of yellow pine. Iron masts and yards are now being introduced.

The "hard-wood" supply of the eastern and middle states is also nearly exhausted. These woods, comprising beech, birch, maple, and chestnut, were extensively used during the early active building times, and are still used to some extent in the timbers, beams, and planking of vessels; but there is very little of that timber left, and it cannot now be relied upon as a resource of any value for the ship-building industry. It is true that a large area of primitive forest land exists in the northern part of Maine, covering from 12,000 to 14,000 square miles of territory. Professor Sargent says that the timber is principally black spruce, with some scattered second growth pine and scattering bodies of hard wood, of which the yellow birch and the sugar maple are the most valuable, and it is possible that the future construction of railroads may make this region a factor of some importance in the future of the shipping industry in Maine, but the prospect is that the northern forests of the state will not become accessible for many years to come, as the logs are too heavy to drive down the rivers, and there is now no other way of getting them out. It ought, perhaps, to be mentioned that there is much hard wood in the north of Michigan.

A good ship-building wood, which was not much used by the early builders but has been put into ships extensively of late years, is the larch, variously called "hackmatack" and "tamarack". The wood of this tree is light colored, tough, buoyant, and durable, and a large vessel built completely of this wood would carry at least 300 tons more freight than an oak-built ship. It is not strong enough, however, to be used in parts of ships exposed to stress, and the uses for which it has been found most valuable are for knees, stanchions, and top timbers. The hackmatack has the valuable peculiarity of being free from acids which will corrode iron bolts driven through it. It holds iron with a tenacious grip. In these respects it is far superior to oak, and on account of its buoyancy, tenacity, and durability nearly all the Atlantic ship-yards use it, when it can be obtained, in the tops of vessels, as the cargo-carrying power is slightly increased and the center of gravity of the ship is kept low. On the northern coast the larch is sometimes from 80 to 100 feet in height, with the trunk sometimes 2 and 3 feet in diameter, and always grows in the swamps. A considerable body of this timber exists scattered through the northern counties of Maine, but it is so far away from the railroads that it is inaccessible. The larch is a tree of quick growth. A tract of it once cleared off springs up again immediately, and in about ten or fifteen years' time the trees are large enough for knees for the smaller class of vessels. There is apparently no reason why larch may not be relied upon for a long period for the use to which it is now chiefly put.

Spruce, too, like all other forest trees of the north Atlantic coast, is fast disappearing. It has never been used within the limits of the United States to any great extent in ship-building except for the light spars of vessels, but in the Canadian provinces forests are found of coast-spruce strong, tough, and durable which have been extensively utilized for the construction of vessels. The timber is cheap, and a ship when built of it is a good carrier and of remarkable durability for one constructed of so soft a timber. A number of small vessels built in the eastern part of Maine have also been constructed largely of spruce, but that is believed to be the only locality in the whole of the United States where spruce has been so used. For the light spars of vessels this wood is invaluable, as it is as light as white pine or cedar and is elastic and strong. A great deal of it was exported in the colonial days to England, and even at the present time a large number of European vessels are supplied with spruce spars from America, but the timber is now scarce. The chief sources of supply are Canada, Maine, New Hampshire, Vermont, northern New York, and West Virginia. A system prevails in Maine of cutting only the large trees from the spruce woods, leaving the smaller ones; and as the tree is one of rapid growth, the woods can be profitably worked at intervals of from fifteen to twenty-five years.

One other ship-building wood grows upon the Atlantic coast in limited supply, and has been used to some extent for a hundred years. This is the live-oak of Florida, a timber so durable that a ship built of it would last a hundred years, but so heavy as to make its use undesirable. A great deal of this timber was utilized during the twenty years following 1840 in navy vessels, steam propellers, and large clipper ships, particularly in the bows and sterns. Two large vessels have been built on Long Island within the last five years with live-oak frames, but experience has proved that vessels into which this wood enters to any considerable extent are inferior cargo carriers. Live-oak vessels have, as a rule, changed hands faster than those built of any other wood. There is a good deal of this timber left in Florida, but no one wants it.

Speaking in a general way, it must be admitted that the supply of valuable ship-building timber on the Atlantic coast has been materially impaired by the past two centuries of steady pillaging; and it is diminishing now so fast that wooden ships are likely to rise materially in price in the course of the next twenty years. If relief is to be looked for from any quarter, it is probable that it will come from the far northwest, on the Pacific coast.

Washington territory and Oregon, west of the Cascade mountains, are covered with the heaviest continuous belt of forest growth now existing in the United States, and perhaps in the world. Perhaps the single exception to this remark is the magnificent redwood belt of the California ranges. Nine-tenths of the forests first named are the yellow or red fir. There is a valuable cedar and several varieties of pine are scattered among the firs; there are also hemlock, spruce, a poor quality of oak, and some laurel. The tide-land spruce of that region makes excellent knees, and the laurel supplies stem pieces and other parts of the ship for which hard wood is positively required. The fir is valuable for all the rest of the ship. The trees grow to gigantic size, being from 150 to 300 feet in height, with the trunk from 5 to 8 and even 10 feet in diameter. They grow so straight that the lumbermen often fail, even with the aid of a plumb-line, to discover the slightest deflection from a true perpendicular. The wood is lighter and coarser grained than white oak, but is as strong, elastic, and tough as oak, and when cut at the right season of the year is equally as durable.

This timber first came to the notice of the officers of the United States navy more than thirty years ago. One or two war vessels having been sent into Puget sound to protect the settlers from the Indians, the officers were captivated with the timber, growing as it did from the water's edge as far inland as the eye could reach, and running up even on the sides of the colossal peaks of the region. Word being sent to Washington that it seemed desirable to test the qualities of the wood for ship-building, Admiral Farragut caused a quantity of it to be sent to the navy-yard near San Francisco and special tests to be made, with a view to ascertaining the size of scantling required to construct a vessel of fir having the same strength as though it were built of eastern white oak. Specifications for the sloop-of-war Manzanita were prepared from the results of these experiments. The fir was tested both there and at various eastern yards and found to be a satisfactory material for wooden vessels.

The following is an extract from a report by Constructor George W. Much, of the United States navy, in January, 1879, to Rear-Admiral Rodgers, on this subject:

In compliance with bureau order of October 12, 1878, to furnish the information required in your letter of October 3, 1878, relative to amended specifications for building the screw-steamer Manzanita with the Atlantic coast wood crossed out, also whether the carbolized laurel in the yard schooner Freda remains perfectly sound, etc., I have the honor to report that upon the receipt of the order I instituted inquiries as to the best Pacific coast and other woods that could be obtained in San Francisco for ship-building purposes, and by the information received from old settlers, timber dealers, vessel-owners, ship-builders, shipwrights, and others conversant in timber and timber material, find from their experience that there is no material on this or the Atlantic coast better adapted for outside and inside planking, for keels, keelsons, clamps, bilge strakes, knees, and breast-hooks than the Washington territory yellow fir, or yellow Oregon pine. It has also been adopted for frame timber in all vessels built on the coast for the last ten years, and so far with good results, and I have therefore adopted it in the specifications.

The Washington territory yellow fir or Oregon yellow pine can be readily procured, free from sap or other defects, of any desired size up to 90 feet in length, is in strength fully equal to Atlantic coast white oak, and has fully the same tenacity to hold fastening, and never becomes iron sick as it does when corroded by the acid contained in white oak. The great length of the Washington territory yellow fir saves to the ship-builder in fastening butts and scarfs and gives greater elasticity to the hull, and consequently diminishes the danger of springing a leak. Owing to the straight growth of this timber, there are comparatively but few natural crooks, but by judicious and careful selection the proper growth or shape could be obtained from the larger trees, and, if they were not readily found, the sharper floors, futtocks, and hooks could be built in the same manner as those built at this yard for the United States schooner Freda. For mast and spar timber the Washington territory yellow fir has no superior. Shipwrights and ship-builders of this coast, from their experience in repairs to sail and steam vessels, fully indorse the lasting qualities of this wood. Innumerable instances might be given of vessels built on this coast constructed entirely of Washington territory yellow fir. Some of them built as early as 1857 are still remaining perfectly sound, strong, and staunch.

The length of the fir timber is a strong point in its favor, as from trees 300 feet in height sticks of any required length can be obtained, while on the Atlantic coast oak and hard wood cannot be bought of a greater average length than 45 feet. Plank and logs of 60 feet are costly and hard to get; on the other hand, in the yellow-fir region logs for keels, keelsons, and planking can be obtained of any length that the saw-mills can handle. Keel and keelson pieces from 110 to 120 feet in length are habitually used. In the transfer steamboat Solano, of 3,549 tons, built at Oakland in 1879 and 1880, keelson pieces were used 150 feet long and 24 inches square without a particle of sap, rent, or check, and sound, straight, and free from knots and defects of every kind. In the curved parts of frames no longer sticks can be employed than in the eastern yards, but in all the longitudinal pieces of the ship, upon which the rigidity of the hull depends, the builders find it convenient to use stuff of an average length of 90 feet, and can get all they want of it without extra cost. The long stuff is preferred, because it gives strength and elasticity to the ship, and because it saves much labor in construction, owing to the fewer number of butts.

Professor Sargent says that any estimate of the actual amount of timber standing in the territory is scarcely possible with the existing knowledge of the country; but the area of the forests is enormous, and the quantity of timber to the acre is remarkable. One estimate of the quantity of timber standing, apparently an extravagant one, makes it equal to the whole amount of the wood cut in the United States from the first settlement down to the present time. An important fact about the Pacific fir is that it reproduces itself so fast in its rainy home that it can be made to last almost indefinitely.

A large number of coasting vessels have been built out of Pacific coast fir, and several ships have been constructed for the grain trade with Liverpool. There was a great difference in the length of time for which these vessels respectively lasted. Some speedily decayed, others were sound after twenty years' use, and builders were for a few years greatly puzzled to account for this phenomenon; but attention has been called of late to the time of year at which the timber for the different vessels was cut, and it is now believed that the trouble in the cases of early decay arose entirely from using summer-cut trees. Builders intend hereafter to select fall- and winter-cut timber for their vessels, and the experts of the Pacific coast believe that fir felled when the sap is out of the wood and salted after being put into the vessel will last as long as white oak.

The cost of fir will also have some bearing on the question of iron or wood as a material for sailing vessels. As long as it can be bought for $10 and $12 per thousand board feet or less than $25 or $30 a thousand, while iron costs anything like present prices, the wooden ship will be a cheaper vessel than one of iron.

The following is a statement of the specific gravities and weights of the ship-building woods of the United States, prepared for this report by Professor C. S. Sargent, of Brookline, Massachusetts, chief special agent in charge of forestry statistics of the census of 1880:

Woods.	Specific gravity.	Weight per cubic foot.	Woods.	Specific gravity.	Weight per cubic foot.	Woods.	Specific gravity.	Weight per cubic foot.
		Pounds.			*Pounds.*			*Pounds.*
White oak	0.7438	46.35	Live oak	0.9504	59.23	White laurel	0.6517	40.61
Pitch-pine of New England	0.4957	30.89	Chestnut	0.4504	28.07	Western white cedar	0.4623	28.81
Jersey pine	0.4957	30.89	Locust	0.7333	45.70	Cedar of Puget sound	0.3796	23.64
Southern pine	0.6999	43.62	Rock maple	0.6827	42.53	Alaska cedar	0.4782	29.80
White pine	0.3842	23.94	Black sugar maple	0.6921	43.13	Southern cypress	0.4600	28.67
White cedar	0.3322	20.70	American beech	0.6883	42.89	Madeira wood	0.9533	59.41
Red cedar	0.4926	30.70	Yellow birch	0.6553	40.84	Horse-flesh dogwood	0.8734	54.43
Hemlock	0.4202	26.19	Southern poplar	0.3889	24.23	Mastic	1.0109	63.00
Hackmatack	0.6236	38.86	Yellow fir	0.5155	32.13			
Black spruce	0.4584	28.57	Redwood	0.4208	26.22			

These are the weights of absolutely dry woods; for woods used for ordinary industrial purposes an addition of from 10 to 15 per cent. should be made for moisture remaining in the wood. For ship timber the weights should be corrected by adding about 25 per cent. For instance, white oak partially seasoned weighs on the average 56 pounds per cubic foot, and yellow fir 42 pounds per cubic foot in the ship-yard.

Constructor Samuel H. Pook, of the United States navy, has supplied the following data of actual weights of woods in the ship-yards:

	Weight per cubic foot in pounds.
White oak	56
Pitch-pine	40 to 50
White pine	35
Spruce	33
Maple	40
Beech	49
Live oak	76
Hackmatack	42
Chestnut	36
Hemlock	30
Sycamore	35
White holly	47
White cedar	21
Red cedar	35
Cypress	31
Hickory	53

CHAPTER IX.

STATISTICS OF SHIP-BUILDING.

STATISTICS OF SHIP-BUILDING.

NUMBER, TONNAGE, AND VALUE OF NEW VESSELS, AND NUMBER AND VALUE OF BOATS BUILT DURING THE CENSUS YEAR, BY STATES AND TERRITORIES.

State and Territory.	NEW VESSELS. (a)			BOATS.		CANAL-BOATS. (b)			Value of repairing.	Total value of all products.
	Number built.	Tonnage.	Value.	Number built.	Value.	Number built.	Tonnage.	Value.		
The United States	2,415	498,878	$19,225,714	8,026	$876,999	643	66,707	$1,739,975	$16,697,614	$36,800,327
Alabama									60,000	60,000
Arkansas	3	300	28,000							28,000
California	21	7,361	770,696	200	57,545				969,398	1,797,639
Connecticut	52	11,473	413,009	280	37,200				317,451	767,660
Delaware	55	31,123	1,614,969	100	18,437				529,097	2,162,503
Florida	13	217	25,000	45	16,050				44,000	85,050
Georgia	2	539	17,000							17,000
Illinois	11	1,397	137,300	85	9,050	1	88	8,300	745,743	892,093
Indiana	64	26,524	726,680	52	3,100				80,875	810,655
Iowa	2	860	70,000						42,000	112,000
Kansas	1	178	26,000							26,000
Kentucky	23	2,130	86,215	25	1,000				161,800	249,015
Louisiana	36	1,231	105,525	80	15,600				222,400	343,525
Maine	88	41,396	2,174,650	970	53,818				681,378	2,909,846
Maryland	131	7,499	320,260	133	45,000	60	4,270	84,000	1,423,370	1,788,630
Massachusetts	39	5,605	391,655	3,765	186,727				1,703,284	2,281,666
Michigan	69	15,909	1,390,050	210	13,117				631,469	2,034,636
Minnesota									15,000	15,000
Mississippi	3	33	3,500						2,000	5,500
Missouri	17	3,451	358,487						206,700	565,187
Nebraska	1	52	9,000							9,000
New Hampshire				44	4,440				25,630	30,070
New Jersey	53	7,455	409,714	134	34,460	10	1,010	14,600	940,455	1,384,629
New York	635	76,418	3,145,536	1,221	263,957	441	49,887	1,370,525	4,575,551	7,985,044
North Carolina	8	487	22,650						34,569	57,219
Ohio	55	25,132	1,127,600	91	18,400	1	11	2,300	406,210	1,552,210
Oregon	19	2,162	176,600						29,900	206,500
Pennsylvania	802	204,507	4,676,258	318	47,888	122	10,711	237,450	1,965,324	6,689,470
Rhode Island	17	379	129,000	68	27,610				360,431	517,041
South Carolina	27	1,615	92,900						51,100	144,000
Tennessee	1	48	5,000							5,000
Texas	16	758	55,780						22,000	77,780
Vermont	5	550	17,800			5	550	17,800		17,800
Virginia	26	514	62,050	48	9,800	3	180	5,000	109,174	181,024
Washington	14	1,769	161,600	80	1,900				21,000	184,500
West Virginia	85	16,727	221,230						9,900	231,130
Wisconsin	21	3,079	254,000	77	11,900				310,405	576,305

a Includes wooden and iron vessels and canal-boats.   *b* Included with new vessels.

SHIP-BUILDING INDUSTRY.

NUMBER, TONNAGE, AND VALUE OF NEW VESSELS, AND NUMBER AND VALUE OF BOATS BUILT DURING THE CENSUS YEAR, BY COUNTIES.

States and counties.	NEW VESSELS. (a)			BOATS.		CANAL-BOATS. (b)			Value of repairing.	Total value of all products.
	Number built.	Tonnage.	Value.	Number built.	Value.	Number built.	Tonnage.	Value.		
ALABAMA.										
Mobile									$60,000	$60,000
ARKANSAS.										
Johnson	1	125	$12,000							12,000
Pulaski	1	86	8,000							8,000
Sebastian	1	89	8,000							8,000
Total	3	300	28,000							28,000
CALIFORNIA.										
Alameda	5	5,964	638,296						51,000	689,296
Humboldt	1	347	15,000							15,000
Mendocino									5,500	5,500
San Francisco (city)	15	1,050	117,400	200	$57,545				912,898	1,087,843
Total	21	7,361	770,696	200	57,545				969,398	1,797,639
CONNECTICUT.										
Fairfield	3	68	10,300	34	2,320				11,500	24,120
Hartford									32,600	32,600
Middlesex	2	228	10,000	13	1,625				135,502	147,127
New Haven	34	4,486	128,000	65	6,666				30,660	165,326
New London	13	6,691	264,709	168	26,589				107,189	398,487
Total	52	11,473	413,009	280	37,200				317,451	767,660
DELAWARE.										
Kent	1	400	12,000							12,000
New Castle	44	27,704	1,432,669	100	18,437				523,097	1,974,203
Sussex	10	3,019	170,300						6,000	176,390
Total	55	31,123	1,614,969	100	18,437				529,097	2,162,503
FLORIDA.										
Duval				10	3,050					3,050
Franklin	4	32	3,400							3,400
Hernando	1	19	5,000							5,000
Hillsborough	1	11	1,800							1,800
Levy	1	6	450	15	5,000				6,000	11,450
Manatee	1	13	1,500						5,000	6,500
Marion	1	94	9,000							9,000
Monroe	3	29	2,850	20	8,000				33,000	43,850
Volusia	1	13	1,000							1,000
Total	13	217	25,000	45	16,050				44,000	85,050
GEORGIA.										
Glynn	1	243	8,000							8,000
Telfair	1	296	9,000							9,000
Total	2	539	17,000							17,000
ILLINOIS.										
Alexander									9,860	9,860
Cook	3	138	16,200	85	9,050	1	88	8,300	633,883	659,133
Jasper	1	10	2,000							2,000
Jersey	1	102	12,000							12,000
Massac	3	750	59,500						40,000	99,500
Peoria	2	68	6,600							6,600
Pulaski	1	329	41,000						62,000	103,000
Total	11	1,397	137,300	85	9,050	1	88	8,300	745,743	892,093
INDIANA.										
Clark	28	17,010	489,700	40	2,500				17,000	509,200
Daviess	1	28	2,800							2,800
Floyd	7	5,307	65,700							65,700
Hendricks	1	49	4,500							4,500
Jefferson	6	3,006	110,000						40,000	150,000
Martin	1	28	4,000							4,000
Perry									2,500	2,500
Switzerland	1	28	4,000							4,000
Tippecanoe	1	29	3,000							3,000
Vanderburgh	17	1,016	38,980	12	600				21,375	60,955
Warrick	1	23	4,000							4,000
Total	64	26,524	726,680	52	3,100				80,875	810,655

a Includes wooden and iron vessels and canal-boats.   b Included with new vessels.

STATISTICS OF SHIP-BUILDING.

NUMBER, TONNAGE, AND VALUE OF NEW VESSELS, ETC.—Continued.

States and counties.	NEW VESSELS. (a)			BOATS.		CANAL-BOATS. (b)			Value of repairing.	Total value of all products.
	Number built.	Tonnage.	Value.	Number built.	Value.	Number built.	Tonnage.	Value.		
IOWA.										
Dubuque	2	860	$70,000						$42,000	$112,000
KANSAS.										
Leavenworth	1	178	26,000							26,000
KENTUCKY.										
Barren	1	23	3,000							3,000
Boyd	3	135	15,000	25	$1,000				8,000	24,000
Franklin	1	60	6,500							6,500
Jefferson	1	30	30,000						15,000	45,000
Kenton	16	1,861	29,715						58,800	88,515
McCracken									80,000	80,000
Union	1	21	2,000							2,000
Total	23	2,130	86,215	25	1,000				161,800	249,015
LOUISIANA. (c)										
Calcasieu	3	86	13,925							13,925
Catahoula	1	11	6,000							6,000
Claiborne	1	18	8,000							8,000
Iberville	3	13	950							950
Jefferson	2	35	6,500							6,500
Orleans	7	250	25,050	80	15,600				222,400	263,050
Rapides	1	84	9,000							9,000
Saint Landry	1	21	8,000							8,000
Saint Mary	9	603	18,300							18,300
Saint Tammany	6	88	7,600							7,600
Tangipahoa	1	13	1,500							1,500
Terrebonne	1	9	700							700
Total	36	1,231	105,525	80	15,600				222,400	343,525
MAINE.										
Aroostook				80	2,000					2,000
Cumberland	8	7,125	401,442	225	11,950				189,718	603,110
Hancock	10	1,580	84,480	124	5,435				85,784	175,699
Knox	9	6,297	306,550	79	6,395				133,014	445,959
Lincoln	5	1,477	78,600	14	1,135				32,264	111,999
Penobscot				130	4,896				57,321	62,217
Sagadahoc	32	20,223	986,758	58	10,640				79,530	1,076,928
Waldo	1	350	14,000	15	900				18,755	33,655
Washington	10	838	61,100	201	8,776				71,992	141,868
York	13	3,506	241,720	44	1,691				13,000	256,411
Total	88	41,396	2,174,650	970	53,818				681,378	2,909,846
MARYLAND.										
Allegany	59	4,140	80,600			59	4,140	$80,600	30,500	111,100
Anne Arundel									4,000	4,000
Baltimore (city)	23	2,162	136,210	80	23,900				1,284,970	1,445,080
Calvert									5,300	5,300
Cecil	1	130	3,400			1	130	3,400		3,400
Dorchester	13	374	31,400	6	2,300				18,200	51,900
Harford	1	22	3,000						25,000	28,000
Queen Anne	1	6	900							900
Saint Mary's	2	30	3,500							3,500
Somerset	9	121	10,850	20	8,000				7,200	26,050
Talbot	11	135	14,100	12	4,800				11,200	30,100
Wicomico	6	161	14,800	15	6,000				16,000	36,800
Worcester	5	218	21,500						21,000	42,500
Total	131	7,499	320,260	133	45,000	60	4,270	84,000	1,423,370	1,788,630
MASSACHUSETTS.										
Barnstable				72	14,075				45,823	59,898
Bristol	1	12	1,000	235	28,047				202,739	231,786
Dukes				6	1,910				47,569	49,479
Essex	17	1,761	131,050	2,951	73,799				180,485	385,334
Middlesex				46	7,500					7,500
Norfolk	2	938	48,000	259	14,850					62,850
Plymouth				6	1,171				2,500	3,671
Suffolk	19	2,894	211,605	170	43,375				1,224,168	1,479,148
Worcester				20	2,000					2,000
Total	39	5,605	391,655	3,765	186,727				1,703,284	2,281,666
MICHIGAN.										
Allegan	1	23	3,500							3,500
Alpena	1	6	1,500							1,500
Berrien	4	409	41,200							41,200
Huron	6	80	6,800							6,800
Iosco	1	403	18,000							18,000

a Includes wooden and iron vessels and canal-boats.   b Included with new vessels.   c Parishes.

SHIP-BUILDING INDUSTRY.

NUMBER, TONNAGE, AND VALUE OF NEW VESSELS, ETC.—Continued.

States and counties.	NEW VESSELS. (a)			BOATS.		CANAL-BOATS. (b)			Value of repairing.	Total value of all products.
	Number built.	Tonnage.	Value.	Number built.	Value.	Number built.	Tonnage.	Value.		
MICHIGAN—continued.										
Macomb	4	759	$57,500							$57,500
Manistee	1	22	2,000							2,000
Manitou	1	11	950							950
Mason	1	12	900							900
Muskegon	2	34	4,800							4,800
Ottawa	9	681	87,850						$17,900	105,750
Saginaw	14	5,314	340,550	87	$2,950				71,000	414,500
Saint Clair	7	644	34,900	30	1,992				118,169	155,061
Sanilac				10	2,100					2,100
Van Buren	4	96	4,600							4,600
Wayne	13	7,415	785,000	83	6,075				424,400	1,215,475
Total	69	15,909	1,390,050	210	13,117				631,469	2,034,636
MINNESOTA.										
Washington									15,000	15,000
MISSISSIPPI.										
Hancock	1	17	2,000							2,000
Harrison	2	16	1,500						2,000	3,500
Total	3	33	3,500						2,000	5,500
MISSOURI.										
Butler	1	86	8,000							8,000
Clay	1	29	9,000							9,000
Cole	1	42	7,000							7,000
Gasconade	1	91	9,000							9,000
Howard	2	109	10,475							10,475
Jackson	1	48	15,000							15,000
Saint Louis (city)	10	3,046	300,012						206,700	506,712
Total	17	3,451	358,487						206,700	565,187
NEBRASKA.										
Cass	1	52	9,000							9,000
NEW HAMPSHIRE.										
Rockingham				44	4,440				25,630	30,070
NEW JERSEY.										
Atlantic	4	48	5,100						1,300	6,400
Burlington	6	259	10,400	4	1,820	1	200	$1,800	13,400	25,620
Camden	11	2,139	200,087	26	8,000				230,489	438,576
Cape May	7	396	30,200							30,200
Cumberland	6	1,879	112,300						19,400	131,700
Essex									22,500	22,500
Gloucester	1	19	2,500							2,500
Hudson	2	300	6,000	78	21,050				516,716	543,766
Mercer									31,000	31,000
Middlesex	1	164	9,000						54,750	63,750
Monmouth	10	882	16,800			9	810	12,800	20,000	36,800
Ocean	1	9	1,200	4	1,600					2,800
Union	4	1,360	16,127	22	1,990				30,900	49,017
Total	53	7,455	409,714	134	34,460	10	1,010	14,600	940,455	1,384,629
NEW YORK.										
Albany	7	793	22,800			6	780	18,300	90,000	112,800
Cayuga	1	132	3,600	13	2,850	1	132	3,600	7,350	13,800
Chautauqua	1	124	2,500			1	124	2,500		2,500
Clinton	6	722	24,600			6	722	24,600		24,600
Duchess	4	120	16,300							16,300
Erie	134	16,188	668,390	47	2,800	108	13,189	384,475	495,766	1,166,956
Essex	13	1,709	36,800			13	1,709	36,800	18,000	54,800
Greene	9	2,345	200,300						32,000	232,300
Herkimer									31,400	31,400
Jefferson	6	408	35,800							35,800
Kings	78	11,259	649,995	92	19,241				1,330,552	1,999,788
Lewis	4	160	6,800			4	160	6,800	2,200	9,000
Madison	8	1,052	27,600			8	1,052	27,600	17,387	44,987
Monroe	38	5,035	153,100	48	5,510	37	4,885	147,100		158,610
Montgomery									6,000	6,000
New York	2	18	2,100	642	163,360				1,905,545	2,071,005
Niagara	58	6,911	233,700			58	6,911	233,700	29,700	263,400
Oneida	22	2,196	62,900			20	1,931	50,900	21,476	84,376
Onondaga	7	850	23,800	12	1,100	7	850	23,800	5,800	30,700
Ontario				24	11,720					11,720
Orange	6	724	126,000						57,400	183,400
Oswego	33	4,517	113,200	22	1,190	31	4,117	92,400	31,173	145,563
Queens	1	8	1,200							1,200
Richmond	13	1,582	100,000	12	1,400				87,400	188,800
Rockland	3	130	21,000						9,000	30,000
Saint Lawrence				30	4,000				5,467	9,467
Saratoga	12	1,560	38,000			12	1,560	38,000	11,000	49,000
Schenectady									5,500	5,500
Schuyler	6	739	33,500	20	800	6	739	33,500		34,300
Seneca	1	130	3,500			1	130	3,500	4,600	8,100

a Includes wooden and iron vessels and canal-boats. b Included with new vessels.

STATISTICS OF SHIP-BUILDING.

NUMBER, TONNAGE, AND VALUE OF NEW VESSELS, ETC.—Continued.

States and counties.	NEW VESSELS. (a)			BOATS.		CANAL-BOATS. (b)			Value of repairing.	Total value of all products.
	Number built.	Tonnage.	Value.	Number built.	Value.	Number built.	Tonnage.	Value.		
NEW YORK—continued.										
Suffolk	18	2,567	$147,750	124	$31,040				$131,188	$309,978
Sullivan	18	1,367	21,950			18	1,367	$21,950	8,000	29,950
Tompkins	24	2,938	86,000			24	2,938	86,000		86,000
Ulster	73	5,634	157,700			57	3,697	70,400	188,847	346,547
Warren				50	2,000					2,000
Washington	23	2,894	64,600			23	2,894	64,600	6,000	70,600
Wayne									3,000	3,000
Westchester	6	1,606	60,051	85	16,946				33,800	110,797
Total	635	76,418	3,145,536	1,221	263,957	441	49,887	1,370,525	4,575,551	7,985,044
NORTH CAROLINA.										
Beaufort	5	395	14,800						2,069	16,869
Brunswick									15,500	15,500
Craven	1	10	900							900
Dare									6,000	6,000
Pamlico	1	11	950							950
Pasquotank									11,000	11,000
Pitts	1	71	6,000							6,000
Total	8	487	22,650						34,569	57,219
OHIO.										
Ashtabula	1	6	1,000							1,000
Brown	1	23	6,000							6,000
Columbiana	1	44	9,000							9,000
Cuyahoga	3	4,940	286,000	36	4,200				228,050	518,250
Defiance									1,200	1,200
Erie	4	1,503	114,000	23	6,300				9,000	129,300
Fairfield									3,000	3,000
Hamilton	18	13,305	470,000	(c)	2,000				94,700	566,700
Jefferson	8	1,447	9,000							9,000
Lawrence	4	435	41,500						9,000	50,500
Lorain	6	776	60,000							60,000
Lucas	4	832	59,300	32	5,900				35,100	100,300
Scioto	1	1,351	11,000							11,000
Stark									5,000	5,000
Summit	1	11	2,300			1	11	2,300	21,160	23,460
Washington	3	459	58,500							58,500
Total	55	25,132	1,127,600	91	18,400	1	11	2,300	406,210	1,552,210
OREGON.										
Benton	1	23	2,800							2,800
Clackamas									12,000	12,000
Clatsop	1	9	3,000							3,000
Columbia	1	16	3,000							3,000
Coos	1	51	3,000							3,000
Multnomah	11	1,574	63,300						7,900	71,200
Wasco	4	489	101,500						10,000	111,500
Total	19	2,162	176,600						29,900	206,500
PENNSYLVANIA.										
Allegheny	503	132,978	652,840	80	5,600				191,400	849,840
Armstrong (d)			8,000							8,000
Beaver	9	3,332	234,400							234,400
Bucks	3	270	8,400			3	270	8,400	3,000	11,400
Carbon	13	1,176	23,400			13	1,176	23,400		23,400
Clarion (d)			28,580							28,580
Columbia	3	221	24,000			3	221	24,000		24,000
Dauphin				20	700					700
Delaware	5	10,611	1,800,699	9	1,500				4,600	1,806,799
Erie				6	1,500				8,000	9,500
Luzerne	1	90	2,200			1	90	2,200		2,200
Perry	3	276	7,000			3	276	7,000		7,000
Philadelphia	28	10,351	1,487,769	203	38,588				1,741,624	3,267,981
Schuylkill	24	3,168	59,100			24	3,168	59,100		59,100
Union	25	2,250	50,600			25	2,250	50,600		50,600
Washington	135	36,524	226,520						8,000	234,520
Wayne	48	3,110	60,050			48	3,110	60,050	5,400	65,450
York	2	150	2,700			2	150	2,700	3,300	6,000
Total	802	204,507	4,676,258	318	47,888	122	10,711	237,450	1,965,324	6,689,470
RHODE ISLAND.										
Bristol	16	283	115,000	6	540				19,800	135,340
Newport				40	13,370				215,000	228,370
Providence				10	5,700				125,631	131,331
Washington	1	96	14,000	12	8,000					22,000
Total	17	379	129,000	68	27,610				360,431	517,041

a Includes wooden and iron vessels and canal boats. b Included with new vessels. c Number not given. d Bottoms only.

SHIP-BUILDING INDUSTRY.

NUMBER, TONNAGE, AND VALUE OF NEW VESSELS, ETC.—Continued.

States and counties.	NEW VESSELS. (a)			BOATS.		CANAL-BOATS. (b)			Value of repairing.	Total value of all products.
	Number built.	Tonnage.	Value.	Number built.	Value.	Number built.	Tonnage.	Value.		
SOUTH CAROLINA.										
Beaufort									$3,400	$3,400
Charleston	27	1,615	$92,900						47,700	140,600
Total	27	1,615	92,900						51,100	144,000
TENNESSEE.										
Shelby	1	48	5,000							5,000
TEXAS.										
Calhoun									3,000	3,000
Chambers	2	23	2,250							2,250
Denton	1	8	450							450
Galveston	6	84	7,100							7,100
Harris	4	590	36,500						19,000	55,500
Matagorda	2	32	2,480							2,480
Orange	1	21	7,000							7,000
Total	16	758	55,780						22,000	77,780
VERMONT.										
Addison	3	330	11,000			3	330	$11,000		11,000
Franklin	1	110	3,800			1	110	3,800		3,800
Rutland	1	110	3,000			1	110	3,000		3,000
Total	5	550	17,800			5	550	17,800		17,800
VIRGINIA.										
Campbell									4,000	4,000
Elizabeth City	5	44	9,600	22	$3,600				8,000	21,200
Fairfax	1	7	600						13,474	14,074
Halifax				6	1,600					1,600
Henrico	3	180	5,000			3	180	5,000	18,500	23,500
Isle of Wight	1	16	1,100							1,100
Mathews	3	19	2,400							2,400
Middlesex	2	81	13,500							13,500
Nansemond	1	14	1,800							1,800
Norfolk	3	67	16,300						42,200	58,500
Northumberland	4	63	8,600	20	4,600				13,000	26,200
York	3	29	3,150						10,000	13,150
Total	26	514	62,050	48	9,800	3	180	5,000	109,174	181,024
WASHINGTON TERRITORY.										
Clallam	1	43	3,500							3,500
Clarke	1	48	6,000							6,000
Island	1	6	800							800
Jefferson	4	745	80,000							80,000
King	4	840	57,500						21,000	78,500
Pacific	1	15	2,000							2,000
Pierce	1	38	2,800							2,800
Thurston				80	1,900					1,900
Walla Walla	1	34	9,000							9,000
Total	14	1,769	161,600	80	1,900				21,000	184,500
WEST VIRGINIA.										
Braxton			5,280							5,280
Jackson	4	1,341	73,000							73,000
Kanawha	51	9,145	31,100						3,900	35,000
Mason	14	4,603	61,300						6,000	67,300
Ohio	9	730	27,550							27,550
Pleasant	6	720	5,000							5,000
Tyler	1	188	18,000							18,000
Total	85	16,727	221,230						9,900	231,130
WISCONSIN.										
Brown	3	604	59,000						24,000	83,000
Dane				25	2,000					2,000
Door	3	134	18,000							18,000
La Crosse	3	300	28,000						17,600	45,600
Manitowoc	7	1,382	81,000						24,000	105,000
Milwaukee	3	621	61,000	32	3,400				237,305	301,705
Racine	1	14	5,000						7,500	12,500
Sheboygan	1	24	2,000							2,000
Walworth				20	6,500					6,500
Total	21	3,079	254,000	77	11,900				310,405	576,305

a Includes wooden and iron vessels and canal-boats.   b Included with new vessels.

STATISTICS OF SHIP-BUILDING.

NUMBER, TONNAGE, AND VALUE OF IRON VESSELS BUILT AND REPAIRED DURING THE CENSUS YEAR, BY COUNTIES.

States and counties.	NEW VESSELS.			Value of repairs.	Total value of all products.
	Number built.	Tonnage.	Value.		
The United States	67	31,347	$5,006,193	$1,298,545	6,304,838
DELAWARE.					
New Castle	22	8,925	1,262,800	440,545	1,703,345
MARYLAND.					
Baltimore (city)	1	55	17,500	160,000	177,500
MASSACHUSETTS.					
Suffolk				80,000	80,000
MICHIGAN.					
Wayne	3	1,533	387,500		387,500
MISSOURI.					
Saint Louis (a)	7	2,740	241,000		241,000
NEW JERSEY.					
Camden	4	382	75,875	29,000	104,875
NEW YORK.					
Erie	4	150	15,000	27,000	42,000
Orange	2	529	74,000		74,000
Total	6	679	89,000	27,000	116,000
PENNSYLVANIA.					
Allegheny	5	550	84,000		84,000
Delaware	5	10,611	1,792,699		1,792,699
Philadelphia	14	5,872	1,145,919	562,000	1,707,919
Total	24	17,033	3,022,618	562,000	3,584,618

a Includes city of Saint Louis.

SHIP-BUILDING INDUSTRY.

NUMBER AND TONNAGE OF VESSELS, NUMBER OF ESTABLISHMENTS, CAPITAL, AVERAGE VALUE OF

A—AGGREGATE.

	States and Territories.	Boats.	Vessels repaired, as reported.	New vessels.	Tonnage of new vessels.	No. of establishments.	Capital.	Average number of hands employed.	Total amount paid in wages on vessels in the ship-yard.
		Number.	Number.	Number.			Dollars.		Dollars.
	The United States	8,026	16,507	2,415	498,878	2,188	20,979,874	21,345	12,713,813
1	Alabama					1	25,000	25	22,500
2	Arkansas			3	300	3	2,500	25	3,600
3	California	200		21	7,361	62	1,806,923	534	589,564
4	Connecticut	280	840	52	11,473	94	334,300	500	256,849
5	Delaware	100		55	31,123	18	935,200	1,576	900,322
6	Florida	45		13	217	48	30,750	46	33,580
7	Georgia			2	539	2	3,000	4	2,250
8	Illinois	85		11	1,397	28	457,000	465	247,395
9	Indiana	52		64	26,524	23	194,250	312	211,736
10	Iowa			2	860	1	25,000	75	37,000
11	Kansas			1	178	1	1,000	11	1,900
12	Kentucky	25		23	2,130	11	88,450	157	92,171
13	Louisiana	80		36	1,231	38	152,100	218	113,526
14	Maine	970	1,687	88	41,396	379	811,750	1,967	838,559
15	Maryland	133	712	131	7,499	166	1,606,535	1,178	657,789
16	Massachusetts	3,765	3,269	39	5,605	276	1,765,450	1,328	804,571
17	Michigan	210		69	15,909	72	476,775	1,537	745,933
18	Minnesota					1	10,000	16	8,000
19	Mississippi			3	33	3	2,500	4	2,860
20	Missouri			17	3,451	14	247,900	293	196,005
21	Nebraska			1	52	1	300	9	1,400
22	New Hampshire	44	8			15	15,330	26	12,243
23	New Jersey	134	2,680	53	7,455	93	943,070	930	548,807
24	New York	1,221	6,469	635	76,418	457	3,944,100	4,661	2,907,129
25	North Carolina			8	487	11	15,400	38	19,256
26	Ohio	91		55	25,132	54	423,050	773	414,360
27	Oregon			19	2,162	14	63,300	85	77,150
28	Pennsylvania	318		802	204,507	125	5,797,731	3,298	2,279,629
29	Rhode Island	68	840	17	379	22	227,700	318	194,662
30	South Carolina			27	1,615	16	46,300	94	55,990
31	Tennessee			1	48	1	500	6	600
32	Texas			16	758	16	23,350	43	30,170
33	Vermont			5	550	3	20,700	12	4,400
34	Virginia	48	2	26	514	65	185,960	146	75,526
35	Washington	80		14	1,769	11	33,000	62	51,298
36	West Virginia			85	16,727	19	55,000	99	51,510
37	Wisconsin	77		21	3,079	24	208,700	474	223,573

B—NEW VESSELS.

	States and Territories.	Boats.	Vessels repaired, as reported.	New vessels.	Tonnage of new vessels.	No. of establishments.	Capital.	Average number of hands employed.	Total amount paid in wages on vessels in the ship-yard.
	The United States			2,415	498,878	640	8,777,150	10,039	5,616,071
1	Arkansas			3	300	3	2,500	25	3,600
2	California			21	7,361	13	45,050	181	199,485
3	Connecticut			52	11,473	8	34,700	211	106,400
4	Delaware			55	31,123	12	904,400	1,105	623,997
5	Florida			13	217	13	2,150	9	7,030
6	Georgia			2	539	2	3,000	4	2,250
7	Illinois			11	1,397	8	20,250	50	24,960
8	Indiana			64	26,524	16	146,450	246	172,186
9	Iowa			2	860	(a)	5,000	20	11,000
10	Kansas			1	178	1	1,000	11	1,900
11	Kentucky			23	2,130	5	15,300	28	16,721
12	Louisiana			36	1,231	27	9,900	34	21,350
13	Maine			88	41,396	51	433,200	1,390	576,502
14	Maryland			131	7,499	37	100,300	208	96,405
15	Massachusetts			39	5,605	26	83,200	217	116,560
16	Michigan			69	15,909	47	178,600	920	431,058
17	Mississippi			3	33	2	1,500	2	1,360
18	Missouri			17	3,451	10	59,900	168	103,705
19	Nebraska			1	52	1	300	9	1,400
20	New Jersey			53	7,455	30	309,000	227	115,488
21	New York			635	76,418	142	736,250	1,742	884,887
22	North Carolina			8	487	6	4,400	12	5,056
23	Ohio			55	25,132	21	214,350	429	232,613
24	Oregon			19	2,162	12	47,000	64	57,950
25	Pennsylvania			802	204,507	58	5,184,200	2,221	1,525,120
26	Rhode Island			17	379	2	40,500	63	38,000
27	South Carolina			27	1,615	9	13,700	54	32,530
28	Tennessee			1	48	1	500	6	600
29	Texas			16	758	15	18,050	24	15,970
30	Vermont			5	550	3	20,700	12	4,400
31	Virginia			26	514	20	8,500	44	20,180
32	Washington			14	1,769	8	24,000	49	37,898
33	West Virginia			85	16,727	18	48,000	87	45,350
34	Wisconsin			21	3,079	13	61,300	167	82,160

a Included in "Repairing of vessels".

STATISTICS OF SHIP-BUILDING.

NUMBER OF HANDS EMPLOYED, AMOUNT OF WAGES PAID, MATERIALS USED, AND PRODUCTS.

A—AGGREGATE.

				PRINCIPAL MATERIALS.							
Hard pine.	White pine.	White oak.	Knees.	Total quantity of lumber, including other kinds.	Iron.	Yellow metal and brass.	Duck.	Manila rope.	Hemp cordage.	Total value of all materials.	Total value of all products.
Feet. 39,327,372	*Feet.* 47,506,048	*Feet.* 69,701,360	*Number.* 97,192	*Feet.* 179,873,966	*Pounds.* 125,701,922	*Pounds.* 7,669,826	*Yards.* 4,684,464	*Pounds.* 1,996,163	*Pounds.* 1,125,131	*Dollars.* 19,736,358	*Dollars.* 36,800,327
30,000				30,000	40,000	20,000				25,000	60,000	1
32,000	24,000			171,000	176,000	3,100	700	900		21,700	28,000	2
		196,000	1,621	6,580,000	2,092,656	1,058,730	151,453	73,840	36,880	959,349	1,797,639	3
2,777,000	604,080	722,900	3,320	4,793,450	1,042,156	60,800	85,870	38,981	41,142	430,425	767,660	4
1,966,500	1,886,500	2,217,800	4,651	6,411,800	13,045,744	135,866	65,602	67,097	74,804	964,275	2,162,503	5
95,100		38,800		176,400	138,160	800	19,520	6,530	200	43,250	85,050	6
95,000	8,000	14,000		117,000	90,000	1,200	550	750		13,700	17,000	7
	1,234,500	3,631,800	45	5,137,300	1,130,400	7,250	761,350	2,580		492,010	892,093	8
	1,569,100	4,878,300		7,046,400	3,173,600	47,900	28,800	36,300		529,840	810,655	9
	160,000	300,000		460,000	139,000	4,000	1,600	1,250		62,000	112,000	10
	30,000	60,000		90,000	72,000	1,000	400	380		23,000	26,000	11
2,500	1,352,500	1,451,000	40	3,291,000	569,699	3,700	2,250	2,350		126,550	249,015	12
233,100		72,500		423,600	362,230	5,100	85,030	7,120	680	162,405	343,525	13
13,882,112	3,064,208	5,193,710	26,560	25,866,351	9,981,416	467,956	601,298	446,862	373,712	1,935,857	2,909,846	14
4,596,700	3,430,200	2,376,500	3,440	10,536,400	3,299,358	514,554	408,940	118,920	151,600	884,299	1,788,630	15
2,197,760	2,065,860	1,877,650	8,750	6,958,745	2,955,965	1,044,611	423,275	94,235	125,000	1,173,640	2,281,666	16
	2,482,600	6,122,600	6,383	8,636,200	9,479,730	48,300	147,776	84,320	19,650	1,089,985	2,034,636	17
		8,000		19,000	11,600		610	430	150	2,500	15,000	18
9,000										1,950	5,500	19
	978,000	2,165,500		3,336,500	2,421,260	8,000	4,600	4,150		313,392	565,187	20
	15,000	23,000		38,000	18,000	400	200	300		7,000	9,000	21
10,000	39,600	16,400	70	74,000	19,300		10,900			14,369	30,070	22
1,827,800	1,665,300	2,274,300	5,620	6,279,900	2,455,048	211,958	87,940	47,687	58,316	649,194	1,384,629	23
7,652,800	10,461,000	14,535,900	23,103	35,905,020	16,292,176	3,072,264	811,130	267,121	34,477	4,055,637	7,985,044	24
232,000	13,000	25,000	310	270,000	124,400		2,600	1,300	1,560	32,075	57,219	25
40,000	1,937,000	7,793,500	2,518	10,166,500	7,635,020	74,900	157,750	100,350	16,300	985,960	1,552,210	26
		12,500	125	836,000	420,700	5,200	3,210	8,500	2,080	124,400	206,500	27
2,099,300	10,960,800	7,908,900	6,055	24,321,600	43,810,621	763,487	639,580	523,520	162,400	3,610,367	6,689,470	28
185,000	178,300	190,600	1,330	726,900	952,058	65,000	4,100	5,400		266,858	517,041	29
584,600	10,400	40,100	436	680,100	220,600	900	16,080	2,810		55,250	144,000	30
8,000	3,000	18,000		29,000	28,000	300	200	300		4,100	5,000	31
278,100	8,300	167,100		459,500	129,500	14,750	8,180	13,840	18,590	40,340	77,780	32
		120,400		63,800	184,200	52,000			1,420	9,200	17,800	33
493,000		30,300	102	190,600	183,125			9,270	7,240	4,350	74,578	181,024	34
		16,000	147	890,000	519,700	8,500	7,000	6,600	6,700	3,800	121,300	184,500	35
	2,093,000	1,228,000		3,363,000	389,300	3,200	3,900	6,400		162,300	231,130	36
	1,081,100	3,755,600	1,635	4,848,200	2,231,400	6,500	134,500	16,020	1,000	268,303	576,305	37

B—NEW VESSELS.

Hard pine.	White pine.	White oak.	Knees.	Total quantity of lumber, including other kinds.	Iron.	Yellow metal and brass.	Duck.	Manila rope.	Hemp cordage.	Total value of all materials.	Total value of all products.	
29,653,232	33,072,968	52,461,950	69,903	131,234,191	99,296,779	1,294,808	670,704	1,374,618	736,931	11,944,212	19,225,714	
32,000	24,000			171,000	176,000	3,100	700	900		21,700	28,000	1
		101,000	1,615	3,880,000	1,811,156	51,650	20,653	33,540	16,880	548,618	770,696	2
2,445,000	154,080	446,000	1,965	3,467,600	817,676	28,300	17,385	26,331	38,142	276,550	413,009	3
1,881,500	1,853,500	2,029,800	4,101	6,100,800	11,390,744	135,866	46,602	67,097	74,804	758,289	1,614,969	4
38,100		34,800		77,900	54,400	800	2,020	2,350	200	17,450	25,000	5
95,000	8,000	14,000		117,000	90,000	1,200	550	750		13,700	17,000	6
	212,500	611,800	45	859,300	365,900	7,050	1,350	2,580		100,890	137,300	7
	1,434,100	4,578,300		6,611,400	2,971,100	47,900	13,800	36,300		500,290	726,680	8
	160,000	280,000		440,000	115,000	4,000	1,600	1,250		53,000	70,000	9
	30,000	60,000		90,000	72,000	1,000	400	380		23,000	26,000	10
2,500	512,500	261,000		981,000	329,699	3,700	2,250	2,350		62,150	86,215	11
223,100		72,500		375,100	360,030	4,300	7,130	6,320	680	73,080	105,525	12
13,166,072	2,327,038	4,686,600	21,823	23,295,811	8,806,343	321,202	228,738	413,962	335,512	1,532,346	2,174,650	13
527,200	1,321,200	1,581,500	1,690	3,429,900	1,252,448	3,700	25,240	37,660	31,600	201,545	320,260	14
1,066,760	347,550	767,150	2,857	2,280,460	1,266,986	19,291	31,345	38,750	43,000	255,361	391,655	15
	1,577,200	5,229,600	4,473	6,806,900	8,321,570	46,500	51,996	83,940	19,650	842,115	1,390,050	16
9,000		8,000		19,000	11,600		610	430	150	1,450	3,500	17
	278,000	335,500		628,500	1,871,260	8,000	4,600	4,150		231,392	358,487	18
	15,000	23,000		38,000	18,000	400	200	300		7,000	9,000	19
1,122,500	430,700	1,240,800	3,409	2,862,400	1,568,794	26,185	26,750	42,267	58,316	248,561	409,714	20
5,892,000	7,833,600	10,862,800	16,691	26,431,820	9,919,842	48,681	45,510	150,931	34,477	1,921,523	3,145,536	21
232,000	13,000	25,000	310	270,000	124,400		2,600	1,300	1,560	14,875	22,650	22
40,000	1,779,000	7,415,500	2,248	9,594,500	6,682,800	58,800	35,550	98,730	16,300	821,550	1,127,600	23
		12,500	125	836,000	420,700	5,200	3,210	8,500	2,080	114,300	176,600	24
1,919,800	10,071,500	7,372,100	5,240	22,516,000	36,721,231	380,733	60,285	256,040	37,400	2,706,107	4,676,258	25
60,000	79,000	63,000	990	375,000	448,000	52,000	2,600	3,400		65,500	129,000	26
469,600	10,400	16,100	436	535,100	163,600	900	3,080	2,810		37,550	92,900	27
8,000	3,000	18,000		29,000	28,000	300	200	300		4,100	5,000	28
258,100	8,300	157,100		429,500	113,500	14,750	8,180	13,840	18,590	34,940	55,780	29
		120,400		63,800	184,200	52,000			1,420	9,200	17,800	30
165,000	16,300	98,200	641	284,000	133,900		6,870	6,360	4,350	31,500	62,050	31
		16,000	147	856,000	509,100	7,000	6,600	6,700	3,800	114,100	161,600	32
	2,063,000	1,198,000		3,303,000	367,300	3,200	3,900	6,400		159,600	221,230	33
	390,100	2,668,000	955	3,058,100	1,941,700	6,500	9,500	16,020	1,000	140,880	254,000	34

SHIP-BUILDING INDUSTRY.

NUMBER AND TONNAGE OF VESSELS, NUMBER OF ESTABLISHMENTS, CAPITAL, AVERAGE

C—REPAIRING OF VESSELS.

	States and Territories.	Boats. Number.	New vessels. Number.	Tonnage of new vessels.	Boats built. Number.	No. of establishments.	Capital. Dollars.	Average number of hands employed.	Total amount paid in wages on vessels in the ship-yard. Dollars.
	The United States					812	11,882,059	10,671	6,730,136
1	Alabama					1	25,000	25	22,500
2	California					40	1,754,423	326	368,746
3	Connecticut					22	279,900	255	136,520
4	Delaware					5	25,800	465	272,713
5	Florida					6	25,700	25	18,600
6	Illinois					17	435,450	408	218,635
7	Indiana					5	47,000	63	37,950
8	Iowa					1	20,000	55	26,000
9	Kentucky					5	73,000	127	75,000
10	Louisiana					9	139,700	173	85,176
11	Maine					100	346,775	520	238,380
12	Maryland					70	1,497,125	931	542,529
13	Massachusetts					140	1,586,925	974	610,917
14	Michigan					17	290,700	603	307,943
15	Minnesota					1	10,000	16	8,000
16	Mississippi					1	1,000	2	1,500
17	Missouri					4	188,000	125	92,300
18	New Hampshire					7	11,930	22	10,048
19	New Jersey					48	621,700	679	419,992
20	New York					192	3,126,550	2,750	1,908,892
21	North Carolina					5	11,000	26	14,200
22	Ohio					28	202,600	333	174,142
23	Oregon					2	16,300	21	19,200
24	Pennsylvania					48	599,281	1,044	733,795
25	Rhode Island					8	172,000	234	144,927
26	South Carolina					7	32,600	40	23,460
27	Texas					1	5,300	19	14,200
28	Virginia					13	175,800	89	49,648
29	Washington					2	8,000	12	12,400
30	West Virginia					1	7,000	12	6,160
31	Wisconsin					6	145,500	297	135,663

D—BOATS.

	States and Territories.	Boats.	New vessels.	Tonnage of new vessels.	Boats built.	No. of establishments.	Capital.	Average number of hands employed.	Total amount paid in wages on vessels in the ship-yard.
	The United States				8,026	736	320,665	635	367,606
1	California				200	9	7,450	27	21,333
2	Connecticut				280	64	19,700	34	13,929
3	Delaware				100	1	5,000	6	3,612
4	Florida				45	29	2,900	12	7,950
5	Illinois				85	3	1,300	7	3,800
6	Indiana				52	2	800	3	1,600
7	Kentucky				25	1	150	2	450
8	Louisiana				80	2	2,500	11	7,000
9	Maine				970	228	31,775	57	23,677
10	Maryland				133	59	9,110	39	18,855
11	Massachusetts				3,765	110	95,325	137	77,094
12	Michigan				210	8	7,475	14	6,932
13	New Hampshire				44	8	3,400	4	2,195
14	New Jersey				134	15	12,370	24	13,327
15	New York				1,221	123	81,300	169	113,350
16	Ohio				91	5	6,100	11	7,605
17	Pennsylvania				318	19	14,250	33	20,714
18	Rhode Island				68	12	15,200	21	11,735
19	Virginia				48	32	1,660	13	5,698
20	Washington				80	1	1,000	1	1,000
21	Wisconsin				77	5	1,900	10	5,750

E—OCEAN, COAST, AND RIVER VESSELS.

	States and Territories.	Boats.	New vessels.	Tonnage of new vessels.	Boats built.	No. of establishments.	Capital.	Average number of hands employed.	Total amount paid in wages on vessels in the ship-yard.
	The United States	7,240	731	159,325		1,645	16,806,599	14,284	9,092,538
1	Alabama					1	25,000	25	22,500
2	California	200	21	7,361		62	1,806,923	534	589,564
3	Connecticut	280	52	11,473		94	334,300	500	256,849
4	Delaware	100	55	31,123		18	935,200	1,576	900,322
5	Florida	45	13	217		48	30,750	46	33,580
6	Georgia		2	539		2	3,000	4	2,250
7	Louisiana	80	28	864		31	147,900	203	102,626
8	Maine	970	88	41,396		379	814,750	1,967	838,559
9	Maryland	133	71	3,229		159	1,587,535	1,103	624,539
10	Massachusetts	3,765	39	5,605		276	1,765,450	1,328	804,571
11	Mississippi		3	33		3	2,500	4	2,860
12	New Hampshire	44				15	15,330	26	12,243
13	New Jersey	134	43	6,445		74	821,170	787	469,762
14	New York	1,061	159	22,574		275	2,601,850	2,821	2,041,988
15	North Carolina		8	487		11	15,400	38	19,256
16	Oregon		19	2,162		14	63,300	85	77,150
17	Pennsylvania	232	33	20,962		55	5,324,231	2,588	1,890,673
18	Rhode Island	68	17	379		22	227,700	318	194,662
19	South Carolina		27	1,615		16	46,300	94	55,090
20	Texas		16	758		16	23,350	43	30,170
21	Virginia	48	23	334		63	184,660	132	71,126
22	Washington	80	14	1,769		11	33,000	62	51,298

STATISTICS OF SHIP-BUILDING. 263

NUMBER OF HANDS EMPLOYED, AMOUNT OF WAGES PAID, MATERIALS USED, ETC.—Continued.

C—REPAIRING OF VESSELS.

Hard pine.	White pine.	White oak.	Knees.	Total quantity of lumber, including other kinds.	Iron.	Yellow metal and brass.	Duck.	Manila rope.	Hemp cordage.	Total value of all materials.	Total value of all products.	
Feet.	*Feet.*	*Feet.*	*Number.*	*Feet.*	*Pounds.*	*Pounds.*	*Yards.*	*Pounds.*	*Pounds.*	*Dollars.*	*Dollars.*	
9,279,340	13,048,370	16,505,620	23,527	45,355,100	26,016,654	6,355,383	3,965,105	586,800	388,200	7,422,914	16,697,614	
30,000				30,000	40,000	20,000				25,000	60,000	1
		89,000	6	2,654,000	277,700	1,007,080	130,000	40,000	20,000	393,992	969,398	2
330,000	409,000	258,500	1,135	1,233,500	200,800	32,500	56,165	2,000	3,000	136,789	317,451	3
85,000	30,000	180,000	550	295,000	1,617,000		19,000			195,325	529,097	4
41,000		4,000		68,000	66,000		13,000			18,000	44,000	5
	1,010,000	3,000,000		4,240,000	763,000		760,000			388,840	745,743	6
	135,000	300,000		435,000	202,500		15,000			28,050	80,875	7
		20,000		20,000	24,000					9,000	42,000	8
	840,000	1,190,000		2,310,000	240,000					64,300	161,800	9
							76,000			84,325	222,400	10
716,040	519,870	423,520	4,497	2,220,100	1,130,443	146,354	371,740	32,200	38,750	376,917	681,378	11
3,834,000	2,097,000	787,000	1,750	6,832,000	2,041,150	510,374	380,000	80,000	120,000	666,296	1,423,370	12
1,130,000	1,048,700	871,800	3,405	3,539,300	1,620,450	1,024,620	380,300	46,100	82,000	836,478	1,703,284	13
	866,000	870,000	1,610	1,761,000	1,150,000	1,800	95,000			243,347	631,469	14
										2,500	15,000	15
										500	2,000	16
	700,000	1,830,000		2,708,000	550,000					82,000	206,700	17
10,000	23,000	8,000	50	49,000	6,500		10,900			12,284	25,630	18
705,300	1,210,100	1,010,900	2,199	3,331,200	879,204	185,473	60,000	5,000		384,058	940,455	19
1,758,000	2,431,700	3,464,900	6,060	8,822,900	6,255,829	3,007,718	762,000	114,500		2,021,964	4,575,551	20
										17,200	34,569	21
	108,000	361,000	270	497,000	933,000	16,000	120,000			155,760	406,210	22
										10,100	29,900	23
178,000	820,000	505,000	775	1,683,000	7,081,500	381,964	578,000	267,000	125,000	883,895	1,965,324	24
125,000	77,000	112,000	250	314,000	498,078	13,000				189,183	360,431	25
115,000		24,000		145,000	57,000		13,000			17,700	51,100	26
20,000		10,000		30,000	16,000					5,400	22,000	27
202,000	14,000	91,000	290	307,000	47,500	8,500				40,538	109,174	28
				18,000	9,000					6,800	21,000	29
	30,000	30,000		60,000	22,000					2,700	9,900	30
	679,000	1,065,000	680	1,752,000	288,000		125,000			123,673	310,405	31

D—BOATS.

Hard pine.	White pine.	White oak.	Knees.	Total lumber.	Iron.	Yellow metal and brass.	Duck.	Manila rope.	Hemp cordage.	Total value materials.	Total value products.	
394,800	1,384,710	733,790	3,762	3,284,675	388,489	19,635	48,655	34,745		369,232	876,999	
		6,000		46,000	3,800		800	300		16,739	57,545	1
2,000	41,000	18,400	220	92,350	23,680		12,320	10,650		17,086	37,200	2
	3,000	8,000		16,000	38,000					10,661	18,437	3
16,000		8,000		30,500	17,760		4,500	4,180		7,800	16,050	4
	12,000	20,000		38,000	1,500	200				2,280	9,050	5
										1,500	3,100	6
										100	1,000	7
10,000		500		48,500	2,200	800	1,900	800		5,000	15,600	8
	217,300	83,590	240	350,440	44,630	400	820	700		26,594	53,818	9
235,500	12,000	8,000		274,500	5,760	480	3,700	1,260		16,458	45,000	10
1,000	669,610	238,700	2,488	1,138,985	68,529	700	11,630	9,385		81,801	186,727	11
	39,400	23,000	300	68,400	8,160		780	380		4,523	13,117	12
	16,600	8,400	20	25,000	12,800					2,085	4,440	13
	24,500	22,600	12	86,200	7,050	300	1,190	420		16,575	34,460	14
2,800	195,700	208,200	352	650,300	116,505	15,865	3,620	1,690		112,150	263,957	15
	50,000	17,000		75,000	19,220	100	2,200	1,620		8,650	18,400	16
1,500	69,300	31,800	40	122,600	7,890	790	1,295	480		20,365	47,888	17
	22,300	15,600	90	37,900	5,980		1,500	2,000		12,175	27,610	18
126,000		1,400		129,900	1,725		2,400	880		2,540	9,800	19
				16,000	1,600					400	1,900	20
	12,000	22,600		38,100	1,700					3,750	11,900	21

E—OCEAN, COAST, AND RIVER VESSELS.

Hard pine.	White pine.	White oak.	Knees.	Total lumber.	Iron.	Yellow metal and brass.	Duck.	Manila rope.	Hemp cordage.	Total value materials.	Total value products.	
38,501,272	16,434,348	19,999,260	75,093	91,580,066	85,876,577	7,403,526	3,184,138	1,402,242	1,088,434	13,011,784	25,149,750	
30,000				30,000	40,000	20,000				25,000	60,000	1
		196,000	1,621	6,580,000	2,092,656	1,058,730	151,453	73,840	36,880	959,349	1,797,639	2
2,777,000	604,080	722,900	3,320	4,793,450	1,042,156	60,800	85,870	38,981	41,142	430,425	767,660	3
1,966,500	1,886,500	2,217,800	4,651	6,411,800	13,045,744	135,866	65,602	67,097	74,804	964,275	2,162,503	4
95,100		38,800		176,400	138,160	800	19,520	6,530	200	43,250	85,050	5
95,000	8,000	14,000		117,000	90,000	1,200	550	750		13,700	17,000	6
134,100		39,500	40	240,600	102,230	1,400	83,630	4,870	680	115,905	279,525	7
13,882,112	3,064,208	5,193,710	26,560	25,866,351	9,981,416	467,956	601,298	446,862	373,712	1,935,857	2,909,846	8
4,593,700	2,175,200	1,454,500	3,422	8,356,400	2,644,358	514,354	408,940	106,340	151,600	814,799	1,674,130	9
2,197,760	2,065,860	1,877,650	8,750	6,958,745	2,955,965	1,044,611	423,275	94,235	125,000	1,173,640	2,281,666	10
9,000		8,000		19,000	11,600		610	430	150	1,950	5,500	11
10,000	39,600	16,400	70	74,000	19,300		10,900			14,369	30,070	12
1,776,800	1,421,600	1,938,400	5,165	5,649,300	2,319,483	203,958	87,940	46,737	58,316	583,264	1,214,829	13
7,145,200	2,748,500	4,547,300	14,765	16,022,420	9,334,277	3,064,014	595,170	166,290	29,730	2,700,146	5,441,588	14
232,000	13,000	25,000	310	270,000	124,400	2,600	1,300	1,560		32,075	57,219	15
		12,500	125	836,000	420,700	5,200	3,210	8,500	2,080	124,400	206,500	16
2,091,300	2,180,500	1,092,400	3,450	5,776,200	39,533,149	725,887	600,600	303,830	162,000	2,524,654	5,063,680	17
185,000	178,300	190,600	1,330	726,900	952,058	65,000	4,100	5,400		266,858	517,041	18
584,600	10,400	40,100	436	680,100	220,600		16,080	2,810		55,250	144,000	19
278,100	8,300	167,100		459,500	129,500	14,750	8,180	13,840	18,590	40,340	77,780	20
418,000	30,300	190,600	931	645,900	159,125	8,500	9,270	6,640	4,350	70,978	172,024	21
		16,000	147	890,000	519,700	7,000	6,600	6,700	3,800	121,300	184,500	22

SHIP-BUILDING INDUSTRY.

NUMBER AND TONNAGE OF VESSELS, NUMBER OF ESTABLISHMENTS, CAPITAL, AVERAGE

F—NORTHERN LAKES.

	States.	Boats.	New vessels.	Tonnage of new vessels.	No. of establishments.	Capital.	Average number of hands employed.	Total amount paid in wages on vessels in the ship-yard.
		Number.	*Number.*			*Dollars.*		*Dollars.*
	The United States	629	142	30,752	199	1,865,325	3,352	1,664,917
1	Illinois	85	2	50	19	352,300	339	176,975
2	Michigan	210	69	15,909	72	476,775	1,537	745,933
3	New York	160	35	3,957	59	592,500	629	321,081
4	Ohio	91	18	8,057	26	246,050	439	231,905
5	Pennsylvania	6			1	10,000	8	4,200
6	Wisconsin	77	18	2,779	22	187,700	400	184,823

G—WESTERN RIVERS.

	States.	Boats.	New vessels.	Tonnage of new vessels.	No. of establishments.	Capital.	Average number of hands employed.	Total amount paid in wages on vessels in the ship-yard.
	The United States	157	899	242,094	155	1,227,500	1,996	1,183,072
1	Arkansas		3	300	3	2,500	25	3,600
2	Illinois		8	1,259	7	102,000	118	65,720
3	Indiana	52	64	26,524	23	194,250	312	211,736
4	Iowa		2	860	1	25,000	75	37,000
5	Kansas		1	178	1	1,000	11	1,900
6	Kentucky	25	23	2,130	11	88,450	157	92,171
7	Louisiana		8	367	7	4,200	15	10,900
8	Minnesota				1	10,000	16	8,000
9	Missouri		17	3,451	14	247,900	293	196,005
10	Nebraska		1	52	1	300	9	1,400
11	Ohio		36	17,064	14	155,000	266	153,420
12	Pennsylvania	80	647	172,834	50	320,400	520	310,360
13	Tennessee		1	48	1	500	6	600
14	West Virginia		85	16,727	19	55,000	99	51,510
15	Wisconsin		3	300	2	21,000	74	38,750

H—CANAL-BOATS.

	States.	Boats.	New vessels.	Tonnage of new vessels.	No. of establishments.	Capital.	Average number of hands employed.	Total amount paid in wages on vessels in the ship-yard.
	The United States		643	66,707	189	1,080,450	1,713	773,286
1	Illinois		1	88	2	2,700	8	4,700
2	Maryland		60	4,270	7	19,000	75	33,250
3	New Jersey		10	1,010	19	121,900	143	79,045
4	New York		441	49,887	123	749,750	1,211	544,060
5	Ohio		1	11	14	22,000	68	29,035
6	Pennsylvania		122	10,711	19	143,100	182	74,396
7	Vermont		5	550	3	20,700	12	4,400
8	Virginia		3	180	2	1,300	14	4,400

I—IRON VESSELS. (a)

	States.	Boats.	New vessels.	Tonnage of new vessels.	No. of establishments.	Capital.	Average number of hands employed.	Total amount paid in wages on vessels in the ship-yard.
	The United States		67	31,347	16	7,497,000	4,262	2,732,599
1	Delaware		22	8,925	2	800,000	1,252	753,953
2	Maryland		1	55	2	1,000,000	223	134,000
3	Massachusetts				2	500,000	60	35,500
4	Michigan		3	1,533	1	100,000	240	155,600
5	Missouri		7	2,740	1	30,000	120	78,412
6	New Jersey		4	382	1	200,000	72	43,600
7	New York		6	679	2	62,000	77	46,000
8	Pennsylvania		24	17,033	5	4,805,000	2,218	1,485,534

a Also included with preceding classes.

STATISTICS OF SHIP-BUILDING.

NUMBER OF HANDS EMPLOYED, AMOUNT OF WAGES PAID, MATERIALS USED, ETC.—Continued.

F—NORTHERN LAKES.

				PRINCIPAL MATERIALS.							
Hard pine.	White pine.	White oak.	Knees.	Total quantity of lumber, including other kinds.	Iron.	Yellow metal and brass.	Duck.	Manila rope.	Hemp cordage.	Total value of all materials.	Total value of all products.
Feet.	Feet.	Feet.	Number.	Feet.	Pounds.	Pounds.	Yards.	Pounds.	Pounds.	Dollars.	Dollars.
3,000	5,951,300	18,967,700	13,733	25,172,600	19,175,755	86,000	1,398,176	155,956	41,697	2,642,455	4,870,645
....	458,500	1,777,300	27	2,241,800	506,500	650	760,000	150	....	356,220	650,833	1
....	2,482,600	6,122,600	6,383	8,636,200	9,479,730	48,300	147,776	84,320	19,650	1,089,985	2,034,636	2
3,000	1,421,600	3,145,500	3,186	4,764,200	2,906,825	8,250	215,960	16,746	4,747	455,307	848,321	3
....	585,000	4,365,500	2,502	4,958,500	4,211,020	23,800	140,600	39,470	16,300	476,400	796,650	4
....	2,500	1,200	....	3,700	280	....	540	150	....	3,600	9,500	5
....	1,001,100	3,555,600	1,635	4,568,200	2,071,400	5,000	133,300	15,120	1,000	260,943	530,705	6

G—WESTERN RIVERS.

181,500	16,008,600	20,619,000	....	41,684,100	15,141,519	170,950	102,150	322,310	....	2,856,745	4,450,587
32,000	24,000	115,000	....	171,000	176,000	3,100	700	900	....	21,700	28,000	1
....	766,000	1,830,500	....	2,861,500	622,400	6,400	1,350	2,430	....	133,190	232,960	2
....	1,569,100	4,878,300	....	7,046,400	3,173,600	47,900	28,800	36,300	....	529,840	810,655	3
....	160,000	300,000	....	460,000	139,000	4,000	1,600	1,250	....	62,000	112,000	4
....	30,000	60,000	....	90,000	72,000	1,000	400	380	....	23,000	26,000	5
2,500	1,352,500	1,451,000	....	3,291,000	569,699	3,700	2,250	2,350	....	126,550	249,015	6
99,000	....	33,000	....	183,000	260,000	3,700	1,400	2,250	....	46,500	64,000	7
....	....	....	....	....	....	....	....	....	....	2,500	15,000	8
....	978,000	2,165,500	....	3,336,500	2,421,260	8,000	4,600	4,150	....	313,392	565,187	9
....	15,000	23,000	....	38,000	18,000	400	200	300	....	7,000	9,000	10
40,000	1,346,000	3,408,000	....	5,182,000	3,419,600	51,100	17,150	60,700	....	494,200	701,700	11
....	7,592,000	4,908,700	....	15,352,700	3,692,660	36,650	38,400	203,700	....	923,113	1,355,340	12
8,000	3,000	18,000	....	29,000	28,000	300	200	300	....	4,100	5,000	13
....	2,093,000	1,228,000	....	3,363,000	389,300	3,200	3,900	6,400	....	162,300	231,130	14
....	80,000	200,000	....	280,000	160,000	1,500	1,200	900	....	7,360	45,600	15

H—CANAL-BOATS.

641,600	9,111,800	10,115,400	8,366	21,437,200	5,508,071	9,350	....	115,655	....	1,225,374	2,329,345
....	10,000	24,000	18	34,000	1,500	200	....	....	....	2,600	8,300	1
3,000	1,255,000	922,000	18	2,180,000	655,000	200	....	12,580	....	69,500	114,500	2
51,000	243,700	335,900	455	630,600	135,565	8,000	....	950	....	65,930	169,800	3
504,600	6,290,900	6,843,100	5,152	15,118,400	4,051,074	....	....	84,085	....	900,184	1,695,135	4
....	6,000	20,000	16	26,000	4,400	....	....	180	....	15,360	53,860	5
8,000	1,185,800	1,906,600	2,605	3,189,000	584,532	950	....	15,840	....	159,000	260,950	6
....	120,400	63,800	102	184,200	52,000	....	....	1,420	....	9,200	17,800	7
75,000	....	....	....	75,000	24,000	....	....	600	....	3,600	9,000	8

I—IRON VESSELS. (a)

2,254,000	3,353,000	639,100	....	6,663,100	54,326,737	501,332	47,000	51,450	31,400	2,851,073	6,394,838
723,000	1,264,000	207,000	....	2,425,000	11,981,186	118,945	17,800	15,700	8,000	692,435	1,703,345	1
....	5,000	1,000	....	6,000	468,000	400	....	250	....	28,000	177,509	2
....	....	....	....	196,000	....	....	....	....	....	35,000	80,000	3
....	285,000	40,000	....	325,000	4,502,000	16,000	2,400	1,500	....	187,000	387,500	4
....	122,000	41,500	....	163,500	1,585,000	4,000	2,500	1,500	....	153,000	241,000	5
3,000	34,000	2,000	....	39,000	1,220,000	15,600	800	1,800	....	39,200	104,875	6
....	56,000	17,000	....	76,000	875,000	5,000	1,100	900	....	55,000	116,000	7
1,528,000	1,587,000	330,600	....	3,628,600	33,499,551	341,387	22,400	29,800	23,400	1,661,438	3,584,618	8

a Also included with preceding classes.

INDEX TO REPORT ON SHIP-BUILDING.

A.

	Page.
Adoption of the screw-wheel for towing-boats at ocean ports	149
Alabama, statistics of fishing vessels owned in	2
Alaska, fishing canoes of	40, 42, 43
Alaska, state of the vessel-building industry in	136, 137
Alaska, statistics of fishing vessels owned in	2
Alaskan war canoe	42
Alexandria, Virginia, the ship-yards of	128, 129
Allegheny City, Pennsylvania, state of the vessel industry in	187
Allegheny river. (See Western rivers.)	
Alpena, Michigan, fishing boats at	43
Amboy, New Jersey, oyster skiffs at	32
American clippers	72
American coasting and lake steamers and tugs, general adoption of the screw propeller in	149, 153, 160, 167
American lines of packet ships, origin and success of	68
American war vessels, early	86, 106, 108, 115
Amesbury, Massachusetts, vessel building at	107, 108
Annamessex, Maryland, the Methodist canoe of	35
Annapolis, Maryland, state of the industry at	127
Apalachicola, Florida, character of the fishing boats of	38
Arizona, ship work in	131
Aroostook river, Maine, batteau building on the	96
Ashtabula, Ohio, fishing boats	43
Astoria, Oregon, first vessel on the Pacific coast built at	133
Astoria, Oregon, present vessel building at	165
Athens, New York, vessel building at	120, 161
Atlantic coast ship-yards, bevel saw in	103, 110, 123, 126

B.

Baltimore, Maryland, canoes for oystering and trading at	35
Baltimore, Maryland, clipper sailing vessels of	74, 84, 126
Baltimore, Maryland, iron-ship yard in	214
Baltimore, Maryland, state of the ship-building industry at	126
Banker fishing schooner	12
Barge and vessel building at New Haven, Connecticut	114
Barge building at California, Pennsylvania	186
Barge building at Charleston and Coalburg, West Virginia	190
Barge building at Elizabeth and McKeesport, Pennsylvania	187
Barge building at Monongahela City, Pennsylvania	186, 187
Barge building at Rocky Hill, Connecticut	114
Barge building at Six-Mile Ferry, Pennsylvania	187
Barge building at Steubenville, Ohio	188
Barges, coal, in Maryland under construction	127
Barges, coal, in New Jersey under construction	121
Barges, coal, on Long Island sound	112, 114
Barges, grain, on the Columbia river	165
Barges, ice, on the Hudson river	120
Barges on western rivers, kinds of, used, and where built	181, 186
Barges on western rivers, number and tonnage of	176
Barnegat, New Jersey, state of the ship-building industry at	122
Bath, Maine, cost of hackmatack knees at	103
Bath, Maine, fishing schooners built at	13, 101
Bath, Maine, state of the ship-building industry at	101
Bath, Maine, whaling propellers of	28
Batteau building on the Aroostook river, Maine	96
Bay City, Michigan, boat and vessel building at	43, 172
Bay Shore, New York, vessel building at	119
Beaufort, North Carolina, vessel building at	130
Beech. (See Hard wood.)	
Belfast, Maine, vessel building at	98

	Page.
Belle Port, New York, vessel building at	119
Belle Vernon, Pennsylvania, steamboat and barge building at	186
Bell's Ferry, North Carolina, vessel building at	130
Bent frames and bent knees, experiments made with	94
Bethel, Delaware, vessel building at	125
Bevel saw in Atlantic coast ship-yards	103, 110, 123, 126
Bevel saw in popular use on the northern lakes	170–172
Bevel saw in ship-yards on the Pacific coast	132, 135
Bevel saw used by Donald McKay	87
Beverly, Massachusetts, fishing-boat building at	20, 109
Birch. (See Hard wood.)	
Black Rock, Connecticut, marine railway at	114
Block Island, Rhode Island, discovered by Adrian Blok	46
Block Island, Rhode Island, fishing boats of	9
Blok, Adrian, discovery of Block Island, Rhode Island, by	46
Blue Hill, Maine, vessel building at	97
Blue Point, New York, vessel building at	119
Boat and barge building at Dravosburg, Pennsylvania	187
Boat- and ship-yards of Huron, Ohio	43, 139
Boat and vessel building at Bay City, Michigan	43, 172
Boat and vessel building at Bridgeport, Connecticut	30, 114
Boat and vessel building at Essex, Massachusetts	20, 30, 114, 103, 160
Boat and vessel building at Salisbury, Massachusetts	20, 107
Boat and vessel building at Toledo, Ohio	43, 140
Boat and vessel building at Tuckerton and West Creek, New Jersey	34, 122
Boat building at Charlotte, New York	43
Boat building at Erie, Pennsylvania	43
Boat building at Greenfield, Pennsylvania	186
Boat building at Groton, Connecticut	30
Boat building at Mattapoisett, Massachusetts	111
Boat building at Martha's Vineyard, Massachusetts, decay of	111
Boat building at Patchogue, New York	119
Boat building at Port Republic, New Jersey, decay of	122
Boat building at Port Townsend, Washington territory	134
Boat building at Racine, Wisconsin	43
Boat building at Rice's Landing, Pennsylvania	186
Boat building at Rockport, Massachusetts	109
Boat building at Rocky River and Sandusky, Ohio	43
Boat building at Sanilac, Michigan	43
Boat building at Sheboygan, Wisconsin	43
Boat building at Somers' Point, New Jersey, decay of	122
Boat building at Vermillion, Ohio	44
Boat building at Wellfleet, Massachusetts, decay of	111
Boat-building industry at Malden, New York, decay of	120
Boat-building industry of Gloucester, Massachusetts, state of	109
Boats and boat building of Provincetown, Massachusetts	23, 111
Boats, building of, in Maine coast towns	96, 99
Boats built during the census year, number and value of, by counties	254–258
Boats built during the census year, number and value of, by states and territories	253
Boats, decay of building, in New England towns	108, 111, 112
Boats, fishing, in the United States	1–45
Boats, produce	183
Boothbay, Maine, building and repairing of vessels at	100
Boothbay, Maine, fishing schooners built at, for Gloucester, Massachusetts	13
Boothbay, Maine, fishing steamers built at	18, 160
Boston, Massachusetts, colonial vessel-building at	50
Boston, Massachusetts, iron-ship yards at	200, 201
Boston, Massachusetts, pioneer vessel for the trade of	46
Boston, Massachusetts, sailing clippers of	73–82

	Page.
Boston, Massachusetts, United States navy-yard at, description of	235
Boston, Massachusetts, vessel building at, at the present time	110, 160
Boston, Massachusetts, whaling boats and vessels owned at	23
Boston, Massachusetts, wood sloops of the early settlers of	9, 47
Bradford, Massachusetts, vessel building at	108
Bremen and Brewer, Maine, vessel building at	98, 99
Bridgeport, Connecticut, boat and vessel building at	30, 114
Brigantine, evolution of the, from the ketch	61
Brigantines, statistics of the number of, built in the New England colonies	50
Bristol, Maine, vessel building at	99
Bristol, Rhode Island, steam yachts built at	160
Broad Creek, Maryland, vessel building at	128
Broad-horn. (*See* Barges; Western rivers.)	
Brookline, Maine, vessel building at	97
Brooklyn navy-yard, description of	236
Brooklyn, New York. (*See* New York.)	
Brownsville, Pennsylvania, steamboat and barge building at	186
Brunswick, Maine, vessel building at	104
Bucksport, Maine, vessel building at	97
Buffalo, New York, canal-boat building at	230
Buffalo, New York, iron-ship yard at	218, 219
Buffalo, New York, vessel building at	169
Bug-eye, description of a	35
Builders of steamboats and steamships at New York	116
Building and repairing at New London, Connecticut	113
Building and repairing of vessels at Boothbay and East Boothbay, Maine	100
Building of iron ships in the United States	196–222
Building of steamboats and steamships in the United States at the present time	112, 160
Building of vessels at Medford, Massachusetts, after the war of 1812	110
Burning of the steam frigate Missouri	156

C.

Cairo, Illinois, vessel-building resources of	194
Calais, Maine, vessel building at	96
California fishing vessels, statistics of	2
California, iron-ship work in	214, 215
California, Pennsylvania, barge building at	186
California, timber of	131, 248
California, vessel building in	131, 162
Cambridge, Maryland, vessel building at	127
Camden, Maine, vessel building at	96
Camden, New Jersey, vessel building at	123, 162, 202
Canal-boat building at Buffalo, New York	230
Canal-boat yards at Rondout, New York	223
Canal-boats, steam	228, 230–232
Canal navigation and boat building of Illinois	231
Canal navigation and boat building of Maryland	232
Canal navigation and canal-boats of New Jersey	232
Canal navigation and canal-boats of New York	223
Canal navigation and canal-boats of Ohio	230
Canal navigation and canal-boats of Pennsylvania	232
Canal navigation and canal-boats of Virginia	233
Canals and canal-boats, history of	223–233
Canoe building at Point Lookout, Maryland	35
Canoe building at York, Virginia	38
Canoes, fishing, of Virginia	34
Canoes for oystering and trading at Baltimore, Maryland	35
Canoes in New England colonies	5, 22, 28
Canoes on Chesapeake bay	34
Canoes on Puget sound and in Alaska	42
Canvas. (*See* Sails.)	
Cape Cod, Massachusetts, vessel building on	22, 112
Caravel, sail plan of a	5
Carpenters' measurement, origin of	50
Cat-rigged boats	32
Cedar in frame timbers of large vessels	89, 156
Cedar Keys, Florida, fishing vessels of	38
Cedar planking in fishing boats	21, 23, 32
Cedar, Puget sound canoes hewn from logs of	42
Cedar, specific gravity of	249
Cedar trees in New Jersey	121
Cedar trees in Washington territory and Oregon	248
Ceiling of grain vessels	104, 118, 127
Celilo, Oregon, steamboat work at	165

	Page.
Character of the fishing boats of Apalachicola, Florida	38
Charleston, South Carolina, ship work at	130
Charleston, West Virginia, barge building at	190
Charlestown, Massachusetts, colonial vessel-building at	47
Charlestown, Massachusetts, United States navy-yard at, description of the	235
Charlotte, New York, boat building at	43
Chebacco boats, origin of, at Essex, Massachusetts	7
Chesapeake bay, canoes on	34
Chester, Pennsylvania, iron-ship yard at	205
Chestnut, Indian canoes in New England made of	28
Chestnut, specific gravity of	249
Chestnut timbers in Connecticut and New York vessels	113, 115, 119, 120
Chestnut, use of, in large steamers at New York city	151, 156
Chicago, Illinois, iron-ship yard at	221
Chicago, Illinois, iron tug built at	221
Cincinnati, Ohio, steamboat and barge building at	190
City Island, New York, vessel building and repairing at	120
Clayton, New York, vessel building at	43, 169
Cleveland, Ohio, fishing boats built at	43
Cleveland, Ohio, iron-ship yard at	219
Cleveland, Ohio, vessel building at	169
Clipper sailing vessels, builders of, at Boston	110
Clipper sailing vessels, builders of, at New York	116
Clipper sailing vessels of Baltimore	74, 86, 126
Clipper sailing vessels on the northern lakes	137
Clipper sailing vessels, origin and evolution of the, of the United States	72
Clipper sailing vessels, scantling of famous	87
Clipper sailing vessels, time made by celebrated	85
Clipper schooner, the New England	12, 13
Clippers, sailing, of Massachusetts	73
Coal barges in Maryland under construction	127
Coal barges in New Jersey under construction	121
Coal barges on Long Island sound	112, 114
Coal-boats of western rivers, use of hemlock in	182, 183
Coalburg, West Virginia, barge building at	190
Coal schooners superseded by coal barges	112, 114, 124
Coasting schooners	93
Cohasset, Massachusetts, vessel building at	111
Colonial building of merchant vessels in Massachusetts	47, 50
Colonial fishermen, early, use of lugger by	6
Colonial fishing ventures of Massachusetts	3
Colonial fleet of war vessels at the capture of Louisburg	10
Colonial merchantmen as war vessels, heavy armament of	59
Colonial ship-building of Medford, Massachusetts	46
Colonial ship-building of New York	48
Colonial vessel building at Boston, Massachusetts	50
Colonial vessel building at Charlestown, Massachusetts	47
Columbia river steamboats, iron shrouds or hog-chains in	164
Competition for trade between sail and steam vessels, prospect of	141
Composite vessels	160
Connecticut and New York vessels, chestnut timbers in	113, 115, 119, 120
Connecticut, early ship-building of	48
Connecticut, fishing boats of, described	28
Connecticut, statistics of fishing vessels of	2
Connecticut, vessel building of, greatly decayed	113, 161
Coosaw, South Carolina, vessel building at	130
Coos bay, Oregon, vessel building at	133
Coppering of vessels at the principal Atlantic ports	104, 111, 118, 124, 127
Coppering of vessels, origin and object of the practice of, and how the metal is put on	27
Copper, quantity of, used in the ship-building industry in the census year	261
Cordage for the United States navy made at the Charlestown navy-yard	235
Cordage of canal-boats	230
Cordage of Gloucester fishing schooners	14
Cordage of the clipper Great Republic	90
Cordage, outfits of, obtained in the great cities	104, 108, 122, 124, 127
Cordage, wire standing, on the northern lakes	138
Cos Cob, Connecticut, vessel repairing at	115
Cost of iron ships, per register ton, in England	142
Cotton ships	65
Covington, Kentucky, steamboat and barge work at	190
Crisfield, Maryland, fishing boats of	33
Cundy's harbor, Maine, dory building at	20
Cutler, Maine, vessel building at	96
Cypress, specific gravity of	249

INDEX TO REPORT ON SHIP-BUILDING. 269

	Page.
Cypress tree abundant on the lower Ohio	193
Cypress, use of, in New Orleans luggers	39
Cypress, use of, in the steamboat Natchez	190

D.

	Page.
Dalles, Oregon, steamboat work at the	165
Damariscotta, Maine, vessel building at	100
Decay of ship-building at East Machias, Maine	96
Decay of vessel building in Connecticut	113, 161
Delaware river, vessel building and repairing on the	123
Delaware, statistics of fishing vessels of	2
Delaware, vessel building in	124
Dennysville, Maine, vessel building at	100
Description of a bug-eye	35
Description of a ketch	6
Description of a model barge	184, 185
Description of the Brooklyn navy-yard	236
Description of the long-boat of the Potomac river	128
Description of the navy-yards of the United States	234–241
Description of the New London (Connecticut) navy-yard	236
Description of the Norfolk navy-yard	240
Description of the Pensacola navy-yard	240
Description of the Portsmouth navy-yard	235
Description of the Washington navy-yard	238–240
Description of towing-boats	149, 163, 165, 175, 191, 202
Description of whaling vessels and boats	22–28
Detroit, Michigan, vessel building at	171
Discovery bay, Washington territory, vessel building at	134
Dogwood, specific gravity of	249
Dories, description of	19–21
Dory building at Cundy's harbor, Maine	20
Dory building at Newburyport, Massachusetts	20
Dravosburg, Pennsylvania, boat and barge building at	187
Dry-docks at United States navy-yards	235, 237, 240, 241
Dry-docks, hulls of northern lake steamers converted into	166
Dry-docks, large, at San Francisco	132
Dry-docks, location of principal, on the Atlantic coast	104, 111, 118, 123–125, 127
Dry-docks on the Erie canal	229, 230
Dry-docks on the northern lakes	169, 171, 173
Dry-docks, small, on the Monongahela river	187
Duxbury, Massachusetts, vessel building at	111

E.

	Page.
Early experiments with the paddle-wheel	144, 147
East Boothbay, Maine, building and repairing of vessels at	100
East Deering, Maine, vessel building at	104
East Machias, Maine, decay of ship-building at	96
Eastport, Maine, vessel building at	96, 160
East Saginaw, Michigan, vessel building at	172
Elizabeth City, North Carolina, vessel building at	130
Elizabeth, Pennsylvania, barge building at	187
Elizabethport, New Jersey, repairing at	121
Ellsworth, Maine, vessel building at	97
Engine shops of Louisville, Kentucky	191
Erie canal, dry-docks on the	229, 230
Erie, Pennsylvania, boat building at	43
Essex, Connecticut, boat and vessel building at	30, 114
Essex, Massachusetts, building of clipper fishing schooners at	12
Essex, Massachusetts, origin of Chebacco boats at	7
Essex, Massachusetts, state of boat and vessel building at	20, 108, 160
European fishing expeditions to Maine	3, 4
Evansville, Indiana, steamboat building at	192
Evolution of the brigantine from the ketch	61
Experiments made with bent frames	94
Exportation of spars to England in colonial times	104, 105

F.

	Page.
Fairhaven, Connecticut, fishing boats at	29, 32, 114
Fairhaven, Massachusetts, whale boats built at	23
Ferry-boats at New York	162
Fir knees in use on the Pacific coast	134, 135, 163, 165
First schooner in America	12
First screw frigate in the world built at New York	149
First vessel in America built at Stage island, Maine	46
First vessel on the Pacific coast built at Astoria, Oregon	133

	Page.
Fishing-boat building at Beverly, Massachusetts	20, 109
Fishing boats and vessels	1–45
Fishing boats and vessels of New London, Connecticut	23, 30
Fishing boats at Alpena, Michigan	43
Fishing boats at Ashtabula and Cleveland, Ohio	43
Fishing boats at Fairhaven, Connecticut	29, 32, 114
Fishing boats at Gloucester, Massachusetts	20, 21
Fishing boats at Marquette, Michigan	43, 44
Fishing boats of Block Island, Rhode Island	9
Fishing boats of Crisfield, Maryland	33
Fishing boats of Long Island, New York	17, 22
Fishing boats of New Haven, Connecticut	29
Fishing boats of the northern lakes	43–45
Fishing canoes and bug-eyes of Maryland	34, 35
Fishing canoes of Alaska	40, 42, 43
Fishing canoes of Puget sound	40
Fishing canoes of Virginia	34
Fishing craft built at Lorain, Ohio	43
Fishing fleet of Illinois, statistics of the	2
Fishing schooners and sloops of Florida	39
Fishing schooners built at Bath, Maine	13, 101
Fishing schooners built at Boothbay, Maine, for Gloucester, Massachusetts	13
Fishing schooners of New England and New York	12
Fishing smacks of New York described	17, 20
Fishing steamers built at Boothbay, Maine	18, 160
Fishing vessels at Marblehead, Massachusetts	108
Fishing vessels at Port Norris and Salem, New Jersey, repair of	123
Fishing vessels of Cedar Keys, Florida	38
Fishing vessels of Florida, description of	38
Fishing vessels of Gloucester, Massachusetts	12
Fishing vessels of Nantucket, Massachusetts	22, 111
Fitch, John, screw propeller invented by	144
Flat-boats of western rivers	176, 181
Flat-iron boat built at Connecticut	29
Florida, description of fishing vessels of	38
Florida fishing vessels, live oak used to some extent in	39
Florida fishing vessels, use of mastic in	39
Florida, statistics of fishing vessels of	2
Frames of northern lake vessels, strapping of	140, 168, 173
Frames of ocean and river vessels, strapping of	67, 88, 89, 102, 152, 156, 163
Frames of vessels, strapping of, origin of the practice of, in Europe	67
Frederica, Delaware, vessel building at	125
Freedom, Pennsylvania, steamboat building at	187
Freeport, Maine, vessel building at	104
Freighting-ships (sailing)	66
Friendship, Maine, vessel building at	99
Frigates. (See War vessels.)	
Fulton, Robert, part taken by, in the early construction of steam vessels	145, 146
Fulton's pioneer steam frigate of the world	146

G.

	Page.
Galveston, Texas, vessel building at	130
General description of oyster boats	28–38
Georgetown, Maine, vessel building of	100
Georgetown, South Carolina, vessel building of	130
Georgia, statistics of fishing vessels of	2
Georgia, timber supply of	243, 246
Georgia, vessel building of	130
Gibraltar, Michigan, vessel building of	171
Gildersleeve's Landing, Connecticut, vessel building of	113
Gloucester, Massachusetts, first vessel of the schooner rig built at	11
Gloucester, Massachusetts, fishing boats built at	20, 21
Gloucester, Massachusetts, fishing vessels of	12
Gloucester, Massachusetts, state of the boat-building industry at	109
Gloucester, Virginia, oyster canoes at	38
Goodspeed's Landing, Connecticut, repairing of steamboats at	114
Grain barges on the Columbia river	165
Grain vessels, ceiling of	104, 118, 127
Grand Haven, Michigan, vessel building at	173
Great Kanawha river. (See Western rivers.)	
Greenbank, New Jersey, vessel building at	34, 122
Green Bay, Wisconsin, vessel building at	43, 174
Greenfield, Pennsylvania, boat building at	186
Greenport, New York, vessel building at	119
Groton, Connecticut, boat building at	30

270 INDEX TO REPORT ON SHIP-BUILDING.

	Page.
Growth in the size of sailing vessels after 1820	70
Gum tree, specific gravity of	249
Gum tree, supply of	129, 193
Gum tree, use of, for keels, etc.	102, 129

H.

	Page.
Hackmatack knees, cost of, at Bath, Maine	103
Hackmatack knees in New England vessels	26, 88, 90, 97, 99, 102, 108
Hackmatack, specific gravity of	249
Hackmatack, supply of, in the United States	257
Hackmatack timbers in frames of vessels	28, 87, 96-98, 102, 104, 111, 151, 156
Hard wood found in the forests of New Jersey	121
Hard wood, price of, in Maine	98, 103, 113
Hard wood, specific gravity of	249
Hard wood, supply of, in the United States	247
Hard wood, use of, in bottoms of canal-boats	224-227, 229
Hard wood, use of, in frames of ocean and Hudson river vessels	25, 87, 97, 102, 107
Hard wood, use of, in keels of ocean vessels	12, 25, 87, 89, 102, 107, 108
Harrington, Maine, vessel building at	97
Haverhill, Massachusetts, vessel building at	107
Havre de Grace, Maryland, vessel building at	127
Hemlock employed in ceiling vessels for grain cargoes at New York	118
Hemlock flooring employed in northern lake vessels	138
Hemlock, specific gravity of	249
Hemlock, use of, in canal-boats	224
Hemlock, use of, in coal-boats of western rivers	182, 183
Herreshoff steam yachts	160
History of canals and canal-boats	223-233
History of steamboats and steamships in the United States	144-195
History of the building of sailing vessels in the United States	46-95
Holly, specific gravity of	249
Hudson river, ice barges on the	120
Hudson river steamboats, iron shrouds or hog-chains in	150, 151
Hudson river vessels, ocean and, use of hard wood in frames of	25, 87, 97, 102, 107
Hulls of northern lake steamers converted into dry-docks	166
Humboldt bay, California, vessel building at	132
Huntingdon, New York, vessel building at	120
Huron, Ohio, boat- and ship-yards of	43, 139
Hyannis, Massachusetts, vessel work at	111

I.

	Page.
Ice barges on the Hudson river	120
Idle ship-yards of Newburyport, Massachusetts	107
Illinois, canal navigation and boat building of	231
Illinois, statistics of the fishing fleet of	2
Illinois, steamboat yards and marine railways of, on the Ohio river	193
Importation of iron in early times	64
Indiana, statistics of fishing boats of	2
Indiana, steamboat yards of, on the Ohio river	191
Indian canoes in New England made of chestnut	28
Indianola, Texas, vessel building at	130
Iowa, steamboat yards of	194
Ipswich, Massachusetts, vessel building at	108
Iron and steel vessels built at Pittsburgh, Pennsylvania	215, 216
Iron bolts, etc., prices of, for fastening	103, 229
Iron-clads. (See War vessels.)	
Iron, importation of, in early times	64
Iron, pig, angle, and plate, prices of	196, 197, 199
Iron, pounds of, in the fastenings of a fishing boat	21, 25
Iron, pounds of, in the fastenings of canal-boats	224, 227
Iron, pounds of, in the fastenings of western river barges	182, 183, 187
Iron sailing vessels	142, 200, 203, 207
Iron-ship building at Philadelphia	202
Iron-ship building at Wyandotte, Michigan	221, 222
Iron-ship building in New Jersey	202
Iron-ship work at San Francisco, California	214, 215
Iron-ship yard at Baltimore, Maryland	214
Iron-ship yard at Buffalo, New York	218, 219
Iron-ship yard at Chester, Pennsylvania	205
Iron-ship yard at Chicago, Illinois	221
Iron-ship yard at Cleveland, Ohio	219
Iron-ship yard at Marcus Hook, Pennsylvania	208
Iron-ship yard at Saint Louis, Missouri	217, 218
Iron-ship-yard, principal, of Michigan	221, 222
Iron-ship yards at Boston, Massachusetts	200, 201
Iron-ship yards at Wilmington, Delaware	208-213

	Page.
Iron-ship yards of Maryland	214
Iron-ship yards of New York	196, 197, 201
Iron-ship yards of Pennsylvania	202
Iron ship yards of the northern lakes	218-222
Iron ships, building of, in the United States	196-222
Iron ships, cost of, per register ton, in England	142
Iron ships, plant for building, at the United States navy-yards	235, 237, 241
Iron ships, tendency in favor of, in various parts of the United States	143, 160, 161, 171, 174
Iron shops in United States navy-yards	235, 236, 238, 239, 241
Iron shrouds or hog-chains in Columbia river steamboats	164
Iron shrouds or hog-chains in Hudson river steamboats	150, 151
Iron shrouds or hog-chains in western river steamboats	179, 184, 185, 188, 192, 193
Iron strapping of frames of northern lake vessels	140, 168, 172
Iron strapping of frames of vessels built on the ocean coasts	67, 88, 89, 102, 152, 156, 163
Iron, tons of, in the fastenings, etc., of ocean vessels	92, 126, 128, 163
Iron, tons of, in the fastenings of northern lake vessels	140, 170
Iron, weight of	198, 199
Ironton, Ohio, vessel building at	190
Iron towing-boats at Saint Louis	217
Iron vessels built and repaired during the census year, number, tonnage, and value of, by counties	259
Iron vessels built on the western rivers	216-218
Iron war vessels built at Pittsburgh	216
Islip, New York, vessel building at	119

J.

	Page.
Jefferson, Cairo, and Saint Louis, a few propeller towing-boats at	191, 194
Jeffersonville, Indiana, large steamboat yards at	191
Jersey City, New Jersey, ship and repair yards of	121
Jew's rafts	108
Jiggers	7

K.

	Page.
Kennebunkport, Maine, vessel building of	18, 65, 105, 160
Kentucky, vessel building of	190
Ketch, description of a	6
Ketch, statistics of building the, in colonial years	59
Kettle-bottom ships	65
Key West, Florida, fishing vessels of	38
Kinds of barges used on western rivers, and where built	181, 186
Kinds of timber used in spars	97, 98, 102, 111, 122, 135, 156, 246, 247
Kittery, Maine, United States navy-yard at	235
Kittery, Maine, vessel building of	105
Knees, bent, experiments with	94
Knees, cost of hackmatack, in Bath, Maine	103
Knees, fir, in use on the Pacific coast	131, 133, 135
Knees, hackmatack, in ocean vessels	26, 88, 90, 97, 99, 102, 108
Knees, northern lake vessels built without	168, 175
Knees, number of, in a vessel	90, 103
Knees, oak, in use in former years	88, 89, 99, 102, 156
Knees, oak, now in use in the middle Atlantic states	122, 123

L.

	Page.
Lateen sail on ancient vessels	5
Lateen sail on San Francisco fishing boats	40
Lateen sail, transition of the, to modern forms	7, 9
Laurel, specific gravity of	249
Laurel, use of, in Pacific coast vessels	131, 133, 135, 163
League Island navy-yard, repair work at the	236
Leesburg, New Jersey, vessel building at	122
Lines of some of the famous clippers of Donald McKay	75-82
List of ships built by Donald McKay	72
Live oak, a poor quality of, in California	131
Live oak, specific gravity of	249
Live oak, supply of, in the United States	248
Live oak used to some extent in Florida for ship-building	39
Live oak, use of, in frames of northern vessels	132, 133, 156
Locust, specific gravity of	249
Locust trees on Long Island, New York	119
Locust, use of, for treenails	89, 102
Locust, use of, in frame timbers of vessels	102
Long-boat of the Potomac river, description of the	128
Long Island, New York, fishing boats of	17, 21
Long Island, New York, vessel building on	119

INDEX TO REPORT ON SHIP-BUILDING.

	Page.
Long Island sound, coal barges on	112, 114
Lorain, Ohio, fishing craft built at	43
Louisiana, statistics of fishing boats of	2
Louisiana, vessel building of	130, 194
Louisville, Kentucky, engine shops of	191
Lugger for fishing and fruit trade in Louisiana	39
Lugger, use of, by early colonial fishermen	6
Lynchburg, Texas, vessel building at	130

M.

McKay, Donald, lines of some of the famous clippers of	75–82
McKay, Donald, list of ships built by	72
McKeesport, Pennsylvania, barge building at	187
Machiasport, Maine, vessel building at	96
Madeira wood, use of	39, 249
Madison, Connecticut, vessel building at	114
Madison, Indiana, vessel building at	191
Maine coast towns, boat building in	96, 99
Maine, European fishing expeditions to	3, 4
Maine, Pacific coast lumber vessels built in	134
Maine, present state of the ship-building industry in	96, 105
Maine, statistics of fishing vessels of	2
Maine, steamboat building in	160
Malden, New York, decay of the boat-building industry at	120
Manitowoc, Wisconsin, vessel building at	43, 137, 174
Maple. (See Hard wood.)	
Marblehead, Massachusetts, fishing vessels at	108
Marcus Hook, Pennsylvania, iron-ship yard at	208
Mare Island navy-yard, value of buildings at the	241
Marietta, Ohio, steamboat building at	190
Marine City, Michigan, vessel building at	171
Marine railway at Black Rock, Connecticut	114
Marine railway, largest, on the Atlantic coast	113
Marine railway, pioneer, in America	109
Marine railways in the southern states	130
Marine railways in United States navy-yards	235, 238
Marine railways, New England	96–100, 104, 105, 109, 111–115
Marine railways on the middle Atlantic coast	118–121, 123, 124, 127–129
Marine railways on the Pacific coast	132, 136
Marine railways on western rivers	187, 190–194
Marquette, Michigan, fishing boats at	43, 44
Martha's Vineyard, Massachusetts, decay of boat-building at	111
Maryland, canal navigation and boat building of	232
Maryland, coal barges in, under construction	127
Maryland, fishing canoes and bug-eyes of	34, 35
Maryland, iron-ship yards of	214
Maryland, present vessel building of	126
Maryland, statistics of fishing vessels of	3
Maryland, timber supply of	87, 128, 244
Massachusetts, colonial building of merchant vessels in	47, 50
Massachusetts, colonial fishing ventures of	3
Massachusetts, present state of the ship-building industry in	107
Massachusetts, sailing clippers of	73
Massachusetts, statistics of fishing vessels of	3
Massachusetts, steamer building in	160
Massachusetts, wood and fishing sloops of	9
Mastic, specific gravity of	249
Mastic, use of, in Florida fishing vessels	39
Matagorda, Texas, ship-building at	130
Mattapoisett, Massachusetts, boat-building at	111
Mauricetown and May's Landing, New Jersey, ship-yards of	122
Measurement of a ship of 1695 contracted to be built	60
Measurement, old and new, in the United States	64
Measurement, origin of carpenters'	50
Medford, Massachusetts, building of vessels at, after the war of 1812	110
Medford, Massachusetts, colonial ship-building of	46
Methodist canoe of Annamessex, Maryland	35
Metropolis, Illinois, steamboat work at	193
Michigan, principal iron-ship yard of	221, 222
Michigan, statistics of fishing vessels of	3
Michigan, steamer and vessel building in	171
Michigan, timber supply of	171–173, 245, 247
Middle Atlantic coast, marine railways on	118–121, 123, 124, 127–129
Middle Haddam and Middletown, Connecticut, decay of ship-building at	114
Milford and Milton, Delaware, vessel building at	125
Milwaukee, Wisconsin, vessel building at	43, 173

	Page.
Minnesota, statistics of fishing vessels of	3
Minnesota, steamboat building in	194
Mississippi river. (See Western rivers.)	
Mississippi, statistics of fishing vessels of	3
Missouri river. (See Western rivers.)	
Missouri, steamboat building in	194
Missouri, timber supply of	195, 245
Model barge, description of a	184, 185
Model of a French frigate copied by American builders	64
Monongahela City, barge building at	186
Monongahela river. (See Western rivers.)	
Monongahela river, small dry-docks on the	187
Mound City, Illinois, yard and marine railway at	193
Mount Clemens, Michigan, vessel building at	171
Mystic, Connecticut, decay of ship-building at	113

N.

Nantucket, Massachusetts, fishing vessels of	22, 111
Navigation laws	63, 64
Navy-yards of the United States, description of the	234–241
New Albany, Indiana, steamboat and barge yards of	192
New Bedford, Massachusetts, burning of vessels and boats of, by British	10, 22
New Bedford, Massachusetts, vessel building of, at the present time	111
New Bedford, Massachusetts, whaling vessels and boats of	22
New Berne, North Carolina, vessel work at	130
New Brunswick, New Jersey, vessel building at	122
Newburgh, New York, work at the ship-yards of	120, 161, 202
Newburyport, Massachusetts, dory building at	20
Newburyport, Massachusetts, idle ship-yards of	107
New England colonies, canoes in	5, 22, 28
New England colonies, statistics of the number of brigantines built in the	50
New England marine railways	96–100, 104, 105, 109, 111–115
New England towns, decay of boat-building in	108, 111, 112
New England vessels, hackmatack knees in	26, 88, 90, 97, 99, 102, 108
New Hampshire, ship-building of	105
New Hampshire, statistics of fishing vessels of	3
New Haven, Connecticut, barge and vessel building at	114
New Haven, Connecticut, fishing boats of	29
New Jersey, canal navigation and canal-boats of	232
New Jersey, cedar trees in	121
New Jersey, iron-ship building in	202
New Jersey, statistics of fishing vessels of	3
New Jersey, vessel building of, at the present time	121
New London, Connecticut, building and repairing at	113
New London, Connecticut, fishing boats and vessels of	23, 30
New London navy-yard, description of	236
New Orleans, Louisiana, vessel and boat building at	39, 130, 162, 194
Newport, Rhode Island, decay of ship and boat building at	112
Newport, Rhode Island, whaling vessels of	22, 23
New vessels built during the census year, number, tonnage, and value of, by counties	254–258
New vessels built during the census year, number, tonnage, and value of, by states and territories	253
New York, canal navigation and canal-boats of	223
New York city, construction of packet ships at	116
New York city, steam vessels at	161
New York, colonial ship-building of	48
New York ferry-boats	162
New York, fishing smacks of, described	17, 20
New York, iron-ship yards of	196, 197, 201
New York, packets and clipper ships of	68, 73
New York, present state of the ship-building industry of	115
New York, statistics of fishing vessels of	3
New York, steamer building, for the trade of the lakes, at	169
New York, timber supply of	119, 120, 225, 229, 245, 247
Noank, Connecticut, ship-yard and marine railway at	113
Noank, Connecticut, steamers built at	18, 161
Norfolk navy-yard, description of	240
Norfolk, Virginia, trading and fishing boats of	35, 129
Norfolk, Virginia, vessel building and repairing at	129
North Carolina, present state of the vessel-building industry in	130
North Carolina, statistics of fishing vessels of	3
Northern lake schooners, three-, four-, and five-masters	138–140
Northern lake vessels built without knees	138, 170
Northern lake vessels, iron strapping of frames of	140, 168, 173

272 INDEX TO REPORT ON SHIP-BUILDING.

	Page.
Northern lakes, bevel saw in popular use on the	170–172
Northern lakes, dry-docks on the	169, 171, 173
Northern lakes, fishing boats of	43–45
Northern lakes, iron-ship yards of	218–222
Northern lakes, ship-carpenters from New York sent to, in the war of 1812	116
Northern lakes, statistics of fishing vessels of	2
Northern lakes, steamer building on the	149, 166
Northern lakes, timber supply of	171–173, 245, 246
Northern lakes, vessel building on the	137
Northport, New York, vessel building at	120
North Weymouth, Massachusetts, vessel building at	111
Noted war vessels which have been built at the United States navy-yards	235, 237, 240
Number and tonnage of barges on western rivers	176
Number and tonnage of sailing vessels in the United States	46
Number and tonnage of vessels, number of establishments, capital, average number of hands employed, amount of wages paid, materials used, and value of products, by states and territories	260–265
A—Aggregate	260, 261
B—New vessels	260, 261
C—Repairing of vessels	262, 263
D—Boats	262, 263
E—Ocean, coast, and river vessels	262, 263
F—Northern lakes	264, 265
G—Western rivers	264, 265
H—Canal-boats	264, 265
I—Iron vessels	264, 265
Number and value of boats built during the census year, by counties	254–258
Number and value of boats built during the census year, by states and territories	253
Number of knees in a vessel	90, 103
Number, tonnage, and value of iron vessels built and repaired during the census year, by counties	259
Number, tonnage, and value of new vessels built during the census year, by counties	254–258
Number, tonnage, and value of new vessels built during the census year, by states and territories	253
Nyack, New York, vessel building at	120

O.

Oak knees in use in former years	60, 88, 90, 102, 156
Oak knees now in use in the middle United States	122, 125
Oakland, California, vessel building at	132, 162
Oak. (See White oak.)	
Oak, white, bent knees and timbers of	94
Oak, white, cost of, in England	142, 143
Oak, white, failure of the native supply of, in England	242
Oak, white, general supply of, of the United States now failing	243
Oak, white, on the western rivers	151, 178, 179, 182, 186–188, 190–193, 195
Oak, white, preferred for frame timber in Maine	97, 98, 102, 138, 169, 171–174
Oak, white, supply of, in the Atlantic States	105, 107, 113, 119, 120, 122, 124, 126, 128, 171
Oak, white, use of, in canal-boats	223, 227, 231, 232
Oak, white, use of, in fishing schooners	12, 13, 15
Oak, white, use of, in large ocean vessels	25, 60, 61, 64, 87, 89, 156, 161
Ocean and Hudson river vessels, use of hard wood in frames of	25, 87, 97, 102, 107
Ocean vessels, hackmatack knees in	26, 88, 90, 97, 99, 102, 108
Ocean vessels, use of hard wood in keels of	12, 25, 87, 89, 102, 107, 108
Ogdensburg, New York, vessel building at	43, 169
Ohio, canal navigation and canal-boats of	230
Ohio river. (See Western rivers.)	
Ohio, statistics of fishing vessels of	3
Ohio, steamboat and barge building in, for the western rivers	190
Ohio, vessel building in, for the northern lakes	140, 169
Old and new measurement in the United States	64
Oregon City, Oregon, vessel building at	165
Oregon pine. (See Yellow fir.)	
Oregon, statistics of fishing vessels of	3
Oregon, timber supply of	161, 248
Oregon, vessel-building industry in	133, 163–165
Origin and object of the practice of the coppering of vessels, and how the metal is put on	27
Origin of sloops in the United States	9
Oswego, New York, vessel and boat building at	43, 169, 225
Outfits of cordage obtained in the great cities	104, 108, 122, 124, 127

	Page.
Outfits of sails, where usually bought	104, 108, 122–127
Oxford, Maryland, repairs of vessels at	128
Oyster boats, general description of	28–38
Oyster canoes at Gloucester, Virginia	38
Oyster canoes of Pocosin, Virginia	38
Oyster skiffs at Amboy, New Jersey	32

P.

Pacific coast lumber vessels built in Maine	134
Pacific coast, marine railways on the	132, 136
Pacific coast vessels, use of laurel in	131, 133, 136, 163
Packet lines on the Atlantic	68
Packets and clipper ships of New York	68, 73
Packet ships, construction of, at New York city	116
Packet ships, origin and success of the American lines of	68
Paddle-wheel, early experiments with the	144, 147
Pamrapo, New Jersey, yacht building at	121
Patchogue, New York, boat building at	119
Peculiarities of northern lake vessels	137
Pennsylvania, canal navigation and canal-boats of	232
Pennsylvania, iron-ship yards of	202
Pennsylvania, statistics of fishing vessels of	3
Pennsylvania, steamboat and barge building in, for the western rivers	186
Pensacola navy-yard, description of	240
Perth Amboy, New Jersey, vessel building at	121
Philadelphia, iron-ship building at	202
Philadelphia, vessel building and repairing at	123, 162
Phippsburg, Maine, ship-yard at	101
Pig, angle, and plate iron, prices of	196, 197, 199
Pine, white, exportation of, to England	104, 105
Pine, white, general supply of, in the United States	247
Pine, white, used for decking and cabins	25, 60, 61, 64, 87, 89, 156, 162
Pine, white, use of, in boats and canoes	12, 20, 29, 31, 43
Pine, white, use of, for masts and spars	97, 99, 102, 111, 127, 132, 138, 246, 247
Pine, yellow, abundant supply of, in Virginia	128, 246
Pine, yellow, a native of New Jersey	121, 122
Pine, yellow, general supply of, in the United States	246
Pine, yellow, introduction of, to northern ship-yards	64, 87
Pine, yellow, used in Virginia for canoes	34
Pinkie stern in early New England fishing and trading boats	6, 7
Pinkie stern in model barges on the western rivers	184
Pinkie stern in San Francisco fishing boats	40
Pinkie stern in wooden fishing boats of Chesapeake bay	38
Pinkies, statistics of the building of, in the New England colonies	50
Pinnace	5
Pioneer marine railway in America	109
Pioneer vessel for the trade of Boston, Massachusetts	46
Pitch-pine. (See Yellow pine.)	
Pittsburgh, Pennsylvania, iron and steel vessels built at	215, 216
Pittsburgh, Pennsylvania, pioneer western river steamboat built at	176
Pittsburgh, Pennsylvania, present steamboat and barge building of	187
Planking, cedar, in fishing-boats	21, 23, 32
Plant for building iron ships at the United States navy-yards	235, 237, 241
Pocomoke City, Maryland, ship-yards at	128
Pocosin, Virginia, oyster canoes of	38
Point Lookout, Maryland, canoe building at	35
Poplar, specific gravity of	249
Poplar, use of, in western river boats	179, 180, 184, 185, 187, 188, 190, 193
Port Blakeley, Washington territory, ship-building at	135
Port Gamble, Washington territory, ship-building at	134
Port Huron, Michigan, vessel repairing at	172
Port Jefferson, New York, vessel building at	119
Portland, Maine, vessel and boat building at	20, 104, 160
Portland, Oregon, steamboat building at	165
Port Ludlow, Washington territory, vessel building at	133
Port Madison, Washington territory, vessel building at	134
Port Norris, New Jersey, repair of fishing vessels at	123
Port Republic, New Jersey, decay of boat-building at	122
Portsmouth navy-yard, description of	235
Portsmouth, New Hampshire, ship-building at	105
Port Townsend, Washington territory, boat-building at	134
Pounds of iron in the fastenings of a fishing-boat	21, 25
Pounds of iron in the fastenings of canal-boats	224, 227
Pounds of iron in the fastenings of western river barges	182, 183, 187
Present vessel building at Astoria, Oregon	165
Prices of iron bolts, etc., for fastening	103, 229

INDEX TO REPORT ON SHIP-BUILDING.

	Page.
Prices of pig, angle, and plate iron	196, 197, 199
Privateers in and after the Revolution	62, 63, 115
Privateers. (*See* War vessels.)	
Produce boats	183
Propellers. (*See* Screw-propellers.)	
Provincetown, Massachusetts, boats and boat-building of	23, 111
Puget sound canoes hewn from logs of cedar	42
Puget sound, canoes on, and in Alaska	42
Puget sound, fishing canoes of	40
Puget sound, ship-building industry of	133
Puget sound, timber supply of	131, 134, 136, 248

Q.

Quaint fishing boats at San Francisco, California	40

R.

Racine, Wisconsin, boat-building at	43
Rappahannock, the ship	70
Redwood timber	132, 248
Repair work at Saint Michael's, Maryland	124
Repair work at Savannah, Georgia	130
Repair work at Sayville, New York	119
Repair work at Sharptown, Maryland	128
Repair work at the League Island navy-yard	238
Repair work at Whitehaven, Maryland	128
Rhode Island, early whaling vessels of	22
Rhode Island, statistics of fishing vessels of	3
Rhode Island, vessel building industry of	112, 160
Rice's Landing, Pennsylvania, boat-building at	186
Richmond, Maine, vessel-building at	101
Rockland, Maine, ship-yards and marine railways of	97
Rockport, Massachusetts, boat-building at	109
Rocky Hill, Connecticut, barge-building at	114
Rocky River, Ohio, boat-building at	43
Rondout, New York, canal-boat yards at	223
Rondout, New York, vessel building at	120, 161
Rowley, Massachusetts, vessel-building at	108
Rye, New York, yacht-building at	120

S.

Saco, Maine, decay of ship-building at	105
Sag Harbor, New York, early whaling boats of	22
Sag Harbor, New York, present vessel building of	119
Sailing clippers of Boston, Massachusetts	73-82
Sailing vessels, growth in the size of, after 1820	70
Sailing vessels, history of the building of, in the United States	46-95
Sailing vessels, iron	142, 200, 203, 207
Sailing vessels, number and tonnage of, in the United States	46
Sail, lateen, and its transition to modern forms	4, 7, 9
Sail-lofts in navy-yards	235, 237, 239
Sail plan of a Block Island boat	10
Sail plan of a caravel	5
Sail plan of a cat-rigged boat	33
Sail plan of a fishing schooner	17, 19
Sail plan of a fishing sharpie	31, 44
Sail plan of a ketch	8
Sail plan of a northern lake schooner	139, 140
Sail plan of a pink or Chebacco boat	9
Sail plan of a snow or brig	61
Sail plan of a square topsail sloop	11
Sail plan of a whaling bark	26
Sail plan of Chesapeake bay boats	36, 37
Sail plan of the clipper Great Republic, showing modern division of the topsails	91
Sail plan of the clipper Sovereign of the Seas, showing old-fashioned topsails	76
Sails, division of topsails into upper and lower	86
Sails, outfits of, usually bought in the large cities	104, 108, 122-127
Sails, yards of canvas, on Gloucester fishing schooners	15
Sails, yards of canvas, on various vessels	89, 94, 135, 139
Saint George's harbor, Maine, vessel repairing at	99
Saint Joseph, Michigan, vessel building at	173
Saint Louis, iron-ship yard at	217, 218
Saint Louis, vessel building at	194
Saint Michael's, Maryland, repair work at	124
Salem, Massachusetts, early vessel building of	47
Salem, Massachusetts, present state of the industry at	109
Salem, New Jersey, repairs of fishing vessels at	123
Salem, Oregon, steamboat building at	164
Salisbury, Maryland, vessel repairing at	128
Salisbury, Massachusetts, boat and vessel building at	20, 107
Sandusky and Sanilac, Ohio, boat-building at	43
San Francisco, California, iron-ship work at	214, 215
San Francisco, California, quaint fishing-boats at	40
San Francisco, California, vessel-building at	131, 162
Savannah, Georgia, repair work at	130
Sayville, New York, repair work at	119
Schooners, coal, superseded by coal-barges	112, 114, 124
Schooners, coasting, three- and four masters	93
Schooners, fishing, of Florida	39
Schooners, fishing, of New England and New York	12
Schooners for the wood trade of the Potomac	128
Schooners, northern lake, three-, four-, and five-masters	138-140
Scituate, Massachusetts, decay of ship-building at	111
Screw propeller as auxiliary power in whalers	28
Screw propeller, experiment by John Cox Stevens of a	145
Screw propeller, general adoption of, in American coasting and lake steamers and tugs	149, 153, 160, 167
Screw propeller introduced into canal-boats	228, 230-232
Screw propeller invented by John Fitch, an American	144
Screw propeller, size of, in various vessels	160, 173, 191, 202, 203, 265
Screw propeller, successful experiments with, by Ericsson	148
Shallop	5, 6
Sharpie	22, 30, 43
Sharptown, Maryland, repair work at	128
Sheboygan, Wisconsin, boat-building at	43
Ship and boat building at Newport, Rhode Island, decay of	113
Ship and repair yards at Jersey City, New Jersey	121
Ship-building at Matagorda, Texas	130
Ship-building at Middle Haddam and Middletown, Connecticut, decay of	114
Ship-building at Mystic, Connecticut, decay of	113
Ship-building at Port Blakeley, Washington territory	135
Ship-building at Port Gamble, Washington territory	134
Ship-building at Portsmouth, New Hampshire	105
Ship-building at Saco, Maine, decay of	105
Ship-building at Scituate, Massachusetts, decay of	111
Ship-building at Thomaston, Maine	98
Ship-building at Waldoboro' and Wiscasset, Maine, decay of	100
Ship-building industry in Maine, present state of the	96-105
Ship-building industry in Massachusetts, present state of the	107
Ship-building industry of New York, present state of the	115
Ship-building industry of Puget sound	133
Ship-building industry, quantity of copper used in, in the census year	261
Ship-building of New Hampshire	105
Ship-building of Yarmouth, Maine	104
Ship of 1695, measurement of a, contracted to be built	60
Ship work at Charleston, South Carolina	130
Ship work in Arizona	131
Ship-yard and marine railway at Noank, Connecticut	113
Ship-yards and marine railways of Rockland, Maine	97
Ship-yards at Alexandria, Virginia	128, 129
Ship-yards at Phippsburg, Maine	101
Ship-yards at Pocomoke City, Maryland	128
Ship-yards of May's Landing and Mauricetown, New Jersey	122
Ship-yards of Newburgh, New York, work at the	121, 161, 202
Ship-yards on the Pacific Coast, bevel saw in	132, 135
Side-wheel of western river boats	177, 180
Side-wheels employed on early passenger boats on the northern lakes	166
Side-wheels used at New York city	145-147, 155
Six-Mile Ferry, Pennsylvania, barge building at	187
Skiffs	29, 32
Slave ships	126
Sloops, employment of, in the trade of Massachusetts bay	47
Sloops, fishing, in Florida	39
Sloops, large size of early trading	62, 115, 145
Sloops, origin of, in the United States	9
Sloops, whaling	22
Snags and snag-boats	195
Snows	50, 61
Solomon's Island, Maryland, vessel building of	38, 128
Somers' Point, New Jersey, decay of boat building at	122
South Carolina, statistics of fishing vessels of	3
South Carolina, timber supply of	243, 245, 246

INDEX TO REPORT ON SHIP-BUILDING.

	Page.
South Carolina, vessel building and repairing in	130
Southern states, marine railways in the	130
South Norwalk, Connecticut, vessel and boat building at	30, 115, 160
Spars, exportation of, to England in colonial times	104, 105
Spars, kinds of timber used in	97, 99, 102, 111, 127, 132, 138, 246, 247
Spars of Gloucester fishing schooner	14
Spars of northern lake schooners	138, 140
Spars of northern lake fishing sharpies	44
Spars of Pacific coast vessels	135
Spars of the clipper-ship Champion of the Seas	89
Spars of the clipper-ship Great Republic	90
Spars of whaling barks	26
Spars, topmast, fidded abaft the lower mast	86
Specific gravity of cedar	249
Specific gravity of chestnut	247
Specific gravity of cypress	249
Specific gravity of dogwood	249
Specific gravity of hackmatack	249
Specific gravity of hard wood	249
Specific gravity of hemlock	249
Specific gravity of holly	249
Specific gravity of laurel	249
Specific gravity of live oak	249
Specific gravity of locust	249
Specific gravity of mastic	249
Specific gravity of poplar	249
Specific gravity of the gum tree	249
Spruce	247, 248
Stage island, Maine, building of first vessel in America at	46
Staten Island, New York, vessel building on	119
State of the ship-building industry at Baltimore, Maryland	126
State of the ship-building industry at Barnegat, New Jersey	122
State of the ship-building industry at Bath, Maine	101
State of the vessel industry in Allegheny City, Pennsylvania	187
Statistics of building the ketch in colonial years	50
Statistics of California fishing vessels	2
Statistics of fishing boats of Indiana	2
Statistics of fishing boats of Louisiana	2
Statistics of fishing vessels of Connecticut	2
Statistics of fishing vessels of Delaware	2
Statistics of fishing vessels of Florida	2
Statistics of fishing vessels of Georgia	2
Statistics of fishing vessels of Maine	3
Statistics of fishing vessels of Maryland	3
Statistics of fishing vessels of Massachusetts	3
Statistics of fishing vessels of Michigan	3
Statistics of fishing vessels of Minnesota	3
Statistics of fishing vessels of Mississippi	3
Statistics of fishing vessels of New Hampshire	3
Statistics of fishing vessels of New Jersey	3
Statistics of fishing vessels of New York	3
Statistics of fishing vessels of North Carolina	3
Statistics of fishing vessels of Ohio	3
Statistics of fishing vessels of Oregon	3
Statistics of fishing vessels of Pennsylvania	3
Statistics of fishing vessels of Rhode Island	3
Statistics of fishing vessels of South Carolina	3
Statistics of fishing vessels of the northern lakes	2
Statistics of fishing vessels of Virginia	3
Statistics of fishing vessels of Washington territory	3
Statistics of fishing vessels of Wisconsin	3
Statistics of fishing vessels owned in Alabama	2
Statistics of fishing vessels owned in Alaska	2
Statistics of the building of pinkies in the New England colonies	50
Statistics of the fishing fleet of Illinois	2
Statistics of the number of brigantines built in the New England colonies	50
Steamboat and barge building at Belle Vernon, Pennsylvania	186
Steamboat and barge building at Brownsville, Pennsylvania	186
Steamboat and barge building at Cincinnati, Ohio	190
Steamboat and barge building in Pennsylvania for the western rivers	186
Steamboat and barge building of Pittsburgh, Pennsylvania, present	187
Steamboat and barge building on the western rivers	174
Steamboat and barge work at Covington, Kentucky	190
Steamboat and barge yards of New Albany, Indiana	192
Steamboat building at Evansville, Indiana	192
Steamboat building at Freedom, Pennsylvania	187

	Page.
Steamboat building at Marietta, Ohio	190
Steamboat building at Salem, Oregon	164
Steamboat building in Maine	160
Steamboat building in Minnesota	194
Steamboat building in Missouri	194
Steamboat work at Celilo, Oregon	165
Steamboat work at Metropolis, Illinois	193
Steamboat work at The Dalles, Oregon	165
Steamboat yards and marine railways of Illinois on the Ohio river	193
Steamboat yards, large, at Jeffersonville, Indiana	191
Steamboat yards of Indiana on the Ohio river	191
Steamboat yards of Iowa	194
Steamboats and steamships, builders of, at New York	116
Steamboats and steamships, building of, at the present time in the United States	112, 160
Steamboats and steamships, history of, in the United States	144–105
Steamboats and steamships, present competition between, and sail vessels	141
Steamboats and steamships sent out by the English to compete with American sailing packets	70
Steamboats, steamships, and steam fishing vessels	18, 28, 45
Steam canal-boats	228, 230–23
Steam vessels at New York city	161
Steam vessels, early construction of, part taken by Robert Fulton in the	145, 146
Steam yachts built at Bristol, Rhode Island	160
Steamer and vessel building in Michigan	171
Steamer building for the trade of the lakes at New York	169
Steamer building in Massachusetts	160
Steamer building in Wisconsin	173
Steamer building on the northern lakes	149, 166
Steamers built at Noank, Connecticut	18, 161
Stern-wheels introduced on western rivers	152, 176, 180
Stern-wheels on the Pacific coast	136, 164
Stern-wheel steamboats, towing boats on the western rivers by means of	185
Steubenville, Ohio, barge-building at	188
Stevens, John Cox, experiment by, of a screw propeller	145
Strapping of frames of northern lake vessels	140, 168, 173
Strapping of frames of ocean and river vessels	67, 88, 89, 102, 152, 156, 163
Strapping of frames of vessels, origin of the practice of, in Europe	67
Surf-boats	21

T.

	Page.
Taunton, Massachusetts, coal barges of	111
Tennessee river. (*See* Western rivers.)	
Texas, statistics of fishing vessels of	3
Texas, vessel-building industry in	130
Thomaston, Maine, ship-building of	98
Timber supply of California	131, 248
Timber supply of Georgia	243, 246
Timber supply of Maryland	87, 128, 244
Timber supply of Michigan	171–173, 245, 247
Timber supply of New York	119, 120, 225, 229, 245, 247
Timber supply of Oregon	161, 248
Timber supply of Puget sound	131, 134, 136, 248
Timber supply of South Carolina	243, 245, 246
Timber supply of the northern lakes	171–173, 245, 246
Timber supply of Virginia	34, 87, 128, 244, 246
Timber supply of Washington territory	134, 163, 248
Toledo, Ohio, boat and vessel building of	43, 140
Tonnage duties	63, 65, 66
Tons of iron in the fastenings, etc., of ocean vessels	92, 126, 128, 163
Tons of iron in the fastenings of northern lake vessels	140, 170
Topmast spars fidded abaft the lower mast	86
Towing-boats at Jefferson, Cairo, and Saint Louis	191, 194
Towing-boats described	149, 163, 165, 175, 191, 202
Towing-boats, iron, at Saint Louis	217
Towing-boats on the northern lakes	138
Towing boats on the western rivers by means of stern-wheel steamboats	185
Towing-boats, original steamboats in England intended for	144
Towing-boats, the screw-wheel adopted for, at ocean ports in America	149
Towing-boats, western river, how built	187–189
Trading and fishing boats of Norfolk, Virginia	35, 129
Treenail machines	87, 110
Tuckerton, New Jersey, boat and vessel building at	34, 122
Tuckahoe, New Jersey, vessel building at	122
Tugs. (*See* Towing-boats.)	

INDEX TO REPORT ON SHIP-BUILDING.

U.

	Page.
United States navy, cordage for the, made at the Charlestown navy-yard	235
United States navy-yard at Boston, Massachusetts, description of	235
United States navy-yard at Charlestown, Massachusetts, description of the	235
United States navy-yard at Kittery, Maine, description of	235
United States navy-yards, dry-docks at the	235, 237, 240, 241
United States navy-yards, iron shops in	235, 236, 238, 239, 241
United States navy-yards, marine railways in	235, 238
United States, supply of hard wood in the	247
Use of gum tree for keels, etc	102, 129

V.

	Page.
Value of buildings at the Mare Island navy-yard	241
Vermillion, Ohio, boat-building at	43
Vessel and boat building at Bay City, Michigan	43, 172
Vessel and boat building at New Orleans, Louisiana	39, 130, 162, 194
Vessel and boat building at Oswego, New York	43, 169, 225
Vessel and boat building at South Norwalk, Connecticut	30, 115, 160
Vessel-building and repairing at City Island, New York	120
Vessel building and repairing at Norfolk, Virginia	129
Vessel building and repairing at Philadelphia	123, 162
Vessel building and repairing in South Carolina	130
Vessel building and repairing on the Delaware river	123
Vessel building at Amesbury, Massachusetts	107, 108
Vessel building at Athens, New York	120, 161
Vessel building at Bay Shore, New York	119
Vessel building at Beaufort, North Carolina	130
Vessel building at Belfast, Maine	98
Vessel building at Belle Port, New York	119
Vessel building at Bell's Ferry, North Carolina	130
Vessel building at Bethel, Delaware	125
Vessel building at Blue Hill, Maine	97
Vessel building at Blue Point, New York	97
Vessel building at Boston, Massachusetts, at the present time	110, 160
Vessel building at Bradford, Massachusetts	108
Vessel building at Bremen and Brewer, Maine	98, 99
Vessel building at Bristol, Maine	99
Vessel building at Broad Creek, Maryland	128
Vessel building at Brookline, Maine	97
Vessel building at Brunswick, Maine	104
Vessel building at Bucksport, Maine	97
Vessel building at Buffalo, New York	169
Vessel building at Calais, Maine	96
Vessel building at Cambridge, Maryland	127
Vessel building at Camden, Maine	96
Vessel building at Camden, New Jersey	123, 162, 202
Vessel building at Cape Cod, Massachusetts	22, 112
Vessel building at Clayton, New York	43, 169
Vessel building at Cleveland, Ohio	169
Vessel building at Cohasset, Massachusetts	111
Vessel building at Coosaw, South Carolina	130
Vessel building at Coos Bay, Oregon	133
Vessel building at Cos Cob, Connecticut	115
Vessel building at Cutler, Maine	96
Vessel building at Damariscotta and Damaysville, Maine	100
Vessel building at Detroit, Michigan	171
Vessel building at Discovery bay, Washington territory	134
Vessel building at Duxbury, Massachusetts	111
Vessel building at East Deering, Maine	104
Vessel building at Eastport, Maine	96, 160
Vessel building at East Saginaw, Michigan	172
Vessel building at Elizabeth City, North Carolina	130
Vessel building at Ellsworth, Maine	97
Vessel building at Frederica, Delaware	125
Vessel building at Freeport, Maine	104
Vessel building at Friendship, Maine	99
Vessel building at Galveston, Texas	130
Vessel building at Georgetown, Maine	100
Vessel building at Georgetown, South Carolina	130
Vessel building at Gibraltar, Michigan	171
Vessel building at Gildersleeve's Landing, Connecticut	115
Vessel building at Grand Haven, Michigan	173
Vessel building at Greenland, New Jersey	34, 122
Vessel building at Green Bay, Wisconsin	43, 174

	Page.
Vessel building at Greenport, New York	119
Vessel building at Harrington, Maine	97
Vessel building at Haverhill, Massachusetts	107
Vessel building at Havre de Grace, Maryland	127
Vessel building at Humboldt bay, California	132
Vessel building at Huntingdon, New York	120
Vessel building at Indianola, Texas	130
Vessel building at Ipswich, Massachusetts	108
Vessel building at Ironton, Ohio	190
Vessel building at Islip, New York	119
Vessel building at Kennebunkport, Maine	18, 66, 105, 160
Vessel building at Kittery, Maine	105
Vessel building at Leesburg, New Jersey	122
Vessel building at Lynchburg, Texas	130
Vessel building at Machiasport, Maine	96
Vessel building at Madison, Connecticut	114
Vessel building at Madison, Indiana	191
Vessel building at Manitowoc, Wisconsin	43, 137, 174
Vessel building at Marine City, Michigan	171
Vessel building at Milford and Milton, Delaware	125
Vessel building at Milwaukee, Wisconsin	43, 173
Vessel building at Mount Clemens, Michigan	171
Vessel building at New Bedford, Massachusetts, at the present time	111
Vessel building at New Brunswick, New Jersey	122
Vessel building at Northport, New York	120
Vessel building at North Weymouth, Massachusetts	111
Vessel building at Nyack, New York	120
Vessel building at Oakland, California	132, 162
Vessel building at Ogdensburg, New York	43, 169
Vessel building at Oregon City, Oregon	135
Vessel building at Perth Amboy, New Jersey	121
Vessel building at Richmond, Maine	101
Vessel building at Rondout, New York	120, 161
Vessel building at Rowley, Massachusetts	108
Vessel building at Sag Harbor, New York	119
Vessel building at Saint Joseph, Maryland	173
Vessel building at Saint Louis, Missouri	194
Vessel building at Salem, Massachusetts	47
Vessel building at San Francisco, California	131, 162
Vessel building at Solomon's Island, Maryland	32, 128
Vessel building at Tuckahoe, New Jersey	122
Vessel building at Wallula, Oregon	135
Vessel building at Washington, North Carolina	130
Vessel building at Wheeling, West Virginia	168
Vessel building at Wilmington, Delaware	124, 162
Vessel building of Georgia	130
Vessel building of Kentucky	190
Vessel building of Louisiana	130, 194
Vessel building of Maryland, present	126
Vessel building of New Jersey at the present time	121
Vessel building of Oregon	133
Vessel building on Long Island, New York	118
Vessel building on Staten Island, New York	119
Vessel-building industry in Alaska, state of the	136, 137
Vessel-building industry in Oregon	133, 162, 163
Vessel-building industry in Rhode Island	112, 160
Vessel-building industry in Texas	130
Vessel-building industry in Virginia	129
Vessel-building industry in North Carolina, present state of the	130
Vessel building in Ohio for the northern lakes	140, 169
Vessel building in Washington territory	131, 133, 162
Vessel building on the northern lakes	137
Vessel-building resources of Cairo, Illinois	194
Vessel industry in Allegheny City, Pennsylvania, state of the	187
Vessel repairing at Saint George's harbor, Maine	96
Vessel work at Hyannis, Massachusetts	112
Vessel work at New Berne, North Carolina	130
Vessels at Oxford, Maryland, repair of	128
Vessels built on the ocean coasts, iron strapping of frames of	67, 88, 89, 90
	152, 156, 160
Virginia, canal navigation and canal-boats of	22
Virginia, fishing canoes of	24
Virginia, statistics of fishing vessels of	3
Virginia, timber supply of	74, 84, 128, 247
Virginia, vessel-building industry in	129

W.

	Page.
Waldoboro', Maine, decay of ship-building at	100
Wallula, Oregon, vessel building at	165
War vessels built at New York on foreign account	86, 152, 153
War vessels built at private yards for the government in 1861	234
War vessels built on the lakes in the war of 1812	116
War vessels, colonial fleet of, at the capture of Louisburg	10
War vessels, early American	86, 106, 108, 115
War vessels, heavy armament of colonial merchantmen as	59
War vessels, iron, built at Pittsburgh	216
War vessels, noted, which have been built at the United States navy-yards	235, 237, 240
Washington navy-yard, description of	238–240
Washington, North Carolina, vessel building at	130
Washington territory and Oregon, cedar trees in	248
Washington territory, canoes of Puget sound	42
Washington territory, statistics of fishing vessels of	3
Washington territory, timber supply of	134, 163, 248
Washington territory, vessel building in	131, 133, 163
Weight of iron	198, 199
Wellfleet, Massachusetts, decay of boat-building at	111
West Creek, New Jersey, boat and vessel building at	34, 122
Western river boats, use of poplar in	179, 180, 184, 185, 187, 188, 190, 193
Western rivers, barges on, number and tonnage of	176
Western river steamboats, iron shrouds or hog-chains in	179, 184, 185, 188, 192, 193
Western river towing-boats, how built	187–189
Western rivers, flat-boats of	176, 181
Western rivers, iron vessels built on the	216–218
Western rivers, kinds of barges used on, and where built	181, 186
Western rivers, marine railways on	187, 190–194
Western rivers, steamboat and barge building on	174
West Virginia, vessel building of	188
Whale boats built at Fairhaven, Massachusetts	23
Whaling boats and vessels owned at Boston, Massachusetts	23
Whaling boats of Sag Harbor, New York, early	22
Whaling sloops	22
Whaling vessels and boats, description of	22–28
Whaling vessels and boats of New Bedford, Massachusetts	22
Whaling vessels, early, of Rhode Island	22
Whaling vessels of Newport, Rhode Island	22, 23
Whaling propellers of Bath, Maine	28
Wharf-boats	175
Wheeling, West Virginia, decline of vessel building at	188
Whitehaven, Maryland, repair work at	128
White oak, bent, knees and timbers	94
White oak, cost of, in England	142, 143
White oak, failure of the native supply of, in England	242
White oak, general supply of, in the United States now failing	243
White oak on the western rivers	151, 178, 179, 182, 186–188, 190–193, 195
White oak preferred for frame timber in Maine	97, 98, 102, 138, 169, 171–174
White-oak supply in the Atlantic states	105, 107, 113, 119, 120, 122, 124, 126, 128, 171
White oak, use of, in canal-boats	223, 227, 231, 232
White oak, use of, in fishing schooners	12, 13, 15
White oak, use of, in large ocean vessels	25, 60, 61, 64, 87, 89, 156, 161
White pine, exportation of, spar timber to England	104, 105
White pine, general supply of, in the United States	247
White pine used for decking and cabins	25, 60, 61, 64, 87, 89, 156, 162
White pine, use of, for masts and spars	97, 99, 102, 111, 127, 132, 138, 246, 247
White pine, use of, in boats and canoes	12, 20, 29, 31, 43
Wilmington, Delaware, iron-ship yards at	208–213
Wilmington, Delaware, wooden-vessel building at	124, 162
Wire standing cordage on the northern lakes	138
Wiscasset, Maine, decay of ship-building at	100
Wisconsin, statistics of fishing vessels of	3
Wisconsin, steamer building in	173
Wood and fishing sloops of Massachusetts	9
Wood sloops of the early settlers of Boston, Massachusetts	9, 47
Wyandotte, Michigan, iron-ship building at	221, 222

Y.

	Page.
Yacht building at Pamrapo, New Jersey	121
Yacht building at Rye, New York	120
Yard and marine railway at Mound City, Illinois	193
Yards of canvas sails on various vessels	15, 89, 94, 135, 139
Yarmouth, Maine, ship-building of	104
Yellow pine, abundant supply of, in Virginia	128, 246
Yellow pine a native of New Jersey	121, 122
Yellow pine, general supply of, in the United States	246
Yellow pine, introduction of, to northern ship-yards	64, 87
Yellow pine used in Virginia for canoes	34
York, Virginia, canoe-building at	38